Lecture Notes in Computer Science

Lecture Notes in Artificial Intelligence 15920

Founding Editor

Jörg Siekmann

Series Editors

Randy Goebel, *University of Alberta, Edmonton, Canada*
Wolfgang Wahlster, *DFKI, Berlin, Germany*
Zhi-Hua Zhou, *Nanjing University, Nanjing, China*

The series Lecture Notes in Artificial Intelligence (LNAI) was established in 1988 as a topical subseries of LNCS devoted to artificial intelligence.

The series publishes state-of-the-art research results at a high level. As with the LNCS mother series, the mission of the series is to serve the international R & D community by providing an invaluable service, mainly focused on the publication of conference and workshop proceedings and postproceedings.

Tianqing Zhu · Wanlei Zhou · Congcong Zhu
Editors

Knowledge Science, Engineering and Management

18th International Conference, KSEM 2025
Macao, China, August 4–7, 2025
Proceedings, Part II

 Springer

Editors
Tianqing Zhu
City University of Macau
Macau, China

Wanlei Zhou
City University of Macau
Macau, China

Congcong Zhu
City University of Macau
Macau, China

ISSN 0302-9743　　　　　　　ISSN 1611-3349　(electronic)
Lecture Notes in Artificial Intelligence
ISBN 978-981-95-3051-9　　　ISBN 978-981-95-3052-6　(eBook)
https://doi.org/10.1007/978-981-95-3052-6

LNCS Sublibrary: SL7 – Artificial Intelligence

Preface

On behalf of the Conference Committee, we are pleased to present the proceedings of the 18th International Conference on Knowledge Science, Engineering and Management (**KSEM 2025**), held at the Wynn Palace, Macau Special Administrative Region, China, from August 4–7, 2025. KSEM 2025 was the eighteenth event in this well-established series of conferences, founded by Academician Ruqian Lu, which is recognized as a premier international forum for the exchange of research in artificial intelligence, data science, knowledge engineering, AI safety, large language models, and related frontier areas. Over the years, KSEM has provided an important venue for disseminating both theoretical advances and practical innovations, fostering interdisciplinary collaboration between academia and industry.

This year, KSEM 2025 received 354 submissions from authors around the world. Following a rigorous single-blind peer-review process, with an average of 2.82 reviews received per submission, involving 342 Program Committee members and external reviewers, 106 regular papers, 66 short papers, and 16 workshop papers were accepted for inclusion in these proceedings and will be submitted for EI indexing. In addition to the contributed papers, the program featured keynote lectures by distinguished scholars, as well as workshops and tutorials on emerging research topics, offering valuable opportunities for academic exchange and collaboration.

Among the accepted papers, the following were selected for the **Best Paper Awards**:

- *Masked Aggregation Learning for Enhancing Distributed Gradient Boosting Decision Trees* Yuting Zha, Chao Lin, Xinyi Huang, and Dugang Liu
- *Label Inference Attacks against Federated Unlearning* Wei Wang, Xiangyun Tang, Yajie Wang, Yijing Lin, Tao Zhang, Meng Shen, Dusit Niyato, and Liehuang Zhu

The **Best Student Paper Awards** went to:

- *LVLM-FDA: Protecting Large Vision-language Models via Fast Detection of Malicious Attempts* Boxu Chen, Chaoyi Wang, Le Yang, Ziwei Zheng, Cong Wang, Qian Wang, and Chao Shen
- *FATFI: A Framework to Generate Adversarial Traffic with Feature Interpretability* Yikang Wang, Weina Niu, Dujuan Gu, Qingjun Yuan, Jiacheng Gong, Shuangqi Gan, Xin Lin, and Xiaosong Zhang

We would like to express our sincere gratitude to all authors for their valuable contributions, and to the Program Committee members and reviewers for their professional and timely evaluations. We also warmly thank all the volunteers who supported the conference at various stages.

We further extend our appreciation to the following chairs for their invaluable contributions:

- **General Chairs:** Wanlei Zhou, Zhi Jin, Aniello Castiglione
- **Program Chairs:** Tianqing Zhu, Gang Li, Congcong Zhu, Lucia Cimmino

- **Local Chairs:** Wenjian Liu, Minghao Wang, Huajie Chen
- **Publication Chairs:** Lefeng Zhang, Youyang Qu
- **Workshop Chairs:** Jia Gu, Bo Liu, Chi Liu
- **Publicity Chairs:** Yu Huang, Minfeng Qi

We were so honored to have many renowned scholars be part of this conference. Finally, we would like to thank all speakers, authors, and participants for their great contribution to and support for the success of KSEM 2025.

August 2025

Tianqing Zhu
Wanlei Zhou
Congcong Zhu

Committees

General Chairs

Wanlei Zhou	City University of Macau, China
Zhi Jin	Peking University, China
Aniello Castiglione	University of Salerno, Italy

Program Chairs

Tianqing Zhu	City University of Macau, China
Gang Li	Deakin University, Australia
Congcong Zhu	City University of Macau, China
Lucia Cimmino	University of Salerno, Italy

Local Chairs

Wenjian Liu	City University of Macau, China
Minghao Wang	City University of Macau, China
Huajie Chen	City University of Macau, China

Publication Chairs

Lefeng Zhang	City University of Macau, China
Youyang Qu	Shandong Computer Science Center, China

Workshop Chairs

Jia Gu	City University of Macau, China
Bo Liu	University of Technology Sydney, Australia
Chi Liu	City University of Macau, China

Publicity Chairs

Yu Huang	Peking University, China
Minfeng Qi	City University of Macau, China

Contents – Part II

Noise-Resistant Federated Open Set Recognition

Hahn Gao[1], Yang Liu[1(✉)], Zixuan Qin[1], and Wou Ou[2]

[1] College of Intelligence and Computing, Tianjin University, Tianjin 300350, China
{hahngao,yangliuyl,qinzixuan1958}@tju.edu.cn
[2] HIAS, University of Chinese Academy of Sciences, Zhejiang 310024, China
wuou@ucas.ac.cn

Abstract. Open domain adaptation is a significant area of research that transcends the limitations of closed domain adaptation. Although numerous effective methods have been developed in recent years, it remains essential to address challenges such as data security and noisy labels within the source domain dataset, as these issues frequently arise in real-world applications. To tackle these concerns, we propose Noise-Resistant Federated Learning (NRFed). First, we integrate federated learning to ensure data security by keeping the data on local clients. Next, we incorporate Bayesian Neural Networks (BNNs), which enable local clients to assess their own uncertainty and achieve weighted aggregation, thereby reducing the impact of noisy clients. To further address the issue of noisy labels, we implement a confidence-based label correction technique that purifies the noisy training dataset. Finally, extensive experiments conducted on the Office-31 and Office-Home datasets demonstrate that NRFed effectively mitigates issues related to noisy labels.

Keywords: open domain adaptation · noisy label · federated learning · uncertainty · label correction

1 Introduction

In many practical machine learning tasks, obtaining labeled training data is often limited due to the high associated costs. Although numerous publicly available labeled image datasets exist, images collected from the internet often differ significantly from those required for specific tasks. Task-specific images may vary from training datasets in terms of angles, scenes, and other factors, placing them in distinct domains, commonly referred to as the source domain and the target domain. While traditional domain adaptation methods were initially developed with practical applications, they typically assume that the categories in both the source and target domains are identical, an assumption that clearly deviates from reality. In many real-world scenarios, the target domain contains categories absent in the source domain, resulting in misclassification. This challenge is addressed by open set domain adaptation (OSDA), which recognizes and circumvents the restrictive assumptions of closed domain adaptation [1].

T. Zhu et al. (Eds.): KSEM 2025, LNAI 15920, pp. 1–13, 2026.
https://doi.org/10.1007/978-981-95-3052-6_1

However, the complexity of real-world data extends beyond these challenges. As noted earlier, obtaining labeled data is both costly and difficult. In large datasets, label errors are inevitable due to human mistakes and other factors. Moreover, in an attempt to quickly amass large volumes of training data, cost-effective methods like automated image labeling via machine learning models are often employed. Unfortunately, these methods tend to introduce significant label noise, which can severely affect the learning of source domain knowledge and degrade the performance of domain adaptation.

Existing methods propose many effective solutions for noisy training dataset. These methods of Learning with Noisy Labels (LNL) [2] can be broadly categorized into three main methods. The first method, filtering strategies [3,4], identifies samples with noisy labels using thresholds or techniques like pre-training or clustering [5,6], often based on loss magnitude [2]. However, this method is unreliable as high-loss samples may contain crucial boundary information, and removing them can result in the loss of important insights. The second method assumes a fixed noise distribution in the dataset [7]. While estimating and correcting noise can improve data quality, real-world noise often deviates from these assumptions. The third method mitigates the impact of noisy labels by employing techniques such as model ensembling [8], interpolation training [9], or data augmentation [10], though these methods increase computational demands.

On the other hand, existing OSDA methods rely on shared data between the source and target domains. However, in real-world applications, data often cannot be shared due to privacy concerns, which causes traditional domain adaptation approaches to fail. Federated learning (FL) offers an effective solution to this challenge by allowing clients to participate in the aggregation process through the submission of locally trained model updates to a central server, without sharing any local training data [11]. Although some studies have explored federated learning models to address this issue and successfully achieve OSDA tasks [12,13], they often overlook the quality of the source domain's training data and fail to adequately handle noisy labels.

To safeguard data privacy and address label noise in source domain datasets within open set scenarios, we propose a robust open set domain adaptive federated learning model, NRFed. This method mitigates privacy and security concerns associated with data sharing in OSDA by leveraging federated learning models. It also enhances resistance to noisy labels through improvements in both the local training and federated aggregation stages. During local training, each client uses a confidence-based label correction method to refine its dataset, identifying and correcting potentially noisy samples based on their confidence scores. In the federated aggregation phase, BNNs are introduced to allow local clients to assess their own uncertainty [14]. Each client generates an uncertainty score using BNNs and uploads this score along with model updates to the server. The server then selectively aggregates these updates, enabling the global model to achieve near-optimal performance while minimizing the impact of label noise.

Our main contributions are summarized as follows:

- This method addresses practical machine learning challenges by effectively tackling real-world issues such as open sets, data privacy, and noisy labels, thereby enhancing its ability to handle real-world tasks more effectively.
- This method incorporates BNNs to allow local clients to quantify their own uncertainty, thereby optimizing the global model through weighted aggregation based on this uncertainty.
- This method effectively corrects noisy labels while preserving more dataset information compared to simply removing noisy samples. Moreover, it is versatile and can be integrated into existing machine learning frameworks.

2   Methodology

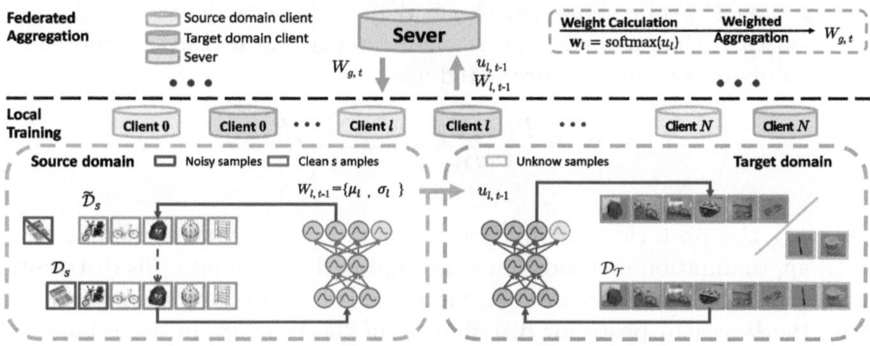

Fig. 1. NRFed Framework Illustration.

The primary goal of NRFed is to address a critical challenge in machine learning: the presence of label noise in both training and open-set datasets, while ensuring data security. As illustrated in Fig. 1, in the local training phase, each source domain client maintains a confidence score to every sample and corrects the labels in their dataset to obtain a clear source domain dataset. Simultaneously, the target domain client employs the source domain model trained on the clean dataset to delineate between known and unknown categories. In the federated aggregation phase, to prevent noisy labels from spreading to other clients, underperforming clients are penalized. We introduce BNNs, which replace fixed network weights with Gaussian distributions. During prediction, the BNNs sample from each Gaussian distribution to generate weight values, drawing multiple samples to produce a range of prediction outcomes that reflect prediction uncertainty. The server then utilizes this uncertainty for weighted aggregation of client models to form the global model.

2.1   Preliminaries

NRFed facilitates the collaboration of distributed source domain clients to train a global model for OSDA tasks in target domain clients, while ensuring that client data remains local. In our formulation, let $\mathcal{D}_\mathcal{S} = \{\mathcal{D}_l\}_{l=1}^N$ represent the N source domain clients, where $\mathcal{D}_l = \{(x_s^i, y_s^i)\}_{i=1}^{n_l}$ denotes the set of n_l labeled examples. Furthermore, the target domain client possesses n_t unlabeled examples, denoted as $\mathcal{D}_\mathcal{T} = \{x_t^j\}_{j=1}^{n_t}$. Since local training datasets are collected independently by each client, unknown categories arise solely during the domain adaptation phase, indicating that local training datasets face primarily label noise issues.

2.2   BNNs for OSDA

To measure uncertainty, we introduce BNNs in the OSDA task. BNNs incorporate prior assumptions and compute the posterior distribution $P(W|\mathcal{D})$ of the weights W rather than restricting the solution to argmax values. Consequently, the predictive distribution of a predicted label $\hat{y}$ for a test data point $\hat{x}$ is expressed as $P(\hat{y}|\hat{x}) = \mathbb{E}_{P(W|\mathcal{D})}[P(\hat{y}|\hat{x}, W)]$. This necessitates calculating an expectation each time a prediction is made. According to Bayes' theorem, the posterior probability can be represented as:

$$P(W|\mathcal{D}) = \frac{P(W, \mathcal{D})}{P(\mathcal{D})} = \frac{P(\mathcal{D}|W)P(W)}{P(\mathcal{D})}. \tag{1}$$

Deriving the posterior distribution presents a significant challenge. Consequently, approximation methods must be employed to estimate this distribution. As noted by Graves [15], variational inference is a viable approach for approximating the Bayesian posterior distribution of the weights. In accordance with the variational method, an approximate distribution $q(W|\theta)$ is defined, with q aiming to closely resemble the true posterior $P(W|\mathcal{D})$. Here, $\theta = \{\mu, \sigma\}$ represents the Gaussian distribution parameters of W. This reformulates the task of deriving a posterior distribution into an optimization challenge focused on identifying the optimal θ:

$$\begin{aligned}
\theta^* &= \arg\min \int q \log \frac{q}{P(W)P(\mathcal{D}|W)} dW \\
&= \arg\min KL[q\|P(W)] - \mathbb{E}_q[\log(P(\mathcal{D}|W)].
\end{aligned} \tag{2}$$

where the KL divergence can also be viewed as a loss function:

$$\mathcal{L}_{KL} = KL[q\|P(W)] = \int q \log \frac{q}{P(W)} dW. \tag{3}$$

To fully leverage the model's prior knowledge, the loss function of BNNs employs the Evidence Lower Bound (ELBO) loss function, which comprises two components. One component is the conventional neural network loss function, utilizing the Negative Log-Likelihood Loss $\mathcal{L}_{nll}$. The other component is the

KL divergence, which integrates the model's prior knowledge. Therefore, the complete $\mathcal{L}_{ELBO}$ can be expressed as:

$$\mathcal{L}_{ELBO} = \mathcal{L}_{nll} + \beta\mathcal{L}_{KL}, \quad \beta = \frac{2^{n_l-(b+1)}}{2^{n_l}-1}, \tag{4}$$

where b denotes the batch size.

2.3 Local Training

Due to the distribution of source and target data across different clients, the parameters of the source domain model must be transferred to the target domain. Each source domain client has a Bayesian generator G^l and a classifier C^l, both of which are uploaded to the target domain client and subsequently to the server for aggregation. For OSDA, C^l outputs a $(K+1)$-dimensional vector, where K represents known categories and the final dimension indicates the probability of unknown categories. During local training, the source domain client employs confidence-based label correction to refine noisy labels, while the target domain client utilizes adversarial techniques to establish boundaries for unknown categories.

Label Correction. This method aims to maximize the preservation of critical information while minimizing the interference caused by label noise. Let $f \in \mathbb{R}^D$ represent the feature extracted by G^l, where D denotes the dimensionality of the feature space. If $\mathbf{W} \in \mathbb{R}^{D \times K}$ represents the weights of C^l, then $\mathbf{W}$ functions as the class prototype matrix, with $\mathbf{W}_c \in \mathbb{R}^D$ serving as the prototype for class c. The similarity between feature f^i and prototype $\mathbf{W}_c$ is expressed as $z(c; x^i) = (\mathbf{W}_c)^\top f^i$, representing the logit of a linear classifier. For each source domain client example x_s^i, the confidence of class c can be denoted as:

$$v_c^i = \frac{e^{z(c;x_s^i)}}{\sum_{c=1}^{K} e^{z(c;x_s^i)}}. \tag{5}$$

The higher the confidence level, the greater the certainty that the model classifies the sample into a particular category.

During local training, each client computes the per-category confidence at each epoch, accumulating these values across categories. Upon convergence, labels are corrected using the accumulated confidence V^i. In the final round of local training, the model evaluates the confidence for each sample. If the highest confidence category V_c^i differs from the labeled category $V_{y_s^i}^i$, it indicates the presence of a noisy label. The label is then corrected to the category corresponding to the highest V_c^i, which the model identifies as the most accurate. Thus, the new labels $\tilde{y}^i$ can be represented as:

$$\tilde{y}_s^i = \begin{cases} \arg\max\limits_c V_c^i, & \text{if } \max V_c^i > V_{y_s^i}^i \\ y_s^i, & \text{else.} \end{cases} \tag{6}$$

Previous studies indicate that a model's memory of noisy labels increases as training converges, making early-stage correction most effective for focusing on clean samples. Consequently, this method corrects labels at the early stage while shielding still-noisy samples in later stages. To preserve boundary knowledge, the model first learns boundary information before memorizing noisy samples, followed by selective learning on the corrected data. Since relying solely on loss values for label detection may overlook important boundary details, a dual evaluation criterion is employed. This criterion combines the loss function with $v^i_{\tilde{y}^i_s}$ for selection. Samples with high loss but critical boundary information are retained, while those with high loss and low confidence across categories are identified as noisy. Thus, the final clean dataset $\tilde{\mathcal{D}}$ is formed using this approach.

$$\tilde{\mathcal{D}} = \{x^i_s | v^i_{\tilde{y}^i_s} > \tau_v \text{ and } \mathcal{L}_{ELBO}(x^i_s) < \tau_l\}. \tag{7}$$

As training progresses, the memory strength of models for samples increases. However, as training converges, the model reinforces erroneous memories of noisy labels. To address this issue, the thresholds for selecting noisy samples are dynamically defined as $\tau_l(t)$ and $\tau_v(t)$ in each global epoch t.

$$\tau_l(t+1) = \lambda(\tau_l(t)) + (1-\lambda) \max \mathcal{L}_{ELBO}(x^i_s; t+1), \tag{8}$$

$$\tau_v(t+1) = \lambda(\tau_v(t)) + (1-\lambda) \max v^i_{c,t+1}, \tag{9}$$

where $\tau_l(0) = 0$ and $\tau_v(0) = n_l$.

When a sample simultaneously exhibits both a high loss and low confidence, the local client identifies the label of x^i as polluted, suggesting it is not a critical boundary sample. Consequently, the model disregards such samples, thereby biasing the model toward training on cleaner datasets.

Unknown Category Detection. After learning from the source domain, the source domain client transfers model information to the target domain client. The target domain client utilizes its own dataset to establish the boundary of unknown categories through generative adversarial learning. Here, C^l builds boundary between known and unknown categories, while G^l aims to deceive C^l. During this process, G^l aligns target domain samples with the source domain or classifies x^j_t as an unknown category. This method helps establish a boundary to distinguish unknown categories, enabling the model to recognize unseen samples as unknown rather than misclassifying them. The target client uses its unlabeled data $\mathcal{D}_\mathcal{T} = \{x^j_t\}^{n_t}_{j=1}$ with binary cross-entropy loss and a gradient reversal layer. The adversarial loss for the source domain is:

$$L_{adv}(W_{G^l}, W_{C^l}) = \sum_{j=1}^{n_t} \ell_{ce}\left(C^l(G^l(x^j_t; W_{G^l}), W_{C^l}), y^{j|K+1}_t\right), \tag{10}$$

where ℓ_{ce} represents the binary cross-entropy loss, and W_{G^l} and W_{C^l} denote the weights of the generator and classifier. With reference to the above analysis, the updates for the generator and classifier are given by:

$$(W_{G^l})^{t+1} = (W_{G^l})^t - \nabla L_{ELBO}(W_{G^l}) + \nabla L_{adv}(W_{G^l}), \tag{11}$$

$$(W_{C^l})^{t+1} = (W_{C^l})^t - \nabla L_{ELBO}(W_{C^l}) - \nabla L_{adv}(W_{C^l}). \tag{12}$$

The updated model parameters will be used for aggregating the federated global model in this round.

2.4 Uncertainty-Driven Federated Aggregation

Traditional Federated Averaging (FedAvg) [11] aggregates all clients with the same weight, overlooking client disparity and resulting in suboptimal global model outcomes. By assigning aggregation weights based on client uncertainty values, our method addresses this issue. In this work, the traditional network is replaced with BNNs. As described in Sect. 2.2, BNNs view the predictive output $\hat{y}$ for an unseen sample $\hat{x}$ as a predictive distribution $P(\hat{y}|\hat{x}, \mathcal{D})$, so,

$$\mathbb{E}_q[P(\hat{y}|\hat{x}, \mathcal{D})] = \int q P_W(y|x) \mathrm{d}W \approx \frac{1}{M} \sum_{m=1}^{M} P_{W_m}(\hat{y}|\hat{x}), \tag{13}$$

where M is the predefined number of samples. This estimator allows us to evaluate the uncertainty of our predictions by the definition of variance, hence called predictive variance and denoted as Var:

$$\mathrm{Var}(P(\hat{y}|\hat{x})) = \mathbb{E}_q[\hat{y}\hat{y}^\top] - \mathbb{E}_q[\hat{y}]\mathbb{E}_q[\hat{y}]^\top, \tag{14}$$

where $\mathbb{E}_q[\hat{y}] = \mathbb{E}_{q_\theta(\hat{y}|\hat{x})}[\hat{y}]$.

To better measure the impact of label noise on the model and distinguish between data quality and poor model performance, it is necessary to separate aleatoric uncertainty from epistemic uncertainty. Therefore, the Var can be decomposed as:

$$\mathrm{Var}(P(\hat{y}|\hat{x})) = \underbrace{\frac{1}{M} \sum_{m=1}^{M} \mathrm{diag}(\hat{p}_m) - \hat{p}_m \hat{p}_m^\top}_{\text{aleatoric}(u^a)} + \underbrace{\frac{1}{M} \sum_{m=1}^{M} (\hat{p}_m - \bar{p})(\hat{p}_m - \bar{p})^\top}_{\text{epistemic}(u^e)}, \tag{15}$$

where $\bar{p} = \frac{1}{M} \sum_{m=1}^{M} \hat{p}_m$ and $\hat{p}_m = \mathrm{Softmax}(z(\hat{x}))$.

Aleatoric uncertainty pertains to the quality of training data, often stemming from noisy labels or class imbalances, whereas epistemic uncertainty relates to model performance. Elevated aleatoric uncertainty indicates substantial noise within the dataset, while heightened epistemic uncertainty signifies inadequate model performance. In contrast to traditional federated learning, this approach necessitates that clients upload not only their local model parameters W_s from each training round but also their uncertainty to optimize aggregation.

Table 1. OS (%) and OS* (%) with Different Noise Rates on Office-31 Dataset Under IID Setting

Category		OSDA methods				Denoise FL			Ours
Method		FedAvg	SHOT	FedLoGe	FOSDA	FedNed	FedNoRo	RoFed	NRFed
(η^l, η^u)	Task	OS OS*	OS OS*	OS OS*	OS OS*	OS OS*	OS OS*	OS OS*	OS OS*
	A→D	85.8 92.0	72.1 78.7	86.1 96.1	90.3 96.3	85.3 91.5	86.1 90.8	90.6 96.6	**91.8 97.3**
	D→A	71.6 72.5	58.3 63.2	73.5 73.9	73.2 76.1	70.0 72.1	73.9 76.5	75.6 77.6	**77.9 80.2**
(0.2,0.4)	A→W	87.0 91.4	75.5 81.5	87.2 91.1	89.8 97.6	82.4 89.2	88.9 95.1	**93.2** 98.6	92.8 **99.4**
	W→A	75.0 76.4	69.8 76.0	76.1 76.2	75.6 78.6	74.2 76.8	74.4 77.2	76.7 79.5	**77.9 80.1**
	D→W	91.5 92.9	82.6 89.6	83.2 85.8	93.2 97.3	87.0 87.6	86.7 92.0	87.3 94.4	**96.5** 97.5
	W→D	95.3 97.9	93.0 99.3	94.0 98.3	93.6 **100.0**	95.3 98.0	91.8 96.8	96.0 99.3	**97.0** 99.3
	A→D	83.8 89.1	58.5 62.5	85.0 93.0	82.3 88.2	82.8 89.5	85.1 88.0	89.4 94.5	**90.6 96.3**
	D→A	68.4 68.9	54.5 70.3	70.0 69.8	71.4 73.9	65.0 63.2	66.5 68.1	71.3 72.2	**73.0 74.8**
(0.3,0.5)	A→W	78.6 81.8	63.1 68.4	82.7 86.0	85.6 93.3	73.9 80.4	88.0 93.3	**92.6** 97.1	91.3 **98.6**
	W→A	72.0 71.8	61.1 66.3	74.0 74.5	68.2 69.0	67.6 69.0	73.3 75.7	**80.4 81.5**	75.5 78.4
	D→W	79.2 77.4	64.4 69.5	72.1 71.4	90.1 **92.3**	85.2 84.5	84.0 88.1	89.0 92.2	**91.7** 90.9
	W→D	88.3 88.9	83.1 90.0	89.5 92.6	92.5 97.0	92.0 96.5	93.8 96.8	**95.2 98.3**	94.1 94.7
	A→D	45.5 48.5	40.0 40.8	62.6 64.2	64.4 69.6	57.2 62.0	52.0 53.3	**71.5 76.5**	69.0 71.3
	D→A	45.7 45.4	34.3 36.6	56.8 54.5	46.8 49.3	57.8 58.2	58.5 61.8	54.4 54.9	**65.2 68.2**
(0.5,0.7)	A→W	46.7 47.6	48.0 50.2	56.8 58.0	57.5 62.3	47.8 52.2	47.2 50.2	**76.1 78.7**	71.6 76.8
	W→A	46.3 46.9	30.9 31.3	56.4 55.3	48.5 51.2	53.0 56.2	51.1 52.7	49.6 53.5	**69.3 70.8**
	D→W	58.0 55.6	43.1 46.1	62.0 63.0	68.4 72.9	65.6 64.4	63.7 65.8	66.5 71.4	**76.2 73.9**
	W→D	71.1 71.4	80.0 86.7	68.4 70.5	82.0 85.2	77.3 77.8	67.8 73.5	78.5 78.3	**90.9 91.4**

After the server receives the client model and its corresponding uncertainty, it first calculates the aggregation weights $\mathbf{w}_l$ based on their uncertainty and then obtains the global model W_g of the current round through weighted aggregation:

$$\mathbf{w}_l = \mathrm{softmax}(-u_l) = \mathrm{softmax}(-\epsilon u_l^a + (\epsilon - 1)u_l^e), \tag{16}$$

$$W_g = \sum_{l=1}^{N} \mathbf{w}_l W_l. \tag{17}$$

The global model thus obtained will favor the results of clients that performed better in the current round of federated learning, while mitigating the impact of clients heavily affected by contamination. This method brings the aggregated result closer to the desired outcome. Finally, the aggregated W_g is sent back to each client, marking the completion of one round of federated learning.

3   Experiments

In this section, we first validate the effectiveness of our method under different noise rates. Then, we conduct ablation experiments for the optimization method.

3.1   Experimental Setup

Baselines. We compare NRFed with seven baselines. For fair comparison, the method was compared with optimization methods for OSDA methods and federated learning methods resistant to data noise (Denoise FL). (1)FedAvg [11] is a classical federated learning method that does not employ data enhancement and is designed for scenarios with noisy labels. (2)SHOT [16] utilizes pseudo-labeling for target adaptation in source-free unsupervised domain adaptation. (3)FOSDA [12] adopts a class-based approach for global model aggregation. (4)FedLoGe [17] enhances both local and global models by employing personalized aggregation through representation learning and classifier alignment. (5)FedNed [18] identifies noisy clients and applies knowledge distillation rather than discarding them. (6)RoFed [19] aggregates models using class-wise centroids to manage noisy labels. (7)FedNoRo [20] develops a noise-robust method by selecting and training noisy clients through specific strategies.

Training Setting. To accurately simulate real-world noise conditions, we refer to [20], which employs heterogeneous instance-dependent noise (H-IDN) capable of modeling complex and realistic label noise. We assume that the local noise rate, denoted as η_i, follows a uniform distribution $U(\eta^l, \eta^u)$ for each client. To ensure a fair comparison, it is crucial that all methods are standardized when testing different strategies. The number of clients, N, is set at 10. In the label correction phase, the hyperparameter λ is fixed at 0.5, while during the aggregation phase, ϵ is set to 0.8. Additionally, the predetermined sample size, denoted as M, is established at 40. We utilize two evaluation metrics: overall average accuracy (OS) and average accuracy among known categories (OS*),

$$\text{OS*} = \frac{1}{K} \sum_{k=1}^{K} \frac{|x_t \in \mathcal{D}_{tk} \wedge \hat{y}_k = y_k|}{|\mathcal{D}_{tk}|}, \text{OS} = \frac{1}{K+1} \sum_{k=1}^{K+1} \frac{|x_t \in \mathcal{D}_{tk} \wedge \hat{y}_k = y_k|}{|\mathcal{D}_{tk}|}, \tag{18}$$

where $\hat{y}$ is the predicted result and $\mathcal{D}_{tk}$ is the test dataset with the label y_k.

3.2   Results

As illustrated in Table 1, NRFed demonstrates superior performance in comparison to existing methods on the Office-31 dataset across various noise rates. Under the IID setting, our method achieves an average OS of 88.98% for noise rates ranging from 0.2 to 0.4, surpassing the next best method by 2.42%. When the noise rate increases to between 0.5 and 0.7, our method maintains its superiority, attaining an average OS of 73.7%, which is 7.6% higher than the suboptimal methods OS of 66.1%. This demonstrates that NRFed remains effective in resisting noisy labels, with its stability offering a particularly significant advantage in high-noise scenarios.

Methods designed for instance-irrelevant noise [18] demonstrate reduced performance when confronted with H-IDN noise. Moreover, techniques that focus

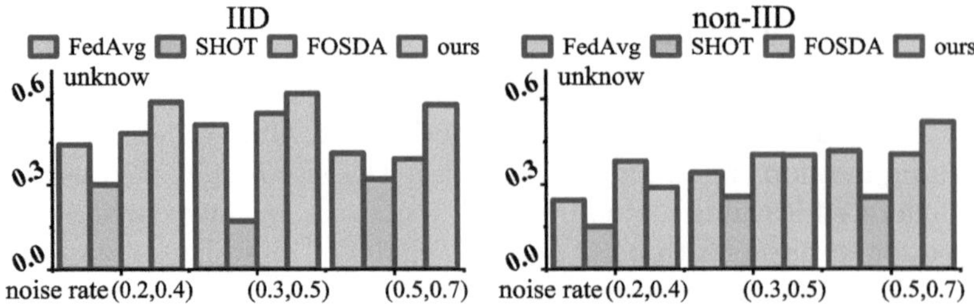

Fig. 2. Unknown Category Learning Performance.

solely on selecting and excluding noisy samples or clients prove less effective than those aimed at correcting noisy labels. Thus, merely disregarding noisy data is inadequate for developing an effective model, underscoring the importance of label noise correction. Furthermore, as illustrated in Fig. 2, NRFed excels at identifying newly emerged unknown category samples in the test dataset across both IID and non-IID settings, while also ensuring superior identification of known categories. This reinforces NRFed's performance advantage over alternative methods in identifying unknown categories.

3.3   Ablation Study

Label Correction. To validate the noisy label correction capability of NRFed, we utilize the $A \to D$ task with a noise rate of $(\eta^l, \eta^u) = (0.5, 0.7)$ on the Office-31 dataset. Figure 3 illustrates the selection and correction results: "SUM" is the total noisy samples, while $W \to R$, $W \to W$, and $R \to W$ indicate corrections from wrong to right, wrong to wrong, and right to wrong, respectively. Most noisy labels are corrected accurately, with only a few misclassifications remaining or at risk of being misclassified, which may be addressed in subsequent iterations.

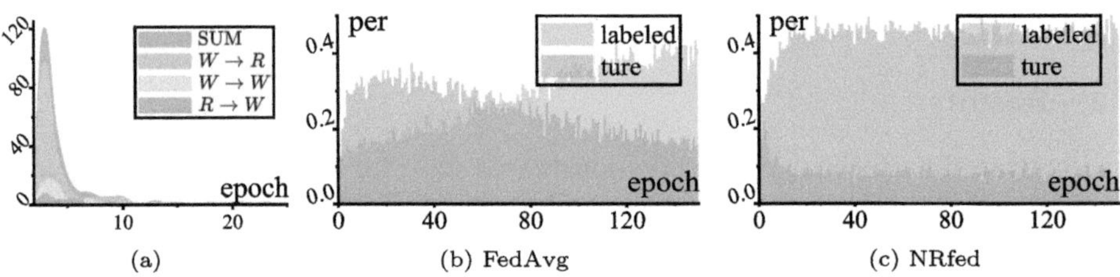

Fig. 3. Plot (a) shows noisy label correction effects; (b) and (c) examine the network's memorization behavior.

Figures 3 b and 3 c show the percentages of noisy samples predicted as either the correct category or incorrectly labeled categories by various methods within the task. Neural networks tend to memorize noisy labels early in the training process, which diminishes the effectiveness of subsequent corrections during later stable phases. Therefore, correcting labels prior to noise memorization is essential to minimize its impact. This proactive approach ensures that the model learns accurate label information from the outset.

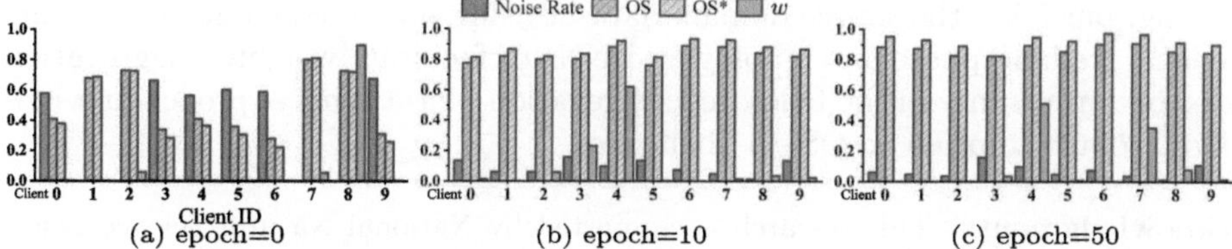

Fig. 4. Validation of aggregation weight rationality.

NRFed uses aggregation weights informed by uncertainty to mitigate the impact of low-performing clients, as demonstrated in Fig. 4. This method effectively captures client performance at each epoch through an uncertainty. Initially, the weights prioritize higher-performing clients, thereby enhancing the global model's performance. As the model stabilizes, the disparity in uncertainty diminishes, reflecting an overall improvement for all clients.

Table 2. OS (%) and OS* (%) of Different optimise.

Task	A→D		D→A	
Method	OS	OS*	OS	OS*
FedAvg	45.5	48.5	45.7	45.4
Opt Aggregation Only	53.1	56.8	48.0	51.6
Denoise Only	67.7	70.0	56.1	56.7
NRFed	**69.0**	**71.3**	**65.2**	**68.2**

We experimentally verify our findings on representative tasks with noise rates of $(\eta^l, \eta^u) = (0.2, 0.4)$. As illustrated in Table 2, the results demonstrate enhancements in both optimization components compared to the baseline method, FedAvg. Particularly noteworthy is the substantial improvement observed with the combined approach of local label correction and uncertainty-driven federated aggregation. This indicates that optimizing local label correction for label noise is crucial for overall optimization.

4   Conclusion

While the OSDA problem offers a practical framework, real-world scenarios frequently involve source domain data with noisy labels due to various factors. Our method recognizes the existence of label noise in the source domain data and addresses this challenge within a federated learning environment that emphasizes data security. Specifically, NRFed optimizes two critical stages of federated learning: purifying the source domain dataset using predicted confidence during the local training phase and employing BNNs to facilitate weighted aggregation based on uncertainty in the federated aggregation phase. This approach provides a more robust solution to OSDA challenges.

Acknowledgments. This research is supported by National Natural Science Foundation of China [No.62476194, U23B2049].

References

1. Busto, P.P., Gall, J.: Open set domain adaptation. In: IEEE International Conference on Computer Vision, pp. 754–763 (2017)
2. Han, B., et al.: Co-teaching: robust training of deep neural networks with extremely noisy labels. In: Advances in Neural Information Processing Systems, pp. 8536–8546 (2018)
3. Northcutt, C., Jiang, L., Chuang, I.: Confident learning: estimating uncertainty in dataset labels. J. Artifi. Intell. Res. **70**, 1373–1411 (2021)
4. Cheng, H., Zhu, Z., Li, X., Gong, Y., Sun, X., Liu, Y.: Learning with instance-dependent label noise: a sample sieve approach. ArXiv abs/2010.02347 (2020)
5. Li, Y., Han, H., Shan, S., Chen, X.: Disc: Learning from noisy labels via dynamic instance-specific selection and correction. In: IEEE/CVF Conference on Computer Vision and Pattern Recognition, pp. 24070–24079 (2023)
6. Wu, Z.F., Wei, T., Jiang, J., Mao, C., Tang, M., Li, Y.F.: Ngc: a unified framework for learning with open-world noisy data. In: IEEE/CVF International Conference on Computer Vision, pp. 62–71 (2021)
7. Liu, Y., Guo, H.: Peer loss functions: learning from noisy labels without knowing noise rates. In: International Conference on Machine Learning, pp. 6226–6236 (2020)
8. Li, J., Socher, R., Hoi, S.C.: Dividemix: learning with noisy labels as semi-supervised learning. ArXiv abs/2002.07394 (2020)
9. Ortego, D., Arazo, E., Albert, P., O'Connor, N.E., McGuinness, K.: Multi-objective interpolation training for robustness to label noise. In: IEEE/CVF Conference on Computer Vision and Pattern Recognition, pp. 6606–6615 (2021)
10. Karim, N., Rizve, M.N., Rahnavard, N., Mian, A., Shah, M.: Unicon: combating label noise through uniform selection and contrastive learning. In: IEEE/CVF Conference on Computer Vision and Pattern Recognition, pp. 9676–9686 (2022)
11. McMahan, B., Moore, E., Ramage, D., Hampson, S., y Arcas, B.A.: Communication-efficient learning of deep networks from decentralized data. In: Artificial Intelligence and Statistics Conference, pp. 1273–1282 (2017)

12. Qin, Z., Yang, L., Gao, F., Hu, Q., Shen, C.: Uncertainty-aware aggregation for federated open set domain adaptation. IEEE Trans. Neural Netw. Learn. Syst., 1–15 (2022)
13. Kulshreshtha, K., Goel, B., Kanyal, H.S., Singhal, V.: Federated learning in the era of privacy preservation: a comprehensive review and future directions. In: 2024 2nd International Conference on Disruptive Technologies, pp. 763–768. IEEE (2024)
14. Blundell, C., Cornebise, J., Kavukcuoglu, K., Wierstra, D.: Weight uncertainty in neural network. In: International Conference on Machine Learning, pp. 1613–1622 (2015)
15. Graves, A.: Practical variational inference for neural networks. Adv. Neural Inf. Process. Syst. **24** (2011)
16. Liang, J., Hu, D., Feng, J.: Do we really need to access the source data? source hypothesis transfer for unsupervised domain adaptation. In: International Conference on Machine Learning, pp. 6028–6039 (2020)
17. Xiao, Z., et al.: Fedloge: joint local and generic federated learning under long-tailed data. ArXiv abs/2401.08977 (2024)
18. Lu, Y., et al.: Federated learning with extremely noisy clients via negative distillation. ArXiv abs/2312.12703 (2023)
19. Yang, S., Park, H., Byun, J., Kim, C.: Robust federated learning with noisy labels. IEEE Intell. Syst. **37**, 35–43 (2022)
20. Wu, N., Yu, L., Jiang, X., Cheng, K.T., Yan, Z.: Fednoro: towards noise-robust federated learning by addressing class imbalance and label noise heterogeneity. In: International Joint Conference on Artificial Intelligence, pp. 4424–4432 (2023)

Graph Representation-Aware Online Aggregations over Knowledge Graph

Jingyi Qiu[1], Aibo Song[1(✉)], Tongwei Liu[2], Tianbo Zhang[1], Yongjian Wang[1], and Kun Zhao[3]

[1] School of Computer Science and Engineering, Southeast University, Nanjing, China
`{jingyi_qiu,absong,tianbozhang,kingyongjian}@seu.edu.cn`
[2] School of Cyber Science and Engineering, Southeast University, Nanjing, China
`twliu@seu.edu.cn`
[3] Nari Technology Co., Ltd., Nanjing, China
`zhaokun@sgepri.sgcc.com.cn`

Abstract. Knowledge graphs, as databases that represent knowledge in a graph structure, offer abundant resources for numerous applications. This paper is dedicated to the online aggregations tailored for knowledge graphs. Online aggregations refer to execute aggregate queries in real-time through factoid query processing and unbiased sampling, their efficiency and accuracy are often limited by the factoid queries. To overcome these hurdles, this paper proposes online aggregations incorporated with graph representations. We first design a graph representation model that fuses long-neighbor attention to provide better representations for the online aggregations on knowledge graph. Furthermore, a distribution feature elimination of representations for unbiased sampling and a two-stage sample pruning for irrelevant samples filtering are designed, thereby reducing the computation for the aggregate queries. By merging online aggregations with graph representations, an unbiased estimators are introduced, along with the confidence interval of the estimated result on the samples. Experimental results demonstrate that our model can efficiently return effective aggregate query results with guaranteed relative error, successfully tackling existing challenges for online aggregations on knowledge graphs.

Keywords: Graph representation · Knowledge graph · Online aggregations · Long-neighbor attention · Distribution feature elimination

1 Introduction

Knowledge graphs abstract real-world knowledge into a graph format, with nodes representing entities and edges denoting relationships. In recent years, knowledge graphs are increasingly revealing their potential across various applications and

T. Zhu et al. (Eds.): KSEM 2025, LNAI 15920, pp. 14–27, 2026.
https://doi.org/10.1007/978-981-95-3052-6_2

driving industry growth [1]. Querying serves as a core between databases and downstream tasks, attracting significant attention in knowledge graph research.

Knowledge graph queries fall into factoid queries and aggregate queries. Factoid queries retrieve precise information based on specific attributes or keywords, returning entities that match the query conditions, such as "query the horror movies released in 2020". In contrast, aggregate queries focus on statistical analyses for entities that satisfy query conditions, often utilizing aggregate operations like SUM, COUNT and AVG to uncover the distribution of the dataset, e.g., "calculate the average score of horror movies released between 2015 and 2020". Aggregate queries play a vital role in practical applications, with query logs containing a substantial portion of aggregate queries [2]. Yet, their execution often relies on numerous factoid queries, which undoubtedly increases the time complexity of the querying process. In fact, users often do not require an absolutely precise answer but rather preferring a quick and credible approximate answer. To this end, online aggregations have been developed, which involve unbiased sampling to execute factoid queries, result estimation and the accuracy verification. The detailed workflow is depicted in Fig. 1.

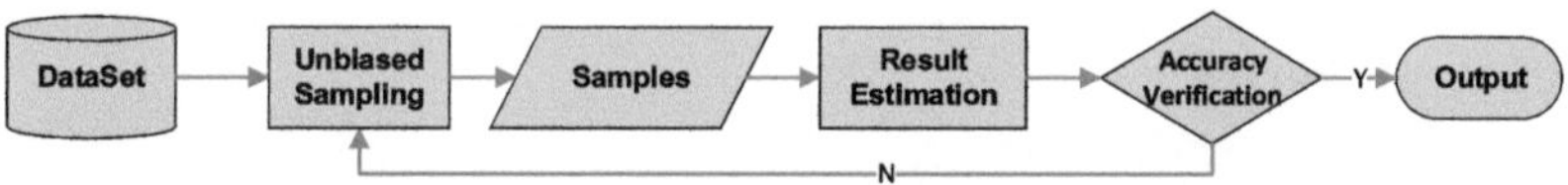

Fig. 1. The basic architecture of online aggregations

Existing methods of online aggregations cannot be directly applicable to the knowledge graph due to two primary reasons: Firstly, knowledge graphs are stored as triples, which make it challenging to conduct unbiased sampling. Most current graph-based sampling algorithms prefer high-degree nodes, leading to inaccurate estimations and poor performance. Secondly, result estimation and accuracy verification are challenging but crucial for accurate aggregate querying. The inherent difficulty in estimating results and analyzing accuracy guarantees stems from the absence of unbiased sampling. Biased result estimation and accuracy verification methods may result in a complete scan of the data, thereby significantly impacting the efficiency of online aggregation.

To address the above limitations, this study employs graph representation models that embed entities and relationships into a low-dimensional vector space. This embedding strategy reduces computational requirements while preserving structural and semantic information for large-scale knowledge graphs. Initially, we explore a graph representation model that fuses long-neighbor attentions, incorporating rich contextual information from multi-hop neighborhoods to boost the model's expressiveness. Consequently, we propose an online aggregation model for knowledge graphs that leverages graph representations, enabling the rapid calculation for aggregate queries. We design an unbiased sampling strategy specifically for knowledge graph representations. Subsequently, we efficiently prune the low-quality nodes from unbiased samples based on the representations. Then we design unbiased estimators and derive confidence intervals for the estimated results. The main contributions are listed as follows:

- We propose a graph representation model for online aggregations, which introduces long-neighbor attentions into the graph attentions mechanism, resulting in learned representations integrating more extensive and long-term information.
- We present a graph representation-aware online aggregations algorithm, which achieves unbiased sampling and sample pruning, finally providing estimated results and confidence interval to guarantee the effectiveness of queries.
- Extensive experiments are designed to validate the effectiveness of the graph representations and online aggregation algorithm proposed in this paper.

The organization of this paper is as follows: Sect. 2 discusses the current research in online aggregations and graph representations. Section 3 introduces the methodology proposed in this paper. Sections 4 and 5 present the experimental results and the conclusion of this study, respectively.

2   Related Work

Online Aggregations. In relational data, online aggregations research has focused on reusing historical results [3] and sharing samples [4] to enhance efficiency. For online aggregations in knowledge graph, earlier methods fall into RQL/SPARQL-based [5] and subgraph matching-based techniques [6]. However, these methods are not only influenced by the quality and response time of factoid query results but also fail to effectively evaluate the quality of query results. With the emergence of graph representation model, some researchers have started to explore the use of graph representations to address aggregate query problems. Literature [7] proposes an approximate query method for COUNT queries on incomplete graph data, which estimates inaccessible nodes based on accessible ones, but struggles to measure result accuracy. Overall, current research on knowledge graph online aggregations heavily relies on factoid query results, lacking robust methods for ensuring result accuracy.

Graph Representations. Graph representations refer to embed nodes and relationships into a low-dimensional vector space, greatly facilitating the effective utilization of graph structure for downstream tasks. Early methods utilized adjacency matrices and matrix factorization to conduct node representations [8,9]. However, matrix-based limitations in time and space complexity hinder their scalability to large graphs. Inspired by word embedding in natural language processing, graph representation methods based on translational invariance have emerged, such as TransE [10] and its variant models [11–13]. Nevertheless, they always face limitations in fully exploring the rich semantic information within nodes. To address this issue, researchers have incorporated attentions mechanisms to optimize node representations by weighting the information of neighbor nodes, such as GAT [14], HAN [15] and GC-LSTM [16]. In general, those methods leverages multi-layer neural networks to deeply mine the potential semantic information of the graph. Nonetheless, only directly connected nodes are considered in the single-layer networks, making it difficult to capture hidden relationships between multi-hop nodes.

3   Methodology

This section presents the graph representation-aware online aggregations over knowledge graph. By incorporating graph representations into the online aggregations, our method efficiently provides aggregate query results with confidence interval. The framework of the model is shown in Fig. 2. Initially, a graph representation model that integrates long-neighbor attentions is devised to embed the knowledge graph into vectors. Secondly, a distributed feature elimination algorithm is utilized to randomize the representations, achieving efficient unbiased graph sampling. Based on the graph representations, low-quality samples that do not satisfy the query conditions are rapidly pruned by two stages. Correct answers meeting query conditions are extracted from the remaining samples using the knowledge graph and utilized to estimate results of the aggregate query. Additionally, a confidence interval is proposed as a guarantee of the accuracy. The process is then iteratively refined to improve the effectiveness of the aggregate query until the user's requirements are satisfied.

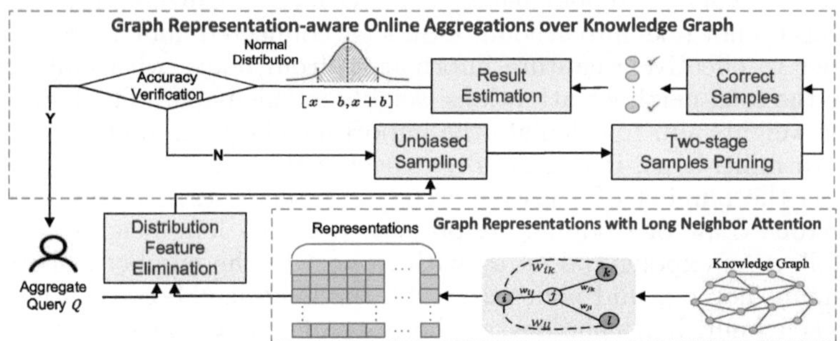

Fig. 2. The framework of graph representation-aware online aggregations

3.1   Graph Representations with Long-Neighbor Attentions

This paper initially transforms knowledge graph into a flexible and computationally convenient vector form through graph representations. Graph attentions mechanisms stand out among other graph representation models due to their iterative updating of node features through weighted aggregation of neighbor nodes, resulting in improved performance. Nonetheless, this approach disregards the relationships between multi-hop nodes and focuses on directly connected nodes within a single-layer neural network, which also contains abundant contextual information. To tackle this problem, we investigate a graph representation model that incorporates long-neighbor attention, aiming to boost the model's expressive capabilities. We start by providing important definitions.

Definitions. Given a knowledge graph $G(V, E, \phi)$, where V and E represents the node set and the edge set, respectively. The function $\phi : V \to \Pi$ denotes the mapping function of node types, where Π is the set of node types, i.e., $\forall v \in V$, $\phi(v) \in \Pi$. As for graph representations, for $\forall v \in V$, there is a function f that can transform the node v as a F-dimensional vector, i.e., $f(v) = \mathbf{h}_v$, where the symbol $\mathbf{h}_v$ denotes the representation of node v.

Long-neighbor Attentions Model. We first present the existing graph attentions network. For $\forall u, v \in G$, the attentions weight w_{uv} represents the importance of node v to node u, i.e., $w_{uv} = \mathsf{LeakyReLU}(\mathbf{a}^T[\mathbf{h}_u||\mathbf{h}_v])$ if $(u, v) \in E$, otherwise $w_{uv} = 0$. Here, $\mathbf{a} \in \mathbb{R}^{2F}$ represents a single-layer feedforward neural network with trainable parameters, $\mathsf{LeakyReLU}(\cdot)$ denotes the nonlinear activation function. Symbol $||$ represents the concatenated operations between vectors.

Existing graph attentions mechanisms can adaptively capture the weights of different neighbor information and better handle complex relationships between nodes. However, they only consider the features of directly connected neighbors and neglect the indirectly connected nodes. As illustrated in graph attentions module in Fig. 2, only the node pairs with the solid lines have attentions' weight, i.e., the directly connected node pairs (i, j), (j, k), (j, l). Current graph attentions mechanisms do not take into account indirectly connected node pairs (i, k), (i, l).

In order to effectively capture information from nodes with multi-hops, we introduce the long-neighbor attentions weights in this paper. The long-neighbor attentions weights aim to calculate the importance between nodes that are connected with multi-hops. It is generally expected that attentions weights should decrease as the number of hops between nodes increases. Drawing inspiration from Newton's Law of Cooling, we propose that the long-neighbor attentions weights follow an exponential decay with respect to the number of hops. Given the maximum hop d_M and nodes $u, v \in G$, the long-neighbor attentions weight w'_{uv} for each multi-hop neighbor at the hops of $d_{uv} < d_M$ can be calculated as $w'_{uv} = w_{uv} \times e^{-\gamma \cdot d_{uv}}$. The parameter γ is the hop decay coefficient. Subsequently, the attentions weights are normalized using softmax function and the representation $\mathbf{h}_u$ for node u is generated.

$$a_{uv} = \mathsf{Softmax}(w'_{uv}) = \frac{e^{w'_{uv}}}{\sum_{v' \in \mathcal{N}_u} e^{w'_{uv'}}}, \quad \mathbf{h}_u = \mathsf{Sigmod}(\sum_{v \in \mathcal{N}_u} a_{uv}\mathbf{h}_v) \tag{1}$$

where $\mathcal{N}_u$ denotes the set of neighbor nodes of node u. The graph neural network leverages a multi-head attentions mechanism to conduct N iterations to update a_{uv} and $\mathbf{h}_u$. Finally, we obtain the representation of the node by calculating the average the representations of each iterations, i.e.,

---

Algorithm 1: Graph Representation-aware Online Aggregations

Input: Knowledge Graph G, Graph Representations $\mathbf{H}_G$, Aggregate Query Q, User Input Relative Error ϵ, Confidence Level $1 - \alpha$
Output: Estimated Result x, Confidence Interval $[x - b, x + b]$

1 $\tilde{\mathbf{H}}_G = \mathsf{DFE}(\mathbf{H}_G)$;
2 $S \leftarrow \emptyset$, $R \leftarrow \emptyset$, $x \leftarrow 0$;   // Initialization
3 **while** $b > x \cdot \epsilon/(1 + \epsilon)$;   // Result Verification
4 **do**
5     $\Delta R \leftarrow \mathsf{RandomSampling}(\tilde{\mathbf{H}}_G)$, $R \leftarrow R \cup \Delta R$;
6     $\Delta S \leftarrow \mathsf{TwoStagePrune}(\mathbf{H}_G, Q, \Delta R)$;
7   Collect correct answers $\Delta S'$ from pruned ΔS;
8   Calculate local result by Eq (2) ;   // Local Estimation
9   Update global result by Eq (3);   // Global Estimation
10   Estimate result x by Eq (4);
11    $b \leftarrow \mathsf{accuracyVerify}(x, \alpha, \epsilon)$;   // Confidence Interval
12 **return** $x, [x - b, x + b]$

$\mathbf{h}_u = \mathsf{Sigmod}(\frac{1}{N} \sum_{n=1}^{N} \sum_{v \in \mathcal{N}_u} a_{uv}^n \mathbf{h}_v^n)$, where a_{uv}^n and $\mathbf{h}_v^n$ are the value of a_{uv} and $\mathbf{h}_v$ in the n-th iterations. The loss function is designed to ensure that the graph representation model can accurately predict the types of the node. In this paper, we employ the cross entropy loss. Based on this, new representations expand the aggregation scope of nodes only within a single layer, i.e., only a single layer enables the model to capture deeper structural and semantic information in the knowledge graph.

Long-neighbor attentions is indispensable for aggregate queries due to the numerous multi-hop relations between entities in such queries. Consider the query "Count papers from VLDB authored by individuals from China." This query requires locating a subgraph in G structured as "VLDB-paper-author-China." Graph representations with long-neighbor attentions facilitate the easier retrieval of the correct match of the paper type node. Both the representations of the VLDB and China display higher similarities with the representations of the correct paper node, despite the two-hop distance between China and the correct paper node. Long-neighbor attentions ensures that the representations preserve nodes with multi-hops, which is advantageous for efficient querying.

3.2   Graph Representation-Aware Online Aggregations Algorithm

If applying the random sampling, the structure of knowledge graphs frequently causes the collected samples to inadequately fulfill the query conditions. However, conduct graph sampling leads to difficulties in setting unbiased estimators for estimating results on samples. To address this, this paper constructs a graph representation-aware online aggregations algorithm for knowledge graphs. The algorithm is outlined in Alg. 1, and its steps are listed as follows:

- To achieve the unbiased sampling on graph structures, we have designed a Distribution Feature Elimination (DFE) algorithm based on the representations, which enables an efficient unbiased sampling for graphs (lines 1–5);

- A two-stage samples pruning is devised for each sample, rapidly filtering out low-quality ones based on connectiviy, thereby enhancing the efficiency (line 6);
- To ensure accuracy, we design unbiased estimators and provide the confidence interval of the estimated results (lines 7–11).

Distribution Feature Elimination of Representations. Typically, unbiased samples are obtained through random sampling from graph. Nonetheless, this approach suffers from low efficiency and affects the overall query performance. To tackle this problem, we have developed a DFE algorithm in this section. This algorithm preserves sample randomness while transforming random node sampling into sequential sampling, resulting in an efficient unbiased graph sampling. All the representations are divided by the type of nodes. Assuming we have a representations $\mathbf{H}_G^\pi$ for type π (each row stores a representation of a node with type π) and an initial partition granularity U_j, the DFE algorithm proceeds with the following detailed steps, depicted in Fig. 3.

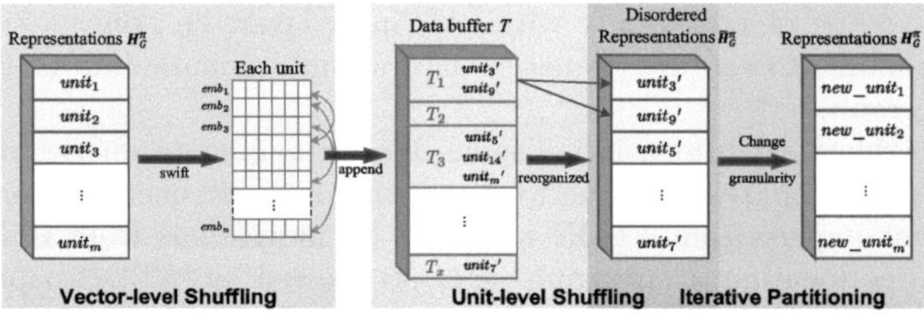

Fig. 3. Distribution feature elimination of representations

- Vector-level shuffling. It divides all the representations into $m = \lceil |\mathbf{H}_G^\pi|/U_j \rceil$ units of equal capacity. Each unit is then sequentially processed by scanning through its vectors and randomly swapping each vector $\mathbf{h}$ with another random vector $\mathbf{h}'$ until the end of the unit is reached. This shuffling disrupts the order of vectors within the units, thus ensuring the randomness of the data in each unit.
- Unit-group shuffling. Once the data within each unit has been disordered, this unit is appended to a randomly select data buffer. After all the units have been appended in the data buffer, they are reorganized in the buffer set $T = \{T_1, T_2, \cdots, T_x\}$ because units are allocated into the randomly selected data buffer, ensuring the random distribution of units within $\mathbf{H}_G^\pi$.
- Iterative partitioning. It resets a suitable unit size U_{j+1} and repeats the above process, partitioning the representations $\mathbf{H}_G^\pi$ for K times with varying granularities to achieve complete randomization of the representation distribution.

After obtaining the fully randomized representations, our module initiates the sampling process from a random starting point and sequentially extracts multiple unsampled units from the unit groups. These units constitute the sample set R for the following online aggregations.

Two-stage Samples Pruning. This section aims to prune nodes from the unbiased sample set R that do not satisfy the query conditions. We propose a pruning model to eliminate low-quality nodes based on their representations. In general, nodes in a query are highly interconnected in G. For instance, given the query "Identifying authors who have co-authored papers with Carsten Lutz and Philippe Hanschke," let $C_Q = \{\mathsf{CarstenLutz}, \mathsf{PhilippeHanschke}\}$ denote the set of known nodes, and t_Q represent the target author node. The correct t_Q must be connected to all nodes in C_Q. For $\forall v \in R$, if v is connected to all known nodes, it is likely a correct match. However, determining the existence of paths between v and each known node is challenging. Thus, we utilize graph representations to evaluate connectivity and remove samples lacking paths to all known nodes. The pruning process consists of two stages.

Stage 1: This stage filters nodes irrelevant to the query by representation distances. The target node t_Q's correct match should connect with all known nodes in C_Q, so the nodes presenting high similarity to C_Q are probable matches for t_Q. Graph representations with long-neighbor attentions effectively fuse multi-hops node connectivity, making them ideal for similarity calculations. In this paper, node similarity is quantified by the reciprocal of the total Euclidean distance between representations, defined as $\mathsf{sim}(v, C_Q) = 1/\sum_{c \in C_Q} ||\mathbf{h}_v - \mathbf{h}_c||_2$. K-means clustering segregates similarities into two clusters. The lower similarity cluster is pruned, while the other proceeds to the next stage.

Stage 2: It is challenging to directly filter samples based solely on vector distances. To address this issue, we proposes a connectivity model based on Deep Neural Network (DNN) to make a secondary pruning on sampled nodes. The connectivity model aims to solve a binary classification problem, determining whether there is connectivity between a given query node v and each known node $c \in C_Q$. The pruning model aims to train a DNN $\varphi(\cdot)$. The DNN takes the concatenation of feature vectors $[\mathbf{h}_u || \mathbf{h}_v]$ of two nodes u and v as input, i.e., $\varphi([\mathbf{h}_u || \mathbf{h}_v])$. Then it outputs the probability of the existence of a path between u and v, thereby achieving the classification task of node connectivity. The loss function of the model employs the binary cross entropy loss.

3.3   Result Estimation and Veritification

In this section, we will estimate results based on the unbiased sample R by iteratively adding samples to it. Firstly, we perform the local estimation for the new samples ΔR. Subsequently, these local results are aggregated into the global estimation, which utilizes the entire unbiased sample R to estimate the query result. Following this, we calculate the confidence interval of the estimated result. If the estimated result meets the accuracy requirements, it is output; otherwise, the process proceeds to the next round of sampling, result estimation and accuracy verification. The detailed steps are as follows.

Local Estimation. In each iteration, the newly acquired sample set is derived via a two-stage pruning process and returned to G to check if they satisfy the query condition. If they do, the samples are added into the correct sample set $\Delta S'$. During the each round, we first calculate the local estimator as follows.

$$
\begin{aligned}
\mathsf{count}(\Delta S') &= |\Delta S'| \\
\mathsf{sum}(\Delta S') &= \sum_{s_i \in \Delta S'} \mathsf{value}(s_i; Q_a) \\
\Delta\chi^2 &= \sum_{\forall s_i \in \Delta S'} \mathsf{value}(s_i; Q_a)
\end{aligned}
\tag{2}
$$

where $\mathsf{value}(s_i; Q_a)$ is the value of the query attributes Q_a for sample s_i. $\Delta\chi^2$ is the sum squares of the values in $\Delta S'$ on the query attribute, which is also calculated as a local estimator.

Global Estimation. After computing the local estimator for the r-th round, they are aggregated with the results from the previous $r-1$ rounds to calculate the global estimator:

$$
\begin{aligned}
\mathsf{sum}_r(S') &= \mathsf{sum}(\Delta S') + \mathsf{sum}_{r-1}(S') \\
\mathsf{count}_r(S') &= \mathsf{count}(\Delta S') + \mathsf{count}_{r-1}(S') \\
\chi_r^2 &= \Delta\chi^2 + \chi_{r-1}^2
\end{aligned}
\tag{3}
$$

where S' denotes the set of all correct samples, $\mathsf{sum}_r(S')$ represents the global estimator for the SUM operation computed from the first r rounds. Given the unbiased estimators for the SUM, COUNT and AVG operations, denoted as x_{sum}, x_{count} and x_{avg}, their estimated results are presented based on the random sampling as follows.

$$
\begin{aligned}
x_{\mathsf{sum}} &= \frac{|\mathbf{H}_G^\pi|}{|R|} \cdot \mathsf{sum}(S') \\
x_{\mathsf{count}} &= \frac{|\mathbf{H}_G^\pi|}{|R|} \cdot \mathsf{count}(S') \\
x_{\mathsf{avg}} &= \frac{x_{\mathsf{sum}}}{x_{\mathsf{count}}}
\end{aligned}
\tag{4}
$$

Accuracy Verification. To determine whether the current sample has produced an accurate enough result that meets the user's requirements, this paper will calculate the confidence interval of the estimated result x. Given the unbiased estimator, the expectation of the estimated result is $E(x) = \bar{x}$, where $\bar{x}$ is the true result. For the variance of the estimated result, the estimator χ_r^2 from global estimator is substituted into Eq. (5) to obtain the variance σ^2 of the query result, which is based on the $\sigma^2 = E(x^2) - [E(x)]^2$:

$$
\sigma_{\mathsf{op}}^2 =
\begin{cases}
\dfrac{\chi_r^2}{\mathsf{count}_r(S')} - x_{\mathsf{avg}}^2, & \mathsf{op=avg} \\[2ex]
\dfrac{\chi_r^2}{|R|} \cdot |\mathbf{H}_G^\pi|^2 - x_{\mathsf{sum}}^2, & \mathsf{op=count} \\[2ex]
\dfrac{\mathsf{count}_r(S')}{|R|} \cdot |\mathbf{H}_G^\pi| - x_{\mathsf{count}}^2, & \mathsf{op=count}
\end{cases}
\tag{5}
$$

According to the Central Limit Theorem, we have:

$$
P\{|x - \bar{x}| \le b\} = P\left\{ \left| \frac{\sqrt{|R|}(x - \bar{x})}{\sigma} \right| \le \frac{b\sqrt{|R|}}{\sigma} \right\} = 2 \times \Phi\left(\frac{b\sqrt{|R|}}{\sigma} - 1 \right)
\tag{6}
$$

where the function $\Phi(\cdot)$ represents the probability distribution function of the standard normal distribution. Given the confidence level $1 - \alpha$, we can calculate the half width of the confidence interval, i.e., $b = \frac{\sigma}{|R|}\Phi^{-1}(1 - \frac{\alpha}{2})$.

Given the acceptable relative error ϵ that user inputs, the error bound b for the current result x can be calculated. If the error bound b satisfies $b \leq (x \cdot \epsilon)/(1 + \epsilon)$, the current result meets the user's requirements [17], meaning that the exact result $\bar{x}$ falls within the confidence interval $[x - b, x + b]$ with a probability of $100(1-\alpha)\%$. If $b > (x \cdot \epsilon)/(1+\epsilon)$, additional sampling and $(r+1)$-th round are necessary to enhance the result's accuracy until $b \leq (x \cdot \epsilon)/(1 + \epsilon)$.

Table 1. The performance of node classification

Model	Cora		CiteSeer		Pubmed	
	Accuracy	Micro-F1	Accuracy	Micro-F1	Accuracy	Micro-F1
DeepWalk	0.764	0.772	0.679	0.681	0.776	0.768
graphSAGE	0.775	0.781	0.681	0.687	0.776	0.768
GCN	0.802	**0.807**	0.678	0.684	0.769	0.755
GAT	0.791	0.786	0.702	0.682	0.778	0.773
Ours	**0.808**	0.805	**0.710**	**0.697**	**0.787**	**0.784**

4 Evaluation

4.1 Experiment Settings

Systems. In this paper, the system is configured with an Intel®CoreTM i7-8700 CPU 3.20GHz, two NVIDIA RTX 2080Ti GPUs, 32GB of memory, and a 1TB disk. The code is written in Python 3.10.

Dataset. The datasets used in this study cover two main areas: graph representations and online aggregations. For graph representations, three datasets are employed, i.e., Cora[1] CiteSeer[2] and Pubmed[3] As for the knowledge graph for online aggregations, there are two datasets for evaluation: (1) DBLP[4] A knowledge graph containing 26,128 nodes and 119,783 edges; (2) Movielens-1M[5]: A knowledge graph includes movie actors, movie style, user rating information, etc. It consists of 10,477 nodes and 1,000,000 edges.

Baseline. To validate the effectiveness of the graph representation incorporating the long-neighbor attention, we choose DeepWalk [18], GCN [19], graphSAGE [20] and GAT [14] as baselines, which includes the traditional methods

---

[1] https://relational.fit.cvut.cz/dataset/CORA.
[2] http://csxstatic.ist.psu.edu/about/data.
[3] http://www.ncbi.nlm.nih.gov/pubmed.
[4] https://dblp.uni-trier.de.
[5] https://movielens.org.

and novel methods. To assess the efficacy of the online aggregations, we choose the graph query model VF2 [21] and the state-of-the-art graph query model GrandIso2 [22] as baselines.

Parameter Setting. We set the representation dimension to $F = 64$ and the hop decay coefficient to $\gamma = 0.55$. For online aggregations, the confidence level is set to $1 - \alpha = 0.9$, the acceptable relative error $\epsilon = 0.1$.

4.2   Performance of Graph Representations

Performance of Node Classification This section evaluates the performance of the proposed graph representations on node classification. Table 1 presents the experimental results with the best results highlighted in bold. The results demonstrate that our method achieves Micro F1 scores of around 80% on all three datasets. The comparison reveals that the classification performance of our model surpasses existing graph representation models. Only 0.01 Micro F1 improvement induces disproportionately larger enhancement in final query outcomes. This underscores the effectiveness of our approach in integrating long-neighbor attention.

Performance of Cluster Visualization. This experiment conducts a clustering visualization experiment on the Cora. Different cluster groups are color-coded, and nodes are projected onto a two-dimensional space via t-SNE, as shown in Fig. 4. Our proposed graph representation model divides the nodes into seven distinct clusters, with nodes in each cluster being more tightly grouped. Conversely, the GCN and GAT models show inter-cluster mixing and the nodes in clusters by graphSAGE and DeepWalk are more scattered. The comparative results reveal the advantage of our proposed model in node clustering.

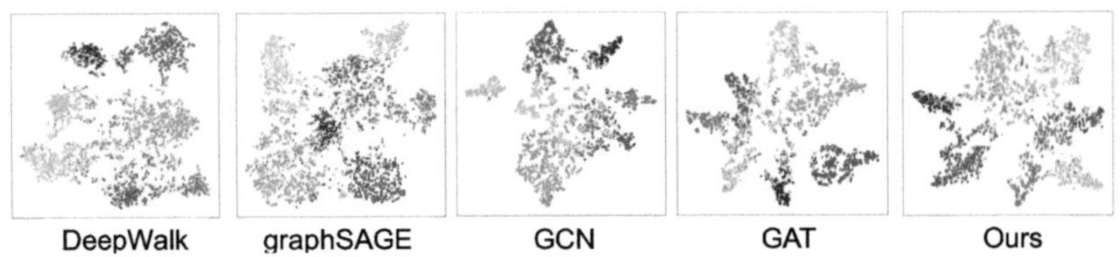

Fig. 4. The performance of cluster visualization on Cora

4.3   Performance of Online Aggregations

For experiments on online aggregations, We randomly generated 300 queries of the same format as shown in Table 2 to conduct experiments. For the DBLP, we sampled queries with the same pattern as Q1, while for the Movielens, we sampled queries with the same pattern as Q2 and Q3.

Table 2. The format of aggregate queries

Index	Operation	Example
Q1	COUNT	How many authors has been published on VLDB?
Q2	SUM	What is the total score of comedy films released between 2000 and 2005?
Q3	AVG	What is the average film critic score for dramas released in 2010?

Table 3. The performance of online aggregations

Model	Q1-shaped		Q2-shaped		Q3-shaped	
	Relative Error	Time	Relative Error	Time	Relative Error	Time
VF2	0%	0.004 s	0%	5.573 s	0%	4.208 s
GrandIso	5.69%	0.011 s	9.62%	3.279 s	4.37%	1.594 s
Ours	1.83%	0.004 s	2.21%	2.964 s	1.95%	1.307 s

The performance and time of the online aggregations are presented in Table 3. The results indicate that our model maintains a relative error of approximately 2.2% or less, providing more accurate results compared to GrandIso. Although our model presents a higher relative error than that of VF2, it offers approximate query results with guaranteed accuracy within a shorter response time. It is noteworthy that the time of our model on Movielens is significantly longer compared to DBLP. This is due to the higher density of the Movielens compared to DBLP, which increases computational complexity.

Effect of Distribution Feature Elimination. To validate the DFE, this study first conducted visual experiments on the distribution of Movielens before and after DFE execution. Figure 5 indicates that following the DFE algorithm, the distributions of both the number of movie viewers and the average rating scores within different data units have become more uniform.

We also implement an ablation model of DFE on online aggregations. The evaluation focuses on sampling ratio and sampling time, with results showcased in Fig. 6. Figure 6 (a) demonstrates that incorporating DFE reduces the sample size for accurate query results to approximately 10%, demonstrating that DFE ensures more unbiased samples. Figure 6 (b) compares sampling response times for each round between traditional methods and unbiased sampling with DFE. The results show over a 1ms reduction in sampling time per round with

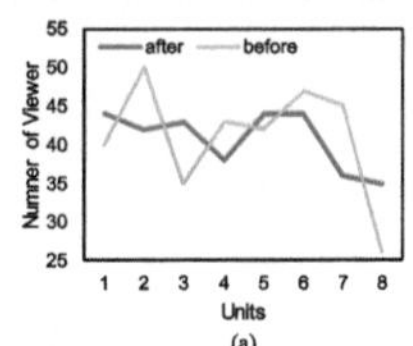
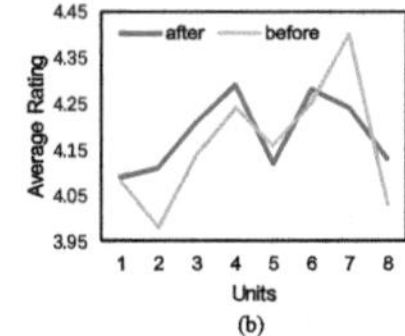
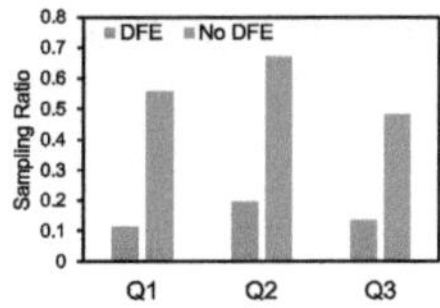
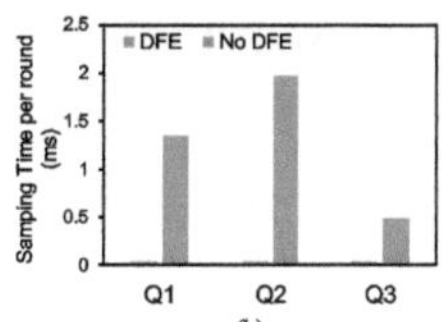

Fig. 5. (a) The number of viewer for movies in each units; (b) The average rating for movies in each units.

Fig. 6. (a) Effect of DFE on sampling ratio; (b) Effect of DFE on sampling time.

Table 4. The effects of confidence level

Confidence	Q1-shaped		Q2-shaped		Q3-shaped	
Level	Relative Error	Time	Relative Error	Time	Relative Error	Time
80%	4.96%	0.001 s	5.83%	0.751 s	4.20%	0.316 s
85%	3.28%	0.002 s	3.69%	1.647 s	3.08%	0.559 s
90%	1.83%	0.004 s	2.21%	2.964 s	1.95%	1.307 s
95%	0.55%	0.019 s	1.26%	8.703 s	0.68%	4.988 s
98%	0.47%	0.045 s	0.75%	13.948 s	0.52%	10.397 s

DFE, significantly cutting down the overall response time. In summary, the DFE notably reduces sampling overhead and validates the query's efficiency.

Effect of Confidence Level. The setting of confidence level influences the relative error and time of online aggregations. In this section, experiments were conducted with confidence levels set at 80%-98% as shown in Table 4.

According to Table 4, higher confidence level yields more precise results, but excessively increases sampling rounds, thereby affecting the query efficiency. A confidence level of 80% results in shorter time but at the expense of a higher relative error in the model. Although the confidence level above 98% can marginally decrease the relative error, it also leads to a substantial increase in response time. As a result, the confidence level is set to 90% in our model.

5   Conclusion

Knowledge graph aims for both efficient and effective online aggregations. Current approaches, still encounter limitations such as inefficient graph index and results' accuracy guarantees. To tackle these limitations, this study introduces an online aggregation approach tailored for knowledge graph based on graph representations. Firstly, we construct a graph representation model that incorporates long-neighbor attention, converting the knowledge graph into a vector form that fuses multi-hop nodes' semantics. Moreover, we design an online aggregation model based on graph representations to conduct unbiased sampling and provide accuracy guarantees efficiently. Experiments show the effectiveness and efficiency of our proposed method.

Disclosure of Interests. The authors have no competing interests to declare that are relevant to the content of this article.

References

1. Yang, S., Han, F., Wu, Y., Yan, X.: Fast top-k search in knowledge graphs. In: ICDE, pp. 990–1001 (2016)
2. Bonifati, A., Martens, W., Timm, T.: An analytical study of large SPARQL query logs. VLDB J. **29**(2), 655–679 (2020)

3. Wu, S., Ooi, B. C., Tan, K. L.: Continuous sampling for online aggregation over multiple queries. In: SIGMOD, pp. 651–662 (2010)
4. Agarwal, S., Mozafari, B., Panda, A., Milner, H., Madden, S., Stoica, I.: BlinkDB: queries with bounded errors and bounded response times on very large data. In: EuroSys, pp. 29–42 (2013)
5. Zou, L., Özsu, M.T., Chen, L., Shen, X., Huang, R., Zhao, D.: GStore: a graph-based SPARQL query engine. VLDB J. **23**(4), 565–590 (2014)
6. Hu, X., Dang, D., Yao, Y., Ye, L.: Natural language aggregate query over RDF data. Inf. Sci. **454–455**, 363–381 (2018)
7. Li, Y., Ge, T., Chen, C. X.: Online indices for predictive top-k entity and aggregate queries on knowledge graph. In: ICDE, pp. 1057–1068 (2020)
8. Koren, Y., Bell, R., Volinsky, C.: Matrix factorization techniques for recommender systems. Computer **42**(8), 30–37 (2009)
9. Roweis, S.T., Saul, L.K.: Nonlinear dimensionality reduction by locally linear embedding. Science **290**(5500), 2323–2326 (2000)
10. Bordes, A., Usunier, N., Garcia-Duran, A., Weston, J., Yakhnenko, O.: Translating embeddings for modeling multi-relational data. In: NIPS, pp. 2787–2795 (2013)
11. Wang, Z., Zhang, J., Feng, J., Chen, Z.: Knowledge graph embedding by translating on hyperplanes. In: AAAI, pp. 1112–1119 (2014)
12. Lin, Y., Liu, Z., Sun, M., Liu, Y., Zhu, X.: Learning entity and relation embeddings for knowledge graph completion. In: AAAI, pp. 2181–2187 (2015)
13. Ji, G., He, S., Xu, L., Kang, L., Zhao, J.: Knowledge graph embedding via dynamic mapping matrix. In: ACL&IJCNLP, pp. 687–696 (2015)
14. Velikovi, P., Cucurull, G., Casanova, A., Romero, A., Liò, P., Bengio, Y.: Graph attention networks. In: ICLR, (2018)
15. Wang, X., et al.: Heterogeneous graph attention network. In: WWW, pp. 2022–2032 (2019)
16. Chen, J., Wang, X., Xu, X.: GC-LSTM: graph convolution embedded LSTM for dynamic network link prediction. Appl. Intell. **52**(7), 7513–7528 (2022)
17. Wang, Y., Khan, A., Xu, X., Jin, J., Hong, Q., Fu, T.: Aggregate queries on knowledge graphs: fast approximation with semantic-aware sampling. In: ICDE, pp. 2914–2927 (2022)
18. Perozzi, B., Al-Rfou, R., Skiena, S.: Deepwalk: online learning of social representations. In: KDD, pp. 701–710 (2014)
19. Kipf, T. N., Welling, M.: Semi-supervised classification with graph convolutional networks. In: ICLR, (2017)
20. Hamilton, W., Ying, Z., Leskovec, J.: Inductive representation learning on large graphs. In: NIPS, pp. 1024–1034 (2017)
21. Cordella, L.P., Foggia, P., Sansone, C., Vento, M.: A (sub) graph isomorphism algorithm for matching large graphs. IEEE Trans. Pattern Anal. Mach. Intell. **26**(10), 1367–1372 (2004)
22. Matelsky, J.K., et al.: DotMotif: an open-source tool for connectome subgraph isomorphism search and graph queries. Sci. Rep. **11**, 13045 (2021)

LWMUNet: Enhancing Semantic Segmentation with Learnable Linked Sliding-Window Serialization

Sizhe Yang, Yutao Qin, and Wei Ren(✉)

School of Computer and Information Science, Southwest University,
Chongqing, China
`oicq@swu.edu.cn`

Abstract. Semantic segmentation requires both precise pixel-level labeling and the ability to capture long-range dependencies. Traditional CNNs struggle with global context modeling, while transformers rely on patch embeddings to reduce their quadratic computational costs, sacrificing fine-grained details. Recently, Mamba has emerged as a promising paradigm for long-range dependency modeling with linear complexity. However, its standard serialization disrupts spatial locality, limiting its effectiveness for image-based tasks. To address these limitations, we propose Linked Window Mamba UNet (LWMUNet), which introduces a novel Linked Sliding-Window Serialization (LSWS) mechanism. LSWS transforms the entire image into a single sequence while preserving spatial locality, ensuring both pixel-level precision and global context retention. Furthermore, to accommodate the diverse locality requirements across tasks, we develop Learnable LSWS (L2SWS), enabling adaptive window configurations. The serialized sequence is then processed by Linked Window Mamba, which serves as the encoder of LWMUNet. Experimental results on MoNuSeg, GlaS, and ISIC-2018 demonstrate that LWMUNet surpasses all baselines, achieving Dice scores of 81.27, 92.09, and 91.21, along with superior IoU and HD95 metrics.

Keywords: Semantic Segmentation · Mamba · UNet · Overlapping Sliding-Window · Serialization · Learnable Configuration

1 Introduction

Semantic segmentation plays a crucial role in computer vision, aiming to label each pixel in an image with a specific category, providing a detailed understanding of the image's content [7]. Traditional CNNs-based models struggle with long-range dependencies due to their limited receptive fields [19]. Transformer-based models [25] excel at capturing long-range context but suffer from quadratic complexity. They have to package pixels into patches [23] to reduce the computational cost, leading to the loss of fine-grained pixel-level details.

T. Zhu et al. (Eds.): KSEM 2025, LNAI 15920, pp. 28–39, 2026.
https://doi.org/10.1007/978-981-95-3052-6_3

Recently, structured state space sequence models (SSMs) [6] (e.g., Mamba [4]) have emerged as a powerful long-sequence modeling approach with linear complexity in terms of input size. However, many Mamba-based models continue to rely on the transformer's patch embedding approach. With Mamba, actually, we could directly model all the pixels in the whole image, preserving pixel-level precision while also capturing long-range contextual dependencies. However, this introduces another challenge: traditional serialization methods along coordinate axes, disrupt the inherent spatial locality of the image, making it challenging for Mamba to model the image effectively [28].

In this paper, we propose Linked Window Mamba UNet (**LWMUNet**) for semantic segmentation, incorporating the core innovation of Linked Sliding-Window Serialization (**LSWS**). LSWS partition the image into overlapping windows then serializes them into a window sequence. Pixels inside each window are serialized into subsequences, and then concatenated in the order of window sequence . Furthermore, to address the variable scope of locality across tasks, we introduce Learnable LSWS (**L2SWS**), enabling the model to autonomously adapt window configurations. Based on that, we designed Linked Window Mamba (LWMamba), a novel Mamba that processes the sequences generated by L2SWS. LWMUNet incorporates LWMamba in its encoder, resulting in improved segmentation outcomes.

Main contributions of this paper are as follows:

(1) **Linked Sliding-Window Serialzation (LSWS):** We introduce a novel serialzation method which serializes the all the pixels in the image into one single sequence, preserving pixel-level details while maintaining locality in the sequence.
(2) **Lernable LSWS (L2SWS):** We further design a learnable mechansim for LSWS, which enables the model to autonomously learn and adapt the window configuration, providing strong cross-task adaptability.
(3) **Linked Window Mamba Unet (LWMUNet):** We propose Linked Window Mamba UNet (LWMUNet), a U-Net architecture that utilizes Linked Window Mamba as its encoder. Simulations on three benchmark datasets: GlaS [22], MoNuSeg [13], and ISIC-2018 [3] show that LWMUNet achieves state-of-the-art performance in terms of Dice scores, IoU, and HD95, demonstrate its ability to capture fine-grained local details while modeling long-range dependencies

2   Related Work

2.1   Limitation of Mamba's Traditional Serialization

As an efficient sequence model, the key to applying Mamba to computer vision tasks is how to serialize an image into a sequence [10]. As illustrated in Fig1(a) and (b), serialization alog one coordinate axis causes the loss of relationship in another, which results in the disruption of spatial locality. Various Mamba variants have attempted to address this issue. VMamba [16] scans images both

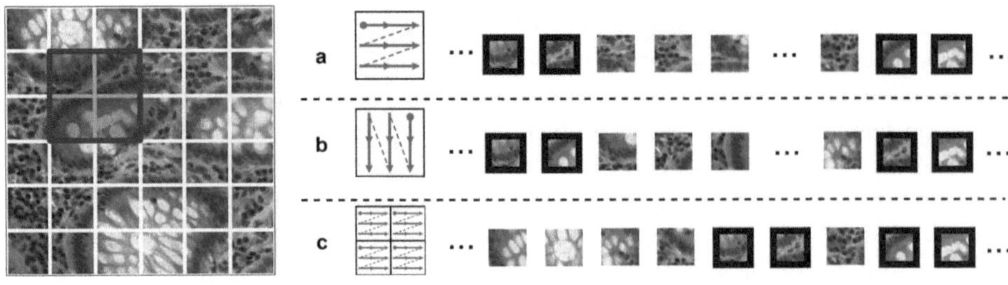

Fig. 1. Illustration of serialzation methods. (a) and (b): Traversing the entire row or column axis resuls in significant distances for neighboring pixels within the same semantic region (e.g., the cell in the image). (c) the windowed serialization without Overlapping enhances the ability to capture local dependencies, but still lacks interactions between the windows.

horizontally and vertically to preserve the 2D structure but still struggles with large or complex images. LocalMamba [10] divides the image into smaller, individual windows without overlapping, enhancing local feature preservation but lacking inter-window interactions, which limits the capture of long-range dependencies.

2.2   The Locality Varies in Different Tasks

The scope of locality in semantic segmentation differs across tasks, primarily due to variations in object size and distribution [9]. For instance, as shown in tab2, in the MoNuSeg [13] dataset, which involves nucleus segmentation, the task requires precise localization of small, densely packed nuclei, emphasizing fine-grained pixel-level details. In the GlaS [22] dataset, gland segmentation necessitates capturing local boundaries and larger structural details, highlighting the need for localized information within a broader context. Lastly, in the ISIC-2018 [3] dataset, skin lesion segmentation requires attention to both local texture details and larger shape information to distinguish lesions from healthy skin. These examples illustrate how the focus on locality varies across tasks, requiring different window scales and strides to maintain it.

3   Method

In this section, we first introduce the Linked Sliding-Window Serialization (LSWS) mechanism, which processes the image through overlapping sliding-window sampling, window serialization, and pixel serialization. Then, we present the Learnable LSWS (L2SWS), which adaptively adjusts window configurations to suit different datasets. Finally, we detail the Linked Window Mamba UNet (LWMUNet), a UNet architecture using Linked Window Mamba as its encoder.

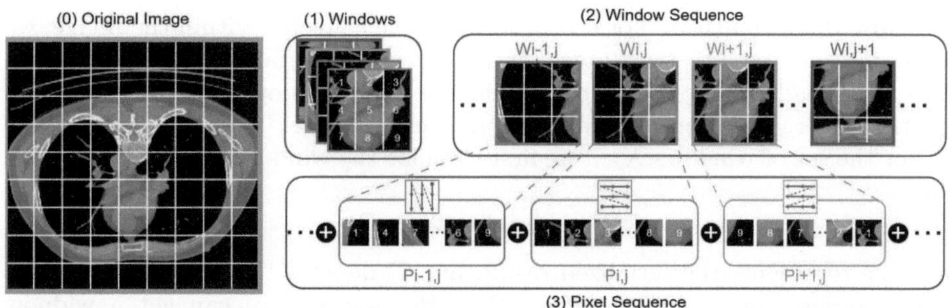

Fig. 2. The process of the Linked Sliding-Window Serialization mechanism (LSWS): (0) The original window waiting to be serialized.   (1) The windows sampled by sliding-window mechanism.   (2) The window is serialized into a window sequence   (3) The pixels internal each window are serialized into subsequences. After that, the pixel-subsequences are concatenated into one single sequence in the order of window.

3.1 Linked Sliding-Window Serialization (LSWS)

As shown in Fig. 2, the Linked Sliding-Window Serialization (LSWS) mechanism consists of three main steps: Firstly, we sample the windows from the input feature map by Overlapping Sliding-Window mechanism. Next, the windows are serialized into window-sequence in a specific order. Finally, the pixels inside each window are serialized into subsequences, then concatenated in the order of the window-sequence.

Overlapping Sliding-Window Sampling As show in Fig2 (1), we begin by extracting windows from the input feature map using an Overlapping Sliding-Window Sampling mechanism. Given an input feature map $X \in \mathbb{R}^{H \times W}$, we apply the sliding window operation to obtain a set of windows:

$$X_{\mathrm{sw}} = \mathrm{slide}(X, K, S) \tag{1}$$

where K represents the window size and S denotes the stride. Specifically, each window W_{ij} is defined by its position in the feature map as:

$$W_{i,j} = [(i-1) \cdot S : (i-1) \cdot S + K, \quad (j-1) \cdot S : (j-1) \cdot S + K] \tag{2}$$

This operation generates a collection of overlapping windows from the input feature map, ensuring spatial continuity between neighboring windows. The overlap between two consecutive windows, W_{ij} and W_{kl}, is computed as:

$$O_{W_{ij}, W_{kl}} = [\max(0, K - (k-i) \cdot S), \max(0, K - (l-j) \cdot S)] \tag{3}$$

where $O_{W_{ij}}$ and $O_{W_{kl}}$ represent the overlapping region between the two windows.

Window Serialization. For serialization of the elements within the image, we divide the process into two stages: external window serialization, which represents the broader sampling direction, and internal window serialization, which governs the organization of details within each window.

For the set of windows X_{sw}, we first serialize the windows in a specific direction:

$$W = \text{Serialize}(X_{sw}, \mathcal{D}) \tag{4}$$

Here, $\mathcal{W}$ represents the serialized result, and $\mathcal{D}$ denotes the serialization direction or order. For example , when $\mathcal{D} = $ Horizontal , we can get a widnow sequence of $[W_{1,1} \quad W_{1,2} \quad W_{1,3} \ldots W_{2,1} \quad W_{2,2} \ldots]$, and when $\mathcal{D} = $ Vertical, $[W_{1,1} \quad W_{2,1} \quad W_{3,1} \ldots W_{1,2} \quad W_{2,2} \ldots]$.

Pixel Serialization and Window Linking. Next, we serialize the pixels into subsequences within each window independently. For a given window $W_{i,j}$, we have:

$$P_{i,j} = \text{Serialize}(W_{i,j}, d) \tag{5}$$

where $P_{i,j}$ represents the serialized pixel subsequence and d denotes the serialization direction. For instance , given $d = $ Horizontal, $P_{i,j} = [p_{i,j} \ p_{i+1,j} \cdots p_{i+K,j+K}]$, and for $d = $ Vertical Reversed , the W_{ij} is serialized into $[p_{i+K,j+K}; p_{i+K,j+K-1} \cdots p_{i,j}]$

Afterward, we concatenate the independent pixel subsequences P , and the order of the subsequence $P_{i,j}$ is determined by $\mathcal{W}$:

$$\mathcal{P} = \text{concat}(P_{i_1,j_1}, P_{i_2,j_2} \cdots) \tag{6}$$

This produces the final pixel sequence $\mathcal{P}$. By now, the windows are linked together, and the entire image is serialized into **ONE** single sequence. In summary , the process can be formulated as :

$$\mathcal{P} = LSWS(X, K, S, \mathcal{D} + d) \tag{7}$$

where $\mathcal{D}+d$ represents the Window-level serialzation direction and the Pixel-level serialzion direction.

3.2   Learnable LSWS (L2SWS)

In LSWS, the use of the Overlapping Sliding-Window Sampling mechanism allows us to effectively preserve the locality of the final sequence. However, the required scope of locality may vary across different datasets. Therefore, selecting the appropriate window configuration becomes a crucial task.

To adaptively adjust the window scale and stride, we first pre-define several window configurations (*window-scale, stride*):

$$\text{Choices} = \{(56, 28), (28, 14), (14, 7), (7, 1), (5, 1), (4, 2), (3, 1), \ldots\} \tag{8}$$

Following the principle of DARTS [14], we transform the discrete selection process into a continuous domain, allowing for the use of softmax probabilities to represent the selection of window configurations :

$$y = \sum_{c \in \mathcal{C}} \frac{\exp(\alpha_c)}{\sum_{c' \in \mathcal{C}} \exp(\alpha_{c'})} \text{LWMamba}_{w_c}(x) \tag{9}$$

where α denotes the learnable param, $\mathcal{C}$ represents the Choices, and $LWMamba$ is the Mamba model utilize LSWS mechanism to operate on image, which we will explain in the next section.

This mechanism enables the simultaneous optimization of both the network parameters and the window selection variable α. The window configuration with the highest selection probability is then chosen. So the entire process can be formulated as follow:

$$\mathcal{P} = L2SWS(X, \mathcal{D} + d) = LSWS(X, K_l, S_l, \mathcal{D} + d) \tag{10}$$

where K_l and S_l represents the learned window size and stride .

3.3 Linked Window Mamba UNet (LWMUNet)

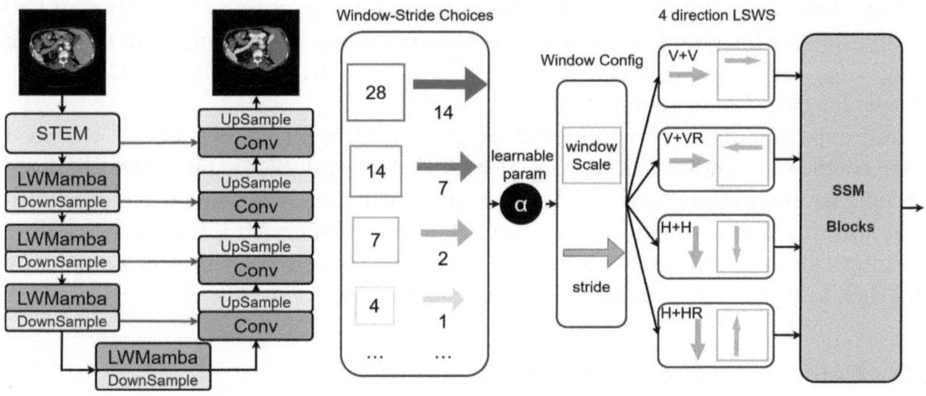

Fig. 3. Left: the architecture of Linked Window Mamba UNet (LWMUNet) Right: the inner process of Linked Window Mamba (LWMamba).

Following the classic UNet architecture, the overview of Linked Window Mamba UNet (**LWMUNet**) is illustrated on the left side of Fig. 3. Let F_l represent the feature map at the l-th layer of the encoder, where l denotes the layer index. The STEM layer, which comprises convolution, normalization, activation, and pooling operations, performs an initial extraction of raw image information. Given an input image $F_{\text{in}} \in \mathbb{R}^{C \times W \times H}$, the STEM layer encodes it into the feature map $F_0 \in \mathbb{R}^{64 \times \frac{H}{2} \times \frac{W}{2}}$. At each subsequent level, the feature map size is reduced by half, and the number of channels doubles, such that for the l-th layer, $F_l \in \mathbb{R}^{(64 \times 2^l) \times \frac{H}{2^{l+1}} \times \frac{W}{2^{l+1}}}$.

The most distinguish feature of LWMUNet lies in its encoder, Linked Window Mamba (**LWMamba**). The inner process of LWMamba is shown in the right part of Fig3. Firstly, a suitable window configuration for LSWS is chosen by the learnable param,   Next, LSWS is used to serialize the image in four directions, including Horizontal + Horizontal, Horizontal + Horizontal Reverse, Vertical + Vertical, and Vertical + Vertical Reverse (window direction + pixel direction). At last, each sequences is modeled individually by Mamba's SSM blocks, and then added together to construct the output Y:

$$Y = \sum_{dir \in Dir} SSM(L2SWS(X, dir)) \tag{11}$$

where Dir represents the four serialization directions mentioned before.

4   Experiments

4.1   Datasets and Implementation Details

We evaluate the proposed Linked Window Mamba UNet with other methods on three widely used datasets: MoNuSeg [13], GlaS [22], and ISIC-2018 [3], whose features have been detailed in the related work. GlaS contains 85 training and 80 testing images for gland segmentation. MoNuSeg has 30 training and 14 testing images for multi-organ nuclei segmentation. ISIC-2018 includes 2,594 training images for skin lesion segmentation.

All experiments were conducted on an NVIDIA RTX 4090 GPU. We used Dice coefficient, Intersection over Union (IoU), and 95% Hausdorff distance (HD95) as evaluation metrics. To prevent overfitting, we applied random flipping and rotation augmentations. The Adam optimizer with a Cosine Annealing learning rate schedule was used, and the loss function combines cross-entropy and dice loss. All input images were resized to 224×224 [26].

4.2   Comparisons of Model Performances

This section provides the simulation results of segmentation accuracy and cost between LWMUNet and the baseline networks on GlaS (165 samples) [22], MoNuSeg (44 samples) [13], and ISIC-2018 (2000+ samples) [3]. The metrics are Dice, IoU and HD95 for segmentation accuracy and Floating-point Operations (Flops), number of parameters (param) and inference time (inf-time) for system cost. Additionally, the optimal window configurations for each dataset, learnet by the L2SWS mechanism, are also detailed in this section.

Table 1. Comparison of Dice, IoU, and HD95 scores across MoNuSeg, GlaS, and ISIC-2018 datasets, and Flops, Param, and Inference Time for different networks

Networks	Flops (G)	param (M)	inf-time(ms)	MoNuSeg			GlaS			ISIC-2018		
				Dice	IoU	HD95	Dice	IoU	HD95	Dice	IOU	HD95
U-Net [20]	9.347	7.767	2.735	77.27	63.51	5.58	85.45	74.78	15.3	88.01	80.65	14.57
MultiResUNet [12]	20.563	78.461	17.580	77.19	64.14	3.34	88.73	80.89	8.87	88.72	81.01	12.7
TransUNet [2]	52.774	56.702	17.511	78.53	65.05	3.34	88.42	80.40	9.10	88.47	80.95	12.02
MedT [24]	44.196	131.572	14.717	77.46	63.37	6.74	85.92	75.47	16.02	87.67	80.03	15.28
SwinUNet [1]	6.126	27.168	7.564	76.32	62.09	2.77	89.58	81.04	8.27	88.45	80.75	12.75
UCTransNet [26]	32.984	66.242	18.629	79.68	67.16	2.72	90.18	81.86	7.55	89.18	83.54	12.37
ACCUnet [11]	34.757	16.876	20.625	75.20	61.76	4.48	88.61	75.24	12.96	87.75	81.99	13.69
VMUnet [21]	7.517	44.274	15.721	79.10	65.95	4.02	86.68	76.23	11.17	89.04	83.75	12.81
SwinUMamba [15]	18.958	28.731	14.157	78.85	65.82	3.85	86.54	76.11	10.25	88.88	83.73	13.01
LKM-Unet [27]	18.596	8.024	9.298	80.24	66.26	3.03	90.98	80.15	7.41	89.99	84.57	11.45
Ours	15.391	6.649	14.254	**81.27**	**68.44**	**2.62**	**92.09**	**81.93**	**6.58**	**91.21**	**84.72**	**9.96**

Table 2. Window Configurations for Different Datasets and Stages, the Configurations Are Represented in the Format of (Window-Scale , Stride)

Stages	MoNuSeg	GlaS	ISIC
1	4,2	28,14	56,28
2	4,2	16,8	28,14
3	14,7	14,7	14,7
4	3,1	7,1	7,1

Simulation Results on Network Accuracy and Cost. Table 1 presents the performance of LWMUNet across three datasets, demonstrating its superior segmentation capabilities. LWMUNet achieves higher **Dice** scores than the second-best model, surpassing it by 1.03 on MoNuSeg, 1.11 on GlaS, and 1.22 on ISIC-2018, which highlights its ability to maintain high consistency with the ground truth. For **IoU**, which reflects object detection ability, it outperforms UCTransNet by 1.28 on MoNuSeg , 0.07 on GlaS and LKM-UNet by 0.15 on ISIC-2018, indicating robust segmentation performance. Additionally, LWMUNet achieves the lowest **HD95** values across all datasets (6.58 on GlaS, 2.62 on MoNuSeg, and 9.96 on ISIC-2018), demonstrating superior edge precision.

Regarding system cost ,with 15.391G Flops, 6.649M parameters, and an inference time of 14.254ms, LWMUNet balances computational efficiency and segmentation accuracy, making it a practical choice for real-world applications.

The Optimal Window Configuration Learned by L2SWS. LWMUNet's strong performance is largely attributed to the adaptive L2SWS mechanism, which dynamically learns the optimal window configurations for each dataset (see Table 2). For **MoNuSeg**, L2SWS prioritizes fine-grained localization by employing smaller windows with larger strides in the early stages, then transitions to larger windows with smaller strides to capture broader contextual relationships. For **GlaS**, it initially sets a window scale of 28 with a stride of 14 to model global structures before refining local details with progressively smaller windows. For **ISIC-2018**, L2SWS follows a consistent halving strategy, ensuring that window sizes remain proportional to the downsampled feature maps. In the final stage, it further refines segmentation by enhancing local interactions between adjacent windows.

In summary, the L2SWS mechanism endows LWMUNet with the ability to adaptively tailor window configurations to the specific needs of each dataset, thereby enhancing its segmentation performance across diverse tasks.

4.3   Ablation Study

Table 3. Comparison of Different Serialization Methods

Operation			Result		
Window	Overlap	Link	MoNu	GlaS	ISIC
			77.31	89.56	88.83
✓			80.29	90.34	89.02
✓	✓		80.62	90.96	89.30
✓		✓	81.08	91.28	90.11
✓	✓	✓	**81.27**	**92.09**	**91.21**

Table 4. LWMamba encoder vs. other backbones

Backbones	MoNuSeg	GlaS	ISIC
UNet-encoder [20]	77.27	85.45	88.01
ResNet34 [8]	77.70	87.15	88.15
ViT [5]	76.21	86.93	88.21
Swin [17]	76.32	88.58	88.36
ConvNeXt [18]	80.37	90.83	88.27
VMamba [16]	79.10	86.68	89.04
LWMamba	**81.27**	**92.09**	**91.21**

Effectiveness of Linked Sliding-Window Serialization. The LSWS mechanism is composed of three key strategies: (1) utilizing local windows to maintain spatial locality in images, (2) overlapping sampling to enhance interactions between adjacent windows, and (3) linking pixel subsequences in the order of the window sequence to form a single sequence, enabling Mamba to leverage its long-term modeling capabilities. The ablation study results in Table 3 demonstrate the incremental improvements brought by each component.

As shown in Table 3, serializing the entire row or column axis without local windows results in the poorest performance across all three datasets. Next, by applying local windows to serialize the image, a significant improvement is observed, highlighting the importance of preserving locality in semantic segmentation.

Building on the windowed serialization, we further investigate the impact of overlapping and linking. Both methods lead to noticeable performance gains on all datasets. Finally, by integrating all strategies, we construct the Linked Sliding-Window Serialization mechanism, which achieves the best results.

Effectiveness of Serialization Directions in LWMamba. In the Linked Window Mamba, we implement the LSWS with four specific serialization directions (window direction + pixel direction): Horizontal + Horizontal, Horizontal + Horizontal Reverse, Vertical + Vertical, and Vertical + Vertical Reverse.

To explore the impact of these serialization directions, we conducted experiments at two levels. As shown in Table 5, serializing only horizontally or vertically results in a noticeable drop in accuracy. In Table 6, "forward" means the pixel direction is the same as the window's (e.g., Horizontal + Horizontal), while "reverse" means the opposite (e.g., Vertical + Vertical Reverse). Using only forward or reverse directions fails to achieve satisfactory performance. By combining all four directions, LWMamba can effectively capture the spatial structure, leading to improved segmentation results.

Table 5. LWMamba's Serialization Directions at the Window Level

Direction	MoNuSeg	GlaS	ISIC
Horizontal	80.67	91.85	90.58
Vertical	80.73	91.70	90.54
H + W	81.27	92.09	91.21

Table 6. LWMamba's Serialization Directions at the Pixel Level

Direction	MoNuSeg	GlaS	ISIC
forward	80.87	91.43	90.12
reverse	80.71	91.39	90.05
f + r	81.27	92.09	91.21

Effectiveness of LWMamba's Encoder. LWMUNet employs LWMamba as its encoder. We compare LWMamba with other widely-used backbones to evaluate its advantages. The results are summarized in Table 4.

The compared encoders include popular and classic backbones. UNet's encoder, ResNet34 and ConvNeXt are convolutional backbones; ViT, Swin are transformer-based backbones; VMamba is the newly proposed Mamba backbone The baseline model for comparison is UNet, a widely adopted architecture in image segmentation.

As shown in Table 4, LWMamba achieves the highest Dice scores on all three datasets, with 81.27 on MoNuSeg, 92.09 on GlaS, and 91.21 on ISIC. These results demonstrate the superior performance of LWMamba compared to other backbones. Notably, LWMamba outperforms the second-best model by a significant margin on the large-scale ISIC-2018 dataset, highlighting its effectiveness in handling complex segmentation tasks.

5   Conclusion

In this paper, we introduced Linked Window Mamba UNet (LWMUNet), a novel architecture that leverages our innovative Linked Sliding-Window Serialization (LSWS) mechanism to convert the entire image into a unified sequence while preserving spatial locality. Additionally, our Learnable LSWS (L2SWS) adapts window configurations to meet diverse task requirements. By processing this sequence with the Linked Window Mamba encoder within a UNet framework, LWMUNet achieves superior segmentation performance on multiple benchmarks, as demonstrated by our extensive experimental results.

References

1. Cao, H., et al.: Swin-unet: Unet-like pure transformer for medical image segmentation. In: Proceedings of the European Conference on Computer Vision Workshops (ECCVW) (2022)
2. Chen, J., et al.: Transunet: rethinking the u-net architecture design for medical image segmentation through the lens of transformers. Medical Image Analysis **97**, 103280 (2024). https://doi.org/10.1016/j.media.2024.103280, https://www.sciencedirect.com/science/article/pii/S1361841524002056
3. Codella, N., et al.: Skin lesion analysis toward melanoma detection 2018: A challenge hosted by the international skin imaging collaboration (isic) (2019). https://arxiv.org/abs/1902.03368
4. Dao, T., Gu, A.: Transformers are SSMs: generalized models and efficient algorithms through structured state space duality. In: International Conference on Machine Learning (ICML) (2024)
5. Dosovitskiy, A., et al.: An image is worth 16x16 words: Transformers for image recognition at scale. ICLR (2021)
6. Gu, A., Goel, K., Ré, C.: Efficiently modeling long sequences with structured state spaces. In: The International Conference on Learning Representations (ICLR) (2022)
7. Guo, Y., Liu, Y., Georgiou, T., Lew, M.S.: A review of semantic segmentation using deep neural networks. Int. J. Multimed. Inform. Retrieval **7**, 87–93 (2018)
8. He, K., Zhang, X., Ren, S., Sun, J.: Deep residual learning for image recognition. In: Proceedings of the IEEE Conference on Computer Vision and Pattern Recognition, pp. 770–778 (2016)
9. Hodgson, M.E.: What size window for image classification? a cognitive perspective. PE & RS- Photogram. Eng. Remote Sens. **64**(8), 797–807 (1998)
10. Huang, T., Pei, X., You, S., Wang, F., Qian, C., Xu, C.: Localmamba: visual state space model with windowed selective scan. arXiv preprint arXiv:2403.09338 (2024)
11. Ibtehaz, N., Kihara, D.: Acc-unet: A completely convolutional unet model for the 2020s. In: Greenspan, H., Madabhushi, A., Mousavi, P., Salcudean, S., Duncan, J., Syeda-Mahmood, T., Taylor, R. (eds.) Medical Image Computing and Computer Assisted Intervention – MICCAI 2023, pp. 692–702. Springer Nature Switzerland (2023)

12. Ibtehaz, N., Rahman, M.S.: Multiresunet: rethinking the u-net architecture for multimodal biomedical image segmentation. Neural Netw. **121**, 74–87 (2020)
13. Kumar, N., et al.: A multi-organ nucleus segmentation challenge. In: International Conference on Medical Image Computing and Computer-Assisted Intervention (MICCAI) (2017)
14. Liu, H., Simonyan, K., Yang, Y.: Darts: Differentiable architecture search. arXiv preprint arXiv:1806.09055 (2018)
15. Liu, J., et al.: Swin-umamba: Mamba-based unet with imagenet-based pretraining. arXiv preprint arXiv:2402.03302 (2024)
16. Liu, Y., et al.: Vmamba: visual state space model. Adv. Neural. Inf. Process. Syst. **37**, 103031–103063 (2025)
17. Liu, Z., et al.: Swin transformer: Hierarchical vision transformer using shifted windows. In: Proceedings of the IEEE/CVF International Conference on Computer Vision, pp. 10012–10022 (2021)
18. Liu, Z., Mao, H., Wu, C.Y., Feichtenhofer, C., Darrell, T., Xie, S.: A convnet for the 2020s. In: Proceedings of the IEEE/CVF Conference on Computer Vision and Pattern Recognition, pp. 11976–11986 (2022)
19. Romero, D., et al.: Towards a general purpose cnn for long range dependencies in nd. Workingpaper (Jun 2022), first two authors contributed equally to this work
20. Ronneberger, O., Fischer, P., Brox, T.: U-net: Convolutional networks for biomedical image segmentation. In: Medical Image Computing and Computer-Assisted Intervention (MICCAI), pp. 234–241 (2015). https://doi.org/10.1007/978-3-319-24574-4_28
21. Ruan, J., Li, J., Xiang, S.: Vm-unet: Vision mamba unet for medical image segmentation (2024). https://arxiv.org/abs/2402.02491
22. Sirinukunwattana, K., et al.: Gland segmentation in colon histology images: the glas challenge contest. In: International Conference on Medical Image Computing and Computer-Assisted Intervention (MICCAI) (2017)
23. Trockman, A., Kolter, J.Z.: Patches are all you need? arXiv preprint arXiv:2201.09792 (2022)
24. Valanarasu, J.M.J., Oza, P., Hacihaliloglu, I., Patel, V.M.: Medical transformer: gated axial-attention for medical image segmentation. In: de Bruijne, M., et al. (eds.) MICCAI 2021. LNCS, vol. 12901, pp. 36–46. Springer, Cham (2021). https://doi.org/10.1007/978-3-030-87193-2_4
25. Vaswani, A., et al.: Attention is all you need. In: Advances in Neural Information Processing Systems. vol. 30 (2017). https://papers.nips.cc/paper/7181-attention-is-all-you-need
26. Wang, H., Cao, P., Wang, J., Zaiane, O.R.: Uctransnet: rethinking the skip connections in u-net from a channel-wise perspective with transformer. Proceedings of the AAAI Conference on Artificial Intelligence **36**(3), 2441–2449 (Jun 2022). https://doi.org/10.1609/aaai.v36i3.20144, https://ojs.aaai.org/index.php/AAAI/article/view/20144
27. Wang, J., Chen, J., Chen, D.Z., Wu, J.: LKM-UNet: large Kernel Vision Mamba UNet for Medical Image Segmentation . In: proceedings of Medical Image Computing and Computer Assisted Intervention – MICCAI 2024. vol. LNCS 15008. Springer Nature Switzerland (October 2024)
28. Xu, R., Yang, S., Wang, Y., Cai, Y., Du, B., Chen, H.: Visual mamba: a survey and new outlooks (2024)

A Trusted Federated Learning Scheme for Distributed GAN Model Training

Jinge Ma[1,2,3], Zixuan Wang[1], Mingke Chen[1], and Wei Ren[1,4(✉)]

[1] School of Computer Science, China University of Geosciences, Wuhan, China
`20211003691mjg@cug.edu.cn`
[2] Key Laboratory of Data Intelligence and Advanced Computing in Provincial Universities, Soochow University, Soochow, China
[3] Key Laboratory of Data Protection and Intelligent Management (Sichuan University), Sichuan, China
[4] Provincial Key Laboratory of Multimodal Perceiving and Intelligent Systems, Jiaxing University, Jiaxing, China
`weirencs@cug.edu.cn`

Abstract. This paper presents a blockchain-based incentivised federated learning GAN model developed to enhance privacy, security and efficiency in collaborative training setups. The framework allows multiple participants to collaboratively train a robust model while maintaining privacy. The blockchain ensures that the distribution of rewards is transparent and immutable, thereby increasing the security of the system. The experimental results demonstrate the effectiveness of our approach in protecting privacy, resisting complex attacks, and improving training efficiency through dynamic rewards. It also examines the impact of different reward values on training outcomes and validates the effectiveness of the incentive mechanism. Future research will investigate the potential of advanced cryptography to enhance the security and integrity of blockchain transactions, with the aim of extending the model to multi-task learning, thereby broadening its applicability across domains and larger datasets.

Keywords: Federated learning · GAN · Blockchain · Security

1 Introduction

In the era of big data, the demand for training deep models is rapidly increasing. Deep learning plays a key role in applications such as medical diagnostics, financial risk analysis, and personalised recommendations. However, efficiently training models without exposing sensitive data remains a major challenge, especially in multi-party collaborations. Federated learning addresses this by enabling participants to train models locally and share parameters instead of raw data, preserving privacy while improving model generalisation.

Generative adversarial networks (GANs) use a generator and a discriminator in an adversarial setup to produce realistic data. In sensitive domains like medical

T. Zhu et al. (Eds.): KSEM 2025, LNAI 15920, pp. 40–52, 2026.
https://doi.org/10.1007/978-981-95-3052-6_4

imaging and finance, centralised data storage is impractical. Federated GANs allow distributed training across nodes without sharing raw data, enhancing privacy. However, they remain vulnerable to security threats such as backdoor attacks. In this study, we experimentally compare federated GANs with existing methods, including MGAN [2], FedGAN [3], and FL-GAN [4]. Results show our method significantly outperforms others in resisting backdoor attacks.

For instance, federated learning and blockchain now enable banks to detect and block fraudulent transactions in real-time while protecting customer privacy. Federated GANs allow multiple financial institutions to collaboratively train anti-fraud models without data sharing. However, compliance costs, operational complexity, and data heterogeneity remain major challenges. Blockchain technology offers a solution with its immutability and transparency, enabling secure model updates and data exchanges. Smart contracts further automate model deployment, enhancing efficiency and reducing fraud risk.

This paper presents a blockchain-based incentivised federated learning GAN model that enhances security, incentivisation and efficiency:

1. **Enhanced Security for Federated GAN**: Integrates specific protocols to defend against threats such as backdoor attacks, validated through comparative experimentation.
2. **Blockchain-Based Misbehavior Avoidance**: Encourages participation by rewarding data owners and trainers per training iteration, ensuring transparency and security via blockchain.
3. **Optimization of Resources and Training Efficiency**: Proposes dynamic resource allocation based on rewards, improving training efficiency and resource use, confirmed by experiments.

The rest of the paper is organised as follows: Sect. 2 reviews related work. In Sect. 3, the proposed method is presented. The experimental results and analysis are presented in Sect. 4. Section 5 concludes the paper.

2   Related Work

Federated Learning, Blockchain, and Generative Adversarial Networks represent key advancements in modern machine learning and secure computing.

FL enables multiple clients to collaboratively train models while keeping data local, preserving privacy. It optimises a global loss function based on the average of individual client losses [5]. FedAvg [6] initiated distributed learning but struggled with non-IID data. Methods like SCAFFOLD [7], FedFix [8], and momentum-based techniques [9] improved robustness and convergence. Recent works on federated bilevel optimisation (FedMBO) further enhanced training efficiency. Overviews by Bonawitz et al. [10] and adaptive communication strategies [11] have improved scalability. Applications in healthcare [12] underscore FL's relevance to privacy-preserving machine learning.

Blockchain ensures decentralised and secure data management via cryptographically linked blocks and consensus mechanisms. Smart contracts automate agreements but face security risks. Tools like DefectChecker [13] and Oyente help identify vulnerabilities [14]. With the rise of NFTs, new issues have emerged, addressed by tools such as NFTGuard. Protocol-level security of Bitcoin and Ethereum remains a focus [15,16]. Strengthening blockchain security is essential for trust and resilience.

GANs transform generative modelling by training a generator G and a discriminator D adversarially [17]. Innovations like StyleGAN [18] introduced fine-grained image control, while disentangled representations and transformer-based editing improved flexibility. Techniques like Wasserstein GANs [19] enhanced fidelity and diversity. These advances have expanded the capabilities of controllable and realistic data generation.

Collectively, FL, blockchain, and GANs exemplify the evolution of distributed, secure, and generative computing, addressing critical needs for privacy, security, and creativity in modern data-driven applications.

3   Proposed Method

In this article, we propose a blockchain-based incentivised federated learning GAN. In this section, we first present the overall structure of the model, and then provide detailed descriptions of the various participating parties.

3.1   Notations

We list the notations used throughout this paper in Table 1.

Table 1. Used notations and their meanings.

Notation	Meaning
Reward_t	Reward value paid by the client at the tth iteration
t	Number of times a client updates using the returned gradients
N	Number of valid generators trained by collaborators
Gen^t	Client's generator model at the tth update
score_i^t	The center's score for the ith valid generator
gradient_i^t	The updated gradient for the ith valid generator compared to Gen^t
Deadline^t	Deadline for the tth iteration
$D(\cdot)$	Apply dropout and add noise to the model
$\text{train}_i(\cdot)$	Collaborator i trains on local data
$F(\cdot)$	Set of quantitative metrics
$f_i(\cdot)$	The ith quantitative metric
$\text{valid}(\cdot)$	Generator validity check function

3.2   Overview

Figure 1 depicts the framework of our proposed model, which comprises three types of participants: n client models, m collaborator models, a trusted central server, and a central ledger. Each client and collaborator model has at least one generator and one discriminator. Each participant's local data has similar but different distribution characteristics. In the event that a client attempts to use its generator to generate data with characteristics similar to those observed in a collaborator's data, direct training on the collaborator's dataset is not feasible due to privacy concerns. In such a scenario, the involvement of the central server is required.

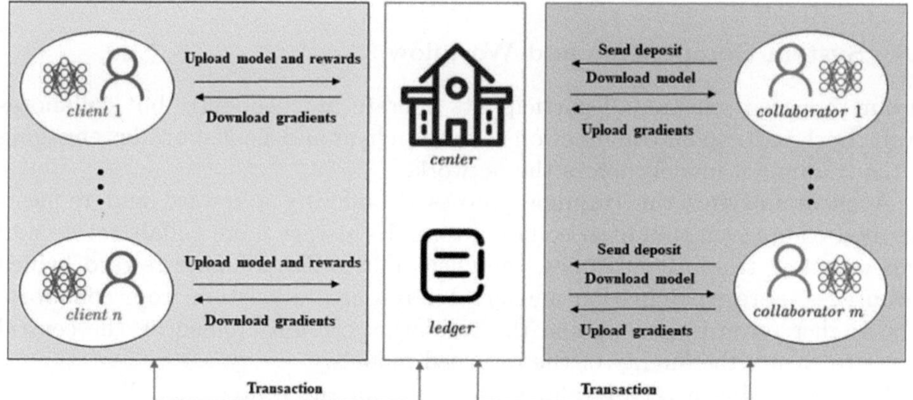

Fig. 1. The overview of our proposed framework.

The training process is as follows:

Initial Setup: The client initially sends their generator model along with a certain amount of digital currency as a reward to the central server.

Central Server Processing: Upon receipt of the generator and reward, the central server records the transaction and then applies dropout and noise to the generator before awaiting requests from collaborating parties.

Collaborator Participation: Collaborators can actively request to join the training by first sending a certain amount of digital currency as a deposit and requesting a client's generator from the central server.

Generator Handoff: The central server records the transaction, sends the processed generator back to the collaborator, and informs them of the reward amount provided.

Local Training by Collaborators: Collaborators utilise the discriminator and generator prepared for the corresponding client to train on their local datasets, adjusting their resource allocation based on the size of the reward. Following training, the trained generator is sent back to the central server.

44   J. Ma et al.

Central Server validity and Reward Distribution: Upon receipt, the central server initially assesses the validity of the generator on a range of qualitative metrics. If a sufficient number of valid generators are received or the deadline is reached, the server transmits all the gradients back to the client. The central server then distributes the rewards to the collaborators based on the performance of their generators on various metrics, with the distribution and transaction details recorded on the blockchain.

In our methodology, the reward value provided by the client directly determines the validity of the training. Higher reward values incentivise collaborators to allocate more resources, allowing them to earn a larger share of the rewards. Additionally, a higher reward value also leads the central server to apply stricter criteria when assessing the validity of the generators returned by collaborators.

3.3   System Components and Workflow

In our proposed scheme, all participants operate independently but collaboratively. Each participant can function as both a client and a collaborator, engaging in the training of models across the network.

A client initiates the training process by offering a reward and requesting model improvements from collaborators. To attract more collaborators and achieve better training outcomes, the client must offer a higher reward, which encourages more participation and greater resource allocation from collaborators. Higher rewards also tighten the validation criteria applied by the central server to ensure the quality of the returned models.

Upon receiving a set of valid gradients from the center, the client is also furnished with corresponding scores that reflect the quality of the training. A higher score indicates better training quality. Clients calculate the weights for aggregation using the formula:

$$w_i = \frac{score_i}{\sum_{j=1}^{N} score_j},$$

where $score_i$ is the score of the ith gradient and N is the total number of gradients. Using these weights, the client updates its model as follows:

$$\text{Gen}^{t+1} = \text{Gen}^t + \sum_{i=1}^{N} w_i \times \text{gradient}_i, \tag{1}$$

where Gen^t is the client's generator model at iteration t, and gradient_i represents the ith valid gradient.

Collaborators first estimate whether they can complete the training before the deadline. If not, they abstain from training. Otherwise, they proceed and adjust their resource investment based on the reward size—the higher the reward, the more computational resources (e.g., training threads and iterations) are allocated.

The central server acts as the trusted authority responsible for model distribution, validation, transaction recording, and blockchain management. It evaluates the quality of generator models by comparing the generated data with real data using quantitative metrics such as Wasserstein Distance, Maximum Mean Discrepancy (MMD), and 1-Nearest Neighbor Distance. Since the center lacks its own local dataset, it receives de-identified data from clients and collaborators to protect privacy.

Before training begins, the center collects an equal quantity of de-identified data from all parties. Upon receiving a model and reward from a client, it records the transaction and applies dropout and noise to the model:

$$\text{Gen}' = D(\text{Gen}^t). \tag{2}$$

The center then evaluates the processed model:

$$F(\text{Gen}^t) = \{f_1(\text{Gen}^t), f_2(\text{Gen}^t), \ldots, f_k(\text{Gen}^t)\}, \tag{3}$$

where each f_j denotes a different metric.

Collaborators submit a deposit along with their training request. The center records the transaction and sends the processed model Gen' to the collaborator. After local training, the collaborator returns the updated model:

$$\text{model}_i = \text{train}_i(\text{Gen}'), \tag{4}$$

and the center evaluates the model:

$$F(\text{model}_i) = \{f_1(\text{model}_i), f_2(\text{model}_i), \ldots, f_k(\text{model}_i)\}. \tag{5}$$

The center determines the validity of each model using:

$$f_j(\text{model}_i) \leq \text{valid}(\text{reward}, t) \times f_j(\text{Gen}^t), \quad (j = 1, \ldots, k), \tag{6}$$

where $\text{valid}(\text{reward}, t)$ is a decreasing function that tightens the acceptance criteria as the reward and training iteration t increase.

If a model passes validation, it is accepted as a valid generator. Otherwise, if no valid generators are obtained by the deadline, the center refunds the client and records the event.

For valid generators, the center calculates a set of improvements:

$$Y_i = \text{valid}(\text{reward}_t, t) \times F(\text{Gen}^t) - F(\text{model}_i) = \{y_{i_1}, y_{i_2}, \ldots, y_{i_k}\}. \tag{7}$$

The Y_i vectors are then standardized:

$$\begin{cases} \mu_i = \frac{1}{N} \sum_{j=1}^{k} y_{i_j} \\[2ex] \sigma_i = \sqrt{\frac{1}{N} \sum_{j=1}^{k} (y_{i_j} - \mu_i)^2} \\[2ex] s_{i_j} = \frac{y_{i_j} - \mu_i}{\sigma_i} \\[2ex] x_{i_j} = \sigma(s_{i_j}) = \frac{1}{1 + e^{-s_{i_j}}} \\[2ex] (i = 1, \ldots, N; \quad j = 1, \ldots, k) \end{cases} \tag{8}$$

where x_{i_j} represents the normalized improvement.

Each collaborator's score is then calculated as:

$$\text{score}_i = \sum_{j=1}^{k} x_{i_j}. \tag{9}$$

The gradient for each valid model is computed as $\text{gradient}_i = \text{model}_i - \text{Gen}^t$. The center returns these gradients and scores to the client and distributes rewards proportionally:

$$\text{money}_i = \text{reward}_t \times \frac{\text{score}_i}{\sum_{j=1}^{k} \text{score}_j}. \tag{10}$$

Finally, the center records the outcomes on the blockchain to ensure transparency and traceability. The detailed procedure is summarised in Algorithm 1.

4   Experimental Results and Analysis

In our experiments, we used three datasets: MNIST, CIFAR-10, and ISIC. Both client and collaborator models were based on GANs. We first generated visual samples for qualitative analysis, then performed Hidden-Trigger Backdoor Attacks on our models and existing federated GANs to compare quantitative metrics. Finally, we adjusted reward values to analyse metric trends during training, evaluating the impact of rewards on training efficiency.

4.1   Visualization

During training, one client model and three collaborator models were established, with a maximum reward value of 50. All collaborator models were assumed to be non-malicious. The dataset was evenly divided into four subsets, with each party assigned an equal share. Additionally, 10% of each party's data was sent as non-private data to a trusted central server for collaborator validation.

Figure 2 shows the generated samples on the MNIST and CIFAR-10 datasets. Specifically, Fig. 2 and Fig. 3 present handwritten digit samples at 15 and 30 epochs, respectively. As epochs increased, sample quality improved, although digits with greater curvature, such as 2, 5, and 8, remained relatively blurry. Figure 5c and Fig. 5d display samples from the CIFAR-10 dataset at 25 and 50 epochs. Increased epochs enhanced visual clarity, with Fig. 5d showing noticeable improvement over Fig. 4, though some blurriness persisted.

4.2   Resistant to Backdoor Attacks

Hidden Trigger Backdoor Attacks [1] involve introducing seemingly normal but actually contaminated data during training. This data appears consistent with target category images in pixel space but aligns with source images modified by a trigger in feature space. This allows the backdoor to activate under specific

---

Algorithm 1: Process of the scheme

Input: All collaborators send the same amount of **non-private data** to the center (used for verification)
Output: Updated generator models
for *each client in Clients* **do**
  for $t = 0$ *to* T **do**
    $Center \leftarrow (Gen^t, reward_t)$;   // *client* sends to Center
    Initialize *list* ;   // Store indices of valid collaborator generators
    Center: ;
      $Gen' \leftarrow D(Gen^t)$;   // Apply dropout and noise
      Record transaction, compute $F(Gen^t)$;   // Using Eq. 3
    for *each* $i = 0$ *to* m *in parallel* **do**
      $collaborator_i \rightarrow$ Center: (request, deposit) ;
      $Center \rightarrow collaborator_i: Gen'$;
      while $TRUE$ **do**
        $collaborator_i \rightarrow$ Center: $model_i$;   // Eq. 4
        Compute $F(model_i)$;   // Center side
        if $GetCurrentTime() > Deadline_t$ **then**
            break ;
        else if *Satisfies Eq. 6* **then**
            $list$.append(i) ;
            break ;
        else
            $Gen' \leftarrow model_i$;
            continue ;

    for *each* i *in list* **do**
      $Y_i \leftarrow$ Calculate Eq. 7 with $(Gen^t, model_i)$;
      $gradient_i \leftarrow (model_i - Gen^t)$;
    if $list.length == 0$ **then**
      $Center \rightarrow client: reward_t$;   // Return reward
      break ;
    for *each* i *in list* **do**
      $X_i \leftarrow$ Calculate Eq. 8 with Y ;   // Normalization
      $score_i \leftarrow \sum_{j=1}^{k} x_{i_j}$;   // Eq. 9
      $money_i \leftarrow reward_t \times \frac{score_i}{\sum_{j=1}^{k} score_j}$;   // Eq. 10
      $Center \rightarrow collaborator_i: money_i$;
      Record on blockchain ;
    $Center \rightarrow client: \{gradient_1, \cdots, gradient_N\}$;
    $Center \rightarrow client: \{score_1, \cdots, score_N\}$;
    $Gen^{t+1} = Gen^t + \sum_{i=1}^{N} w_i \times gradient_i$;   // Update using Eq. 1

---

conditions, causing the model to operate according to the attacker's intent while appearing normal during regular operations.

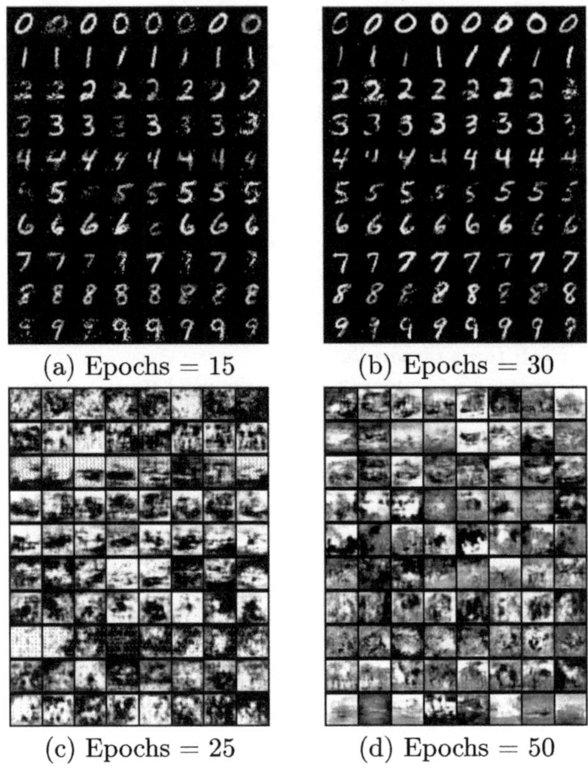

(a) Epochs = 15   (b) Epochs = 30

(c) Epochs = 25   (d) Epochs = 50

Fig. 2. Samples generated on the MNIST (top row) and CIFAR-10 (bottom row) datasets at different epochs.

Table 2. Quantitative comparison of backdoor attack defenses. ↑ indicates better with larger values, ↓ indicates better with smaller values.

	Our Method	MGAN	FEDGAN	Global FL-GAN
MMD ↓	0.02222	0.01613	**0.01612**	0.03175
Wasserstein ↓	1.24975	2.20202	1.86665	**1.17152**
1-NN ↓	**37.0889**	88.8016	76.8652	55.5127
KID ↓	**0.18899**	0.58614	0.45657	0.23130
FID ↓	**299.258**	505.878	472.419	310.296
IS ↑	**2.9576**	1.3614	1.4922	1.3560

Table 2 compares our method with MGAN [2], FedGAN [3], and FL-GAN [4] in defending against Hidden Trigger Backdoor Attacks on the ISIC dataset. Each method was tested with two normal clients and one malicious client, assuming the central server had access to all model datasets.

Our method outperforms the others on most metrics, particularly KID, FID, and IS, indicating better image quality and diversity under attack. It also achieves the lowest 1-NN Distance (37.0889), suggesting stronger feature similarity to the original data and resilience against malicious feature embedding.

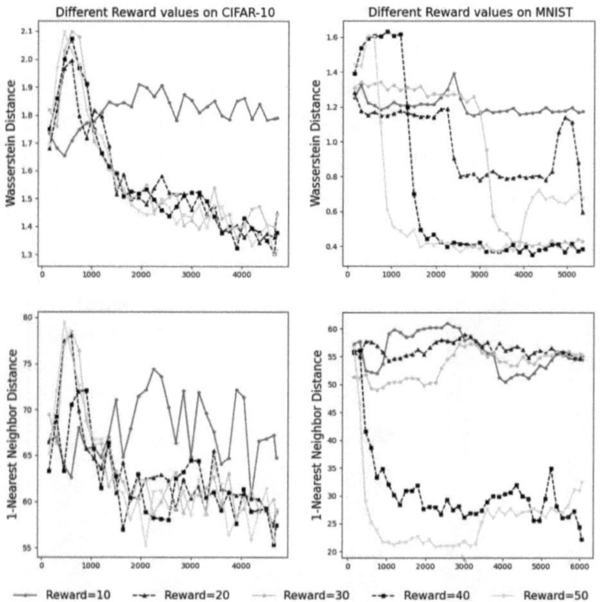

Fig. 3. The impact of different reward values on Wasserstein Distance and 1-Nearest Neighbor Distance on the CIFAR-10 and MNIST datasets.

4.3 Quantitative Analysis of Reward Incentive Validity

To evaluate the effectiveness of reward incentives, one client model, three collaborator models, and a trusted server were set up. The server accessed only non-private portions of the data. Experiments were conducted on the MNIST and CIFAR-10 datasets with reward values set at 10, 20, 30, 40, and 50. Four metrics were used for evaluation: Wasserstein Distance, Maximum Mean Discrepancy (MMD), 1-Nearest Neighbor Distance, and runtime.

Figure 3 shows that higher reward values lead to faster convergence of Wasserstein Distance and 1-NN Distance on both datasets. On CIFAR-10, except for reward 10, the results were largely consistent across different values. In later training stages, fluctuations increased as it became harder for collaborators to meet the training criteria. If they failed to do so before the deadline, the client received no effective feedback.

Table 3 shows that as reward values increase, MMD mean values slightly decrease on both datasets, while variance remains low, indicating stable training performance without significant fluctuations.

Table 3. The impact of different reward values on MMD in CIFAR-10 and MNIST. μ is the mean, and σ^2 is the variance.

Reward Values	MNIST		CIFAR-10	
	$\mu + 0.152$	σ^2	$\mu + 1.52 \times 10^{-4}$	σ^2
10	6.86×10^{-4}	3.92×10^{-5}	4.79×10^{-8}	9.08×10^{-13}
20	2.03×10^{-6}	6.90×10^{-11}	6.81×10^{-8}	1.07×10^{-12}
30	1.31×10^{-6}	8.28×10^{-11}	5.09×10^{-8}	6.94×10^{-13}
40	1.05×10^{-6}	3.45×10^{-10}	8.39×10^{-8}	4.12×10^{-12}
50	8.36×10^{-7}	5.51×10^{-12}	3.16×10^{-8}	3.22×10^{-13}

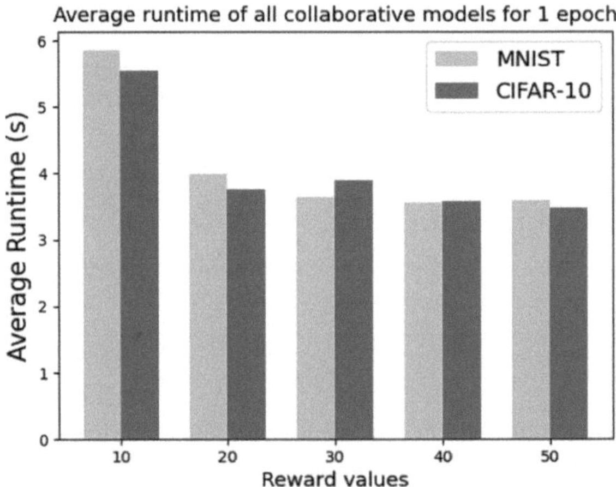

Fig. 4. The average runtime of all collaborative models for 1 epoch under different reward values on the MNIST and CIFAR-10 datasets.

Figure 4 shows that increasing reward values effectively reduces training time, with the most significant drop observed when increasing the reward from 10 to 20, confirming the motivational effect of rewards on training efficiency.

5 Conclusion

This paper introduces a blockchain-based incentivized federated learning model using GAN to enhance privacy, security, and efficiency in collaborative training. Our model effectively addresses key challenges in federated learning, such as data privacy and participant incentives.

Experimental results show that the model excels in maintaining data privacy and resisting complex backdoor attacks. Quantitative measures indicate superior performance in image quality, diversity, and authenticity, reflected in low KID, FID, and 1-NN scores. Additionally, increased reward values are directly linked to improved performance, validating the incentive design.

Future work could explore more advanced encryption techniques to enhance blockchain security and expand the model to support multi-task learning, increasing its applicability across various domains and larger datasets.

Acknowledgement. The research was financially supported by the Key Laboratory of Data Intelligence and Advanced Computing in Provincial Universities, Soochow University (No. KJS2409), Provincial Key Laboratory of Multimodal Perceiving and Intelligent Systems, Jiaxing University (No. MPIS202416), the Key Laboratory of Data Protection and Intelligent Management, Ministry of Education, Sichuan University and also the Fundamental Research Funds for the Central Universities (No. SCU2023D008), and the CCF-NSFOCUS Kun-Peng Scientific Research Fund (No. CCFNSFOCUS2023009).

References

1. Saha, A.e.a.: Hidden trigger backdoor attacks. In: AAAI Conference on Artificial Intelligence (2020)
2. Hoang, Q.e.a.: Mgan: training generative adversarial nets with multiple generators. In: International Conference on Learning Representations (2018)
3. Rasouli, M.e.a.: Fedgan: Federated generative adversarial networks for distributed data. arXiv:2006.07228 (2020)
4. Jin, R.e.a.: Backdoor attack is a devil in federated gan-based medical image synthesis. In: Int. Workshop on Simulation and Synthesis in Medical Imaging (2022)
5. Konecný, J.e.a.: Federated learning: Strategies for improving communication efficiency. arXiv:1610.05492 (2016)
6. McMahan, B.e.a.: Communication-efficient learning of deep networks from decentralized data. In: Artificial Intelligence and Statistics (2017)
7. Karimireddy, S.e.a.: Scaffold: Stochastic controlled averaging for federated learning. In: International Conference on Machine Learning (2020)
8. Fraboni, Y.e.a.: A general theory for federated optimization with asynchronous and heterogeneous clients updates. J. Mach. Learn. Res. (2023)
9. Cheng, Z.e.a.: Momentum benefits non-iid federated learning simply and provably. arXiv:2306.16504 (2023)
10. Bonawitz, K.e.a.: Towards federated learning at scale: system design. In: Proceedings of the Machine Learning Systems (2019)
11. Reddi, S.e.a.: Adaptive federated optimization. arXiv:2003.00295 (2020)
12. Li, J.e.a.: A federated learning based privacy-preserving smart healthcare system. IEEE Trans. Industrial Informatics (2021)
13. Chen, J.e.a.: Defectchecker: automated smart contract defect detection by analyzing EVM bytecode. IEEE Trans. Software Engineering (2021)
14. Atzei, N.e.a.: A survey of attacks on ethereum smart contracts (sok). In: International Conference on Principles of Security and Trust (2017)
15. Tschorsch, F.e.a.: Bitcoin and beyond: a technical survey on decentralized digital currencies. IEEE Commun. Surv. Tutorials (2016)
16. Gervais, A.e.a.: On the security and performance of proof of work blockchains. In: ACM SIGSAC Conference on Computer and Communications Security (2016)
17. Goodfellow, I.e.a.: Generative adversarial nets. In: Adance Neural Information Processing Systems (2014)

18. Karras, T.e.a.: A style-based generator architecture for generative adversarial networks. In: IEEE/CVF Conference on Computer Vision and Pattern Recognition (2019)
19. Arjovsky, M.e.a.: Wasserstein generative adversarial networks. In: International Conference on Machine Learning (2017)

Multimodal Sentiment Analysis with Modality-Robust and -Biased Representations and Distance-Aware Contrastive Learning

Lang Shen[1], Qifei Zhang[1(✉)], Wenjuan Li[2], Minfeng Lu[3], and Xiubo Liang[1]

[1] School of Software, Zhejiang University, Ningbo 315000, Zhejiang, China
`cstzhangqf@zju.edu.cn`
[2] School of Information Science and Technology, Hangzhou Normal University, Hangzhou 311121, Zhejiang, China
[3] School of Modern Information Technology, Zhejiang Polytechnic University of Mechanical and Electrical Engineering, Hangzhou 310053, Zhejiang, China

Abstract. Multimodal Sentiment Analysis (MSA) leverages information from multiple modalities to predict sentiment labels. However, existing approaches often suffer from the challenge of fitting spurious correlations between multimodal features and sentiment labels, with varying degrees of spurious correlations across different modalities. To address this issue, we propose MbrCL, a novel framework that integrates dynamic fusion and distance-aware contrastive learning. The dynamic fusion process is carried out in three steps: (1) disentangling robust and biased features within each modality, (2) estimating the degree of bias using the biased features, and (3) determining implicit and dominant modalities based on bias weights. Implicit modalities are employed to guide the computation of inter-modal correlations. Subsequently, the multimodal features are utilized to compute mixed-modal correlations through our proposed distance-aware contrastive learning, which incorporates affective label distance information. Finally, we identify sentiment-related information using a self-attention mechanism based on mixed-modal correlations and robust features extracted from visual and audio modalities. Experimental results on CMU-MOSI and CMU-MOSEI demonstrate that our model achieves state-of-the-art performance by effectively eliminating the interference of spurious correlations, leading to more accurate sentiment predictions.

Keywords: Multimodal Sentiment Analysis · Contrastive Learning · Feature Decoupling

1 Introduction

During the past two decades, Sentiment Analysis (SA) has seen widespread application across various domains, ranging from consumer product evaluation to

T. Zhu et al. (Eds.): KSEM 2025, LNAI 15920, pp. 53–68, 2026.
https://doi.org/10.1007/978-981-95-3052-6_5

national security. Early research mainly focused on analyzing emotions through users' textual comments [9,16]. However, relying solely on text-based modalities often introduces challenges such as ambiguity and contextual vagueness [2,37]. With the rise of social media platforms, individuals increasingly express their emotions using multimodal information, such as videos and audio [8,19–21]. The inherent cross-modal consistency and complementarity of these multimodal inputs provide richer semantic information for sentiment analysis.

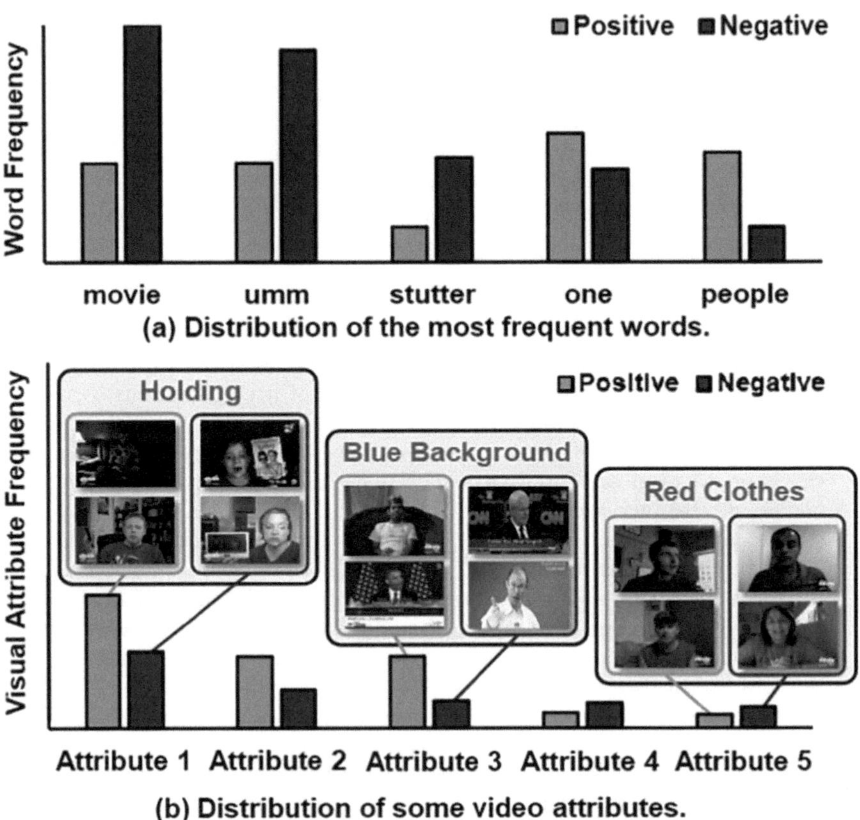

Fig. 1. The distribution of the top-5 most frequent words and visual attributes.

Previous research in multimodal sentiment analysis (MSA) has mainly focused on two aspects: representation learning and multimodal fusion. In terms of representation learning, methods such as adversarial learning [12] and multitask learning [6] have been explored to align and map features from different modalities into a shared representation space. Furthermore, self-supervised learning [33] has been employed to enhance unimodal representations, allowing their integration into fusion models for improved feature learning. On the multimodal fusion front, existing studies have adopted sophisticated fusion mechanisms to capture cross-modal relationships, including tensor-based fusion [34] and graph-based fusion [1]. Furthermore, several studies have explored integrating modalities through pre-trained transformers such as BERT [4] and XLNet [32] to improve the representation and fusion of multimodal features [18,27].

Despite these advances, existing MSA models often struggle with spurious correlations between multimodal features and affective labels. For example, as illustrated in Fig. 1, the word "movie" in Fig. 1(a) and the attribute "blue background" in Fig. 1(b) exhibit strong correlations with negative and positive sentiment labels, respectively. However, these features are unreliable indicators of sentiment. Due to shortcut bias [5], MSA models are prone to learning such spurious correlations, which can lead to suboptimal predictions. Sun et al. [22] highlighted the issue of false correlations between textual features and emotional labels. However, spurious correlations are not exclusive to the textual modality. Similar challenges exist in the video and audio modalities, further complicating the learning process in multimodal sentiment analysis.

In this paper, we propose a novel framework, MrbCL, which incorporates a dynamic fusion strategy to address the challenges of spurious correlations in multimodal sentiment analysis (MSA). The core of the dynamic fusion strategy lies in estimating the bias for each sample through the following three steps: (1) separating robust features (i.e., emotionally-relevant features such as smiles) and biased features (i.e., emotionally-irrelevant features such as blue backgrounds) within each modality; (2) leveraging biased features to estimate sample bias; and (3) identifying the modality with the highest bias weight as the implicit modality (i.e., the modality with the strongest spurious correlation, which will not directly contribute to the final decision), while treating the other two modalities as dominant modalities.

To effectively separate multimodal features for bias estimation, we design three pairs of robust extractors and bias extractors, with each pair dedicated to extracting robust and biased features for a specific modality. While previous studies have commonly employed generalized cross-entropy (GCE) loss [38] to train bias extractors and amplify bias for estimation, GCE loss is not directly applicable to MSA tasks, as these are often framed as regression rather than classification problems [34]. To address this limitation, we propose a novel generalized mean absolute error (GMAE) loss, specifically tailored to remove biased features in regression-based MSA tasks. The estimated bias weight for each biased feature is then computed as the absolute error between the output of the bias extractor and the ground-truth sentiment label. The key intuition here is that biased features with stronger spurious correlations tend to exhibit smaller absolute errors, while less biased features show larger errors. These estimated bias weights are subsequently utilized to adjust the mean absolute error (MAE) loss via inverse probability weighting (IPW), thereby enabling robust feature training.

In our fusion strategy, implicit modalities play a unique role by guiding inter-modal learning indirectly. To achieve this, we design a transformer-based attention module [26] to compute correlations between modalities. Specifically, the transformer takes the implicit modality as the input key-value pair and the dominant modalities as queries. In our framework, the implicit modality is excluded from directly influencing sentiment predictions. Instead, it serves as an indirect guide for learning inter-modal correlations. This design ensures that the influence of implicit modalities is constrained to facilitate better cross-modal learning without directly contributing to sentiment analysis.

The fused multimodal features are further processed through distance-aware contrastive learning to compute mixed-modal correlations. These correlations, combined with the robust features from each dominant modality, are then utilized for final sentiment prediction.

Extensive experiments on two public datasets, MOSEI and MOSI, demonstrate the effectiveness and superiority of our proposed framework in mitigating spurious correlations and enhancing sentiment prediction performance.

The main contributions are summarized as follows:

(1) We propose the MrbCL framework, which introduces a novel Generalized Mean Absolute Error (GMAE) loss to disentangle robust features and biased features. By estimating the bias weights of different modalities, our framework dynamically identifies explicit and implicit modalities, effectively addressing spurious correlations in multimodal sentiment analysis.
(2) We introduce a distance-aware contrastive learning mechanism, which incorporates emotional label distance information to explore and model the mixed-modal correlations among the three modalities, enhancing the effectiveness of inter-modal interactions.
(3) Extensive experiments conducted on two widely-used benchmark datasets, MOSEI and MOSI, demonstrate that the proposed MrbCL framework achieves state-of-the-art performance.

2   Related Works

2.1   Multimodal Sentiment Analysis

In recent years, significant progress has been made in multimodal sentiment analysis (MSA), with numerous studies exploring various approaches. Prior research has primarily focused on two key aspects: representation learning and multimodal fusion. For representation learning, previous studies have employed various strategies, including shift-based models that adjust textual representations based on aligned nonverbal behaviors such as audio and visual modalities [28], shared subspace learning models that map all modalities into modality-invariant and modality-specific representations simultaneously [6], and self-supervised models that generate unimodal labels using self-supervised learning strategies and train models through multitask learning [33]. In terms of multimodal fusion, existing approaches can be categorized based on the stage at which fusion occurs. Early fusion strategies combine features from different modalities at an initial stage [18, 24, 27, 31, 35], while late fusion strategies first learn intra-modal representations and then perform inter-modal fusion at a later stage [3, 11, 34]. Despite the successes achieved by these studies, they often fail to address the issue of spurious correlations between multimodal features and sentiment labels.

2.2   Contrastive Learning

Contrastive learning is an emerging method for self-supervised learning. Its fundamental concept involves bringing the anchor and positive samples closer, while pushing away the anchor and negative samples. In the MSA task, recent works adopt supervised contrastive learning to explore the interactions between or among different modalities. To reduce modality gap in MSA, Mai et al. [13] proposed a hybrid contrastive learning framework. Similarly, Lin et al. [10] proposed a novel hierarchical graph contrastive learning framework, which performs intra-modal and inter-modal graph contrastive learning.

3   Methods

In this section, we present the detailed modules of our MrbCL framework shown in Fig. 2.

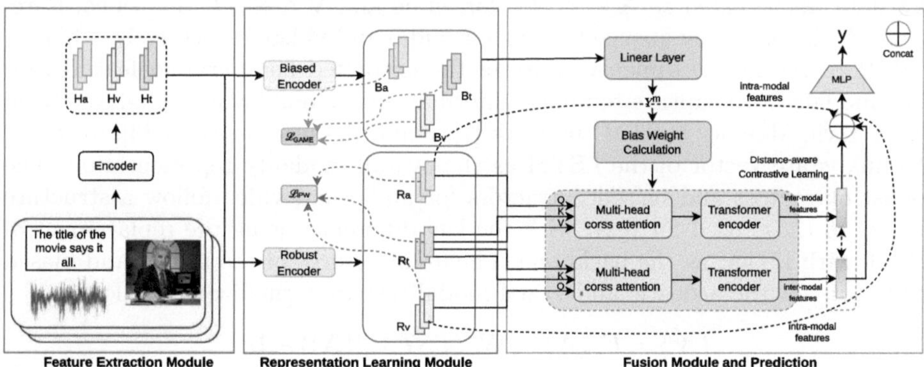

Fig. 2. Overview of our proposed MrbCL. We disentangle robust and biased features within each modality, and calculate the bias weights through the biased features to dynamically determine the implicit modality (In the architecture diagram, the implicit modal assumption is the textual modal.) and dominant modalities. Subsequently, we leverage inter-modal and mixed-modal correlations through a transformer-based attention mechanism and distance-aware contrastive learning. Finally, emotional information is identified based on features derived from the mixed-modal correlations and the robust features extracted from the visual and audio modalities, ensuring a comprehensive and accurate sentiment representation.

3.1   Disentangled Representation Learning

Robust and Biased Extractors. To extract robust and biased features in each modality, we present three pairs of the robust extractors E_R^m and biased extractors E_B^m, $m \in \{t, a, v\}$.

Extractors for Textual Modality. For the textual modality, we leverage the remarkable success of large pre-trained transformer-based language models by employing BERT as the backbone to extract textual representations from raw text. Consistent with prior studies [18], we select the first [CLS] token from the last layer of BERT as the overall textual representation. To further refine the features, we utilize linear layers to project the representations into a low-dimensional semantic space. The raw text T is then passed through the textual robust extractors and textual biased extractors, which generate the robust and biased latent vectors of the text, denoted as $\mathbf{v}_\kappa^t$. The overall structures of the textual robust and biased extractors are formalized as follows:

$$\mathbf{v}_\kappa^t = E_\kappa^t(T) = \mathbf{W}_\kappa^t(BERT_\kappa^t(T)) + \mathbf{b}_\kappa^t, \tag{1}$$

where $\kappa \in \{R, B\}, \mathbf{v}_\kappa^t \in \mathbb{R}^{d_s}, \mathbf{W}_\kappa^t \in \mathbb{R}^{d_s \times d_t}, \mathbf{b}_\kappa^t \in \mathbb{R}^{d_s}$, d_s and d_t denote the dimensions of the latent vectors and BERT's output.

Extractors for Acoustic and Visual Modalities. For the acoustic and visual modalities, we utilize hand-crafted features extracted by Yu et al. [33] from the raw data, represented as $\mathbf{A} \in \mathbb{R}^{l_a \times d_a}$ for audio and $\mathbf{V} \in \mathbb{R}^{l_v \times d_v}$ for video. Here, l_a and l_v denote the sequence lengths for audio and video, respectively, while d_a and d_v represent the dimensionality of the extracted hand-crafted features for each modality. To capture temporal information, we employ a single-layer Long Short-Term Memory (LSTM) network [7]. Following prior work [6,33], we select the final state vector of the LSTM as the overall modality representation. The robust extractors and biased extractors for audio and video follow a structure similar to those used for text, with the key difference being the replacement of BERT with LSTM as the backbone. The architectures of the robust and biased extractors for the acoustic and visual modalities are formalized as follows:

$$\begin{cases} \mathbf{v}_\kappa^a = E_\kappa^a(\mathbf{A}) = \mathbf{W}_\kappa^a(LSTM_\kappa^a(\mathbf{A})) + \mathbf{b}_\kappa^a, \\[2ex] \mathbf{v}_\kappa^v = E_\kappa^v(\mathbf{V}) = \mathbf{W}_\kappa^v(LSTM_\kappa^v(\mathbf{V})) + \mathbf{b}_\kappa^v, \end{cases} \tag{2}$$

where $\mathbf{v}_\kappa^{a/v} \in \mathbb{R}^{d_s}$ denote the robust and biased latent vectors of audio and video, $\mathbf{W}_\kappa^{a/v} \in \mathbb{R}^{d_s \times d'_{a/v}}, \mathbf{b}_\kappa^{a/v} \in \mathbb{R}^{d_s}$, and $d'_{a/v}$ are the dimension of the output of LSTM.

GMAE Loss. To enhance the ability of biased extractors to capture high-quality biased features, we propose the Generalized Mean Absolute Error (GMAE) loss. It is well-known that biased features are easier to learn compared to robust features during the early stages of training [14]. Building on this observation, prior studies have utilized Generalized Cross-Entropy (GCE) [38] loss to train biased models by amplifying the learning of "easier" biases. Specifically, GCE loss encourages biased models to focus on "easier" samples, where there is strong agreement between the model's predictions and the labels, thereby amplifying the model's inherent "prejudice." This is because, in the early training stages, "easier" samples are more likely to contain spurious correlations, allowing the model to make more accurate predictions for such biased samples. However, GCE loss is designed specifically for classification tasks and is not directly applicable to regression tasks like MSA. To address this limitation, we develop the GMAE loss, which is tailored to amplify the biases in regression-based tasks. The proposed GMAE loss is formulated as follows:

$$\begin{cases} Y_B^m = \mathbf{w}_B^m \mathbf{f}_B^m + b_B^m, \\ \mathcal{L}_{GMAE}^m(Y, Y_B^m) = -2\ln(e^{|Y-Y_B^m|} + 1) + 2|Y - Y_B^m|, \end{cases} \tag{3}$$

where $\mathbf{w}_R^m \in \mathbb{R}^{1 \times d_s}$ and $b_B^m \in \mathbb{R}$ are trainable parameters. To calculate GMAE loss, we forward the biased features for prediction, $Y_B^m \in \mathbb{R}$ are the sentiment predictions based on biased features $\mathbf{f}_B^m$.

The gradient of the GMAE loss up-weights the gradient of MAE loss when the sample has a low absolute value between the prediction and the label as follows,

$$\nabla \mathcal{L}_{GMAE}(Y, Y_B^m) = \frac{2}{1 + e^{|Y-Y_B^m|}} \nabla \mathcal{L}_{MAE}(Y, Y_B^m). \tag{4}$$

We assign greater weights to samples that are predicted well by the biased model, i.e., the lower $|Y - Y_B^m|$, the higher $\frac{2}{1+e^{|Y-Y_B^m|}}$. In addition, GMAE loss is able to keep the gradient weight between 0 and 1, which avoids gradient explosion and makes the training process more stable. To sum up, by GMAE loss, a sample with an "easier" biased feature could gain low absolute value and high gradient weight while training, which helps the biased model amplify the "prejudice".

IPW-Enhanced MAE Loss. For the regression task, existing studies mostly utilize MAE loss as follows,

$$\mathcal{L}_{MAE} = |Y - \tilde{Y}|. \tag{5}$$

However, Mean Absolute Error (MAE) loss treats all samples equally, regardless of whether they contain bias or not. When training with MAE loss, robust extractors cannot effectively focus on unbiased samples, as they also acquire biased features from biased samples. To address this issue, it is crucial to train robust extractors to emphasize learning from unbiased samples. The challenge lies in the fact that robust extractors are unable to identify which samples are unbiased, making it difficult to extract robust features directly. A widely used approach to address this problem is Inverse Probability Weighting (IPW) [17], which assigns smaller weights to samples with strong bias during training. By doing so, the robust extractors are guided to focus more on learning the robust features of unbiased samples. To this end, we adopt an IPW-enhanced MAE loss, which re-weights the MAE loss based on the estimated bias weights. This approach allows the robust extractors to prioritize unbiased samples during training. The re-weighted IPW-MAE loss is formulated as follows:

$$\mathcal{L}_{IPW} = \mathcal{L}_{MAE} \cdot \frac{1}{P(x|Bias(x)) + 1}. \tag{6}$$

This IPW implies that if a sample $x = [T, A, V]$ is more likely associated with its biased features, we should underweight the loss to discourage such a biased sample. We calculate $P(x|Bias(x))$ as follows,

$$P(x|Bias(x)) \propto \psi(Y, Y_B^m) \cdot (|Y - \tilde{Y}|), \tag{7}$$

where $\psi(\cdot)$ is illustrated in Eq. 8, and $|Y - \tilde{Y}|$ is the absolute value without gradients.

3.2 Dynamic Fusion

Bias weight Calculation. The biased extractors are trained with amplifying the "prejudice" by GMAE loss so that biased models are good at utilizing biased features for prediction. The more precisely the biased model predicts, the more biased the sample is. Thus, we employ the absolute value calculated between the prediction and the label to measure how much each modality is likely to be biased. The smaller the absolute value, the larger the bias in the modality. Then, we estimate the bias weight of a sample by calculating the minimum or average value of absolute value in each modality and taking the inverse as follows,

$$\begin{cases} \psi_{min}(Y, Y_B^m) = \frac{1}{\min(|Y-Y_B^t|,|Y-Y_B^a|,|Y-Y_B^v|)}, \\ \\ \psi_{avg}(Y, Y_B^m) = \frac{1}{\arg(|Y-Y_B^t|,|Y-Y_B^a|,|Y-Y_B^v|)}, \end{cases} \tag{8}$$

where $\psi(\cdot)$ denotes the bias weight estimation function of a sample, the larger the bias weight is, the more bias a sample has. We regard the two equations in Eq. 8 as $MinStrategy$ and $AvgStrategy$ respectively. We consider that $MinStrategy$ selects the most biased modality to indicate how much a sample is biased and $AvgStrategy$ estimates the bias degree of a sample based on the biased degree of the three modalities simultaneously.

Our dynamic fusion module, utilizes the implicit modality to implicitly guide the inter-modal learning. We perform the inter-modal fusion with a cross-attention module and a transformer encoder [26]. The cross-attention function has three input matrices, Q as query, K as key, and V as value. The standard attention function is formulated as

$$Att(Q, K, V) = \sigma\left(\frac{QW^{(Q)}(KW^{(K)})^\mathsf{T}}{\sqrt{d}}\right) VW^{(V)}, \tag{9}$$

where $W^{(Q)}, W^{(K)}$ and $W^{(V)}, \sigma$ are the linear projection weight matrices of Q, K and V, and the softmax activation function, respectively, and d is the common dimension for three modalities.

Inspired by [24], we explore the inter-modal correlation by involving both the implicit and explicit modalities in the attention operation. The three matrices in our fusion module are from the primary and secondary modalities. Thus the attention function in our fusion module becomes

$$Att(Q^s, K^p, V^p) = \sigma\left(\frac{Q^s W^{(Q^s)}(K^p W^{(K^p)})^\mathsf{T}}{\sqrt{d}}\right) V^p W^{(V^p)}, \tag{10}$$

where the superscripts s and p indicate that the matrices are from the explicit modality and the implicit modality. In other words, we use explicit modalities (Suppose they are audio and visual) as the query and the implicit modality (Suppose it is the text) as key and value in the attention module to enforce the modality invariance on the common space of queries and key-value pairs, as well as reduce the distribution gap between modalities. Finally, we obtain two fusion features, h^{at} and h^{vt}. The former is for the fusion of audio and text, and the latter is for the fusion of visual and text.

As the implicit modality is used as key and value, we reinforce the explicit modality by attending to the correlated elements of the implicit modality in our fusion. Thus the distribution mismatch between different modalities is well bridged. In addition, the implicit modality in our fusion module does not have an independent branch and will not be directly involved in the final prediction. This means that information in the implicit modality can only be propagated forward through the fusion regarding the similarity of the distribution between the modalities. Thus, the shortcut from the implicit modality to the final prediction will be cut off and the distribution of the explicit modality will be forced closer to the implicit modality to obtain more task-relevant information.

3.3 Distance-Aware Contrastive Learning

We apply contrastive learning to mixed-modal features, which are fused with text, to calculate the mixed-modal correlations, as shown in Fig. 3. Previous methods using supervised contrastive learning typically treat the MSA task as a classification problem by dividing sentiment labels into discrete classes and sampling positive and negative samples based on the classes. However, these methods

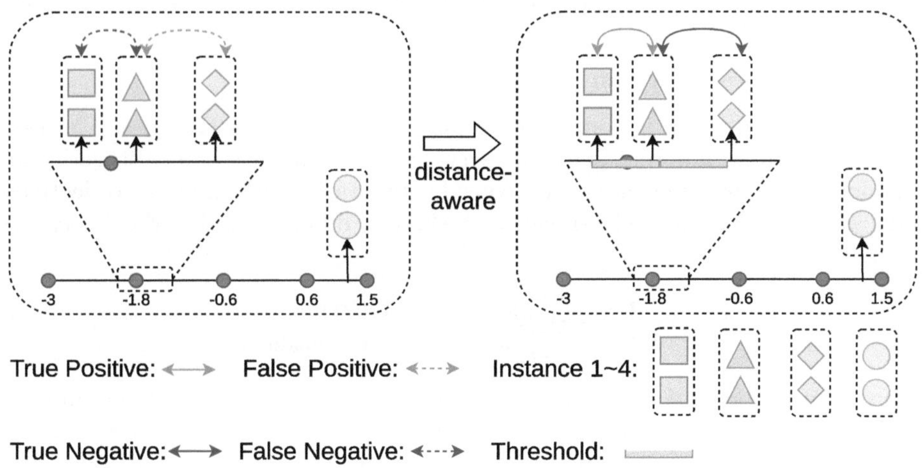

Fig. 3. The distance-aware contrastive learning is proposed to avoid sampling false positive and negative samples by introducing distance information of sentiment labels into traditional contrastive learning.

ignore the continuous nature of sentiment labels and the distance information between them, which can lead to the sampling of false positive and negative samples. For example, the label of instance 2 ($ins.2$) is closer to instance 1 ($ins.1$) than instance 3 ($ins.3$). However, traditional methods would treat $ins.2$ and $ins.3$ as a positive pair and $ins.2$ and $ins.1$ as a negative pair because the labels of $ins.2$ and $ins.3$ are in the same segment. Zolfaghari et al. [39] exclude false negative samples in contrastive learning according to input embeddings. Inspired by this, we introduce distance information of labels into our distance-aware contrastive learning, which allows us to avoid both false positive and negative samples. When it comes to classification tasks, it is important to note that our loss will degenerate into a regular contrastive loss. We select positive and negative samples based on the distance between their labels within a batch. Specifically, we calculate the label distance between the anchor sample and the other samples in the batch. Samples with label distances less than a threshold c are considered positive samples, while those with distances greater than c are considered negative samples.

Formally, the distance-aware contrastive loss $\mathcal{L}_{DACL}$ (based on InfoNCE [15]) can be derived as

$$\mathcal{L}_{DACL}(h_i^{at}, h_i^{vt}) = -\log \frac{\sum_{j \in P} \exp(\Phi(h_i^{vt}, h_j^{at})/\tau)}{\sum_{k \notin P} \exp(\Phi(h_i^{vt}, h_k^{at})/\tau)}, \tag{11}$$

where Φ is a cosine similarity scoring function, T is the temperature, h^{vt} is the fused feature of visual and text, h^{at} is the fused feature of audio and text, P represents the index set of positive samples that are selected based on label distance, and i, j, k represent the indices of different samples. We consider using different fusion pairs as anchors, so the final contrastive loss $\mathcal{L}_{CL}$ is

$$\mathcal{L}_{CL} = \mathcal{L}_{DACL}(h_i^{at}, h_i^{vt}) + \mathcal{L}_{DACL}(h_i^{vt}, h_i^{at}). \tag{12}$$

3.4   Objectives Function

Our objective function is composed of task loss and contrastive loss. The task loss is designed for different tasks and serves as the primary training objective for our model. In our experiments, we consider two tasks with different objectives: a regression task and a classification task. For different tasks, the losses are calculated as

$$\mathcal{L}_{task} = \begin{cases} \frac{1}{N} \sum_i^N |\hat{y}_i - y_i| & \text{for regression} \\ -\frac{1}{N} \sum_i^N y_i \log \hat{y}_i & \text{for classification} \end{cases} \tag{13}$$

where N is the size of a minibatch, y_i and $\hat{y}_i$ represent the true label and the predicted label of the ith sample. For each branch, we use the task loss to guide its training. After the dynamic fusion module, we use the contrastive loss $\mathcal{L}_{CL}$ between the inter-modal features which is described in Eq. 12. The final objective function can be represented as

$$\mathcal{L} = \mathcal{L}_{task} + \lambda \mathcal{L}_{IPW} + \alpha \mathcal{L}_{GAME} + \beta \mathcal{L}_{CL}, \tag{14}$$

where λ, α and β are the weight of IPW loss, GAME loss and the contrastive loss.

4 Experiments

4.1 Datasets

We evaluate our approach on two widely used multimodal sentiment analysis datasets: CMU-MOSI [37] and CMU-MOSEI [1]. CMU-MOSI contains 2,199 opinion segments. Each sample is annotated with a sentiment score on the scale ranging from negative to positive [−3, 3]. CMU-MOSEI comprises 23,453 annotated video clips from 1,000 speakers, each annotated with a sentiment scale from −3 to 3. In our experiments, we utilize the segmentation methods offered by the CMU-Multimodal SDK [36].

4.2 Evaluation Criteria

Following the previous works [6,30,33], we utilize four evaluation metrics to assess the performance of the proposed model. Specifically, we report binary classification accuracy (Acc-2) task and weighted F1 score (F1-Score) for the classification task as well as mean absolute error (MAE) and Pearson correlation (Corr) for the regression task. For Acc-2 and F1-Score, we use the segmentation marker -/- to report the results, with the left score representing "negative/non-negative" classification and the right score representing "negative/positive" classification.

4.3 Comparison with Baselines

To evaluate the rationality and effectiveness of our method, we compare the proposed model with the following recent and competitive baselines: LMF [11], MFM [25], ICCN [23], MISA [6], Self-MM [33], and FDMER [29].

The results compared with baselines on the two datasets are presented in Tables 1 and 2. We have the following observations. Our MrbCL achieved state-of-the-art or comparable results on all metrics on the MOSEI and MOI datasets. Notably, our model shows a significant improvement on the MOSEI dataset, possibly because the larger dataset allows the model to learn more correlations between modes and align them more efficiently.

Table 1. The Experiment Results on CMU-MOSEI

Model	MAE	Corr	Acc-2	F1-Score
LMF	0.623	0.677	-/82.0	-/82.1
MFM	0.568	0.717	-/84.5	-/84.3
ICCN	0.565	0.713	-/84.2	-/84.2
MISA	0.555	0.756	83.6/85.5	83.8/85.3
Self-MM	0.530	0.765	82.81/85.17	82.53/85.30
FDMER	0.536	0.773	86.1/-	85.8/-
MrbCL	**0.528**	**0.787**	**85.23/86.16**	**85.26/85.95**

Table 2. The Experiment Results on CMU-MOSI

Model	MAE	Corr	Acc-2	F1-Score
LMF	0.917	0.695	-/82.5	-/82.4
MFM	0.877	0.706	-/81.7	-/81.6
ICCN	0.860	0.710	-/83.0	-/83.0
MISA	0.783	0.761	81.8/83.4	81.7/83.6
Self-MM	0.713	0.798	84.00/85.98	84.42/85.9
FDMER	0.724	0.788	84.6/-	84.7/-
MrbCL	**0.703**	**0.804**	**85.13/86.0**	**85.08/85.91**

Table 3. Ablation Study on the CMU-MOSEI dataset

Model	MAE	Corr	Acc-2	F1-Score
MrbCL	**0.528**	**0.787**	**85.23/86.16**	**85.26/85.95**
text as implicit	0.533	0.765	83.2/85.7	83.4/85.5
audio as implicit	0.542	0.758	82.80/85.10	82.82/85.33
visual as implicit	0.538	0.761	83.09/85.46	83.14/85.28
w/o-$\mathcal{L}_{IPW}$	0.539	0.762	82.73/85.19	83.42/85.23
w/o-$\mathcal{L}_{GAME}$	0.541	0.765	82.87/85.33	83.45/85.37
w/o-$\mathcal{L}_{CL}$	0.538	0.769	82.96/85.23	83.37/85.16

4.4 Ablation Studies

We conduct a detailed analysis of each component of our framework. These components include dynamic fusion (rows 2-4), Representation Learning (rows 5, 6) and Distance-aware contrastive learning (row 7). All these ablation experiments are performed on the MOSEI dataset. The results of the ablation study are shown in Table 3.

Specified Modality as Implicit Guidance. In our framework, we dynamically select the most biased mode as the recessive mode because we believe that the degree of false correlation of the three modes is constantly changing. Rows 3, 4, and 5 compare the performance of models that use text, audio, and visual modes as recessive modes, and all three show worse results than row 1. These results show that dynamic selection of implicitly guided modes is more effective in reducing spurious correlations.

w/o-$\mathcal{L}_{IPW}$ and w/o-$\mathcal{L}_{GAME}$. After employing the model w/o-$\mathcal{L}_{IPW}$, we can see the performance drops significantly. This phenomenon shows assigning a small weight to a sample with a strong bias for debiasing is indeed indispensable. The setting of w/o-$\mathcal{L}_{GAME}$ obtains worse results than the original model. This is because our proposed GMAE loss can train a model to be biased by amplifying the prejudice. However, the model trained with standard MAE loss not only exploits the biased attribute but also partially learns the robust attribute, which can hurt the debiasing ability of our overall algorithm by estimating the bias of each modality inaccurately.

Distance-Aware Contrastive Learning. With the help of contrastive learning, our framework is able to further obtain mixed-modality correlations. In row 8 of Table 3, we demonstrate the impact of removing the distance-aware contrastive loss on the performance of the model. Our results show that removing this loss will decrease the model's performance in all metrics. Despite the drop, the performance of the model is still comparable to other state-of-the-art methods. This indicates that our preferential fusion strategy is effective, and contrastive learning can further build mixed-modality correlations to improve performance on this basis.

Fig. 4. Two testing cases of the baseline (i.e., Self-MM) and MrbCL on the *neg./pos.* results.

4.5   Case Study

To gain more insights into our model, we randomly selected two cases to explain how the spurious correlations in video modality affect the traditional MSA model and why MrbCL is able to handle such spurious correlations in the testing set. We illustrated the binary *neg./pos.* results of Self-MM and MrbCL on two testing samples from MOSI datasets in Fig. 4.

For instance, in Case 1, the video features a woman with a smile and a white background. Through manual analysis, we found 43 videos in the training set with a white background, among which 17 had positive sentiment labels and 26 had negative sentiment labels. The white background represents a superficial attribute that models can easily capture, leading to spurious correlations with sentiment labels. As a result, traditional MSA models struggle to mitigate these spurious correlations and often predict Case 1 as negative sentiment. In contrast, MrbCL effectively handles such biased cases by focusing on robust features, such as the woman's smile, for sentiment prediction. This highlights MrbCL's strong debiasing ability. A similar observation is evident in Case 2, further validating the effectiveness of the model in reducing the impact of spurious correlations.

5   Conclusion

In this work, we address the issue of spurious correlations between multimodal data and sentiment labels. To mitigate this problem, we propose a novel framework with a dynamic multimodal fusion strategy. Our framework disentangles robust and biased features across textual, acoustic, and visual modalities and estimates bias weights to select an implicit modality, which serves as an indirect guide for multimodal learning. Additionally, we introduce a distance-aware contrastive learning method to capture mixed-modal correlations by leveraging the distance information of sentiment labels. Finally, we evaluate our proposed MrbCL framework on two benchmark MSA datasets, where it consistently outperforms state-of-the-art methods, demonstrating its effectiveness and robustness.

References

1. Bagher Zadeh, A., Liang, P.P., Poria, S., Cambria, E., Morency, L.P.: Multimodal language analysis in the wild: CMU-MOSEI dataset and interpretable dynamic fusion graph. In: Proceedings of the 56th Annual Meeting of the Association for Computational Linguistics (Volume 1: Long Papers) (2018). https://doi.org/10.18653/v1/p18-1208
2. Chen, Y., Yuan, J., You, Q., Luo, J.: Twitter sentiment analysis via bi-sense emoji embedding and attention-based LSTM. In: Proceedings of the 26th ACM International Conference on Multimedia, pp. 117–125 (2018). https://doi.org/10.1145/3240508.3240533
3. Dai, W., Cahyawijaya, S., Liu, Z., Fung, P.: Multimodal end-to-end sparse model for emotion recognition. In: Proceedings of the 2021 Conference of the North American Chapter of the Association for Computational Linguistics: Human Language Technologies (2021). https://doi.org/10.18653/v1/2021.naacl-main.417
4. Devlin, J., Chang, M.W., Lee, K., Toutanova, K.: Bert: pre-training of deep bidirectional transformers for language understanding. In: Proceedings of the 2019 Conference of the North (2019). https://doi.org/10.18653/v1/n19-1423
5. Geirhos, R., et al.: Shortcut learning in deep neural networks. Nat. Mach. Intell. 665–673 (2020). https://doi.org/10.1038/s42256-020-00257-z
6. Hazarika, D., Zimmermann, R., Poria, S.: Misa: modality-invariant and -specific representations for multimodal sentiment analysis. In: Proceedings of the 28th ACM International Conference on Multimedia. Cornell University (2020)

7. Hochreiter, S., Schmidhuber, J.: Long short-term memory. Neural Comput. 1735–1780 (1997). https://doi.org/10.1162/neco.1997.9.8.1735
8. Hu, J., Fang, Q., Qian, S., Xu, C.: Multi-modal attentive graph pooling model for community question answer matching. In: Proceedings of the 28th ACM International Conference on Multimedia, pp. 3505–3513 (2020). https://doi.org/10.1145/3394171.3413711
9. Lei, X., Qian, X., Zhao, G.: Rating prediction based on social sentiment from textual reviews. IEEE Trans. Multimedia 1910–1921 (2016). https://doi.org/10.1109/tmm.2016.2575738
10. Lin, Z., et al.: Modeling intra-and inter-modal relations: hierarchical graph contrastive learning for multimodal sentiment analysis
11. Liu, Z., Shen, Y., Lakshminarasimhan, V.B., Liang, P.P., Bagher Zadeh, A., Morency, L.P.: Efficient low-rank multimodal fusion with modality-specific factors. In: Proceedings of the 56th Annual Meeting of the Association for Computational Linguistics (Volume 1: Long Papers) (2018). https://doi.org/10.18653/v1/p18-1209
12. Mai, S., Hu, H., Xing, S.: Modality to modality translation: an adversarial representation learning and graph fusion network for multimodal fusion. In: Proceedings of the AAAI Conference on Artificial Intelligence, pp. 164–172 (2020). https://doi.org/10.1609/aaai.v34i01.5347
13. Mai, S., Zeng, Y., Zheng, S., Hu, H.: Hybrid contrastive learning of tri-modal representation for multimodal sentiment analysis. IEEE Trans. Affect. Comput. 1 (2022). https://doi.org/10.1109/taffc.2022.3172360
14. Nam, J., Cha, H., Ahn, S., Lee, J.H., Shin, J.: Learning from failure: de-biasing classifier from biased classifier. In: Neural Information Processing Systems (2020)
15. Oord, A., Li, Y., Vinyals, O.: Representation learning with contrastive predictive coding. arXiv:1807.03748 (2018)
16. Pang, B., Lee, L.: A sentimental education. In: Proceedings of the 42nd Annual Meeting on Association for Computational Linguistics - ACL 2004 (2004). https://doi.org/10.3115/1218955.1218990
17. Qi, J., Tang, K., Sun, Q., Hua, X.S., Zhang, H.: Class is invariant to context and vice versa: on learning invariance for out-of-distribution generalization (2022)
18. Rahman, W., et al.: Integrating multimodal information in large pretrained transformers. In: Proceedings of the 58th Annual Meeting of the Association for Computational Linguistics (2020). https://doi.org/10.18653/v1/2020.acl-main.214
19. Soleymani, M., Garcia, D., Jou, B., Schuller, B., Chang, S.F., Pantic, M.: A survey of multimodal sentiment analysis. Image Vis. Comput 3–14 (2017). https://doi.org/10.1016/j.imavis.2017.08.003
20. Sun, T., Jing, L., Wei, Y., Song, X., Cheng, Z., Nie, L.: Dual consistency-enhanced semi-supervised sentiment analysis towards COVID-19 tweets
21. Sun, T., Wang, C., Song, X., Feng, F., Nie, L.: Response generation by jointly modeling personalized linguistic styles and emotions. ACM Trans. Multimed. Comput. Commun. Appl. **18**(2), 1–20 (2022). https://doi.org/10.1145/3475872
22. Sun, T., Wang, W., Jing, L., Cui, Y., Song, X., Nie, L.: Counterfactual reasoning for out-of-distribution multimodal sentiment analysis. In: Proceedings of the 30th ACM International Conference on Multimedia (2022). https://doi.org/10.1145/3503161.3548211
23. Sun, Z., Sarma, P., Sethares, W., Liang, Y.: Learning relationships between text, audio, and video via deep canonical correlation for multimodal language analysis. In: Proceedings of the AAAI Conference on Artificial Intelligence, pp. 8992–8999 (2020). https://doi.org/10.1609/aaai.v34i05.6431

24. Tsai, Y.H.H., Bai, S., Liang, P.P., Kolter, J.Z., Morency, L.P., Salakhutdinov, R.: Multimodal transformer for unaligned multimodal language sequences. In: Proceedings of the 57th Annual Meeting of the Association for Computational Linguistics (2019). https://doi.org/10.18653/v1/p19-1656
25. Tsai, Y.H.H., Liang, P.P., Zadeh, A., Morency, L.P., Salakhutdinov, R.: Learning factorized multimodal representations. In: International Conference on Learning Representations (2019). https://openreview.net/forum?id=rygqqsA9KX
26. Vaswani, A., et al.: Attention is all you need. In: Neural Information Processing Systems (2017)
27. Wang, D., Liu, S., Wang, Q., Tian, Y., He, L., Gao, X.: Cross-modal enhancement network for multimodal sentiment analysis
28. Wang, Y., Shen, Y., Liu, Z., Liang, P.P., Zadeh, A., Morency, L.P.: Words can shift: dynamically adjusting word representations using nonverbal behaviors. In: Proceedings of the AAAI Conference on Artificial Intelligence, pp. 7216–7223 (2019). https://doi.org/10.1609/aaai.v33i01.33017216
29. Yang, D., Huang, S.: Disentangled representation learning for multimodal emotion recognition
30. Yang, J., Yu, Y., Niu, D., Guo, W., Xu, Y.: Confede: contrastive feature decomposition for multimodal sentiment analysis
31. Yang, K., Xu, H., Gao, K.: CM-Bert. In: Proceedings of the 28th ACM International Conference on Multimedia (2020). https://doi.org/10.1145/3394171.3413690
32. Yang, Z., Dai, Z., Yang, Y., Carbonell, J., Salakhutdinov, R., Le, Q.: XLNet: generalized autoregressive pretraining for language understanding
33. Yu, W., Xu, H., Yuan, Z., Wu, J.: Learning modality-specific representations with self-supervised multi-task learning for multimodal sentiment analysis. In: Proceedings of the AAAI Conference on Artificial Intelligence, pp. 10790–10797 (2022). https://doi.org/10.1609/aaai.v35i12.17289
34. Zadeh, A., Chen, M., Poria, S., Cambria, E., Morency, L.P.: Tensor fusion network for multimodal sentiment analysis. arXiv:1707.07250 (2017)
35. Zadeh, A., Liang, P.P., Mazumder, N., Poria, S., Cambria, E., Morency, L.P.: Memory fusion network for multi-view sequential learning. In: Proceedings of the AAAI Conference on Artificial Intelligence (2022). https://doi.org/10.1609/aaai.v32i1.12021
36. Zadeh, A., Liang, P.P., Poria, S., Vij, P., Cambria, E., Morency, L.P.: Multi-attention recurrent network for human communication comprehension. In: Proceedings of the AAAI Conference on Artificial Intelligence (2022). https://doi.org/10.1609/aaai.v32i1.12024
37. Zadeh, A., Zellers, R., Pincus, E., Morency, L.P.: Mosi: multimodal corpus of sentiment intensity and subjectivity analysis in online opinion videos. arXiv:1606.06259 (2016)
38. Zhang, Z., Sabuncu, M.: Generalized cross entropy loss for training deep neural networks with noisy labels. In: Advances in Neural Information Processing Systems (2018)
39. Zolfaghari, M., Zhu, Y., Gehler, P., Brox, T.: CrossCLR: cross-modal contrastive learning for multi-modal video representations. In: 2021 IEEE/CVF International Conference on Computer Vision (ICCV) (2021). https://doi.org/10.1109/iccv48922.2021.00148

DeNoiseFood Dataset with ECAMixDNet: An Efficient Denoising Framework for Complex Textured Food Images

Xin Yuan, Yonghui Chen[✉], Fupan Wang, Ruiying Wang, and Weijie Tang

School of Computer Science and Technology, Southwest University of Science and Technology, Mianyang, China
{yuanxin,wangruiying}@mails.swust.edu.cn,
{chenyonghui,wangfp}@swust.edu.cn

Abstract. Food image denoising faces dual challenges of preserving complex textures while suppressing noise. To address limitations of traditional methods—including fixed receptive fields struggling to capture multi-scale features and up-sampling processes lacking effective noise suppression causing texture blur—this study proposes ECAMixDNet, a hybrid network integrating Swin-Transformer with CNN decoders. The framework introduces a CAMixer dynamic encoding module that adaptively captures irregular food texture features through self-adjusting mechanisms. For feature reconstruction, we innovatively design an Efficient Channel-Aware Mixed Up-sampling (ECAMixUp) method to achieve multi-scale channel noise suppression, effectively reducing high-frequency artifacts. To overcome data scarcity in food denoising research, we constructed the first paired noise-clean food image dataset, DeNoiseFood. Experiments demonstrate that ECAMixDNet preserves critical texture details and color fidelity on DeNoiseFood, outperforming baseline models in PSNR/SSIM metrics. Cross-domain validation on the SIDD dataset confirms its generalization capability, providing robust technical support for food recognition, nutritional analysis, and related applications. The code for this paper can be found at: https://github.com/YX-yy/ECAMixDNet.

Keywords: Food Image Denoising · Dynamic Coding · Efficient Channel-aware Mixed Up-sampling · DeNoiseFood · ECAMixDNet

1 Introduction

Food images serve as the core data carrier for food recognition and nutritional analysis, and their texture clarity and detail integrity directly impact the accuracy of downstream tasks. However, noise contamination during the acquisition process can lead to blurred key textures and edge distortion, necessitating efficient denoising methods. Supervised deep learning methods have made significant progress in denoising natural images: Zhang et al. [1] constructed an end-to-end framework through batch normalization and residual connections; Anwar et al. [2] introduced channel attention to enhance noise sensitivity modeling; MIRNet [3] and MPRNet [4] utilized cascaded attention modules

© The Author(s), under exclusive license to Springer Nature Singapore Pte Ltd. 2026
T. Zhu et al. (Eds.): KSEM 2025, LNAI 15920, pp. 69–82, 2026.
https://doi.org/10.1007/978-981-95-3052-6_6

to expand the model's capacity. However, the inherent inductive bias of CNNs limits their ability for global modeling. The introduction of Transformers (such as SUNet [5] and TECDNet [6]) enhances representational capacity but still presents two major drawbacks:

(1) The preprocessing stage relies on fixed receptive field convolutions, which inadequately capture multi-scale features of irregular textures in food images;
(2) The Up-sampling process lacks a channel noise suppression mechanism, making it prone to introducing high-frequency artifacts. To address this, we propose an efficient channel-aware hybrid denoising network model (ECAMixDNet) based on a collaboration between Swin Transformer and CNN. The core innovations include two aspects:
(1) The introduction of the CAMixer dynamic encoding module [7], which uses a learnable attention mechanism to achieve adaptive capture of multi-scale textures in food images, breaking the static kernel weight limitation of traditional convolutions;
(2) The proposal of an efficient channel-aware hybrid Up-sampling (E-CAMixUp) mechanism, which applies multi-scale channel noise suppression during the feature reconstruction phase, effectively reducing the likelihood of high-frequency artifact generation.

Although existing food image datasets such as Food-101 [8] and Food-172 [9] are widely used for classification tasks, their noise characteristics and the severe lack of paired data significantly hinder supervised denoising research. Therefore, we constructed a food-specific noise dataset, DeNoiseFood, by synthesizing noise at three different levels, covering multiple typical food categories with paired images to support model training.

Experimental results show that the proposed method outperforms several state-of-the-art supervised image denoising methods on the DeNoiseFood dataset. Visualization results verify the advantages of this method in maintaining features such as food image textures and high color sensitivity. Cross-domain generalization experiments on the publicly available SIDD dataset also demonstrate the effectiveness of the proposed method.

2   Related Work

2.1   Food-Specific Noise Dataset DeNoiseFood

The food image dataset constructed in this study consists of two parts:

(1) The original clean images were obtained from the professional photography website Snapper.com, and a total of 150 high-resolution ($\geq 1920 \times 1080$) images were selected, covering diversified food categories such as Chinese and Western food, desserts, etc., and all of the images were captured by a professional photographer under a standardized lighting environment, with accurate image reproduction and clear texture details.

(2) The noise synthesis method adopts a controlled noise injection strategy [10] to superimpose three different Gaussian-pepper hybrid noises on each original image, with the standard deviation of the Gaussian noise set to σ =5/10/15 and the density of the pepper noise corresponding to 5%/10%/15%.

The noise synthesis process is realized by the random noise generation module, and finally a dataset containing 450 noisy images (150 × 3) is formed, whose noise intensity gradient covers light (σ=5), medium (σ =10) and heavy (σ =15) contamination scenarios, which can simulate the composite noise pattern introduced by the sensor thermal noise, low light gain and transmission compression in the shooting of real food products.

This construction strategy not only preserves the high texture complexity and color sensitivity of food images, but also provides a systematic benchmark for robustness validation through the design of multilevel noise intensities. Example of DeNoiseFood is shown in Fig. 1.

Fig. 1. Graphical representation of the DeNoiseFood dataset

2.2 U-Net Architecture Network Based on Swin-Transformer

The use of Swin-Transformer to build networks shaped like U-net architectures [11] is a common approach in image restoration tasks, which captures long-range dependencies and multi-scale spatial features through the hierarchical design of Swin Trans-former modules. The architecture employs a symmetric encoder-decoder structure equipped with jump connections, where each stage builds the Swin Transformer layer through a shift window-based self-attention mechanism to model local and global contextual associations.

In the encoding path, the feature map is progressively down-sampled and the channel dimensions are extended to realize the extraction of hierarchical representations, while the corresponding decoding path employs an Up-sampling operation and combines with the Swin Transformer module to bridge the underlying texture features with the higher-level semantic information through jump connections to progressively recover the high-resolution details.

This design supports effective feature fusion across scales, especially for reconstructing clean images that need to preserve fine-grained details, and inherits the strong adaptability of the U-Net-like framework, which can integrate the attention mechanism or the hybrid convolutional-Transformer module to cope with diverse degradation modes in the denoising task of real scenes. This type of architecture is schematized in Fig. 2.

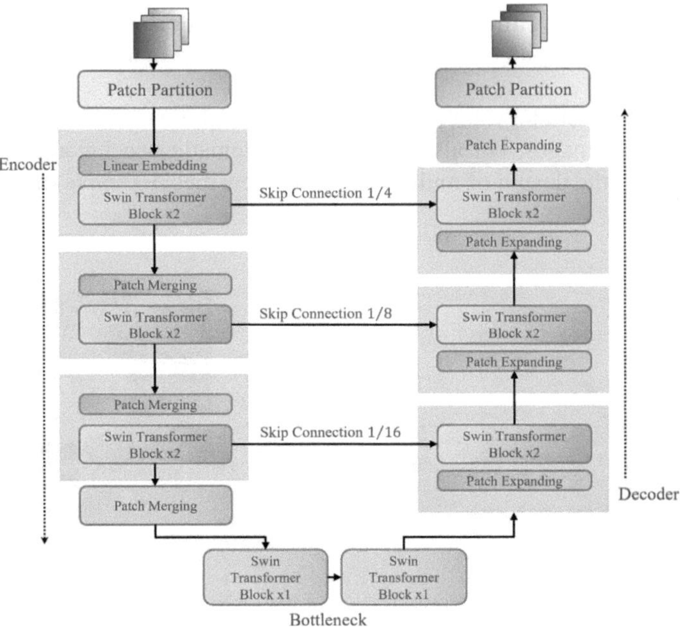

Fig. 2. U-net architecture network based on Swin-Transformer

2.3   Commonly Used Up-Sampling Methods in CV

Up-sampling techniques play an important role in vision tasks for reconstructing high-resolution features from low-resolution representations.

Bilinear interpolation estimates pixel values by weighted averaging of neigh-boring pixels, which is computationally efficient but prone to produce excessively smooth output. Transpositional convolution [12] is able to adaptively recover spatial details by sampling the feature map on a learnable kernel, but may trigger checker-board grid artifacts. Subpixel convolution [13] converts channel features to spatial dimensions through periodic channel rearrangement, which improves resolution with-out introducing training parameters, but still fails to effectively address tessellation artifacts. Dynamic Up-sampling (DUpsample) [14] utilizes a learnable content-aware matrix to maintain semantic consistency to reduce the probability of tessellation artifacts to some extent.

Although these methods are widely used in tasks such as super-resolution and image restoration, for the specific task of food noise image denoising, the lack of a suppression mechanism for the difference in noise distribution between channels still makes it easy to introduce artifacts in the reconstruction stage.

3 Denoising Methods: ECAMixDNet

3.1 CAMixer Dynamic Encoding Module

To address the problem of inadequate extraction of multilevel texture features of food images due to the use of fixed sense field convolution in the image preprocessing stage, the CAMixer module is introduced in this paper, as shown schematically in Fig. 3.

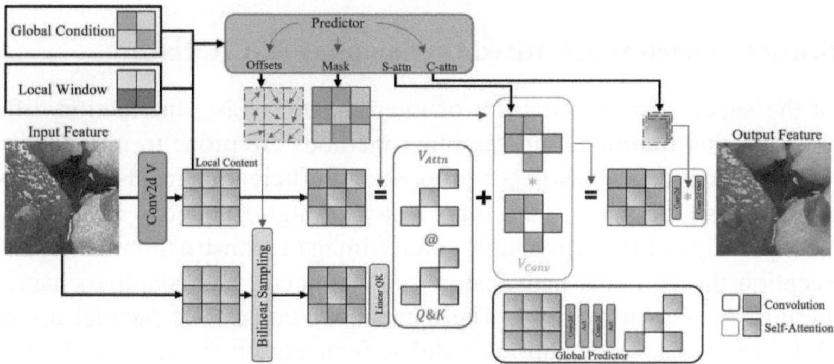

Fig. 3. CAMixer dynamic coding module

CAMixer contains three main components, the predictor module, the attention branch, and the convolution branch. The learnable predictor improves the representation of the convolution by generating multiple bootstraps, including offsets for window warping, masks for categorizing windows, and convolutional attention for giving dynamic properties to the convolution, which adaptively adjusts the attention to include more useful textures.

Given the input feature $X \in R^{C \times H \times W}$, the predictor first obtains the local condition $C_l = V$, the global condition $C_g \in R^{2 \times H \times W}$, and the linear positional encoding $C_w \in R^{2 \times H \times W}$ through point-by-point convolutional projection and initial global prediction to generate the shared intermediate feature map F. Subsequently, it generates the offset map, the mixing mask, and the simplified spatial/channel attention:

$$\begin{cases} F = f_{\text{head}}\left(C_l, C_g, C_w\right), \\ \hat{F} = f_{\text{reduce}}\left(F\right) \in R^{\frac{HW}{M^2} \times M^2}, \\ \Delta p = r \cdot f_{\text{offsets}}\left(F\right) \in R^{2 \times H \times W}, \\ m = \hat{F} W_{\text{mask}} \in R^{\frac{HW}{M^2} \times 1}, \\ A_s = f_{\text{sa}}(F) \in R^{1 \times H \times W}, \\ A_c = f_{\text{ca}}(F) \in R^{C \times 1 \times 1} \end{cases} \tag{1}$$

where Δp is a content-dependent offset matrix used to distort the window by a more complex structure; r is a scalar controlling the offset range; $\hat{F}$ is an intermediate feature for dimensionality reduction rearrangement, M is the attention window size; m is a mask used to decide whether to use attention or convolution to compute the cropped window; and A_s and A_c are the spatial and channel attention, respectively, used to augment convolutional branching.

The CAMixer module regulates the content-aware mixing by controlling the self-attention percentage: when $\gamma = 1$, CAMixer uses a combination of self-attention and convolution to use the attention mechanism for regions with high texture complexity, and when $\gamma = 0$ CAMixer degenerates to using pure convolution for regions with simple textures, which balances the computational complexity while avoiding fixed The problem of inadequate multi-level texture feature extraction for food images by sensory field convolution.

3.2 Efficient Channel-Aware Mixed Up-Sampling (E-CAMixUp)

Aiming at the suppression mechanism of inter-channel noise distribution differences and the problem that traditional up-sampling methods are prone to introduce artifacts in the reconstruction stage, this paper proposes an efficient channel-aware mixed up-sampling mechanism oriented to the suppression of high-frequency artifacts, which is synergistically designed to realize high-quality image reconstruction under multiscale noise perception through dual-path feature reconstruction and adaptive channel interaction filtering. As shown in Fig. 4. The mechanism consists of parallel up-sampling paths and dynamic channel attention modules, focusing on the cross-scale noise coupling problem in the feature fusion process [15].

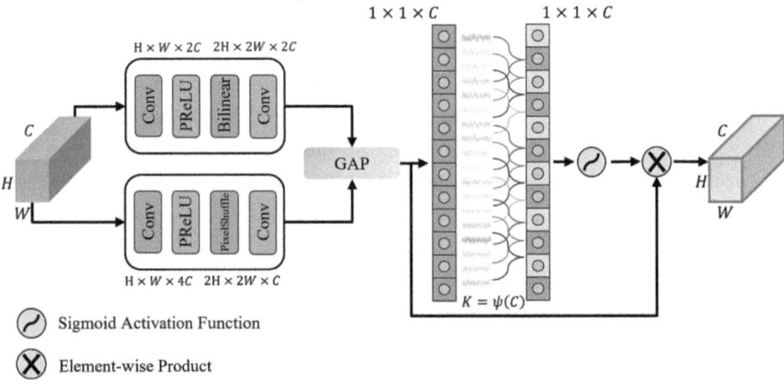

Fig. 4. Efficient Channel-Aware Mixed Up-sampling (Efficient CAMixUp)

To mitigate the checkerboard effect induced by sampling on a single path while preserving multiscale feature diversity, discontinuous changes in local structure are captured in the high-frequency detail reconstruction branch by a pixel reorganization operation (Subpixel Convolution) [16], and in the low-frequency smoothing reconstruction branch by using an interpolating kernel-learning affine transformation (Bilinear Up-sampling) [13] to maintain global continuity. The dual path outputs are fused by element-by-element weighting to generate preliminary up-sampled feature X_{up}:

$$X_{up} = \alpha \odot \text{Subpixel}(X) + (1 - \alpha) \odot \text{Bilinear}(X) \tag{2}$$

where the dynamic weights $\alpha \in [0, 1]^C$ are adaptively generated from the channel dimensions to balance the high/low frequency information contributions from different channels.

A dynamic channel-aware filtering module is designed to address the potential high-frequency noise and cross-scale interference in the up-sampled features as well as the insufficient coverage of the convolution kernel leading to over-localization in the case of a large number of channels.

Firstly, the cross-scale channel descriptor $g \in R^{2C}$ is generated by multiscale statistical aggregation of the initial up-sampled features X_{up}, which is pooled hierarchically (global average pooling and local maximum pooling), and then after sparse channel interaction, a one-dimensional convolution kernel is used to achieve nonlinear mapping between channels, and the kernel size k is dynamically adjusted based on the number of channels C:

$$k = \left\lceil \frac{\log_2(C)}{\gamma} + \frac{b}{\gamma} \right\rceil, (\gamma = 2, b = 1) \tag{3}$$

Subsequently, channel attention weights $\omega \in R^C$ are generated using a Sigmoid function and multiplied channel-by-channel with the up-sampled features:

$$X_{out} = X_{up} \otimes \sigma(\text{Conv}\,1D(g; k)) \tag{4}$$

The E-CAMixUp method is heterogeneous feature synergistic, and the dual-path up-sampling introduces channel-level dynamic weights a to realize the adaptive fusion of high-frequency details and low-frequency smoothing, and at the same time enhances the ability of recognizing cross-scale noise patterns through the joint design of hierarchical pooling and adaptive convolution kernel, and the grayscale heatmap of the feature response of the up-sampling using the E-CAMixUp method is shown in Fig. 5. The figure shows that The problem of blurring of features such as food image edges and textures due to the introduction of artifacts in the reconstruction stage is effectively mitigated.

3.3 Efficient Channel-Aware Mixed Denoising Network (ECAMixDNet)

The general structure of the ECAMixDNet model is shown in Fig. 6, where a degraded image $I \in R^{3 \times H \times W}$, where H is input, where H and W denote the height and width of the image, respectively, and 3 is the number of channels of the image (i.e., RGB image), and the image is subjected to a two-stage stacked CAMixer module to learn content-aware mixing information:

$$\begin{cases} X_0 = \text{Conv}_{3 \times 3}(I) \in R^{C \times H \times W}, (C = 32), \\ C_g = \text{Predictor}(X_0) = \text{Conv}_{1 \times 1}(\text{LeakyReLU}(\text{Conv}_{3 \times 3}(X_0))), \\ X_0^{\text{enhanced}} = \text{CAMixer}_2(\text{CAMixer}_1(\text{Concat}(X_0, C_g))), \end{cases} \tag{5}$$

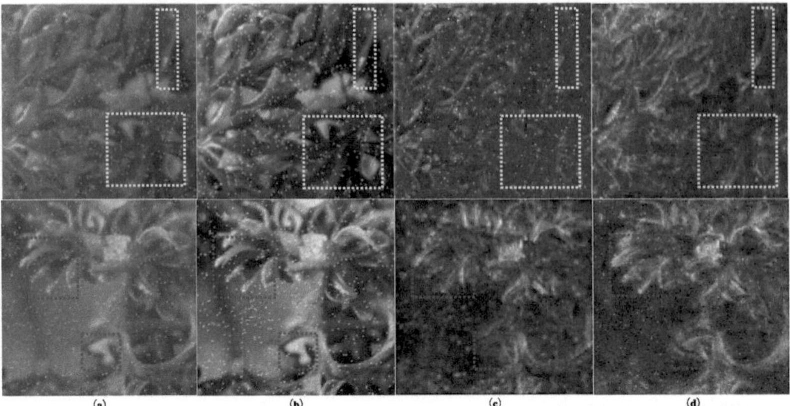

Fig. 5. (a) (b) feature heat maps and feature gray heat maps before inputting the coding layer for the top and bottom two different images, respectively, and (c) (d) gray heat maps using conventional convolutional up-sampling and using efficient channel-aware mixed up-sampling in the feature reconstruction stage of the second layer of the decoder, respectively. (Color figure online)

It also combines residual linking and normalization operations to further extract features and maintain the stability of the network, and the generated feature maps go to the subsequent encoder module for further feature extraction.

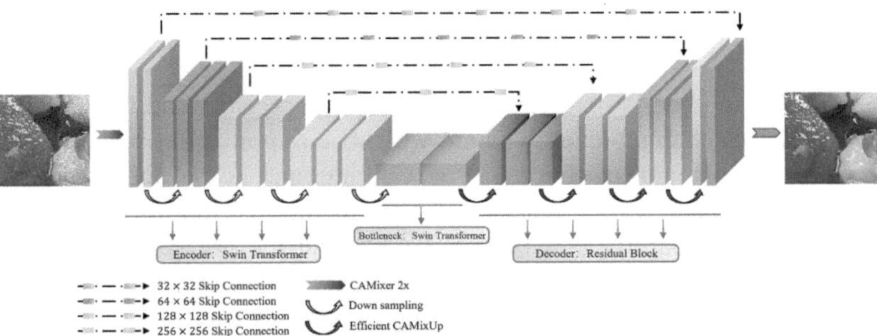

Fig. 6. Efficient Channel-Aware Mixed Denoising Networks

ECAMixDNet's encoder employs four stages, each of which includes a feature transform module and a down-sampling module. The feature transform module uses stacked Swin Transformer blocks and incorporates the RBF (Radial Basis Function) attention [6] mechanism for feature extraction. These modules efficiently capture the multi-scale features in the image and thus help in recovering the actual content in the input image. Each encoder stage also uses a 4 × 4 convolutional layer (stride = 2) for down-sampling, compressing the spatial resolution and extending the channel capacity. The encoder functions as in Eq. (6):

$$X_i = E_i\left(X_{i-1}\right), i = 1, 2, 3, 4 \tag{6}$$

where E_i denotes the $i-th$ encoder stage and $X_i \in R^{2^i C \times \frac{H}{2^i} \times \frac{W}{2^i}}$ is the feature embedding after processing in each encoder stage.

After the four stages of the encoder, ECAMixDNet uses a bottleneck layer, which consists of a Swin Transformer block, to extract high-level global features X_4. The bottleneck layer plays a key role in the model to help capture global image information.

ECAMixDNet's decoder progressively recovers high-resolution images through four stages. Each decoder stage contains an efficient channel-aware mixed up-sampling module and a Residual Block. The efficient channel-aware mixed up-sampling module solves the suppression mechanism of the noise distribution difference between channels, which is easy to introduce artifacts in the reconstruction stage, and further improves the image recovery quality.

The input feature embedding $Y_i \in R^{\frac{C}{2^i} \times 2^i H \times 2^i W}$ from each decoder stage is spliced with the feature $X_i \in R^{2^i C \times \frac{H}{2^i} \times \frac{W}{2^i}}$ from the encoder stage of the same level and fed into the residual block for feature transformation. The residual block consists of two 3×3 convolutional layers and uses an Identity Connection. This design is more efficient than the Swin Trans-former block computation and at the same time can effectively recover the details of the image.

$$\begin{cases} Y_{i-1} = E_- \, \text{CAMixUP}\left(Y_i\right), i = 4, 3, 2, 1, \\ D_i = \text{Conv}_{3\times3}\left(\text{LeakyReLU}\left(\text{Conv}_{3\times3}\left(Y_{i-1}, X_{i-1}\right)\right)\right), i = 4, 3, 2, 1, \end{cases} \tag{7}$$

where D_i denotes the $i-th$ decoder stage, Y_i and X_{i-1} are the inputs of the $i-th$ decoder stage and the features passed from the $i-th$ encoder, respectively.

After the four decoder stages, ECAMixDNet maps the output P_{out} to the denoised image $I^{'} \in R^{3 \times H \times W}$ through a 3×3 convolutional layer and sums it with the input image I to obtain the final denoised image:

$$I^{'} = I + R \tag{8}$$

where R is the denoised residual image and $I^{'}$ is the final denoised image.

The loss function ECAMixDNet uses Charbonnier loss as a training objective to optimize the denoising effect:

$$L(I, \hat{I}) = \sqrt{\left(I' - \hat{I}\right) + \varepsilon^2} \tag{9}$$

where, $\hat{I}$ is the clean food image, $\varepsilon \in 10^{-3}$.

4   Experiments

In order to evaluate the performance of the model in the experiments, this paper validates the effectiveness of the proposed model (ECAMixDNet) in the task of food image denoising by comparing it with the mainstream denoising methods on the DeNoise-Food dataset with three different noise levels, using PSNR, which is used in the field of image denoising to measure the quality of the image restoration, and SSIM, which is used in the field of image denoising to measure the similarity of the structure of the image. While in order to cover the ablation analysis and cross-domain generalizability, this paper also conducts ablation experiments on the DeNoiseFood dataset with a noise level of 5, and cross-domain generalizability comparisons on the image denoising public dataset SIDD, to validate the model performance in terms of quantitative metrics, and multidimensionality of visual quality.

The training set of each of the three DeNoiseFood datasets with different noise levels contains 15,000 pairs of noisy-clean image slices with a fixed input resolution of 128×128 pixels, and all models are trained for 600 epochs using the AdamW optimizer with the initial learning rate set to $2 \times 10^\wedge - 4$, which is lowered to $1 \times 10^\wedge - 7$ by the cosine annealing strategy, and training Data enhancement was enforced by MixUp technique for linear combination of each batch of data, experiments were performed on NVIDIA RTX 4090D GPUs.

4.1   ECAMixDNet vs. Other Models

Quantitative Experiments. ECAMixDNet is compared with four image denoising methods, DnCNN [1], BM3D [17], Uformer [18], and TECDNet, in three DeNoiseFood datasets with different noise levels. Although ECAMixDNet is slightly more complex than some lightweight methods, its significant improvement in recovery quality at common noise levels offsets the minor computational cost associated with its complexity. As shown in Table 1, the quality of visual restoration of different denoising methods in pollution scenes with noise intensity gradient of light ($\sigma = 5$), medium ($\sigma = 10$) and heavy ($\sigma = 15$) respectively.

Table 1. Comparison of different models under three DeNoiseFood datasets with different noise levels

Method	DeNoiseFood($\sigma = 5$)		DeNoiseFood($\sigma = 10$)		DeNoiseFood($\sigma = 15$)	
	PSNR(dB)	SSIM	PSNR(dB)	SSIM	PSNR(dB)	SSIM
DnCNN	36.70	0.91	34.61	0.88	32.74	0.82
BM3D	38.10	0.94	35.66	0.9	34.43	0.87
Uformer-S	42.56	0.96	39.96	0.94	38.56	0.93
TECDNet	42.57	0.96	39.96	0.94	38.56	0.93
ECAMixDNet	**42.78**	**0.97**	**40.12**	**0.95**	**38.65**	**0.94**

Qualitative Experiment. The visualization of the denoising effect of the five models is shown in Fig. 7, and the PSNR of ECAMixDNet is much higher than that of BM3D and DnCNN regardless of the noise intensity, from which it can be seen that the image denoised by BM3D and DnCNN still retains some noise, especially for the removal of pretzel noise is not effective, and at the same time, it causes visible distortion near the sharp edges. The latest methods Uformer, TECDNet and the ECAMixDNet model in this paper can effectively remove noise, but ECAMixDNet benefits from different feature preprocessing methods and up-sampling methods to better preserve the food image texture, which leads to an increase in its PSNR by 0.1–0.3 dB.

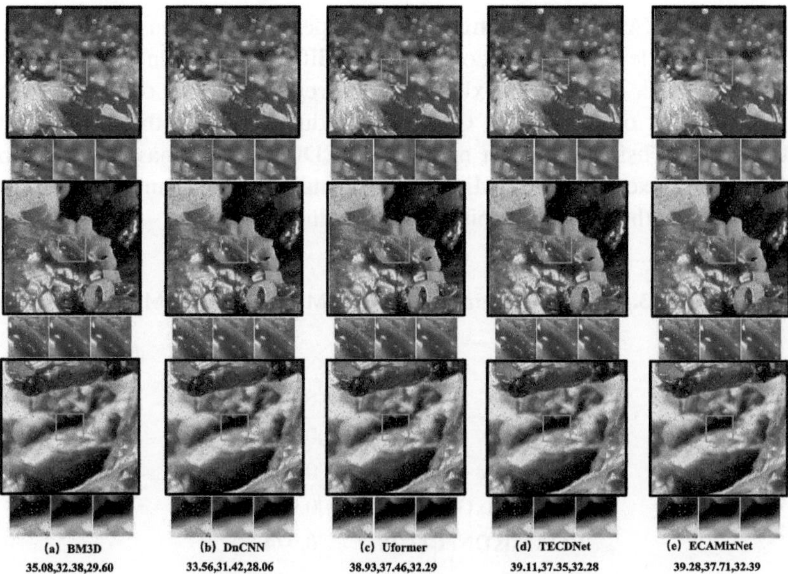

Fig. 7. Visualization of the denoising effect of the five models, the noise intensity of each image from top to bottom is 5/10/15, respectively, and the three small graphs below each image are the noise image, the denoised image, and the original image, respectively, and the bottom value represents the PSNR value of the model under the three noise intensities.

4.2 Ablation Experiment

CAMixer Stacking Layer Selection Experiment. On the DeNoiseFood dataset with a noise level of 5, we compared the differences in denoising performance between stacking one, two, and three layers of CAMixer modules with different computational complexities, as shown in Table 2. With only one layer of CAMixer module the results are not satisfactory due to the lack of accuracy in global conditional tensor characterization and the similar level of predictor's attention to the global, whereas the effect of stacking three layers is close to that of stacking two layers, but the computational complexity is increased by 0.18 G. Therefore, we choose to stack two layers of CAMixer module.

Table 2. CAMixer Stacking Layer Selection Experiment

Method	DeNoiseFood($\sigma = 5$)		
	PSNR(dB)	SSIM	MACs(G)
Conventional	42.49	0.953	21.90
+CAMixer	42.42	0.951	22.08
+CAMixer 2x	42.65	**0.967**	22.24
+CAMixer 3x	**42.66**	**0.967**	**22.42**

CAMixer and E-CAMixUp Combination Experiments. On the DeNoiseFood dataset with a noise level of 5, we compared the difference in denoising performance between the CAMixer and E-CAMixUp modules, respectively. In our experiments, we set up two versions: one using the CAMixer module and the other applying the E-CAMixUp module, using the latest method, TECDNet, as the baseline, as shown in Table 3. Both CAMixer and E-CAMixUp, either individually or in combination, have positively improved the overall denoising performance.

Table 3. Ablation experiments with CAMixer and E-CAMixUp

Method	DeNoiseFood($\sigma = 5$)	
	PSNR (dB)	SSIM
TECNet	42.57	0.963
+CAMixer	42.65	0.967
+E-CAMixUp	42.70	0.968
ECAMixDNet	**42.78**	**0.974**

4.3   Cross-Domain Generalizability Experiments

We evaluate the performance of ECAMixDNet in removing real noise on the SIDD dataset [19]. It is compared with seven state-of-the-art denoising methods including DnCNN, BM3D, RIDNet, MPRNet, MIRNet, Uformer and TECDNet. The performance of ECAMixDNe on the SIDD dataset is shown in the Table 4, demonstrating its cross-domain generalization.

Table 4. Experiments on cross-domain generalizability of SIDD datasets

Method	SIDD Dataset	
	PSNR (dB)	SSIM
DnCNN	23.66	0.583
BM3D	25.65	0.685
RIDNet	38.71	0.951
MPRNet	39.71	0.958
MIRNet	39.72	0.959
Uformer-S	**39.77**	**0.970**
TECDNet	**39.77**	**0.970**
ECAMixDNet	**39.77**	**0.970**

5   Conclusion

In this study, we designed the ECAMixDNet efficient channel-aware hybrid denoising network, which maintains a good denoising performance on the DeNoiseFood dataset with three different noise levels, and demonstrates the same excellent performance of ECAMixDNet in removing real noise through cross-domain generalizability experiments on the public image denoising dataset SIDD. Meanwhile, a noise-clean food image dataset DeNoiseFood is created for food image denoising task, which provides pairwise data support for the subsequent related research in the field of food image denoising, in addition, through the ablation experiments, it verifies the important role of the E-CAMixUp up-sampling method in eliminating the tessellated artifacts to enhance the denoising performance of the model. Although the current method we designed has a better denoising effect on the DeNoiseFood dataset, due to the rich diversity of food image types cannot be completely exhausted, so we will continue to improve the coverage scenarios of the dataset in future work to further verify the generality of the method in this paper.

References

1. Zhang, K., Zuo, W., Chen, Y., et al.: Beyond a gaussian denoiser: residual learning of deep CNN for image denoising. IEEE Trans. Image Process. **26**(7), 3142–3155 (2017)
2. Anwar, S., Barnes, N.: Real image denoising with feature attention. In: Proceedings of the IEEE/CVF International Conference on Computer Vision, pp. 3155–3164 (2019)
3. Zamir, S.W., et al.: Learning enriched features for real image restoration and enhancement. In: Vedaldi, A., Bischof, H., Brox, T., Frahm, J.-M. (eds.) ECCV 2020. LNCS, vol. 12370, pp. 492–511. Springer, Cham (2020). https://doi.org/10.1007/978-3-030-58595-2_30
4. Zamir, S.W., Arora, A., Khan, S., et al.: Multi-stage progressive image restoration. In: Proceedings of the IEEE/CVF Conference on Computer Vision and Pattern Recognition, pp. 14821–14831 (2021)
5. Fan, C.M., Liu, T.J., Liu, K.H.: SUNet: swin transformer UNet for image denoising. In: 2022 IEEE International Symposium on Circuits and Systems (ISCAS), pp. 2333–2337. IEEE (2022)
6. Zhao, M., Cao, G., Huang, X., et al.: Hybrid transformer-CNN for real image denoising. IEEE Signal Process. Lett. **29**, 1252–1256 (2022)
7. Wang, Y., Liu, Y., Zhao, S., et al.: CAMixerSR: only details need more "attention". In: Proceedings of the IEEE/CVF Conference on Computer Vision and Pattern Recognition, pp. 25837–25846 (2024)
8. Bossard, L., Guillaumin, M., Van Gool, L.: Food-101 – Mining discriminative components with random forests. In: Fleet, D., Pajdla, T., Schiele, B., Tuytelaars, T. (eds.) ECCV 2014. LNCS, vol. 8694, pp. 446–461. Springer, Cham (2014). https://doi.org/10.1007/978-3-319-10599-4_29
9. Chen, J., Ngo, C.W.: Deep-based ingredient recognition for cooking recipe retrieval. In: Proceedings of the 24th ACM International Conference on Multimedia, pp. 32–41 (2016)
10. Akbar, S.A., Verma, A.: Analyzing noise models and advanced filtering algorithms for image enhancement. arXiv preprint arXiv:2410.21946 (2024)
11. Ronneberger, O., Fischer, P., Brox, T.: U-Net: Convolutional networks for biomedical image segmentation. In: Navab, N., Hornegger, J., Wells, W.M., Frangi, A.F. (eds.) MICCAI 2015. LNCS, vol. 9351, pp. 234–241. Springer, Cham (2015). https://doi.org/10.1007/978-3-319-24574-4_28

12. Long J, Shelhamer, E., Darrell, T.: Fully convolutional networks for semantic segmentation. In: Proceedings of the IEEE Conference on Computer Vision and Pattern Recognition, pp. 3431–3440 (2015)
13. Shi, W., Caballero, J., Huszár, F., et al.: Real-time single image and video super-resolution using an efficient sub-pixel convolutional neural network. In: Proceedings of the IEEE Conference on Computer Vision and Pattern Recognition, pp. 1874–1883 (2016)
14. Liu, R., Deng, H., Huang, Y., et al.: Decoupled spatial-temporal transformer for video inpainting. arXiv preprint arXiv:2104.06637 (2021)
15. Wang, Q., Wu, B., Zhu, P., et al.: ECA-Net: efficient channel attention for deep convolutional neural networks. In: Proceedings of the IEEE/CVF Conference on Computer Vision and Pattern Recognition, pp. 11534–11542 (2020)
16. Cao, H., et al.: Swin-UNet: UNet-like pure transformer for medical image segmentation. arXiv preprint arXiv:2105.05537 (2021)
17. Dabov, K., Foi, A., Katkovnik, V., et al.: Image denoising by sparse 3-D transform-domain collaborative filtering. IEEE Trans. Image Process. $16(8)$, 2080–2095 (2007)
18. Wang, Z., Cun, X., Bao, J., et al.: Uformer: a general U-shaped transformer for image restoration. In: Proceedings of the IEEE/CVF Conference on Computer Vision and Pattern Recognition, pp. 17683–17693 (2022)
19. Abdelhamed, A., Lin, S., Brown, M.S.: A high-quality denoising dataset for smartphone cameras. In: Proceedings of the IEEE Conference on Computer Vision and Pattern Recognition, pp. 1692–1700 (2018)

Leveraging Language Model and Knowledge Tracing for Personalized Question Generation

Zhongwei Yin[1], Li Li[1]([✉]), Xiaofei Xu[2], Yao Li[1], and Hao Zhou[1]

[1] School of Computer and Information Science, Southwest University, Chongqing, China
lily@swu.edu.cn, yssssss@email.swu.edu.cn
[2] School of Computing Technologies, RMIT University, Melbourne, Australia

Abstract. Automatic Question Generation (QG) in NLP research has garnered significant attention, aimed at assisting educators in improving classroom performance and promoting the adoption of intelligent education systems. However, few studies have addressed the critical challenge of controlling difficulty levels, particularly at the fine-grained, individual student level required for adaptive education. To achieve personalized question generation, we explored the integration of language models with knowledge tracing models, resulting in the development of the Language-Deep-Knowledge-Tracing (LDKT) model. This model can extract students' textual interaction histories and represent their knowledge states, allowing for accurate predictions of their performance on new questions. Subsequently, the Difficulty-Controllable Question Generation (DCQG) model is guided to generate questions that align with the target difficulty, using datasets processed by the LDKT model. Both automated metrics and human evaluations have demonstrated the effectiveness of our proposed modules. The LDKT model achieved a maximum AUC of 0.77, while the DCQG model attained a minimum difficulty deviation RMSE of 3.96, both showing improvements over baselines. Further studies indicate that our work provides more options for modern intelligent education and advances the digitalization of teaching.

Keywords: Question Generation · Controllable Difficulty · Adaptive Education · Knowledge Tracing · Language Model

1 Introduction

Question generation, as a popular field within NLP, has diverse applications: enhancing machine reading comprehension performance [5], facilitating human-computer dialogues [18], and advancing intelligent education [7]. Notably, generating questions in educational settings has drawn much attention. This includes tasks like cloze generation [9], reading comprehension question generation [6], distractor generation [14], and question-answer joint generation [11]. These methods

© The Author(s), under exclusive license to Springer Nature Singapore Pte Ltd. 2026
T. Zhu et al. (Eds.): KSEM 2025, LNAI 15920, pp. 83–95, 2026.
https://doi.org/10.1007/978-981-95-3052-6_7

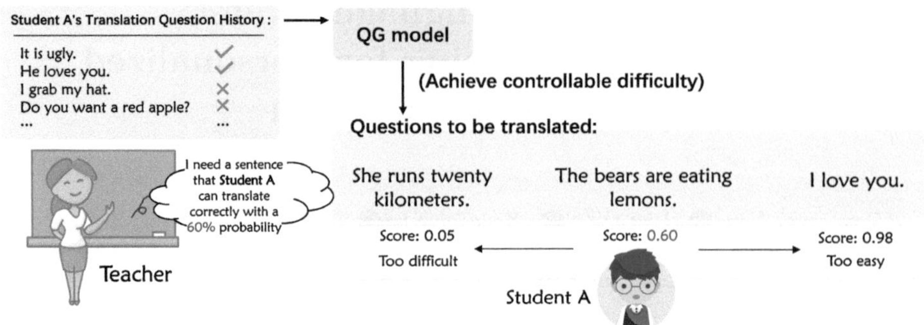

Fig. 1. The demand scenario of individualized education for customized problem difficulty (taking translation task as an example). We define the difficulty score in terms of the accuracy rate, ranging from 0 to 1, with higher values indicating easier questions.

are employed to assist teachers in enhancing students' classroom performance, aligning with the contemporary needs of intelligent education.

In practical applications, beyond ensuring the quality of generated results (e.g., relevance and fluency), the difficulty level of the questions is also a critical factor. Exam questions must possess an appropriate difficulty level to effectively gauge students' knowledge mastery, thereby allowing educators to formulate effective subsequent learning strategies. In this regard, several studies have attempted to control the difficulty of generated questions, but definitions differ. For example, Gao et al. [3] used the accuracy of the question-answering model to reflect question difficulty, while Fei et al. [2] controlled the difficulty by adjusting the number of chain jumps between reasoning entities involved in the questions.

Although difficulty may have varying evaluation criteria across different contexts, according to Confucius' principle of "teaching in accordance with individual aptitude", the difficulty level should be tailored to each student's unique circumstances to achieve personalized educational programs. Figure 1 shows that achieving this goal requires obtaining students' historical data. Research in the Knowledge Tracing (KT) field [1] models and predicts students' knowledge mastery by tracking each student's interaction history. However, most data and models are designed for vector formats and lack the processing of textual knowledge content. Srivastava et al. [15] leveraged the language model to extract textual learning data to generate questions of specified difficulty for individual students. However, this approach relies solely on end-to-end training with GPT-2 [12], lacking effective techniques in the KT domain to handle sequential data.

In this paper, we attempt to integrate language models (LM) with the Deep Knowledge Tracing (DKT) model [10] to analyze the textual interaction history of students. This information is then used to assist in training the QG model, enabling personalized difficulty control for each student and enhancing educational effectiveness, as shown in Fig. 2. Firstly, to thoroughly exploit the latent information within student interaction data, we developed a Difficulty Finder and a Unified Encoder to provide the model with structured inputs. Then, we designed a pre-trained Language model-driven DKT module (LDKT) that learns and merges students' knowledge states with question representations, thereby predicting their accuracy in solving new problems, which can be interpreted as difficulty scores. Subsequently, this KT model serves as a constraint to guide the QG model in generating questions whose actual difficulty closely aligns with the target difficulty, utilizing our designed mixed loss function. Finally, through comprehensive experiments and comparative analysis with baseline models, we achieved promising results. In summary, our contributions are as follows:

1. We design a Difficulty Finder and a Unified Encoder, integrating the capabilities of LM and DKT to learn from students' text-based question-answer interactions, thereby effectively predicting their accuracy in responding to new questions.
2. We provide the QG model with critical difficulty evaluation information from the calibrated KT model, enabling personalized and controllable difficulty in question generation through the formulated mixed loss function.
3. Our model shows superior results on the datasets, enhancing performance on both automatic metrics and human evaluations, thus meeting the requirements of practical educational scenarios.

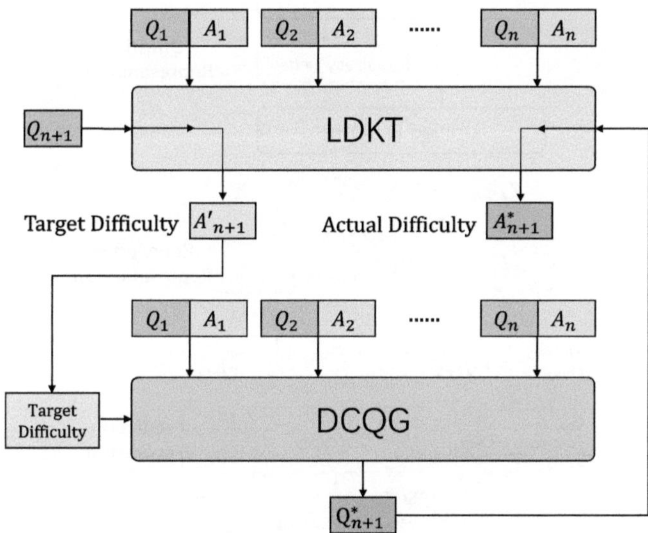

Fig. 2. Overview of framework for personalized difficulty-controllable question generation, which consists of two task stages.

2 Methods

Our work aims to achieve personalized difficulty control in question generation. Formally, given the historical interaction data with text information for the student, denoted as $Q_1/A_1 \sim Q_n/A_n$, and the teacher-defined target difficulty d, the task is to generate a question with a difficulty level that matches the student's proficiency, as defined by Eq. 1.

$$\begin{cases} S = (Q_1, A_1, Q_2, A_2, \cdots, Q_n, A_n) \\ Q^* = \underset{Q}{\mathrm{argmax}} \log P_{\theta_{QG}}(Q|d, S) \end{cases} \tag{1}$$

The interaction history is utilized to represent the student's state S. Inspired by Srivastava et al. [15], we optimize the QG model ($P_{\theta_{QG}}$) through the formulation of two specific tasks. As shown in Fig. 2, the KT model predicts the accuracy of a student facing new questions Q_{n+1} by learning the state S. Under proper calibration, the predicted accuracy A'_{n+1} can be interpreted as the difficulty score d, which, together with S, guides the QG model to generate questions whose actual difficulty A^*_{n+1} closely aligns with the target difficulty. We will introduce the KT and QG modules in Sects. 2.1 and 2.2, respectively.

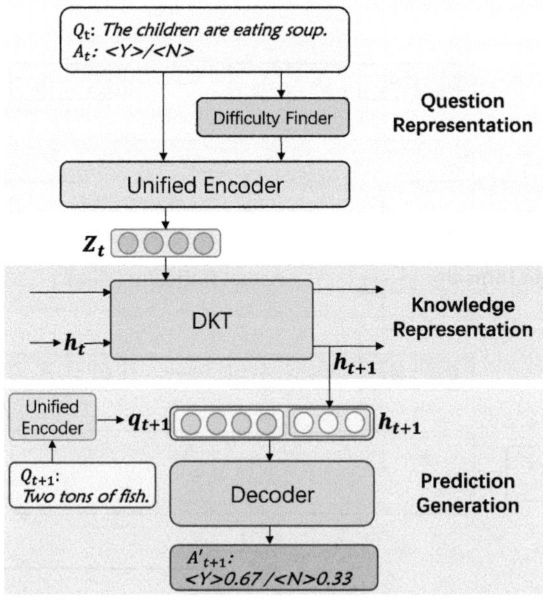

Fig. 3. Overview of our proposed LDKT model.

2.1 Language-Deep-Knowledge-Tracing (LDKT)

Conventional KT models struggle to learn textual information from the question data, and incorporating LM can address this challenge. Inspired by Liu et al. [8], who validated the feasibility of aligning code representations with students' knowledge states, we propose the LDKT model, as shown in Fig. 3. In the Question Representation phase, to extract information from the students' question-answer sequences, we introduce the Difficulty Finder and the Unified Encoder components to structure input text and obtain representation vectors. Subsequently, we utilize temporal models in the Knowledge Representation module to update the students' real-time knowledge states. Finally, during decoding, we combine the representation of the current new question, denoted as q_{t+1}, to predict the student's response accuracy A'_{t+1}.

Difficulty Finder: Question datasets are typically collected from classes or schools, where students are part of a similar distribution. The responses of these students to particular questions often indicate the relative difficulty of those questions. Based on this observation, we designed a Difficulty Finder. This component extracts the average accuracy rates from the historical performance of other students on the current question, mapping these rates to a difficulty score ranging from 0 to 1, which is subsequently employed to inspire the model. Questions with sparse data will be assigned a default difficulty score, which is the mode from the available data.

Unified Encoder: Given our task scenario and the diversity of educational questions, we can leverage the language understanding capabilities of the LM to establish a unified input layer. By using labels such as <QU>, <AN>, and <DI> to denote individual questions, answers, and difficulty retrieval, respectively, we concatenate these elements into a text sequence. Beginning-of-sequence (<BOS>) and end-of-sequence (<EOS>) tokens are then used to delineate a complete student response history. Notably, this approach is extendable to incorporate additional information, such as distractors and background context, by augmenting the LM with labels that convey specific meanings.

After processing the question data, we use the pre-trained encoder to obtain the representation vector Z_t for the current question-answer pair $Q_t A_t$. As shown in Fig. 3, for all response histories Z_0 to Z_t of the student, our designed knowledge representation module estimates the student's knowledge mastery level. This module updates the student's current knowledge state h_{t+1} using the DKT [10] model, which is concise and efficient, making it particularly suitable for scenarios lacking information, such as knowledge points.

$$h_{t+1} = DKT(h_t, Z_t) \tag{2}$$

This state can be synchronously updated based on subsequent questions, reflecting changes in the student's knowledge level. Following this, to predict the accuracy of the student's response to question Q_{t+1}, we fine-tuned the pre-trained decoder and developed an alignment function to integrate the question representation q_{t+1} with the knowledge state h_{t+1}. In practice, we compared three alignment methods for vector fusion—addition, gating, and linear combination:

- Addition: $q_{t+1} + h_{t+1}$
- Gating: $\alpha \cdot q_{t+1} + (1 - \alpha) \cdot h_{t+1}$

- Linear combination: $q_{t+1} + \boldsymbol{A} \cdot \boldsymbol{h}_{t+1} + \boldsymbol{b}$

Here, α is the hyperparameter controlling gating, while $\boldsymbol{A}$ and $\boldsymbol{b}$ are learnable parameters. The fused vector subsequently serves as input for the generator to predict the response accuracy.

2.2 Difficulty-Controllable Question Generation (DCQG)

DCQG faces its greatest challenge in defining and labeling difficulty. Our solution utilizes the predicted scores of the calibrated LDKT model as a substitute. By removing the last question in the input sequence, the predicted score serves as the target difficulty to guide the QG model in aligning with the difficulty level of the pending question. In Fig. 2, the data processed by the same Difficulty Finder and Unified Encoder from Sect. 2.1 function as the input for QG.

However, employing the target difficulty merely as an input label to conduct the model is insufficient and overly reliant on the encapsulated pre-trained language model. To enhance the constraints on difficulty information, we devised a mixed loss function that builds upon the existing supervised loss of the generation model. The generated results from the QG model are fed back into the LDKT to predict the actual difficulty, with the deviation from the expected target difficulty employed as additional penalization information, shown in Eq. 3.

$$\mathcal{L}_{QG} = \sum_{i=1}^{|D|} \sum_{t=t_g+1}^{|X^i|} -\beta_1 \cdot logP_{\theta_{QG}}(X_t^i|X_{<t}^i) + \beta_2 \cdot (d_{target}^i - d_{actual}^i)^2 \qquad (3)$$

The independent dataset D, augmented with target difficulty by the LDKT, comprises X^i, which represents the interaction history of the i-th student sample. We employ the <G> token to signal model ($P_{\theta_{QG}}$) the starting point for generating a question, which is positioned at the t_g-th location in X^i. The actual difficulty and target difficulty of the generated results are denoted as d_{actual}^i and d_{target}^i, respectively. Ultimately, two additional hyperparameters β_1 and β_2, are introduced to balance the influence of the two loss components.

3 Experiments and Results

3.1 Datasets and Baselines

Due to the absence of student interaction data in QG datasets and the predominance of question IDs instead of question texts in KT datasets, we chose the Second Language Acquisition Modeling Shared Task dataset [13] to evaluate model's performance. This dataset contains sequential records of translation questions and responses from Spanish and French learners. The preprocessed dataset comprises around 60,000 sequence entries, which are divided into train/dev/test sets in an 8:1:1 ratio. The distribution of learners for the two languages is treated as separate sub-datasets, which are used to evaluate our models independently.

We primarily compare our method with two baseline models: LM-KT [15] and FS-KT [16]. The former approach solely leverages the language capabilities of GPT-2, using students' historical interaction as the prompt text for straightforward prediction. The latter approach, tailored for educational scenarios within a classroom setting of 50 students, has incorporated methods such as self-control loss and Top-P sampling to enhance few-shot learning.

We employ AUC to evaluate the predictive performance of the KT module, which represents the area under the receiver operating characteristic curve, ranging from 0 to 1. A value closer to 1 indicates superior predictive performance, while a value near 0.5 suggests minimal predictive value. For the QG module, we assess its effectiveness in difficulty control and question quality using both custom automated metrics (detailed in Sect. 3.5) and human evaluation.

3.2 Implementation Details

We implement our model in PyTorch and conduct training using two GTX-3090Ti GPUs. Considering limited computational resources, we primarily fine-tuned two pre-trained language models: GPT-2 and GLM-4-9B [4]. The former has the same parameter scale as the two baseline models, ensuring a fair comparison. The latter is an open-source large language model (LLM) released in 2024, which we implemented through LoRA fine-tuning. Besides, the DKT model is implemented using Bi-LSTM, featuring a simple and efficient structure that can be well adapted to the PLM, with an input dimension of 968 and a hidden layer dimension of 768. The model's learning rate is set to 5e-5.

Table 1. Experimental results of our KT model and baselines.

Models (**Spanish**)	AUC (seen)	AUC (unseen)
LM-KT	0.74 ± .0002	0.76 ± .002
FS-KT (50 students)	0.69 ± .0002	0.66 ± .003
Standard DKT	0.67 ± .0002	0.68 ± .002
Qwen2.5 (14B)	0.61 ± .0002	0.59 ± .003
Our Model (GPT-2)	**0.76 ± .0001**	**0.77 ± .002**
Our Model (GLM-4)	0.76 ± .0002	0.76 ± .003
Models (**French**)	AUC (seen)	AUC (unseen)
LM-KT	0.73 ± .0002	0.70 ± .002
FS-KT (50 students)	0.68 ± .0002	0.68 ± .003
Standard DKT	0.62 ± .0001	0.60 ± .002
Qwen2.5 (14B)	0.60 ± .0002	0.58 ± .003
Our Model (GPT-2)	**0.75 ± .0002**	0.72 ± .002
Our Model (GLM-4)	0.74 ± .0002	**0.73 ± .002**

3.3   Comparison of LDKT Model

Table 1 presents the primary comparison results of the KT models. Here, "unseen" refers to test set questions that are not part of the training set and have never been encountered by any student, highlighting the model's ability to generalize to new problems. Firstly, the AUC statistics indicate that for both types of language learners, our model slightly outperforms the baseline models at the same parameter scale (GPT-2), achieving up to a 2.9% improvement over LM-KT and up to 16.7% over FS-KT. This demonstrates that our approach, which integrates PLM and DKT models, effectively learns students' knowledge states from textual interaction history and enhances prediction accuracy. Secondly, Standard DKT omits the question text information, using ID numbers to represent questions, as is traditional in the DKT field. This approach diverges significantly from the upstream tasks in the language model's pretraining phase, preventing the full utilization of its potential, resulting in poorer performance.

Additionally, we deployed the large language model Qwen2.5-14B [17] and performed few-shot learning for this text-based KT task, providing 10 positive and 10 negative samples. Statistical analysis revealed that the performance on both sub-datasets was poor, indicating that relying solely on LLM is insufficient. Even with large-scale parameters, current LLMs still lack the ability to effectively extract complex temporal information from long-sequence data. In contrast, our model addresses this challenge by ingeniously integrating the DKT. Finally, comparing the practical performance of our model on GPT-2 and GLM-4, we found that despite the increase in parameter size (from 1.5B to 9B), the improvement in AUC was not significant. Since the dataset focuses on beginner-level translation tasks, it lacks a deep assessment of reasoning and comprehension. Thus, both GPT-2 and GLM-4 can fully understand the information.

Table 2. Experimental results of ablation and alignment analysis for LDKT

LDKT		Spanish		French	
		AUC (seen)	AUC (unseen)	AUC (seen)	AUC (unseen)
Ablation	-w/o DKT	0.72 ± .0002	0.73 ± .003	0.71 ± .0003	0.69 ± .003
	-w/o Difficulty Finder	0.74 ± .0003	0.75 ± .003	0.72 ± .0003	0.70 ± .003
	-Question Only	0.67 ± .0002	0.58 ± .003	0.65 ± .0003	0.62 ± .002
Alignment	Addition	0.72 ± .0002	0.70 ± .003	0.71 ± .0003	0.69 ± .002
	Gating	**0.76 ± .0001**	**0.77 ± .002**	**0.75 ± .0002**	**0.72 ± .002**
	Linear combination	0.75 ± .0002	0.76 ± .003	0.73 ± .0003	0.71 ± .003

3.4   Ablation and Alignment Analysis of LDKT

Table 2 presents the ablation experiments and the comparison of alignment schemes in LDKT (based on GPT-2). Specifically, the ablation experiments assess the effects of removing the DKT module, the Difficulty Finder module, and the interaction history (Question Only). We observe several conclusions from these results. Firstly, our introduction of DKT and the Difficulty Finder both help improve the model's performance. These components assist in modeling students' knowledge states from historical information and question difficulty, thereby enhancing prediction accuracy. Secondly, the "Question Only" results are notably poor, indicating that capturing student states from interactions is crucial for prediction. Finally, the gating achieves relatively optimal results among the three alignment schemes for knowledge state and question representation, with $\alpha = 0.3$ determined through grid search.

3.5 Automatic Evaluation of DCQG

Since our scenario is open-domain, unlike reading comprehension-based QG, commonly used metrics like $BLEU_n$ are not applicable. We designed automatic evaluation metrics to demonstrate that the QG model is tailored to individual students and target difficulty. For student samples unseen by the model, we set nine target difficulty scores ranging from 0.1 to 0.9 and generated 30 questions for each level. Finally, we evaluated the actual difficulty using the calibrated LDKT model, with the Root Mean Squared Error (RMSE) between the target and actual difficulty scores reflecting the effectiveness of difficulty control. A smaller RMSE indicates that the generated questions more closely align with the target difficulty. The statistical results are shown in Table 3.

Table 3. Automatic evaluation of QG.

Models	RMSE↓	
	Spanish	French
LM-KT	6.62	6.22
Our Model	**4.84**	**3.96**
-w/o History	16.03	14.98
-w/o Difficulty Info	21.68	20.55

Firstly, when using the same GPT-2, our DCQG reduces the relevant metrics by 26.9% and 36.6% compared to LM-KT, demonstrating its positive impact on difficulty control. Next, we conducted ablation studies by removing the student's interaction history from the prompts (-w/o History) and eliminating difficulty control information (-w/o Difficulty Info), including the target difficulty and the difficulty deviation penalty. The results indicate that achieving high-quality personalized question generation is inseparable from students' individual information and the teacher-specified target requirements.

Finally, since the DCQG model relies on the loss function in Eq. 3 for precise difficulty control, we conducted a grid analysis on β_1 and β_2 to explore optimal balance parameter settings. As shown in Fig. 4, by combining the results and taking into account the practical significance implied by the formula, we ultimately set β_1 and β_2 to 0.6 and 0.4, respectively.

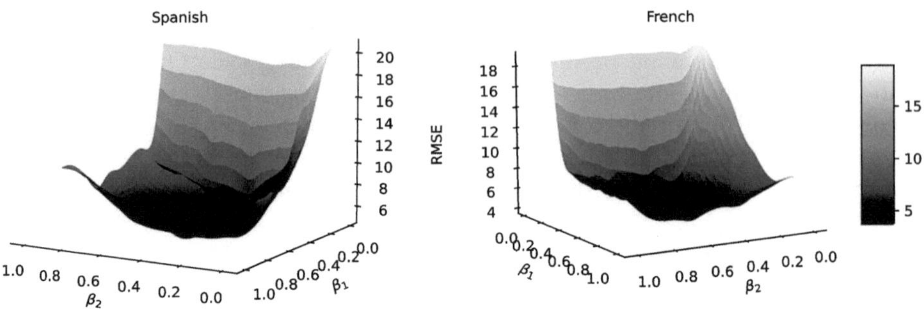

Fig. 4. Analysis of β_1 and β_2.

3.6   Human Evaluation of DCQG

Furthermore, relying solely on automated metrics for evaluating QG does not capture fluency and students' subjective perceptions, making human evaluation an essential standard in the field of text generation. We invited five participants, all of whom hold a bachelor's degree or higher from Chinese universities and have passed the CET-6 examination. Considering that the dataset focuses on open-domain translation tasks, we evaluated the model-generated results from the following three aspects:

- Fluency (F): Assesses the grammatical correctness and smoothness of the generated questions.
- Diversity (D1): Evaluates the variety of the generated outputs and their suitability for open-domain scenarios.
- Difficulty Alignment (D2): Measures the alignment between the generated questions and the target difficulty level.

We assigned a score of 1 to 5 for each criterion and asked the participants to evaluate 100 anonymized generated samples. Overall, the statistical results exhibited robust consistency, with the average scores presented in Table 4. It can be observed that our proposed DCQG model, by deeply learning from student interaction history and comprehensively perceiving difficulty control information, outperformed the two baseline models and achieved the best overall performance across the three human evaluation criteria.

Furthermore, to further demonstrate the difficulty control capability, we had the complete DCQG model generate 20 questions for each of the nine target difficulty levels (0.1–0.9). Subsequently, the participants were asked to estimate the target difficulty based on the generated questions. For each target difficulty

Table 4. Human evaluation results of QG.

Models	Spanish			French		
	F	D1	D2	F	D1	D2
LM-KT	3.77	3.81	3.80	**3.83**	3.58	3.75
FS-KT (50 students)	3.62	3.85	3.85	3.74	3.68	3.68
Our Model	**3.80**	3.88	**4.12**	3.72	**3.70**	**4.08**
-w/o History	2.98	3.44	3.02	3.05	3.35	2.90
-w/o Difficulty Info	3.66	**3.90**	1.92	3.54	3.66	1.36

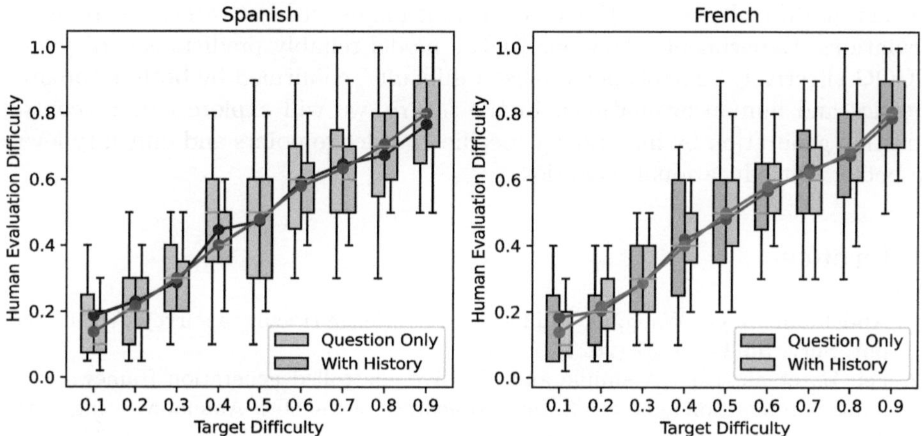

Fig. 5. Statistical chart of human difficulty assessment.

level, we provided 10 samples containing only the question itself (Question Only) and 10 samples including student history (With History). The corresponding statistical results are presented in Fig. 5. We observed that regardless of whether the participants were aware of the student history, the manually estimated difficulty values for the DCQG model exhibited a high degree of alignment with the target difficulty. When the participants had full access to the student history, the variance in the manually estimated difficulty values significantly decreased and converged towards the target difficulty. This aligns well with the practical requirements of personalized difficulty control.

4   Limitation

The task we focus on is in the open domain, lacking control over specific sentence structures or vocabulary (particular knowledge points in KT). Therefore, when educators aim to assess students' mastery of a particular knowledge point, our model may fail to meet this requirement. Additionally, due to the lack of multidisciplinary datasets with student interaction history, our model has limitations in terms of generalization. It cannot be effectively validated or further improved on data from non-language disciplines such as mathematics and science. This issue requires further exploration in future research.

5 Conclusion

In this study, we combine language models with knowledge tracing for personalized question difficulty. Our model comprises two components: LDKT and DCQG. The LDKT model analyzes student interactions to estimate knowledge levels and forecast question accuracy. It then aids the DCQG model by supplying the actual difficulty of questions, ensuring it aligns with set targets by reducing deviations. Experiments show our LDKT model reliably predicts accuracy, and DCQG effectively controls personalized difficulty, confirmed by both automated metrics and human evaluations. In the future, we will explore how to control question generation by integrating specific knowledge points and difficulty levels to better suit educational scenarios.

References

1. Abdelrahman, G., Wang, Q., Nunes, B.: Knowledge tracing: a survey. ACM Comput. Surv. **55**(11), 1–37 (2023)
2. Fei, Z., et al.: Cqg: A simple and effective controlled generation framework for multi-hop question generation. In: Proceedings of the 60th Annual Meeting of the Association for Computational Linguistics (Volume 1: Long Papers), pp. 6896–6906 (2022)
3. Gao, Y., Bing, L., Chen, W., Lyu, M.R., King, I.: Difficulty controllable generation of reading comprehension questions. In: Kraus, S. (ed.) Proceedings of the Twenty-Eighth International Joint Conference on Artificial Intelligence, IJCAI 2019, Macao, China, August 10-16, 2019, pp. 4968–4974. ijcai.org (2019)
4. GLM, T., et al.: Chatglm: A family of large language models from glm-130b to glm-4 all tools. arXiv preprint arXiv:2406.12793 (2024)
5. Jauhar, S.K., Turney, P., Hovy, E.: Tables as semi-structured knowledge for question answering. In: Proceedings of the 54th Annual Meeting of the Association for Computational Linguistics (Volume 1: Long Papers), pp. 474–483 (2016)
6. Jia, X., Zhou, W., Sun, X., Wu, Y.: Eqg-race: examination-type question generation. In: Proceedings of the AAAI . Conference on Artificial Intelligence, vol. 35, pp. 13143–13151 (2021)
7. Kurdi, G., Leo, J., Parsia, B., Sattler, U., Al-Emari, S.: A systematic review of automatic question generation for educational purposes. Int. J. Artif. Intell. Educ. **30**, 121–204 (2020)
8. Liu, N., Wang, Z., Baraniuk, R., Lan, A.: Open-ended knowledge tracing for computer science education. In: Proceedings of the 2022 Conference on Empirical Methods in Natural Language Processing (2022)
9. Matsumori, S., Okuoka, K., Shibata, R., Inoue, M., Fukuchi, Y., Imai, M.: Mask and cloze: automatic open cloze question generation using a masked language model. IEEE Access **11**, 9835–9850 (2023)

10. Piech, C., et al.: Deep knowledge tracing. In: Advances in Neural Information Processing Systems, vol. 28 (2015)
11. Qu, F., Jia, X., Wu, Y.: Asking questions like educational experts: Automatically generating question-answer pairs on real-world examination data. In: Proceedings of the 2021 Conference on Empirical Methods in Natural Language Processing, pp. 2583–2593 (2021)
12. Radford, A., Wu, J., Child, R., Luan, D., Amodei, D., Sutskever, I., et al.: Language models are unsupervised multitask learners. OpenAI blog **1**(8), 9 (2019)
13. Settles, B., Brust, C., Gustafson, E., Hagiwara, M., Madnani, N.: Second language acquisition modeling. In: Proceedings of The Thirteenth Workshop on Innovative Use of Nlp for Building Educational Applications, pp. 56–65 (2018)
14. Shuai, P., Li, L., Liu, S., Shen, J.: QDG: a unified model for automatic question-distractor pairs generation. Appl. Intell. **53**(7), 8275–8285 (2023)
15. Srivastava, M., Goodman, N.: Question generation for adaptive education. In: Proceedings of the 59th Annual Meeting of the Association for Computational Linguistics and the 11th International Joint Conference on Natural Language Processing (Volume 2: Short Papers), pp. 692–701 (2021)
16. Wang, Y., Li, L.: Difficulty-controlled question generation in adaptive education for few-shot learning. In: International Conference on Advanced Data Mining and Applications, pp. 584–598. Springer (2023)
17. Yang, A., et al.: Qwen2.5 technical report. arXiv preprint arXiv:2412.15115 (2024)
18. Zhang, Z., Li, G., Huang, G., Li, J.: A study of human-computer interaction and intimacy in the era of big data and artificial intelligence. In: 5th International Conference on Computer Information Science and Application Technology (CISAT 2022). vol. 12451, pp. 1245–1251. SPIE (2022)

MFTP: Multi-round Feedback for Dynamic Travel Itinerary Optimization

Yunfei Lu[1], Peng Jin[2,3], Yifan Zhang[1], Lingjiao Xu[2,3], Bing Wang[1], and Xingyuan Chen[2,3]($\boxtimes$)

[1] School of Computer Science and Software Engineering, SouthWest Petroleum University, Chengdu, Sichuan, China
{202321000526,202322000592,wang_bing}@swpu.edu.cn
[2] Sichuan Provincial Key Laboratory of Philosophy and Social Science for Language Intelligence in Special Education, Leshan, Sichuan, China
jandp@pku.edu.cn
[3] Key Lab of Internet Natural Language Processing of Sichuan Provincial Education Department, Leshan, Sichuan, China
chenxingyuan000@gmail.com

Abstract. Multi-day travel itinerary planning is increasingly vital for personalised tourism, yet it poses significant challenges due to complex constraints like budget, time, and user preferences. Traditional planning methods, unable to process natural language directly, often fail to capture user intent accurately. While Large Language Models (LLMs) enable natural language understanding, single-agent systems built upon them frequently exhibit hallucinations, leading to logical inconsistencies and poor constraint adherence in complex scenarios. To address these issues, we propose the Multi-round Feedback Travel Planner (MFTP), an intelligent multi-agent framework that enhances planning through iterative feedback and cooperative optimisation. MFTP integrates intent parsing, planning and evaluation agents. The parsing module structures user requirements, the planning agent drafts an initial itinerary, and the evaluation agent validates constraints across multiple dimensions, with iterative interplay refining the plan. Experiments on the TravelPlanner dataset demonstrate MFTP's superiority over baseline methods, significantly enhancing pass rates and constraint satisfaction, and effectively resolving logical conflicts and constraint violations in multi-day travel planning. Code can be found at https://github.com/lsnuNLP/ems

Keywords: Travel Planning · Multi-Agent Collaboration · Large Language Models · Iterative Optimization

1 Introduction

In recent years, the rapid recovery of international tourism [1] and the widespread adoption of smart travel technologies have significantly increased the demand for personalised itinerary planning. LLMs, with their strong natural language

© The Author(s), under exclusive license to Springer Nature Singapore Pte Ltd. 2026
T. Zhu et al. (Eds.): KSEM 2025, LNAI 15920, pp. 96–107, 2026.
https://doi.org/10.1007/978-981-95-3052-6_8

understanding and generation capabilities [2], demonstrate potential in this field, such as crafting initial plans from user queries. Building on this, LLM-based agents integrated with external tools enhance technical capabilities [3], while multi-agent systems, leveraging collaboration and role specialisation [4], provide innovative approaches to complex travel requirements.

Despite these advances, applying LLMs to personalized itinerary suggestions often results in logical inconsistencies, budget overruns, and day mismatches [5]. As shown in Fig. 1, existing methods lack awareness of plan flaws, such as unreasonable scheduling or cost exceedances, and their fixed reasoning patterns struggle to adapt to the diversity and complexity of user demands. These short-comings stem from single-model reliance on rigid reasoning modes—akin to the psychological "mental set" phenomenon [6]—limiting flexibility in novel scenarios. Thus, a multi-agent system is needed to deeply understand user intent and iteratively refine plan defects, improving accuracy and practicality [7].

To address these challenges, we propose a model-independent, **M**ulti-round **F**eedback **T**ravel **P**lanning framework (MFTP) that surpasses traditional direct planning limitations through multi-agent collaboration. In MFTP, intent parsing first decodes user inputs—e.g., identifying a low-intensity preference from "relaxed sightseeing"—followed by coordinated optimization among agents with predefined roles. For instance, when an evaluation agent detects a "budget overrun", it feeds back to the planning agent, which adjusts activities to meet constraints. Unlike single-model direct planning, MFTP's dynamic feedback and agent interplay ensure plans align closely with user needs. Experiments on the TravelPlanner dataset, using models like Qwen 2.5-32B against direct planning baselines, validate MFTP's effectiveness, showing superior performance in commonsense constraints (e.g., varied dining styles) and hard constraints (e.g., budget limits). The main contributions of this paper are as follows:

- We introduce a novel framework that leverages multi-agent collaboration and iterative feedback to improve itinerary quality. By integrating intent parsing, planning, and evaluation agents, MFTP ensures precise constraint adherence and logical consistency in multi-day travel planning.
- Experimental results demonstrate that MFTP outperforms traditional direct and CoT planning methods on the TravelPlanner dataset, achieving significant improvements in pass rates and constraint satisfaction for complex travel queries.
- MFTP's adaptability and efficiency lay a foundation for personalized smart tourism services, enabling smaller-parameter models to deliver customized itineraries with performance comparable to larger, advanced systems.

2 Related Work

2.1 Traditional Planning Methods

Travel itinerary planning has been widely studied, with researchers developing mathematical models to generate optimal tour paths under spatiotemporal

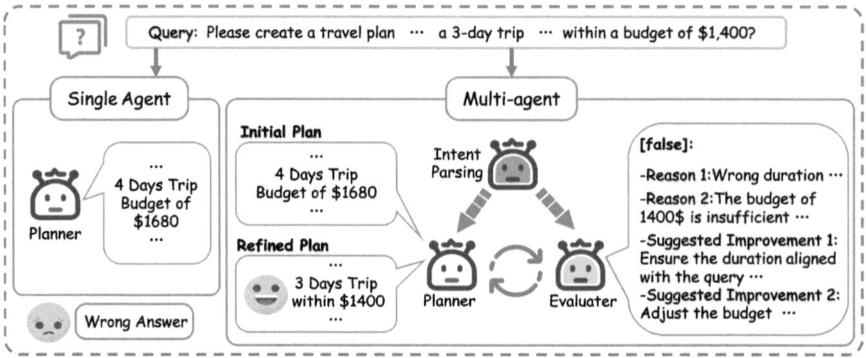

Fig. 1. Comparison of multi-agent and single-agent systems in travel itinerary planning. The multi-agent system can iteratively refine itineraries for complex constraints. The single-agent system fails to adjust plans for mismatches in travel days or budget, lacking feedback for improvement.

constraints. Multiple computational paradigms, such as dynamic programming, heuristic search, and metaheuristic algorithms, have emerged, each approach strives to strike a balance between path length and the coverage of points of interest. Gavalas et al. [8] systematically reviewed the Tourist Trip Design Problem, identifying the core challenge: transforming discrete POI nodes into a continuous tour plan that meets users' personalized needs while respecting real-world constraints [9]. To improve planning quality, methods like crowdsourcing, social networks, and case-based reasoning have been used to model user preferences, integrating other travellers' experiences for more tailored outcomes. Tenemaza et al. [10] applied genetic algorithms to optimize itinerary schemes, while Keyder et al. [11] proposed a soft constraint framework to ease rigid constraints, though limitations persist in defining objectives and capturing user needs.

2.2   Planning with LLMs

Recent advances in LLMs, such as ChatGPT [12], have drawn attention to their potential in itinerary planning. Studies suggest LLMs can enhance travel experiences by understanding user needs. Yet, quantitative evaluations show that these models struggle with complex tasks, particularly in coordinating multiple time nodes for long-span itineraries, leading to incoherent or conflicting plans [5]. LLMs also face challenges in balancing multiple constraints to produce optimal solutions and adapting to dynamic environments, as they cannot easily integrate external information for real-time adjustments. Even advanced models like GPT-4 exhibit limitations in multi-constraint, long-span planning. To address these issues, researchers have employed strategies like Chain of Thought [13], task decomposition [14], and reflection mechanisms [15], improving the quality and reliability of generated itineraries.

2.3 Planning with Intelligent Agents

Intelligent agents have made significant strides in addressing complex planning, challenges through task decomposition, multi-step reasoning, and tool integration [16]. Systems like AutoGPT [17] exemplify their potential in orchestrating intricate plans. LLM-driven agents typically employ a modular architecture, consisting of Memory, Tool-use, and Planning components, which enhances their capacity to formulate effective strategies [18]. The memory module retains critical context for extended planning, while tool use enables real-time adaptation to external inputs. These capabilities empower agents to surpass single-agent constraints, facilitating collaborative planning for sophisticated tasks. For instance, Li et al. [19] introduced a role-playing framework that leverages prompts to align agent plans with human goals, and Wang et al. [20] proposed a group discussion model, enhancing planning precision through prompt-guided reasoning. Similarly, Liu et al. [21] developed a dynamic team selection approach with adaptable communication, yielding robust planning outcomes across varied scenarios.

3   Method

In this section, we present MFTP, our iterative optimisation framework driven by dynamic feedback. The central objective of this framework is to enhance the performance of language-based intelligent agents in complex travel planning tasks through a closed-round process of understanding, planning, evaluation, and corrective feedback. The framework comprises three core modules: (1) a user intent parsing and transformation module, (2) a planning agent based on an LLM, and (3) a rule-based, role-specific evaluation agent. As illustrated in Fig. 2, this framework progressively approaches the optimal solution for complex travel planning tasks through multiple rounds of feedback and refinement.

3.1 Definition of the MFTP Framework

The MFTP framework proposed in this paper is a feedback-based, multi-iterative travel planning method. The core concept of this framework is to generate high-quality travel plans through the close collaboration of user intent understanding, a planning agent, and an evaluation-feedback agent, combined with predefined optimization strategies. Specifically, the framework takes user needs as its starting point. Given an initial user input q, the framework generates a feasible plan through the following steps:

Input Transformation: The intention parsing module U parses the raw input q and converts it into a structured intention representation $I_0 = U(q)$ encapsulating user preferences, constraints, and priority labels. This representation includes explicit details such as destination, date, transportation, and budget, extracted from unstructured natural language input. The process aims to clearly delineate user requirements, maximising the model's output adherence to specified constraints.

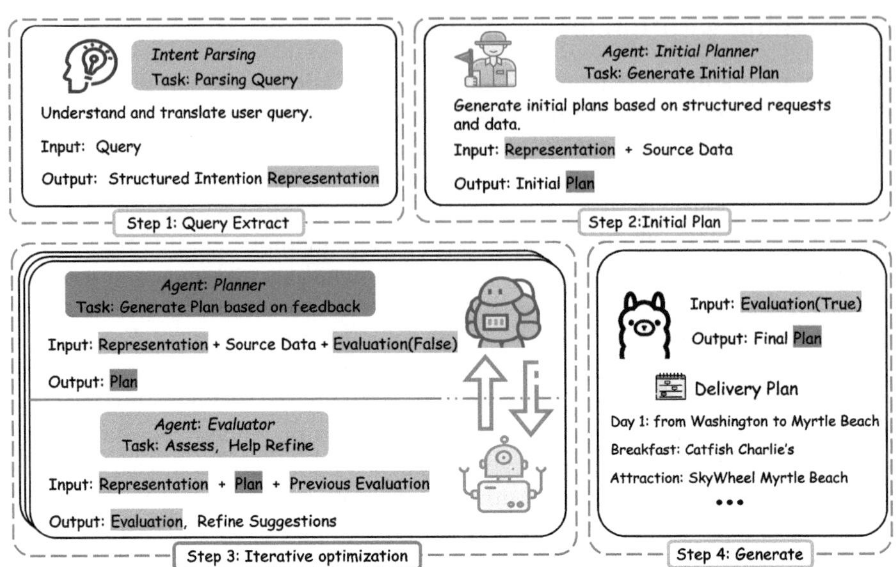

Fig. 2. Architecture of the MFTP framework, depicting Dual-Agent interaction, Intent Parsing, and Iterative Feedback Optimization.

Initial Plan Generation: The planning agent P generates an initial plan $P_0 = P(I_0)$ based on the structured intention I_0. The objective of this step is to produce a preliminary travel planning draft according to the user's initial requirements.

Constraint Evaluation: The evaluation agent E, powered by a LLM, conducts constraint verification on the current plan P_t, producing evaluation results by integrating the current plan with prior assessment outcomes $E(P_{t-1})$. This fusion is formalized as:

$$F_t = E(P_t \mid E(P_{t-1})) \tag{1}$$

where F_t denotes the evaluation outcome, conditioned on the previous result. If the agent confirms the plan meets all criteria—such as dates, destination, budget, and group size—and maintains logical consistency, F_t yields [true], indicating approval. Otherwise, it outputs [false] with concise reasons (e.g., misaligned dates) and structured improvement suggestions. The criteria reflect general user intent, not tied to specific metrics.

Feedback Iteration: If the evaluation outcome F_t does not yield [true] , indicating the current plan P_t fails to fully satisfy user requirements, the planning agent P initiates iterative optimization. using feedback from the evaluation agent generates an improved plan:

$$P_{t+1} = P(I_0 \mid F_t) \tag{2}$$

This process harnesses the interplay between evaluation and planning agents to enhance the final itinerary, refining it based on structured critiques in F_t.

Termination Condition: The planning process concludes when the evaluation outcome F_t yields [true], indicating full compliance with user requirements, or when the iteration count reaches the preset maximum $T = T_{\max}$. In the latter case, the final plan $P_{T_{\max}}$ is output as the result.

The Algorithm 1 encapsulates the whole process:

Algorithm 1. Multi-round Feedback Travel Planner (MFTP)

1: **Input:** User query q
2: **Output:** Final travel plan P_t
3: Initialize $I_0 = U(q)$ $P_0 = P(I_0)$ $F_0 = E(P_0)$
4: **for** $t = 1$ **to** $T_{\max}$ **do**
5:     $P_t = P(I_0 \mid F_{t-1})$ // Update plan based on feedback
6:     $F_t = E(P_t \mid E(P_{t-1}))$ //Evaluate based on the previous assessment
7:     **if** F_t indicates a valid plan **then**
8:         **Return** P_t
9:     **else**
10:         $P_{t+1} = P(I_0 \mid F_t)$
11:     **end if**
12: **end for**
13: **Return** P_t

3.2   Implementation of Core Module

Intent Parsing Module: This module uses a one-shot prompt to convert user input q into a standardized JSON format. A predefined template with an example (e.g., "Plan a 3-day trip...") guides the LLM to extract key details: cities in order, exact or vague dates, budget, and specific requests (e.g., non-stop flights) as other requirements. Unspecified fields are marked as null. The example-driven prompt ensures structured intent extraction for planning.

Planner Agent: This module uses the LLM's planning capabilities via in-context learning with a role-based prompt (e.g., "You are a proficient planner"). It combines the user query q, prior feedback $E(P_{t-1})$, and input data into a prompt template. The LLM creates a detailed travel plan, including specifics like flight numbers, restaurant names, and accommodations, based only on the input. The output follows a structured format (e.g., daily breakdowns with city, transportation, etc.), aligning with q and commonsense constraints.

Evaluator Agent: This LLM-based module evaluates the current travel plan P_t against the user query q and prior feedback $E(P_{t-1})$ using a structured prompt. It checks for alignment with q (e.g., dates, destination, budget) and logical consistency, outputting [true] if satisfied. If not, it returns [false] with brief reasons (e.g., budget exceeded) and structured suggestions (e.g., lower dining costs). Inputs include P_t, $E(P_{t-1})$, and q, ensuring precise feedback in a predefined format for iterative refinement in MFTP.

4   Experiments

In this section, we rigorously evaluate leading LLMs and established planning strategies using the TravelPlanner dataset under a sole-planning mode. We assume all planning information is readily available, enabling the planner agent to directly craft a plan from the data.

4.1   Travel Planner Dataset

The TravelPlanner benchmark dataset, employed in this study, assesses the multi-constraint planning abilities of language agents in intricate real-world contexts. Tailored to travel planning tasks, it offers a rigorous testing platform by replicating real-world scenarios encompassing transportation, accommodations, attractions, dining, and diverse user demands. In the following, we outline its composition, constraint design, and evaluation methodology.

Dataset Composition: 1) Query-Plan Pairs: This dataset comprises 1,225 manually annotated query-plan pairs, segmented into nine difficulty levels based on travel duration and constraint count. Longer travel periods entail visiting more cities, while ambiguous destinations heighten the agent's challenge in selecting plans that meet user needs. 2) Tools and Sandbox Environment: To maintain experimental consistency, the dataset provides a static database containing nearly 4 million records, accessible via six specialized tools such as flight search, restaurant search, and distance calculation.

Constraint Design: 1) Environmental Constraints: When critical information, such as sold-out flights, is unavailable, the agent must adapt its planning strategy dynamically. 2) Commonsense Constraints: These encompass itinerary logic and diversity rules (e.g., avoiding repetition in attractions or meal types). 3) Hard Constraints: Explicit user-specified constraints—including duration, budget, accommodation preferences, traveller count, and transportation modes—require strict adherence.

Evaluation Methods: 1) Delivery Rate: Assess whether the agent can produce a complete plan within a constrained 30-step process. 2) Constraint Pass Rate: Evaluates compliance with commonsense and hard constraints, using Micro and Macro strategies to measure individual constraint satisfaction and overall adherence, respectively.
The Micro Pass Rate is formalized as follows:

$$\text{Micro Pass Rate} = \frac{\sum_{p \in P} \sum_{c \in C_p} \mathbb{1}_{\text{passed}(c,p)}}{\sum_{p \in P} |C_p|} \tag{3}$$

The Macro Pass Rate is formalized as follows:

$$\text{Macro Pass Rate} = \frac{\sum_{p \in P} \mathbb{1}_{\text{passed}(c,p)}}{|P|} \tag{4}$$

3) Final Pass Rate: The proportion of generated plans meeting all constraints concurrently, reflecting the agent framework's ability to deliver realistic, standards-compliant itineraries.

4.2   Baselines

To comprehensively evaluate the proposed framework's effectiveness, we conducted multi-dimensional comparative experiments. For baseline selection, we experimented with several advanced language models across diverse parameter scales and architectures, benchmarking Qwen-2.5, Mixtral-8x7B-MoE, Gemini Pro and GPT-3.5-Turbo. These models span billions to trillions of parameters, covering both mixture-of-experts models and inference architectures, effectively representing the current diversity of LLMs.

At the reasoning strategy level, we systematically incorporated mainstream planning strategies into the study, including:

Direct: This approach leverages prompts to guide the model in producing outputs directly, prioritising efficiency and simplicity for tasks requiring straightforward responses.

Chain-of-Thought: This method enhances multi-step reasoning clarity and coherence by breaking problems into explicit reasoning chains, with its reasoning ability demonstrated in mathematical and semantic tasks [13].

Given the reliance of complex travel itinerary planning on long contexts and the capacity of extended context windows to reduce planning errors from information truncation, we chose models with at least 32K-token context windows for our experiments.

4.3   Experimental Results

Table 1. Performance Evaluation of Planner-Evaluator Combinations (GPT-3.5-Turbo, Mixtral-8 × 7B-MoE and Gemini Pro Data from [5])

	Delivery Rate	Commonsense Pass Rate		Hard Constraint Pass Rate		Final Pass Rate
		Micro	Macro	Micro	Macro	
Validation (#180)						
$\text{Direct}_{GPT-3.5-Turbo}$	100	60.2	4.4	11.0	2.8	0
$\text{COT}_{GPT-3.5-Turbo}$	100	66.3	3.3	11.9	5.0	0
$\text{Direct}_{Mixtral-8} \times 7B-MoE$	100	68.1	5.0	3.3	1.1	0
$\text{Direct}_{GeminiPro}$	93.9	65.0	8.3	9.3	4.4	0.6
$\text{Direct}_{Qwen-2.5-32B}$	100	73.4	5.56	11.91	5.0	0.56
$\text{CoT}_{Qwen-2.5-32B}$	100	76.18	9.44	18.57	10.0	1.11
$\textbf{MFTP}_{\textbf{Qwen-2.5-32B}}$**(Ours)**	**100**	**78.33**	**11.67**	**22.14**	**11.11**	**2.23**
Test (#1,000)						
$\text{Direct}_{GPT-3.5-Turbo}$	100	59.5	2.7	9.5	4.4	0.6
$\text{COT}_{GPT-3.5-Turbo}$	100	64.4	2.3	9.8	3.8	0.4
$\text{Direct}_{Mixtral-8} \times 7B-MoE$	99.3	67.0	3.7	3.9	1.6	0.7
$\text{Direct}_{GeminiPro}$	93.7	64.7	7.9	10.6	4.7	2.1
$\text{Direct}_{Qwen-2.5-32B}$	99.9	72.9	7.1	15.85	9.8	1.67
$\text{CoT}_{Qwen-2.5-32B}$	99.7	73.36	8.4	16.29	10.9	2.1
$\textbf{MFTP}_{\textbf{Qwen-2.5-32B}}$ **(Ours)**	99.9	**75.02**	9.3	**21.09**	14.0	3.0

Comparison results between MFTP and baseline methods are presented in Table 1, evaluated using TravelPlanner metrics: delivery rate, constraint pass rate (Micro and Macro), and final pass rate. Compared to the Direct method, MFTP significantly improves the final pass rate (by 1.67%) and hard constraint pass rate (by 10.23% Micro and 6.11% Macro) on the validation set with the Qwen-2.5 model. Against the Chain-of-Thought method, MFTP with Qwen-2.5 enhances the delivery rate and constraint pass rate on the validation set, each by over 1%, demonstrating superior constraint handling. Additionally, citing from [5], MFTP with the Qwen-2.5-32B achieves performance surpassing GPT-3.5-Turbo, Mixtral-8 × 7B, and Gemini Pro, showcasing its ability to optimize smaller models to outperform complex, large-parameter architectures.

The ablation experiment results, shown in Fig. 3 as bar charts, quantify each module's contribution to framework performance. We designed four comparative tests: (1) baseline method; (2) variant with the understanding module alone; (3) variant with the iterative optimization mechanism alone; (4) full MFTP framework. Results reveal that the understanding module significantly boosts compliance with commonsense constraints, while the iterative optimization mechanism markedly improves alignment with user preferences. Further analysis shows the complete MFTP framework, integrating both modules, significantly outperforms the baseline in commonsense pass rate, hard constraint pass rate, and final pass rate, confirming each component's individual contribution and the critical synergy driving overall performance gains.

4.4   Ablation Experiment

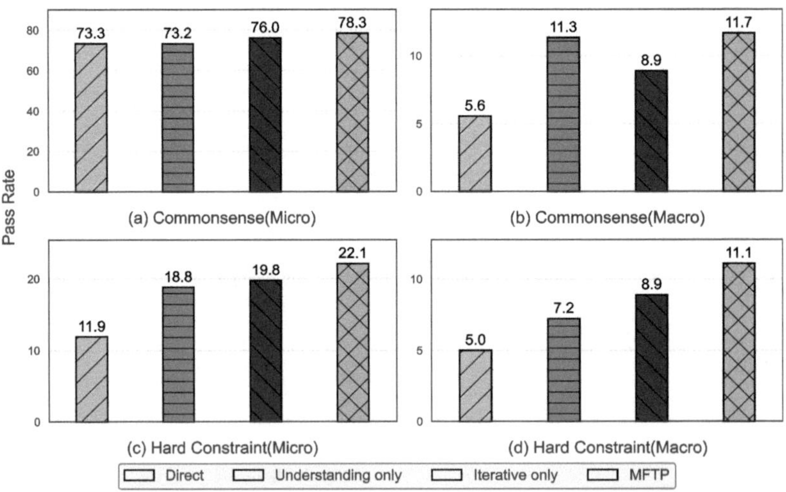

Fig. 3. Comparison of pass rates across different methods.

To further validate the iterative feedback method and assess its performance across iteration counts, we conducted ablation experiments targeting 0 to 5 iterations, as shown in Fig. 4. Results indicate that most pass rate metrics rise from 0 to 3 iterations but decline at 4 to 5 iterations. Thus, we selected 4 iterations as the optimal configuration, balancing performance gains and computational cost. Due to time and model usage constraints, we capped the maximum iterations at 5.

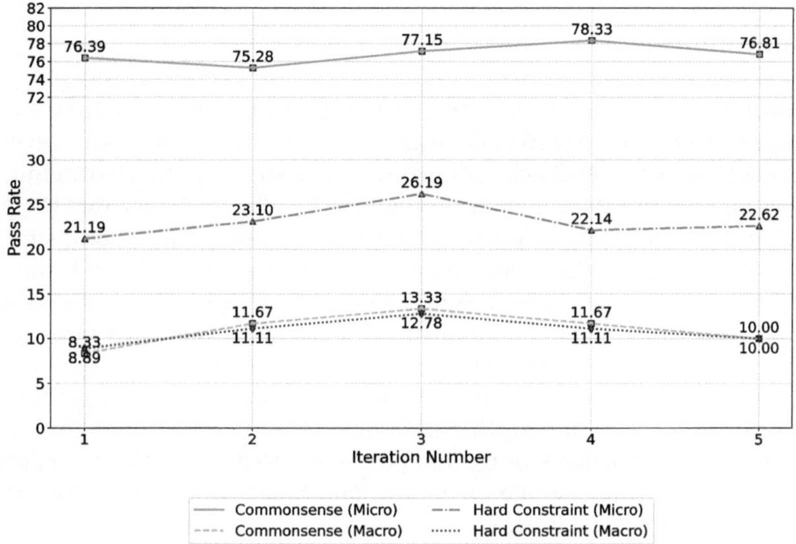

Fig. 4. Ablation study of MFTP pass rates across 0 to 5 iterations for Commonsense and Hard Constraint metrics.

4.5 Analysis of Planner-Evaluator Parameter Impact

Experiments investigating the impact of parameter sizes on MFTP's planner and evaluator were conducted using the validation set with various model combinations. As the Delivery Rate consistently reached 100% across all configurations, it is omitted from the results. Table 2 presents the remaining metrics, which indicate that performance is optimized when both agents employ the same model. When a small-parameter agent plans and a large-parameter agent evaluates, the latter's complex feedback often disrupts the former's simpler output, reducing commonsense and hard constraint pass rates—for instance, failing to meet diverse dining requirements. Conversely, when a large-parameter agent handles planning and a small-parameter agent performs evaluation, the planning exhibits high quality with robust commonsense pass rates, while the smaller agent provides focused feedback, such as budget adjustments tailored to user needs, further improving the final itinerary quality.

Table 2. Performance Evaluation of Planner-Evaluator Combinations

Planner	Evaluator	Commonsense Pass Rate		Hard Constraint Pass Rate		Final Pass Rate
		Micro	Macro	Micro	Macro	
LLaMA-3.1-8B	LLaMA-3.1-8B	74.58	4.44	7.86	2.22	0
LLaMA-3.1-8B	Qwen-2.5-32B	66.67	6.11	6.6	2.22	0
Qwen-2.5-32B	LLaMA-3.1-8B	77.15	8.89	20.71	9.44	1.11
Qwen-2.5-32B	Qwen-2.5-32B	78.33	11.67	22.1	11.11	2.23

5 Conclusions

This paper proposes MFTP, a practical multi-agent framework that enhances multi-agent systems' ability to understand and adapt to user needs in travel planning through iterative feedback optimization and an intent understanding module. Experimental results demonstrate that MFTP effectively narrows the performance gap between small-parameter models and complex, large-parameter models in travel planning tasks, achieving gains without additional fine-tuning, thus significantly reducing hardware resource demands. Empirical studies on models like LLaMA-3.1 and Qwen-2.5 confirm MFTP's effectiveness in boosting performance. Despite these improvements, the framework falls short in fully meeting diverse user demands and adhering to hard constraints, suggesting future research should focus on integrating data more effectively, clarifying users' hard constraints, and optimizing storage and processing to improve the model's understanding of needs, enhance plan accuracy, and boost user satisfaction, thereby elevating MFTP's practical value.

Acknowledgements. This research was supported by the Central Guidance for Local Science and Technology Development Fund Projects (No.2024ZYD0268).

References

1. World Tourism Organization (UN Tourism): World tourism barometer (May 2024). https://doi.org/10.18111/wtobarometereng.2024.22.1.2
2. Zhao, W.X., et al.: A survey of large language models. arXiv preprint arXiv:2303.18223 **1**(2) (2023)
3. Qin, Y., et al.: Toolllm: Facilitating large language models to master 16000+ real-world apis. arXiv preprint arXiv:2307.16789 (2023)
4. Wang, L., et al.: A survey on large language model based autonomous agents. Front. Comp. Sci. **18**(6), 186345 (2024)
5. Xie, J., et al.: Travelplanner: a benchmark for real-world planning with language agents. arXiv preprint arXiv:2402.01622 (2024)
6. Jersild, A.T.: Mental set and shift. No. 89, Columbia university (1927)
7. Du, Y., Li, S., Torralba, A., Tenenbaum, J.B., Mordatch, I.: Improving factuality and reasoning in language models through multiagent debate. In: Forty-first International Conference on Machine Learning (2023)

8. Gavalas, D., Konstantopoulos, C., Mastakas, K., Pantziou, G.: A survey on algorithmic approaches for solving tourist trip design problems. J. Heuristics **20**(3), 291–328 (2014). https://doi.org/10.1007/s10732-014-9242-5

9. Tang, Y., et al.: Itinera: Integrating spatial optimization with large language models for open-domain urban itinerary planning, pp. 1413–1432 (2024)

10. Tenemaza, M., Luján-Mora, S., De Antonio, A., Ramirez, J.: Improving itinerary recommendations for tourists through metaheuristic algorithms: an optimization proposal. IEEE Access **8**, 79003–79023 (2020)

11. Keyder, E., Geffner, H.: Soft goals can be compiled away. J. Artif. Intell. Res. **36**, 547–556 (2009)

12. OpenAI: Introducing chatgpt by openai (2022). https://openai.com/blog/chatgpt

13. Wei, J., et al.: Chain-of-thought prompting elicits reasoning in large language models. Adv. Neural. Inf. Process. Syst. **35**, 24824–24837 (2022)

14. Yao, S., et al.: React: synergizing reasoning and acting in language models. In: International Conference on Learning Representations (ICLR) (2023)

15. Shinn, N., Cassano, F., Gopinath, A., Narasimhan, K., Yao, S.: Reflexion: language agents with verbal reinforcement learning. Adv. Neural. Inf. Process. Syst. **36**, 8634–8652 (2023)

16. Li, A., Xie, Y., Li, S., Tsung, F., Ding, B., Li, Y.: Agent-oriented planning in multi-agent systems. arXiv preprint arXiv:2410.02189 (2024)

17. Significant Gravitas: AutoGPT. https://github.com/Significant-Gravitas/AutoGPT

18. Weng, L.: LLM-powered autonomous agents. lilianweng.github.io (Jun 2023). https://lilianweng.github.io/posts/2023-06-23-agent/

19. Li, G., Hammoud, H., Itani, H., Khizbullin, D., Ghanem, B.: Camel: communicative agents for "mind" exploration of large language model society. Adv. Neural. Inf. Process. Syst. **36**, 51991–52008 (2023)

20. Wang, Q., Wang, Z., Su, Y., Tong, H., Song, Y.: Rethinking the bounds of LLM reasoning: Are multi-agent discussions the key? In: Ku, L.W., Martins, A., Srikumar, V. (eds.) Proceedings of the 62nd Annual Meeting of the Association for Computational Linguistics (Volume 1: Long Papers), pp. 6106–6131. Association for Computational Linguistics, Bangkok, Thailand (Aug 2024). https://doi.org/10.18653/v1/2024.acl-long.331, https://aclanthology.org/2024.acl-long.331/

21. Liu, Z., Zhang, Y., Li, P., Liu, Y., Yang, D.: A dynamic LLM-powered agent network for task-oriented agent collaboration. In: First Conference on Language Modeling (2024)

GraphRAG-KM: An Automated Framework for Transforming Industrial Documents into Ontology and Conceptual Models

Duyun Wang[1], Peilin Han[1], Shmuel Tyszberowicz[2,1], Mingyue Zhang[1], and Bo Liu[1(✉)]

[1] Southwest University, Chongqing, China
liubocq@swu.edu.cn
[2] Afeka Academic College of Engineering, Tel-Aviv, Israel

Abstract. With the increasing complexity of industrial systems, efficiently extracting and modelling knowledge from massive technical standards documentation has become a major challenge. This paper presents GraphRAG-KM, an automated framework for accurately converting unstructured industrial documents into structured ontology (OWL) and conceptual (UML) models. The framework integrates multi-layered technologies, including MinerU, retrieval-augmented generation (RAG), large language models (LLMs), and K-Means clustering, to precisely extract entities, relationships, and hierarchical structures. Specifically, MinerU and OCR preprocess PDF documents into structured Markdown texts, which are then semantically enriched by GraphRAG via targeted retrieval and indexing. Subsequently, LLMs infer implicit attributes and relationships, thereby enhancing semantic completeness. Meanwhile, K-Means clustering identifies latent associative relations, which significantly improves model completeness and semantic depth. Experimental evaluations on the MIL-STD-6016 standard demonstrate that GraphRAG-KM achieves a knowledge extraction accuracy of 94.7%, significantly outperforming traditional LLMs methods (approximately 30%). Reading efficiency improved by 58.66% in readability assessments, and comprehension accuracy increased by 29.2% compared to traditional reading methods. Furthermore, automated modelling efficiency improved by 6.75 times compared to manual methods. GraphRAG-KM thus represents an effective solution for intelligent, scalable, and efficient knowledge management in industrial engineering contexts.

Keywords: Information Extraction · Industrial Document Analysis · Ontology Modelling · GraphRAG · Model-Based System Engineering

1 Introduction

High-end manufacturing industries, such as military communications, aerospace, and equipment manufacturing, heavily rely on standardised industrial documents

T. Zhu et al. (Eds.): KSEM 2025, LNAI 15920, pp. 108–120, 2026.
https://doi.org/10.1007/978-981-95-3052-6_9

for the design, development, and maintenance of engineering systems [1,2]. These documents contain key technical specifications and implementation guidelines, which are important in supporting system engineering practices [3].

In recent years, system engineering has shifted from document-based development to model-based system engineering (MBSE) [4]. However, as industrial systems grow more complex, their associated documents become voluminous and difficult to manage, posing challenges to MBSE adoption. For example, industrial documents often contain detailed specifications and technical standards, such as the MIL-STD-6016 protocol [5] used by the U.S. Army to define Link 16, which exceeds 6,000 pages in length. Managing such large-scale documents remains a major constraint for MBSE development.

Large Language Models (LLMs) have significantly improved text analysis automation [6] but still struggle with document information extraction due to limited context windows and the risk of generating inaccurate content [7]. Retrieval-Augmented Generation (RAG) [8] addresses these challenges by incorporating external knowledge bases, retrieving relevant fragments, and incorporating them as additional context. Thus, enhancing comprehension and reliability in industrial text processing.

MinerU is an open-source tool for extracting structured data from unstructured PDFs [9] but lacks knowledge representation and reasoning. *GraphRAG* [10], a Retrieval-Augmented Generation (RAG) method, improves knowledge retrieval but cannot capture multi-layer logical relationships.

The GraphRAG-KM framework that we have developed (illustrated in Fig. 1) offers the following contributions: (1) *One-step extraction of key entities and relationships:* Integrates MinerU and GraphRAG for direct extraction of key entities and relationships from PDFs, storing results in Parquet format to enhance data structuring. (2) *Leveraging LLMs for Attribute Completion and Relationship Inference:* Uses LLMs to enrich entity attributes and object properties, improving ontology and conceptual modelling. (3) *Optimising K-Means Clustering for Hierarchical Relationship Modelling:* Employs K-Means clustering to identify missing associative logical relationships, improving knowledge structure completeness. (4) *Establishing a Unified Conversion Process from Industrial Documents to Ontology and Conceptual Models:* Develops an automated pipeline for unstructured text parsing and structured storage, supporting ontology (OWL)[1] and conceptual model (UML) consistency and reusability.

To evaluate our approach, we applied the GraphRAG-KM framework to a case study based on Link 16, as specified in the MIL-STD-6016 standard, and conducted experiments to validate its effectiveness and efficiency in modelling tactical chain knowledge.

2   Related Work

With the advancement of industrial technology, there is an increasing demand for informatisation, intelligence, and automation in the industrial sector. Model-

---

[1] OWL (Web Ontology Language), see https://www.w3.org/OWL/.

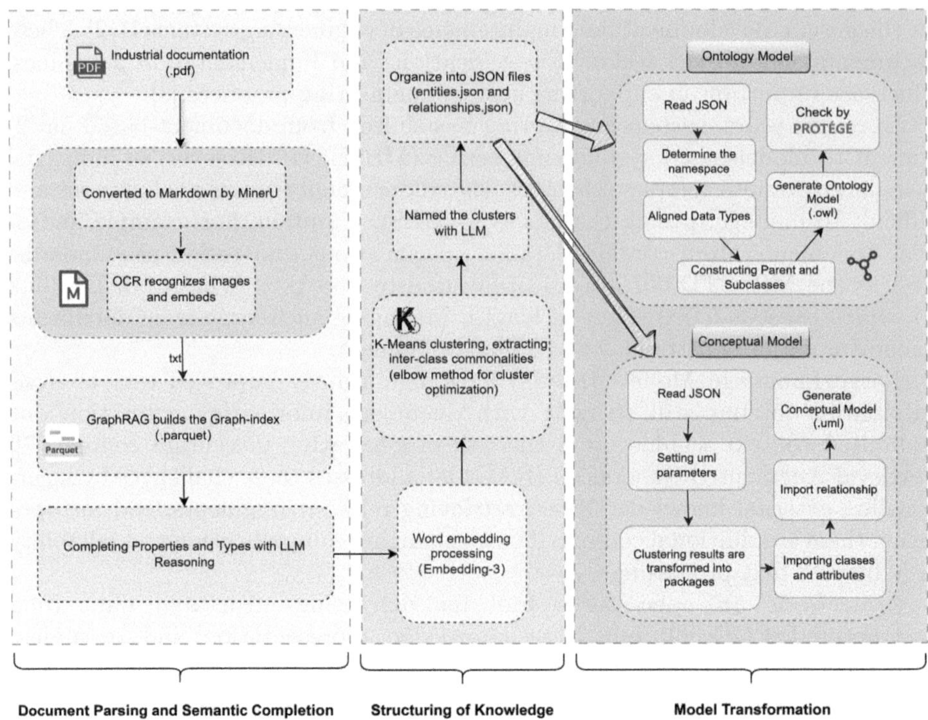

Fig. 1. FlowChart Of GraphRAG-KM.

Based System Engineering (MBSE) plays a crucial role in achieving this goal by transforming traditional documents into models that emphasise Process, Method, Tool, and Environment (PMTE) integration [11].

In recent years, document parsing technologies have advanced significantly. For example, Wang Bing et al. [9] developed MinerU. This document recognition tool integrates Optical Character Recognition (OCR), table recognition, and formula parsing to convert industrial standard documents into structured data. However, its functionality is limited to text extraction and lacks semantic modelling capabilities. Consequently, the extracted information still requires further relational analysis to derive meaningful knowledge.

Microsoft's GraphRAG, developed by Darren Edge et al. [10], combines retrieval-augmented generation (RAG) with knowledge graphs, using graph-based indexing to improve the precision of LLMs in answering long-document questions.

The research of Kumar et al. [12] explores the application of K-means clustering in the OWL domain, where semantic clustering is used to identify shared concepts and optimise knowledge structures. However, this approach relies on external knowledge bases (e.g., WordNet) and lacks adaptive modelling capabilities for previously unknown concepts. This limitation poses challenges when applying the method to industrial document-based knowledge modelling.

Abolhasani et al. [13] attempted to extract knowledge graphs from documents; however, their results failed to effectively achieve category clustering and logical relationship construction, nor did they produce a complete ontology model.

3 Methodology

This section introduces the framework structure of our proposed approach, providing a detailed description of each step, process, and the key algorithms used. The framework has been implemented as an open source project on GitHub (https://github.com/GraphRAG-KM/GraphragKM).

3.1 Overview of the Methodology

This study proposes a knowledge modelling framework based on GraphRAG-KM, as illustrated in Fig. 1. The proposed method enables the extraction of conceptual and ontological models from industrial documents through a fully automated process, facilitating an efficient transformation from unstructured text to structured knowledge.

The proposed approach explicitly divides the processing pipeline into three key phases: *document parsing and semantic completion, knowledge structuring,* and *model transformation.*

1. *Document Parsing and Semantic Completion*: The system employs a multi-layered information processing technique to extract core concepts and relationships from industrial standard documents. Additionally, an indexing mechanism is incorporated to enhance the organisation and accessibility of extracted information.
2. *Structuring of Knowledge*: The extracted information is systematically structured to establish hierarchical relationships among concepts. This process optimises logical coherence and ensures alignment with knowledge representations of the industrial system.
3. *Model Transformation*: This phase focuses on transforming the structured knowledge into formal representations, such as UML and OWL models. These representations facilitate system modelling and knowledge management, enhancing their applicability in industrial domains.

The entire process emphasises automation and intelligence, leveraging RAG, LLMs, and K-means clustering to ensure the precision of document parsing and the completeness of knowledge modelling. Furthermore, this method provides a standardised conversion process from industrial documents to ontologies and conceptual models, enhancing the practical application of MBSE in complex industrial systems. By implementing this approach, researchers and engineers can efficiently transform unstructured standard documents into structured knowledge, offering a more intelligent and scalable solution for industrial knowledge management and system design (Fig. 3).

3.2 Document Parsing and Semantic Completion

We propose an automated method for extracting core concepts, entities, and relationships from unstructured industrial documents, transforming them into structured data for subsequent modelling.

Industrial documents often contain complex terms, images, and tables, making precise extraction difficult. To address this, we integrate MinerU, OCR, and GraphRAG to enhance semantic completeness and data structuring.
The workflow consists of: (1) *Industrial Document Processing.* Industrial PDFs containing text, tables, and images are preprocessed using MinerU, converting them into Markdown (MD) format. EasyOCR extracts textual content from images, reintegrating it into the Markdown document for a unified representation. (2) *Index Construction.* GraphRAG indexes the Markdown document by segmenting content and structuring key concepts and relationships into a graph-based format. The indexed data is stored in '.parquet' files, with entities in 'entities.parquet' and relationships in 'relationships.parquet'. (3) *Semantic Completion.* A large language model (Deepseek-v3) [14] enhances knowledge completeness by inferring missing attributes and data types for entities in 'entities.parquet' and deducing implicit semantic relationships from 'relationships.parquet', enriching logical associations.

This workflow automates the transformation of industrial PDFs into a structured data frame of class and relationship definitions, laying the groundwork for further entity clustering via K-Means, complementing GraphRAG's entity identification.

3.3 Structuring of Knowledge

Using clustering algorithms, this phase uncovers implicit entity commonalities and latent relationships within the document, thereby enhancing data hierarchy and logical clarity.

Since the initial index constructed by GraphRAG does not fully reveal implicit associations between classes, this study introduces the K-Means clustering algorithm to analyse entity similarities comprehensively. Utilising the Embedding-3 model from Bigmodel, the entity and relationship information completed by LLMs is vectorised through word embeddings. The optimal number of clusters k is determined by computing the silhouette coefficient. K-Means clustering is then applied to automatically analyse the data, identifying potential logical commonalities among concepts and supplementing the relationships omitted in the indexing phase.

The primary goal of K-Means clustering is to minimise intra-cluster variance, optimising the following loss function:

$$J = \sum_{i=1}^{n} \sum_{k=1}^{K} \mathbf{1}(c_i = k)\|x_i - \mu_k\|^2 \tag{1}$$

where n is the number of data points, K the number of clusters, c_i the cluster label for data point x_i, and μ_k the centroid of cluster k.

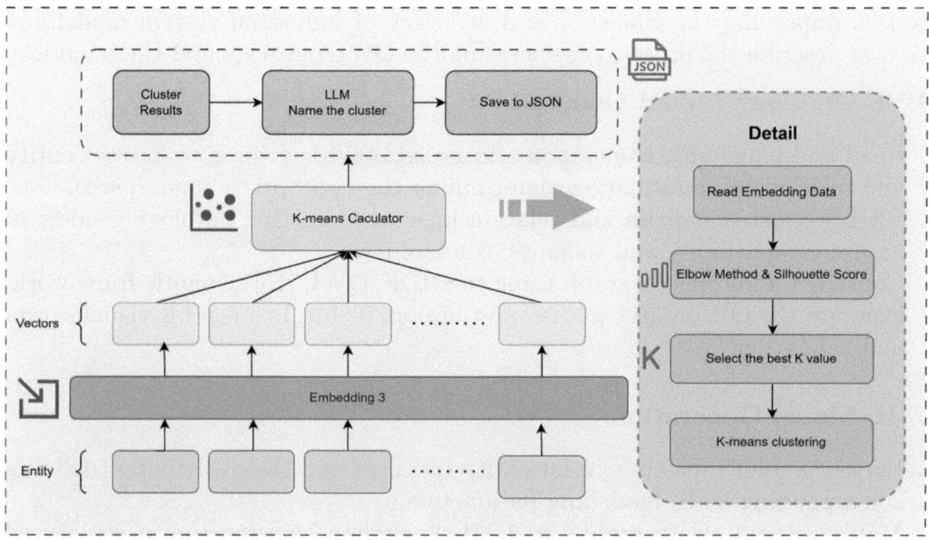

Fig. 2. K-means Detailed Process.

To determine the optimal number of clusters K, the silhouette coefficient evaluates clustering performance. For each data point i, it is computed as:

$$s(i) = \frac{b(i) - a(i)}{\max(a(i), b(i))} \tag{2}$$

where $a(i)$ is the average intra-cluster distance of i, and $b(i)$ the average distance from i to the nearest neighbouring cluster. The overall silhouette coefficient S is:

$$S = \frac{1}{n} \sum_{i=1}^{n} s(i) \tag{3}$$

This metric helps identify the optimal K, ensuring well-separated and compact clusters. The optimal k value can be selected by computing the silhouette coefficient, ensuring that the clustering results achieve better separation and compactness, thereby further revealing the latent relationships between entities. The detailed workflow is illustrated in Fig. 2.

3.4   Model Transformation

The model transformation phase aims to automatically generate both OWL ontology models and UML conceptual models based on the optimised JSON files from the clustering process. This dual approach addresses the needs of industrial knowledge management and system design. Through a standardised conversion process, this study enables the automated mapping of structured knowledge to models, improving the efficiency and accuracy of industrial system modelling. We now describe the process of generating the OWL ontology and UML models.

OWL Ontology Model Generation:

1. Read and parse `entities.json` and `relationships.json` to extract entity and relationship information, determining the appropriate namespaces.
2. Align extracted entities and relationships with existing ontology models to ensure compatibility and semantic consistency.
3. Construct a knowledge graph using the RDF/OWL [15] semantic framework, generate the OWL ontology file, and import it into Protégé for visualisation and validation.

UML Model Generation:

1. Parse the JSON files to extract entity concepts and their attributes, defining corresponding UML modelling parameters.
2. Map clustered entity groups to UML `Packages`, constructing a structured UML class diagram.
3. Parse relationship information from JSON files to define class associations, ensuring the integrity of the UML model for software development and system analysis.

4   Validation of GraphRAG-KM Effectiveness

To empirically evaluate the effectiveness of the GraphRAG-KM framework in industrial document parsing, ontology modelling, and conceptual modelling, this study aims to address the following research questions (RQs):

- **RQ1 (Structured Knowledge Extraction Capability)**: Can GraphRAG-KM improve the accuracy of extracting structured knowledge from unstructured industrial documents (e.g., MIL-STD-6016)? How does it perform in entity recognition, relationship extraction, and hierarchical modelling compared to direct LLM-based parsing?
- **RQ2 (Readability of Ontology and Conceptual Models)**: Do the ontology (OWL) and conceptual models (UML) generated by the framework comply with semantic standards? To what extent do they enhance the comprehension speed and accuracy of document content for participants without prior knowledge?
- **RQ3 (Automation Efficiency in Knowledge Extraction and Modelling)**: How does GraphRAG-KM perform in extracting knowledge and converting it into ontology/conceptual models? Compared to traditional manual modelling, does it improve efficiency and reduce development time?

Experimental Dataset. This study selects the MIL-STD-6016 standard document as the experimental dataset, focusing on sections related to core components of tactical data links (e.g., Sect. 4.1 of the MIL-STD-6016). This is a tactical data link protocol defined by the U.S. Department of Defence, specifying message formats, operational procedures, and system interoperability standards. With its highly structured technical content, it serves as an appropriate test case for knowledge extraction and ontology modelling.

Experimental Baseline. Due to the absence of a unified standard between ontology and conceptual models, this study adopts an expert-driven manual modelling approach as the baseline, applied to randomly selected document sections. During the accuracy evaluation, results are validated by expert manual inspection, where conceptual consistency is considered correct.

Experimental Method. The GraphRAG-KM framework is employed to parse selected document sections, converting them into *structured knowledge* and automatically generating both *ontology models* (OWL) and *conceptual models* (UML). This case study enables a comparative evaluation with expert-driven manual models, facilitating the analysis of GraphRAG-KM's advantages in knowledge extraction, ontology construction, and conceptual modelling. Furthermore, it validates its applicability in processing industrial standard documents.

4.1 Evaluation of RQ1

To evaluate the effectiveness of the GraphRAG-KM framework in extracting structured knowledge, this experiment involves two stakeholder groups: domain experts and knowledge engineering researchers. The evaluation incorporates both objective and subjective metrics.

- *Subjective Metrics*: A questionnaire-based survey is used to assess domain experts' perceptions of the Completeness, accuracy, and interpretability of the structured knowledge generated by GraphRAG-KM.
- *Objective Metrics*: These include the number of correctly identified entities and the accuracy of relation extraction.

Experimental Setup. The experimental subject is a set of randomly selected sections from the MIL-STD-6016 standard document, containing definitions and operational procedures for tactical data link (TDL) core components.

Structured knowledge models are evaluated using a blind evaluation approach, where models generated by different methods are randomly mixed and assessed by 8 participants:

- Generated by GraphRAG-KM.
- Generated by GraphRAG-KM without K-means clustering.
- Directly extracted by LLMs (various models).
- Manually constructed by domain experts.

Each expert evaluates the models without knowing their source, following the criteria below, using a *Likert scale (1–7)* [16]:

1. *Completeness*: Are the extracted entities and relations comprehensive?
2. *Consistency*: Does the classification and inheritance structure comply with established norms?
3. *Relation Accuracy*: Are the extracted relations aligned with the document definitions?

The correctness column in Table 1 is calculated using the following formula, representing the proportion of entities and relations in the current model that are considered correct when using the expert model as a reference.

$$\text{Correctness} = \frac{\text{Number of Correct Entities}}{\text{Number of Expert Model Entities}} \times 100\% \qquad (4)$$

The evaluation scores are summarised in Table 1. The data presented in the table represents the average performance of the same method across different test sections.

Table 1. Comparison of Completeness, Consistency, and Accuracy Across Methods

Method	Completeness	Consistency	Relation Accuracy	Correctness
Manually Model	6.88	7.00	6.88	100%
GraphRAG-KM	6.62	6.75	6.75	94.7%
GraphRAG-KM(No KM)	6.00	6.38	6.25	90.6%
ChatGPT-o1	4.62	4.62	3.38	33.3%
ChatGPT-4o	3.67	4.12	3.25	28.5%
Deepseek-r1	4.50	4.25	3.62	32.4%
Deepseek-v3	3.25	3.75	2.88	22.3%

The experimental results indicate that the GraphRAG-KM framework significantly enhances the accuracy of structured knowledge extraction from unstructured industrial documents, outperforming traditional LLM-based parsing methods in entity recognition, relation extraction, and hierarchical modelling. Additionally, K-means clustering plays a crucial role in establishing logical relationships and optimising category classification.

4.2   Evaluation of RQ2

In this experiment, we evaluate the readability of ontology models (OWL) and conceptual models (UML) generated by the GraphRAG-KM framework, as well as their impact on participants' comprehension speed and accuracy.

Experimental Setup. We invited a group of participants with no prior knowledge. To ensure that their comprehension was not affected by unfamiliarity with file structures, we first provided them with instructions on understanding the structure of JSON, using *Protégé*[2] to view OWL ontology models, and interpreting UML conceptual models.

A controlled experiment was conducted using randomly selected sections from MIL-STD-6016B. The participants were divided into four groups:

1. *Control Group (C)*: Directly reads the selected sections.
2. *Experimental Group (T1)*: Reads the ontology (OWL) and conceptual model (UML) generated by GraphRAG-KM.
3. *Experimental Group (T2)*: Reads the ontology (OWL) and conceptual model (UML) generated by GraphRAG-KM without using the K-means algorithm.
4. *Experimental Group (T3)*: Reads the JSON generated by GraphRAG-KM.

All participants read the assigned materials independently, without access to external resources or discussions during the experiment. After reading, they complete the same questionnaire, which assesses their understanding of overall concepts rather than memorisation of details, and their accuracy is recorded. The evaluation is conducted using both subjective and objective metrics.

- *Subjective Metrics*: Assessed using a Likert scale (1–7), evaluating participants' perceptions of model readability and knowledge structure consistency. Additionally, qualitative feedback is collected through interviews to discuss the strengths and limitations of the GraphRAG-KM-generated structured knowledge.
- *Objective Metrics*: Measured by reading time and comprehension accuracy.

Table 2. Readability, Knowledge Structure, & Comprehension Performance Evaluation

Group	Readability	Knowledge Structure	Time	Comprehension Accuracy
C	2.12	1.88	25:12	65.3%
T1	6.38	6.75	8:26	94.5%
T2	6.12	6.12	10:09	88.8%
T3	4.62	5.38	15:49	72.6%

The experimental results (see Table 2) demonstrate that GraphRAG-KM framework significantly improves the efficiency of participants with no prior knowledge. Under the same conditions, it reduces reading time by 67.12% and improves comprehension accuracy by 44.72% compared to directly reading industrial documents.

---

[2] Protégé (https://protege.stanford.edu/) is a free, open-source tool for editing and viewing ontology models.

In the interview feedback, participants stated that compared to the original documents, the automatic modelling approach presents knowledge in a more intuitive and readable manner, thereby reducing the learning cost of professional documentation.

4.3   Evaluation of RQ3

In this experiment, we assess the performance of the GraphRAG-KM framework in the knowledge extraction process and transformation into ontology/conceptual models. The evaluation compares the framework's efficiency against manual modelling performed by domain experts, measuring the degree of automation and improvements in modelling efficiency.

A *time-based comparative experiment* is conducted, where the time required to complete the same task using two different methods is recorded, and the efficiency improvement rate is calculated.

1. *Control Group (C)*: Knowledge engineering researchers manually analyse selected sections of the MIL-STD-6016 standard document to construct OWL ontology and UML conceptual models.
2. *Experimental Group (T)*: The GraphRAG-KM framework is used for automated parsing, entity recognition, relation extraction, modelling, and optimisation.

Evaluation Metrics

- *Modelling Time*: Measures the time required to generate OWL and UML models, comparing the differences with manual modelling.
- *Overall Efficiency Improvement*: Calculates the automation improvement rate of GraphRAG-KM based on experimental data.

Table 3. Comparison of GraphRAG-KM and Expert Modelling Time Across Examples

Data	Pages	GraphRAG-KM Time	Expert Time
Example 1	51	9:36	20:24
Example 2	76	10:43	34:52
Example 3	95	15:51	41:03
Example 4	407	50:31	7:32:05 (combined)

The experimental results in Table 3 indicate that the conversion efficiency of the GraphRAG-KM framework is 6.75 times faster than traditional manual modelling on a per-page basis. Moreover, this advantage becomes more pronounced in large-volume documents, as the human brain struggles to process extensive information and sustain continuous work over long periods. Our study significantly reduces the time required for knowledge extraction and transformation, substantially improving overall efficiency.

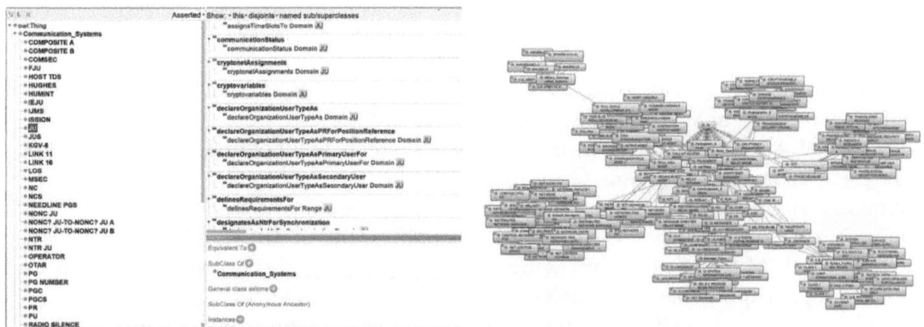

Fig. 3. GraphRAG-KM - Ontology Model Visualisation.

5 Conclusion

We developed an automated knowledge extraction and modelling framework called GraphRAG-KM in the research. By integrating MinerU document parsing technology, GraphRAG semantic indexing, and K-means clustering optimisation, the framework effectively achieves efficient automated transformation from industrial standards documents to OWL ontology models and UML conceptual models. Experimental results demonstrate that this approach significantly improves the efficiency and accuracy of extracting structured knowledge from industrial documents. In future research, we will explore more advanced semantic completion techniques and clustering methods, optimising mechanisms to identify implicit logical relationships, thus enhancing the logical completeness and applicability of the resulting models.

References

1. Wang, H., et al.: A review of military knowledge models. IOP Conf. Ser. Mater. Sci. Eng. **768**, 072060 (2020)
2. Souri, E., et al.: Integrating manufacturing knowledge with design process to improve quality in the aerospace industry. Procedia CIRP **84**, 374–379 (2019)
3. Logan, P., et al.: Documents are an essential part of model based systems engineering. In: INCOSE International Symposium, vol. 22, no. 1, pp. 1899–1913 (2012)
4. Adedjouma, M., et al.: From document-based to model-based system and software engineering (2016)
5. U.S. Department of Defense: Mil-std-6016: Tactical data link (tdl) standards (2024). https://www.document-center.com/standards/show/MIL-STD-6016. Accessed 15 Mar 2025
6. Zubiaga, A.: Natural language processing in the era of large language models. Front. Artif. Intell. **6**, 1350306 (2024)
7. Rawte, V., et al.: A survey of hallucination in large foundation models. arXiv preprint arXiv:2309.05922 (2023)
8. Gao, Y., et al.: Retrieval-augmented generation for large language models: a survey. arXiv preprint arXiv:2312.10997 **2** (2023)

9. Wang, B., et al.: MinerU: an open-source solution for precise document content extraction. arXiv preprint arXiv:2409.18839 (2024)
10. Edge, D., et al.: From local to global: a graph rag approach to query-focused summarization. arXiv preprint arXiv:2404.16130 (2024)
11. Estefan, J.A., et al.: Survey of model-based systems engineering (MBSE) methodologies. Incose MBSE Focus Group **25**(8), 1–12 (2007)
12. Kumar, R.L., et al.: Semantics based clustering through cover-kmeans with ontovsm for information retrieval. Inf. Technol. Control **49**(3), 370–380 (2020)
13. Abolhasani, M.S., et al.: Leveraging LLM for automated ontology extraction and knowledge graph generation. arXiv preprint arXiv:2412.00608 (2024)
14. Liu, A., et al.: Deepseek-v3 technical report. arXiv preprint arXiv:2412.19437 (2024)
15. Decker, S., et al.: The semantic web: the roles of XML and RDF. IEEE Internet Comput. **4**(5), 63–73 (2000)
16. Joshi, A., et al.: Likert scale: explored and explained. Br. J. Appl. Sci. Technol. **7**(4), 396 (2015)

MPN: Leveraging Multilingual Patch Neuron for Cross-Lingual Model Editing

Nianwen Si[1,2](✉) ⓘ, Heyu Chang[2] ⓘ, Wei-Qiang Zhang[1] ⓘ,
and Wenlin Zhang[2] ⓘ

[1] Department of Electronic Engineering, Tsinghua University, Beijing, China
`snw1608@163.com, wqzhang@tsinghua.edu.cn`
[2] Information Engineering University, Zhengzhou, China

Abstract. Large language models are known for encoding a vast amount of factual knowledge, but they often become outdated due to the ever-changing nature of external information. A promising solution to this challenge is the utilization of model editing methods to update the knowledge in an efficient manner. However, the majority of existing model editing techniques are limited to monolingual frameworks, thus failing to address the issue of cross-lingual knowledge synchronization for multilingual models. To tackle this problem, we propose a simple yet effective method for cross-lingual model editing, which trains **multilingual patch neuron (MPN)** to encode cross-lingual knowledge. This approach can be easily adapted to existing approaches to enhance their cross-lingual editing capabilities. We conduct experiments on the XNLI dataset and a self-constructed XFEVER dataset. Experimental results demonstrate that the proposed method achieves improved performance in cross-lingual editing without excessive modifications on the original methodology, thereby showcasing its user-friendly characteristics.

Keywords: Model editing · Large language model · Knowledge update · Cross-lingual · Model fine-tuning

1 Introduction

Large language models (LLMs) [5,30] have made remarkable progress and become a forefront technology in natural language processing recently. With their extensive factual knowledge learnt during pretraining and fine-tuning, LLMs are often compared to knowledge bases. However, the presence of erroneous knowledge in training data and the ever-changing nature of real-world information can result in issues such as knowledge truncation and errors within LLMs. Therefore, it is crucial to regularly modify and update the model's knowledge to address these challenges.

One natural approach to updating a model's knowledge is to retrain it on new corpora. Unfortunately, this method has significant computational costs, as LLMs require extensive resources, including compute power and time. An advanced approach is parameter-efficient fine-tuning [8,10], but it has the risk of overfitting and catastrophic forgetting. More recently, researchers have introduced model editing methods that allow for calibrating specific knowledge without affecting other aspects of the model, showing promise in addressing these challenges. These methods can be categorized into three groups: 1) Fine-tuning based methods [3,6,7,9,11], which fine-tune some model parameters to encode specific knowledge while constraining changes to unrelated knowledge; 2) Hypernetwork based methods [4,19,28], which use a hypernetwork to predict the parameter changes needed for specific inputs; and 3) Locate-then-edit [14,17,18,21,32], which identify neurons related to specific knowledge and fine-tune them to modify their semantic expression.

However, these methods primarily focus on monolingual editing and overlook the cross-lingual transferability of the editing results. For example, when editing a model with English examples, the edited model may provide updated responses in English but still offer outdated answers in other languages, as shown in Fig. 1. Since most large models encode knowledge in multiple languages, cross-lingual editing is a highly relevant problem that necessitates simultaneous updating knowledge across multiple languages.

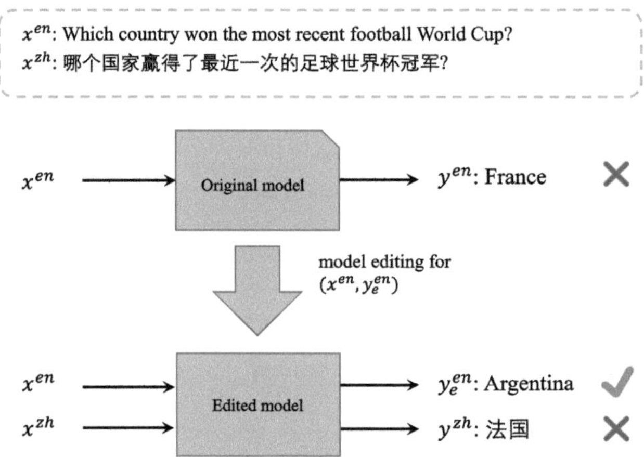

Fig. 1. Monolingual model editing fails in cross-lingual scenario.

Currently, only a few works have explored the cross-lingual effects of model editing. Bi-zsRE [31] assessed the cross-lingual capabilities of existing monolingual editing methods using English and Chinese datasets. The results showed that the cross-lingual generalizability of existing methods was unsatisfactory. LiME [36] leveraged the language anisotropic characteristics of multilingual models to adaptively learn a language-specific mask for methods like KnowledgeEditor [4] and MEND [19] using hypernetworks. This approach improved cross-lingual editing effectiveness, but it requires modifications to the editing method and is limited to hypernetwork-based methods. AMIG [1] focus solely on English-Chinese editing and ignore the generalization to other languages. It adopts a locate-then-edit framework by identifying knowledge neurons using multilingual integrated gradients [27] and then editing those neurons. Similar approaches, such as LU-LAFNs [41], follow comparable strategies. However, recent study reveals that updating knowledge by identifying and editing neurons has limited cross-lingual effectiveness due to the inconsistency of multilingual knowledge in models [25]. More recently, ReMaKE [33] maintains a multilingual knowledge base and integrates multilingual knowledge retrieval from this base into the in-context learning based model editing method IKE [42]. Despite the improvement in cross-lingual editing performance compared to monolingual IKE, ReMaKE does not fundamentally rectify the knowledge representation of the model.

The challenge of cross-lingual model editing mainly lies in the language gap that exists between different languages. This means that when editing a model for one language, the same fact described in another language may not change as well. Previous researches on cross-lingual transfer in multilingual models have struggled with this issue. Explicit multilingual fine-tuning methods, such as tuning the language adapters for various languages with multilingual datasets, have been used to bridge the language gap [22–24]. Inspired by this, we propose **multilingual patch neuron (MPN)**, a straightforward yet effective method for editing multilingual model. It only needs to modify the data sampler during the training process of the existing editing method. By using English examples alongside any parallel corpus as input, the MPN can greatly improve the cross-lingual ability of the existing monolingual editing method without extra modifications of the editing method itself.

The main contributions of this paper are as follows:

- We reveal that existing fine-tuning based editing methods possess a certain degree of cross-lingual editing effect. This effect is not derived from the editing method itself, but rather from the inherent cross-lingual transfer ability of the multilingual model.
- We introduce a straightforward yet practical cross-lingual editing method named MPN based on Transformer-patcher [11], which has good versatility and can be extended to other fine-tuning based editing methods. Without increasing any complexity, it endows the monolingual editing methods with the ability to perform cross-lingual editing while maintaining the original effectiveness.
- We evaluate the cross-lingual capability of MPN on two multilingual datasets, XFEVER and XNLI. The results demonstrate that our method effectively enhances cross-lingual editing, achieving an average improvement of over 13% across the five languages in the XFEVER dataset and approximately 14% across the fourteen languages in the XNLI dataset.

2   Related Work

2.1   Model Editing

Current model editing methods can be divided into three main categories:

Methods Based on Fine-Tuning. The simplest way is to fine-tune the whole model directly on the new knowledge, but this will inevitably affect the existing knowledge of the model and cause catastrophic forgetting. Research on the internal representation of transformer shows that the feed-forward neural network (FFN) layer in transformer block is the main location to encode factual knowledge [3,7]. Building upon this, a variety of model editing methods based on fine-tuning FNN layer are proposed, such as knowledge neuron [3], CaliNet [6], GRACE [9], and Transformer-patcher [11]. By fine-tuning a sum number of additional parameters added to the model, it is able to learn new knowledge and minimize the impact on existing knowledge. In addition, several locate-then-edit methods have been proposed, including ROME [17], MEMIT [18], PMET [14], WISE [32], and FiNE [21]. These methods involve identifying key neurons associated with particular pieces of knowledge and then adjusting these neurons as necessary to modify or update the factual knowledge stored within the model.

Methods Based on Hypernetwork. The so-called hypernetwork refers to an additional network used to predict the updates of the parameters in target network. The main idea of hypernetwork based method involves training an editor (hypernetwork) using a dataset of new knowledge, allowing it to learn how to edit knowledge and maintain generalization and locality of new knowledge. When providing new facts, the trained editor can automatically predict the necessary parameter updates for editing these facts. Examples of methods based on hypernetwork include KnowledgeEditor [4], MEND [19], and MALMEN [28]. KnowledgeEditor employs an LSTM as the editor, while MEND utilizes tensor decomposition to reduce the parameter size of the editor network, thereby simplifying the training process. MALMEN formulates the parameter shift aggregation as the least square problem, subsequently updating the model parameters using the normal equation.

Methods Based on In-Context Learning . Methods such as IKE [42] and MemPrompt [15] treat the model as a black box and leveraged its few-shot prompt learning ability to rectify knowledge. In this approach, the model is prompted using the input question, and new knowledge is provided alongside as a demonstration. These methods rely on the large model's excellent reasoning ability and perform well in the inferential generalization of editing results. For example, models like LLaMA-2 [30] process strong chain-of-thought reasoning ability, enabling them to decompose multi-hop question into sub-problems with answers during the inference process. However, if the format of sub-question decomposition is inconsistent with expectations, the editing effect will be limited.

In addition, several other methods are proposed like SERAC [20], MELO [39], Knowledge Circuit [38], and knowledge graph-based editing [16,40]. Despite these advances, challenging issues in this field are not well solved, such as cross-lingual generalization, reasoning on editing results, and sustainable editing. This paper mainly focuses on the cross-lingual editing problem.

2.2   Cross-Lingual Transfer

Cross-lingual transfer refers to the ability of a model trained on one language to improve its performance on corresponding tasks in another language. Multilingual models possess cross-lingual transfer ability due to their implicit unified knowledge representation across different languages [35]. However, this often results in a "transfer gap" where the task performance in the target language is generally worse than that in the source language. In traditional cross-lingual transfer methods, the common approach is to fine-tune the model directly on the source language for downstream tasks and then test it on the task set of the target language. In this case, low-resource languages and languages that are far from the source language tend to have poorer transfer performance on downstream tasks, resulting in a more pronounced transfer gap. Currently, The adapter is the mainstream method for cross-lingual transfer, with language-specific adapter and task adapter being two commonly used adapters that enable the model to adapt to both language and task [22–24].

To make model editing methods also capable of cross-lingual capabilities, LiME [36] proposes a language anisotropy model editing method and tests its effectiveness on XNLI [2] and mLAMA datasets [12]. However, this method is only applicable to hypernetwork-based editing methods and requires modifications to the details of the editing method. AMIG [1] introduces a language-independent knowledge neuron method, considering only the generalization between English and Chinese. However, multilingual models like mBERT [5] typically contain over 100 languages, thus this method cannot cover most languages in large models. Bi-zsRE [31] translates the zsRE dataset [4,13] into Chinese with the API interfaces of gpt-3.5-turbo and gpt-4 to create a bilingual version of Chinese-English. Then, it tests the mutual transfer effects of existing seven editing methods between English editing and Chinese editing. This work also has limited coverage of language types and does not investigate how to improve cross-lingual editing.

3   Cross-Lingual Model Editing

3.1   Task Definition

Model editing aims to update the knowledge embedded in a trained model, enabling the incorporation of new knowledge without retraining from scratch. Three key requirements must be met during this process: reliability, generality, and locality [37]. Formally, given the original model $f(.;\theta)$ to be edit, where θ denotes the model parameters. The goal is to find a new model $f(.;\theta')$ that satisfies reliability based on $f(.;\theta)$, while also ensuring generality and locality.

Reliability. Reliability refers to the successful editing of an example. For an example to be edited $(x_{edit}^{en}, y_{edit}^{en})$, where x_{edit}^{en} represents the input in English description and y_{edit}^{en} represents the corresponding output, reliability requires the edited model $f(.; \theta')$ to meet the following criteria:

$$f(x_{edit}^{en}; \theta') = y_{edit}^{en} \tag{1}$$

In classification tasks, y_{edit}^{en} is a classification label. In question-answering tasks, y_{edit}^{en} denotes an output answer. Reliability is typically measured using the task loss during the model's training. For classification models, cross-entropy loss or KL loss is commonly used, e.g., $CrossEntropy(f(x_{edit}^{en}; \theta), y_{edit}^{en})$.

Generality. In monolingual editing, generality requires that the edited model can accurately predict semantically rephrased examples. For the rephrased example $(x_{rephrase}^{en}, y_{edit}^{en}) \in R(x_{edit}^{en}, y_{edit}^{en})$, the following are needed:

$$f(x_{rephrase}^{en}; \theta') = y_{edit}^{en}, \quad \forall x_{rephrase}^{en} \in R \tag{2}$$

While for cross-lingual editing, generality should be extended to parallel expression in different languages in order to achieve cross-lingual generalizability. For example, the model edited on English data needs to consider not only generalize to English rephrases but also to cross-lingual parallel data. Therefore, for parallel example $(x_{parallel}^{l}, y_{edit}^{l}) \in P(x_{edit}^{en}, y_{edit}^{en})$, where l denotes the any other language expect English, the following are needed:

$$f(x_{parallel}^{l}; \theta') = y_{edit}^{en}, \quad \forall x_{rephrase}^{l} \in P \tag{3}$$

Locality. Locality denotes that the newly added knowledge does not affect the original knowledge stored in the model. To achieve locality, for unrelated example $(x', y') \in L(x_{edit}^{en}, y_{edit}^{en})$, where (x', y') denotes the semantically unrelated example to $(x_{edit}^{en}, y_{edit}^{en})$, the following are needed:

$$f(x'; \theta') = y', \forall x' \in L \tag{4}$$

LiME [36] defines locality as irrelevant knowledge across languages. However, the storage of knowledge of different languages in multilingual models is not balanced, and a certain piece of knowledge encoded in a high-resource language not necessarily exist in a low-resource language. Since English examples are primarily used for editing in this work, we only consider irrelevant knowledge from English corpora and not from other language.

3.2   Monolingual Baseline

In the realm of cross-lingual transfer learning for multilingual models, fine-tuning stands out as the most effective methodology, which entails augmenting the training process with additional language-specific adapters to facilitate multilingual training [22–24]. When it comes to model editing, fine-tuning is also the most direct approach to acquiring new knowledge by adjusting certain parameters within the model. Transformer-patcher is one of these methods that add additional neuron for editing new knowledge sequentially into the model [11].

Transformer-patcher fine-tunes the final FFN layer of a model, treating this layer as a key-value pair and add new pairs to store new knowledge. It emphasizes sequential and sustainable editing, learning only one piece of knowledge at a time. For each new piece of knowledge, a new key-value pair (i.e. patch) is created and physically separated from the neurons of the original FFN neuron to minimize interference with the existing knowledge. The structure of the FFN layer with the added patch neuron is depicted in Fig. 2.

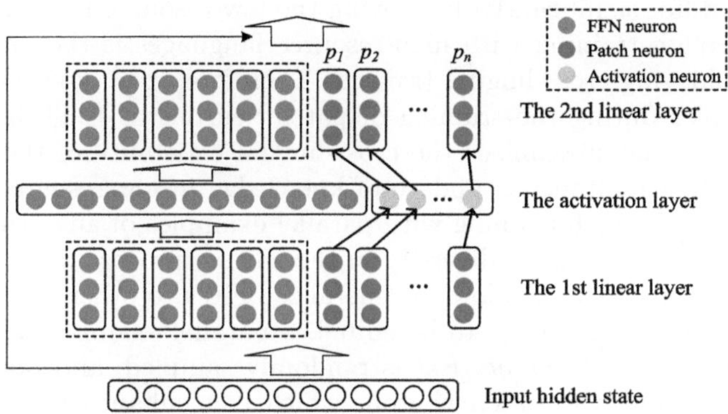

Fig. 2. The FFN layer mainly consists of two linear layers. The blue neurons represent the original model neurons and remain frozen during training. The red neurons are added patch neurons, which are trainable. (Color figure online)

From the perspective of key and value pair of knowledge neuron, the first and second linear layer of the FFN layer can be denoted as K and V, respectively [3,7]. Given the input vector q to the FFN layer, the output $\mathrm{FFN}(q)$ can be calculated as follows:

$$a = \sigma(q \cdot K + b_k) \tag{5}$$

$$\mathrm{FFN}(q) = a \cdot V + b_v \tag{6}$$

while σ denotes the activation function, e.g. GLUE. a is the activation of the first linear layer. For each example to be edited, a key-value pair will be added alongside the last FFN layer. Specifically, k_p and b_p is added with the first linear layer, and v_p is added with the second linear layer. Then, the new forward process of the updated FFN layer can be formalized as follows:

$$[a, a_p] = \sigma(q \cdot [K, k_p] + [b_k, b_p]) \tag{7}$$

$$\mathrm{FFN}'(q) = [a, a_p] \cdot \begin{bmatrix} V \\ v_p \end{bmatrix} + b_v = \mathrm{FFN}(q) + a_p \cdot v_p \tag{8}$$

Finally, the output $\text{FFN}'(\boldsymbol{q})$ is obtained which contains the calibration because of the added $a_p \cdot \boldsymbol{v_p}$. To ensure efficacy, the patch neuron should be maximally activated by the example to be edited. While for locality, memory loss on unrelated examples sampled from the training and test set is utilized.

3.3 Multilingual Patch Neuron

To improve cross-lingual editing effectiveness, we propose to use English examples as the primary input combined with any other parallel corpora to train multilingual patch neuron (i.e. MPN), enabling the patch to obtain the cross-lingual transfer ability. The reasons behind this is twofold: Firstly, while various languages in a multilingual model share the same semantic representation space, their abilities differ significantly. Improving the low-resource language ability of the model through training with high-resource languages is the most common method for achieving cross-lingual transfer. Therefore, it is essential to employ English examples during the training of patch neurons as English serves as a central language that maximizes the cross-lingual capability of the patch, and better drives the simultaneous update of knowledge in low-resource languages. Secondly, pairing English training with parallel examples of any other language can further enhance linguistic diversity in the editing process, resulting in multilingual patch neurons that allow to generalize better to other languages.

Specifically, for $(x_{edit}^{en}, y_{edit}^{en})$ to be edited, a parallel example $(x_{edit}^{l}, y_{edit}^{l})$ in another language $l \in language\_list$ is randomly sampled, and both examples are used for training the patch neuron, which can enhance the cross-lingual generalization ability of the patch. The loss function is formalized as following:

$$loss = CrossEntropy(f(x_{edit}^{en}, x_{edit}^{l}; \theta'), y_{edit}^{en}, y_{edit}^{l}) \tag{9}$$

MPN only requires modifying the input of the Transformer-patcher without altering other components, which improves the cross-lingual generalization of the patch in a simple way. MPN differs from LiME in that LiME requires complete correspondence between parallel corpora of different languages for training, whereas we use weaker parallel corpora with less stringent requirements. Additionally, since only the input needs to be modified, MPN can be easily extended to other fine-tuning based editing methods to improve their cross-lingual editing effectiveness.

4 Experiments

4.1 Settings

Model. We use bert-base-multilingual-uncased [5] from Huggingface as the target multilingual model, which comprises 12 transformer blocks and supports 102 languages. Following the default settings of Transformer-patcher [11], we edit the final FFN layer of the model.

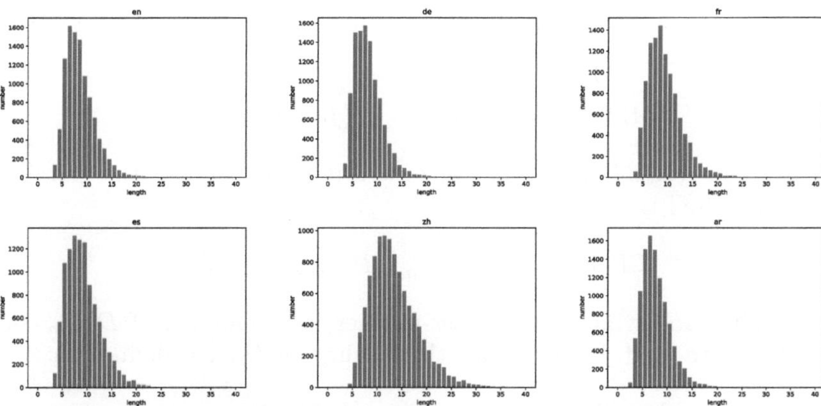

Fig. 3. Sentence length distribution for six languages (en, de, fr, es, zh, and ar) on the XFEVER dataset.

Datasets. We conduct experiments on two knowledge-intensive datasets, including FEVER [29] and XNLI [2]. For FEVER dataset, we follow previous work by splitting its training set into a ratio of 0.8:0.1:0.1 for training set D_{train}, validation set D_{val}, and editing set D_{edit}. This results in 83,972/10,496/10,496 examples, respectively. We use examples in D_{edit} to edit the target model. The original development set is retained as the test set D_{test} for testing locality, containing 10,444 examples. To perform cross-lingual editing, we use machine translation models to expand D_{edit} into multiple language versions $D_{parallel}$, including German (de), French (fr), Spanish (es), Chinese (zh), and Arabic (ar). The final dataset is denoted as XFEVER.

For XNLI dataset, it is a multilingual natural language inference dataset containing parallel corpora in 15 languages. Each sample comprises a premise and a hypothesis, and the task is to determine their entailment relationship: {entailment, neutral, contradiction}. It includes both high-resource languages like English (en) and low-resource languages like Swahili (sw), allowing for testing the transferability of editing methods for low-resource languages. We train the model using multiNLI dataset [34] containing 392,702 training examples. The development and test sets of XNLI dataset contain 2,490 and 5,010 examples for each language. The development set is used to determine the optimal trained model, and the test set is used to edit the model.

Evaluation Metrics. For reliability, it refers to the success rate on editing set D_{edit} , which is defined as:

$$\text{Reliability} = E_{(x,y)\sim D_{edit}}[I(f(x;\theta') = y)] \tag{10}$$

where I is the indicator function.

For generality, we use the English rephrase set $D_{rephrase}$ from XFEVER dataset to examine monolingual generalizaiton (MLG). While for XNLI dataset, we do not calculate the MLG since it does not contain rephrase data. MLG is formally defined as:

$$\mathrm{MLG} = E_{(x,y)\sim D_{rephrase}}[I(f_t(x;\theta') = y)] \tag{11}$$

To examine cross-lingual generalization (CLG), we use the parallel set $D_{parallel}$ and CLG is defined as:

$$\mathrm{CLG} = E_{(x,y)\sim D_{parallel}}[I(f_t(x;\theta') = y)] \tag{12}$$

For locality, following Transformer-patcher, a proportion of D_{train} and all test set D_{test} are used. For example, the locality on D_{test} is defined as:

$$\mathrm{Locality}_{\mathrm{test}} = E_{(x,y)\sim D_{test}}[I(f_t(x;\theta') = y)] \tag{13}$$

4.2 Implement Details

Fine-Tuning Model on XFEVER Dataset. To construct a cross-lingual model editing dataset, we translate the editing set of FEVER dataset used in [4,11] into five languages: de, fr, es, zh, and ar. The translated field is"input", and the resulting dataset is called XFEVER, which contains six languages: en, de, fr, es, zh, and ar, covering three different language families. The average sentence length in above six languages is 8.2, 7.8, 8.9, 8.8, 13.2, and 7.4. The distribution of sentence length is shown in the Fig. 3. The hyperparameters for training the initial model are set as shown in Table 1. We select the model that performs best on the validation set, with an accuracy of 88.11%.

Table 1. Datasets and hyperparameter settings for training the original model on XFEVER and XNLI

Hyper-parameters	XFEVER	XNLI
train set	83,972	392,702
validation set	10,496	2490
editing set	10,496	5010
test set	10,444	–
epoch	20	3
batch_size	128	64
learning rate	3e-5	3e-5
max_length	32	128
weight_decay	0.01	0.01
warmup_updates	500	500
eps	0.1	0.1

Fine-Tuning Model on XNLI Dataset. We fine-tune the mBERT model on MultiNLI training set (a total of 392,702 examples) and use the English version of XNLI development set (a total of 2490 examples) as the criterion for selecting the best model. Details of XNLI dataset and hyperparameters settings for training the original model is listed in Table 1. We set the batch size to 64 and the epoch to 3. Finally, we select the best model with an accuracy of 0.750 on training set and 0.828 on development set. This accuracy is comparable to the official report of the mBERT model.

4.3   Results on XFEVER Dataset

Table 2 shows the experimental results on XFEVER dataset. Patch Num. denotes the number of added patches. Reliability denotes the accuracy on English editing set. MLG (monolingual generalization) denotes the generalization on English rephrase examples. CLG (cross-lingual generalization) denotes the generalization on cross-lingual parallel examples. Locality denotes the impact on unrelated English examples sampled from training set and test set.

As shown in Table 2, the original model has a locality of 93.05 on training set and 77.08 on test set, with an accuracy of 88.07 on editing set. For other languages, the original model itself has cross-lingual generalization ability to some extent. This is primarily due to the shared representation space inherent in language models across different languages. When fine-tuning the mBERT model for specific downstream task using only English example, the resulting model retains ability to perform same task in other languages. This further validates the cross-lingual capabilities of language models.

Table 2. Results on XFEVER dataset

Models/Methods	Patch Num.	Reliability (en)	MLG	CLG						Locality	
				de	fr	es	zh	ar	Avg.	Train	Test
Original model	0	88.07	84.86	85.32	85.92	85.96	82.73	81.69	84.32	93.05	77.08
Fine-tuning based methods											
Fine-tuning [4]	0	83.72	78.65	83.77	83.99	85.83	72.86	70.91	79.47	87.15	74.81
Fine-tuning+KL [4]	0	87.47	83.20	82.86	82.61	82.82	81.04	78.07	81.48	**92.79**	77.51
T-patcher [11]	1207	98.75	90.34	90.42	91.54	92.21	83.02	82.11	87.86	92.48	**77.81**
Hypernetwork based methods											
ENN [26]	0	99.83	95.00	92.18	93.16	93.18	87.23	82.38	89.63	90.52	77.09
KnowledgeEditor [4]	0	92.18	84.45	81.49	82.15	81.41	78.42	76.97	80.09	91.29	77.21
MEND [19]	0	**99.88**	**97.87**	97.20	97.47	97.64	89.65	87.82	93.96	92.15	76.89
MPN (only)	2519	99.20	94.33	94.97	95.34	95.34	86.10	82.85	90.92	92.26	77.06
MPN (all)	4598	99.29	93.05	**98.39**	**98.45**	**98.58**	**95.53**	**95.30**	**97.25**	92.31	77.04

While for editing methods, we compared the following methods: 1) **Fine-tuning based methods**, which edits the last FNN layer and uses cross-entropy loss as a constraint. Fine-tuning+KL denotes the utilization of KL loss. It can be observed that simple fine-tuning cause suboptimal performance on various test metrics because of forgetting problems. T-patcher [11] trains monolingual patch neurons with English examples and tests the generalization on other languages. The Reliability value of T-patcher is 98.75, and it can generalize to de, fr, and es, achieving CLG values over 90.42. This demonstrates that T-patcher also possesses some cross-lingual ability, but there is still a significant transfer gap. For languages from different families, such as ar and zh, their CLG values only increase from 81.69/82.73 to 82.11/83.02, indicating that generalization across different language families cannot be achieved. 2) **Hypernetwork based methods**: These approaches leverage hypernetworks to dynamically adjust model parameters. For instance, MEND [19] integrates meta-learning with hypernetworks, achieving the average CLG (93.96) and MLG (97.87), particularly excelling in closely related languages (e.g., de/fr/es with CLG >97%). ENN [26] balances reliability (99.83) and cross-lingual generalization (CLG Avg. 89.63) but struggles with distant languages (e.g., ar/zh). While these methods mitigate catastrophic forgetting, their effectiveness diminishes for linguistically divergent languages, highlighting persistent cross-family transfer gaps. 3) **MPN**, which trains multilingual patch neuron using English example along with sampled example from another language. When using the English example and the sampled example as conditions to judge whether the current input needs editing, i.e. MPN (only), the average CLG improvement is about 6.6%. This suggests that the multilingual patch neuron trained in this manner has good cross-lingual generalization. When using examples from six language corresponding to the current input as conditions, i.e. MPN (all), the average CLG improvement increases to about 13%. Furthermore, the MLG and Locality values of the MPN method are also satisfactory, indicating its effectiveness.

4.4   Results on XNLI Dataset

For XNLI dataset, the experimental results are shown in Table 3. It can be seen that the accuracy of the original model on editing set is 81.66, but its cross-lingual generalization effect is not ideal, with Thai (th) performing the worst due to the absence of th during mBERT's pre-training. The low-resource language sw also exhibits poor cross-lingual generalization which is only 49.82. For editing method, after editing with Fine-tuning, the cross-lingual generalization on editing set further decreases. T-patcher improves the cross-lingual generalization effect to some extent, but since its editing does not specifically optimize for cross-lingual characteristics, the improvement is limited, with only about a 1% increase in average CLG value compared to the original model. However, for MPN, there is an increase of 13.8% on average CLG than that of the original model. This indicates that MPN can significantly improve the cross-lingual editing effect.

Table 3. Results on XNLI dataset

Models/Methods	Patch Num.	Reliability (en)	CLG															Locality
			ar	bg	de	el	es	fr	hi	ru	sw	th	tr	ur	vi	zh	Avg.	
Original model	0	81.66	63.75	69.90	70.92	66.95	74.53	72.61	61.00	69.38	49.82	34.95	62.24	58.50	66.21	66.11	63.35	81.81
Fine-tuning [4]	0	75.79	56.03	61.04	63.69	58.88	68.00	65.37	53.99	60.68	46.07	35.35	54.19	52.14	58.98	55.99	56.46	76.51
T-patcher [11]	954	**99.66**	64.33	71.44	73.71	67.70	79.44	76.21	61.32	70.68	50.08	35.11	62.59	58.82	66.91	66.27	64.62	**81.65**
MPN (all)	2254	99.40	**78.86**	**86.13**	**87.56**	**82.91**	**90.82**	**89.46**	**75.39**	**84.99**	**58.04**	**35.67**	**76.59**	**71.88**	**80.64**	**81.22**	**77.15**	81.16

4.5   Discussion

To directly observe the generalization effect of editing methods on multiple languages, we collect 722 examples from XFEVER editing set across six languages where the original model made incorrect predictions. These examples formed the editing set. The results are presented in Table 4. It is evident that while Fine-tuning performs well on these examples, it significantly disrupts the locality of both the training and test sets. T-patcher exhibits improved locality but falls short in achieving cross-lingual generalization, particularly for zh and ar, where the edited knowledge does not generalize effectively. In contrast, the proposed MPN demonstrates strong cross-lingual generalization as well as good locality.

Table 4. Results on the set of examples where predictions in six languages are incorrect on XFEVER editing set.

Models/Methods	Patch Num.	Reliability	MLG	CLG						Locality	
				de	fr	es	zh	ar	Avg.	Train	Test
Original model	0	0	0	0	0	0	0	0	0	93.05	77.08
Fine-tuning [4]	45	99.45	96.72	96.95	94.74	95.43	98.61	96.12	96.37	9.85	26.26
T-patcher [11]	710	**97.65**	66.26	57.62	64.96	68.84	5.96	10.80	41.64	92.36	**77.10**
MPN (all)	711	97.51	**75.73**	**98.89**	**99.58**	**99.58**	**98.89**	**99.17**	**99.22**	**92.43**	77.03

5   Conclusion

This paper explores the cross-lingual generalization of model editing and introduces a method for cross-lingual editing using multilingual patch neurons. This approach minimally alters the original editing method by incorporating cross-lingual sampling at the input to enhance its cross-lingual editing capability. Our findings suggest that the fine-tuning based editing methods, such as Fine-tuning and Transformer-patcher, demonstrate some degree of cross-lingual generalization. This capability mainly arises from the cross-lingual transferability of multilingual models rather than the editing methods. To this end, this study trains multilingual patch neurons through cross-lingual sampling at the input of editing methods, resulting in better cross-lingual editing result.

Acknowledgments. This work was generously supported by Natural Science Foundation of Henan (No. 252300420990), Science and Technology Research Project of Henan Province (No. 252102211040) and National Natural Science Foundation of China (62276153). We sincerely appreciate the constructive feedback from the anonymous reviewers on an earlier draft of this work.

References

1. Chen, Y., Cao, P., Chen, Y., Liu, K., Zhao, J.: Journey to the center of the knowledge neurons: discoveries of language-independent knowledge neurons and degenerate knowledge neurons. arXiv preprint arXiv:2308.13198 (2023)
2. Conneau, A., et al.: XNLI: evaluating cross-lingual sentence representations. arXiv preprint arXiv:1809.05053 (2018)
3. Dai, D., Dong, L., Hao, Y., Sui, Z., Chang, B., Wei, F.: Knowledge neurons in pretrained transformers. arXiv preprint arXiv:2104.08696 (2021)
4. De Cao, N., Aziz, W., Titov, I.: Editing factual knowledge in language models. arXiv preprint arXiv:2104.08164 (2021)
5. Devlin, J., Chang, M.W., Lee, K., Toutanova, K.: Bert: pre-training of deep bidirectional transformers for language understanding. arXiv preprint arXiv:1810.04805 (2018)
6. Dong, Q., Dai, D., Song, Y., Xu, J., Sui, Z., Li, L.: Calibrating factual knowledge in pretrained language models. arXiv preprint arXiv:2210.03329 (2022)
7. Geva, M., Schuster, R., Berant, J., Levy, O.: Transformer feed-forward layers are key-value memories. arXiv preprint arXiv:2012.14913 (2020)
8. Han, Z., Gao, C., Liu, J., Zhang, J., Zhang, S.Q.: Parameter-efficient fine-tuning for large models: a comprehensive survey (2024)
9. Hartvigsen, T., Sankaranarayanan, S., Palangi, H., Kim, Y., Ghassemi, M.: Aging with grace: lifelong model editing with discrete key-value adaptors. arXiv preprint arXiv:2211.11031 (2022)
10. Hu, E.J., et al.: LoRA: low-rank adaptation of large language models (2021)
11. Huang, Z., Shen, Y., Zhang, X., Zhou, J., Rong, W., Xiong, Z.: Transformer-patcher: one mistake worth one neuron. arXiv preprint arXiv:2301.09785 (2023)
12. Kassner, N., Dufter, P., Schütze, H.: Multilingual lama: investigating knowledge in multilingual pretrained language models. arXiv preprint arXiv:2102.00894 (2021)
13. Levy, O., Seo, M., Choi, E., Zettlemoyer, L.: Zero-shot relation extraction via reading comprehension. arXiv preprint arXiv:1706.04115 (2017)
14. Li, X., Li, S., Song, S., Yang, J., Ma, J., Yu, J.: PMET: precise model editing in a transformer. arXiv preprint arXiv:2308.08742 (2023)
15. Madaan, A., Tandon, N., Clark, P., Yang, Y.: Memory-assisted prompt editing to improve GPT-3 after deployment. arXiv preprint arXiv:2201.06009 (2022)
16. Markowitz, E., et al.: K-edit: language model editing with contextual knowledge awareness (2025)
17. Meng, K., Bau, D., Andonian, A., Belinkov, Y.: Locating and editing factual associations in GPT. Adv. Neural. Inf. Process. Syst. **35**, 17359–17372 (2022)
18. Meng, K., Sharma, A.S., Andonian, A., Belinkov, Y., Bau, D.: Mass-editing memory in a transformer. arXiv preprint arXiv:2210.07229 (2022)
19. Mitchell, E., Lin, C., Bosselut, A., Finn, C., Manning, C.D.: Fast model editing at scale. arXiv preprint arXiv:2110.11309 (2021)

20. Mitchell, E., Lin, C., Bosselut, A., Manning, C.D., Finn, C.: Memory-based model editing at scale. In: International Conference on Machine Learning, pp. 15817–15831. PMLR (2022)
21. Pan, H., et al.: Precise localization of memories: a fine-grained neuron-level knowledge editing technique for LLMs (2025)
22. Parović, M., Ansell, A., Vulić, I., Korhonen, A.: Cross-lingual transfer with target language-ready task adapters. arXiv preprint arXiv:2306.02767 (2023)
23. Parović, M., Glavaš, G., Vulić, I., Korhonen, A.: Bad-x: bilingual adapters improve zero-shot cross-lingual transfer. In: Proceedings of the 2022 Conference of the North American Chapter of the Association for Computational Linguistics: Human Language Technologies, pp. 1791–1799 (2022)
24. Pfeiffer, J., Vulić, I., Gurevych, I., Ruder, S.: Mad-x: an adapter-based framework for multi-task cross-lingual transfer. arXiv preprint arXiv:2005.00052 (2020)
25. Qi, J., Fernández, R., Bisazza, A.: Cross-lingual consistency of factual knowledge in multilingual language models. arXiv preprint arXiv:2310.10378 (2023)
26. Sinitsin, A., Plokhotnyuk, V., Pyrkin, D., Popov, S., Babenko, A.: Editable neural networks. arXiv preprint arXiv:2004.00345 (2020)
27. Sundararajan, M., Taly, A., Yan, Q.: Axiomatic attribution for deep networks. In: International Conference on Machine Learning, pp. 3319–3328. PMLR (2017)
28. Tan, C., Zhang, G., Fu, J.: Massive editing for large language models via meta learning. arXiv preprint arXiv:2311.04661 (2023)
29. Thorne, J., Vlachos, A., Christodoulopoulos, C., Mittal, A.: FEVER: a large-scale dataset for fact extraction and VERification. In: Walker, M., Ji, H., Stent, A. (eds.) Proceedings of the 2018 Conference of the North American Chapter of the Association for Computational Linguistics: Human Language Technologies, Volume 1 (Long Papers), pp. 809–819. Association for Computational Linguistics, New Orleans, Louisiana (2018)
30. Touvron, H., et al.: Llama: open and efficient foundation language models. arXiv preprint arXiv:2302.13971 (2023)
31. Wang, J., Liang, Y., Sun, Z., Cao, Y., Xu, J.: Cross-lingual knowledge editing in large language models. arXiv preprint arXiv:2309.08952 (2023)
32. Wang, P., et al.: WISE: rethinking the knowledge memory for lifelong model editing of large language models. Adv. Neural. Inf. Process. Syst. **37**, 53764–53797 (2024)
33. Wang, W., Haddow, B., Birch, A.: Retrieval-augmented multilingual knowledge editing. arXiv preprint arXiv:2312.13040 (2023)
34. Williams, A., Nangia, N., Bowman, S.R.: A broad-coverage challenge corpus for sentence understanding through inference. arXiv preprint arXiv:1704.05426 (2017)
35. Wu, S., Conneau, A., Li, H., Zettlemoyer, L., Stoyanov, V.: Emerging cross-lingual structure in pretrained language models. arXiv preprint arXiv:1911.01464 (2019)
36. Xu, Y., Hou, Y., Che, W., Zhang, M.: Language anisotropic cross-lingual model editing. arXiv preprint arXiv:2205.12677 (2022)
37. Yao, Y., et al.: Editing large language models: problems, methods, and opportunities. arXiv preprint arXiv:2305.13172 (2023)
38. Yao, Y., et al.: Knowledge circuits in pretrained transformers. arXiv preprint arXiv:2405.17969 (2024)
39. Yu, L., Chen, Q., Zhou, J., He, L.: MELO: enhancing model editing with neuron-indexed dynamic LoRA. arXiv preprint arXiv:2312.11795 (2023)

40. Zhang, M., Ye, X., Liu, Q., Ren, P., Wu, S., Chen, Z.: Knowledge graph enhanced large language model editing. In: Al-Onaizan, Y., Bansal, M., Chen, Y.N. (eds.) Proceedings of the 2024 Conference on Empirical Methods in Natural Language Processing, pp. 22647–22662. Association for Computational Linguistics, Miami, Florida, USA (2024)
41. Zhang, X., et al.: Multilingual knowledge editing with language-agnostic factual neurons. In: Rambow, O., Wanner, L., Apidianaki, M., Al-Khalifa, H., Eugenio, B.D., Schockaert, S. (eds.) Proceedings of the 31st International Conference on Computational Linguistics, pp. 5775–5788. Association for Computational Linguistics, Abu Dhabi, UAE (2025)
42. Zheng, C., et al.: Can we edit factual knowledge by in-context learning? arXiv preprint arXiv:2305.12740 (2023)

AD^2-pFed: Personalized Federated Learning Based on Adaptive Bilateral Distillation with Diffusion Models

Zhenhao Wang[1,2], Xin Wang[1,2]([envelope]), Yongwei Tang[1,2,3], Dongrun Li[1,2], Ming Yang[1,2], and Xiaoming Wu[1,2]

[1] Key Laboratory of Computing Power Network and Information Security, Ministry of Education, Shandong Computer Science Center, Qilu University of Technology (Shandong Academy of Sciences), Jinan 250014, China
`{10431240019,10431230017}@stu.qlu.edu.cn`, `{yangm,wuxm}@sdas.org`,
`xinwang@qlu.edu.cn`
[2] Shandong Provincial Key Laboratory of Industrial Network and Information System Security, Shandong Fundamental Research Center for Computer Science, Jinan 250014, China
[3] School of Mechanical Engineering, Key Laboratory of High Efficiency and Clean Mechanical Manufacture, Ministry of Education, Shandong University, Jinan 250061, China
`tangyw@sdas.org`

Abstract. Federated learning is a distributed machine learning framework that enables local participants to collaboratively train a global model without sharing their data. However, the presence of heterogeneous data among clients, coupled with the growing demand for user-specific customization, renders a single global model inadequate for such scenarios. This makes personalized federated learning (pFL) a promising research direction. Existing pFL methods often prioritize model personalization at the expense of generalization. To address this issue, we propose a pFL framework based on adaptive bilateral distillation with diffusion models, termed AD^2-pFed, which aims to balance the personalization and generalization capabilities of client models. AD^2-pFed employs adaptive mutual learning and ensemble learning on the client side to facilitate knowledge transfer between private and shared models. On the server side, global pseudo-data, generated from aggregated local generators trained using diffusion models, is used as distillation samples to dynamically fine-tune the initial global model in each iteration, capturing diverse knowledge from clients. Extensive experiments on three benchmark datasets demonstrate that AD^2-pFed consistently outperforms baseline methods under varying data heterogeneity scenarios.

Keywords: Personalized federated learning · Non-IID data · Knowledge distillation · Ensemble learning

1   Introduction

Federated learning (FL) is a distributed machine learning framework that enables collaborative model training while preserving data privacy through the iterative aggregation of local models on a central server. Traditional FL methods, such as FedAvg [1] and FedProx [2], focus on training global models with robust generalization capabilities. However, statistical heterogeneity—such as non-independent and identically distributed (non-IID) data and imbalanced distributions [3]—poses significant challenges to achieving globally generalized models. Furthermore, a single global model often fails to accommodate the personalized requirements of individual users.

In recent years, personalized federated learning (pFL) has emerged as a solution that tailors models for each client while preserving the generalization of the global model, thereby addressing both data heterogeneity and personalization requirements [3]. The existing body of research on pFL can be categorized into the following aspects:

(1) **Local training of a single global model.** Methods such as Per-FedAvg [4] leverage meta-learning to optimize initialization parameters, enabling models to quickly adapt to personalized requirements. Model decoupling approaches, like FedRep [5], share feature extractors between the server and clients to capture global knowledge, while training personalized heads using local data. These methods generally require all clients to adopt the same model architecture.

(2) **Local training of additional personalized models.** Approaches such as Ditto [6] and pFedMe [7] decouple the optimization of global and personalized models, aiming to balance generalization and personalization. The performance of these algorithms is highly sensitive to the choice of regularization parameters, which, if improperly tuned, can disrupt this balance.

(3) **Multi-center FL.** This approach aggregates similar clients to generate multiple global models, each tailored to specific client groups. For example, FedAMP [8] uses message-passing mechanisms to adaptively compute model similarity, while FedCluster [9] clusters similar clients for group-wise optimization, improving intra-group performance. However, during the aggregation process, these methods are constrained by their reliance on learning exclusively from similar models, which limits their generalization capability post-aggregation.

(4) **Federated knowledge distillation (FKD).** Knowledge distillation facilitates the transfer of knowledge from teacher models to student models, enabling knowledge exchange between local and global models [10–13]. This approach not only addresses the challenge of heterogeneous model architectures across clients [10] but also enhances the transfer of both personalized and generalized knowledge [12]. Given these advantages, we adopt FKD as the foundation of our study.

Various FKD approaches have been proposed in the literature, yet these methods still exhibit certain limitations. For instance, FedDF [14] and Fed-

Gen [15] leverage auxiliary datasets for knowledge transfer, while FedFTG [16], DaFKD [17], and FedTweet [13] use pseudo-data to fine-tune global models. Fed-NTD [18] investigates the influence of non-local data features on global models. However, these methods often prioritize model generalization excessively, sometimes at the cost of personalization. Federated mutual learning (FML) [10], which employs mutual distillation between global and local models, addresses this issue by preserving the adaptability of local models while maintaining the generalization capability of the global model. This approach mitigates some limitations of traditional FKD methods. Representative FML-based methods, such as FedKD [11], which incorporates loss-guided mechanisms, and FedAPEN [12], based on ensemble learning, have shown promising results. Nevertheless, these FML-based approaches face challenges in effectively regulating distillation intensity while adaptively balancing model personalization and generalization. Additionally, the diversity of local data is not always fully accounted for in these methods.

To address the limitations of existing FKD methods, we propose AD^2-pFed, a novel pFL framework based on adaptive bilateral distillation with diffusion models. AD^2-pFed employs adaptive ensemble learning to regulate the proportion of personalized and shared models during the loss-guided mutual distillation process, while simultaneously accounting for client data diversity. On the server side, the local generators—trained using client data—are dynamically aggregated to generate global pseudo-data, which further fine-tunes the initially aggregated global shared model via distillation. A diffusion model is utilized as the generator to mitigate the mode collapse issue commonly associated with generative adversarial networks (GANs), thereby enhancing the quality and stability of the generated data. Our main contributions are as follows:

- We propose the AD^2-pFed approach, which leverages personalized and shared models for mutual learning and ensemble learning, facilitating an adaptive balance between model generalization and personalization.
- We design a distillation-based fine-tuning strategy for the global model to effectively integrate diverse client knowledge, where the distillation samples are generated by dynamically aggregated local generators trained using diffusion models.
- We conduct extensive experiments on multiple datasets, demonstrating that AD^2-pFed consistently outperforms baseline methods across varying levels of data heterogeneity, highlighting its effectiveness.

2   Preliminary and Problem Formulation

Consider a learning task where each data sample x and its corresponding ground-truth label y on the i-th client are drawn from a specific distribution $(x, y) \sim \mathcal{D}_i$. In a pFL problem, N clients train N individualized models $W = \{w_1, w_2, \ldots, w_N\}$, where each model w_k is tailored to the data X_k of the corresponding client. Let $p^{w_k} = f_{w_k}(x)$ represent the prediction of a model w_k on input x, and $L(p^{w_k}, y)$ denote the loss function between p^{w_k} and y. The training objective for the local models is defined as:

$$\min_{w_1, w_2, \ldots, w_N} L^W := \frac{1}{N} \sum_{k=1}^{N} \frac{1}{|X_k|} \sum_{x \in X_k} L(p^{w_k}, y). \tag{1}$$

We adopt FML as the underlying paradigm to address the considered pFL problem. The goal of FML is to train a private model and a shared model using the same dataset, with each model acting as a teacher to facilitate knowledge transfer between them. This knowledge transfer is achieved by computing the Kullback-Leibler (KL) divergence between the soft predictions p^w and p^s of the two models on the local training dataset. The corresponding optimization objective is given by:

$$\min_{w} \mathcal{L}_{ML}^{w} := \mathcal{L}_{CE}(p^w, y) + \mathcal{D}_{KL}(p^w \| p^s), \tag{2}$$

$$\min_{s} \mathcal{L}_{ML}^{s} := \mathcal{L}_{CE}(p^s, y) + \mathcal{D}_{KL}(p^s \| p^w). \tag{3}$$

Here, $\mathcal{L}_{CE}(\cdot)$ represents the cross-entropy loss, which measures the discrepancy between the model's predicted distribution and the true labels, ensuring classification accuracy. Meanwhile, $\mathcal{D}_{KL}(\cdot)$ quantifies the divergence between the two predicted distributions, facilitating knowledge transfer between the shared model s and the private model w.

To enhance the richness of client data in heterogeneous data environments, we employ diffusion models to generate data with improved quality and stability. The core idea behind diffusion models is to learn the data distribution by applying forward noise injection and reverse denoising, which enables the generation of high-quality samples. In our framework, the diffusion model on each client serves as a local generator trained with the local dataset D_i. The training objective for the local generator is defined as:

$$\mathcal{L}_{\text{simple}} = \mathbb{E}_{t, x_0, \epsilon} \left[\| \epsilon - \epsilon_k(x_t, t) \|^2 \right], \tag{4}$$

where $\mathcal{L}_{\text{simple}}$ represents the mean squared error loss, t denotes the diffusion time step, ϵ represents Gaussian noise, and ϵ_k is the noise predicted by the neural network θ_k. Through iterative optimization, θ_k learns to predict ϵ_k, progressively approximating ϵ and restoring data that aligns with the original distribution x_0. In the following, we use g_k to denote the local generator of the k-th client.

3   Methodology

The overall workflow of AD^2-pFed is illustrated in Fig. 1. Clients use their local data to independently train local generators, private models, and shared models. The private and shared models are trained using adaptive mutual learning (AML) and adaptive ensemble learning (AEL), respectively, while the local generator is trained with a local diffusion model. After training, private models remain on the local devices, while the shared models are uploaded to the server for aggregation. On the server side, a dynamic weighting strategy is employed to aggregate the shared models and local generators, obtaining the global model and global generator, respectively. This strategy adjusts the aggregation weights based on the similarity between the initially data-volume-based global model and the local shared models, ensuring a more precise integration of client knowledge. Pseudo-data generated by the global generator is then used as distillation samples to transfer knowledge from the dynamically aggregated local shared models to the global model, completing the fine-tuning process. The detailed steps of the proposed algorithm are provided in Algorithm 1.

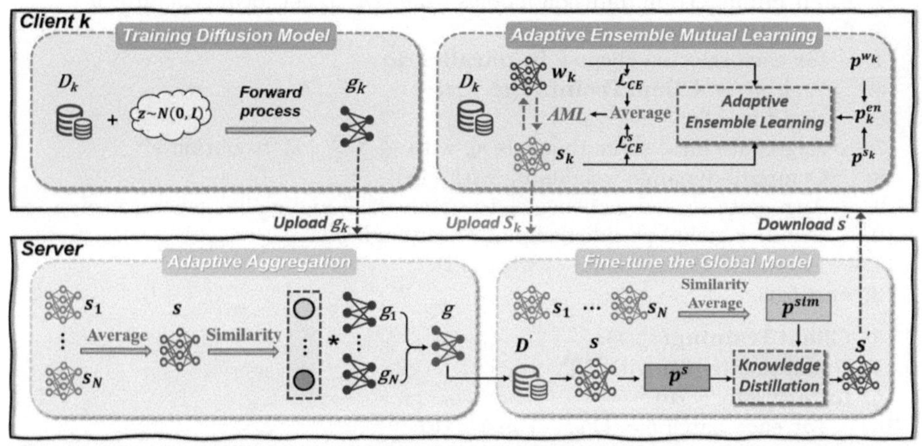

Fig. 1. AD^2-pFed's workflow.

3.1 Adaptive Mutual Learning

In this subsection, we propose an AML approach that adjusts learning intensity based on the loss values of local and global models. Since the effectiveness of FML is closely tied to the reliability of model predictions, unreliable predictions can distort the learning process. Higher prediction reliability increases learning intensity, while lower reliability decreases it. To achieve this, we control the learning intensity by considering the combined prediction losses of the private model w_k and the shared model s_k, as formulated below:

$$\mathcal{L}_d = \frac{\mathcal{D}_{KL}\big(\log(\text{softmax}(p^{w_k})), \text{softmax}(p^{s_k})\big)}{\text{Loss}_{CE} + \text{Loss}_{CE}^s}, \tag{5}$$

$$\mathcal{L}_s = \frac{\mathcal{D}_{KL}\big(\log(\text{softmax}(p^{s_k})), \text{softmax}(p^{w_k})\big)}{\text{Loss}_{CE} + \text{Loss}_{CE}^s}. \tag{6}$$

Here, p^{w_k} and p^{s_k} represent the soft predictions obtained by the private model w_k and the shared model s_k, respectively, when trained on the local dataset $\mathcal{D}_i$. In addition, Loss_{CE} denotes the prediction loss of the private model, while Loss_{CE}^s represents the prediction loss of the shared model.

Algorithm 1: AD^2-pFed

---

1 **Input**: Number of communication rounds T, number of clients N, learning rate η, number of local epochs E, local datasets $\{\mathcal{D}_k\}$, batch size b.

2 **Output**: Final private models w_k^T.

  1: **Server**: Initialize global model s^0 and ask clients to initialize w_k^0.

  2: **Each client**: Train diffusion models using $\mathcal{D}_k$ to get local generator g_k.

  3: **for** $t = 1$ to T **do**

  4:     **for** each selected client k **in parallel do**

  5:       $s_k^t, g_k \leftarrow$ **ClientTraining**(s^{t-1}, t)

  6:     **end for**

  7:     Aggregate local shared models s_k^t with $\frac{1}{N}\sum_{k=1}^{N} s_k^t$ to obtain s^t;

  8:     Compute dynamic weights β_k^t with (13);

  9:     Aggregate s_k^t and g_k using β_k^t to obtain s_t^{sim} and global generator g^t;

  10:    Produce global pseudo samples $\mathcal{D}'$ through g^t;

  11:    Fine-tune global model s^t with (14).

  12: **end for**

  13: **ClientTraining**(s_k^t, t):

  14: Update λ_k^t by (9) with X_k^λ;

  15: **for** $e = 1$ to E **do**

  16:    **for** each batch $b = \{x_k, y_k\}$ in $\mathcal{D}_k$ **do**

  17:      $L_{CE}(s_k^t), L_{CE}(w_k^t) \leftarrow$ CrossEntropyLossFunction

  18:      Compute AML losses L_d and L_s for s_k^t and w_k^t with (5) and (6);

  19:      Compute AEL loss L_{en} for s_k^t and w_k^t with (10);

  20:      Update private model w_k^t and shared model s_k^t with (11) and (12).

  21:    **end for**

  22: **end for**

  23: **return** s_k^t and g_k to server

3.2 Adaptive Ensemble Learning

In this subsection, we propose an adaptive ensemble learning method that dynamically adjusts the weights of the shared and private models to balance generalization and personalization. In traditional ensemble learning methods, the penalty parameter λ is fixed and identical across all clients. However, in real-world scenarios, the distance between each client's local data distribution and the global data distribution center may vary. To address this issue, we propose learning a personalized penalty parameter $\lambda_k \in [0,1]$ for each client, enabling better adaptation to local data distributions and achieving an improved balance between personalized and generalized knowledge. Specifically, a larger λ_k gives more weight to the private model in the final result, while a smaller λ_k increases the influence of the shared model.

The penalty parameters for all clients are denoted as $\mathcal{T} = \{\lambda_1, \ldots, \lambda_N\}$. The optimization objective of AD^2-pFed with respect to $\mathcal{T}$ is

$$\min_{s, \mathcal{W}, \mathcal{T}} \frac{1}{N} \sum_{k=1}^{N} \frac{1}{|X_k|} \sum_{x \in X_k} \mathcal{L}[\lambda_k \cdot p^{w_k} + (1 - \lambda_k) \cdot p^{s_k}, y]. \tag{7}$$

The soft label p_k^{en} of the ensemble prediction for each client is defined as:

$$p_k^{\text{en}} = \lambda_k \cdot p^{w_k} + (1 - \lambda_k) \cdot p^{s_k}. \tag{8}$$

During the training of λ_k, private models tend to overfit the local training dataset, which can cause λ_k to approach 1 if trained directly on it. To address this, we randomly sample 10% of the local training data, denoted as $X_k^{'a}$ to train λ_k. Based on the ensemble prediction p^{en} generated by the shared and private models, the update rule for λ_k is:

$$\lambda_k \leftarrow \lambda_k - \eta \frac{\partial \mathcal{L}_{CE}(p_k^{\text{en}}, y)}{\partial \lambda_k}, \tag{9}$$

where η is the learning rate, and the parameter λ_k is updated iteratively using stochastic gradient descent. The final adaptive ensemble learning loss function is given by:

$$\mathcal{L}_{\text{en}} = \mathcal{L}_{CE}(p_k^{\text{en}}, y). \tag{10}$$

Thus, we construct the total loss functions for the private model w_k and the shared model s_k during local training:

$$\mathcal{L}^{w_k} = \mathcal{L}_{CE}(p^{w_k}, y) + \mathcal{L}_d + \mathcal{L}_{\text{en}}, \tag{11}$$

$$\mathcal{L}^{s_k} = \mathcal{L}_{CE}(p^{s_k}, y) + \mathcal{L}_s + \mathcal{L}_{\text{en}}. \tag{12}$$

3.3   Global Model Fine-Tuning

In this subsection, we propose a knowledge distillation-based method to fine-tune the global model without requiring additional data. In scenarios with significant cross-client non-IID data distributions, traditional weighted aggregation methods may fail to capture the necessary data diversity and provide limited insight into the data distributions of individual clients. In our proposed method, the server first aggregates the shared models s_k from each client to obtain an initial global model by computing $s = \frac{1}{N} \sum_{k=1}^{N} s_k$.

To generate global pseudo-data that is representative of the global data distribution, we dynamically aggregate the local generators. Direct aggregation based solely on data volume may not yield a generator that effectively represents the global distribution. To address this, we guide the aggregation process using cosine similarity, which evaluates the consistency between local and global model updates, ensuring that local models with similar optimization trajectories contribute more to the global update. The cosine similarity between each local shared model s_k and the data-volume-based global model s is calculated as: $\mathrm{Cos}(s_k, s) = \frac{s_k \cdot s}{\|s_k\| \|s\|}$. The cosine similarities are then normalized to obtain a dynamic weight β_k:

$$\beta_k = \frac{\mathrm{Cos}(s_k, s)}{\sum_{k=1}^{N} \mathrm{Cos}(s_k, s)}. \tag{13}$$

The local generators g_k are aggregated using dynamic weights β_k to produce a global generator $g = \sum_{k=1}^{N} \beta_k \cdot g_k$. Similarly, s_k are aggregated utilizing β_k, resulting in $s^{\mathrm{sim}} = \sum_{k=1}^{m} \beta_k \cdot s_k$, which enables the global shared model to incorporate more information. Finally, using the integrated model s^{sim} as the teacher model and the current global shared model s as the student model, knowledge distillation is performed with global pseudo-data $(x', y') \sim \mathcal{D}'$ generated by the global generator g. The fine-tuning process of s using s^{sim} is as follows:

$$s' = \arg\min_{s} \mathcal{L}_{KD}^{s} \left(s^{\mathrm{sim}}, s\right). \tag{14}$$

Since the pseudo-data generated by local generators does not retain any specific original samples, the dynamically aggregated global generator and its resulting global pseudo-data still preserve client privacy.

4   Experiments

4.1   Experimental Setup

Datasets and Data Heterogeneity. We evaluate the AD^2-pFed framework on three datasets: FashionMNIST, CIFAR-10, and CIFAR-100. Two non-IID scenarios are considered:

1) **Pathological non-IID**: We assign unbalanced data across $2/2/10$ classes to each client from a total of $10/10/100$ classes in the FashionMNIST, CIFAR-10, and CIFAR-100 datasets, respectively.
2) **Practical non-IID**: We adopt the Dirichlet distribution-based partitioning method. By controlling the parameter α, the data distribution across clients varies from highly non-IID to nearly IID. We evaluate α values of 0.05, 0.1, 0.5 and 1 for detailed analysis. The client data is divided into 75% training set and 25% test set.

Implementation Details. 1) Evaluation of the personalization capability of local models: We compare AD^2-pFed against several baselines, including FedAvg, FedProx, FML, Per-FedAvg, FedKD, FedTweet, FedAMP, and FedAPEN. In this evaluation, the training and test sets of the clients have the same distribution. 2) Evaluation of the generalization performance of the global model: We assess the generalization performance of AD^2-pFed in comparison with FedAMP, Per-FedAvg, FML, FedKD, and FedAPEN. In this case, the training and test sets of the clients follow different distributions. 3) Ablation studies: We conduct ablation studies to evaluate the contribution of different components of the proposed framework. These experiments are performed under both pathological and practical non-IID ($\alpha = 0.1$) settings. In these settings, FashionMNIST and CIFAR10 use a CNN with two convolutional layers and one fully connected layer for training, while CIFAR-100 utilizes a CNN with three convolutional layers and one fully connected layer. The learning rate for FedAvg and FedProx is set to 0.1 across all datasets. For FML, PerFedAvg, FedKD, FedTweet, FedAMP, FedAPEN, and AD^2-pFed, the learning rate is set to 0.005 for FashionMNIST and CIFAR-10, and 0.05 for CIFAR-100. The number of local epochs is set to 3 for all methods, and the batch size is fixed at 32. All other experimental settings are kept consistent across methods to ensure fair comparisons. Test accuracies are reported as the average performance across all clients.

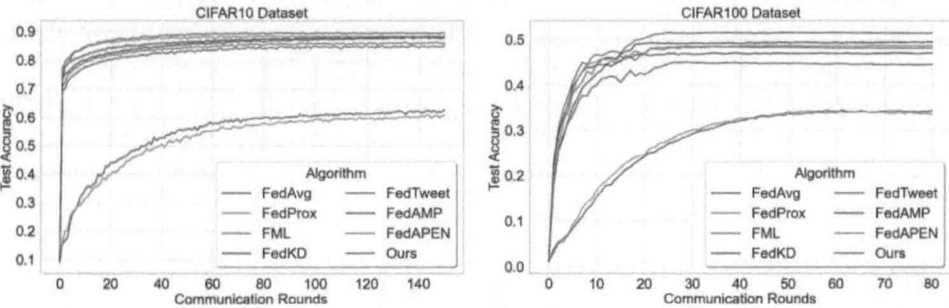

Fig. 2. Accuracy curves on CIFAR-10 and CIFAR-100 under practical non-IID setting with $\alpha = 0.1$.

4.2 Personalized Performance Comparison

Table 1 presents the test accuracy of all methods across three datasets, two heterogeneous scenarios, and four levels of heterogeneity. It is observed that as the level of data heterogeneity increases, the performance of pFL-related algorithms (FML, Per-FedAvg, FedKD, FedTweet, FedAMP, FedAPEN, AD^2-pFed) improves, while traditional FL algorithms (FedAvg, FedProx) experience a decline, with performance dropping to approximately half of that seen in personalized algorithms under extreme heterogeneity. This may be attributed to the adverse effects on global model generalization. AD^2-pFed outperforms other personalized algorithms in most scenarios, except under the CIFAR-10 practical non-IID setting with $\alpha = 0.05$, where its accuracy is 0.15% lower than that of FedAMP. Furthermore, AD^2-pFed demonstrates lower performance variation across all settings, particularly under high heterogeneity, highlighting its robustness and stability in handling heterogeneous scenarios.

Figure 2 presents the accuracy curves of two image datasets under the practical non-IID scenario with $\alpha = 0.1$. The accuracy of FedAvg and FedProx increases slowly due to the absence of personalized models, which limits their ability to adapt to local data distributions and results in slower

146   Z. Wang et al.

Table 1. Accuracy on FashionMNIST, CIFAR-10, and CIFAR-100 under Pathological Non-IID and Practical Non-IID settings.

	Method	Pathological Non-IID	Practical Non-IID			
		non-IID	$\alpha = 1$	$\alpha = 0.5$	$\alpha = 0.1$	$\alpha = 0.05$
FashionMNIST	FedAvg	79.20 ± 0.204	90.20 ± 0.042	89.56 ± 0.032	84.56 ± 0.095	81.26 ± 0.456
	FedProx	78.65 ± 0.187	90.02 ± 0.048	89.43 ± 0.033	84.75 ± 0.097	80.88 ± 0.325
	FML	98.03 ± 0.016	87.34 ± 0.145	90.38 ± 0.155	95.42 ± 0.086	96.09 ± 0.215
	Per-FedAvg	95.78 ± 0.015	85.79 ± 0.166	88.01 ± 0.156	92.84 ± 0.055	95.21 ± 0.223
	FedKD	98.15 ± 0.016	87.88 ± 0.165	91.69 ± 0.163	95.88 ± 0.069	97.26 ± 0.234
	FedTweet	96.41 ± 0.021	86.02 ± 0.187	88.64 ± 0.156	93.43 ± 0.088	96.02 ± 0.284
	FedAMP	98.78 ± 0.023	89.46 ± 0.147	91.54 ± 0.171	96.26 ± 0.086	98.17 ± 0.246
	FedAPEN	99.03 ± 0.015	90.11 ± 0.169	92.38 ± 0.156	96.62 ± 0.086	97.69 ± 0.215
	AD^2-pFed	$\mathbf{99.43 \pm 0.011}$	$\mathbf{91.02 \pm 0.171}$	$\mathbf{92.76 \pm 0.156}$	$\mathbf{97.38 \pm 0.075}$	$\mathbf{98.56 \pm 0.214}$
CIFAR-10	FedAvg	56.50 ± 0.128	68.97 ± 0.035	66.80 ± 0.044	59.89 ± 0.086	55.23 ± 0.123
	FedProx	56.24 ± 0.132	68.45 ± 0.041	66.32 ± 0.051	59.74 ± 0.085	55.21 ± 0.121
	FML	86.56 ± 0.054	63.47 ± 0.055	67.70 ± 0.076	87.87 ± 0.120	93.52 ± 0.162
	Per-FedAvg	84.56 ± 0.052	61.56 ± 0.058	64.62 ± 0.077	84.22 ± 0.103	90.31 ± 0.173
	FedKD	88.45 ± 0.048	63.77 ± 0.061	67.82 ± 0.080	88.23 ± 0.091	93.81 ± 0.160
	FedTweet	85.34 ± 0.065	62.28 ± 0.036	65.17 ± 0.035	84.99 ± 0.127	91.12 ± 0.202
	FedAMP	89.21 ± 0.057	66.47 ± 0.078	69.11 ± 0.104	89.34 ± 0.111	$\mathbf{94.12 \pm 0.173}$
	FedAPEN	89.43 ± 0.048	68.12 ± 0.044	70.92 ± 0.048	89.21 ± 0.091	93.77 ± 0.160
	AD^2-pFed	$\mathbf{90.32 \pm 0.052}$	$\mathbf{69.31 \pm 0.052}$	$\mathbf{71.26 \pm 0.075}$	$\mathbf{89.68 \pm 0.105}$	93.97 ± 0.135
CIFAR-100	FedAvg	30.59 ± 0.049	36.59 ± 0.033	35.19 ± 0.027	33.40 ± 0.044	30.23 ± 0.044
	FedProx	30.92 ± 0.045	35.78 ± 0.031	34.56 ± 0.028	33.18 ± 0.045	29.68 ± 0.051
	FML	49.55 ± 0.063	33.45 ± 0.031	36.23 ± 0.032	47.56 ± 0.059	57.86 ± 0.069
	Per-FedAvg	46.32 ± 0.061	30.17 ± 0.033	33.16 ± 0.036	44.23 ± 0.062	54.99 ± 0.085
	FedKD	50.47 ± 0.053	33.47 ± 0.030	36.01 ± 0.029	47.58 ± 0.057	58.46 ± 0.076
	FedTweet	47.11 ± 0.065	30.81 ± 0.039	33.79 ± 0.035	45.10 ± 0.064	55.61 ± 0.081
	FedAMP	51.55 ± 0.064	36.07 ± 0.029	38.42 ± 0.035	49.09 ± 0.052	59.17 ± 0.083
	FedAPEN	51.47 ± 0.053	36.79 ± 0.037	39.01 ± 0.035	48.68 ± 0.057	58.66 ± 0.077
	AD^2-pFed	$\mathbf{52.25 \pm 0.050}$	$\mathbf{37.88 \pm 0.34}$	$\mathbf{40.23 \pm 0.025}$	$\mathbf{51.45 \pm 0.048}$	$\mathbf{59.83 \pm 0.075}$

convergence. In contrast, personalized algorithms (FML, FedKD, FedTweet, FedAMP, FedAPEN, and AD^2-pFed) achieve convergence within 20 communication rounds, highlighting their superiority in handling heterogeneous data. Among these, AD^2-pFed consistently outperforms the other baseline algorithms in terms of test accuracy.

4.3   Generalization Performance Comparison

This section evaluates the generalization performance of four baseline algorithms (FedAMP, Per-FedAvg, FML, FedKD, FedAPEN) and our proposed AD^2-pFed on the CIFAR-10 and CIFAR-100 datasets. Unlike personalized testing, generalization testing ensures that all clients share the same distribution and quantity of test data. As shown in Fig. 3, the performance of the global model improves with increasing values of α, highlighting the significant impact of data heterogeneity on generalization. AD^2-pFed outperforms the baseline algorithms across various levels of heterogeneity. For CIFAR-10, accuracy stabilizes when α exceeds

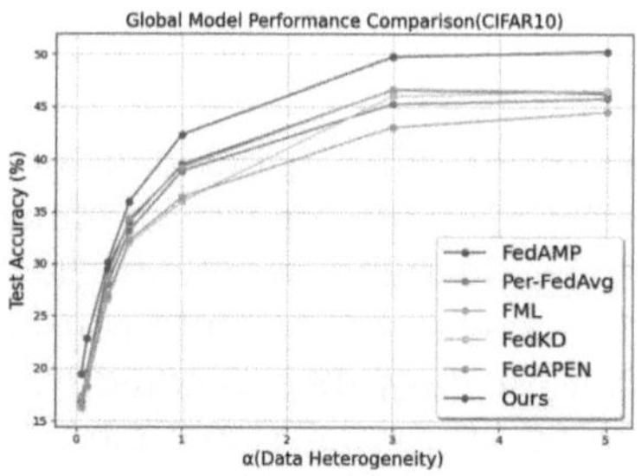
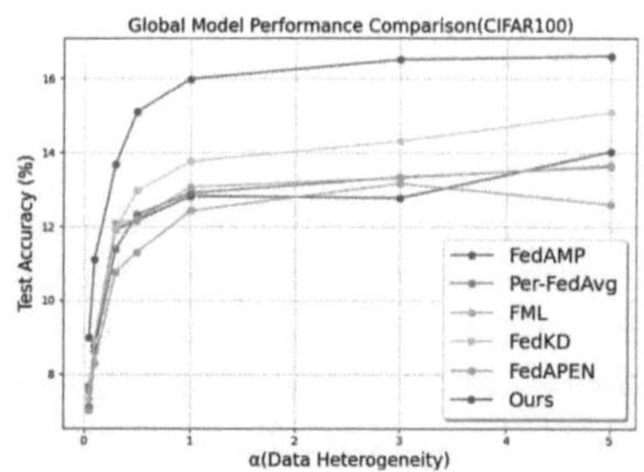

Fig. 3. Accuracy curves with varying levels of heterogeneity.

3, reaching optimal performance across all algorithms, while for CIFAR-100, accuracy gradually stabilizes once α surpasses 1.

4.4 Ablation Study

Table 2. Ablation study on FashionMNIST, CIFAR-10, and CIFAR-100 datasets under pathological and practical non-IID ($\alpha = 0.1$) settings.

Dataset	FashionMNIST		CIFAR-10		CIFAR-100	
	Pathological	Practical	Pathological	Practical	Pathological	Practical
w/o AML	82.36	87.18	62.18	64.78	36.54	37.89
w/o DFT	98.17	96.61	89.11	88.26	51.27	50.07
w/o ADG	96.26	95.56	87.34	86.16	49.14	46.23
w/o AEL	95.61	95.04	86.01	85.67	48.44	45.11
AD^2-pFed	**99.43**	**97.38**	**90.32**	**89.68**	**52.25**	**51.45**

Table 2 demonstrates the effectiveness of each key component in AD^2-pFed, with the following analysis:

1) w/o AML (adaptive mutual learning): Removing mutual distillation eliminates the support provided by the auxiliary global model, reducing AD^2-pFed to a fine-tuned version of FedAvg, which results in a significant drop in accuracy. **2) w/o DFT (distillation fine-tuning)**: Similarity-based fine-tuning enables the global model to capture the client data distribution. Removing this component leads to a decline in model performance. **3) w/o ADG (adaptive distillation guidance)**: Without adaptive distillation guidance, unreliable predictions from intermediate models may mislead the knowledge transfer process, which in turn reduces the performance of private models. **4) w/o AEL (adaptive ensemble learning)**: Adaptive ensemble learning dynamically adjusts personalization parameters based on data heterogeneity, enhancing mutual learning. Its removal significantly degrades the performance of private models.

5   Conclusion

This paper proposes a pFL method called AD^2-pFed, which is based on adaptive bilateral distillation with diffusion models. The method employs loss-function-guided mutual learning and adaptive ensemble learning locally to facilitate knowledge transfer between private and shared models. Additionally, considering the diversity of local data distributions, global pseudo-data generated by diffusion models is used as distillation samples to fine-tune the global model. This approach improves the performance of personalized models while preserving the generalization capability of the global model. Extensive experiments across various datasets and settings have demonstrated the effectiveness of the proposed method. In future work, we aim to explore a pFL framework based on bilateral distillation under heterogeneous scenarios involving both label and domain shifts.

Acknowledgement. This work was supported in part by the Taishan Scholars Program under Grant tsqn202408239, in part by the Shandong Provincial Nature Science Foundation of China under Grant ZR2024MF100, in part by the NSFC under Grant 62402256, and in part by the QLU/SDAS Pilot Project for Integrated Innovation of Science, Education, and Industry under Grant 2024ZDZX08.

References

1. McMahan, B., Moore, E., Ramage, D., Hampson, S., Arcas, B.A.: Communication-efficient learning of deep networks from decentralized data. In: Artificial Intelligence and Statistics, pp. 1273–1282. PMLR (2017)
2. Li, T., Sahu, A.K., Zaheer, M., Sanjabi, M., Talwalkar, A., Smith, V.: Federated optimization in heterogeneous networks. Proc. Mach. Learn. Syst. **2**, 429–450 (2020)
3. Tan, A.Z., Yu, H., Cui, L., Yang, Q.: Towards personalized federated learning. IEEE Trans. Neural Netw. Learn. Syst. **34**(12), 9587–9603 (2022)
4. Fallah, A., Mokhtari, A., Ozdaglar, A.: Personalized federated learning with theoretical guarantees: a model-agnostic meta-learning approach. Adv. Neural. Inf. Process. Syst. **33**, 3557–3568 (2020)
5. Collins, L., Hassani, H., Mokhtari, A., Shakkottai, S.: Exploiting shared representations for personalized federated learning. In: International Conference on Machine Learning, pp. 2089–2099. PMLR (2021)
6. Li, T., Hu, S., Beirami, A., Smith, V.: Ditto: fair and robust federated learning through personalization. In: International Conference on Machine Learning, pp. 6357–6368. PMLR (2021)
7. T Dinh, C., Tran, N., Nguyen, J.: Personalized federated learning with moreau envelopes. In: Advances in Neural Information Processing Systems, vol. 33, pp. 21394–21405 (2020)
8. Huang, Y., et al.: Personalized cross-silo federated learning on non-IID data. In: Proceedings of the AAAI Conference on Artificial Intelligence, vol. 35, pp. 7865–7873 (2021)

9. Sattler, F., Müller, K.-R., Samek, W.: Clustered federated learning: model-agnostic distributed multitask optimization under privacy constraints. IEEE Trans. Neural Netw. Learn. Syst. **32**(8), 3710–3722 (2020)
10. Shen, T., et al.: Federated mutual learning. arXiv preprint arXiv:2006.16765 (2020)
11. Chuhan, W., Fangzhao, W., Lyu, L., Huang, Y., Xie, X.: Communication-efficient federated learning via knowledge distillation. Nat. Commun. **13**(1), 2032 (2022)
12. Qin, Z., Deng, S., Zhao, M., Yan, X.: Fedapen: personalized cross-silo federated learning with adaptability to statistical heterogeneity. In: Proceedings of the 29th ACM SIGKDD Conference on Knowledge Discovery and Data Mining, pp. 1954–1964 (2023)
13. Wang, Y., Wang, W., Wang, X., Zhang, H., Xiaoming, W., Yang, M.: Fedtweet: two-fold knowledge distillation for non-IID federated learning. Comput. Electr. Eng. **114**, 109067 (2024)
14. Lin, T., Kong, L., Stich, S.U., Jaggi, M.: Ensemble distillation for robust model fusion in federated learning. In: Advances in Neural Information Processing Systems, vol. 33, pp. 2351–2363 (2020)
15. Zhu, Z., Hong, J., Zhou, J.: Data-free knowledge distillation for heterogeneous federated learning. In: International Conference on Machine Learning, pp. 12878–12889. PMLR (2021)
16. Zhang, L., Shen, L., Ding, L., Tao, D., Duan, L.-Y.: Fine-tuning global model via data-free knowledge distillation for non-IID federated learning. In: Proceedings of the IEEE/CVF Conference on Computer Vision and Pattern Recognition, pp. 10174–10183 (2022)
17. Wang, H., Li, Y., Xu, W., Li, R., Zhan, Y., Zeng, Z.: Dafkd: domain-aware federated knowledge distillation. In: Proceedings of the IEEE/CVF Conference on Computer Vision and Pattern Recognition, pp. 20412–20421 (2023)
18. Lee, G., Jeong, M., Shin, Y., Bae, S., Yun, S.-Y.: Preservation of the global knowledge by not-true distillation in federated learning. Adv. Neural. Inf. Process. Syst. **35**, 38461–38474 (2022)

FATDyG: A Dynamic Network Link Prediction Framework for Time, Space, and Frequency Awareness

Rong Qian, Zihao Wang[✉], Yuchen Zhou, and Yuyi Tian

Beijing Electronic Science and Technology Institute, Beijing 100070, China
wzhzyzx@163.com
https://www.besti.edu.cn/

Abstract. Dynamic networks are widely utilized in social media, biological networks, and various other fields. Accurate prediction of their link evolution is crucial for understanding dynamic behaviors. However, existing methods still face several challenges in link prediction. First, effectively capturing long-term dependencies in time-series modeling remains difficult, and existing approaches struggle to adapt to irregular time intervals. Second, the ability to extract frequency characteristics in non-stationary signals is limited, making it difficult to capture local abrupt changes and periodic patterns in dynamic networks. To address these issues, we proposes the Frequency-Aware Transformer for Dynamic Graphs (FAT-DyG) framework. Specifically, a time-difference-aware GRU is employed to capture short-term dependencies while adapting to irregular time intervals. Meanwhile, long-term dynamic relationships are modeled using the global attention mechanism of the Transformer. Additionally, discrete cosine transform (DCT) is leveraged to extract periodic features in the frequency domain, and dynamic frequency selection is introduced to enhance the fusion of long- and short-term features. Experiments on seven real-world dynamic network datasets demonstrate that FATDyG outperforms existing methods in link prediction tasks. Compared to baseline approaches, FATDyG achieves up to 3.52% and 1.22% improvements in Average Precision (AP) and the Area Under the Receiver Operating Characteristic Curve (AUC-ROC) respectively, validating its effectiveness.

Keywords: Dynamic Networks · Link Prediction · Time-difference-aware GRU · Transformer · Discrete cosine transform · Deep Learning

1 Introduction

Dynamic network link prediction aims to forecast future connections between nodes based on historical network interaction data and has significant applications in social networks, recommendation systems, bioinformatics, and other fields [1]. Unlike static networks, where the topology remains unchanged, dynamic networks evolve over time. Therefore, link prediction in dynamic networks requires not only structural information between nodes but also an understanding of temporal evolution patterns to accurately predict future connections.

© The Author(s), under exclusive license to Springer Nature Singapore Pte Ltd. 2026
T. Zhu et al. (Eds.): KSEM 2025, LNAI 15920, pp. 150–165, 2026.
https://doi.org/10.1007/978-981-95-3052-6_12

The development of dynamic network link prediction techniques has transitioned from traditional methods to deep learning approaches. Early methods, including matrix factorization, probabilistic models, spectral analysis, and time series models, achieved some success on small-scale networks. However, they generally suffer from high computational complexity and limited capacity to capture high-dimensional nonlinear features. To overcome these limitations, deep learning-based methods have emerged, including autoencoder (AE)-based approaches, recurrent neural networks (RNNs), generative adversarial networks (GANs), and graph neural networks (GNNs). These methods effectively extract complex features in dynamic networks. However, most of them rely on sequential modeling in the time domain and overlook periodic patterns in the frequency domain. Additionally, these sequence-based time-domain methods often struggle with the vanishing gradient problem, leading to poor performance in modeling long-term dependencies. To address these shortcomings, recent studies have explored frequency-domain characteristics, such as capturing periodic and long-term dependency patterns in dynamic graphs using Fast Fourier Transform (FFT) [2]. However, FFT assumes global stationarity and fails to localize time-varying features. As a result, it struggles to capture non-stationary abrupt changes and transient patterns in dynamic networks. Moreover, existing methods have not fully exploited frequency characteristics in dynamic graph tasks and lack a dedicated frequency enhancement mechanism suitable for dynamic graph modeling.

To overcome the above challenges, this paper proposes a novel dynamic graph modeling framework, Frequency-Aware Transformer for Dynamic Graphs (FATDyG). FATDyG innovatively integrates temporal and frequency-domain modeling and captures local dynamics of irregularly spaced sequences using a time-difference-aware gated recurrent unit (GRU) [3]. Additionally, the global attention mechanism of the Transformer [4] is incorporated to model long-term dependencies, addressing the limitations of traditional models in capturing extended interactions and handling abrupt events. Furthermore, we design a dynamic frequency enhancement module based on the Discrete Cosine Transform (DCT) [5] to adaptively extract periodic features and local abrupt changes in the frequency domain. By leveraging learnable weights, this module enables multi-scale fusion of long- and short-term features, significantly improving prediction accuracy and robustness in complex dynamic scenarios. Experiments on seven real-world dynamic network datasets demonstrate that FATDyG achieves state-of-the-art (SOTA) performance under transductive settings, as well as across multiple negative sampling strategies. The key contributions of this paper are as follows:

1. We propose a time-difference-aware GRU mechanism and integrate it with a Transformer to effectively address the challenges of long-term dependency modeling and irregular interval adaptation in traditional time-series models.
2. We design a dynamic frequency enhancement module based on DCT, which accurately captures key frequency-domain features and periodic patterns, leveraging them to enhance long- and short-term feature representations.
3. Extensive experiments across seven datasets and multiple experimental settings show significant performance improvements. FATDyG achieves a maximum AP improvement of 3.52% and an AUC-ROC improvement of 1.22%, verifying the superiority of our framework.

2 Related Work

2.1 Traditional Methods for Dynamic Network Link Prediction

Traditional methods primarily include matrix decomposition, probabilistic models, spectral clustering, and time series analysis. Matrix decomposition captures the topological evolution of dynamic networks through low-dimensional embeddings. For instance, Gao, Denoyer, and Gallinari [6] proposed a graph-regularized matrix decomposition method that integrates multi-source information to predict link probabilities. Ahmed et al. [7] introduced a non-negative matrix factorization approach to construct matrix factors that incorporate critical network features, proving its convergence and correctness. Ma, Sun, and Qin [8] leveraged graph communicability to perform matrix decomposition for each network snapshot, obtained feature matrices, and then folded them for link prediction. However, matrix decomposition methods often lead to high computational costs and have limited capability in capturing high-dimensional feature correlations.

Probabilistic models focus on statistically modeling dynamic network evolution. Sarkar, Chakrabarti, and Jordan [9] adopted a non-parametric approach to link prediction under the assumption that links are independent, determined by the characteristics of nodes and their neighbors. Ahmed and Chen [10] reformulated the link prediction problem as a random walk process, computing similarity scores between nodes and their neighbors. Lakshmi and Bhavani [11] introduced a dynamic network co-occurrence probability into collaborative networks, constructing Markov random fields to predict links. While probabilistic models effectively capture the evolutionary patterns of dynamic networks, they suffer from high computational complexity when applied to large-scale networks.

Spectral clustering methods analyze network evolution based on the graph Laplacian matrix. Fang, Kohram, and Ralescu [12] employed spectral theory and low-rank approximation to track the evolution of node features. Wu, Chang, and Liao [13] proposed a spectral graph theory-based method for dynamic network link prediction, utilizing a finite impulse response filter model to track the evolution of latent eigenvectors for each node. Although spectral clustering methods can effectively track network evolution and predict dynamic links, they are difficult to scale to complex dynamic networks and involve significant computational overhead.

In recent years, time series analysis has been increasingly applied to dynamic network link prediction, yielding promising results. Rossetti et al. [14] introduced a supervised learning approach that integrates dynamic social network analysis, time series forecasting, feature selection, and network community structure to predict future interactions, restricting predictions to links between users from the same social background. Ozcan and Oguducu [15] proposed a multivariate time series-based link prediction model that incorporates dynamic network evolution, node similarity, and connectivity information, leveraging covariance structures and link emergence patterns to accurately predict new and recurring links. Time series-based methods perform well in predicting links for networks where significant changes occur within specific time intervals. However, most of these methods fail to capture the global topological features of the network and face challenges in modeling the nonlinear temporal evolution patterns of dynamic networks.

2.2 Deep Learning Methods for Dynamic Network Link Prediction

Deep learning methods significantly enhance the modeling capabilities of dynamic networks through nonlinear mapping and end-to-end learning, especially when handling datasets with complex nonlinear properties. In early studies, Rahman et al. [16] proposed an autoencoder-based framework to generate node embeddings by optimizing encoding problems, but it struggled with modeling long-term dependencies. Goyal et al. [17] applied deep autoencoders to capture the connectivity trends of dynamic graphs, yet their approach lacked adaptability to sudden interactions. With the introduction of RNNs, GANs, and GNNs, dynamic graph representation learning has seen significant breakthroughs. Pareja et al. [18] used RNNs to update the parameters of Graph Convolutional Networks (GCNs), enabling adaptive adjustments over time to capture the temporal variations in dynamic graph data. However, discretizing time intervals could lead to information loss. Rossi et al. [19] designed a memory module to store temporal change information, enhancing the model's ability to learn dynamic graph structures, but their approach faced limitations in modeling global dependencies. Kumar, Zhang, and Leskovec [20] introduced a dual-RNN structure to capture the temporal evolution of node embeddings, effectively modeling short-term interactions, but their method was susceptible to the vanishing gradient problem when handling long-term dependencies. Trivedi et al. [21] combined RNNs with sequential point processes to model continuous-time dynamic interactions, improving local dynamics capture but showing limited ability to represent high-dimensional nonlinear features. Lei et al. [22] optimized weighted dynamic network prediction using a generator-discriminator structure, yet training stability remained a challenge.

Currently, attention mechanisms are widely used in processing temporal features. Xu et al. [23] introduced time encoding and a graph attention mechanism to enable temporally-aware neighbor aggregation, but their approach had limited capacity for capturing periodic patterns in non-stationary signals. Wang et al. [24] leveraged Transformer models and a dual-flow encoder to aggregate spatiotemporal information, achieving global dependency modeling, but their approach was highly sensitive to hyperparameters and computationally expensive. Yu et al. [25] integrated neighbor co-occurrence encoding with sequence partitioning and employed Transformers to model long-range dependencies, yielding promising results but exhibiting sensitivity to the negative sampling strategy.

Additionally, there exist lightweight hybrid approaches. Poursafaei et al. [25] proposed a lightweight link prediction method based on edge storage and similarity retrieval, allowing link prediction without explicit model training, yet its reliance on strong assumptions about historical interactions limited adaptability to complex dynamic scenarios. Cong et al. [27] utilized a multi-layer perceptron (MLP) structure for feature mixing to achieve efficient dynamic graph modeling, but their method lacked the capability to capture long-term nonlinear dependencies. Wang et al. [28] introduced a causal anonymous walk sampling approach to extract local structural information and capture causal relationships within node neighborhoods, but their sampling strategy proved less robust in sparse networks. Tian, Qi, and Guo [29] integrated frequency enhancement techniques to improve prediction performance by capturing periodic patterns through frequency domain analysis; however, their method heavily relied on the assumption that the data exhibited periodic behavior.

Although these methods have made significant progress in capturing temporal dynamics, most dynamic graph models still exhibit limitations in leveraging node information, particularly when handling long sequence node interactions, and struggle with comprehensive global dynamic modeling.

3   Method

This section provides a detailed description of the FATDyG model. As illustrated in Fig. 1, the FATDyG framework consists of six key components: encoding layer, temporal capture layer, global feature fusion layer, frequency enhancement layer, aggregation layer, and link prediction layer. By employing hierarchical feature extraction, fusion, and enhancement, the model enables efficient representation learning for dynamic networks.

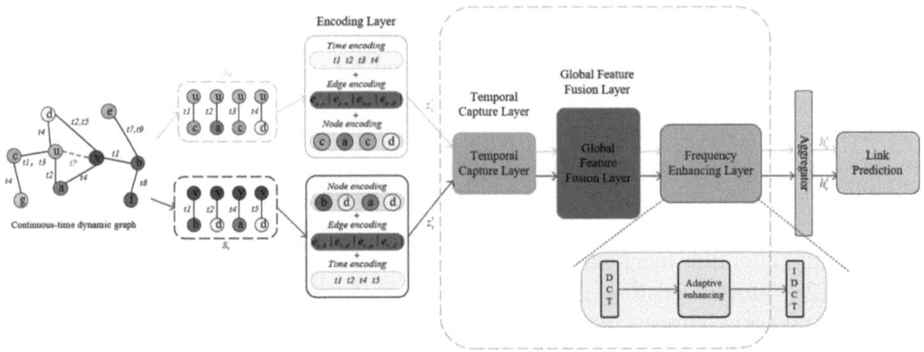

Fig. 1. The overview of FATDyG.

3.1   Encoding Layer

The model processes a node pair (u, v) and a target timestamp (t) as input. First, we sample L first-hop historical neighbors for each node, sorted chronologically to construct two interaction sequences S_u^t and S_v^t. Zero-padding is applied if a node has fewer than L historical neighbors. These sequences are then processed through an encoding layer that simultaneously embeds node features (structural attributes), link characteristics (interaction types/weights), and temporal information (timestamp encoding). The layer hierarchically fuses these three information dimensions through feature concatenation and nonlinear transformations.

Node/Edge Encoding: In dynamic graphs, both nodes and edges often carry associated feature information. To compute embeddings for interactions, it is sufficient to extract the intrinsic features of neighboring nodes and edges from the interaction sequence S_*^t, where $*$ can be either u or v. Similar to existing methods, nodes and edges are encoded as $Z_{*,N}^{t} \in \mathbb{R}^{L \times d_N}$ and $Z_{*,E}^{t} \in \mathbb{R}^{L \times d_E}$ respectively, where d_N and d_E represent the dimensions of node and edge embeddings.

Time Encoding: Time encoding is employed to map constant timestamps to vectors $Z_{*,T}^{t} \in \mathbb{R}^{L \times d_T}$, where d_T is the dimension of time embeddings. Specifically, the widely adopted time encoding function $\cos(t_n \omega)$ is used, where $\omega = \{\alpha^{-(i-1)/\beta}\}_{i=1}^{d_T}$ is employed to encode timestamps. Here, α and β are hyperparameters designed such that when i approache d_T, $t_{\max} \times \alpha^{-(i-1)/\beta}$ approaches 0. The cosine function is then applied to project these values into the range of $[-1, +1]$. Notably, relative timestamps, rather than absolute timestamps, are used for encoding. In other words, if the timestamp of the sampled interaction is t_0, and the specific timestamp for link prediction is t, the effective relative time encoding function becomes $\cos((t_n - t)\omega)$. It is important to note that ω remains constant and is not updated during training. Subsequently, the concatenated encodings for nodes are summed as $Z_*^{t} = Z_{*,N}^{t} + Z_{*,E}^{t} + Z_{*,T}^{t} \in \mathbb{R}^{L \times d}$.

3.2 Temporal Capture Layer

To address the shortcomings of existing RNN methods in modeling irregular time intervals, an improved GRU unit is proposed. By introducing time-difference awareness, this unit enhances the ability to model irregular time intervals. Compared to the standard GRU, our approach utilizes γ_n to control the decay of information, making the model more suitable for processing dynamic data with uneven time distributions.

$$\gamma_n = \exp(-\lambda \cdot \Delta t_n) \tag{1}$$

where γ_n is a learnable parameter that adaptively adjusts the historical state weights, effectively modeling interaction sequences with irregular time intervals. Δt_n represents the time difference between adjacent interactions and modifies the influence of historical states through exponential decay.

The gated update process of GRU is as follows:

Update and reset gates:

$$r_n = \sigma(W_r \cdot [h_{n-1}; Z_*^{t}[n, :]] + b_r) \tag{2}$$

$$z_n = \sigma(W_z \cdot [h_{n-1}; Z_*^{t}[n, :]] + b_z) \tag{3}$$

where r_n is the reset gate that controls the influence of the previous hidden state h_{n-1} on the current state, while z_n is the update gate that determines the extent to which the past state contributes to the current state update.

Candidate hidden state:

$$\tilde{h}_n = \tanh(W_h \cdot [r_n \odot h_{n-1}; Z_*^{t}[n, :]] + b_h) \tag{4}$$

Here, $\tilde{h}_t$ adjusts the contribution of historical information through the reset gate, and $Z_*^{t}[n, :] \in \mathbb{R}^{d}$ represents the input feature at the current time step.

Hidden state update:

$$h_n = (1 - \gamma_n z_n) \odot h_{n-1} + \gamma_n z_n \odot \tilde{h}_n \tag{5}$$

where γ_n serves as a time-decay factor, affecting the information retention of h_{n-1}, while z_n controls the fusion ratio between new and old information.

Finally, all hidden states h_t across the sequence are concatenated to form $H_{\text{gru}} = [h_1, \ldots, h_L]^T \in \mathbb{R}^{L \times d}$, which serves as the input to the subsequent layers.

3.3 Global Feature Fusion Layer

In dynamic graph modeling tasks, traditional time-series models such as GRU can only capture local temporal dependencies, making it challenging to effectively model global dynamics. To overcome this limitation, this paper introduces a Transformer-based global modeling mechanism to enhance the model's ability to capture long-range dependencies and further improve the accuracy of link prediction. Specifically, a Multi-Head Self-Attention (MHA) mechanism is employed to model global relationships within the graph, thereby obtaining a global feature representation $H_{\text{trans}} \in \mathbb{R}^{L \times d}$.

First, to compute the attention scores, the input H_{gru} is linearly transformed to obtain the query matrix Q, the key matrix K, and the value matrix V.

$$Q = H_{\text{gru}} W^Q, \quad K = H_{\text{gru}} W^K, \quad V = H_{\text{gru}} W^V \tag{6}$$

where $W^Q, W^K, W^V \in \mathbb{R}^{d \times d}$ is a learnable parameter. Then, the attention weights are computed using the scaled dot-product method and normalized with softmax before performing a weighted sum.

$$\text{Attention}(Q, K, V) = \text{Softmax}\left(\frac{QK^{\mathrm{T}}}{\sqrt{d}}\right) V \tag{7}$$

To improve the model's expressiveness, the multi-head self-attention mechanism is employed. In this approach, Q, K, V is split into h independent subspaces, each with a dimension of d / h.

$$Q_i = QW^{Q_i}, \quad K_i = KW^{K_i}, \quad V_i = VW^{V_i} \tag{8}$$

where $W_{Q_i}, W_{K_i}, W_{V_i} \in \mathbb{R}^{d \times (d/h)}$ is the learnable parameter associated with each attention head. After each attention head independently computes attention scores, the results are concatenated and passed through a linear transformation to obtain the final multi-head attention output:

$$H_{\text{mha}} = \text{Concat}(\text{head}_1, \ldots, \text{head}_h) W^O \tag{9}$$

where $W^O \in \mathbb{R}^{d \times d}$ is the output transformation matrix. To further enhance the nonlinear expressiveness of features, a Feedforward Neural Network (FFN) is introduced after the MHA layer. The computation of the FFN is as follows:

$$H_{\text{trans}} = \text{ReLU}(H_{\text{mha}} W_1 + b_1) W_2 + b_2 \tag{10}$$

where $W_1 \in \mathbb{R}^{d \times d}$ and $W_2 \in \mathbb{R}^{d \times d}$ are learnable parameters, and b_1 and b_2 are bias terms. This nonlinear transformation compensates for the attention mechanism's limitations in local feature extraction, thereby improving the overall expressiveness of the model.

3.4 Frequency Enhancing Layer

In this paper, DCT is applied to the frequency enhancement layer, positioned after the temporal capture layer and the global feature fusion layer. This approach not only improves the model's ability to capture both global and local patterns but also optimizes the fusion of long- and short-term features through frequency-domain operations, thereby enhancing overall prediction performance.

DCT is utilized to decompose time-series data into its component frequencies, enabling more efficient extraction of interaction patterns across different frequency ranges. Compared to FFT, DCT operates solely on real numbers, offering higher computational efficiency and being more suitable for energy compression in time-series data, especially when most of the energy is concentrated in low-frequency components.

To better identify key frequencies in historical interaction sequences, a one-dimensional discrete cosine transform is first applied along the time dimension (first dimension) to transform the input historical interaction sequence $H_{\text{trans}} \in \mathbb{R}^{L \times d}$ into the frequency domain:

$$F = \mathrm{DCT}(H_{trans}) \tag{11}$$

where H_{trans} represents the input time-domain sequence data, and $F \in \mathbb{R}^{L \times d}$ is its frequency-domain representation. Each column of F corresponds to the frequency components of a particular feature dimension, while $\mathrm{DCT}(\cdot)$ denotes the one-dimensional discrete cosine transform operation. In the frequency domain, the frequency components are adaptively enhanced through element-wise multiplication with a learnable enhancement tensor $W_f \in \mathbb{R}^{L \times d}$:

$$F_{\text{enhanced}} = F \odot W_f \tag{12}$$

where W_f is a learnable parameter matrix used to adjust the significance of different frequency components, $\odot$ denotes element-wise multiplication (Hadamard product), and $F_{\text{enhanced}} \in \mathbb{R}^{L \times d}$ represents the enhanced frequency-domain representation. Subsequently, an inverse discrete cosine transform (IDCT) is applied to F_{enhanced} to reconstruct the sequence back into the time domain:

$$H_{\text{enhanced}} = \mathrm{IDCT}(F_{\text{enhanced}}) \tag{13}$$

where $\mathrm{IDCT}(\cdot)$ denotes the one-dimensional inverse discrete cosine transform operation, and $H_{\text{enhanced}} \in \mathbb{R}^{L \times d}$ is the enhanced time-domain sequence data.

Finally, a residual connection and Dropout layers are employed to prevent overfitting while preserving the global dynamic characteristics of the temporal data:

$$H_{\text{final}} = H_{\text{trans}} + \mathrm{Dropout}(H_{\text{enhanced}}) \tag{14}$$

3.5 Aggregator Layer

Unlike most methods that aggregate sequences using average pooling, which assumes all historical interactions contribute equally and overlooks the temporal sensitivity and varying importance of key events in dynamic networks, we adopt a weighted aggregation strategy to generate time-aware node representations h_*^t. By dynamically assigning feature importance through learnable weights, our approach focuses on critical events and enhances the model's ability to capture non-stationary dynamics.

$$h_*^t = \text{Sigmoid}(W_{\text{agg}})^T \cdot H_{\text{final}} \tag{15}$$

where $W_{agg} \in \mathbb{R}^L$ is a trainable vector designed to adaptively learn the importance of various interactions.

3.6 Link Prediction Layer

The link prediction result $\hat{y}$ is computed using a two-layer multilayer perceptron (MLP) and transformed into a link probability via softmax, with the input being the concatenation of the two node embedding vectors.

$$\hat{y} = Softmax(MLP(ReLU(MLP([h_u^t \| h_v^t])))) \tag{16}$$

3.7 Loss Function

For link prediction loss, we adopt binary cross-entropy loss function, which is defined as:

$$\mathcal{L} = -\frac{1}{N} \sum_{i=1}^{N} (y_i \log \hat{y}_i + (1 - y_i) \log(1 - \hat{y}_i)) \tag{17}$$

where N is the number of positive/negative samples, y_i represents the ground-truth label of sample i, and $\hat{y}_i$ represents the predicted value.

4 Experiments

4.1 Datasets

In this study, we utilize seven publicly available real-world datasets: Wiki, REDDIT, MOOC, LastFM, Enron, Social Evo, and UCI. The detailed statistical characteristics of the datasets are delineated in Table 1.

The sparsity of the graphs is quantified using the density score, calculated as $\frac{2|E|}{|V|(|V|-1)}$, where $|E|$ and $|V|$ represent the number of edges and nodes in the training set respectively. To ensure a structured evaluation, we split each dataset into three chronological segments for training, validation, and testing, following a 70%-15%-15% ratio.

Table 1. Statistics of the datasets.

Dataset	Nodes	Edges	Unique Edges	Node/Link Feature	TimeGranularity	Duration	density
Wikipeida	9227	157474	18257	0/172	Unixtimestamp	1month	4.30E-03
Reddit	10984	672447	78516	0/172	Unixtimestamp	1 month	8.51E-03
MOOC	7144	411749	178443	0/4	Unixtimestamp	17 month	1.26E-02
LastFM	1980	1293103	154993	0/0	Unixtimestamp	1 month	5.57E-01
Enron	184	125235	3125	0/0	Unixtimestamp	3 years	5.53E + 00
SocialEvo.	74	2099519	4486	0/2	Unixtimestamp	8 months	5.36E + 02
UCI	1899	59835	20296	0/0	Unixtimestamp	196 days	3.66E-02

4.2 Baselines

To evaluate the performance of the proposed method, we compares it with the 10 most advanced existing methods, which are categorized into three groups:

1. Neural network-based modeling methods: JODIE [20], DyRep [21], TGN [19].
2. Methods based on the attention mechanism: TGAT [23], TCL [24], DyGFormer [25].
3. Other methods (heuristic storage, frequency domain, and mixing models): CAWN [28], EdgeBank [26], GraphMixer [27], FreeDyG [29].

4.3 Evaluation Metrics and Experimental Settings

To evaluate the FATDyG framework, we adopt Average Precision (AP) and the Area Under the Receiver Operating Characteristic Curve (AUC-ROC) as evaluation metrics. The link prediction task follows a transductive setting, which focuses on predicting future links between nodes observed during training. To ensure a comprehensive comparison, we also incorporate three negative sampling strategies [26]—random (RND), historical (HIST), and inductive (IND), with the latter two being more challenging.

All models are trained for up to 200 epochs using an early stopping strategy with a patience of 20. The model achieving the highest performance on the validation set is selected for testing. We employ the Adam optimizer for all models, setting the learning rate and batch size to 0.0001 and 200 respectively. The hyperparameter configurations of the baseline methods are kept consistent with their respective papers. For our FATDyG model, we set L to 20, d_T to 100, and both α and β to 10, while the output node feature dimension is set to 172 respectively. Each method is run ten times with different random seeds, and the average performance is reported to mitigate variance.

Table 2. AP for transductive dynamic link prediction with different sampling strategies.

NSS	Datasets	Wikipeida	Reddit	MOOC	LastFM	Enron	SocialEvo.	UCI
rnd	JODIE	96.69 ± 0.25	97.83 ± 0.21	77.20 ± 1.32	68.54 ± 2.95	79.10 ± 0.85	88.12 ± 0.74	87.65 ± 1.85
	DyRep	95.23 ± 0.50	98.17 ± 0.02	79.97 ± 0.82	70.79 ± 1.87	82.02 ± 3.07	88.87 ± 0.30	70.24 ± 0.32
	TGAT	96.95 ± 0.17	98.47 ± 0.03	85.44 ± 0.76	73.76 ± 0.45	72.58 ± 0.79	93.16 ± 0.17	79.55 ± 0.83
	TGN	98.42 ± 0.05	98.67 ± 0.04	89.43 ± 2.95	78.69 ± 2.71	85.33 ± 1.05	93.57 ± 0.17	90.69 ± 0.45
	CAWN	98.65 ± 0.04	99.11 ± 0.01	78.66 ± 0.31	86.58 ± 0.10	89.56 ± 0.09	84.96 ± 0.09	94.35 ± 0.11
	EdgeBank	90.37 ± 0.00	94.86 ± 0.00	57.97 ± 0.00	79.29 ± 0.00	83.53 ± 0.00	74.95 ± 0.00	76.20 ± 0.00
	TCL	96.47 ± 0.16	97.61 ± 0.03	81.12 ± 0.43	65.64 ± 2.52	79.70 ± 0.71	93.13 ± 0.16	88.12 ± 2.73
	GraphMixer	97.17 ± 0.05	97.37 ± 0.01	82.73 ± 0.16	75.64 ± 0.23	81.08 ± 0.73	93.37 ± 0.07	93.50 ± 0.49
	DyGFormer	98.82 ± 0.02	99.11 ± 0.02	87.23 ± 0.45	92.07 ± 0.28	92.47 ± 0.12	94.73 ± 0.01	$\underline{95.76 \pm 0.15}$
	FreeDyG	$\underline{99.26 \pm 0.01}$	$\underline{99.48 \pm 0.01}$	$\underline{89.61 \pm 0.19}$	$\underline{92.15 \pm 0.16}$	$\underline{92.51 \pm 0.05}$	$\underline{94.91 \pm 0.01}$	$\mathbf{96.28 \pm 0.11}$
	FATDyG	$\mathbf{99.52 \pm 0.10}$	$\mathbf{99.76 \pm 0.02}$	$\mathbf{92.10 \pm 0.76}$	$\mathbf{95.67 \pm 0.13}$	$\mathbf{94.12 \pm 0.22}$	$\mathbf{95.72 \pm 0.21}$	95.21 ± 0.42
hist	JODIE	81.19 ± 0.48	80.03 ± 0.36	78.94 ± 1.25	74.35 ± 3.81	69.85 ± 2.70	87.44 ± 6.78	75.24 ± 5.80
	DyRep	78.32 ± 0.71	79.83 ± 0.31	75.60 ± 1.12	74.92 ± 2.46	71.19 ± 2.76	93.29 ± 0.43	55.10 ± 3.14
	TGAT	87.01 ± 0.19	79.55 ± 0.20	82.19 ± 0.62	71.59 ± 0.24	64.07 ± 1.05	95.01 ± 0.44	68.27 ± 1.37
	TGN	86.96 ± 0.36	81.75 ± 0.36	$\underline{87.06 \pm 1.93}$	76.87 ± 4.64	73.91 ± 1.76	94.45 ± 0.56	80.43 ± 2.12
	CAWN	72.38 ± 1.85	80.82 ± 0.45	74.05 ± 0.95	69.86 ± 0.43	64.73 ± 0.36	85.53 ± 0.38	65.30 ± 0.43
	EdgeBank	73.35 ± 0.00	73.59 ± 0.00	60.71 ± 0.00	73.03 ± 0.00	76.53 ± 0.00	80.57 ± 0.00	65.50 ± 0.00
	TCL	88.75 ± 0.27	77.14 ± 0.16	77.06 ± 0.41	59.30 ± 2.31	70.66 ± 0.39	94.74 ± 0.31	80.25 ± 2.74
	GraphMixer	$\underline{90.87 \pm 0.08}$	78.44 ± 0.18	77.77 ± 0.92	72.47 ± 0.49	$\underline{77.98 \pm 0.92}$	94.93 ± 0.31	84.11 ± 1.35
	DyGFormer	82.23 ± 2.54	81.02 ± 0.59	85.85 ± 0.66	$\mathbf{81.57 \pm 0.48}$	75.63 ± 0.73	$\underline{97.38 \pm 0.14}$	82.17 ± 0.82
	FreeDyG	$\mathbf{91.59 \pm 0.57}$	$\mathbf{85.67 \pm 1.01}$	86.71 ± 0.81	79.71 ± 0.51	$\mathbf{78.87 \pm 0.82}$	$\mathbf{97.79 \pm 0.23}$	$\mathbf{86.10 \pm 1.19}$
	FATDyGr	90.23 ± 0.37	$\underline{84.27 \pm 0.22}$	$\mathbf{88.47 \pm 0.53}$	$\underline{80.83 \pm 0.17}$	77.63 ± 0.47	96.14 ± 0.19	$\underline{85.21 \pm 0.23}$
ind	JODIE	75.65 ± 0.79	86.98 ± 0.16	65.23 ± 2.19	62.67 ± 4.49	68.96 ± 0.98	89.82 ± 4.11	65.99 ± 1.40
	DyRep	70.21 ± 1.58	86.30 ± 0.26	61.66 ± 0.95	64.41 ± 2.70	67.79 ± 1.53	93.28 ± 0.48	54.79 ± 1.76
	TGAT	87.00 ± 0.16	89.59 ± 0.24	75.95 ± 0.64	71.13 ± 0.17	63.94 ± 1.36	94.84 ± 0.44	68.67 ± 0.84
	TGN	85.62 ± 0.44	88.10 ± 0.24	77.50 ± 2.91	65.95 ± 5.98	70.89 ± 2.72	95.13 ± 0.56	70.94 ± 0.71
	CAWN	74.06 ± 2.62	$\underline{91.67 \pm 0.24}$	73.51 ± 0.94	67.48 ± 0.77	75.15 ± 0.58	88.32 ± 0.27	64.61 ± 0.48
	EdgeBank	80.63 ± 0.00	85.48 ± 0.00	49.43 ± 0.00	$\mathbf{75.49 \pm 0.00}$	73.89 ± 0.00	83.69 ± 0.00	57.43 ± 0.00
	TCL	86.76 ± 0.72	87.45 ± 0.29	74.65 ± 0.54	58.21 ± 0.89	71.29 ± 0.32	94.90 ± 0.36	76.01 ± 1.11
	GraphMixer	$\underline{88.59 \pm 0.17}$	85.26 ± 0.11	74.27 ± 0.92	68.12 ± 0.33	75.01 ± 0.79	94.72 ± 0.33	80.10 ± 0.51
	DyGFormer	78.29 ± 5.38	91.11 ± 0.40	81.24 ± 0.69	73.97 ± 0.50	77.41 ± 0.89	$\mathbf{97.68 \pm 0.10}$	72.25 ± 1.71
	FreeDyG	$\mathbf{90.05 \pm 0.79}$	90.74 ± 0.17	$\mathbf{83.01 \pm 0.87}$	72.19 ± 0.24	$\underline{77.81 \pm 0.65}$	$\underline{97.57 \pm 0.15}$	$\mathbf{82.35 \pm 0.73}$
	FATDyG	87.75 ± 0.58	$\mathbf{92.84 \pm 0.26}$	$\underline{82.18 \pm 0.68}$	$\underline{74.09 \pm 0.62}$	$\mathbf{78.47 \pm 0.52}$	96.52 ± 0.28	$\underline{81.34 \pm 0.75}$

4.4 Comparison With SOTA

In this section, we compare FATDyG with the previous SOTA methods in transductive settings. Tables 2 and 3 show the Average Precision (AP) and the ROC Characteristic Curve (AUC-ROC) results for each dataset under the transductive settings respectively. To provide a more comprehensive analysis of FATDyG, we report results for all three negative sampling strategies, with the best-performing results highlighted in bold and the second-best results underlined.

The experimental results demonstrate that FATDyG outperforms other baselines in most scenarios, with an average ranking close to 1. The AP and AUC-ROC metrics show maximum improvements of 3.52% and 1.22% respectively.

Table 3. AUC-ROC for transductive dynamic link prediction with different sampling strategies.

NSS	Datasets	Wikipeida	Reddit	MOOC	LastFM	Enron	SocialEvo.	UCI
rnd	JODIE	96.33 ± 0.07	98.31 ± 0.05	83.81 ± 2.09	70.49 ± 1.66	87.96 ± 0.52	92.05 ± 0.46	90.44 ± 0.49
	DyRep	94.37 ± 0.09	98.17 ± 0.05	85.03 ± 0.58	71.16 ± 1.89	84.89 ± 3.00	90.76 ± 0.21	68.77 ± 2.34
	TGAT	96.67 ± 0.07	98.47 ± 0.02	87.11 ± 0.19	71.59 ± 0.18	68.89 ± 1.10	94.76 ± 0.16	78.53 ± 0.74
	TGN	98.37 ± 0.07	98.60 ± 0.06	91.21 ± 1.15	78.47 ± 2.94	88.32 ± 0.99	95.39 ± 0.17	92.03 ± 1.13
	CAWN	98.54 ± 0.04	99.01 ± 0.01	80.38 ± 0.26	85.92 ± 0.10	90.45 ± 0.14	87.34 ± 0.08	93.87 ± 0.08
	EdgeBank	90.78 ± 0.00	95.37 ± 0.00	60.86 ± 0.00	83.77 ± 0.00	87.05 ± 0.00	81.60 ± 0.00	77.30 ± 0.00
	TCL	95.84 ± 0.18	97.42 ± 0.02	83.12 ± 0.18	64.06 ± 1.16	75.74 ± 0.72	94.84 ± 0.17	87.82 ± 1.36
	GraphMixer	96.92 ± 0.03	97.17 ± 0.02	84.01 ± 0.17	73.53 ± 0.12	84.38 ± 0.21	95.23 ± 0.07	91.81 ± 0.67
	DyGFormer	98.91 ± 0.02	99.15 ± 0.01	87.91 ± 0.58	93.05 ± 0.10	93.33 ± 0.13	96.30 ± 0.01	94.49 ± 0.26
	FreeDyG	99.41 ± 0.01	99.50 ± 0.01	89.93 ± 0.35	93.42 ± 0.15	94.01 ± 0.11	**96.59 ± 0.04**	**95.00 ± 0.21**
	FATDyG	**99.66 ± 0.07**	**99.82 ± 0.04**	**91.32 ± 0.77**	**94.60 ± 0.12**	**94.66 ± 0.12**	96.31 ± 0.09	94.78 ± 0.27
hist	JODIE	80.77 ± 0.73	80.52 ± 0.32	82.75 ± 0.83	75.22 ± 2.36	75.39 ± 2.37	90.06 ± 3.15	78.64 ± 3.50
	DyRep	77.74 ± 0.33	80.15 ± 0.18	81.06 ± 0.94	74.65 ± 1.98	74.69 ± 3.55	93.12 ± 0.34	57.91 ± 3.12
	TGAT	82.87 ± 0.22	79.33 ± 0.16	80.81 ± 0.67	64.27 ± 0.26	61.85 ± 1.43	93.08 ± 0.59	58.89 ± 1.57
	TGN	82.74 ± 0.32	81.11 ± 0.19	88.00 ± 1.80	77.97 ± 3.04	77.09 ± 2.22	94.71 ± 0.53	77.25 ± 2.68
	CAWN	67.84 ± 0.64	80.27 ± 0.30	71.57 ± 1.07	67.88 ± 0.24	65.10 ± 0.34	87.43 ± 0.15	57.86 ± 0.15
	EdgeBank	77.27 ± 0.00	78.58 ± 0.00	61.90 ± 0.00	78.09 ± 0.00	**79.59 ± 0.00**	85.81 ± 0.00	69.56 ± 0.00
	TCL	85.76 ± 0.46	76.49 ± 0.16	72.09 ± 0.56	47.24 ± 3.13	67.95 ± 0.88	93.44 ± 0.68	72.25 ± 3.46
	GraphMixer	**87.68 ± 0.17**	77.80 ± 0.12	76.68 ± 1.40	64.21 ± 0.73	75.27 ± 1.14	94.39 ± 0.31	77.54 ± 2.02
	DyGFormer	78.80 ± 1.95	80.54 ± 0.29	87.04 ± 0.35	78.78 ± 0.35	76.55 ± 0.52	97.28 ± 0.07	76.97 ± 0.24
	FreeDyG	82.78 ± 0.30	**85.92 ± 0.10**	88.32 ± 0.99	73.53 ± 0.12	75.74 ± 0.72	**97.42 ± 0.02**	**80.38 ± 0.26**
	FATDyG	84.83 ± 0.34	84.51 ± 0.21	**88.77 ± 0.31**	**80.21 ± 0.13**	77.84 ± 0.23	96.03 ± 0.08	80.11 ± 0.31
ind	JODIE	70.96 ± 0.78	83.51 ± 0.15	66.63 ± 2.30	61.32 ± 3.49	70.92 ± 1.05	90.01 ± 3.19	64.14 ± 1.26
	DyRep	67.36 ± 0.96	82.90 ± 0.31	63.26 ± 1.01	62.15 ± 2.12	68.73 ± 1.34	93.07 ± 0.38	54.25 ± 2.01
	TGAT	81.93 ± 0.22	87.13 ± 0.20	73.18 ± 0.33	63.99 ± 0.21	60.45 ± 2.12	92.94 ± 0.61	60.80 ± 1.01
	TGN	80.97 ± 0.31	84.56 ± 0.24	77.44 ± 2.86	65.46 ± 4.27	71.34 ± 2.46	95.24 ± 0.56	64.11 ± 1.04
	CAWN	70.95 ± 0.95	**88.04 ± 0.29**	70.32 ± 1.43	67.92 ± 0.44	75.17 ± 0.50	89.93 ± 0.15	58.06 ± 0.26
	EdgeBank	81.73 ± 0.00	85.93 ± 0.00	48.18 ± 0.00	**77.37 ± 0.00**	75.00 ± 0.00	87.88 ± 0.00	58.03 ± 0.00
	TCL	82.19 ± 0.48	84.67 ± 0.29	70.36 ± 0.37	46.93 ± 2.59	67.64 ± 0.86	93.44 ± 0.72	70.05 ± 1.86
	GraphMixer	**84.28 ± 0.30**	82.21 ± 0.13	72.45 ± 0.72	60.22 ± 0.32	71.53 ± 0.85	94.22 ± 0.32	74.59 ± 0.74
	DyGFormer	75.09 ± 3.70	86.23 ± 0.51	**80.76 ± 0.76**	69.25 ± 0.36	74.07 ± 0.64	97.51 ± 0.06	65.96 ± 1.18
	FreeDyG	82.74 ± 0.32	84.38 ± 0.21	78.47 ± 0.94	72.30 ± 0.59	77.27 ± 0.61	**98.47 ± 0.02**	75.39 ± 0.57
	FATDyG	82.72 ± 0.88	87.23 ± 0.29	80.49 ± 0.51	73.53 ± 0.42	**78.03 ± 0.43**	98.32 ± 0.22	**76.21 ± 0.71**

Additionally, it is worth noting that in large-scale networks with long time spans, such as MOOC, LastFM, and Enron, FATDyG exhibits more significant performance improvements. This further validates its ability to capture long-term dependencies and handle complex network interactions effectively.

We further compare the performance, training time per epoch (measured in seconds), and trainable parameter size (measured in MB) of FATDyG against baseline methods on the WIKI and MOOC datasets, as shown in Fig. 2. In this figure, the x-axis represents training time, the y-axis denotes average precision (AP), bubble size corresponds to the number of model parameters. The results clearly show that RW-based methods, such as CAWN, not only require significantly longer training time but also have a large number of parameters. On the other hand, simpler models like JODIE, despite having fewer parameters, exhibit a noticeable performance gap compared to the best-performing method. In contrast, FATDyG achieves the best performance while maintaining a relatively small number of trainable parameters and a moderate training time.

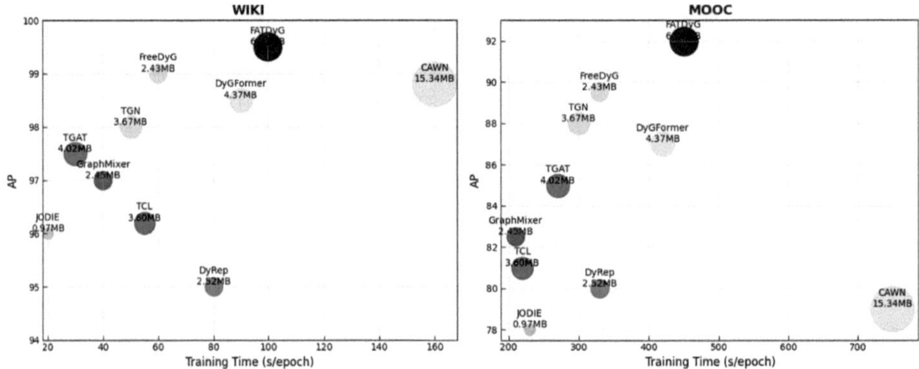

Fig. 2. Comparison of model training efficiency on WIKI and Reddit.

4.5 Ablation Study

We conduct an ablation study on FATDyG to evaluate the effectiveness of its temporal capture layer, global feature fusion layer, and frequency enhancing layer. The models with these components removed are denoted as w/o TC, w/o GFF, and w/o FE respectively. Fig. 3 presents the performance comparison under the transductive random negative sampling setting. All ablated variants exhibit inferior performance across real-world datasets, demonstrating that each module effectively contributes to the model's performance, and their synergy enhances dynamic link prediction.

It is noteworthy that different modules demonstrate varying levels of importance. The model without the global feature fusion layer shows the worst performance, especially in large-scale and long-time-span datasets like MOOC, LastFM, and Enron, where the decline is more evident. This highlights the layer's ability to capture temporal features and its crucial role as the foundation for subsequent frequency-domain processing. Additionally, the frequency-enhancing layer also significantly improves model performance, indicating that operations in the frequency domain are equally critical for the task.

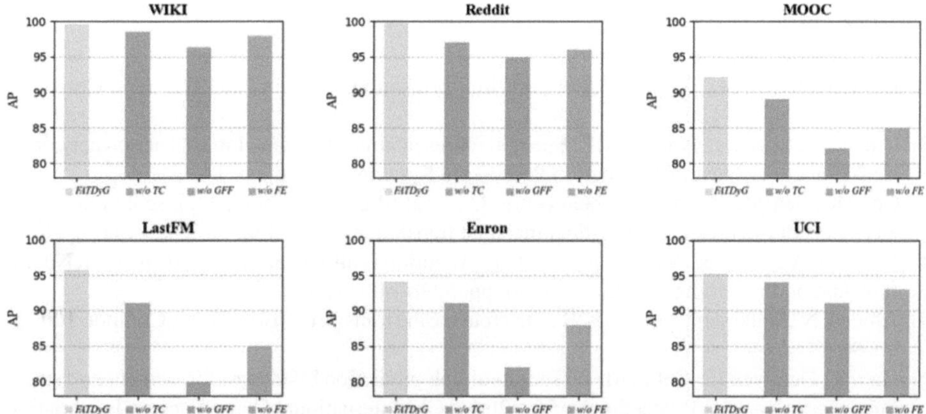

Fig. 3. Ablation study of FATDyG under the transductive random negative sampling setting, where "w/o TC" represents FATDyG without the temporal capturing layer, "w/o GFF" represents FATDyG without the global feature fusion layer, and "w/o FE" represents FATDyG without the frequency enhancing layer.

5 Conclusion

To address the limitations of time-series modeling and the underutilization of frequency-domain information in dynamic network link prediction, this paper proposes FAT-DyG, a dynamic network link prediction framework that integrates temporal, spatial, and frequency-aware components. Specifically, FATDyG innovatively combines a time-difference-aware GRU with a Transformer-based global attention mechanism, effectively modeling long- and short-term dependencies under irregular time intervals. Furthermore, a dynamic frequency enhancement module based on the DCT is designed to accurately capture periodic patterns and local abrupt changes in non-stationary signals through frequency component selection and multi-scale aggregation. This approach overcomes the limitations of traditional methods in capturing long-range dependencies and leveraging frequency-domain features.Experimental results demonstrate that FATDyG consistently outperforms existing methods across multiple real-world dynamic network datasets for link prediction tasks, achieving improvements of up to 3.52% and 1.22% in AP and AUC-ROC scores respectively. Ablation studies further validate the necessity of each module, highlighting their synergistic contributions to enhancing the model's capability in capturing complex dynamic patterns.

Acknowledgement. This work is supported by the National Natural Science Foundation (No. 62406011), the National Natural Science Foundation of China (No. 72104013) and the National Key R&D Program of China (2018YFB1004101).

Disclosure of Interests. The authors have no competing interests to declare that are relevant to the content of this article.

References

1. Lü, L.Y., Ren, X.L., Zhou, T.: Network link prediction: concepts and frontiers. Commun. CCF **12**(4), 12–19 (2016)
2. Rippel, O., Snoek, J., Adams, R.P.: Spectral representations for convolutional neural networks. In: Advances in Neural Information Processing Systems, vol. 28, pp. 1–9 (2015)
3. Cho, K., van Merriënboer, B., Gulcehre, C., et al.: Learning phrase representations using RNN encoder-decoder for statistical machine translation. arXiv:1406.1078 (2014)
4. Vaswani, A., Shazeer, N., Parmar, N., et al.: Attention is all you need. In: Advances in Neural Information Processing Systems, vol. 30, pp. 5998–6008 (2017)
5. Ahmed, N., Natarajan, T., Rao, K.R.: Discrete cosine transform. IEEE Trans. Comput. **100**(1), 90–93 (2006)
6. Gao, S., Denoyer, L., Gallinari, P.: Temporal link prediction by integrating content and structure information. In: Proceedings of the 20th ACM International Conference on Information and Knowledge Management, pp. 1169–1174. ACM, New York (2011)
7. Ahmed, N.M., Chen, L., Wang, Y., et al.: DeepEye: link prediction in dynamic networks based on non-negative matrix factorization. Big Data Min. Anal. **1**(1), 19–33 (2018)
8. Ma, X., Sun, P., Qin, G.: Nonnegative matrix factorization algorithms for link prediction in temporal networks using graph communicability. Pattern Recogn. **71**, 361–374 (2017)
9. Sarkar, P., Chakrabarti, D., Jordan, M.: Nonparametric link prediction in dynamic networks. arXiv:1206.6394 (2012)
10. Ahmed, N.M., Chen, L.: An efficient algorithm for link prediction in temporal uncertain social networks. Inf. Sci. **331**, 120–136 (2016)
11. Jaya Lakshmi, T., Durga, B.S.: Temporal probabilistic measure for link prediction in collaborative networks. Appl. Intell. **47**, 83–95 (2017)
12. Fang, C., Kohram, M., Ralescu, A.L.: Spectral regression with low-rank approximation for dynamic graph link prediction. IEEE Intell. Syst. **26**(4), 48–55 (2011)
13. Wu, T., Chang, C.S., Liao, W.: Tracking network evolution and their applications in structural network analysis. IEEE Trans. Netw. Sci. Eng. **6**(3), 562–575 (2018)
14. Rossetti, G., Guidotti, R., Pennacchioli, D., et al.: Interaction prediction in dynamic networks exploiting community discovery. In: Proceedings of the 2015 IEEE/ACM International Conference on Advances in Social Networks Analysis and Mining, pp. 553–558. ACM, New York (2015)
15. Özcan, A., Öğüdücü, Ş.G.: Multivariate temporal link prediction in evolving social networks. In: Proceedings of the 14th IEEE/ACIS International Conference on Computer and Information Science, pp. 185–190. IEEE, Piscataway (2015)
16. Rahman, M., Saha, T.K., Hasan, M.A., et al.: Dylink2vec: effective feature representation for link prediction in dynamic networks. arXiv:1804.05755 (2018)
17. Goyal, P., Kamra, N., He, X., et al.: Dyngem: deep embedding method for dynamic graphs. arXiv:1805.11273 (2018)
18. Pareja, A., Domeniconi, G., Chen, J., et al.: Evolvegcn: evolving graph convolutional networks for dynamic graphs. In: Proceedings of the AAAI Conference on Artificial Intelligence, vol. 34, no. 04, pp. 5363–5370. AAAI Press, Palo Alto (2020)
19. Rossi, E., Chamberlain, B., Frasca, F., et al.: Temporal graph networks for deep learning on dynamic graphs. arXiv:2006.10637 (2020)
20. Kumar, S., Zhang, X., Leskovec, J.: Predicting dynamic embedding trajectory in temporal interaction networks. In: Proceedings of the25th ACM SIGKDD International Conference on Knowledge Discovery & Data Mining, pp. 1269–1278. ACM, New York (2019)
21. Trivedi, R., Farajtabar, M., Biswal, P., et al.: Dyrep: learning representations over dynamic graphs. In: Proceedings of the International Conference for Learning Representations (2019)

22. Lei, K., Qin, M., Bai, B., et al.: GCN-GAN: a non-linear temporal link prediction model for weighted dynamic networks. In: Proceedings of the IEEE INFOCOM 2019, pp. 388–396. IEEE, Piscataway (2019)

23. Xu, D., Ruan, C., Korpeoglu, E., et al.: inductive representation learning on temporal graphs. arXiv:2002.07962 (2020)

24. Wang, L., Chang, X., Li, S., et al.: TCL: transformer-based dynamic graph modelling via contrastive learning. arXiv:2105.07944 (2021)

25. Yu, L., Sun, L., Du, B., et al.: Towards better dynamic graph learning: new architecture and unified library. In: Advances in Neural Information Processing Systems, vol. 36, pp. 67686–67700 (2023)

26. Poursafaei, F., Huang, S., Pelrine, K., et al.: Towards better evaluation for dynamic link prediction. In: Advances in Neural Information Processing Systems, vol. 35, pp. 32928–32941 (2022)

27. Cong, W., Zhang, S., Kang, J., et al.: Do we really need complicated model architectures for temporal networks? arXiv:2302.11636 (2023)

28. Wang, Y., Chang, Y.Y., Liu, Y., et al.: Inductive representation learning in temporal networks via causal anonymous walks. arXiv:2101.05974 (2021)

29. Tian, Y., Qi, Y., Guo, F.: Freedyg: frequency enhanced continuous-time dynamic graph model for link prediction. In: Proceedings of the12th International Conference for Learning Representations (2024)

Resource Optimization for FPGA-Based SM9 Digital Signature Algorithm

Dezhi An[1], Guifeng Han[1(✉)], Dongli Tan[2], Yujie Shao[2], Jun Lu[1], and Shengcai Zhang[1]

[1] School of Cyber Security, Gansu University of Political Science and Law, Gansu 730070, China
{adz6199,lj6703,zsc6731}@gsupl.edu.cn, hanguifeng@stu.gsupl.edu.cn
[2] School of Computer Science and Technology, Beijing Institute of Technology, Beijing 100081, China
tandongli@bit.edu.cn

Abstract. SM9 digital signature algorithm is a widely applicable cryptographic scheme for user identity verification that demonstrates superior security and scalability, especially for large-scale deployments requiring efficient key management. These characteristics make it a robust solution for diverse applications, particularly in Internet-driven environments. However, it has problems with large resource consumption of Field-Programmable Gate Arrays (FPGA) acceleration. To address this problem, we propose a resource-oriented architecture based on FPGA. This approach optimizes redundant logic units and leverages the sharing processing capabilities of FPGA to handle tasks in a resource-constrained environment. Experimental results demonstrate a 40–75% reduction in resource utilization for critical operations, such as modular inversion and exponentiation, while maintaining acceptable latency.

Keywords: resource optimization · digital signature algorithm · FPGA acceleration · redundant logic unit

1 Introduction

The rise of emerging technologies like IoT and edge computing has significantly increased the speed and scale of data generation, demanding more efficient digital signature algorithms [1,2]. The SM9 algorithm, with its identity-based encryption mechanism, simplifies public key management and enhances system security by avoiding traditional PKI risks [3,4]. However, its high computational complexity limits practical adoption, necessitating hardware acceleration techniques such as FPGA implementation [5,6]. While FPGA acceleration is viable [7,8], the resource-intensive steps in SM9, including identity-to-public key conversion and key generation/signing, consume significant FPGA resources due to complex mathematical operations. This poses challenges in resource-constrained environments, leading to computational shortages, extended response times, and degraded system performance [9].

T. Zhu et al. (Eds.): KSEM 2025, LNAI 15920, pp. 166–177, 2026.
https://doi.org/10.1007/978-981-95-3052-6_13

Current research on digital signature algorithm acceleration focuses on operation optimization and hardware acceleration. Gwoboa Horng optimized DSA by generating $(k, k^{-1} \bmod q)$ pairs [10], while Cheon JH proposed batch verification using w-NAFs for pairing-based signatures [11]. Chafika Benzaid accelerated vBNN-IBS verification in resource-constrained environments [12], and Masada K designed ASIC architectures for elliptic curve mapping and pairing [13]. Z. Feng proposed RapidEC, a GPU-based ECDSA implementation for SM2 [14], and Y Wu optimized SM9's R-ate pairing using a Karatsuba-based multiplier [15]. P. Zhen optimized SM9's Miller loop computations on BN curves [16]. Brooke Lampe and Weizhi Meng surveyed deep learning-based intrusion detection systems for automotive applications, introducing the "can-train-and-test" dataset [17,18]. While these approaches address algorithm and hardware optimization, few consider hardware resource constraints. Conventional designs often use redundant computing units, which can be optimized through unit sharing to reduce FPGA resource consumption. This paper proposes a solution for SM9 acceleration in resource-constrained FPGA environments.

Our key contributions include:

- A resource-sharing architecture for low-frequency modular operations.
- Optimization of twelve-extension field modular multiplication for global resource efficiency.
- Cross-unit resource allocation strategy to reduce DSP utilization by 74%.

2 Background

We describe the main features and basic logic of the SM9 digital signature algorithm in this section. The SM9 cryptographic algorithm is an identification cryptographic algorithm based on elliptic curves including finite fields, elliptic curve point sets, elliptic curve groups, and Jacobian coordinate systems. The SM9 core structure is shown in Fig. 1.

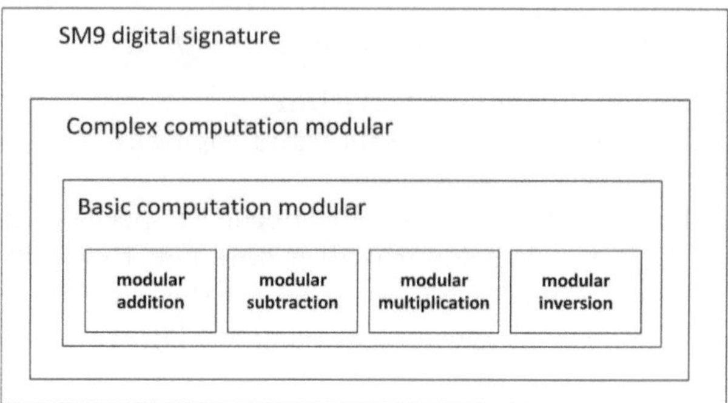

Fig. 1. The main fundamental modules of SM9

2.1 SM9 Digital Signature and Verification Algorithm

SM9 Digital Signature Algorithm, built upon elliptic curve cryptography, leverages Identity-Based Cryptography (IBC) for key computation. That means the strings related to the user's identity can be utilized as public keys. It differs from traditional signature algorithms that select random private keys for calculating public keys, users can assign designated public keys, such as ID number, email, et al., in SM9 and produce private keys via KGC (key generation center). The key generation is divided into master and user key generation, and the master private key is managed by KGC. The bilinear pairings recommended by SM9 include Weil, Tate, Ate, R-ate, et al. Three main parts in SM9 are digital signature algorithm, key agreement algorithm, and encryption/decryption algorithm. The SM9 belongs to bilinear pairs of IBC. Its main algorithms include a digital signature generation algorithm and a verification algorithm based on ECC. Users sign the message digitally with their private keys, and verifiers can generate corresponding public keys by the signers' identifications for reliability verification and check the authenticity, integrity and sender identity of the data. Cryptographic hash functions are applied to compress the sending message and the signed message before generating the signature and verifying the message. The following digital signature generation and verification algorithms come from reference [19].

Digital Signature Generation Algorithm
Let M be the message to be signed. In order to obtain the signature (h, S) of the message M, user A performs the following operations as signer:

A1: Compute the element $g = e(P_1, P_{pub-s})$ in the group G_T;

A2: Generate a random integer $r \in [1, N-1]$;

A3: Compute the element $w = g^r$ in the group G_T, and convert the data type of w to a bit string as specified in reference [3];

A4: Compute the integer $h = H_2(M||w, N)$;

A5: Compute the integer $l = (r - h) mod\ N$; if $l = 0$, go to Step A2;

A6: Compute the element $s = [l]ds_A$ in the group G_1;

A7: Convert the data type of h and S to byte strings, as specified in reference [3]. Output (h, S) as the signature of message M.

Digital Signature Verification Algorithm
To verify the received message M' and its digital signature (h', S'), user B performs the following operations as receiver:

B1: Convert the data type of h' to an integer as specified in reference [3]. Check whether $h' \in [1, N-1]$ holds true. If it does not, the verification fails;

B2: Convert the data type of S' to a point on the elliptic curve, and check whether $S' \in G_1$ holds true as specified in reference [3]. If it does not hold, the verification fails;

B3: Compute the element $g = e(P_1, P_{pub-s})$ in the group G_T;

B4: Compute the element $t = g^h$ in the group G_T;

B5: Compute the integer $h_1 = H_1(ID_A||hid, N)$;

B6: Compute the element $P = [h_1]P_2 + P_{pub-s}$ in the group G_2;

B7: Compute the element $u = e(S', P)$ in the group G_T;

B8: Compute the element $W' = u \cdot t$ in the group G_T. Convert the data type of w to a bit string as specified in reference [3];

B9: Compute an integer $h_2 = H_2(M'||w', N)$ and check whether $h_2 = h'$. If so, the signature is valid. Otherwise, the validation fails.

2.2 SM9 Resource Optimization Potentiality

Compared to other hardware acceleration methods, FPGA is more suitable for accelerating SM9. However, existing SM9 algorithm optimizations on FPGA primarily focus on performance enhancement through techniques such as resource stacking, pre-computation, loop refactoring, decomposition, and simplification. These approaches aim to achieve acceleration based on specific hardware configurations but often overlook resource optimization, leading to a significant increase in system resource consumption. To address this issue, this paper focuses on optimizing resource utilization to ensure the efficient operation of the SM9 algorithm in resource-constrained environments.

3 Resource Optimization for FPGA-Based SM9 Implementation

The SM9 digital signature algorithm involves various operations in multiple finite fields ($F_p, F_{p^2}, F_{p^4}, F_{p^{12}}$), and the four arithmetic modular operations over prime fields (modular addition, modular subtraction, modular multiplication, and modular inversion) serve as the fundamental operation units. The underlying operations of asymmetric cryptographic algorithms like SM9 generally include a large number of modular operations. Modular operations of $F_{p^2}, F_{p^4}, F_{p^{12}}$ are composed of modular operations of F_p, F_{p^2}, F_{p^4} respectively. General modular exponentiation of $F_{p^{12}}$ is based upon modular multiplication of $F_{p^{12}}$. The final modular exponentiation of $F_{p^{12}}$ is composed of both general modular exponentiation of $F_{p^{12}}$ and the four arithmetic modular operations. The point and line function operations of $F_{p^{12}}$ include point doubling and tangent functions, as well as point addition and line functions, all of which are constructed from modular operations of F_{p^2}. Point multiplication of F_p is built from point doubling and point addition operations, which in turn are based on modular operations of F_p. The Frobenius map is primarily composed of modular multiplication of F_p.

3.1 Resource-Oriented Design Within Units

Extension Field Modular Inversion. Modular inversion in an extension field is required only once during the SM9 digital signature process, and this operation does not significantly impact the algorithm's overall performance. Therefore, a resource-oriented framework is designed for the extension field modular inversion. Below is the detailed process of modular inversion. For the modular inversion in a quadratic extension field, the derivation process is as follows:

$$A^{-1} = (a_1 u + a_0)^{-1} = \frac{-a_1}{2a_1^2 + a_0^2} u + \frac{a_0}{2a_1^2 + a_0^2} \tag{1}$$

where $A \in F_{p^2}$ and $a_0, a_1 \in F_p$. A prime field modular multiplication unit, a prime field modular inversion unit, and a prime field modular addition unit are used in quadratic extension field modular inversion.

The quartic extension field modular inversion is derived as follows:

$$A^{-1} = (A_1 v + A_0)^{-1} = \frac{-A_1}{A_0^2 - A_1^2 u} v + \frac{A_0}{A_0^2 - A_1^2 u} \tag{2}$$

where $A \in F_{p^4}$ and $A_0, A_1 \in F_{p^2}$. A quadratic extension field modular inversion unit, a quadratic extension field modular multiplication unit, a quadratic extension modular subtraction unit, and a prime field modular addition unit are used here.

The twelve extension field modular inversion is derived as follows:

$$\begin{aligned}
A^{-1} &= (A_2 w^2 + A_1 w + A_0)^{-1} \\
&= \frac{A_1^2 - A_2 A_0}{(A_1^3 - 3A_2 A_1 A_0)v + A_2^3 v + A_0^3} w^2 + \frac{A_2^2 v - A_1 A_0}{(A_1^3 - 3A_2 A_1 A_0)v + A_2^3 v + A_0^3} w \\
&\quad + \frac{A_0^2 - A_2 A_1 v}{(A_1^3 - 3A_2 A_1 A_0)v + A_2^3 v + A_0^3}
\end{aligned} \tag{3}$$

where $A \in F_{p^{12}}$ and $A_0, A_1, A_2 \in F_{p^4}$. There are multiplications of the quartic extension field with u, v which are $(A_1^3 - 3A_2 A_1 A_0)v$ and $A_2^3 u$ in formula 3. They can be avoided by converting these multiplications to place shifting, modular addition, and modular subtraction which are shown in formula 4. The different operations should be performed in parallel for resource optimization. So, modular addition and modular subtraction can be performed simultaneously with modular multiplication, and multi rounds of modular multiplications can be performed simultaneously with modular inversion.

$$\begin{aligned}
C &= C_1 v + C_0 = (c_3 u + c_2)v + (c_1 u + c_0), \ C \in F_{p^4}, \ C_i \in F_{p^2}, \ C_i \in F_p \\
C_u &= (c_3 u^2 + c_2 u)v + (c_1 u^2 + c_0 u) = (c_2 u - 2c_3)v + (c_0 u - 2c_1) \\
C_v &= C_0 v + C_1 u = (c_1 u + c_0)v + (c_3 u^2 + c_2 u) = (c_1 u + c_0)v + (c_2 u - 2c_3)
\end{aligned} \tag{4}$$

General Modular Exponentiation. The general modular exponentiation can be optimized for resources by utilizing only one twelve extension field modular multiplication unit. Its state machine is shown in Fig. 2. $S0$ is the initial state. The registers are initialized and the computation starts when *in_valid* is high which means the input signal is valid. The square calculation is performed in $S1$.

The state transfers based on r_i in $S2$: $i = i+1$ and the state will be transferred to $S1$ for the next round of square calculation if $r_i = 0$; the state will be transferred to $S3$ if $r_i = 1$. r refers to multiplications of r base numbers. The square output is multiplied by the final result Z accumulatively and saved the result to Z in state $S3$. The loop will be terminated and the output signal will be set to high if $i = l - 1$, then waiting for the next valid input signal. Otherwise, it will continue the loop by jumping to $S1$.

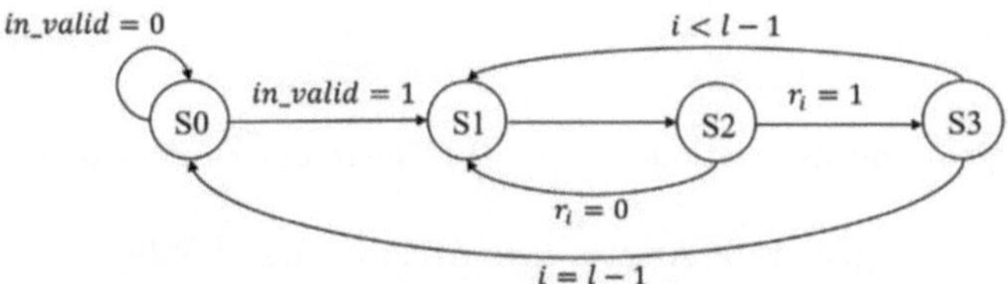

Fig. 2. Resource-Oriented General Modular Exponentiation State Machine

Final Modular Exponentiation. The final modular exponentiation can be optimized based on Frobenius mapping and only one twelve extension field modular multiplication unit is instantiated for final modular exponentiation in resource-oriented design. In detail, the *power*, *mul*_12_0, and *mul*_12_1 are executed serially since the general modular exponentiation is the result of several modular multiplications essentially, so the *power*, *mul*_12_0, and *mul*_12_1 cannot be executed in parallel.

3.2 Cross-Unit Resource-Oriented Design

In the previous section, the twelve extension field modular multiplications are executed in serial within the units of the general modular exponentiation and the final modular exponentiation for resource-oriented design. The limited hardware resources will be overwhelmed if different units are simply concatenated for the SM9 digital signature algorithm. So, it is necessary to design a cross-unit resource-oriented architecture.

From the top-level perspective, the SM9 digital signature algorithm is a series of serial computations, including Miller loop → Frobenius → addition, straight-line function operations and modular multiplication → final modular exponentiation → general modular exponentiation → hash operation → modular subtraction → point multiplication. The Miller loop, final modular exponentiation, and general modular exponentiation are all supported by the twelve extension field modular multiplication module, which consumes over 50% of the DSP resources. Figure 3a shows the unit associations before resource-oriented design, wherein the R-ate bilinear pairing there is a *mul*_12 unit for operations such as $f = f^2$.

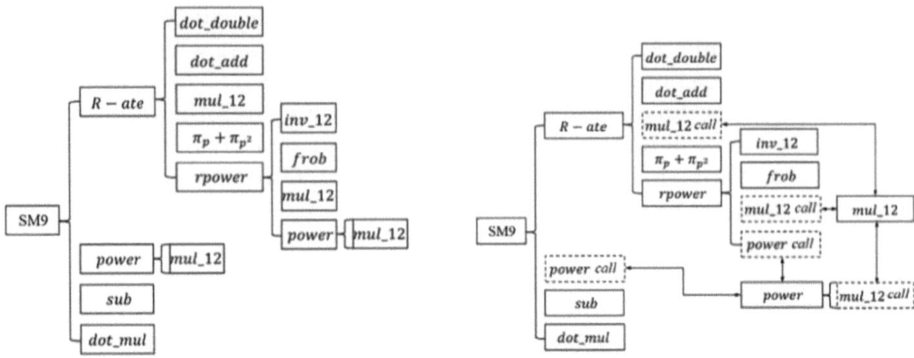

(a) The original unit associations   (b) The resource-oriented unit associations

Fig. 3. Unit Associations Architecture of SM9

The final modular exponentiation (*rpower*) and general modular exponentiation (*power*) contain *mul*_12 separately. The general modular exponentiation in the SM9 top layer also needs the unit for operation. There are at least four *mul*_12 units in the architecture even if only a single *mul*_12 is instantiated in *power* and *rpower* units respectively according to the traditional approach.

For resource optimization, only onea *mul*_12 unit is instantiated at the top level and the R-ate bilinear pairing, general modular exponentiation, and final modular exponentiation do not instantiate it repeatedly. The optimized unit associations are shown in Fig. 3b. The low-level units can call the same physical *mul*_12 unit in the SM9 by adding necessary signals at the interface. The signals include an input valid signal, two operands, an output valid signal, and a result. The input valid signal is responsible for starting the modular multiplication, and the output valid signal notifies the completion of the operation for retrieving the results. The *mul*_12 unit gets operands from different sources based on different input valid signals and outputs the operation results to all connected units which determines whether or not to read the results. A similar global sharing strategy is also applied to the *power* unit.

4   Evaluation

In this section, the simulation tests are implemented to verify the effectiveness of the resource-oriented design. The operation clock cycles and resource utilization are compared before and after resource optimization in the test. The extension field modular inversion, general modular exponentiation, final modular exponentiation, R-ate bilinear pairing, and the SM9 signature process are included.

4.1   Extension Field Modular Inversion

The simulation results for quadratic extension field modular inversion were obtained under two conditions: resource-oriented optimization and unoptimized implementation. Both units were initialized concurrently with a high signal, which then served as an indicator of operational completion for each. In this test, the resource-oriented unit occupied 61 more clock cycles than the unoptimized one, which is equal to two rounds of prime field modular multiplication, or about 13.99% clock cycles of the unoptimized unit. The total basic units occupied by the resource-oriented and the unoptimized quadratic extension field modular inversion are compared in Table 1. The resource-oriented method reduces unit occupation by 40% compared with the unoptimized method.

Table 1. Resource utilization comparison for quadratic extension field modular inversion

method	mul	add	inv
Unoptimized	2	1	2
Resource-oriented	1	1	1

The simulation results for quartic extension field modular inversion were obtained under two conditions: resource-oriented optimization and unoptimized implementation. The experimental conditions are same as above. The total basic units occupied by the resource-oriented and the unoptimized quartic extension field modular inversion are compared in Table 2. The resource-oriented method occupied 128 more clock cycles than the unoptimized one. The extra cycles, which are 24.76% of the unoptimized method, mainly contribute to two rounds of quadratic extension field modular multiplication. By sharing prime field modular multiplication units, our method achieves a 40% reduction in LUT utilization, demonstrating an effective trade-off for resource-constrained systems.

Table 2. The unit utilization comparison of quartic extension field modular inversion between resource-oriented and the unoptimized method

method	mul	add	sub	inv
Unoptimized	10	4	4	2
Resource-oriented	5	3	3	1

The simulation results for quartic extension field modular inversion were obtained under two conditions: resource-oriented optimization and unoptimized implementation. The experimental conditions are same as above. The resource-oriented method occupied 406 more clock cycles than the unoptimized one, which is mainly because of 6 rounds of the quartic extension field modular multiplication. The extra cycles account for 62.65% of the unoptimized way. The total basic units occupied by the resource-oriented and the unoptimized twelve extension field modular inversion are compared in Table 3. The resource-oriented method reduces basic unit occupation by 75% compared with the unoptimized method.

Table 3. The unit utilization comparison of the twelve extension field modular inversion between resource-oriented and unoptimized method

Method	mul	add	sub	inv
Unoptimized	82	38	46	2
Resource-oriented	17	12	12	1

4.2   General Modular Exponentiation

The simulation results of the general modular exponentiation were obtained under two conditions: resource-oriented optimization and unoptimized implementation. The resource-oriented modular exponentiation unit provides the output valid signal. Conversely, the unoptimized general modular exponentiation unit yields two outputs: the output valid signal, square initiation signal. Both the resource-oriented and unoptimized units are initiated simultaneously upon assertion of the initialization signal. The resource-oriented method occupied 647 more clock cycles than the unoptimized one. The extra cycles account for 22.81% of the unoptimized way. The total basic units occupied by the resource-oriented and the unoptimized general modular exponentiation are compared in Table 4. The resource-oriented method reduces basic unit occupation by 50% compared with the unoptimized method.

Table 4. The unit utilization comparison of the general modular exponentiation between resource-oriented and unoptimized method

Method	mul	add	sub	inv
Unoptimized	216	118	90	0
Resource-oriented	108	59	45	0

4.3   Final Modular Exponentiation

The simulation results of the final modular exponentiation were obtained under two conditions: resource-oriented optimization and unoptimized implementation. An output valid signal is generated, accompanying the result of the final modular exponentiation in the resource-oriented method. The resource-oriented method occupied 2724 more clock cycles than the unoptimized one, which is 27.98% of unoptimized method clock cycles. The extra cycles ratio of final modular exponentiation is close to general modular exponentiation since the main computations of final modular exponentiation are concentrated in three instances of general modular exponentiation. The unit utilization comparison of the final modular exponentiation between the resource-oriented and the unoptimized way is shown in Table 5. The resource-oriented final modular exponentiation calls the twelve extension field modular multiplication unit externally instead of instantiating it internally. The resource-oriented method reduces basic unit occupation by 74.17% compared with the unoptimized method.

Table 5. The unit utilization comparison of the final modular exponentiation between resource-oriented and unoptimized method

Method	mul	add	sub	inv
Unoptimized	524	272	224	2
Resource-oriented	135	71	57	1

4.4   R-ate Bilinear Pairing

The simulation results of the final modular exponentiation were obtained under two conditions: resource-oriented optimization and unoptimized implementation. In this simulation, the output valid signals for both the unoptimized and resource-oriented R-ate bilinear pairings were obtained. The resource-oriented method occupied 2724 more clock cycles than the unoptimized one, which is 14.40% of unoptimized method clock cycles. The unit utilization comparison of the final modular exponentiation between the resource-oriented and the unoptimized way is shown in Table 6. The resource-oriented method reduces basic unit occupation by 74.27% compared with the unoptimized method.

Table 6. The unit utilization comparison of the R-ate bilinear pairing between resource-oriented and unoptimized method

Method	mul	add	sub	inv
Unoptimized	669	349	286	2
Resource-oriented	172	89	74	1

4.5   Evaluation with Different Methods

The different optimization methods of SM9 are compared in Table 7. Signature operation is chosen for comparison.

[20] accelerates the performance of SM9 via FPGA. They mainly improve the bilinear pairing and point product algorithms for efficiency. [8] improves the design of modular operations, Frobenius self-homomorphic operations, and point and line functions by resource stacking and schedule optimization. They promote the algorithm parallelism and reduce computation time. [21] aims to reduce

Table 7. The evaluation in different methods

Method	Platform	Frequency(Mhz)	Signature(ms)
[20]	ZYNQ-7000	200	2.21
[8]	Virtex-7	115	3.43
[21]	Virtex-7	129.6	5.9
This paper	Virtex UltraScale+	117.25	0.18

resource utilization and perform the same operation in series, so this method consumes more clock cycles. Their scheme optimizes the sparse multiplication in the Miller loop and reduces the computational load to some extent. Our method has the highest efficiency compared with efficiency-oriented or resource-oriented optimization methods.

5   Conclusions

The proposed resource-oriented optimization framework enables efficient deployment of the SM9 algorithm on FPGAs, particularly in edge computing and IoT scenarios where hardware resources are limited. By strategically reusing modular arithmetic units and implementing cross-unit resource sharing, we reduce DSP consumption significantly while maintaining a competitive signature latency of 0.18 ms. This work bridges the gap between cryptographic security and hardware efficiency, providing a viable solution for next-generation identity-based systems.

Acknowledgments. This work is supported by Lanzhou Science and Technology Program (No. 2023-1-53) and Anning District Science and Technology Program (No. 2024-JB-5).

Disclosure of Interests. The authors have no competing interests to declare that are relevant to the content of this article.

References

1. Al-Absi, M.A., Abdullaev, A., Al-Absi, A.A., Sain, M., Lee, H.J.: Cryptography survey of DSS and DSA. In: Li, L., Pratihar, D.K., Chakrabarty, S., Mishra, P.C. (eds.) Advances in Materials and Manufacturing Engineering. LNME, pp. 661–669. Springer, Singapore (2020). https://doi.org/10.1007/978-981-15-1307-7_75
2. Hou, L., Lin, D., Liu, R.: Hierarchical group signature with verifier-local revocation revisited. Sci. China Inf. Sci. **65**(8), 1–3 (2022)
3. People's Republic of China Cryptography Industry Standard: GM/T 0044.1-2016. Standard. S. Beijing: State Cryptography Administration (2016)
4. Feng, Y., Zhaohui, C.: A survey of SM9 identity cryptography algorithms. J. Inf. Secur. Res. **2**(11), 1008–1027 (2016)
5. Li, M., et al.: High-speed batch verification for discrete-logarithm based signatures via multi-scalar multiplication algorithm. J. Inf. Secur. Appl. **87**, 103898 (2024)

6. Beckwith, L., Nguyen, D.T., Gaj, K.: Hardware accelerators for digital signature algorithms Dilithium and falcon. IEEE Des. Test (2023)
7. Zhang, B., et al.: An efficient SM9 aggregate signature scheme for IoV based on FPGA. Sensors **24**(18), 6011 (2024)
8. Wang, A.T., Guo, B.W., Wei, C.J.: Highly-parallel hardware implementation of optimal ate pairing over Barreto-Naehrig curves. Integration **64**, 13–21 (2019)
9. Liu, X., et al.: More efficient SM9 algorithm based on bilinear pair optimization processing. In: 2020 IEEE 19th International Conference on Trust, Security and Privacy in Computing and Communications (TrustCom), pp. 1704–1710. IEEE (2020)
10. Horng, G.: Accelerating DSA signature generation. Cryptologia **39**(2), 121–125 (2015)
11. Cheon, J.H., Lee, M.-K.: Improved batch verification of signatures using generalized sparse exponents. Comput. Standards Interfaces **40**, 42–52 (2015)
12. Benzaid, C., et al.: Fast authentication in wireless sensor networks. Futur. Gener. Comput. Syst. **55**, 362–375 (2016)
13. Masada, K., Nakayama, R., Ikeda, M.: Hardware acceleration of aggregate signature generation and authentication by BLS signature over BLS12-381 curve. In: 2022 IEEE Symposium in Low-Power and High-Speed Chips (COOL CHIPS), pp. 1–3. IEEE (2022)
14. Feng, Z., et al.: Accelerating elliptic curve digital signature algorithms on GPUs. In: SC22: International Conference for High Performance Computing, Networking, Storage and Analysis, pp. 1–13. IEEE (2022)
15. Wu, Y., Bai, G., Wu, X.: A Karatsuba algorithm based accelerator for pairing computation. In: 2019 IEEE International Conference on Electron Devices and Solid-State Circuits (EDSSC), pp. 1–3. IEEE (2019)
16. Zhen, P., et al.: Research on the miller loop optimization of SM9 bilinear pairings. In: 2017 IEEE 17th International Conference on Communication Technology (ICCT), pp. 138–144. IEEE (2017)
17. Lampe, B., Meng, W.: A survey of deep learning-based intrusion detection in automotive applications. Expert Syst. Appl. **221**, 119771 (2023)
18. Lampe, B., Meng, W.: Can-train-and-test: a curated CAN dataset for automotive intrusion detection. Comput. Secur. **140**, 1–44 (2024). 103777
19. Cryptography Standardization Technical Committee. SM9 Identity-Based Cryptographic Algorithm. Part 1: General, Part 2: Digital Signature Algorithm, Part 3: Key Exchange Protocol, Part 4: Key Encapsulation Mechanism and Public Key Encryption. Cryptography Standardization Technical Committee (2016). https://example.com/path/to/GM_T0044-2016_SM9_identity-based_cryptographic_algorithm
20. Shuai, J.: Design and hardware realization of digital signature system based on SM9 algorithm. Ph.D. thesis. Heilongjiang University (2023)
21. LiJiangfeng. Research on SM9 Algorithm and FPGA Implementation. MA thesis. Xidian University (2021)

Enhancing Pruning Efficiency
via Maximum Prunable Channel Selection
in Tiny Object Detection

Yaxuan Hu[✉]

School of Computer Science, Wuhan University, Wuhan 430072, Hubei, China
`sad123yxhu@gmail.com`

Abstract. Tiny object detection presents significant challenges in computer vision due to inherent limitations such as low-resolution features and insufficient contextual information. While model pruning has emerged as a critical technique for compressing deep neural networks, existing sparse regularization methods often fail to achieve high pruning rates while preserving detection accuracy, especially in YOLO-based architectures. This paper proposes a novel Maximum Prunable Channel Selection (MPCS) algorithm to address the sparsity in pruning YOLOv12 models for tiny object detection. First, we analyze the constraints of conventional sparsity-inducing methods and identify that fixed regularization strategies result in suboptimal channel-wise sparsity distributions. To address this, a cosine-annealed gamma scheduling mechanism is introduced to dynamically adjust the sparsity rate, enabling balanced layerwise regularization. Subsequently, the MPCS algorithm selectively identifies and eliminates redundant channels with maximal prunability scores, thereby decoupling sparsity constraints from the pruning process. Experiments on the benchmark TinyPerson and Visdrone datasets demonstrate that, compared to conventional methods, our approach achieves a 10% improvement in model pruning ratio while maintaining stable detection accuracy. The proposed approach offers a practical solution for deploying lightweight yet accurate detectors in resource-constrained scenarios.

Keywords: Channel Pruning · Model Compression · Channel Selection Algorithm · YOLOv12

1   INTRODUCTION

In recent years, object detection technology has advanced significantly, marked by increasingly deeper and larger models with improved accuracy. However, the growing parameter counts and computational demands of these models pose critical challenges for real-world deployment, particularly on resource-constrained devices like drones or embedded systems. To address this, model pruning has emerged as a pivotal technique for compressing networks while retaining their

T. Zhu et al. (Eds.): KSEM 2025, LNAI 15920, pp. 178–193, 2026.
https://doi.org/10.1007/978-981-95-3052-6_14

detection performance, enabling practical applications in scenarios requiring real-time inference and minimal memory footprints [1, 2].

Existing pruning methodologies are broadly categorized into unstructured pruning and structured pruning. Unstructured pruningÂă(e.g., weight pruning [3]) operates at a granularity smaller than convolutional kernels by zeroing out individual weights based on sparsity thresholds. While theoretically offering high compression ratios, its practical utility is limited by hardware constraints. Structured pruning, particularlyÂăchannel pruning, avoids these limitations by removing entire channels or filters. Classical approaches, such as He et al. [4], combine LASSO regression with least-squares feature map reconstruction to prune redundant channels while minimizing accuracy degradation. Later advancements, including Liu et al. [5], further improved universality by incorporating L1 regularization on the gamma parameters of batch normalization (BN) layers to rank channel importance. These methods achieve competitive pruning ratios but face intrinsic limitations when pushed to extreme compression rates.

In practical deployments of embedded tiny object detection (e.g., aerial imagery analysis), efficiency-accuracy trade-offs are critical. Our initial experiments with YOLOv12 [6] as the baseline model revealed a severe limitation: applying Liu's L1-based channel pruning resulted in a maximum allowable pruning ratio of 65%. Beyond this threshold, entire layers risked being pruned, leading to gradient collapse and irreversible accuracy loss (termed the pruning-restriction problem). This bottleneck stems from uniform sparsity regularization, which inadequately addresses the heterogeneous sensitivity of shallow and deep layers in YOLO architectures. Specifically, shallow layers in tiny object detectors capture fine-grained spatial details essential for recognizing tiny objects; overly aggressive regularization in these layers disproportionately degrades performance. To overcome these limitations, we propose a systematic framework combining dynamic sparsity scheduling and a novel Maximum Prunable Channel Selection (MPCS) algorithm.

Our work makes three key contributions:

- We analyze the inefficacy of uniform L1/L2 regularization in YOLO-based structural pruning, particularly for tiny object detection tasks.
- The proposed MPCS algorithm decouples pruning decisions from rigid sparse constraints, breaking through the limitations of structured pruning ratios and maximizing pruning proportion while ensuring detection accuracy.
- The results on the Tiny-Person and VisDrone datasets show that after applying the MPCS algorithm, the prunable proportion of the model increases to 75%, while the detection accuracy remains largely unchanged, and its memory consumption is further reduced by 15%.

2   RELATED WORK

2.1   Model Sparsification

The sparsification of a model can improve inference speed and reduce storage overhead. Li et al. [7] applied structural sparse regularization to input and output channels in continuous network layers to reduce redundancy with minimal accuracy loss. Wen et al. [8] proposed a structured sparse learning method for structured pruning of models using Group Lasso. Learning a sparse structure reduces computational demand, leading to a hardware speedup. However, utilizing Group Lasso has certain drawbacks.

Zhang et al. [9] used GrOWL regularization to improve it, which not only induces sparsity regularization but also identifies relevant feature groups, thereby reducing the number of free parameters in the network without compromising accuracy. Liu et al. [5] proposed adding L1 regularization to the channel scaling factor to enforce sparsity. This serves as our baseline, to which we add cosine decay to mitigate the issue of a restricted channel pruning ratio.

2.2   Channel Selection Algorithm

Channel selection is a critical step in channel pruning. Researchers have proposed various channel selection algorithms for channel importance estimation from different perspectives.

Two of the most influential early methods, OBD [10] and OBS [11], estimate network weight significance using the second-order derivatives of the loss function with respect to weights (i.e., the Hessian matrix). However, both methods are computationally expensive due to the need to compute the Hessian matrix or its approximation. Pavlo et al. [12] proposed a new criterion based on Taylor expansion, which further reduces computational cost by approximating the change in the loss function caused by pruning network parameters.

Some researchers have focused on feature output constructibility or minimizing the reconstruction error of the pruned network. Thinet [13], proposed by Luo et al., is a well-known method that selects channels for pruning by minimizing the feature reconstruction error. The SNIP algorithm proposed by Yu also leverages reconstruction error, employing a minimization classification network that backpropagates important information to determine the channels to prune. Channel selection is essentially a global channel importance ranking problem. Chin et al. [14] proposed a layer-compensated pruning algorithm that increased detection speed while maintaining detection accuracy. There are also some channel pruning algorithms based on the YOLO model, such as [15–17].

3   Method

This section describes our research methodology, including the investigation of the constrained pruning ratio problem and the proposed maximum prunable channel selection algorithm. Our main contributions are illustrated in Fig. 1, where the highlighted components represent our contributions.

3.1   Sparse Method Analysis

Pruning the YOLOv12 model using the baseline method revealed that the maximum achievable pruning ratio after sparsification was limited to 65% of the

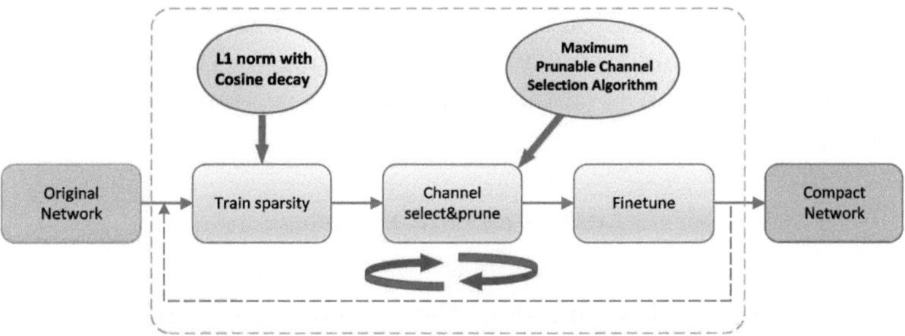

Fig. 1. Pruning process diagram & our contribution

channels. However, a 65% pruning ratio may be insufficient for practical applications. To investigate this limitation, we conducted an in-depth analysis.

Figure 1 illustrates the pruning process, where sparsification serves as the initial step. In the baseline approach, sparsification training is performed by applying L1 regularization to the scale factor γ added to the BN layer to determine channel significance. The BN layer is computed as follows:

$$\hat{z} = \frac{z_{in} - \mu_\delta}{\sqrt{\sigma_\delta^2 + \varepsilon}} \quad ; \quad z_{out} = \gamma\hat{z} + \beta \tag{1}$$

μ_δ and σ_δ denote the mean and standard deviation of the input over mini-batch δ, while β and γ are the trainable scale and shift parameters. Equation 1 indicates that the output size of each channel z_{out} is positively correlated with the scale factor γ. Therefore, we assume that smaller γ values correspond to lower channel importance, allowing us to rank channels accordingly. Channels with γ values approaching zero are prioritized for pruning. As depicted in Fig. 2, the γ values of the BN layer are approximately normally distributed during training, yet many of them concentrate near zero in a sparse manner, making direct pruning infeasible. To address this, L1 regularization is applied to the scale factor γ to promote sparsity and enable effective channel pruning.

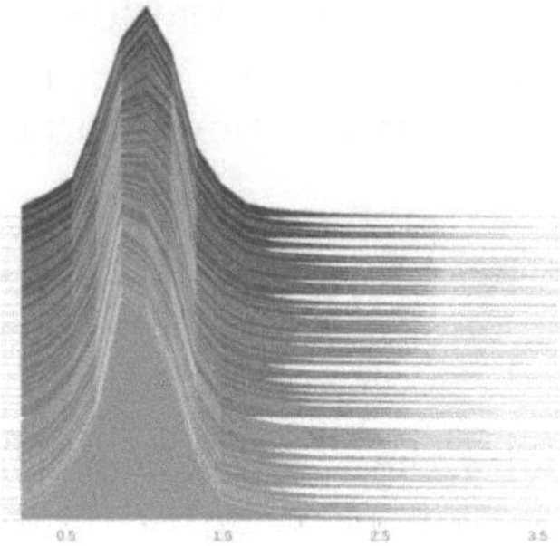

Fig. 2. BN layer gamma parameter distribution

In general, L1 regularization is added after the loss function and serves as a penalty term, promoting sparsity while mitigating overfitting. First, we analyze why L1 regularization is suitable for feature selection, considering the loss function defined in Eq. 2:

$$Loss = L_x + \alpha \sum_{\omega} \|\omega\|_1^1 \tag{2}$$

where L_x represents the loss function, the second term represents the regularization term, α is the regularization coefficient, and ω represents the model parameters. Our objective is to solve $\arg\min_{\omega} L$ under the assumption of a two-dimensional case (i.e., ω_1 and ω_2), where the L1 regularization function is given by $L = |\omega_1| + |\omega_2|$. Using the gradient descent method to solve for L and plot its contour, the L1 regularization function is illustrated in Fig. 3.

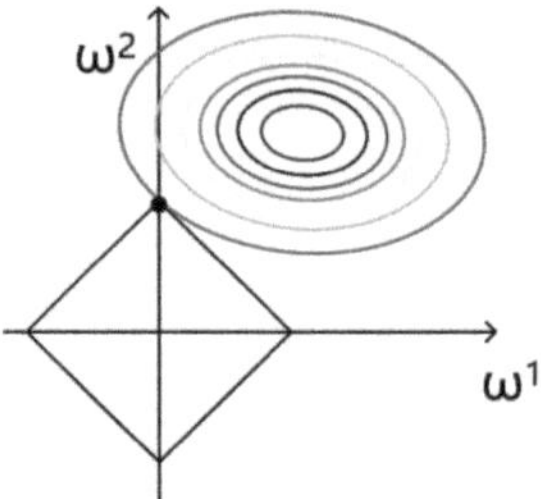

Fig. 3. L1 regularization function

Where the circle denotes the contour line of L_x, the black square represents the L_1 regularization function, and the regularization factor α determines the size of the black square. The optimal solution corresponds to the first intersection point of the curves.

Similarly, the intersection of L_x with the L_1 regularization function is more likely to occur at the corners of the square, where some dimensions tend to be zero (e.g., $\omega_1 = 0$). Consequently, certain features are set to zero, leading to a sparse model suitable for feature selection.

In the baseline method, the loss function incorporating L1 regularization is formulated as follows:

$$Loss = \sum_{(x,y)} l(f(x, W), y) + \lambda \sum_{\gamma} g(\gamma) \tag{3}$$

Here, the first term denotes the training loss, while the second term corresponds to the regularization component. In backpropagation, we obtain:

$$Loss' = \sum l' + \lambda \sum g'(\gamma) = \sum l' + \lambda \sum |\gamma|' = \sum l' + \lambda \sum \gamma * sign(\gamma) \tag{4}$$

Applying L_1 regularization for sparsity training, we obtain the γ parameter distribution of the BN layer, as illustrated in Fig. 7-a. Following sparsity training, most γ values converge to zero. The significance of the channels can then be ranked according to the magnitude of their γ values.

To prevent excessive pruning within each layer, the pruning ratio threshold must be determined. The maximum pruning threshold is computed as the minimum value among the maximum γ values across all layers. The position of this threshold within the global importance ranking is given by:

$$Prune\_Ratio = \frac{Sorted\_Index[\min_{n \in N}(W_{L_n})]}{Total\_Channel\_Num} \tag{5}$$

$$W_{L_n} = \max_{n \in N}(W_{n_i}) \tag{6}$$

Our calculations indicate that the maximum prunable ratio for the YOLOv12s model is 65%. Figure 4 depicts the ratio of the maximum value of each layer to the total number of channels.

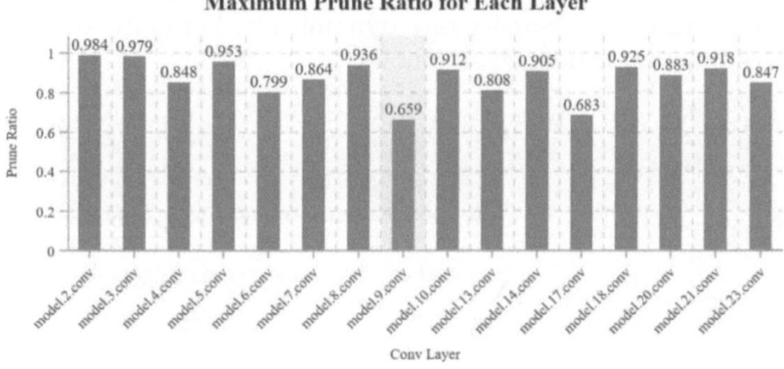

Fig. 4. Maximum prunable percentage of each layer

The maximum value of channels in layer 9 accounts for 65.9% of all channels, as shown in Fig. 4. If the pruning ratio exceeds 65.9%, all channels in layer 9 will be pruned, which is not allowed.

This result is analyzed to determine whether the model's channel pruning ratio can be further improved. The analysis is conducted in terms of the sparsification process, as we utilize the γ parameter for channel importance ranking. Considering that the sparsification parameters may influence the maximum prunable proportion, we conducted experiments with various sparsification parameters. The results are summarized in Table 1.

As shown in Table 1, the maximum prunable ratio of the model varies with different sparsification parameters, indicating that the sparsification parameter affects the proportion of the model that can be pruned. The detailed pruning effects are compared in Chap. 4, where the optimal sparsification parameter of

Table 1. Comparison of prunable proportions of models under different sparsification parameters

Sparse Rate	2×10^{-5}	5×10^{-5}	1×10^{-4}	1.5×10^{-4}	2×10^{-4}
Prune_Ratio (%)	63.4	64.6	65.9	68.5	68.2

1.5×10^{-4} was selected for subsequent experiments. We hypothesize that the addition of L_1 regularization, which induces sparsification in the γ parameters, may be a key factor contributing to the pruning ratio constraint. If the L_1 regularization term is replaced, will the same issue persist? To investigate this, we conducted an experiment replacing L_1 regularization with L_2 regularization. However, the results were unsatisfactory, and the sparsification effect on the γ parameter was even worse. Given that L_2 regularization primarily smooths the weights, it is less effective when directly applied to feature selection.

Can a combination of L_1 and L_2 regularization be beneficial? We explored a mixed sparsification approach that integrates both L_1 and L_2 regularization to induce sparsification in BN layer γ values. Additionally, cosine decay was incorporated to adjust the sparsity rate dynamically. Formally, the mixed regularization loss function is defined as follows:

$$Loss = \sum_{(x,y)} l(f(x, W), y) + \theta \cdot \lambda \sum_{\gamma} g(\gamma) + (1 - \theta) \cdot \lambda \sum_{\gamma} g(\gamma^2) \tag{7}$$

The gradient of the loss function with respect to γ is given by:

$$\frac{\partial L}{\partial \gamma} = \frac{\partial l}{\partial \gamma} + \theta \cdot \lambda \sum \frac{\partial g(\gamma)}{\partial \gamma} + (1 - \theta) \cdot \lambda \sum \frac{\partial g(\gamma^2)}{\partial \gamma} \tag{8}$$

$$L' = \sum l' + \theta \cdot \lambda \sum \gamma \cdot sign(\lambda) + (1 - \theta) \cdot \lambda \sum 2\gamma \tag{9}$$

The first term attenuates the γ values, promoting sparsity, while the second term is proportional to the γ values, ensuring smooth variation in γ. The parameter θ controls the balance between these two effects. The mixed L_1-L_2 sparsification approach is compared with the baseline, and the experimental results are presented in Subsect. 4.2.

During the sparsification process, cosine decay is applied to the sparsification parameter to regulate the sparsity rate of γ values. The formulation is as follows:

$$Sparsity\_Rate = sr \left(\cos^2 \left(\frac{\pi \cdot epoch}{2 \cdot epochs} \right) \cdot 0.9 + 0.1 \right) \tag{10}$$

Figure 5 presents a comparison of sparsity rates between the cosine decay method and the baseline. When using cosine decay, the sparsity rate is higher at the early training stages and gradually decreases towards the end, effectively moderating the training dynamics. The detailed experimental results are provided in Subsect. 4.2.

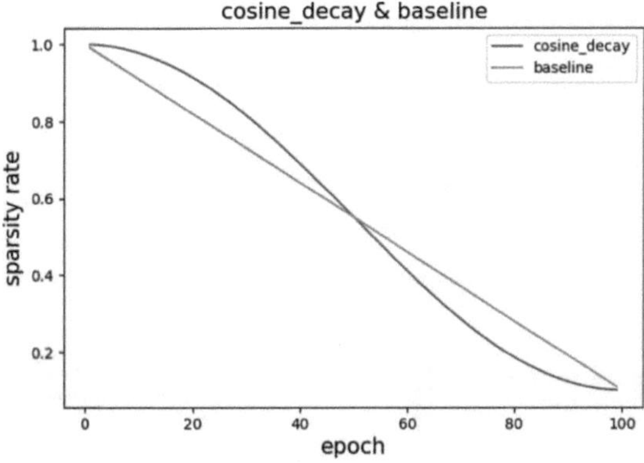

Fig. 5. Comparison of sparsity rate using cosine decay and baseline

3.2   Maximum Prunable Channel Selection (MPCS) Algorithm

In Sect. 3.1, the effects of various sparsity methods are compared, and cosine decay is introduced. The experimental results demonstrate that multiple parameters in the sparsification process can influence the sparsification outcome, thereby imposing constraints on the model's prunable proportion. Utilizing the optimal parameters from multiple experiments and incorporating cosine decay improves the prunable proportion but does not entirely resolve the issue.

To address this, we propose an enhancement to the channel selection algorithm. The pruning ratio restriction problem arises when all channels in a layer are pruned once a certain pruning ratio is exceeded. If the selection of channels can be adjusted to ensure that not every channel in a layer is removed during pruning, this restriction can be fully mitigated. Maintaining some original channels that would otherwise be eliminated necessitates compensatory pruning from other channels. If a method for determining these compensatory channels can be established, the issue can be effectively addressed.

Following the greedy algorithm principle, once the pruning channels are determined, it is ensured that no layer is entirely pruned. If all channels in a layer are about to be pruned, the remaining network layers with sufficient prunable channels compensate accordingly, following specific sequencing rules until the final layer's prunable channels are identified. This guarantees that each layer retains some channels, effectively resolving the pruning ratio restriction problem.

To this end, we propose the Maximum Prunable Channel Selection (MPCS) algorithm. Using the sparsification method described in Sect. 3.1, the γ parameters of the batch normalization (BN) layer are trained to be sparse. The sparsification results are sorted in ascending order, and the corresponding channels are ranked by importance.

The initial number of channels to be pruned in each layer, $P_L(L \in N)$, is determined based on the pruning ratio. To ensure that no layer is completely pruned, we introduce the concept of a minimum number of retained channels,

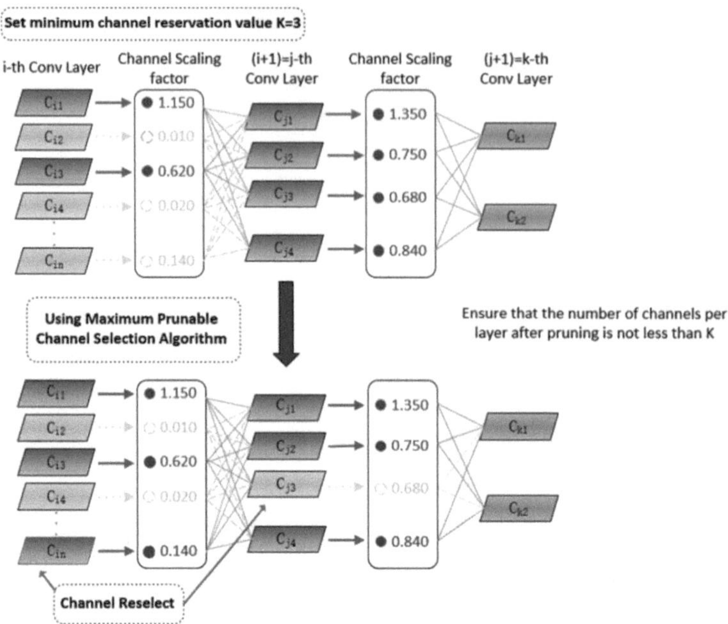

Fig. 6. Example of Maximum Prunable Channel Selection (MPCS) algorithm

k. Let $W_L(L \in N)$ denote the total number of channels in each layer. During layer-wise channel selection, if the number of remaining channels in a layer after pruning is less than k, the number of retained channels is set to k. The updated number of prunable channels is then computed as $P_l = W_L - k$. In this case, $P_L - P_l$ channels are under-pruned, requiring compensation from other layers. The selection of compensatory channels follows an importance-based ordering.

Two compensation strategies are considered: local compensation and global compensation, both evaluated in Sect. 4. Local compensation excludes the network layer in which pruning decisions have already been made and instead selects the least important channels from the remaining layers to adjust the pruning count. Global compensation, on the other hand, considers all channels across the network (except those in the current layer) and compensates by pruning the least important channels first.

Both approaches may lead to scenarios where, after compensation, the number of remaining channels in some layers falls below the minimum retention threshold k. In such cases, the compensation process must be iteratively adjusted until all layers maintain a number of channels greater than k. This iterative adjustment ensures that the pruning ratio restriction problem is fully resolved. A schematic representation of the algorithm is provided in Fig. 6.

The Maximum Prunable Channel Selection algorithm (MPCS) is formally described in Algorithm 1.

Algorithm 1. Maximum Prunable Channel Selection Algorithm(MPCS)

Input: prune ratio c, minimum channel reservation value k, sparsity model S, Channels importance δ, and Number of channels for each layer W_i.

Output: pruned model S' and pruned channel list P.

 1: Sorting δ in ascending order;
 2: Determine the unpruned channels' importance δ_c according to c
 3: Determine the number of initial pruning channel for each layer P_i
 4: Initialize P
 5: **for** $i = 1$ to n **do**
 6:     **if** $W_i - P_i < k$ **then**
 7:         Get $[P_i - (W_i - k)]$ new prune channels P_j by δ_c
 8:         **while** $W_j - P_j > k$ **do**
 9:             $\delta_c \leftarrow \delta_c$ removing these P_j channels
10:             Redetermine $[P_i - (W_i - k)]$ new prune channels P_j
11:         **end while**
12:         $P_i = W_i - k$
13:         P $\leftarrow$ P+P_i
14:     **end if**
15: **end for**
16: Get pruned model S' according to P

In Sect. 4, we determine the experimental value of the minimum retained channels k and validate the feasibility and effectiveness of the proposed MPCS algorithm.

4   Experimental Results

4.1   Metrics and Datasets

The experimental evaluation metrics for comparing different sparsity methods in the first section include the effect of sparsification, the prunable proportion after sparsification, the detection accuracy and speed after pruning, and the model's memory usage. The evaluation metrics for the MPCS algorithm proposed in the second section consist of the pruning ratio, the detection accuracy after pruning, the detection speed, and the model's memory consumption. The datasets we used in this study are the Tiny-Person [18] and Visdrone datasets [19], both of which are widely recognized benchmarks for tiny object detection.

4.2   Experimental Results

First, various experiments on sparsity methods were conducted. Four approaches were employed to train the γ parameters of the BN layer to be sparse: L1 regularization, L1 regularization with cosine decay, a combination of L1 and L2 regularization, and a combination of L1 and L2 regularization with cosine decay. Figure 7 presents a histogram illustrating the trend of γ during sparse training.

Figure 7 demonstrates that when L1 and L2 regularization are combined, the γ parameters become sparse more quickly. However, fewer parameter values are close to zero, which affects the ranking of channel importance. This suggests that combining L1 and L2 regularization may not be optimal for feature selection based on γ parameters. The addition of cosine decay results in a more uniform sparsification of γ, improving parameter sparsification and mitigating the limitation on the pruning ratio.

The pruning ratios of models trained with the four aforementioned sparsity methods are presented in Table 2.

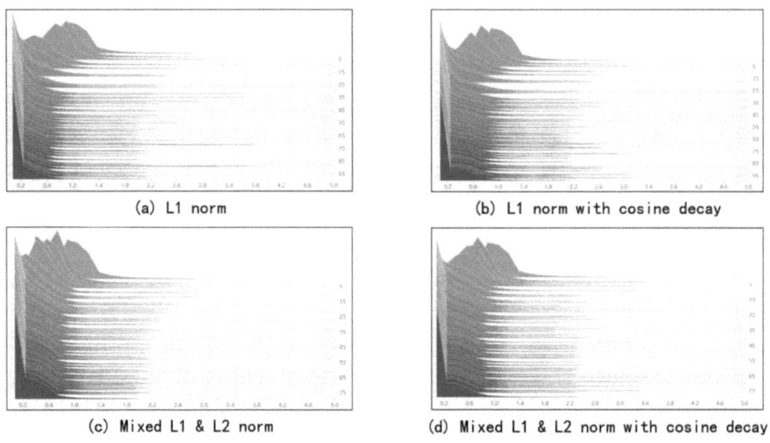

(a) L1 norm   (b) L1 norm with cosine decay

(c) Mixed L1 & L2 norm   (d) Mixed L1 & L2 norm with cosine decay

Fig. 7. Comparison of the trend of gamma values of 4 sparsity method

Table 2. Comparison of the percentage of prunable for different sparsity methods

Sparsity Method	L1 (Cosine decay)	L1	Mixed L1&L2 (Cosine decay)	Mixed L1&L2
Prune_Ratio (%)	68.5	68.8	67.2	67.3

Table 2 indicates that the introduction of cosine decay increases the pruning ratio for both L1 regularization and the mixed L1 and L2 regularization method, highlighting the effectiveness of cosine decay. However, the pruning ratio is slightly lower when mixed L1 and L2 regularization is used compared to L1 regularization alone, suggesting that L2 regularization may not be well-suited for parameter sparsification. Since no significant correlation was observed between the pruning ratio and detection accuracy after pruning, additional experiments were conducted to assess the impact of mixed L1 and L2 regularization and cosine decay on model pruning. The detection results after pruning are shown in Table 3.

Table 3. Comparison of detection results of four sparsity methods after pruning at a 65% pruning ratio

Sparsity Method	L1 (Cosine decay)	L1	Mixed L1&L2 (Cosine decay)	Mixed L1&L2
Tiny-Person mAP	0.517	0.520	0.502	0.506
Visdrone mAP	0.585	0.590	0.573	0.579
Inference Speed	16.8 ms	17.4 ms	18.6 ms	18.1 ms
Model Size	5.97 M	6.08 M	6.27 M	6.20 M

Table 3 reveals that the model's detection accuracy decreases slightly when mixed L1 and L2 regularization is used. However, for both L1 regularization and mixed L1 and L2 regularization, adding cosine decay slightly enhances detection accuracy.

To isolate the effect of the mixing parameter θ, additional experiments were performed with varying θ values, as shown in Table 4.

Table 4. Comparison of pruning effect of different mixing parameters θ

Mixing Parameter	$\theta = 0.5$	$\theta = 0.6$	$\theta = 0.7$	$\theta = 0.8$
Prune_Ratio (%)	54.7	63.6	67.2	67.1
Tiny-Person mAP	0.505	0.514	0.519	0.512
Visdrone mAP	0.570	0.576	0.583	0.574

Table 4 indicates that the highest pruning ratio is achieved at $\theta = 0.7$, and at this value, the model maintains the highest detection accuracy at a 65% pruning ratio. However, the detection accuracy remains slightly lower than that of methods without L2 regularization. Based on these findings, the sparsity method combining L1 and L2 regularization was excluded from subsequent experiments.

The sparsity rate λ also influences pruning performance. Five different values of λ were tested, and the corresponding detection results are displayed in Table 5.

Table 5. Comparison of pruning effects with different sparsity rate

Sparsity Rate	$2 * 10^{-5}$	$5 * 10^{-5}$	$1 * 10^{-4}$	$1.5 * 10^{-4}$	$2 * 10^{-4}$
Prune_Ratio (%)	63.4	64.6	65.9	68.5	68.2
Tiny-Person mAP	0.507	0.513	0.517	0.520	0.510
Visdrone mAP	0.577	0.581	0.590	0.592	0.586

As shown in Table 5, the choice of λ affects both the pruning ratio and post-pruning detection performance. The results indicate that increasing λ improves the fine-tuning effect of the pruned model. Based on these observations, λ was set to $1.5 * 10^{-4}$ for subsequent experiments.

It has been demonstrated that the sparsification method, which employs a combination of L1 and L2 regularization, enhances the rate of parameter sparsity. However, the maximum prunable proportion and the detection accuracy after pruning are slightly lower. The introduction of cosine decay increases the maximum prunable proportion and improves detection accuracy, demonstrating its effectiveness.

Next, experiments were conducted on the maximum prunable channel selection algorithm. Multiple sets of experiments were performed to evaluate the effect of the minimum number of retained channels k, on detection performance. The detection results after 75% pruning are presented in Table 6.

Table 6. Comparison of experimental results for the minimum channel retention number k

Parameter	k=2	k=4	k=8	k=16
Tiny-Person mAP	0.518	0.516	0.511	0.503
Visdrone mAP	0.592	0.587	0.581	0.573
Inference Speed	17.3 ms	17.8 ms	17.1 ms	17.2 ms
Model Size	5.43 MB	5.36 MB	5.31 MB	5.29 MB

Table 6 indicates that the best detection performance is achieved when k=2, corresponding to the largest model size. It is also observed that k does not significantly affect detection speed. Therefore, subsequent experiments were conducted with k=2.

The maximum prunable channel selection algorithm compensates for pruning by replacing channels of lower importance whenever possible. However, the importance of the replaced channels will inevitably be greater than that of the originally pruned channels. Consequently, as k increases, more important channels are replaced, leading to greater accuracy degradation in the pruned model.

Next, two channel compensation strategies—global compensation and local compensation—were compared. The results for a pruning ratio of 70% are presented in Table 7.

Table 7. Comparison of channel global compensation and local compensation

Compensate Method	mAP	Inference Speed	Model Size
Global Re-select in Tiny-Person	0.519	18.1 ms	5.75 MB
Partial Re-select in TinyPerson	0.518	18.3 ms	5.83 MB
Global Re-select in Visdrone	0.587	19.7 ms	5.75 MB
Partial Re-select in Visdrone	0.584	20.4 ms	5.83 MB

The results indicate that there is little difference between the two methods, with global compensation performing slightly better. This is because, in local compensation, the channel retained may be slightly more significant than the one designated for pruning. However, as the number of iterations decreases, the time required for pruning also decreases, allowing for a trade-off between the two methods.

The proposed algorithm does not impose restrictions on the prunable proportion. We pruned the model at ratios ranging from 60%–80%, and the detection accuracy is presented in Table 8.

Table 8. Comparison of pruning results at 60%–80%

Prune Ratio	Baseline	C=0.6	C=0.65	C=0.70	C=0.75	C=0.80
Tiny-Person mAP	0.524	0.524	0.524	0.523	0.518	0.413
Visdrone mAP	0.598	0.598	0.597	0.595	0.588	0.476
Inference Speed	19.4 ms	18.6 ms	18.3 ms	17.6 ms	17.4 ms	17.5 ms
Model Size	18.1 MB	6.57 MB	6.12 MB	5.75 MB	5.23 MB	4.86 MB

Table 8 shows that for pruning ratios between 60% and 70%, the model maintains a detection accuracy of 0.523 and 0.595 in Tiny-person and Visdrone datasets. At a pruning ratio of 70%, memory consumption is reduced to 5.75MB. By balancing detection accuracy, speed, and memory usage, a pruning ratio of 70% is determined to be optimal. This ratio exceeds the maximum pruning ratio achievable without the proposed MPCS algorithm, confirming the algorithm's effectiveness.

Table 9. Comparison the detection results in Tiny-Person and Visdrone datasets of different detectors

Method	Tiny mAP	Visdrone mAP	GFLOPs	Model Size
FasterRCNN [20]	0.473	0.402	492.8	232.2 M
CascadeRCNN [21]	0.547	0.412	739.0	337.6 M
RT-DETR-1 [22]	0.596	0.632	103.8	63.4 M
YOLOv11s [23]	0.521	0.576	21.7	18.4 M
YOLOv11s* [23]	0.521	0.574	11.4	6.32 M
YOLOv11s*+MPCS (Ours)	0.519	0.573	10.9	**5.70 M**
YOLOv12s [6]	0.524	0.598	21.2	18.1 M
YOLOv12s* [6]	0.524	0.597	10.2	6.12 M
YOLOv12s*+MPCS (Ours)	0.523	0.595	**9.8**	**5.75 M**

By removing the pruning ratio restriction using the MPCS algorithm, increasing the pruning ratio does not negatively impact detection accuracy up to a certain threshold. Additionally, model inference speed is improved, and memory usage is significantly reduced, making the approach more suitable for deployment on lightweight devices.

Finally, we apply the MPCS algorithm to YOLOv12s and YOLOv11s for evaluation. The detection results on the two datasets are shown in Table 9. * indicates the use of the baseline pruning algorithm. Tiny mAP indicates the detection results in Tiny-Person dataset.

It can be seen from the table that our algorithm is effective for both YOLOv11 and YOLOv12. Compared with the model without pruning and the one using the baseline pruning algorithm, our approach can further reduce the computational cost and memory usage while keeping the detection accuracy nearly unchanged, proving the robustness and effectiveness of our proposed algorithm once again.

5   Conclusion

To address the issue of restricted pruning ratios in the network slimming method, this paper first analyzes various gamma sparsification methods to identify potential causes of this limitation. Subsequently, a cosine decay method is introduced to mitigate the problem as much as possible and smooth the gamma sparsity. Next, to resolve the issue of restricted pruning ratios, a maximum prunable channel selection (MPCS) algorithm is proposed. This algorithm reselects the channels to be pruned during the baseline selection process, ensuring that not all channels within a layer are pruned simultaneously. Additionally, the minimum number of reserved channels per layer is determined to maintain the detection performance of each layer. After applying the proposed algorithm with a 70% pruning ratio, the model's detection performance remains stable, and its detection speed improves. Compared to the baseline pruning ratio of 60%, the model's memory usage is Reduced by nearly 15%, while detection accuracy remains unchanged. These results demonstrate the feasibility and effectiveness of the proposed MPCS algorithm, making the model more suitable for deployment on lightweight devices. We hope that this paper can provide some insights for advancing research on approaching the theoretical limit of model pruning ratio.

Acknowledgement. This work is supported by the Humanities and Social Sciences Fund of the Ministry of Education of China under Grant No. 24YJAZH042.

References

1. Han, S., Liu, X., Mao, H.: EIE: efficient inference engine on compressed deep neural network. ACM SIGARCH Comput. Archit. News **44**(3), 243–254 (2016)
2. Hu, S., Tang, G., Yu, K., et al.: Embedded YOLO v8: real-time detection of sugarcane nodes in complex natural environments by rapid structural pruning method. Measurement **242**, 116291 (2025)
3. Rathi, N., Panda, P.: STDP-based pruning of connections and weight quantization in spiking neural networks for energy-efficient recognition. IEEE Trans. Comput. Aided Des. Integr. Circuits Syst. **38**(4), 668–677 (2018)

4. He, Y., Zhang, X., Sun, J.: Channel pruning for accelerating very deep neural networks. In: Proceedings of the IEEE International Conference on Computer Vision, pp. 1389–1397 (2017)

5. Liu, Z., Li, J., et al.: Learning efficient convolutional networks through network slimming. In: Proceedings of the IEEE International Conference on Computer Vision, pp. 2736–2744 (2017)

6. Tian, Y., Ye, Q., Doermann. D.: YOLOv12: attention-centric real-time object detectors. arXiv preprint arXiv:2502.12524 (2025)

7. Li, J., Qi, Q., Wang, J., et al.: OICSR: out-in-channel sparsity regularization for compact deep neural networks. In: Proceedings of the IEEE/CVF Conference on Computer Vision and Pattern Recognition, pp. 7046–7055 (2019)

8. Wen, W., Wu, C., Wang, Y., et al.: Learning structured sparsity in deep neural networks. Adv. Neural Inf. Process. Syst. **29** (2016)

9. Zhang, D., Wang, H., Figueiredo, M.: Learning to share: simultaneous parameter tying and sparsification in deep learning. In: International Conference on Learning Representations (2018)

10. LeCun, Y., Denker, J., Solla, S.: Optimal brain damage. Adv. Neural Inf. Process. Syst. **2** (1989)

11. Hassibi, B., Stork, D.: Second order derivatives for network pruning: optimal brain surgeon. Adv. Neural Inf. Process. Syst. **5** (1992)

12. Molchanov, P., Tyree, S., Karras, T., et al.: Pruning convolutional neural networks for resource efficient inference. arXiv preprint arXiv:1611.06440 (2016)

13. Luo, J.H., Wu, J., Lin, W.: ThiNet: a filter level pruning method for deep neural network compression. In: Proceedings of the IEEE International Conference on Computer Vision, pp. 5058–5066 (2017)

14. Chin, T.W., Zhang, C.: Layer-compensated pruning for resource-constrained convolutional neural networks. arXiv preprint arXiv:1810.00518 (2018)

15. Xu, Z., Li, J., Meng, Y., et al.: CAP-YOLO: channel attention based pruning YOLO for coal mine real-time intelligent monitoring. Sensors **22**(12), 4331 (2022)

16. Zhang, R., Lu, Y., Song, Z.: YOLO sparse training and model pruning for street view house numbers recognition. J. Phys. Conf. Ser. **2646**(1), 012025 (2023)

17. Shang, D., Lv, Z., Gao, Z., et al.: Detection of coal gangue by YOLO deep learning method based on channel pruning. Int. J. Coal Prep. Util. **45**(1), 231–243 (2025)

18. Yu, X., Gong, Y., Jiang, N., et al.: Scale match for tiny person detection. In: Proceedings of the IEEE/CVF Winter Conference on Applications of Computer Vision, pp. 1257–1265 (2020)

19. Cao, Y., He, Z., Wang, L., et al.: VisDrone-DET2021: the vision meets drone object detection challenge results. In: Proceedings of the IEEE/CVF International Conference on Computer Vision, pp. 2847–2854 (2021)

20. Ren, S., He, K., Girshick, R., et al.: Faster R-CNN: towards real-time object detection with region proposal networks. IEEE Trans. Pattern Anal. Mach. Intell. **39**(6), 1137–1149 (2016)

21. Cai, Z., Vasconcelos, N.: Cascade R-CNN: delving into high quality object detection. In: Proceedings of the IEEE Conference on Computer Vision and Pattern Recognition, pp. 6154–6162 (2018)

22. Zhao, Y., Lv, W., Xu, S., et al.: DETRs beat YOLOs on real-time object detection. In: Proceedings of the IEEE/CVF Conference on Computer Vision and Pattern Recognition, pp. 16965–16974 (2024)

23. Khanam, R., Hussain, M.: YOLOv11: an overview of the key architectural enhancements. arXiv preprint arXiv:2410.17725 (2024)

A Multimodal Fusion Framework Employing Full-Stage Attention for Survival Prediction

Aolei Liu[1], Junkang Guo[1], Yuhang Wang[1], Jian Liu[1(✉)], Huiyuan Tian[2], Tao Qin[2], Hangrui Xu[1], and Haiyan Wei[1]

[1] School of Computer Science and Information Engineering, Hefei University of Technology, Hefei, China
`{lal,2023110577,wangyuhang,2022217415,2022217594}@mail.hfut.edu.cn`,
`jianliu@hfut.edu.cn`

[2] Zhengzhou University People's Hospital, Henan Provincial People's Hospital, Zhengzhou, China
`{tianhy,qtgoodfreecn}@zzu.edu.cn`

Abstract. Current approaches to multimodal survival analysis based on pathology and genomics often apply attention mechanisms at a single stage, thereby missing fine-grained intra-modal details and cross-modal synergies. We propose a novel framework—**M**ultimodal **F**usion **F**ramework with **F**ull-stage **A**ttention (MFF-FA)—which integrates attention across three stages: feature extraction, modality alignment, and modality fusion. Specifically, we introduce En-UNI for pathology image sampling and representation, and employ attention modules to enhance latent genomic feature interactions. A convolution-based cross-attention module is further developed to model inter-modal correlations between pathology and genomics. Finally, a gating-attention fusion strategy is applied to retain modality-specific characteristics while enhancing their integration. Comparative evaluations demonstrate that MFF-FA outperforms existing state-of-the-art models in predictive accuracy for cancer survival analysis.

Keywords: Multimodal learning · Attention mechanism · Survival analysis · Cross-modality

1 Introduction

Cancer remains a leading cause of mortality worldwide, with patient survival outcomes varying significantly. Accurate survival prediction is essential for guiding personalized treatment. Survival analysis models the time from a defined clinical event to an outcome, providing key prognostic insights [6]. While unimodal data such as genomics or pathology images capture important biological features, they often fail to reflect the full complexity of tumor heterogeneity [15]. Multimodal integration enhances prediction accuracy and deepens our understanding

T. Zhu et al. (Eds.): KSEM 2025, LNAI 15920, pp. 194–206, 2026.
https://doi.org/10.1007/978-981-95-3052-6_15

of tumor biology. Genomic data reveal molecular alterations, while pathology images reflect cellular morphology. Their combination enables the discovery of cross-scale interactions, improving prognostic precision.

Recent advances in feature engineering for pathology images and genomic data have substantially improved cancer survival analysis. Traditional pathology image analysis often depends on manually annotated regions of interest (ROIs), which are low in reproducibility and fail to capture global contextual patterns. To overcome these limitations, the field has shifted towards whole slide image (WSI) analysis, leveraging random patch sampling and pre-trained models such as VGG and ResNet [16]. However, these models—originally trained on natural images—offer limited semantic relevance and interpretability in pathology. In genomic analysis, conventional statistical methods such as t-tests and ANOVA are inadequate for high-dimensional data, hindering effective pattern discovery. As a result, deep neural networks (DNNs), including self-normalizing networks (SNNs) [11], have been increasingly adopted to uncover complex genomic signatures. Additionally, recent studies [4,5] have integrated gene functional information to better elucidate geneâĂŞcancer associations. Nevertheless, capturing intricate biological interactions remains a major challenge, limiting the depth and interpretability of current genomic analyses.

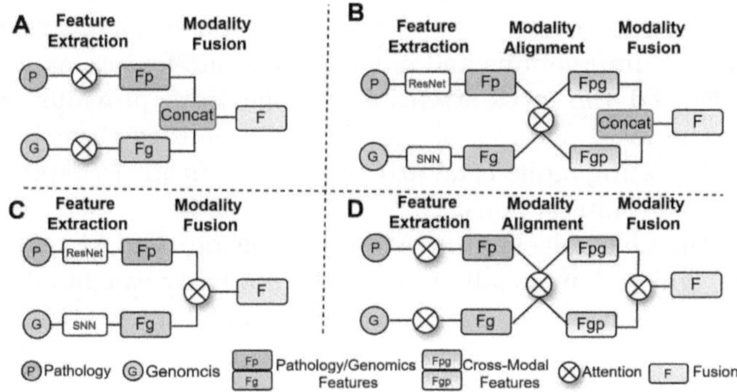

Fig. 1. Attention mechanisms are integrated across key stages of multimodal survival analysis, including A) Feature Extraction, B) Modality Alignment, C) Modality Fusion, and D) Full-Stage, to enhance overall performance.

In multimodal cancer survival prediction, conventional approaches typically integrate genomic data and pathology images via machine learning algorithms or the Cox model to enhance predictive accuracy [8]. However, these methods often fail to capture complex inter-modal interactions. Recent progress in attention mechanisms has shown potential in identifying salient features [18], improving feature extraction, modality alignment, and fusion. Yet, most existing methods apply attention at a single stage, limiting their ability to model deep cross-modal relationships. For instance, in feature extraction (Fig. 1A), the Co-Attention Transformer [4] directs attention to image regions guided by genomic signals but neglects broader cross-modal dynamics. In modality alignment (Fig. 1B), CMTA [21] captures inter-modal correlations, yet lacks fine-grained modeling within each modality. In modality fusion (Fig. 1C), CMFM [19] adaptively adjusts feature weights, but its performance degrades when modalities are incomplete. The key challenge remains: how to incorporate attention across all stages while maintaining both efficiency and robust information flow.

Based on the above observations, we propose MFF-FA (Multimodal Fusion Framework with Full-Stage Attention) for cancer survival prediction, integrating genomic and pathological data (Fig. 1D). Our framework employs attention mechanisms at multiple stages to dynamically capture critical features throughout the multimodal interaction. The main contributions of this work are summarized as follows:

- We propose a Multimodal Fusion Framework with Full-Stage Attention (MFF-FA), which integrates attention mechanisms across three stages— feature extraction, modality alignment, and fusion—to effectively capture and analyze key multimodal information.
- We introduce En-UNI, a multimodal framework that samples pathology images based on entropy, color saturation, and intensity, and leverages a pre-trained UNI model for efficient feature extraction. This design substantially reduces computational overhead while preserving comprehensive global representations. Moreover, we integrate attention mechanisms to highlight geneâĂŞfunction interactions and enhance genomic feature capture.
- We also enhanced the cross-attention module from previous work [21] by focusing on the local features of individual modalities through convolution layers and integrating multi-head attention mechanisms to capture more profound cross-modal interactions.
- We propose the Gate Mechanism Attention Fusion (GMAF) strategy at the fusion stage, which dynamically adjusts the modality weights distribution to enhance information flow and facilitate multimodal integration.

2   Methods

To effectively capture key features in multimodal data, this paper proposes a multimodal fusion framework called Full-Stage Attention (MFF-FA) (Fig. 2). First, we introduce the Full-Stage Attention Mechanism, followed by a detailed explanation of the framework's key components in the Feature Extraction, Modality Alignment, and Modality Fusion stages.

2.1   Full-Stage Attention Mechanism

We introduce attention mechanisms at critical stages—feature extraction, modality alignment, and fusion—to enable efficient interaction between pathology and genomic data. During feature extraction, attention highlights salient features within each modality. A UNI encoder, pre-trained on pathology images via

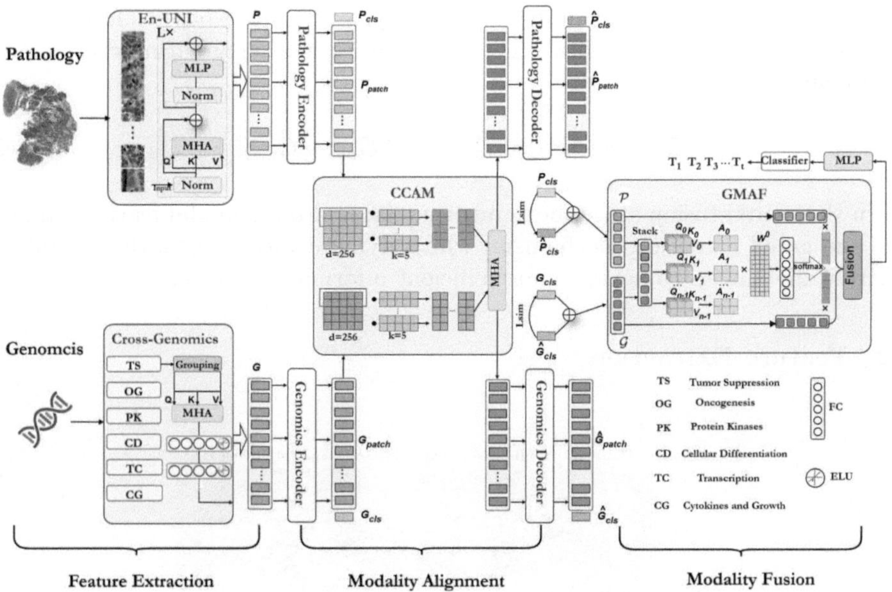

Fig. 2. The MFF-FA framework comprises three key stages. First, an attention mechanism is introduced during feature extraction to emphasize critical unimodal features, resulting in P_{cls} and G_{cls}. Next, a convolutional cross-attention module facilitates inter-modality interaction, producing cross-modal representations $\widehat{P}_{cls}$ and $\widehat{G}_{cls}$. Finally, the GMAF module adaptively weights unimodal and cross-modal features for effective fusion, and a classifier outputs the final survival time prediction.

Vision Transformer (ViT), extracts histopathological features P. Concurrently, multi-head attention captures interactions among genes with diverse biological functions, yielding genomic features G. For modality alignment, we adopt the Nyström Attention strategy from Zhou et al. [21] to reduce computational cost through low-rank approximation.

$$A \approx X_S \left(X_S^T X_S\right)^{-1} X_S^T \tag{1}$$

Let A represent the entire attention matrix, and X_S denote a smaller subset selected from the input sequence. The term $(X_S^T X_S)^{-1}$ refers to the inverse of the inner product of the subset, which is utilized to compute the low-rank approximation.

The Encoder layer generates modality-specific representations for pathology and genomics, denoted as P_{cls} and G_{cls}, respectively. To enhance cross-modal interaction, we introduce a Convolutional Cross-Modal Attention (CCMA) module, where convolution captures local dependencies and refines features for the subsequent multi-head attention. Compared to using multi-head attention alone, this integration improves interaction specificity and relevance. A Decoder layer mirroring the Encoder—further processes the fused features to yield $\widehat{P}_{cls}$ and $\widehat{G}_{cls}$

. To balance intra- and inter-modal consistency, an L1 norm-based similarity loss L_{sim} is applied, preserving intra-modal semantics while regulating cross-modal alignment.

$$L_{\text{sim}} = \left(\left\| P_{\text{cls}} - \widehat{P}_{\text{cls}} \right\|_1 + \left\| G_{\text{cls}} - \widehat{G}_{\text{cls}} \right\|_1 \right) \tag{2}$$

In the modal fusion stage, both intra-modal and inter-modal features are fed into the gated attention mechanism, which dynamically adjusts the weights of different modalities to achieve more efficient information fusion.

2.2   Feature Extraction

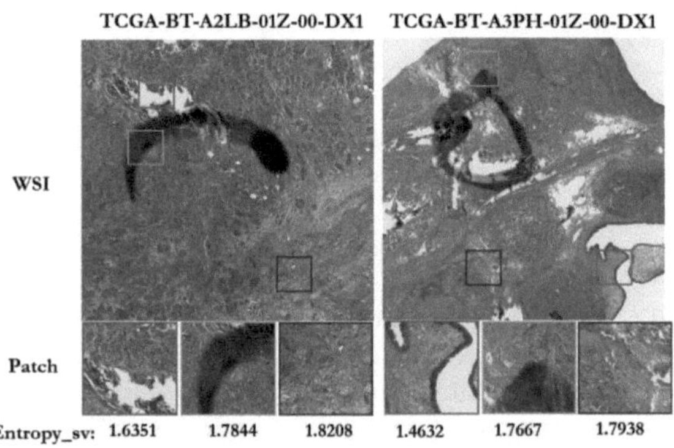

Fig. 3. The Entropy_sv-based sampling strategy combines joint entropy, saturation, and value to efficiently identify semantically representative blocks and accurately detect contaminated regions.

The En-UNI Method for Pathology Images: We adopt the Entropy_sv sampling strategy [12], which integrates key factors such as information entropy, saturation, and color value. This method efficiently locates uncontaminated key regions (Fig. 3). The formula for the calculation is as follows:

$$E = - \sum_{i,j} P_{ij} \log_2 P_{ij}, \tag{3}$$

$$Score = E^2 \cdot \ln(1 + S \cdot V) \tag{4}$$

Here, P_{ij} represents the probability of each grayscale pixel, E denotes the image's entropy, and S and V correspond to the saturation and value components in the HSV color space. The final score is scaled by 1×10^{-3} for comparison.

We extract patch-level features from whole-slide pathology images using the pre-trained UNI model [3], a self-supervised network trained on over 100 million WSIs from diverse tissue types. Specifically, we apply the En-UNI method to obtain representative features from 100 sampled patches per WSI. Each patient's pathology image is represented as a feature matrix $P = \{p_1, p_2, ..., p_M\} \in \mathbb{R}^{M \times d}$, where M is the number of sampled patches, In this paper, M=100.

The Cross-Genomics Module for Genomics: Previous studies [4,14] have classified genes into six functional categories—Tumor Suppression, Oncogenesis, Protein Kinases, Cellular Differentiation, Transcription, Cytokines and Growth— and employed self-normalizing networks (SNN) [11] to extract genomic features. However, this method overlooks the potential interactions between these biological functions.

Genes operate within complex regulatory networks. For instance, gene products such as proteins can influence the expression of other genes [2], and co-expression patterns during biological processes often suggest functional associations [7]. Inspired by multimodal learning, we treat each gene function category as an independent modality and use a multi-head attention mechanism to model their interactions. Specifically, we randomly group the six categories and generate inter-group attention maps to uncover their interrelations and biological implications. This strategy not only enhances our understanding of genomic modalities but also offers novel insights into cancer survival prediction.

Given a set of genomics functions $F = \{F_1, F_2, F_3, F_4, F_5, F_6\}$, it is randomly divided into two subsets F_a, F_b. The interaction attention map A_a, A_b between these subsets is calculated using a multi-head attention mechanism. The computation is defined as follows:

$$A_a(F_a, F_b) = \mathrm{softmax}\left(\frac{Q(F_a) \cdot K(F_b)^T}{\sqrt{d}}\right) \cdot V(F_b), \tag{5}$$

$$A_b(F_b, F_a) = \mathrm{softmax}\left(\frac{Q(F_b) \cdot K(F_a)^T}{\sqrt{d}}\right) \cdot V(F_a) \tag{6}$$

The genomic features of each patient can be represented as $G = Concat(Aa, Ab) = \{g_1, g_2, ..., g_N\} \in \mathbb{R}^{N \times d}$, where N represents the number of biological function categories, In this paper, N=6.

2.3   Modality Alignment

Pathlogy Encoder and Genomics Encoder: According to prior work [21], the pathology encoder integrates a Nyström Attention mechanism and a Pyramid Position Encoding Generator (PPEG), while the genomics encoder employs only Nyström Attention. Two learnable class tokens, P_{cls} and G_{cls} , are introduced to aggregate information from patch features P_{patch} and G_{patch}, respectively. The formula is as follows:

$$P_{\mathrm{cls}}, P_{\mathrm{patch}} = \text{Pathlogy Encoder}(P), \tag{7}$$

$$G_{\mathrm{cls}}, G_{\mathrm{patch}} = \text{Genomics Encoder}(G) \tag{8}$$

Among these, P_{cls} represents the intra-modal features of pathology, while G_{cls} represents the intra-modal features of genomics.

Convolution Cross Attention Module(CCAM): We propose a convolutional cross-attention mechanism to model interactions between P_{cls} and G_{cls}. This module combines 1D convolution and multi-head self-attention to effectively capture cross-modal dependencies. Specifically, 1D convolution layers first extract local patterns within each modality, preserving sequence length through appropriate kernel size K and padding. Then, multi-head self-attention facilitates information exchange between modalities.

Let $P_{\mathrm{patch}} \in \mathbb{R}^{M \times d}$ and $G_{\mathrm{patch}} \in \mathbb{R}^{N \times d}$ denote the input embeddings from pathology and genomics, with sequence lengths M, N and shared embedding dimension $d = 256$, The convolution operation serves as a locality-aware feature extractor prior to cross-attention.

$$y_n = \sum_{k=1}^{K} x_{n+k-1} w_k \quad \text{for} \quad n = 1, 2, \ldots, L - K + 1 \tag{9}$$

Let x_n represent the n-th element in the input sequence, W_k denote the weight of the convolution kernel, and y_n be the output sequence after convolution. The feature representations after convolution are denoted as $P'_{\mathrm{patch}} \in \mathbb{R}^{M \times d}$ and $G'_{\mathrm{patch}} \in \mathbb{R}^{N \times d}$, which represent the local features of the two modes after convolution processing.

The convolution operation captures local dependencies within the input data, enriching the feature representation for the subsequent multi-head self-attention mechanism. This is followed by multi-head self-attention, which enables interaction with the data to extract cross-modal relationships between P'_{patch} and G'_{patch}. The process of multi-head self-attention calculation is as follows:

$$PG'_{\mathrm{patch}} = \mathrm{softmax}\left(\frac{Q(P'_{\mathrm{patch}}) \cdot K(G'_{\mathrm{patch}})^T}{\sqrt{d}} \right) \cdot V(G'_{\mathrm{patch}}), \tag{10}$$

$$GP'_{\mathrm{patch}} = \mathrm{softmax}\left(\frac{Q(G'_{\mathrm{patch}}) \cdot K(P'_{\mathrm{patch}})^T}{\sqrt{d}} \right) \cdot V(P'_{\mathrm{patch}}) \tag{11}$$

PG'_{patch} represents the cross-modal representation learned by pathology from genomics, while GP'_{patch} represents the cross-modal representation learned by genomics from pathology. By doing so, the model can capture complex interactions between different modalities and effectively integrate cross-modal information.

Pathlogy Decoder and Genomics Decoder: To prevent excessive emphasis on modality interactions, which may significantly distort the original features, the decoder mirrors the encoder's structure. This design enables the decoder to restore the original features that were not fed into the CCMA, allowing the model to effectively learn the mapping between cross-modal features.

$$\widehat{P}_{\text{cls}}, \widehat{P}_{\text{patch}} = \text{Pathlogy Decoder}(PG'_{\text{patch}}), \tag{12}$$

$$\widehat{G}_{\text{cls}}, \widehat{G}_{\text{patch}} = \text{Genomics Decoder}(GP'_{\text{patch}}) \tag{13}$$

Among them, $\widehat{P}_{\text{cls}}$ represents the cross-modal feature learned from genomics, while $\widehat{G}_{\text{cls}}$ represents the cross-modal feature learned from pathology.

2.4 Modality Fusion

Cross-modal representations capture inter-modal information, enhancing and recalibrating intra-modal representations. Finally, the integration of intra-modal and cross-modal representations is utilized for survival prediction. The final feature representation of pathology is denoted as $\mathcal{P} = \frac{P_{\text{cls}} + \widehat{P}_{\text{cls}}}{2}$, while the genomics feature is represented as $\mathcal{G} = \frac{G_{\text{cls}} + \widehat{G}_{\text{cls}}}{2}$.

Gate Mechanism Attention Fusion (GMAF): To improve fusion efficiency, we propose the Gate Mechanism Attention Fusion (GMAF) method, illustrated in Fig. 2. Specifically, the features from the two modalities, $\mathcal{P}$ and $\mathcal{G}$, are concatenated to form F_{stack}. A multi-head attention mechanism is then applied to compute the interaction attention map A. Subsequently, a fully connected layer generates gating scores, which are normalized into a probability distribution S via the softmax function. Finally, the modalities are weighted and fused according to this distribution to produce the fused feature F_{fused}.

$$A = \text{MultiHead}(F_{stack}), \tag{14}$$

$$S = \text{softmax}(\text{linear}(A)), \tag{15}$$

$$F_{fused} = S_1 \cdot \mathcal{P} + S_2 \cdot \mathcal{G} \tag{16}$$

Survival prediction is formulated as: $T_1, ...T_t = sigmoid(mlp(F_{fused}))$. In this study, we use the L1 norm to quantify the distance between inter-modal and intra-modal representations. The negative log-likelihood (NLL) [4] survival loss is adopted as the loss function L_{surv} for the survival prediction component. The overall loss function is thus $L_{total} = L_{surv} + \partial L_{sim}$.

3 Experimental Results and Discussion

3.1 Datasets and Implementation Details

We evaluated the proposed method using data from The Cancer Genome Atlas (TCGA), which includes paired genomic data, diagnostic whole-slide images,

Table 1. The performance of different methods on three datasets is summarized, where CG denotes Cross-Genomics. The best and second-best results are highlighted in **bold** and <u>underlined</u>, respectively.

Methods	Modality	Datasets (c-index)		
		BLCA	LUAD	COAD-READ
SNN [11]	Gene Only	0.6243±0.0353	0.6580±0.0445	0.6542±0.0513
SNNTrans [11]		0.6421±0.0140	0.6688±0.0196	0.6873±0.0197
SNNTransCG [11]		0.6564±0.0463	<u>0.6760±0.0280</u>	0.6906±0.0214
AMIL [9]	WSI Only	0.5707±0.0417	0.5700±0.0419	0.6423±0.0778
TransMIL [17]		0.6099±0.0488	0.6044±0.0300	0.6517±0.0943
Porpoise [5]	Gene+WSI	0.6642±0.0258	0.6576±0.0286	0.6247±0.0494
MCAT [4]		0.6624±0.0353	0.6697±0.0359	0.6404±0.0392
DualTrans [21]		0.6656±0.0393	0.6716±0.0348	<u>0.6958±0.0444</u>
CMTA [21]		<u>0.6695±0.0188</u>	0.6663±0.0340	0.6894±0.0245
MoME [20]		0.6344±0.0275	0.6493±0.0167	0.6620±0.0365
MFF-FA (Ours)	Gene+WSI	**0.6995±0.0252**	**0.6883±0.0306**	**0.7269±0.0473**

survival outcomes, and censoring status. The analysis focused on three cancer types—Bladder Urothelial Carcinoma(BLCA) (n = 373), Lung Adenocarcinoma(LUAD) (n = 443), and Colon and Rectum Adenocarcinoma(COAD-READ) (n = 340)—with distinct biological, genetic, and clinical characteristics, providing a solid basis for cross-cancer survival analysis [1,13].

The dataset consisted of 129,700 image patches (224×224) from 1,297 whole-slide images (WSIs). The MFF-FA algorithm was implemented in PyTorch and trained on an NVIDIA A40-40G GPU using the SGD optimizer, with a learning rate of 1×10^{-3}, weight decay of 1×10^{-5}, and a batch size of 1. The hyperparameter ∂ was set to 1. Training was conducted over 30 epochs with 5-fold cross-validation. Survival analysis was assessed using the concordance index (c-index) [10].

Performance Comparison with Unimodal and Multimodal Benchmarks: As shown in Table 1, Our proposed multimodal framework consistently outperforms both unimodal and existing multimodal models across TCGA cancer datasets. As shown in Table 1, it achieves gains of 4.31%, 1.13%, and 3.63% over the best unimodal baselines, highlighting the complementary nature of integrating genomics and pathology. While genomics alone generally surpass pathology due to their richer molecular insights, combining modalities further alleviates the limitations inherent in each. Compared to advanced multimodal approaches such as CMTA, our method yields notable improvements in c-index—by 3.00% (BLCA), 2.20% (LUAD), and 3.75% (COAD-READ)—through full-stage attention mechanisms. These mechanisms progressively emphasize intra-modal representation in early stages and inter-modal interaction in later stages via bidirectional feedback, leading to a more comprehensive understanding of cancer prognosis (Table 2).

Table 2. The experimental results after deleting three key components. CG is the abbreviation of Cross-Genomics. The best results are highlighted in **bold**.

Modules	Datasets (c-index)		
	BLCA	LUAD	COAD-READ
w/o En-UNI	0.6649±0.0449	0.6773±0.0310	0.7044±0.0367
w/o CG	0.6704±0.0399	0.6806±0.0337	0.7098±0.0217
w/o CCAM	0.6892±0.0452	0.6831±0.0174	0.6535±0.0167
w/o GMAF	0.6744±0.0284	0.6849±0.0338	0.7159±0.0278
MFF-FA (ALL)	**0.6995±0.0252**	**0.6883±0.0306**	**0.7269±0.0473**

Table 3. The experimental results after deleting three key components. The best results are highlighted in **bold**.

Stage	Datasets (c-index)		
	BLCA	LUAD	COAD-READ
FE	0.6827±0.0204	0.6773±0.0409	0.7123±0.0241
MA	0.6664±0.0294	0.6736±0.0167	0.6886±0.0395
MF	0.6746±0.0202	0.6769±0.0308	0.7024±0.0336
FE+MA	0.6892±0.0452	0.6849±0.0338	0.7159±0.0278
FE+MF	0.6744±0.0284	0.6831±0.0174	0.6535±0.0167
MA+MF	0.6649±0.0449	0.6773±0.0310	0.7044±0.0367
MFF-FA (ALL)	**0.6995±0.0252**	**0.6883±0.0306**	**0.7269±0.0473**

3.2 Ablation Studies

To evaluate the contribution of each component, we conduct ablation studies using the concordance index (C-index) across three datasets: BLCA, LUAD, and COAD-READ. Removing the En-UNI module—replaced by CLAM—leads to C-index drops of 3.46%, 1.10%, and 2.25%, respectively. Eliminating the Cross-Genomics module results in 2.91%, 0.77%, and 1.71% decreases, indicating that modeling inter-gene relationships enhances biological relevance and predictive accuracy. Replacing the CCAM with Multi-Head Attention yields performance losses of 1.03%, 0.52%, and 7.34%, highlighting the role of local feature extraction and cross-modal interaction. Lastly, substituting the GMAF strategy with basic concatenation reduces performance by 2.51%, 0.34%, and 1.10%, confirming the value of dynamic fusion weighting.

The MFF-FA module integrates attention mechanisms across feature extraction (FE), modality alignment (MA), and fusion (MF) stages. As shown in Table 3, attention removal from any stage leads to noticeable performance degradation. Among individual components, FE yields the greatest benefit, while dual-stage combinations (e.g., FE+MA) further enhance results. Full-stage attention (MFF-FA) consistently achieves the best performance across all datasets, underscoring its effectiveness in capturing both intra- and inter-modal dependencies.

3.3 Survival Analysis

To assess the effectiveness of the MFF-FA model in survival analysis, we performed univariate Kaplan-Meier (KM) estimation. Survival risk scores from the MFF-FA model were used to categorize samples into high- and low-risk groups, and the Log-rank test was employed to evaluate the statistical significance between the survival curves.

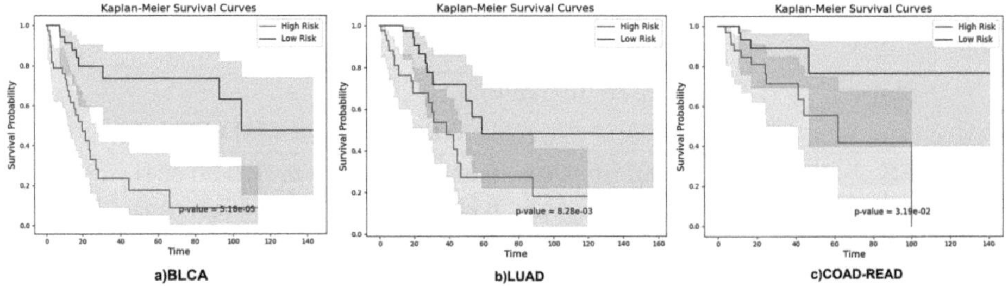

Fig. 4. The Kaplan-Meier (KM) survival curves of MFF-FA on TCGA-BLCA, TCGA-LUAD and TCGA-COAD-READ, survival time is calculated in months.

As shown in Fig. 4, the Log-rank test p-values for multiple cancer datasets were all significantly less than 0.05, indicating a clear survival difference between the high- and low-risk groups. This demonstrates the MFF-FA model's ability to stratify survival risks in cancer patients and underscores its potential to identify crucial survival-related factors, laying a strong foundation for clinical prognostic evaluation.

4   Conclusion

This paper presents a multimodal fusion framework with a full-stage attention mechanism (MFF-FA), which leverages multiple attention stages to effectively capture key features in multimodal data and dynamically adjust modality weights for efficient fusion. During feature extraction, the intra-modality attention mechanism refines single-modality representations, enhancing feature identification accuracy. The cross-modality alignment and fusion mechanism integrates complementary information between modalities, strengthens inter-modality interactions, and improves survival prediction accuracy. To reduce the computational cost of the full-stage attention mechanism, we introduce the En-UNI method, which selects biologically relevant features to enhance both accuracy and efficiency. Experimental results on three TCGA datasets demonstrate that our method outperforms state-of-the-art approaches.

Acknowledgments. This work was supported in part by the Hefei Municipal Natural Science Foundation under Grant (No.HZR2403), Natural Science Research Project of Colleges and Universities in Anhui Province (No.2022AH051889, No.2308085QF227), General Project of Anhui Province Outstanding Young Teachers Cultivation Program in 2024 (No.YQYB2024096).

References

1. Ahmed, K.M., Veeramachaneni, R., et al.: Glutathione peroxidase 2 is a metabolic driver of the tumor immune microenvironment and immune checkpoint inhibitor response. J. Immunother. Canc. (2022)
2. Barabasi, A.L., Oltvai, Z.N.: Network biology: understanding the cell's functional organization. Nat. Rev. Genet. 101–113 (2004)
3. Chen, R.J., Ding, T., et al.: Towards a general-purpose foundation model for computational pathology. Nat. Med. 850–862 (2024)
4. Chen, R.J., Lu, M.Y., et al.: Multimodal co-attention transformer for survival prediction in gigapixel whole slide images. In: Proceedings of the IEEE/CVF International Conference on Computer Vision, pp. 4015–4025 (2021)
5. Chen, R.J., Lu, M.Y., et al.: Pan-cancer integrative histology-genomic analysis via multimodal deep learning. Cancer Cell 865–878 (2022)
6. Cox, D.R.: Regression models and life-tables. J. R. Stat. Soc. Ser. B (Methodological) 187–202 (1972)
7. Han, J.D.J., Bertin, N., et al.: Evidence for dynamically organized modularity in the yeast protein–protein interaction network. Nature 88–93 (2004)
8. Huang, S., Cai, N., et al.: Applications of support vector machine (SVM) learning in cancer genomics. Canc. Genom. Proteom. 41–51 (2018)
9. Ilse, M., Tomczak, J., Welling, M.: Attention-based deep multiple instance learning. In: International Conference on Machine Learning, pp. 2127–2136. PMLR (2018)
10. Kandoth, C., McLellan, M.D., et al.: Mutational landscape and significance across 12 major cancer types. Nature 333–339 (2013)
11. Klambauer, G., Unterthiner, T., Mayr, A., Hochreiter, S.: Self-normalizing neural networks. Adv. Neural Inf. Process. Syst. (2017)
12. Li, L., Pan, H., et al.: PMFN-SSL: self-supervised learning-based progressive multimodal fusion network for cancer diagnosis and prognosis. Knowl.-Based Syst. 111502 (2024)
13. Li, S., Motiño, O., et al.: Protein regulator of cytokinesis 1: a potential oncogenic driver. Molec. Canc. 128 (2023)
14. Liberzon, A., Birger, C., et al.: The molecular signatures database hallmark gene set collection. Cell Syst. 417–425 (2015)

15. Lipkova, J., Chen, R.J., et al.: Artificial intelligence for multimodal data integration in oncology. Canc. Cell 1095–1110 (2022)
16. Lu, M.Y., Williamson, D.F., et al.: Data-efficient and weakly supervised computational pathology on whole-slide images. Nat. Biomed. Eng. 555–570 (2021)
17. Shao, Z., Bian, H., et al.: Transmil: transformer based correlated multiple instance learning for whole slide image classification. Adv. Neural Inf. Process. Syst. 2136–2147 (2021)
18. Vaswani, A.: Attention is all you need. Adv. Neural Inf. Process. Syst. (2017)
19. Wu, X., Shi, Y., Wang, M., Li, A.: Camr: cross-aligned multimodal representation learning for cancer survival prediction. Bioinformatics btad025 (2023)
20. Zheng, H., Wei, D., Zheng, Y.: Mome: mixture of multimodal experts for cancer survival prediction (2024)
21. Zhou, F., Chen, H.: Cross-modal translation and alignment for survival analysis. In: Proceedings of the IEEE/CVF International Conference on Computer Vision, pp. 21485–21494 (2023)

Differentially Private Graph Data Publishing via Feature-Based Community Detection

Zhisong Mo[1], Wen Huang[1], Weixin Zhao[1], Mingxuan Jia[1], Xinrui Li[1], Zhishuo Zhang[2], and Jian Peng[1(✉)]

[1] Sichuan University, Chengdu, China
{mozhisong1,wen,zhaoweixin,jiamx,lixinrui4,jianpeng}@scu.edu.cn
[2] University of Electronic Science and Technology of China, Chengdu, China
202111090814@std.uestc.edu.cn

Abstract. Graph data publishing is essential for numerous applications but raises privacy concerns due to sensitive relationships embedded within the data. Differential privacy is introduced into the Graph data publishing to eliminate privacy concerns. However, existing differentially private graph data publishing method suffer from excessive noise or structural distortions due to random community partitioning. Specifically, data utility does not increase as the privacy budget increases when random partitioning community. To this end, we propose a novel feature-based community detection approach for differentially private graph publishing. Our method leverages structural features extracted from local node neighborhoods to form privacy-aware communities so that data utility continuously increases as privacy budget increases. In other words, our method can overcome the utility growth bottlenecks of existing approaches. Experiments on real-world datasets demonstrate that our method significantly outperforms state-of-the-art methods across multiple structural metrics while maintaining formal privacy guarantees.

Keywords: Differential Privacy · Graph Data Publishing · Feature-Based Clustering · Community Detection · Privacy-Utility Trade-off

1 Introduction

Graph data publishing facilitates numerous analytical tasks across domains such as social networks, communication systems, and biological networks [4,7,8]. These complex relationships enable community detection, influence analysis, recommendation systems, and scientific discovery [4].

However, graph data often contains private information, making direct publication risky [2,17]. Even without explicit identifiers, sophisticated attacks can exploit graph structure and auxiliary information to compromise privacy. Thus, robust privacy-preserving methods are essential.

T. Zhu et al. (Eds.): KSEM 2025, LNAI 15920, pp. 207–219, 2026.
https://doi.org/10.1007/978-981-95-3052-6_16

Traditional approaches include k-anonymity [2] and edge randomization [10], but these lack formal guarantees and remain vulnerable to auxiliary information attacks. Differential privacy (DP) has emerged as the gold standard, preserving privacy regardless of attacker knowledge.

Existing DP graph methods either add noise directly to statistics or adjacency matrices [11,13], or leverage community structures to balance noise and information preservation [16]. Community-based methods like PrivGraph [16] show promise by treating intra- and inter-community edges differently, reducing overall noise while preserving graph properties.

However, community-based methods suffer from structural misalignment with true communities, introducing systemic error that persists regardless of privacy budget. Consequently, utility gains don't scale with relaxed privacy constraints (increasing ε), contradicting theoretical expectations of monotonic improvement.

We introduce a novel DP graph publishing method using feature-driven community detection. Unlike existing solutions, we leverage local structural features from truncated BFS around nodes, capturing rich information with minimal privacy budget. Applying mechanisms to these features rather than random partitions achieves community structures closely approximating intrinsic graph organization, substantially reducing error propagation and improving utility-privacy trade-offs.

Our method ensures monotonic utility increase with privacy budget, aligning with theoretical expectations. By minimizing structural misalignment, additional budget allocations translate directly to utility improvements, overcoming the plateau effect in existing methods.

Our contributions are:

- **Feature-Driven DP Community Detection:** A novel method leveraging node-centric structural features under DP constraints, achieving accurate partitioning and reducing structural inaccuracies from random initialization.
- **Utility Improvement with Increasing Privacy Budget:** Ensuring consistent utility improvement as privacy budget increases, addressing the plateau limitation in existing community-based methods.
- **Comprehensive Empirical Validation:** Extensive experiments on real-world datasets demonstrating substantial outperformance of state-of-the-art methods across privacy budget levels.

2   Related Work

Graph Anonymization. Early anonymization techniques like (k, l)-groupings [2] and link re-identification protection [17] lack formal guarantees and are vulnerable to auxiliary attacks.

DP Graph Publishing. DP graph methods differ in preserving graph features. Wang and Wu [13] used smooth sensitivity for degree distributions, and Wang et al. [14] focused on spectral properties via eigendecomposition. However, existing methods either limit utility by targeting single properties or introduce excessive noise when preserving multiple features.

Community-aware DP Methods. Community-based DP methods exploit graph structure to improve utility. Yuan et al. [16] introduced PrivGraph for noise reduction. These methods typically use random community initialization causing structural misalignment. Our approach addresses this issue by leveraging feature-based initialization for better community alignment.

3 Preliminaries

Differential Privacy. DP [3] ensures minimal impact of a single record on algorithm outputs. Algorithm A satisfies ϵ-DP if for neighboring datasets D, D' differing by one record, and any output T: $\Pr[A(D) \in T] \le e^\epsilon \cdot \Pr[A(D') \in T]$. Common DP mechanisms include Laplace (adds noise from $\mathrm{Lap}(0, GS_f/\epsilon)$) and Exponential (selects outcomes with probability $\propto \exp(\frac{\epsilon}{2GS_q} q(v, o)))$. Composition properties include sequential (budget sum), parallel (max budget for disjoint subsets), and post-processing (maintains DP).

Graph Differential Privacy. Graph DP [1,6,15] protects edge relationships. Graphs $G = (V, E)$ and $G' = (V', E')$ are edge neighbors if they differ by exactly one edge or vertex. Algorithm A satisfies ε-edge DP if for such graphs: $\Pr[A(G) \in T] \le e^\varepsilon \cdot \Pr[A(G') \in T]$.

Breadth-First Search (BFS). BFS explores nodes layer-by-layer from a starting node, capturing local connectivity.

K-means Clustering. K-means clusters dataset $D = \{x_i\}$ into k groups minimizing total intra-cluster variance: $\frac{1}{N} \sum_{j=1}^{k} \sum_{x_i \in O_j} \|x_i - o_j\|^2$, where o_j is centroid of cluster O_j.

Community Detection. The Louvain method [5] detects communities by optimizing modularity: $Q = \sum_C (\frac{\mathrm{in}_C}{2m} - (\frac{\mathrm{tot}_C}{2m})^2)$, where in_C is intra-community edge weight, tot_C total edge weight incident to community C, and m total edge weight.

4 Method

We present our privacy-preserving graph publishing method under edge-level DP that protects individual edges while preserving essential structural properties.

4.1 Overview

As shown in Fig. 1 and Algorithm 1, our method proceeds in five steps: community initialization, super-node construction, refinement, DP extraction, and graph reconstruction.

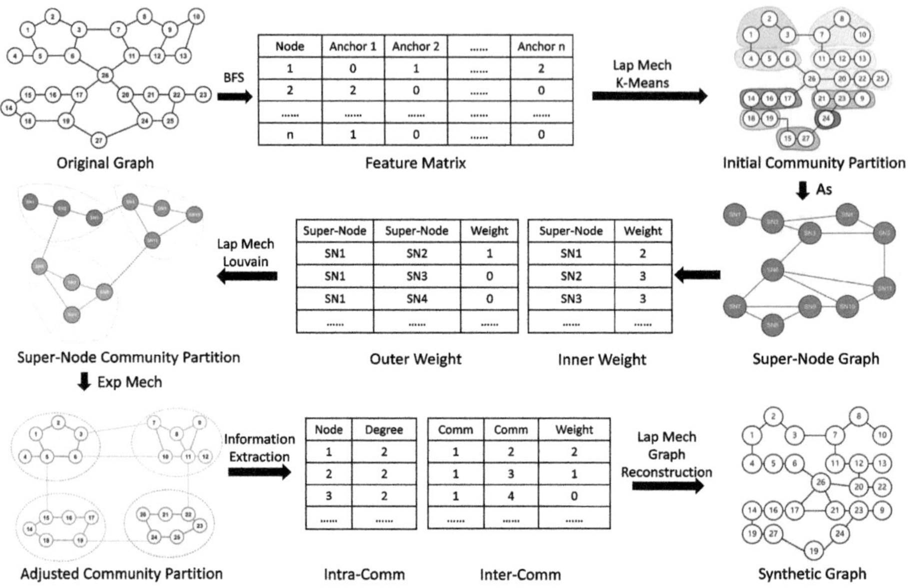

Fig. 1. Overview of our differentially private graph publishing pipeline.

4.2 Method Details

Step 1: Community Initialization via BFS and K-means. Given an undirected graph $G = (V, E)$ with $|V| = n$, we uniformly sample ℓ anchor nodes from V. For each anchor a, we run a BFS restricted to depth $d = 2$. Concretely, for a node v, define $\text{dist}(v, a) = 0$ if $v = a$, 1 if v neighbors a, 2 if v is two hops from a, else ∞.

Stacking each anchor's BFS results forms an $n \times \ell$ feature matrix $\mathbf{F}$. To ensure edge-level DP, we add independent Laplace noise $\text{Lap}(0, 2/\varepsilon_1)$ to each column in $\mathbf{F}$. The factor of 2 in the noise scale accommodates the BFS depth of 2, since removing one edge can alter distances in a local neighborhood. Negative values from the noisy output are clipped to zero. We treat each row of $\mathbf{F}$ as a node embedding and cluster the n nodes into ℓ groups via k-means. Each cluster is then condensed into a single *super-node*, producing an initial coarse partition of G. We capture inter- and intra-cluster connection counts in a super-node adjacency matrix, to which we again add Laplace noise (using ε_1-budget

---

Algorithm 1. Differentially Private Graph Data Publishing

Input: Graph $G = (V, E)$; privacy budget ε; splits $\varepsilon_1, \varepsilon_2, \varepsilon_3, \varepsilon_4$; parameters d, ℓ, k
Output: Sanitized graph $\widehat{G}$

    Step 1: Community Initialization (ε_1)
1: Select ℓ anchor nodes; run BFS to depth d from each
2: Add $\mathrm{Lap}(2/\varepsilon_1)$ noise to distances; form feature matrix $\mathbf{F}$
3: Apply k-means to get super-nodes $\{S_1, \ldots, S_k\}$
    Step 2: Super-Node Graph (ε_2)
4: Build adjacency $\mathbf{W}$ between super-nodes
5: Add $\mathrm{Lap}(1/\varepsilon_2)$ to off-diagonal, $\mathrm{Lap}(2/\varepsilon_2)$ to diagonal
6: Apply Louvain to get partition C_{louvain}
    Step 3: Community Adjustment (ε_3)
7: **for** each node v **do**
8:     Compute modularity gains $\Delta Q_{v \to c}$
9:     Sample new community via $p(c) \propto \exp(\alpha \cdot \Delta Q_{v \to c})$
10: **end for**
    Step 4: Information Extraction (ε_4)
11: Extract inter-community edges with $\mathrm{Lap}(1/\varepsilon_4)$ noise
12: Extract intra-community degrees with $\mathrm{Lap}(2/\varepsilon_4)$ noise
    Step 5: Graph Reconstruction
13: Reconstruct graph from noisy statistics (no additional budget)

---

allocations that distinguish diagonal entries from off-diagonal ones). Finally, we apply a community-detection algorithm (e.g., Louvain) on this noisy super-node matrix to produce our initial partition of the original graph, which serves as the basis for subsequent refinement.

Step 2: Super-Node Graph Construction and Louvain. Following the initial coarse partition from Step 1, suppose we have ℓ super-nodes $\{S_1, \ldots, S_\ell\}$. We now build a smaller, weighted graph $G_{\mathcal{S}} = (\{1, \ldots, \ell\}, E_{\mathcal{S}})$ by forming an $\ell \times \ell$ matrix $\mathbf{W}$, whose entries aggregate edges between (and within) these super-nodes:

$$\mathbf{W}[i, j] = \begin{cases} \sum_{u \in S_i} \sum_{v \in S_j} \mathbf{1}\{(u, v) \in E\}, & i \neq j, \\ \sum_{u, v \in S_i} \mathbf{1}\{(u, v) \in E\}, & i = j. \end{cases}$$

Off-diagonal elements $\mathbf{W}[i, j]$ capture inter-super-node edges, while diagonal elements $\mathbf{W}[i, i]$ record the internal edges within S_i.

To protect edge-level privacy, we separately handle off-diagonal and diagonal entries: *(1) Off-Diagonal:* A single edge modifies exactly one off-diagonal count by at most 1. Thus, each off-diagonal $\mathbf{W}[i, j]$ $(i < j)$ is injected with Laplace noise at scale $\frac{1}{\varepsilon_2}$. We then symmetrize the matrix by copying $\mathbf{W}[i, j]$ to $\mathbf{W}[j, i]$. *(2) Diagonal:* An intra-super-node edge can alter $\mathbf{W}[i, i]$ by up to 2 in an undirected graph, requiring noise at scale $\frac{2}{\varepsilon_2}$. Any negative values after adding noise are clipped to zero. This ensures the final super-node adjacency remains nonnegative, and the total privacy cost for super-node construction is bounded by ε_2.

We treat the noisy matrix $\mathbf{W}$ as the adjacency of $G_{\mathcal{S}}$ and apply Louvain to discover a higher-level community structure. Concretely, Louvain attempts to maximize the modularity $Q = \sum_C \left(\frac{\Sigma_{\text{in}}}{2m} - \left(\frac{\Sigma_{\text{tot}}}{2m} \right)^2 \right)$, where Σ_{in} is the sum of edge weights inside a community C, Σ_{tot} the total edge weight incident to C, and m the sum of all edge weights in $G_{\mathcal{S}}$. After several passes of merging and aggregating super-nodes, Louvain converges to a final set of communities $\{C_1, \ldots, C_{m'}\}$. We then *inherit* these labels back to the original graph by assigning every node in super-node S_i the same label as its parent super-node i. Consequently, each original node receives a refined community label from the differentially private super-node partition.

Step 3: Community Adjustment via Exponential Mechanism. We refine the super-node partition from Step 2 via one (or few) community-adjustment passes. Employing the *exponential mechanism* (EM), nodes probabilistically migrate to better-fitting communities under edge-level DP constraints.

Rationale. Allowing nodes to reconsider community affiliations boosts modularity without overfitting or excessive edge leakage. The EM favors positive modularity gains.

Procedure. Using partition P (Step 2) mapping nodes to communities and budget ε_3 (subdivided if needed): ① *Removal*: Temporarily remove v from c_{old}, reducing current modularity; ② *Candidate Utilities*: For each community c adjacent to v, compute modularity gain $\Delta Q_{v \to c}$; ③ *Exponential Mechanism*: Sample new community c^* with probability $p(c) \propto \exp(\alpha \cdot \Delta Q_{v \to c})$, where α depends on ε_3 and edge contribution sensitivity; ④ *Assignment*: Reassign v to c^*, updating structures. After processing all nodes (1-few iterations), output refined partition P_{refined}.

Privacy Discussion. A single edge alters $\Delta Q_{v \to c}$ by at most a bounded amount (by modularity formula), so EM with scale α enforces ε_3-edge-DP. Repeated passes partition ε_3 via composition, keeping total adjustment budget within ε_3.

Step 4: Information Extraction. After finalizing community assignments, we gather only the *aggregated edge statistics* needed for graph reconstruction, thereby avoiding large-scale noise on the full adjacency matrix. Specifically, we extract:

(1) *Inter-community connections:* For two communities C_i and C_j, let $\mathbf{M}[i,j]$ be the total number of edges connecting nodes in C_i to those in C_j. Storing only the *upper triangular* entries (including the diagonal for intra-community edges), each entry is perturbed with Laplace noise at scale $\frac{1}{\varepsilon_4}$. Negative results are clipped to zero, and the matrix is symmetrized afterward. Since one edge contributes $+1$ to exactly one $\mathbf{M}[i,j]$, the global sensitivity is 1.

(2) *Intra-community degrees:* Within each community C_i, we calculate each node's degree restricted to C_i. An internal edge increments the degree of exactly two nodes, so the sensitivity here is 2. We thus add Laplace noise with scale $\frac{2}{\varepsilon_4}$ for each node's community-internal degree, then clip negatives (and optionally cap large values) to ensure the result is valid. This yields a *noisy* local degree vector for every C_i.

As these two adjacency slices are disjoint, they qualify for *parallel composition* under budget ε_4 (total cost: ε_4). The resulting noisy statistics—post-processed to clip negatives—enable faithful graph reconstruction in the next stage.

Step 5: Graph Reconstruction. Using Step 4's DP statistics, we synthesize the final graph via pure post-processing. Accessing *only* noisy degrees and inter-community edge counts. We reconstruct edges *within* each community C_i using the noisy local degrees: ① *Assign Degrees.* For each node $v \in C_i$, assign its noisy degree $\tilde{d}_v$ and initialize an empty adjacency submatrix $\tilde{A}_{C_i}$. ② *Edge Sampling.* Stochastically connect pairs (u, w) in C_i with probability based on $\hat{d}_u$ and $\hat{d}_w$ (e.g., via thresholding or a Chung–Lu-like method), ensuring the total intra-edges align with $\sum_{v \in C_i} \hat{d}_v / 2$ (up to rounding). ③ *Symmetry and Validation.* Symmetrize $\tilde{A}_{C_i}$ for an undirected subgraph, clipping invalid values to maintain a legal degree sequence.

We link distinct communities (C_i, C_j) using the noisy count $\hat{E}_{ij}$: ① *Random Endpoint Selection.* If $\hat{E}_{ij} > 0$, sample $\hat{E}_{ij}$ node pairs (u, w) where $u \in C_i$, $w \in C_j$. ② *Edge Placement.* Set $\tilde{A}[u, w] = \tilde{A}[w, u] = 1$ for each pair. ③ *No Overlaps.* Cap $\hat{E}_{ij}$ at the maximum feasible cross-community edges to avoid duplicates or self-loops if necessary.

Combining intra- and inter-community edges forms the complete synthetic adjacency matrix $\tilde{A}$. As this relies solely on differentially private summaries, no further privacy budget is consumed. The resulting graph preserves the approximate structure (communities, degrees, inter-community links) inferred in Steps 1–4, maintaining topological features while rigorously safeguarding edge privacy.

4.3   Privacy Analysis

We now show that the entire method achieves ε-Edge Differential Privacy, where $\varepsilon = \varepsilon_1 + \varepsilon_2 + \varepsilon_3 + \varepsilon_4$. Each step consumes its own privacy budget in a sequential manner; within each step, any necessary perturbations are applied on disjoint (parallel) subsets of the adjacency data when possible. We leverage the Laplace and Exponential Mechanisms along with standard composition properties of DP.

Theorem 1 (Overall ε-Edge Differential Privacy). *The proposed method satisfies edge-level DP with total budget $\varepsilon = \varepsilon_1 + \varepsilon_2 + \varepsilon_3 + \varepsilon_4$.*

Proof. We argue that each step is individually ε_i-Edge DP, then rely on the sequential composition property to conclude the overall budget is ε.

Step 1 (ε_1-Edge DP). In community initialization, for each anchor node we gather truncated BFS distances (up to depth 2). Because a single edge can affect the BFS outcome for at most one anchor's distance column by a bounded amount (e.g., by 2), adding Laplace noise at scale proportional to $2/\varepsilon_1$ suffices to protect that column. By parallel composition across anchors, the total cost remains ε_1. The subsequent clustering is post-processing on these noisy features and does not incur additional privacy loss.

Step 2 (ε_2-Edge DP). After forming super-nodes and constructing the $\ell \times \ell$ adjacency matrix $\mathbf{W}$, we add Laplace noise of scale $1/\varepsilon_2$ to each off-diagonal entry and $2/\varepsilon_2$ to diagonal entries, matching the edge-level sensitivities (1 for an inter-super-node edge, 2 for an intra-super-node edge). Hence, any single edge can alter at most one $\mathbf{W}[i,j]$ by an integer amount ≤ 2. The Louvain-based refinement on the perturbed matrix is again post-processing. Thus, Step 2 satisfies ε_2-Edge DP.

Step 3 (ε_3-Edge DP). In the community adjustment phase, nodes are reassigned using the exponential mechanism. Changing a single edge can affect only one node's modularity-based score by a bounded amount when deciding which community yields the best gain. Therefore, running the exponential mechanism with budget ε_3 ensures ε_3-Edge DP for this step, regardless of the order in which nodes are updated. Iterating through all nodes sequentially still uses up to ε_3 in total, not more.

Step 4 (ε_4-Edge DP). Information extraction collects two types of aggregated statistics: ① Inter-community edge counts ($\mathbf{M}[i,j]$), where each edge can contribute up to 1, ② Intra-community degrees for each node, where each edge can increase two nodes' degrees by 1 each (sensitivity 2). These two statistics cover *disjoint* subsets of the adjacency matrix (i.e., off-diagonal vs. within-community edges), so by parallel composition they jointly consume only ε_4. Adding Laplace noise at scales $1/\varepsilon_4$ and $2/\varepsilon_4$ protects these counts under edge-level DP.

Step 5 (No Additional Privacy Cost). The final graph reconstruction is a post-processing procedure that does not access any raw adjacency data, only the noisy outputs of Step 4. Hence, there is no further privacy consumption beyond ε_4.

Overall Composition. Because the above four steps are applied in sequence, their budgets sum up to $\varepsilon = \varepsilon_1 + \varepsilon_2 + \varepsilon_3 + \varepsilon_4$. By the *sequential composition* property of DP, the entire algorithm is thus ε-Edge DP.

5   Experiments

We evaluate our method against four state-of-the-art baselines through extensive experiments.

5.1   Experimental Setup

All experiments were implemented in Python, varying privacy budget ε over predefined ranges with 30 repetitions for statistical significance.

Datasets. We use three benchmark datasets: Chameleon (2,277 nodes, 31,421 edges, density 0.01213; web page network) [12], Facebook (4,039 nodes, 88,234 edges, density 0.01082; social network) [9], and CA-HepPh (12,008 nodes, 118,521 edges, density 0.00164; scientific collaboration) [8].

Evaluation Metrics. We evaluate both global structure and node-level properties using six metrics:

Normalized Mutual Information (NMI) measures structural similarity between original and published graphs: $\mathrm{NMI}(C_1, C_2) = \frac{2 \cdot I(C_1, C_2)}{H(C_1) + H(C_2)}$, where $I(C_1, C_2)$ is mutual information between community partitions.

Modularity Relative Error (Mod Rel) evaluates community structure preservation: $\mathrm{Mod\ Rel} = \frac{|Q_{\mathrm{orig}} - Q_{\mathrm{pub}}|}{Q_{\mathrm{orig}}}$, where Q denotes modularity values.

Eigenvector Centrality Overlap (EVC Overlap) measures preservation of important nodes: $\mathrm{EVC\ Overlap} = \frac{|V_k^{\mathrm{orig}} \cap V_k^{\mathrm{pub}}|}{|V_k^{\mathrm{orig}}|}$, where V_k represents top-k nodes by eigenvector centrality.

Eigenvector Centrality MAE (EVC MAE) quantifies node importance accuracy: $\mathrm{EVC\ MAE} = \frac{1}{n} \sum_{i=1}^{n} |c_i^{\mathrm{orig}} - c_i^{\mathrm{pub}}|$, where c_i are normalized centrality values.

Degree Distribution KL Divergence (Deg KL) measures degree distribution difference: $\mathrm{Deg\ KL} = \sum_d P_{\mathrm{orig}}(d) \log \frac{P_{\mathrm{orig}}(d)}{P_{\mathrm{pub}}(d)}$.

Clustering Coefficient Relative Error (CC Rel) evaluates local density preservation: $\mathrm{CC\ Rel} = \frac{|C_{\mathrm{orig}} - C_{\mathrm{pub}}|}{C_{\mathrm{orig}}}$, where C denotes average clustering coefficients.

Comparison Methods. We compare with four state-of-the-art baselines: **PrivGraph** [16], which leverages community information by differentially privately partitioning nodes into communities and perturbing intra- and inter-community connections separately; **TmF** [11], which adds Laplace noise to the adjacency matrix and selects the top-m noisy entries as edges, where m equals the original edge count; **DER** [1], which relabels nodes to concentrate edges in specific matrix regions, uses quadtree for density estimation, and reconstructs from perturbed densities; and **PrivHRG** [15], which encodes graphs as hierarchical random graphs and applies DP to the hierarchical representation.All baselines are implemented following their original publications using identical privacy parameters for fair comparison.

5.2   Results and Analysis

We present and analyze the experimental results of our differentially private graph data publishing method. We compare our method with baselines on three

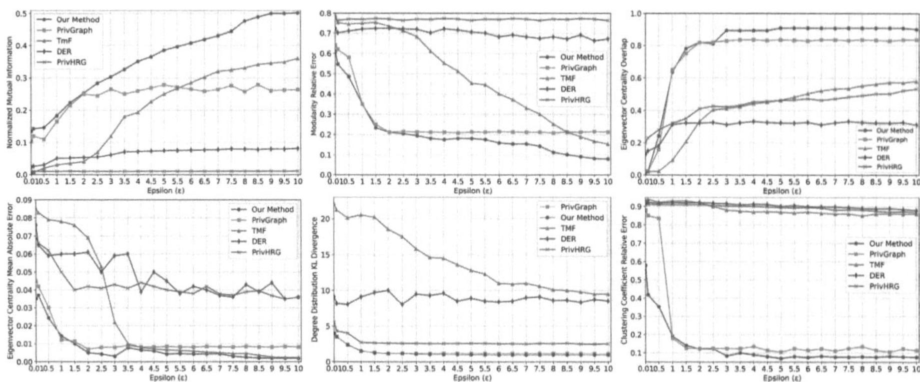

Fig. 2. Performance comparison on **Chameleon** dataset.

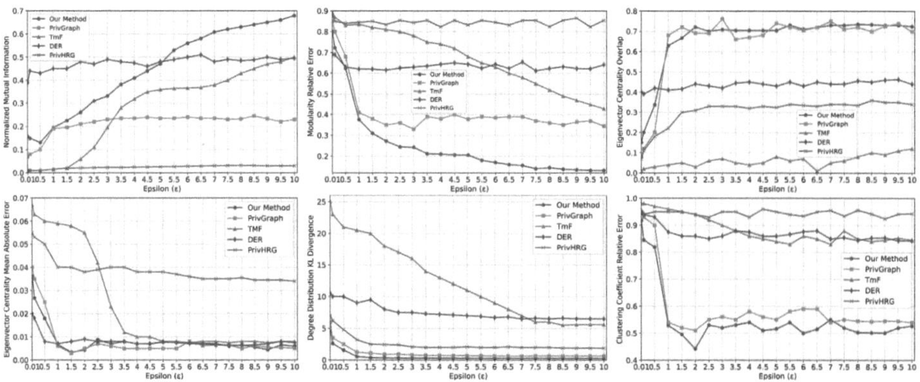

Fig. 3. Performance comparison on **Facebook** dataset.

datasets (Chameleon, Facebook, CA-HepPh) using the six structural preservation metrics described earlier.

As illustrated in Figs. 2, 3 and 4, our method consistently outperforms the baseline methods across most metrics and privacy budgets. The performance improvements can be attributed to our innovative community initialization method, which combines BFS with K-means clustering to generate more meaningful feature matrices and optimized initial community partitions.

Chameleon Dataset Analysis. On the Chameleon dataset, our method demonstrates significant performance advantages across various privacy budgets. For the NMI metric, the value gradually increases as ε grows. At lower ε values, our performance is comparable to PrivGraph but consistently outperforms other methods. When ε exceeds 5, our method shows more than 40% improvement over the best baseline method. Regarding Modularity Relative Error, our method outperforms all other methods across all privacy budgets, with errors

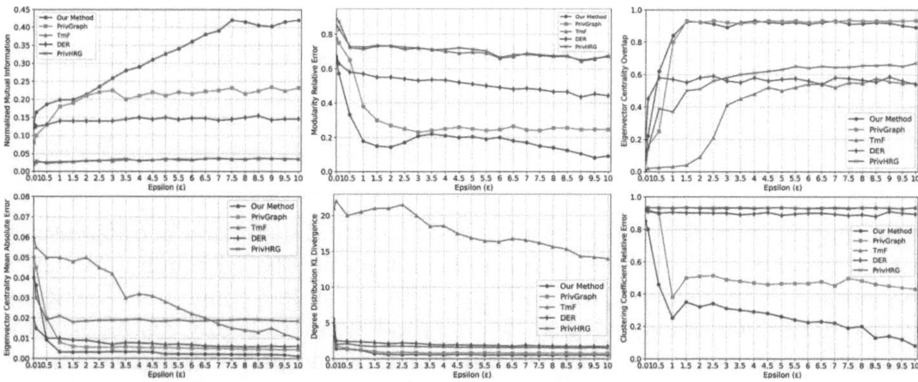

Fig. 4. Performance comparison on **CA-HepPh** dataset.

reduced by over 10% compared to the best-performing baseline when $\varepsilon > 5$. For the EVC Overlap metric, performance steadily improves as ε increases, with our method surpassing the second-best method by approximately 11% when $\varepsilon > 3$. In terms of Clustering Coefficient Relative Error, our method reduces the error by about 40% compared to the second-best performing method when $\varepsilon < 1$.

Facebook Dataset Analysis. For the Facebook dataset, our method demonstrates consistent superiority across key metrics. The NMI values of our method remain consistently higher than all baseline methods throughout the entire privacy budget range. Particularly when $\varepsilon > 5$, our method achieves more than 30% improvement in NMI compared to the second-best performing method. For Modularity Relative Error, we observe a substantial advantage when $\varepsilon > 6$, where our method reduces the error by over 20% compared to the next best baseline. Regarding Eigenvector Centrality Overlap (EVC Overlap), our method shows approximately 10% enhancement over competing methods when $\varepsilon > 3$.

CA-HepPh Dataset Analysis. The CA-HepPh dataset results further confirm the effectiveness of our method. For the NMI metric, our method consistently outperforms all baseline methods across the entire privacy budget range, with particularly significant improvements observed when $\varepsilon > 3$ compared to the second-best performing method. Regarding Modularity Relative Error, our method demonstrates superior performance in both low and high privacy budget regimes: when ε ranges from 0.01 to 2, our method reduces the error by over 20% compared to the second-best baseline, and continues to show significant advantages when $\varepsilon > 6$. For Clustering Coefficient Relative Error, we achieve approximately 40% improvement over the next best method, indicating substantially better preservation of local network structures.

Overall, our differentially private graph data publishing method demonstrates robust performance across diverse graph datasets while ensuring rigorous edge-level DP guarantees. These consistent advantages validate the effectiveness of our feature-based community initialization and multi-phase graph reconstruction strategy.

6 Conclusion

In this paper, we reduce excessive noise and structural distortion in differentially private graph data publishing by introducing a feature-based community detection method. Unlike existing methods that rely on random community partitioning and introduce structural bias, our method extracts highly distinguishable structural features from local node neighborhoods and performs feature clustering under DP constraints, resulting in initial partitions more closely aligned with actual communities. This initial partition significantly reduces the sensitivity of edge and community-level information during subsequent phased noise injection and structural reconstruction, ultimately better preserving the overall structure and important properties of the graph while ensuring edge-level DP.

Experimental results demonstrate that across multiple real-world datasets, compared to traditional random community partitioning and direct adjacency matrix perturbation methods, our method shows significant improvements in degree distribution, clustering coefficient, node centrality, and community quality metrics, with notably more stable structural fidelity in medium to high privacy budget ranges. More importantly, as the privacy budget ε increases, our method consistently achieves better data utility, avoiding the limitation seen in some existing methods where "increasing budget fails to further improve performance."

Acknowledgments. This work was supported by the China Postdoctoral Science Foundation (2024M752210), MOE Liberal Arts and Social Sciences Foundation (24XJCZH004), Key R&D Program of Sichuan Province (2023YFG0115, 2023YFG0112), Sichuan Provincial Industrial Development Fund (2023JB06), and the Sichuan University-Zigong Cooperative Program (2022CDZG-6).

References

1. Chen, R., Fung, B.C., Yu, P.S., Desai, B.C.: Correlated network data publication via differential privacy. VLDB J. **23**, 653–676 (2014)
2. Cormode, G., Srivastava, D., Yu, T., Zhang, Q.: Anonymizing bipartite graph data using safe groupings. Proc. VLDB Endow. **1**(1), 833–844 (2008)
3. Dwork, C., McSherry, F., Nissim, K., Smith, A.: Calibrating noise to sensitivity in private data analysis. In: Halevi, S., Rabin, T. (eds.) TCC 2006. LNCS, vol. 3876, pp. 265–284. Springer, Heidelberg (2006). https://doi.org/10.1007/11681878_14
4. Girvan, M., Newman, M.E.: Community structure in social and biological networks. Proc. Natl. Acad. Sci. **99**(12), 7821–7826 (2002)
5. Guillaume, L.: Fast unfolding of communities in large networks. J. Stat. Mech. Theory Exp. **10**, P1008 (2008)

6. Ji, S., Mittal, P., Beyah, R.: Graph data anonymization, de-anonymization attacks, and de-anonymizability quantification: a survey. IEEE Commun. Surv. Tutor. **19**(2), 1305–1326 (2016)
7. Leskovec, J., Huttenlocher, D., Kleinberg, J.: Signed networks in social media. In: Proceedings of the SIGCHI Conference on Human Factors in Computing Systems, pp. 1361–1370 (2010)
8. Leskovec, J., Kleinberg, J., Faloutsos, C.: Graph evolution: densification and shrinking diameters. ACM Trans. Knowl. Disc. Data (TKDD) **1**(1), 2–es (2007)
9. Leskovec, J., Mcauley, J.: Learning to discover social circles in ego networks. Adv. Neural Inf. Process. Syst. **25** (2012)
10. Li, X., Miao, M., Liu, H., Ma, J., Li, K.C.: An incentive mechanism for k-anonymity in lbs privacy protection based on credit mechanism. Soft. Comput. **21**, 3907–3917 (2017)
11. Nguyen, H.H., Imine, A., Rusinowitch, M.: Differentially private publication of social graphs at linear cost. In: Proceedings of the 2015 IEEE/ACM International Conference on Advances in Social Networks Analysis and Mining 2015, pp. 596–599 (2015)
12. Rozemberczki, B., Allen, C., Sarkar, R.: Multi-scale attributed node embedding. J. Complex Netw. **9**(2), cnab014 (2021)
13. Wang, Y., Wu, X.: Preserving differential privacy in degree-correlation based graph generation. Trans. Data Priv. **6**(2), 127 (2013)
14. Wang, Y., Wu, X., Wu, L.: Differential privacy preserving spectral graph analysis. In: Pei, J., Tseng, V.S., Cao, L., Motoda, H., Xu, G. (eds.) PAKDD 2013. LNCS (LNAI), vol. 7819, pp. 329–340. Springer, Heidelberg (2013). https://doi.org/10. 1007/978-3-642-37456-2_28
15. Xiao, Q., Chen, R., Tan, K.L.: Differentially private network data release via structural inference. In: Proceedings of the 20th ACM SIGKDD International Conference on Knowledge Discovery and Data Mining, pp. 911–920 (2014)
16. Yuan, Q., Zhang, Z., Du, L., Chen, M., Cheng, P., Sun, M.: {PrivGraph}: differentially private graph data publication by exploiting community information. In: 32nd USENIX Security Symposium (USENIX Security 23), pp. 3241–3258 (2023)
17. Zheleva, E., Getoor, L.: Preserving the privacy of sensitive relationships in graph data. In: Bonchi, F., Ferrari, E., Malin, B., Saygin, Y. (eds.) PInKDD 2007. LNCS, vol. 4890, pp. 153–171. Springer, Heidelberg (2008). https://doi.org/10.1007/978-3-540-78478-4_9

Solving the Problem of Task Offloading in Heterogeneous Edge Computing Environments Using Deep Q-Networks and Attention Mechanisms

Huifeng Liu[1,2], Jintao Li[1,2], Hu Zhang[1,2(✉)], Hongjing Yao[3(✉)], Lijuan Xu[1,2], Minghao Shao[1,2], and Hongyu Xu[1,2]

[1] Key Laboratory of Computing Power Network and Information Security, Ministry of Education, Shandong Computer Science Center (National Supercomputer Center in Jinan), Qilu University of Technology (Shandong Academy of Sciences), Jinan, China
[2] Shandong Provincial Key Laboratory of Computing Power Internet and Service Computing, Shandong Fundamental Research Center for Computer Science, Jinan, China
zhanghu@sdas.org
[3] China Railway Jinan Group Co Ltd., Jinan, China
401665874@qq.com

Abstract. In edge computing, offloading tasks from resource-limited devices to nearby edge servers reduces latency and improves efficiency. However, within this environment, performing efficient and energy-saving task offloading remains a challenge due to limited device resources, unstable networks, and diverse demands. In existing research, traditional methods encounter scalability and adaptability issues in dynamic Internet of Things (IoT) environments. Artificial intelligence approaches have shown good adaptive capabilities. However, due to the limited computational and storage resources of edge devices, the complexity of models that can be deployed is restricted. To address these challenges, this paper proposes the DPAQN algorithm, which utilizes Deep Q-Networks (DQN) and incorporates the Progressive Rectangular Window Attention Mechanism (PRWA), aiming to achieve more efficient and energy-saving task offloading strategies. To test the effectiveness of DPAQN, we compare it with five algorithms in terms of multi-objective optimization (TEH). The results indicate that under varying numbers of users and task configurations, DPAQN's overall TEH performance is on average 20.71%–30.39% better than the other five algorithms. Moreover, it works well across different datasets, demonstrating considerable generalization capabilities.

Keywords: Edge Computing · Task Offloading · Attention Mechanism · Deep Q-Networks · Multi-Objective Optimization

1   Introduction

In recent years, edge computing has rapidly emerged as a new computing paradigm. Its core advantage lies in moving data processing and computational tasks to the network edge, closer to end-user devices [1]. This architecture significantly reduces latency and energy consumption during task computation, which is crucial for applications requiring immediate responses. It enables efficient handling of resource-intensive and time-sensitive tasks [2]. Additionally, edge computing helps alleviate the burden on data centers, reduces network congestion, and enhances data security and privacy protection by processing data locally [3]. This setup not only accelerates system response times but also provides a solid foundation for building smarter and more efficient Internet of Things (IoT) applications [4]. Consequently, edge computing shows great potential in task offloading, making it a promising trend for future computing technologies [5].

With the rapid development of edge computing technology, task offloading is becoming a key technique in edge computing. Offloading tasks from IoT terminals to the edge environment can effectively address deficiencies in computational performance and energy efficiency. However, while offloading tasks to the edge environment brings convenience, it also poses a series of challenges:1) How to flexibly schedule the heterogeneous resources of edge servers to accommodate various tasks. 2) How to maintain the flexibility of task offloading strategies amidst network fluctuations and changing user demands to sustain system stability. 3) How to balance performance enhancement with energy savings for sustainable task offloading.

Considering the aforementioned issues, in order to more practically address the problem of task offloading, the contributions of this paper are as follows:

1. Considering the heterogeneity of edge servers and the diversity of users, a task offloading strategy based on the Directed Acyclic Graph (DAG) model is proposed to optimize task offloading in the edge computing environment.
2. To our knowledge, this is the first application of the Progressive Rectangular Window Attention Mechanism (PRWA) to edge computing task offloading, enhancing decision quality. Integrating it with DQN to form the DPAQN algorithm is expected to make new contributions to optimizing task offloading in edge computing environments.
3. The DPAQN algorithm considers task completion time, energy consumption, and throughput, aiming to develop efficient and energy-saving offloading solutions. Comparisons with five other algorithms show that DPAQN enhances the overall performance of task offloading.

The rest of this paper is organized as follows: Related work is reviewed in Sect. 2. Section 3 analyzes the task offloading problem in the edge computing environment. Section 4 discusses the DPAQN algorithm introduced in this paper. Section 5 analyzes the experimental results, and Sect. 6 concludes our work.

2   Related Work

With the rise of edge computing, many scholars have conducted extensive and in-depth research on task offloading in edge computing environments. The research primarily involves two categories of methods: traditional and AI approaches [6].

Traditional Methods . Peng et al. [7] proposed an end-edge-cloud collaborative intelligent computation offloading and resource allocation method (EECCT) for optimizing computation offloading and resource allocation in industrial Internet of Things (IIoT). Nguyen et al. [8] presented a backscatter-assisted orthogonal frequency division multiple access (OFDMA) offloading model and a block coordinate descent (BCD) algorithm to optimize energy and resource allocation for IoT task offloading. Wu et al. [9] introduced an edge-cloud collaborative computing offloading model utilizing an enhanced Particle Swarm Optimization (PSO) algorithm. This model aims to optimize both the latency and energy consumption of mobile devices. Zhang et al. [10] proposed a new task scheduling scheme (GA-EC) based on genetic algorithms for the efficient scheduling of resource-intensive tasks in edge computing environments.

AI Methods . Li et al. [11] proposed models based on Deep Reinforcement Learning (DRL) that take the sum of all delays and energy consumption as the total optimization goal, effectively reducing costs. Xiao et al. [12] proposed a reinforcement learning-based scheme for task offloading in edge computing to optimize performance against jamming and interference by selecting edge devices, transmit power, and offloading rates. Wang et al. [13] proposed an algorithm based on meta-reinforcement learning (MRL) to solve the task offloading problem, which can quickly adapt to new environments with few samples and effectively reduce task latency. Liu et al. [14] proposed a multi-workflow scheduling method based on DQN that can handle the fluctuation of edge service performance over time. Sheng et al. [15] proposed a DRL-based IoT edge computing task scheduling method, showing excellent performance in multiple evaluation metrics. Heidari et al. [16] combined Double Q-learning and Deep Post-Decision State (PDS) learning to propose a novel learning method named D2DPO3 for dynamic computation offloading in IoT edge computing.

Traditional methods are effective for rapid deployment and low complexity due to their simplicity, but they are not well-suited to the dynamics of multi-user and resource-constrained environments. In contrast, AI-based approaches offer real-time decision support in complex and resource-limited scenarios through good adaptability and predictive capabilities, effectively processing high-dimensional data to optimize task offloading. However, AI methods also face challenges in edge computing due to the limited device resources that restrict model complexity, as well as the high demands for robustness and real-time performance caused by network instability and frequent device changes.

We present DPAQN, an AI-based algorithm designed with awareness of resource constraints and network instability in edge environments. It considers practical task offloading scenarios and is experimentally validated.

3   Problem Analysis

3.1   System Model

In the edge computing environment, task offloading is a key optimization issue, involving task allocation between terminal devices and edge servers. Our aim is to achieve efficient and energy-saving task offloading while considering the heterogeneity of edge servers and the diversity of users. The heterogeneity of edge servers is reflected in the varying computing resources, processing speeds, and task offloading requirements, leading to diverse task execution and resource allocation. Additionally, the number of tasks, offloading time, and energy consumption vary across user devices. However, most current research on task offloading methods has overlooked these two points [17].

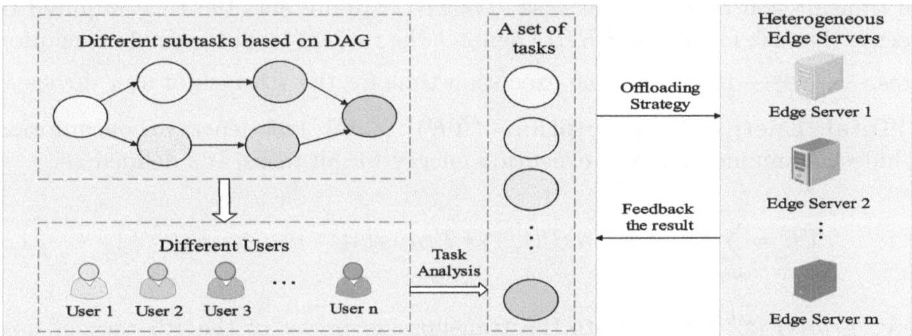

Fig. 1. Overall architecture of task offloading in edge computing environment.

Figure 1 illustrates the architecture of task offloading in the edge computing environment, including various pending subtasks, various user devices, and heterogeneous edge servers. The relationships between subtasks can be represented by a DAG [18], where nodes are tasks and edges show dependencies between subtasks. In the DAG, subtasks without dependency relationships can be executed in parallel, while those with dependencies must be executed sequentially. During the task execution process, subtasks can be dynamically scheduled according to the topology of the DAG to adapt to changes in resources and task execution conditions. Therefore, before user devices send task requests, a detailed analysis of the tasks is conducted through an analyzer, including assessing resource requirements and parsing dependency relationships. Then, based on a predefined offloading strategy, these subtasks are allocated to heterogeneous edge servers, which receive and process tasks based on their characteristics and current status. Finally, the execution results are fed back to the user devices via a feedback mechanism, ensuring accurate and timely data transmission.

3.2 Optimization Problem Statement

Based on the model introduction, the tasks pending for users, represented by the DAG, are offloaded to edge servers with the goal of comprehensively optimizing three metrics: task completion time, energy consumption, and throughput. Below is the formulation of the optimization problem.

(1)Total Task Completion Time (TT). The total completion time of a task includes the transmission time and execution time for all tasks involved. It can be defined as:

$$TT = \sum_{k=1}^{n} \sum_{i=1}^{l} \left(\frac{Data(t_i^{(k)})}{Width(t_i^{(k)})} + \frac{Tlocal(t_i^{(k)})}{RHO} \right) \tag{1}$$

In which, n is the number of users, and l is the number of subtasks for each user. Where $Data(t_i^{(k)})$ is the data size of the ith task for user device k, and $Width(t_i^{(k)})$ denotes the bandwidth allocated to that task. $\frac{Data(t_i^{(k)})}{Width(t_i^{(k)})}$ represents the transmission time for that task. $Tlocal(t_i^{(k)})$ represents the time required to execute the task locally, and RHO denotes the ratio of local to remote execution rates. $\frac{Tlocal(t_i^{(k)})}{RHO}$ represents the execution time for the ith task of user device k.

(2)Total Energy Consumption (TE). Total task energy consumption includes communication and execution energy for all tasks. It's defined as:

$$TE = \sum_{k=1}^{n} \sum_{i=1}^{l} \left(TransP(t_i^{(k)}) * TransT(t_i^{(k)}) + RunE(t_i^{(k)}) \right) \tag{2}$$

Here, $TransP(t_i^{(k)})$ represents the transmission power of the ith task of user device k, and $TransT(t_i^{(k)})$ denotes the communication time of that task. The product of $TransP(t_i^{(k)})$ and $TransT(t_i^{(k)})$ represents the communication energy consumption of the ith task of user device k, namely $CommE(t_i^{(k)})$. $RunE(t_i^{(k)})$ indicates the operational energy consumption of the ith task of user device k, which is predefined based on user settings and task characteristics.

(3) Total Throughput (TH). Here, throughput refers to the number of tasks that the system successfully processes within a given time period. We define the total throughput as TH.

(4)Optimization Objective (TEH). To convert the multi-objective optimization problem into a single-objective optimization problem, the Weighted Sum Method (WSM) is employed. This method normalizes the values of three objectives and combines them into a single goal with weights w_1, w_2, w_3. These weights, where $0 \leq w_i \leq 1$ for $i = 1, 2, 3$ and $w_1 + w_2 + w_3 = 1$, reflect the relative importance of each objective. The total optimization objective function is represented as:

$$\min TEH = w_1 * ||TT|| + w_2 * ||TE|| - w_3 * ||TH|| \tag{3}$$

Here,

$$||TT|| = \frac{TT}{\max(TT_i^{(k)}) * \text{FinishTaskN}} \tag{4}$$

Here, $max(TT_i^{(k)})$ represents the maximum completion time of all finished tasks, and $FinishTaskN$ denotes the number of completed tasks. The calculation method for $||TE||$ and $||TH||$ is analogous. Here, we assign the values of w_1, w_2, w_3 to be 0.25, 0.5, and 0.25, respectively, with the aim of focusing on optimizing the energy consumption of task offloading, while also enhancing the completion time and throughput of the offloaded tasks, striving to establish an energy-efficient and efficient offloading model.

4   Offloading Method

To optimize the aforementioned TEH metrics and achieve more energy-efficient task offloading in edge computing environments, we propose a DPAQN algorithm that combines PRWA with DQN. The foundational framework of the DPAQN algorithm is based on modeling the aforementioned problem as a Markov Decision Process (MDP) to form a DQN-based task offloading algorithm, which then integrates PRWA.

4.1   Task Offloading Based on DQN

In edge computing, task offloading involves migrating computational tasks from user devices to edge servers or nodes for execution. This decision-making process can be modeled as a Markov Decision Process (MDP) represented by a quintuple $\langle s, a, r, p, \gamma \rangle$: s denotes the state space describing the environment's condition. a represents the action space, containing all actions that can be chosen in the current state. r is the immediate reward, reflecting the action's quality based on completion time, energy consumption, and throughput, as shown in Eq. (5). p is the state transition probability that describes the probability of transitioning from one state to another. In task offloading, it involves the probability of tasks transitioning between different offloading decisions. The discount factor γ reflects the significance of immediate and future rewards, ranging from 0 to 1, where 0 indicates that only immediate rewards are considered, and 1 means that long-term rewards are considered equally important as immediate rewards.

$$r = \frac{Throughput}{(TransT(t_i^{(k)}) + RunT(t_i^{(k)})) \times (CommE(t_i^{(k)}) + RunE(t_i^{(k)}))} \tag{5}$$

The process flowchart for task offloading based on DQN is shown in Fig. 2. First, initialize the edge computing environment, DQN parameters, and state s (As shown in Fig. 2(①), which include task characteristics and the status of edge servers. The current state s is used as input, and the action network evaluates the Q-values for all possible actions, selecting the action a with the highest Q-value to be executed (As indicated in Fig. 2 (②). The action a interacts with

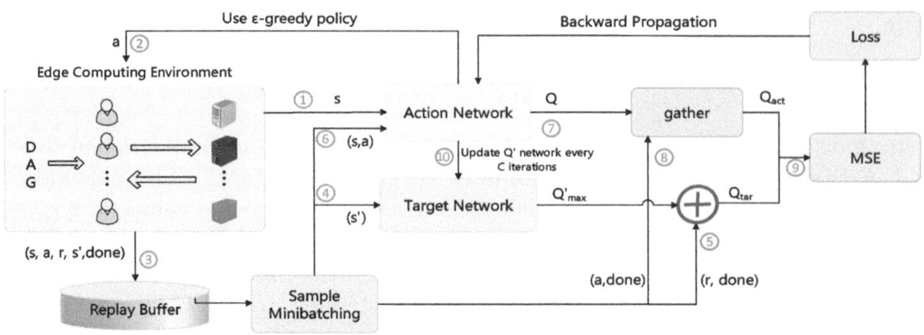

Fig. 2. Flowchart for task offloading based on DQN.

the environment, observes the reward r, and obtains the next state s' and the iteration termination flag *done*. The s, a, r, s', and *done* are then stored in the experience replay buffer (As indicated in Fig. 2 (③) for subsequent learning. A small batch of data is randomly sampled from the experience replay for training.

Taking s' as the input for the target network Q' (As shown in Fig. 2 (④)), calculate the future values $Q'_{\max}$, and then combine them with r and *done* (As indicated in Fig. 2 (⑤) to calculate Q_{tar}. The specific algorithm is provided in Eq. (6), where the value of *done* is either 0 or 1. The action network receives the states s and actions a from the minibatch sampling (As shown in Fig. 2 (⑥), and then the Q-values from the action network (As indicated in Fig. 2 (⑦) are combined with the actions a and *done* from the minibatch sampling (As shown in Fig. 2 (⑧) to obtain the values of Q_{act}. Then, the Mean Squared Error (MSE) loss function is used to calculate the loss between Q_{tar} and Q_{act} (As indicated in Fig. 2(⑨), with the specific algorithm detailed in Eq. (7). Based on the obtained loss, the parameters of the action network are updated through backpropagation, and the parameters of the Q-network are copied to the Q' network every C steps (As shown in Fig. 2 (⑩) to stabilize the training process. Next, it is determined whether the termination condition is met; if the condition is met, the process ends; if not, return to the steps after the initial state and continue execution.

$$Q_{\mathrm{tar}} = r + (1 - \mathrm{done}) * \gamma * Q'_{\max} \tag{6}$$

$$\mathrm{Loss} = \frac{1}{m} \sum_{i=1}^{m} (Q_{\mathrm{tar}} - Q_{\mathrm{act}})^2 \tag{7}$$

4.2 Task Offloading Based on DPAQN

PRWA is a method to boost model performance in deep learning and reinforcement learning. It lets the model focus on different parts of the input when dealing with sequential data. Unlike traditional global attention, PRWA restricts attention to subsets of the input sequence. Thus PRWA can significantly reduce computational load, which is important in resource-constrained environments.

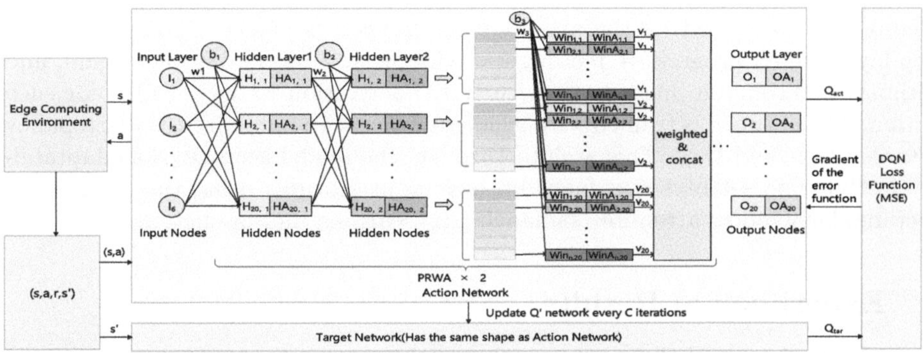

Fig. 3. The overall architecture of the DPAQN model.

The overall structure of the proposed DPAQN algorithm is shown in Fig. 3. PRWA plays its role within the action network and target network of DQN. Given that the overall architecture of DQN has been introduced in Sect. 4.1, we will now detail the aspects related to the incorporation of PRWA. The entire network architecture consists of several neural network layers. The input layer of the network receives feature vectors, processes them through linear transformation and ReLU activation function in the first hidden layer, and passes the output to the second hidden layer. After that, the network introduces the progressive rectangular window attention mechanism, which divides the outputs from the hidden layer into multiple windows and performs weighted sums of features within each window to highlight significant features. The detail of the PRWA is shown in Algorithm 1. This process not only effectively captures local features but also, through progressively processing windows at different positions, enables the model to better adapt to multi-scale feature extraction.

Algorithm 1. Progressive Rectangular Window Attention Mechanism

---

Require: bs: batch_size, len: sequence length, s: window_size, f_dim: feature dimension, $input\_features(bs, len, f\_dim)$: input features

1: Initialize $weighted\_features \leftarrow zeros(b\_s, len, f\_dim)$
2: **for** i from 0 to $len - s$ **do**
3:   $window\_features \leftarrow input\_features[:, i : i + s, :]$
4:   $linear\_features \leftarrow linear\_transform(window\_features)$
5:   $activated\_features \leftarrow \tanh(linear\_features)$
6:   $learnable\_vector \leftarrow initialize\_vector(feature\_dim)$
7:   $dot\_product \leftarrow dot(activated\_features, learnable\_vector)$
8:   $attention\_weights \leftarrow softmax(dot\_product)$
9:   $weighted\_window\_features \leftarrow activated\_features \odot attention\_weights$
10:   $weighted\_features[:, i : i + s, :] \leftarrow weighted\_features[:, i : i + s, :] + weighted\_window\_features$
11: **end for**
12: **return** $weighted\_features$

The output processed by the attention mechanism is passed through two hidden layers and a progressive rectangular window attention layer once again, and ultimately through a linear layer with ReLU activation to output Q_{act} for each action. The network is trained with gradient descent to minimize the discrepancy between Q_{act} and Q_{tar}. This architecture lets the model keep DQN's adaptability in dynamic settings and focus on key input features using the progressive rectangular window attention, enhancing its learning and prediction.

5   Experimental Results

5.1   Experimental Setup

In the experiment, we constructed a dynamic simulation environment for edge computing to study the offloading decisions for user tasks on heterogeneous edge servers. The dataset [19] used is based on the real measurement data of offloaded image recognition computations, while also considering the impact of changes in the network and other system environments in real scenarios on task execution and communication time. Simulation data were generated by adding noise. The environment was initialized with a certain number of users, each of whom was assigned tasks with different attributes, including data transmission size, estimated running time, energy consumption, and CPU resource requirements. Considering that in common scenarios such as industrial automation or enterprise environments, an edge server typically serves a relatively small number of users, we tested eight cases with 20 to 90 users. Specific parameters are detailed in Table 1.   We evaluated the DPAQN algorithm's performance using average

Table 1. Experimental configuration parameters.

Parameters	Description	Value
m	Number of edge servers	4
n	Number of users	20, 30, 40, 50,60,70,80,90
tl	Number of subtasks	1000, 1500, 2000, 2500,3000,3500,4000,4500
Btd	Basic transmitt datasize	8 KB
bw	Total bandwidth	50 Mbps
RHO	Local-to-remote execution rate ratio	2, 4, 6, 8
lr	Learning rate	0.01
γ	Discount factor	0.9

TEH. It was compared with DQN, Double Q-learning, Dueling Deep-Q Network (Dueling DQN), Prioritized Replay and Proximal Policy Optimization (PPO) algorithms. We calculated the improvement in performance in terms of the average value, where the enhancement in average performance can be defined as:

$$\overline{I} = \frac{\overline{\text{TEH}_{\text{other}}} - \overline{\text{TEH}_{\text{DPAQN}}}}{\overline{\text{TEH}_{\text{other}}}} \times 100\% \tag{8}$$

Here, $\overline{\text{TEH}_{\text{other}}}$ and $\overline{\text{TEH}_{\text{DPAQN}}}$ represent the average TEH of other algorithms, and the average TEH obtained by the DPAQN algorithm, respectively.

5.2 Performance Evaluation

We compared the DPAQN algorithm with five other algorithms by testing the TEH metric values for scheduling different numbers of user tasks on four edge servers with varying configurations using the same dataset. As introduced in Sect. 3.2, a smaller TEH value indicates better performance. The TEH values for each algorithm across eight scenarios are shown in Fig. 4.

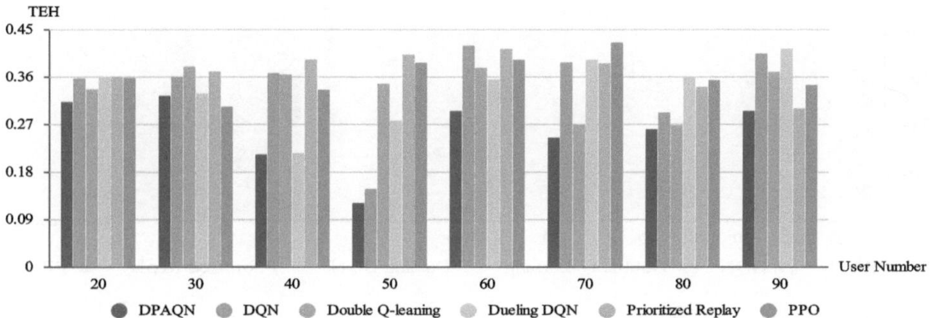

Fig. 4. TEH of six different algorithms under varying numbers of users.

The simulation results indicate that, overall, the DPAQN algorithm outperforms DQN by an average of 24.51096269% in terms of the TEH metric on the four edge servers. It also outperforms Double Q-learning by 23.87575690%, Dueling DQN by 23.52633988%, Prioritized Replay by 30.39486988%, and PPO by 28.82079803%. Our experimental results suggest that the DPAQN algorithm offers certain advantages in optimizing the overall performance of task offloading within edge computing environments.

Specifically, in edge computing environments, network conditions and resource availability are dynamically changing, and the data processed are often sensitive. As a result, the TEH values of different algorithms vary significantly across different user counts. However, in all eight scenarios tested, except when the user count was 20 (where DPAQN's TEH value was slightly higher than that of PPO), the DPAQN algorithm consistently achieved better TEH values than the other five algorithms. Therefore, the DPAQN algorithm is expected to achieve more efficient and energy-saving offloading, and to some extent, optimize the load balancing of edge servers.

To further validate the generalizability of our results, we conducted comparative experiments under different random seeds, and the results are shown in Fig. 5. Overall, in this scenario, DPAQN outperformed DQN by an average of 28.93454619%, Double Q-learning by 20.71041776%, Dueling DQN by 29.19596098%, Prioritized Replay by 28.71283886%, and PPO by 29.46298988%. These results demonstrate the good generalizability of the DPAQN algorithm to some extent. This indicates that the DPAQN algorithm we proposed can, to some extent, alleviate the issues of weak robustness and poor generalizability commonly found in artificial intelligence algorithms.

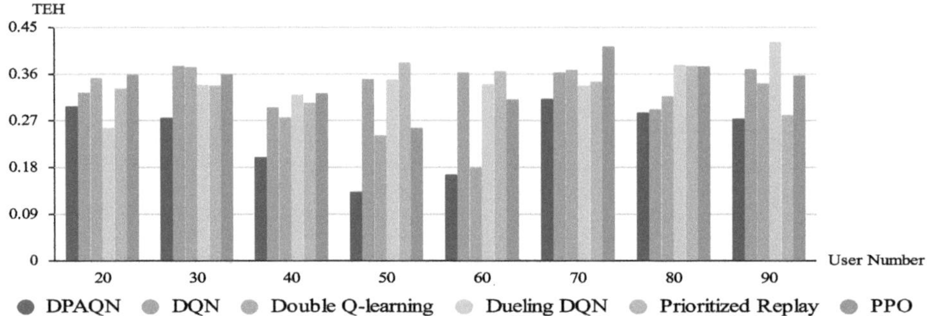

Fig. 5. TEH of six different algorithms under varying numbers of users.

In IIoT, intelligent manufacturing systems need to process large amounts of sensor data for real-time monitoring, predictive maintenance, and quality control. These tasks require low energy consumption, fast completion, and high throughput. The DPAQN algorithm can optimize task offloading strategies by offloading some computationally intensive tasks to edge servers, thereby potentially reducing device energy consumption and increasing task completion speed. For example, in a smart factory, sensors can send data to edge servers for analysis, and the DPAQN algorithm dynamically adjusts offloading decisions based on current network conditions and resource availability. This optimization approach may help reduce device energy consumption and improve system throughput, potentially contributing to the efficiency and intelligence of the production process.

6   Conclusion

This paper takes into account the heterogeneity of edge servers and the diversity of users, and proposes the DPAQN algorithm for the task offloading problem in edge computing environments. It retains the general advantages of AI algorithms while mitigating to some extent, the common instability inherent in AI algorithms. We have conducted experiments on the model considering three metrics: task completion time, energy consumption, and throughput. The experimental results demonstrate the algorithm's good comprehensive performance, which is on average 20.71%-30.39% better than the other five algorithms.

Acknowledgments. This work was supported in part by the National Key R&D Program of China(2023YFB3107305); in part by the Pilot Project for Integrated Innovation of Science, Education, and Industry of Qilu University of Technology (Shandong Academy of Sciences)(2024ZDZX08).

References

1. Feng, C., Han, P., et al.: Computation offloading in mobile edge computing networks: a survey. J. Netw. Comput. Appl. **202**, 103366 (2022)
2. Mao, S., Leng, S., Maharjan, S., Zhang, Y.: Energy efficiency and delay tradeoff for wireless powered mobile-edge computing systems with multi-access schemes. IEEE Trans. Wirel. Commun. **19**(3), 1855–1867 (2019)
3. Wang, C., Yuan, Z., et al.: The security and privacy of mobile edge computing: an artificial intelligence perspective. IEEE Internet Things J. (2023)
4. Qiu, T., Chi, J., et al.: Edge computing in industrial internet of things: architecture, advances and challenges. IEEE Commun. Surv. Tutor. **22**(4), 2462–2488 (2020)
5. Akhlaqi, M.Y., Hanapi, Z.B.M.: Task offloading paradigm in mobile edge computing-current issues, adopted approaches, and future directions. J. Netw. Comput. Appl. **212**, 103568 (2023)
6. Wang, D., et al.: A comprehensive review on internet of things task offloading in multi-access edge computing. Heliyon (2024)
7. Peng, K., Huang, H., et al.: Intelligent computation offloading and resource allocation in IIoT with end-edge-cloud computing using NSGA-III. IEEE Trans. Netw. Sci. Eng. **10**(5), 3032–3046 (2022)
8. Nguyen, P.X., et al.: Backscatter-assisted data offloading in OFDMA-based wireless-powered mobile edge computing for IoT networks. IEEE Internet Things J. **8**(11), 9233–9243 (2021)
9. Wu, J., et al.: Edge-cloud collaborative computation offloading model based on improved partical swarm optimization in MEC. In: 2019 IEEE 25th International Conference on Parallel and Distributed Systems (ICPADS), pp. 959–962. IEEE (2019)
10. Nan, Z., et al.: A new task scheduling scheme based on genetic algorithm for edge computing. Comput. Mater. Continua **71**(1), 1546–2218 (2022)
11. Li, J., Gao, H., Lv, T., Lu, Y.: Deep reinforcement learning based computation offloading and resource allocation for MEC. In: 2018 IEEE Wireless Communications and Networking Conference (WCNC), pp. 1–6. IEEE (2018)
12. Xiao, L., et al.: Reinforcement learning-based mobile offloading for edge computing against jamming and interference. IEEE Trans. Commun. **68**(10), 6114–6126 (2020)
13. Wang, J., et al.: Fast adaptive task offloading in edge computing based on meta reinforcement learning. IEEE Trans. Parallel Distrib. Syst. **32**(1), 242–253 (2020)
14. Liu, H., et al.: Scheduling multi-workflows over edge computing resources with time-varying performance, a novel probability-mass function and DQN-based approach. In: Ku, W.-S., Kanemasa, Y., Serhani, M.A., Zhang, L.-J. (eds.) ICWS 2020. LNCS, vol. 12406, pp. 197–209. Springer, Cham (2020). https://doi.org/10.1007/978-3-030-59618-7_13
15. Sheng, S., Chen, P., Chen, Z., Wu, L., Yao, Y.: Deep reinforcement learning-based task scheduling in IoT edge computing. Sensors **21**(5), 1666 (2021)

16. Heidari, A., et al.: A green, secure, and deep intelligent method for dynamic IoT-edge-cloud offloading scenarios. Sustain. Comput. Inf. Syst. **38**, 100859 (2023)
17. Song, S., Fang, Z., et al.: Semi-online computational offloading by dueling deep-Q network for user behavior prediction. IEEE Access **8**, 118192–118204 (2020)
18. Xue, F., et al.: A deep reinforcement learning based hybrid algorithm for efficient resource scheduling in edge computing environment. Inf. Sci. **608**, 362–374 (2022)
19. Kang, Y., Hauswald, J., et al.:Neurosurgeon: collaborative intelligence between the cloud and mobile edge. ACM SIGARCH Comput. Arch. News **45**(1), 615–629 (2017)

Ant Colony Sampling with Mixture
of Experts for Combinatorial Optimization

Renjie Wang(iD), Helan Liang$^{(\boxtimes)}$(iD), and Fanzhang Li(iD)

School of Computer Science and Technology, Soochow University, Suzhou, China
rjwang0422@stu.suda.edu.cn, {hlliang,lfzh}@suda.edu.cn

Abstract. Recently, neural-guided heuristic algorithms have demonstrated significant advancements in addressing Combinatorial Optimization Problems (COPs). However, these approaches exhibit limitations with respect to their generalizability, and the thoroughness of the exploration within the combinatorial space. In response, this paper introduces the Mixture of Experts Ant Colony Sampler (MoEACS), a nonautoregressive heuristic algorithm guided by deep graph neural network. MoEACS incorporates a Mixture of Experts (MoE) architecture to facilitate the construction of diverse heuristic learners (i.e. experts), thereby diversifying the heuristic generation to enhance the Ant Colony Optimization (ACO) algorithm, an established meta-heuristic algorithm. Furthermore, we propose a novel inference strategy that enhances the search for superior solutions within combinatorial space by preheating the pheromone. Experimental results demonstrate that the MoEACS approach outperforms state-of-the-art (SOTA) ACO across diverse real-world datasets and seven different COPs and achieves performance levels comparable to tailored problem-specific methods in vehicle routing problems. Our source code is available at https://github.com/RenJ-wang/MoEACS.

Keywords: Combinatorial optimization · Deep graph neural networks · Meta-heuristics · Evolutionary computation · Combinatorial search

1   Introduction

Combinatorial optimization (CO) [36] is a crucial domain involving the process of selecting the best solution from a finite set of possible solutions, often under specific constraints. This field plays a significant role in various applications [5].

The Ant Colony Optimization (ACO) algorithm [1,41] is well-suited for effectively solving combinatorial optimization problems (COPs). Pheromone-based positive feedback prioritizes high-quality path exploration in ACO, which integrates problem-specific heuristic information (e.g. distances/costs) with global path-quality insights via pheromones, achieving a dynamic exploration-exploitation trade-off. However, constructing efficient heuristic information and reasonably initializing pheromone matrices remain key challenges in ACO.

T. Zhu et al. (Eds.): KSEM 2025, LNAI 15920, pp. 233–247, 2026.
https://doi.org/10.1007/978-981-95-3052-6_18

To tackle the first concern, contemporary methodologies, exemplified by the emerging DeepACO [41] algorithm and the GFACS [20] algorithm, have harnessed deep graph neural networks to engender heuristic information that was once conventionally devised by experts. Nevertheless, these existing approaches [20,41] fail to consider the node embedding yielded throughout the Graph Neural Network (GNN) [8,17,31] aggregation procedure. As a consequence, the information that demands substantial computational efforts to generate is squandered. In contrast, we capitalize on this information by employing it as input for the gating network of Mixture of Experts (MOE) [7], thereby facilitating decision-making and augmenting the resource utilization efficiency.

Regarding the second matter, pheromone initialization is critical to the performance of the ACO algorithm, as it influences the convergence speed and the quality of the solution. In ACO, the pheromone initialization has evolved from setting a matrix of all ones [20,41] to expert-designed methods [28], and more recently to neural network-based approaches, which are considered a warm-up strategy to accelerate convergence. Among the expert-designed methods [10,42], Bellaachia et al. [3] and Gao et al. [13] used a formula based on the inverse of the node distance, similar to traditional heuristic initialization. This similarity underscores the correlation between heuristic information and pheromone initialization. Expert-designed methods are stable and interpretable but may lack flexibility in complex scenarios. In contrast, neural-based methods [37,38] offer enhanced adaptability to dynamic environments. Our strategy is novel in that it initializes the pheromone matrix with heuristic information derived from neural-based approaches.

Moreover, MoEACS employs unsupervised learning and the non-autoregressive technique, treating COPs as optimization objectives. By integrating the encoder-decoder framework with MoE architecture, it enhances large-scale COPs performance and generates high-quality solutions efficiently.

In conclusion, our **contributions** can be summarized as follows:

i) We propose MoEACS, which synergistically leverages MoE architecture with the deep GNN network. This novel design addresses limitations of traditional ACO, endowing it with enhanced exploratory capabilities within the complex solution space by leveraging the specialized knowledge of multiple 'expert' components.

ii) We propose a novel inference mechanism that accelerates convergence to better solutions during the preparatory stage.

iii) We utilize the previously overlooked node embedding information [20,41] and integrate it into our proposed framework, thus improving the generalization and precision of the algorithm.

2   Related Works

2.1   Ant Colony Optimization

Ant Colony Optimization (ACO) [1] is a nature-inspired metaheuristic that mimics the foraging behavior of ants to find near-optimal paths between their nest and food by using pheromone trails and heuristic information. By mimicking this natural mechanism, ACO is adept at tackling complex optimization problems by directing a colony of artificial ants to explore the solution space and iteratively improve upon the best paths discovered.

For ACO, to enable the direct generation of heuristic rules that can replace expert-designed ones using deep neural networks, Ye et al. [41] introduced Deep-ACO. Furthermore, Kim et al. [20] improved DeepACO with GFACS via off-policy training. However, these methods [20,41] exhibit certain limitations in terms of generalizability and precision. These limitations highlight the need for further refinement to enhance their performance in computational optimization tasks.

2.2   Neural Combinatorial Optimization

Neural Combinatorial Optimization (NCO) [4,14,40] is an interdisciplinary field that employs deep learning techniques to address COPs. NCO has been widely applied to supervised learning [12,22,24,33], reinforcement learning [19,21,23, 27], autoregressive [35], and non-autoregressive algorithms [18].

Supervised learning necessitates labeled data and tends to yield close-to-optimal solutions, yet it typically involves longer training periods. While unsupervised reinforcement learning, which does not require labeled data, often results in relatively less time. The autoregressive algorithm generates sequences by predicting each element sequentially, depending on previously generated elements, while the non-autoregressive algorithm predicts all elements in parallel, often resulting in faster generation. As real-world problems grow in complexity and scale, there is a growing preference in NCO for unsupervised reinforcement learning and non-autoregressive algorithms due to their efficiency.

2.3   Mixture of Experts

Mixture of Experts (MoE) [25,26,29,44] is an ensemble learning architecture that integrates the strengths of various expert models to augment the overall system performance. There exist two primary types of MoE: dense MoE [7], which forwards input to all experts, and sparse MoE [25,43], which transmits input to only a subset of experts.

The emerging MVMoE [43], which integrates sparse MoE layer with attention mechanisms, exhibits versatility and enhanced performance in addressing combinatorial optimization problems. However, the autoregressive nature of MVMoE results in a training time that is considerably longer than that of our MoEACS, posing challenges in applying it to large-scale COPs. Furthermore, experimental studies indicate that the accuracy and generalizability of MVMoE are lower compared to MoEACS under identical conditions.

3 Preliminary

3.1 Combinatorial Optimization Problem

CO is a field of mathematical optimization that involves the selection of the best element from some set of admissible solutions. A COP can be formally described as a triplet $(\mathcal{S}, f, \mathcal{X})$, where $\mathcal{S}$ is the set of all feasible solutions satisfying all constraints, $f : \mathcal{S} \to \mathbb{R}$ is the objective function, and $\mathcal{X}$ is the constraint set. Our goal is to find a solution $s^* \in \mathcal{S}$ such that $f(s^*) = \min_{s \in \mathcal{S}} f(s)$.

We use a canonical COP (e.g. Capacitated Vehicle Routing Problem (CVRP) [6]) as an illustration. A CVRP instance is defined on a graph $\mathcal{G} = (\mathcal{V}, \mathcal{E})$, where the node set $\mathcal{V}$ comprises the depot and customer nodes, and the edge set $\mathcal{E}$ denotes possible paths between nodes. Each node $v_i \in \mathcal{V}$ is located in a two-dimensional space. Each edge $e_{i,j} \in \mathcal{E}$ has associated weight $d_{i,j}$, which represents the distance between nodes v_i and v_j, calculated as $d_{i,j} = |v_i - v_j|^2$.

A CVRP solution denoted as $x(\mathcal{G})$, consists of a set of vehicle routes that start and end at the depot, ensuring that all customers are served. Each route π_k is a sequence of nodes $\pi_k = (\pi_{k1}, \pi_{k2}, \ldots, \pi_{kN}, \pi_{k1})$, where π_{k1} is the depot and $\pi_{k2}, \ldots, \pi_{k(N)}$ are the customers served by vehicle k.

The objective of the CVRP is to find the solution $x(\mathcal{G})$ that minimizes the total distance traveled by all vehicles. Subject to the constraints that each customer is visited exactly once and the load of each vehicle does not exceed its capacity.

3.2 Ant Colony Optimization

The operational mechanism of ACO involves identifying superior solutions through iteratively updating pheromone trails and constructing solutions based on sampling probability. Upon inputting a specific instance $\mathcal{G}$, the ACO algorithm yields an associated heuristic measure matrix $\boldsymbol{\eta}(\mathcal{G}) \in \mathbb{R}^{N \times N}$, and pheromone trails $\boldsymbol{\tau} \in \mathbb{R}^{N \times N}$. Each heuristic measure $\eta_{i,j}(\mathcal{G}) \in \boldsymbol{\eta}(\mathcal{G})$, abbreviated herein as $\eta_{i,j}$ in Eq. (1)), is generated by the MoE framework and quantifies the likelihood of an edge $e_{i,j}$ being selected for inclusion in the solution. Each pheromone trail $\tau_{i,j} \in \boldsymbol{\tau}(\mathcal{G})$ denotes the pheromone concentration on edge $e_{i,j}$, thereby reflecting the quality of the path. We initialize the pheromone matrix via a preheat policy.

Each ant constructs a solution iteratively by selecting the next node with probability:

$$j \in J_k(i) \quad , \quad p^k_{ij}(t) = \frac{[\tau_{ij}(t)]^\alpha [\eta_{ij}]^\beta}{\sum_{l \in J_k(i)} [\tau_{il}(t)]^\alpha [\eta_{il}]^\beta}, \tag{1}$$

where $J_k(i)$ is the set of nodes for ant k is allowed to move to from node v_i, and α and β are hyperparameters that regulate the relative importance of pheromone and heuristic information, both set to 1 in this study.

After all ants have constructed their solutions, each pheromone trail $\tau_{i,j} \in \boldsymbol{\tau}(\mathcal{G})$ is updated as follows:

$$\tau_{ij}(t + 1) = (1 - \rho) \cdot \tau_{ij}(t) + \Delta \tau_{ij}, \tag{2}$$

where ρ is the evaporation rate of pheromone trails and $\Delta\tau_{ij}$ is the amount of pheromone deposited by all ants on edge $e_{i,j}$.

To address the CVRP, each ant in the ACO algorithm constructs a solution path that constitutes an Eulerian circuit, which revisits only the starting point (depot), thereby representing multiple vehicle sub-paths as Hamiltonian circuits. As iterations proceed, ants' pheromone updating and path-selection strategies gradually refine paths, leading to solutions close to the optimal ones.

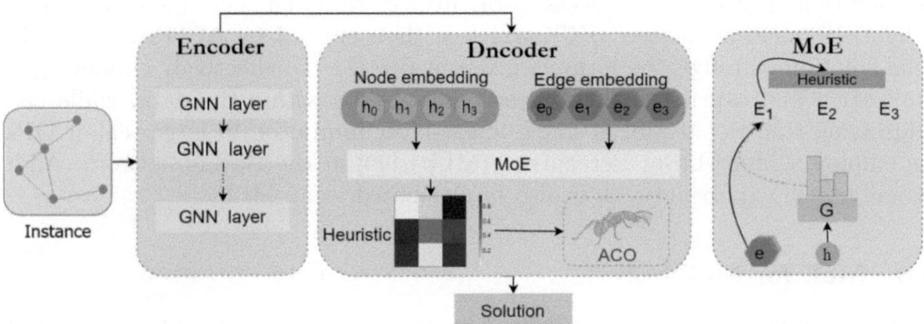

Fig. 1. The overall framework of MoEACS. [Green part]: The encoder processes the input instance to produce node and edge embeddings. In decoding, ACO utilizes MoE-derived heuristic to construct a solution. [Blue part]: Gating network G in MoE layer picks the most suitable expert E by inputting node embedding. The chosen expert E then uses the edge embeddings to generate the heuristic. (Color figure online)

4   Methodology

The MoEACS framework conforms to an encoder-decoder architecture [36], which is shown in Fig. 1.

4.1   Encoder for MoEACS

Within our proposed MoEACS, the encoder instantiated as a deep Graph Neural Network (GNN) [8], is responsible for translating the input graph instance $\mathcal{G}$ into the node and edge embeddings.

The architecture of the GNN, as proposed by Joshi et al. [17] and Qiu et al. [31], consists of 12 layers. For the l-th layer, the node embedding for node v_i is represented by h_i^l and the edge embedding connecting nodes v_i and v_j is expressed as e_{ij}^l. The propagation formula for the network is given as follows:

$$h_i^{l+1} = h_i^l + \alpha(BN(\boldsymbol{U}^l h_i^l + \mathcal{A}_{j\in N_i}(\sigma(e_{ij}^l) \odot \boldsymbol{V}^l h_j^l))), \qquad (3)$$

$$e_{ij}^{l+1} = e_{ij}^l + \alpha(BN(\boldsymbol{P}^l e_{ij}^l + \boldsymbol{Q}^l h_i^l + \boldsymbol{R}^l h_j^l)), \qquad (4)$$

where the square matrix parameters U^l, V^l, P^l, Q^l and R^l are learnable. The SiLU [11] activation function is denoted by α. Batch normalization is abbreviated as BN. $\mathcal{A}_{j \in N_i}$ signifies the mean pooling aggregation operation over the neighborhood of node v_i. σ for sigmoid function, and $\odot$ for point-wise product.

4.2   Decoder for MoEACS

The decoder employs encoder-generated node and edge embeddings to generate the solution. During this process, MoE utilizes these embeddings to construct a heuristic measure matrix $\eta(\mathcal{G})$, which is then applied by ACO to derive the final solution, through the formula given in Eq. (1). To effectively enhance generalization and capture the nonlinear relationships within the data, while also addressing traditional MoE's single linear-layer limitation in large-scale COPs, we employ a Multi-Layer Perceptron (MLP) [30] in the Gating network. Additionally, each expert network is also implemented as an MLP.

4.3   MoE for MoEACS

MoE includes the gating network G and an ensemble of k experts $\{E_1, E_2, ..., E_k\}$. The gating network discriminatively selects the most pertinent expert E_i, which transforms edge embeddings into heuristic matrices. Different experts are routed to various combinatorial spaces, resulting in each expert generating a unique heuristic matrix, thereby enhancing the model's generalizability and adaptability. The relationship between the gating network G and the experts E is determined by Eq. (5).

Precisely, the selection of the expert, as shown in Fig. 1, is achieved through the computation of a similarity score s_i, which is produced by the gating network as $G(h_i) = \text{Softmax}(f(h_i))$, where $f(h_i)$ represents the output of the MLP processing node embedding h_i of node v_i.

A higher similarity score s_i indicates a greater aptitude of the expert. We employ the highest similarity score to identify the most appropriate expert, as described in Eq. (5). This mechanism ensures that the most suitable experts are assigned to process edge embeddings, thereby enhancing the model's overall efficacy and accuracy.

$$\eta = E_i(e), \quad \text{where } i = \text{argmax}\left(\text{Softmax}(G(h))\right), \tag{5}$$

where e corresponds to the edge embeddings, and h represents the node embedding.

For training the gating network, we employ the cross-entropy loss function proposed by Ma et al. [25], where W acts as a coefficient to balance the two terms and the all-ones vector is denoted as $\hat{1}$.

$$\mathcal{L}_{\text{CE}} = \mathbb{E}[-\log(\text{Softmax}(G(h))) - W \cdot \log(\hat{1} - Softmax(G(h)))]. \tag{6}$$

4.4   Pheromone Preheating for MoEACS

The general structure of the preheat policy is illustrated in Fig. 2. As discussed in Para. 4 of the Introduction, the preheat policy models the initial pheromone matrix as $\boldsymbol{\tau}_0 = \boldsymbol{\eta}$, leveraging the similarity between heuristic measures $\boldsymbol{\eta}$ and initial pheromone matrix $\boldsymbol{\tau}_0$. In CVRP, this strategy has been validated experimentally, guiding ants to avoid early stage blind random exploration during the search process, thereby accelerating the convergence speed of the algorithm.

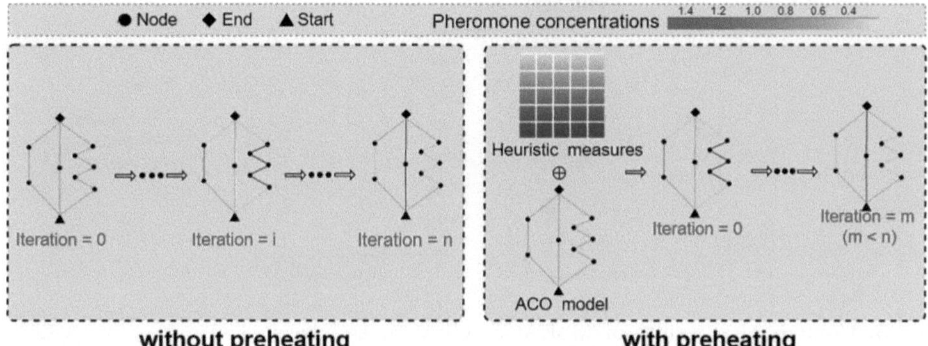

Fig. 2. The schematic compares the ant colony algorithm with and without the preheat policy. The preheat policy employs MoE-generated heuristic measures to initialize pheromone matrix and enhance the ACO model. Trajectory hues reflect pheromone concentrations.

4.5   Training Policy for MoEACS

MoEACS, parameterized by trainable parameters $\boldsymbol{\theta}$, transforms an input graph instance $\mathcal{G}$ into its heuristic measures $\boldsymbol{\eta_\theta}(\mathcal{G})$. The probability of constructing a routing solution $S = \{s_0, s_1, s_2, \ldots, s_m\}$, can be articulated as follows:

$$P(S; \mathcal{G}, \boldsymbol{\eta_\theta}(\mathcal{G})) = \prod_{t=0}^{m-1} P(s_t \mid s_{t+1}; \mathcal{G}, \boldsymbol{\eta_\theta}(\mathcal{G})). \tag{7}$$

Then, we minimized the values of the optimization objectives for both the initial solutions S and those enhanced by the Local Search (LS) [41] operation.

$$\min_{\boldsymbol{\theta}} \mathcal{L}(\boldsymbol{\theta}, \mathcal{G}) = \mathbb{E}_{S \sim P(\cdot; \mathcal{G}, \boldsymbol{\eta_\theta}(\mathcal{G}))}[\, f(S) + C \cdot f(LS(S, f))], \tag{8}$$

where f is an objective function and N denotes the problem scale for COPs. C denotes a coefficient, and its role is identical to that of the W in Eq. (6).

We first simplify the gradient equation (Eq. (10)) for the loss function proposed by [20] by utilizing Eq. (11). Subsequently, the gradient expression

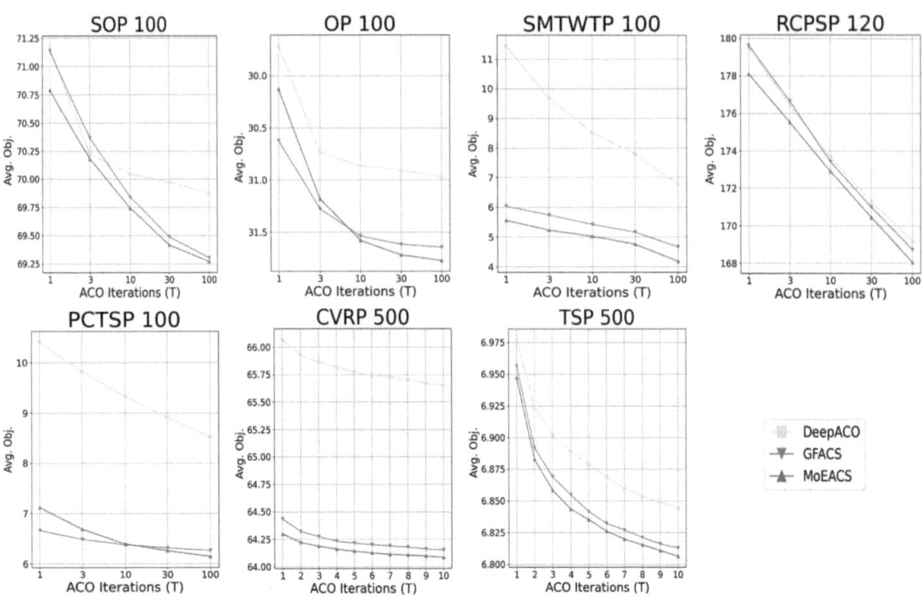

Fig. 3. Comparative results of MoEACS, GFACS, and DeepACO on various COPs. MoEACS outperforms overall neural-guided heuristic baselines. For each task, we plot the average objective value across 100 held-out test instances, except TSP with 128 instances.

(Eq. (9)) is derived by combining the loss term in Eq. (6) with the cross-entropy loss formulated in Eq. (10).

$$\nabla \mathcal{L} = \nabla \mathcal{L}(\boldsymbol{\theta}, \mathcal{G}) + \nabla \mathcal{L}_{\mathrm{CE}}, \tag{9}$$

$$\nabla \mathcal{L}(\boldsymbol{\theta}, \mathcal{G}) = \left\{ E_f(S, \mathcal{G}) \cdot \beta + \nabla_{\boldsymbol{\theta}} \log(P(S; \mathcal{G}, \boldsymbol{\eta_\theta}(\mathcal{G}))) + Z_{\boldsymbol{\theta}}(\mathcal{E}) + \log(2N) \right\}^2, \tag{10}$$

$$E_f(S, \mathcal{G}) = \mathbb{E}[\, (f(S) - avg(\mathcal{G})) + C(f(LS(S, f)) - avg_{LS}(\mathcal{G}))], \tag{11}$$

where $Z_{\boldsymbol{\theta}}$ denotes the feed-forward neural network, following Kim et al. [20]. Let $\mathcal{E}$ represent the edge embeddings derived from the encoding process. β is a hyperparameter that incrementally increases within a specified range throughout the progression of training epochs, thereby progressively emphasizing the influence of $E_f(S, \mathcal{G})$. The expressions $avg(\mathcal{G})$ and $avg_{LS}(\mathcal{G})$ denote the average objective value of the solutions and the solutions after local search (LS), respectively.

5   Experiments

This section evaluates our proposed MoEACS via: 1) comparisons with emerging neural-enhanced heuristic methods on 7 COPs and real datasets; 2) state-of-the-art (SOTA) NCO algorithms for large-scale routing problems; 3) an ablation study, a generalization experiment, and comparisons with the MoE baseline.

Table 1. Performance comparisons between MoEACS and NCO baselines on TSP and CVRP. Results for methods with * are drawn from [9,16,20,41]. We report the average execution time for each instance. Unless otherwise specified, ACO iteration T is set to 10 in neural-based heuristics.

Method	TSP500			TSP1000		
	Obj.	Gap(%)	Time	Obj.	Gap(%)	Time
Concorde	16.55	-	10.7s	23.12	-	108s
LKH-3	16.55	0.02	31.7s	23.14	0.10	102s
AM*	21.46	29.07	0.6s	33.55	45.10	0.5s
POMO*	20.57	24.40	0.6s	30.46	32.00	4.1s
+EAS	18.25	10.29	140s	28.83	24.76	350s
+SGBS	18.86	13.98	318s	28.58	23.41	600s
DIMES*	18.70	12.94	305s	28.66	23.88	600s
SO*	16.94	2.94	15s	23.77	2.80	45s
Pointerformer*	17.14	3.56	14s	24.80	7.30	40s
DeepACO	16.84	1.75	5.8s	23.83	3.07	36s
GFACS	16.82	1.63	5.6s	23.73	2.64	35s
MoEACS(Ours)	**16.81**	**1.57**	5.5s	**23.72**	**2.60**	35s

Method	CVRP500			CVRP1000		
	Obj.	Gap(%)	Time	Obj.	Gap(%)	Time
PyVRP	62.96	-	21.0m	119.29	-	1.4h
LKH-3	63.07	0.18	18.6m	119.52	0.20	2.1h
POMO*	68.69	9.08	2s	145.74	22.14	3s
+ EAS	64.76	2.85	5.0m	126.25	5.83	10.0m
+ SGBS	65.44	3.93	5.2m	127.90	7.21	10.1m
SymNCO*	68.81	9.28	2s	141.82	18.86	3s
+ EAS	64.63	2.65	5.0m	125.58	5.27	10.0m
+ SGBS	65.40	3.87	5.2m	127.53	6.90	10.1m
DeepACO	64.65	2.68	36s	122.15	2.40	1.3m
GFACS	64.19	1.95	36s	121.80	2.11	1.3m
MoEACS (T=5)	64.15	1.89	36s	121.54	1.89	1.3m
MoEACS (T=10)	**64.09**	**1.80**	1.4m	**121.45**	**1.81**	2.9m

Test Setting. We adopted standard datasets that are consistent with Deep-ACO [41] and GFACS [20], ensuring an equitable methodological comparison. Unless otherwise stated, we took the average of three measurements for each test to mitigate stochastic noise.

5.1 Comparisons with ACO Baselines in Various COPs

Benchmark. Following the methods of Kim et al. [20] and Ye et al. [41], we evaluated MoEACS across various COPs, encompassing the Sequential Ordering Problem (SOP), Orienteering Problem (OP), Single Machine Total Weighted Tardiness Problem (SMTWTP), Resource-Constrained Project Scheduling Problem (RCPSP), Prize-Collecting Traveling Salesman Problem

(PCTSP), Capacitated Vehicle Routing Problem (CVRP), and Traveling Salesman Problem (TSP).

Baselines. We employed DeepACO [41] and GFACS [20] as the baseline methods, both of which, akin to our proposed MoEACS, are deep-neural-based algorithms that are grounded in the ACO algorithm and Reinforcement Learning (RL). To ensure a fair comparison, the same number of ants and iterations was utilized for inference across all algorithms.

Results. Figure 3 demonstrates that MoEACS exhibits superior performance compared to both DeepACO and GFACS for all benchmark problems, especially in routing problems. Notably, all three algorithms utilize identical encoders and local search operators, which highlights the critical role of the MoE architecture.

5.2 Comparisons with RL-Based NCO Methods

In this subsection, we evaluated the performance of MoEACS against state-of-the-art RL-based NCO algorithms on large-scale benchmark instances of TSP and CVRP. Comprehensive results are presented in Table 1.

Baselines. Eight SOTA RL-based NCO baselines were employed, including Attention Model (AM) [21], POMO [23], DIMES [31], Select and Optimize (SO) [9], SymNCO [19], DeepACO [41], GFACS [20] and Pointerformer [16]. Furthermore, We used Concorde [2], LKH-3 [15], and PyVRP [39] as heuristic solvers for TSP and CVRP, providing zero-percent gap baselines.

Results. Table 1 illustrates that MoEACS demonstrates competitive performance against existing SOTA RL-based NCO approaches for both TSP and CVRP. Although MoEACS lags marginally behind the SOTA heuristic solvers, it exhibits a significantly faster computation time than both. Furthermore, MoEACS outperforms others RL-based NCO baselines in the gap metric, a superiority particularly evident in the CVRP.

5.3 Comparisons on Real-World Instances

Performance evaluations of MoEACS were conducted against baselines on real-world instances from the TSPLib [32] and CVRPLib-X [34] datasets. The models were trained using different sizes depending on the dataset sizes: 200 for datasets with sizes 100–299, 500 for datasets with sizes 300–699, and 1000 for the remaining datasets, while all other experimental settings were held constant. Results are shown in Table 2. MoEACS outperforms baselines on large TSPLib and CVRPLib instances, yet it slightly underperforms in comparison to GFACS in the small instances. As the problem scale escalates, the performance of GFACS diminishes, highlighting the significance of the MoE architecture.

Table 2. Comparison results on real-world datasets from TSPLib and CVRPLib-x. For N instances in each set, we report the average optimality gap relative to the best-known costs.

Range	N	DeepACO	GFACS	Ours	Range	N	DeepACO	GFACS	Ours
100-299	30	1.25%	1.21%	**1.21%**	100-299	43	3.27%	**2.71%**	2.73%
300-699	10	2.70%	2.60%	**0.96%**	300-699	40	4.22%	3.71%	**1.81%**
700-1350	9	3.93%	3.68%	**3.61%**	700-1001	17	5.07%	4.32%	**4.25%**

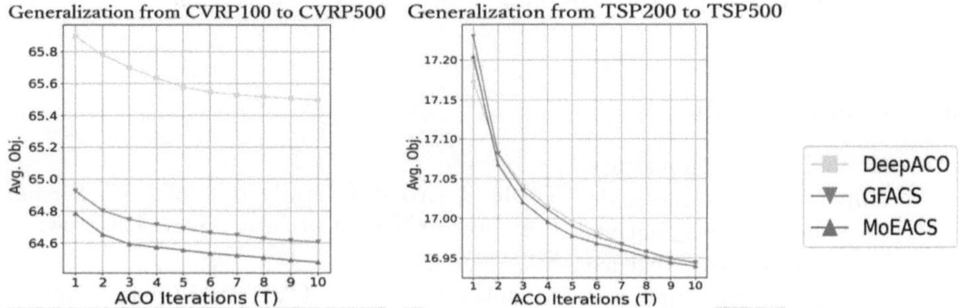

Fig. 4. Results of the generalization experiment. All algorithms were trained on TSP200 and CVRP100, tested on TSP500 and CVRP500 respectively to assess generalization. All other experimental setups remained identical.

5.4 Generalization Experiment

This experiment aimed to assess the generalization performance of the MoEACS algorithm and its comparative neural-based heuristic methods across various problem scales. Specifically, we evaluated generalization by training on TSP200/CVRP100 and testing on TSP500/CVRP500. As illustrated in Fig. 4, MoEACS consistently exhibits stronger generalization than the baseline algorithms on both TSP and CVRP, particularly in the CVRP.

5.5 Comparisons with MoE Baseline in COP

Among recent MoE methods for COPs, MVMoE [43] stands out as a notable approach. MVMoE integrated a Transformer architecture within an encoder-decoder framework, demonstrating competitive performance metrics. For our comparative analysis, we adopted MVMoE as a baseline algorithm, leveraging the dataset originally employed by MVMoE. Both models were trained on CVRP100 and tested across CVRP100/200/500. As indicated in Table 3, our proposed model, MoEACS, significantly outperforms MVMoE in terms of accuracy, while also exhibiting enhanced generalization capabilities. Furthermore, the results highlight that the performance of the MoEACS model is further improved when augmented with the preheat policy.

Table 3. We utilized the same datasets from MVMoE [43] to evaluate the performance of the different models trained on CVRP100 under varying problem scales of CVRP instances.

Method	CVRP100		CVRP200		CVRP500	
	Val.	Gap.(%)	Val.	Gap.(%)	Val.	Gap.(%)
LKH	15.59	0.00	22.02	0.00	30.86	0.00
MVMoE	15.77	1.15	23.09	4.86	37.34	21.00
MoEACS	15.65	0.38	22.31	1.32	31.73	2.82
MoEACS + preheat	15.64	**0.32**	22.29	**1.23**	31.66	**2.59**

5.6 Ablation Study

In this section, an ablation study was conducted on large-scale CVRP to validate the effectiveness of the MoE architecture and preheat policy implemented in the MoEACS. As presented in Table 4, the empirical results confirm that integrating the preheat policy yields improvements in solution quality, while removing the MoE architecture leads to substantially degraded performance.

Table 4. Ablation study of MoEACS. Second row: MoEACS with preheat policy. Last row: E is expert.

Method	CVRP500	CVRP1000
Original	64.11	121.43
w/ + preheat	64.09	121.42
w/{Num.$E = 1$}	64.19	121.80

6 Conclusion

This paper presents MoEACS, a deep-GNN-based heuristic algorithm for combinatorial optimization that integrates the MoE architecture. MoEACS uses the MoE architecture to build diverse heuristic learners generating diverse heuristic measures, enhancing ACO's exploration capabilities. Additionally, we propose a novel inference strategy, known as the pheromone preheat policy, which accelerates algorithm convergence. Future work may extend MoEACS to more COPs or incorporate large language models.

Acknowledgements. This work was supported by the National Natural Science Foundation of China (Grant No. 61672364, 62176172, and 61902269), the National Key R&D Program of China (Grant No. 2018YFA0701700; 2018YFA0701701), and the National Training Program of Innovation and Entrepreneurship for Undergraduates (Grant No. 202410285054Z).

References

1. Abdulghani, B.A., Abdulghani, M.A.: A comprehensive review of ant colony optimization in swarm intelligence for complex problem solving. Acadlore Trans. Mach. Learn. **3**(4), 214–224 (2024)
2. Applegate, D., Bixby, R., Chvátal, V., Cook, W.: Concorde TSP solver. https://www.math.uwaterloo.ca/tsp/concorde/
3. Bellaachia, A., Alathel, D.: A local pheromone initialization approach for ant colony optimization algorithm. In: 2014 IEEE International Conference on Progress in Informatics and Computing, pp. 133–138 (2014)
4. Bello, I., Pham, H., Le, Q.V., Norouzi, M., Bengio, S.: Neural combinatorial optimization with reinforcement learning. arXiv preprint arXiv:1611.09940 (2016)
5. Bernardelli, A. M., et al.: Methods for combinatorial optimization and their applications. Università degli studi di Pavia (2025)
6. Bogyrbayeva, A., Meraliyev, M., et al.: Machine learning to solve vehicle routing problems: a survey. IEEE Trans. Intell. Transp. Syst. (2024)
7. Cai, W., Jiang, J., Wang, F., Tang, J., Kim, S., Huang, J.: A survey on mixture of experts. arXiv preprint arXiv:2407.06204 (2024)
8. Cappart, Q., Ch'etelat, D., Khalil, E.B., Lodi, A., Morris, C., Veličkovi'c, P.: Combinatorial optimization and reasoning with graph neural networks. J. Mach. Learn. Res. **24**(130), 1–61 (2023)
9. Cheng, H., Zheng, H., Cong, Y., Jiang, W., Pu, S.: Select and optimize: learning to solve large–scale TSP instances. In: AISTATS, pp. 1219–1231 (2023)
10. Dai, Q., Ji, J., Liu, C.: An effective initialization strategy of pheromone for ant colony optimization. In: 2009 Fourth International Conference on Bio-Inspired Computing, pp. 1–4 (2009)
11. Elfwing, S., Uchibe, E., Doya, K.: Sigmoid-weighted linear units for neural network function approximation in reinforcement learning. Neural Netw. **107**, 3–11 (2018)
12. Fu, Z.-H., Qiu, K.-B., Zha, H.: Generalize a small pre-trained model to arbitrarily large TSP instances. In: Proceedings of the AAAI Conference on Artificial Intelligence, vol. 35, no. 8, pp. 7474–7482 (2021)
13. Gao, S., Zhong, J., Cui, Y., Gao, C., Li, X.: A novel pheromone initialization strategy of ACO algorithms for solving TSP. In: 2017 13th International Conference on Natural Computation, Fuzzy Systems and Knowledge Discovery (ICNC-FSKD), pp. 243–248 (2017)
14. Garmendia, A.I., Ceberio, J., Mendiburu, A.: Neural combinatorial optimization: a new player in the field. arXiv preprint arXiv:2205.01356 (2022)
15. Helsgaun, K.: An extension of the Lin-Kernighan-Helsgaun TSP solver for constrained traveling salesman and vehicle routing problems, Technical report (2017)
16. Jin, Y., et al.: PointerFormer: deep reinforced multi-pointer transformer for the traveling salesman problem. In: AAAI Conference on Artificial Intelligence (2023)
17. Joshi, C.K., Cappart, Q., et al.: Learning the travelling salesperson problem requires rethinking generalization. arXiv preprint arXiv:2006.07054 (2020)
18. Khalil, E., Dai, H., Zhang, Y., Dilkina, B., Song, L.: Learning combinatorial optimization algorithms over graphs. Adv. Neural Inf. Process. Syst. **30** (2017)
19. Kim, M., Park, J., Park, J.: Sym-NCO: leveraging symmetricity for neural combinatorial optimization. Adv. Neural. Inf. Process. Syst. **35**, 1936–1949 (2022)
20. Kim, M., Choi, S., Son, J., Kim, H.-S., Park, J., Bengio, Y.: Ant colony sampling with GFlowNets for combinatorial optimization. arXiv preprint arXiv:2403.07041 (2024)

21. Kool, W., Van Hoof, H., Welling, M.: Attention, learn to solve routing problems!. arXiv preprint arXiv:1803.08475 (2018)
22. Kwon, Y.-D., Choo, J., Yoon, I., Park, M., et al.: Matrix encoding networks for neural combinatorial optimization. arXiv preprint arXiv:2106.11113 (2021)
23. Kwon, Y.-D., Choo, J., Kim, B., Yoon, I., Gwon, Y., Min, S.: POMO: policy optimization with multiple optima for reinforcement learning. Adv. Neural. Inf. Process. Syst. **33**, 21188–21198 (2020)
24. Luo, F., Lin, X., Liu, F., Zhang, Q., Wang, Z.: Neural combinatorial optimization with heavy decoder: toward large scale generalization. Adv. Neural. Inf. Process. Syst. **36**, 8845–8864 (2023)
25. Ma, L., et al.: Mixture of link predictors on graphs. arXiv preprint arXiv:2402.08583 (2024)
26. Masoudnia, S., Ebrahimpour, R.: Mixture of experts: a literature survey. Artif. Intell. Rev. **42**, 275–293 (2014)
27. Morales, E.F., Escalante, H.J.: A brief introduction to supervised, unsupervised, and reinforcement learning. In: Biosignal Processing and Classification using Computational Learning and Intelligence, pp. 111–129. Elsevier (2022)
28. Neroni, M.: Ant colony optimization with warm-up. Algorithms **14**(10), 295 (2021)
29. Nguyen, H.D., Chamroukhi, F.: Practical and theoretical aspects of mixture-of-experts modeling: an overview. Wiley Interdiscipl. Rev. Data Min. Knowl. Discov. **8**(4), e1246 (2018)
30. Popescu, M.-C., Balas, V.E., Perescu-Popescu, L.: Multilayer perceptron and neural networks. WSEAS Trans. Circ. Syst. **8**(7), 579–588 (2009)
31. Qiu, R., Sun, Z., Yang, Y.: DIMES: a differentiable meta solver for combinatorial optimization problems. Adv. Neural. Inf. Process. Syst. **35**, 25531–25546 (2022)
32. Reinelt, G.: TSPLIB - a traveling salesman problem library. INFORMS J. Comput. **3**, 376–384 (1991). https://api.semanticscholar.org/CorpusID:207225504
33. Sun, Z., Yang, Y.: DIFUSCO: graph-based diffusion solvers for combinatorial optimization. Adv. Neural. Inf. Process. Syst. **36**, 3706–3731 (2023)
34. Uchoa, E., Pecin, D., Pessoa, A.A., Aragão, M.P.D., Vidal, T., Subramanian, A.: New benchmark instances for the capacitated vehicle routing problem. Eur. J. Oper. Res. **257**, 845–858 (2017). https://api.semanticscholar.org/CorpusID:2749712
35. Vinyals, O., Fortunato, M., Jaitly, N.: Pointer networks. In: Advances in Neural Information Processing Systems, vol. 28 (2015)
36. Wang, F., He, Q., Li, S.: Solving combinatorial optimization problems with deep neural network: a survey. Tsinghua Sci. Technol. **29**(5), 1266–1282 (2024)
37. Wang, W., Song, Q., Ji, S., Wang, B.: An improved ant colony algorithm based on competition mechanism of SOM neural network. In: 2023 35th Chinese Control and Decision Conference (CCDC), pp. 2903–2908 (2023)
38. Wang, X., Jin, Y.: An ant colony algorithm assisted by graph neural networks for solving vehicle routing problems. In: Proceedings of the Companion Conference on Genetic and Evolutionary Computation, pp. 5–6. Association for Computing Machinery, Lisbon, Portugal (2023)
39. Wouda, N.A., Lan, L., Kool, W.: PyVRP: a high-performance VRP solver package. INFORMS J. Comput. (2024). https://doi.org/10.1287/ijoc.2023.0055
40. Wu, X., Wang, D., Wen, L., Xiao, Y., Wu, C.: Neural combinatorial optimization algorithms for solving vehicle routing problems: a comprehensive survey with perspectives. arXiv preprint arXiv:2406.00415 (2024)
41. Ye, H., Wang, J., Cao, Z., Liang, H., Li, Y.: DeepACO: neural - enhanced ant systems for combinatorial optimization. Adv. Neural Inf. Process. Syst. **36** (2024)

42. Zheng, Y., Lv, X., Qian, L., Liu, X.: An optimal BP neural network track prediction method based on a GA–ACO hybrid algorithm. J. Marine Sci. Eng. **10**(10), 1399 (2022)
43. Zhou, J., Cao, Z., Wu, Y., Song, W., et al.: MVMoE: multi-task vehicle routing solver with mixture-of-experts. arXiv preprint arXiv:2405.01029 (2024)
44. Zhou, Y., Lei, T., Liu, H., Du, N., et al.: Mixture-of-experts with expert choice routing. Adv. Neural. Inf. Process. Syst. **35**, 7103–7114 (2022)

MSCAN: Multi-scale Context-Aware Network for Multivariate Long-Time Forecasting

Te Xue[1], Yuanfei Deng[1(✉)], Shun Mao[2], Weixing Wang[1], and Meiman Li[1]

[1] School of Artificial Intelligence, Guangdong Open University, Guangzhou, China
fiego.deng@outlook.com, mmli@gdrtvu.edu.cn
[2] South China Normal University, Guangzhou, China
shunm@m.scnu.edu.cn

Abstract. Accurate long-term multivariate time series forecasting is crucial in finance, energy, and traffic management. Despite advances in Transformer-based models, capturing both local structures and long-range dependencies remains challenging. Enhancing multi-scale dependency representation improves forecasting accuracy and stability. This paper introduces MSCAN, which integrates Multi-Scale Dynamic Attention (MSDA) for adaptive dependency modeling and Context-Aware Convolutional Attention (CACA) for refined local feature extraction. By combining attention and convolution, MSCAN effectively models temporal dependencies across multiple resolutions. Experiments on seven benchmark datasets show that MSCAN consistently outperforms existing methods across diverse forecasting tasks.

Keywords: Multivariate time series · Long-Term Forecasting · Attention Mechanism · Context-Aware Representation · Multi-Scale Modeling

1 Introduction

Multivariate time series forecasting (MTSF) has driven advances in smart grids, finance, and industrial automation [1–3]. Unlike univariate forecasting, MTSF captures complex dependencies among multiple variables, enabling more accurate predictions. However, existing models struggle to jointly model local structures and global dependencies, particularly in long-range correlations and dynamic patterns. Recent approaches have improved forecasting accuracy but often lack adaptive mechanisms for efficient multi-scale dependency modeling.

Various models have been developed for MTSF. Statistical methods like Vector Autoregression handle linear dependencies but fail in high-dimensional settings. Recurrent models, such as Long Short-Term Memory (LSTM) and Gated Recurrent Unit (GRU) [4], mitigate vanishing gradients but remain inefficient for long-term forecasting. Transformer-based models [5–8] improve global dependency modeling via self-attention but are computationally expensive. More recent alternatives, such as MLP-based methods (TimeMixer) [9], enhance efficiency but lack multi-scale dependency modeling. Existing models face key challenges: Transformers are computationally expensive and lack local inductive bias, weakening short-term pattern extraction. Simpler models improve efficiency but fail to capture multi-scale dependencies. Many methods also struggle to integrate short-term fluctuations with long-range correlations, limiting their effectiveness in capturing complex temporal structures.

We propose MSCAN, which integrates multi-scale dependency modeling and local feature extraction. Inspired by iTransformer's inverted input embedding, MSCAN preserves temporal structures for better representation. The key contributions are:

- A Context-Aware Convolutional Attention mechanism enhances local feature extraction by integrating static and dynamic contextual modeling, effectively capturing fine-grained short-term dependencies.
- A Multi-Scale Dynamic Attention module fuses information across multiple temporal scales through varied receptive fields, improving the model's ability to capture both short-term fluctuations and long-range dependencies.
- Extensive experiments on ETT, Electricity, Weather, and Traffic show that MSCAN outperforms state-of-the-art models in accuracy and efficiency.

2   Related Work

Modeling long-range dependencies is crucial for time series forecasting. Transformers have significantly improved this aspect, but their quadratic complexity limits scalability. Informer alleviates this via probSparse self-attention, while Nonstationary Transformer [10] applies adaptive normalization to handle statistical variations. ETSformer enhances trend modeling with exponential smoothing, and MR-Transformer [11] integrates adaptive segmentation for long-term forecasting. CNN-based models such as SCINet [12] improve short-term feature extraction but rely on fixed receptive fields, limiting adaptability to dynamic patterns. PWDformer [13] refines temporal fusion through deformable attention, while STTRE [14] introduces spatio-temporal embeddings. N-BEATS [15] employs basis expansion for trend and seasonality modeling, while DeepAR [16] leverages recurrent architectures for probabilistic forecasting. MSCAN builds on these works by integrating CACA for refined local feature extraction and MSDA for adaptive multi-scale dependency modeling, improving both long-term forecasting accuracy and computational efficiency.

3   MSCAN

Given a multivariate time series $X \in \mathbb{R}^{T \times N}$, where T denotes the number of time steps and N the number of variables, the goal is to predict future values over a horizon H. The target sequence is $Y \in \mathbb{R}^{H \times N}$, corresponding to the next H time steps. Time series exhibit both short-term fluctuations and long-range dependencies, requiring models that effectively capture multi-scale patterns. Furthermore, inter-variable relationships dynamically evolve over time, making multivariate feature extraction challenging.

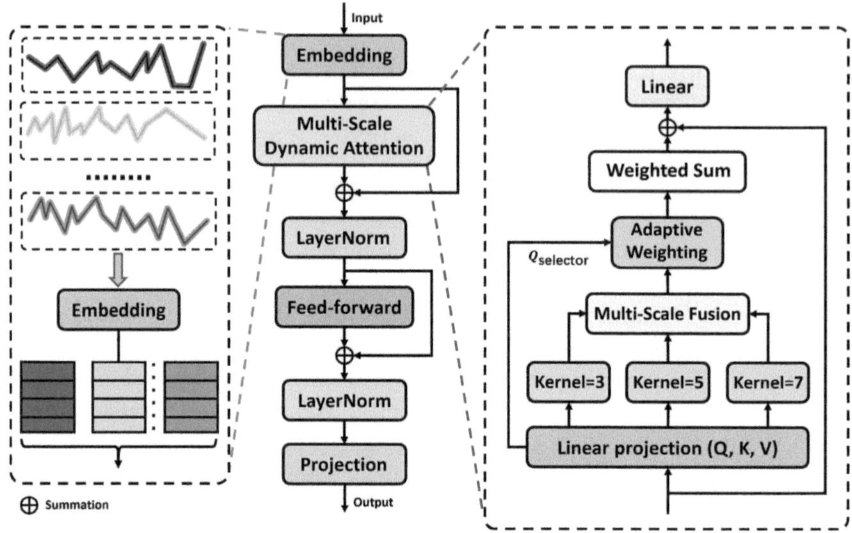

Fig. 1. Architecture of MSCAN. The model consists of three main components: embedding, multi-scale dynamic attention, and multi-scale context-aware convolutional attention.

3.1   Structure Overview

MSCAN integrates MSDA and CACA to enhance long-term forecasting. MSDA captures dependencies across multiple temporal scales, while CACA improves local feature extraction by leveraging static and dynamic context. The overall architecture is illustrated in Fig. 1.

To better preserve temporal structures, MSCAN adopts an inverted input embedding, rearranging the input from time-major (T, N) to variable-major (N, T). This transformation enhances feature extraction before projection:

$$Z_0 = E(\text{Permute}(X)) \in \mathbb{R}^{N \times d}, \tag{1}$$

where $E(\cdot)$ is the embedding function. The encoded sequence passes through L layers of MSDA and CACA:

$$Z_{l+1} = \text{LayerNorm}(\text{MSDA}(Z_l) + Z_l), \quad Y = W Z_L + b, \tag{2}$$

By combining multi-scale attention with context-aware feature extraction, MSCAN effectively models both local and long-range dependencies (Fig. 2).

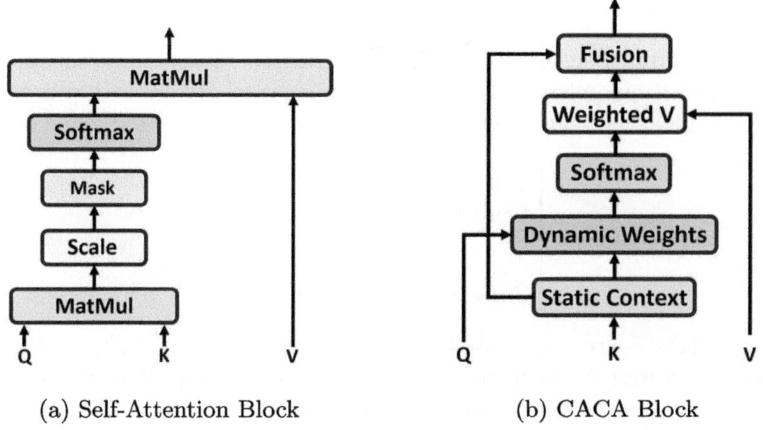

(a) Self-Attention Block   (b) CACA Block

Fig. 2. Comparison of architectures in time-series modeling. (a) Self-attention captures global dependencies. (b) CACA enhances local feature interactions using context-aware convolution.

3.2 Context-Aware Convolutional Attention

CACA enhances local feature extraction by incorporating both static and dynamic contextual modeling. Given a time series input $X \in \mathbb{R}^{T \times d}$, the query (Q), key (K), and value (V) representations are computed as:

$$Q = XW_Q, \quad K = \mathrm{Conv1D}(X, W_K), \quad V = XW_V, \tag{3}$$

where $W_Q, W_V \in \mathbb{R}^{d \times d}$ are learnable projection matrices, and $W_K \in \mathbb{R}^{k \times d}$ encodes local structures. To model static dependencies, a local context representation is extracted:

$$C_s = \sigma(\mathrm{Conv1D}(X, W_K)), \tag{4}$$

where $C_s \in \mathbb{R}^{T \times d}$ captures localized patterns. Meanwhile, a dynamic attention mechanism is introduced to adjust feature importance:

$$A' = \mathrm{Conv1D}([C_s, Q], W_A), \quad A = \mathrm{Softmax}(A'), \tag{5}$$

where $W_A \in \mathbb{R}^{k \times d}$ generates adaptive weights based on both C_s and Q. The final output is a weighted fusion of static and dynamic representations:

$$C_f = A \odot C_s + (1 - A) \odot V, \tag{6}$$

where $\odot$ denotes element-wise multiplication. A residual connection and normalization further stabilize the representation:

$$Z_{\mathrm{CACA}} = \mathrm{LayerNorm}(C_f + X), \tag{7}$$

By dynamically adjusting local dependencies with adaptive attention, CACA improves feature representation, balancing short-term variations with long-range contextual information. This hybrid mechanism enhances both interpretability and forecasting stability.

3.3 Multi-scale Dynamic Attention

MSDA enhances multi-scale dependency modeling by integrating multiple receptive field convolutions with dynamic attention fusion. Given an input sequence $X \in \mathbb{R}^{T \times d}$, multi-scale feature extraction is performed via depth-wise separable convolutions:

$$
X_K = \begin{bmatrix} \mathrm{Conv1D}(X, W_{k_1}) \\ \mathrm{Conv1D}(X, W_{k_2}) \\ \vdots \\ \mathrm{Conv1D}(X, W_{k_m}) \end{bmatrix} \in \mathbb{R}^{T \times m \times d},
\tag{8}
$$

where $W_{k_i} \in \mathbb{R}^{k_i \times d}$ are learnable filters with kernel sizes $\{k_1, k_2, ..., k_m\}$. This allows MSDA to extract both fine-grained and long-range dependencies. Each scale-specific representation undergoes self-attention:

$$
A_K = \mathrm{Softmax}\left(\frac{QK^T}{\sqrt{d}}\right) \in \mathbb{R}^{T \times m \times d},
\tag{9}
$$

where Q, K, V are obtained via linear projections of X. To balance contributions across scales, MSDA introduces adaptive fusion weights:

$$
\alpha_K = \mathrm{Softmax}(\mathrm{Linear}(\mathrm{ReLU}(\mathrm{Linear}(Q)))) \in \mathbb{R}^m,
\tag{10}
$$

The final multi-scale representation is obtained by weighted aggregation:

$$
Z_{\mathrm{MSDA}} = \mathrm{LayerNorm}\left(\sum_i \alpha_{k_i} A_{k_i} V_{k_i} + X\right),
\tag{11}
$$

MSDA is applied iteratively across layers to refine hierarchical temporal representations. Algorithm1 outlines the full computation. By integrating multi-scale feature extraction with adaptive weighting, MSDA effectively captures both short-term fluctuations and long-range dependencies, improving forecasting stability across diverse time horizons.

4 Experiments

4.1 Datasets

To evaluate the proposed model, experiments were conducted on four publicly available time series datasets: Electricity[1], Traffic[2], Weather[3], and Electricity, Transformer Temperature (ETT) [17]. These datasets span electricity consumption, traffic flow, meteorological variables, and industrial monitoring, offering diverse forecasting challenges across different domains.

---

[1] https://archive.ics.uci.edu/ml/datasets/ElectricityLoadDiagrams20112014.
[2] http://pems.dot.ca.gov/.
[3] https://www.ncei.noaa.gov/data/local-climatological-data.

Table 1. We compare competing models for multivariate long-term time series forecasting across forecasting horizons of 96, 192, 336, and 720. *Avg* represents the average performance across these horizons for a comprehensive evaluation.

Models	Metric	MSCAN		iTransformer		PatchTST		Crossformer		TimesMixer		DLinear		MICN		Autoformer		FEDformer	
		MSE	MAE	MSE	MAE	MSE	MAE	MSE	MAE	MSE	MAE	MSE	MAE	MSE	MAE	MSE	MAE	MSE	MAE
ECL	92	0.141	0.235	**0.148**	**0.239**	0.197	0.287	0.213	0.306	0.170	0.262	0.203	0.287	0.198	0.292	0.267	0.368	0.273	0.373
	192	0.158	0.250	**0.167**	**0.258**	0.203	0.295	0.224	0.310	0.185	0.280	0.201	0.290	0.209	0.301	0.333	0.420	0.289	0.384
	336	0.176	0.268	**0.177**	**0.270**	0.213	0.301	0.239	0.326	0.212	0.315	0.217	0.311	0.225	0.323	0.328	0.416	0.301	0.394
	720	**0.215**	**0.304**	0.211	0.301	0.258	0.337	0.273	0.354	0.256	0.377	0.252	0.342	0.258	0.349	0.361	0.506	0.344	0.423
	Avg	0.173	0.264	**0.176**	**0.267**	0.218	0.305	0.237	0.337	0.206	0.308	0.218	0.307	0.222	0.316	0.322	0.427	0.302	0.394
Traffic	92	0.391	0.266	**0.393**	**0.269**	0.460	0.294	0.592	0.340	0.507	0.337	0.630	0.377	0.542	0.329	0.877	0.555	0.778	0.482
	192	**0.414**	0.275	0.413	**0.277**	0.461	0.293	0.611	0.342	0.520	0.348	0.648	0.438	0.553	0.335	0.881	0.546	0.801	0.496
	336	**0.433**	0.281	0.425	**0.283**	0.473	0.298	0.621	0.346	0.522	0.347	0.678	0.460	0.610	0.409	0.891	0.483	0.824	0.507
	720	**0.469**	**0.302**	0.457	0.300	0.501	0.314	0.663	0.366	0.550	0.353	0.704	0.474	0.576	0.385	0.945	0.558	0.835	0.511
	Avg	**0.427**	0.281	0.422	**0.282**	0.474	0.300	0.622	0.349	0.525	0.346	0.665	0.437	0.571	0.364	0.898	0.536	0.810	0.499
weather	92	0.165	0.210	**0.174**	**0.214**	0.184	0.224	0.167	0.244	0.176	0.235	0.256	0.344	0.217	0.283	0.256	0.322	0.307	0.416
	192	0.217	0.252	0.225	**0.258**	0.225	0.261	**0.221**	0.297	0.227	0.288	0.318	0.402	0.247	0.300	0.302	0.365	0.388	0.471
	336	0.268	0.294	0.282	0.300	0.280	**0.299**	**0.279**	0.327	0.290	0.336	0.384	0.462	0.282	0.324	0.337	0.374	0.476	0.531
	720	0.354	0.351	0.358	**0.350**	**0.355**	0.349	0.385	0.395	0.372	0.396	0.462	0.515	0.356	0.368	0.413	0.425	0.561	0.593
	Avg	0.251	0.277	**0.260**	**0.280**	0.261	0.283	0.263	0.316	0.266	0.314	0.355	0.431	0.276	0.318	0.327	0.371	0.433	0.503
ETTh1	92	0.388	0.404	**0.387**	0.405	0.388	0.403	0.415	0.439	0.385	**0.404**	0.462	0.475	0.418	0.435	0.421	0.437	0.458	0.464
	192	0.443	0.436	**0.441**	**0.437**	0.434	0.432	0.478	0.477	0.464	0.447	0.476	0.460	0.478	0.475	0.469	0.468	0.459	0.466
	336	**0.488**	0.459	0.491	**0.463**	0.480	0.464	0.539	0.520	0.554	0.485	0.514	0.480	0.522	0.505	0.513	0.497	0.519	0.506
	720	0.539	0.507	**0.509**	0.494	0.507	0.496	0.858	0.736	0.539	**0.495**	0.568	0.546	0.535	0.526	0.623	0.571	0.537	0.527
	Avg	0.465	0.452	**0.457**	**0.450**	0.452	0.449	0.573	0.543	0.485	0.458	0.505	0.490	0.488	0.485	0.506	0.493	0.493	0.491
ETTh2	92	0.301	0.350	**0.302**	**0.352**	0.309	0.356	0.451	0.474	0.302	0.354	0.333	0.383	0.325	0.378	0.341	0.384	0.342	0.385
	192	0.378	**0.398**	0.380	0.399	**0.379**	0.396	0.502	0.528	0.398	0.414	0.459	0.459	0.480	0.494	0.423	0.436	0.434	0.449
	336	0.427	0.437	**0.424**	0.432	0.441	0.446	0.613	0.602	0.417	**0.435**	0.459	0.459	0.480	0.494	0.447	0.461	0.460	0.471
	720	0.427	0.445	**0.431**	**0.447**	0.433	0.448	0.821	0.715	0.431	0.513	0.689	0.597	0.681	0.588	0.675	0.615	0.496	0.493
	Avg	0.383	**0.408**	**0.384**	0.407	0.391	0.411	0.597	0.580	0.387	0.429	0.521	0.497	0.488	0.483	0.472	0.474	0.433	0.449
ETTm1	92	0.329	0.366	0.342	0.377	0.338	0.371	0.413	0.430	**0.334**	**0.369**	0.346	0.372	0.363	0.416	0.501	0.475	0.457	0.454
	192	0.369	0.387	0.383	0.396	0.370	**0.388**	0.434	0.430	**0.367**	0.410	0.382	0.390	0.411	0.441	0.566	0.497	0.572	0.527
	336	0.402	0.408	0.418	0.418	0.410	**0.409**	0.543	0.508	**0.407**	0.431	0.414	0.414	0.451	0.471	0.541	0.495	0.527	0.501
	720	0.471	**0.448**	0.487	0.457	0.457	0.441	0.599	0.549	**0.469**	0.472	0.473	0.451	0.544	0.538	0.549	0.504	0.674	0.580
	Avg	0.393	0.402	0.408	0.412	**0.394**	**0.402**	0.497	0.479	0.395	0.420	0.403	0.407	0.442	0.467	0.539	0.493	0.557	0.516
ETTm2	92	**0.181**	**0.266**	0.186	0.272	0.180	0.264	0.399	0.432	0.188	0.292	0.191	0.289	0.206	0.316	0.211	0.293	0.210	0.291
	192	**0.246**	**0.306**	0.254	0.314	0.245	0.305	0.556	0.505	0.256	0.339	0.282	0.359	0.352	0.431	0.267	0.326	0.267	0.325
	336	0.308	0.345	0.316	0.351	**0.311**	**0.349**	0.626	0.543	0.321	0.379	0.372	0.421	0.373	0.446	0.331	0.367	0.328	0.366
	720	0.414	0.406	0.414	0.407	0.404	0.400	1.799	1.085	**0.412**	0.440	0.537	0.515	0.577	0.564	0.415	0.408	0.417	0.415
	Avg	**0.287**	**0.331**	0.292	0.336	0.285	0.329	0.845	0.641	0.294	0.362	0.346	0.396	0.377	0.439	0.306	0.349	0.305	0.349
1st Count		20	20	5	5	**9**	**10**	0	0	2	0	0	0	0	0	0	0	0	0

4.2 Baselines and Experiment Setup

We compare MSCAN with state-of-the-art forecasting models, including Transformer-based FEDformer [18], Autoformer, Crossformer [19], iTransformer, and Informer, which improve long-range dependency modeling. PatchTST employs patch-wise representations for feature extraction, while DLinear provides a competitive linear benchmark. We also evaluate TimeMixer, which replaces self-attention with token-mixing MLPs for efficiency, and MICN, which integrates CNNs and Transformers for local-global dependency modeling. MSCAN is tested across four forecasting horizons: 96, 192, 336, and 720 time steps, covering short- to long-term predictions. Performance is measured using Mean Squared Error (MSE) and Mean Absolute Error (MAE):

$$\text{MSE} = \frac{1}{N} \sum_{i=1}^{N} (y_i - \hat{y}_i)^2, \quad \text{MAE} = \frac{1}{N} \sum_{i=1}^{N} |y_i - \hat{y}_i|, \tag{12}$$

where y_i and $\hat{y}_i$ are ground truth and predicted values, and N is the sample count. MSCAN is trained using PyTorch with a batch size of 32 and an initial learning rate of $1e-4$, dynamically adjusted via a scheduling strategy. Early stopping is

---

Algorithm 1 Multi-Scale Dynamic Attention

Require: Input sequence $X \in \mathbb{R}^{T \times d}$, kernel sizes $K = \{3, 5, 7\}$
Ensure: Multi-scale representation Z_{MSDA}
1: **for** $k_i \in K$ **do**
2:     $X_{k_i} \leftarrow \mathrm{Conv1D}(X, W_{k_i})$
3: **end for**
4: $Q, K, V \leftarrow \mathrm{Linear}(X)$
5: **for** $k_i \in K$ **do**
6:     $A_{k_i} \leftarrow \mathrm{Softmax}\left(\frac{QK^T}{\sqrt{d}}\right)$
7:     $V_{k_i} \leftarrow A_{k_i}V$
8: **end for**
9: $\alpha_{k_i} \leftarrow \mathrm{Softmax}(\mathrm{Linear}(\mathrm{ReLU}(\mathrm{Linear}(Q))))$
10: $V_{\mathrm{MSDA}} \leftarrow \sum_{k_i \in K} \alpha_{k_i} V_{k_i}$
11: $Z_{\mathrm{MSDA}} \leftarrow \mathrm{LayerNorm}(V_{\mathrm{MSDA}} + X)$
12: **return** Z_{MSDA}

---

applied if validation performance stagnates for 10 epochs. All experiments run on an NVIDIA GeForce RTX 4070SUPER (12GB) GPU.

Table 2. Robustness of MSCAN performance. The results are obtained from five random seeds.

Dataset Horizon	ECL		Weather		ETTh1	
	MSE	MAE	MSE	MAE	MSE	MAE
92	0.141 ± 0.000	0.235 ± 0.000	0.165 ± 0.001	0.250 ± 0.000	0.389 ± 0.001	0.405 ± 0.000
192	0.158 ± 0.001	0.210 ± 0.001	0.213 ± 0.004	0.252 ± 0.001	0.446 ± 0.002	0.438 ± 0.002
336	0.176 ± 0.001	0.268 ± 0.001	0.269 ± 0.001	0.296 ± 0.001	0.486 ± 0.007	0.457 ± 0.002
720	0.244 ± 0.006	0.303 ± 0.002	0.358 ± 0.004	0.351 ± 0.001	0.536 ± 0.009	0.500 ± 0.010
Dataset Horizon	ETTh2		ETTm1		ETTm2	
	MSE	MAE	MSE	MAE	MSE	MAE
92	0.301 ± 0.001	0.350 ± 0.001	0.328 ± 0.001	0.366 ± 0.001	0.181 ± 0.001	0.265 ± 0.002
192	0.379 ± 0.001	0.398 ± 0.000	0.369 ± 0.001	0.387 ± 0.000	0.248 ± 0.001	0.308 ± 0.002
336	0.422 ± 0.005	0.433 ± 0.003	0.403 ± 0.001	0.410 ± 0.001	0.309 ± 0.001	0.346 ± 0.001
720	0.430 ± 0.003	0.447 ± 0.003	0.471 ± 0.002	0.448 ± 0.001	0.411 ± 0.002	0.404 ± 0.003

4.3   Result and Analysis

Table 1 summarizes the forecasting results, where lower MSE and MAE indicate higher accuracy. The best and second-best performances are highlighted in red and blue, respectively. MSCAN consistently outperforms baselines across datasets and forecasting horizons, demonstrating its ability to capture both local and long-range dependencies. It excels on datasets with complex temporal structures, such as ETT and Traffic, surpassing self-attention and MLP-based models,

Table 3. Ablation of different components of MSCAN in a multivariate long-term prediction task.

Models Metric	ECL		Traffic		Weather		ETTh1		ETTh2		ETTm1		ETTm2	
	MSE	MAE	MSE	MAE	MSE	MAE	MSE	MAE	MSE	MAE	MSE	MAE	MSE	MAE
w/o CA	0,174	0,266	0,904	0,531	0,262	0,282	0,451	0,447	0,388	0,410	0,409	0,414	0,290	0,335
w/o MS	0,182	0,271	0,446	0,293	0,252	0,279	0,459	0,451	0,385	0,409	0,398	0,407	0,288	0,333
MSCAN	0,173	0,264	0,427	0,281	0,251	0,277	0,465	0,452	0,383	0,408	0,393	0,402	0,287	0,331

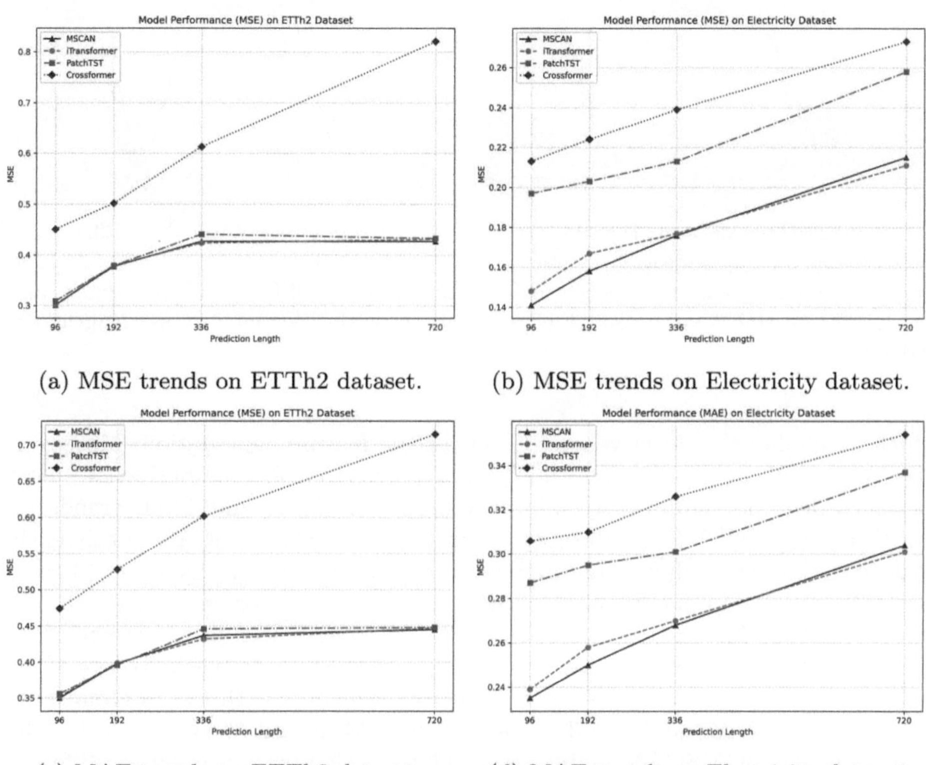

(a) MSE trends on ETTh2 dataset.   (b) MSE trends on Electricity dataset.

(c) MAE trends on ETTh2 dataset.   (d) MAE trends on Electricity dataset.

Fig. 3. MSE and MAE comparison of different models on the Electricity and ETTh2 datasets across prediction lengths.

Table 4. Performance of CACA with different kernel sizes.

Models Metric	ECL		Traffic		Weather		ETTh1		ETTh2		ETTm1		ETTm2	
	MSE	MAE	MSE	MAE	MSE	MAE	MSE	MAE	MSE	MAE	MSE	MAE	MSE	MAE
$k = 3$	0.184	0.273	0.449	0.294	0.253	0.278	0.458	0.449	0.384	0.382	0.403	0.410	0.290	0.334
$k = 5$	0.182	0.271	0.446	0.293	0.252	0.279	0.459	0.451	0.384	0.409	0.398	0.406	0.288	0.333
$k = 7$	0.180	0.270	0.449	0.292	0.251	0.278	0.462	0.453	0.462	0.410	0.396	0.406	0.290	0.334

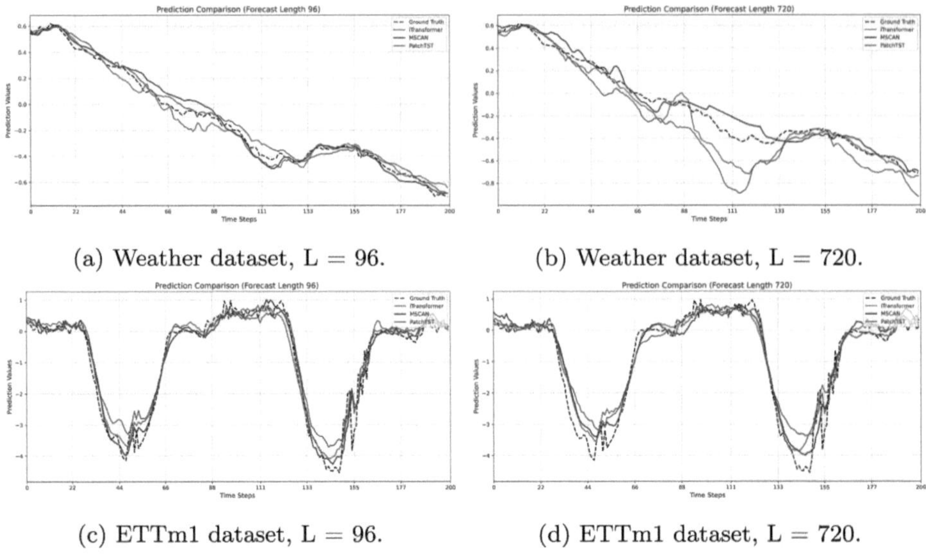

(a) Weather dataset, L = 96.   (b) Weather dataset, L = 720.

(c) ETTm1 dataset, L = 96.   (d) ETTm1 dataset, L = 720.

Fig. 4. Comparison of time series forecasting models (MSCAN, iTransformer, and PatchTST) on the Weather and ETTm1 datasets with different forecast lengths (96 and 720).

which highlights the effectiveness of multi-scale feature aggregation. Moreover, MSCAN maintains stable performance in long-horizon forecasting, where most baselines degrade significantly. Figure 3 shows the MSE and MAE trends on the Electricity and ETTh2 datasets, demonstrating that MSCAN consistently achieves lower errors than other models across prediction lengths. Figure 4 compares the prediction performance of MSCAN with iTransformer and PatchTST across different forecasting horizons. MSCAN consistently provides smoother and more stable predictions, closely aligning with the ground truth. To assess the impact of random initialization, we conduct experiments with five random seeds and report the mean and standard deviation of MSE and MAE (Table 2). The results show that MSCAN maintains a relatively low variance across different datasets and forecasting horizons, suggesting robustness to weight initialization. For most datasets, the standard deviation remains small, indicating consistent performance across multiple training runs.

4.4   Ablation Study

To assess the contributions of CACA and MSDA, we perform ablation experiments by removing each component. Table 3 presents the results, where w/o CA and w/o MS denote MSCAN without CACA and MSDA, respectively. Removing either module degrades performance across all datasets, confirming their importance. The absence of CACA increases errors, emphasizing its role in local feature extraction, while removing MSDA leads to a more significant accuracy drop, par-

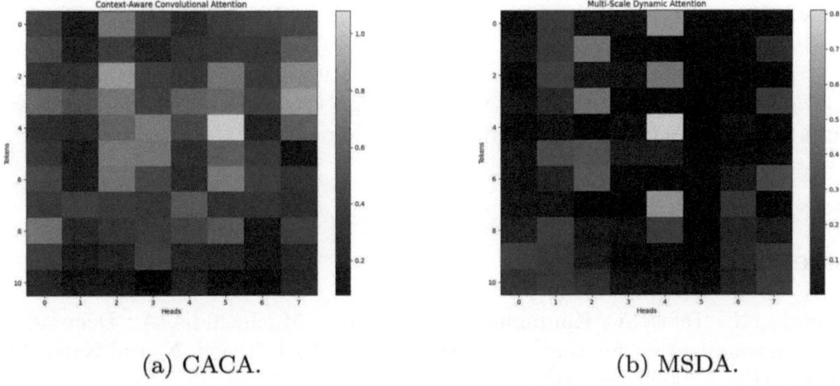

(a) CACA.   (b) MSDA.

Fig. 5. Attention weight distributions of CACA and MSDA. CACA captures local dependencies with a uniform attention spread, while MSDA selectively focuses on key time steps.

ticularly in datasets with complex dependencies like ETT, highlighting its importance in multi-scale modeling. The full MSCAN model consistently achieves the lowest errors, demonstrating the synergy between CACA and MSDA.

Figure 5 compares the attention distributions of CACA and MSDA in MSCAN on the same dataset. CACA maintains a balanced allocation, enhancing short-term feature extraction, while MSDA highlights key time steps, improving long-range modeling. To examine CACA's receptive field impact, we evaluate MSCAN with different kernel sizes ($k = 3, 5, 7$). As shown in Table 4, the performance differences across individual kernel sizes (e.g., k=3, 5, 7) are relatively small, suggesting that no single temporal scale dominates the modeling capability. However, the full MSDA module, which combines multiple receptive fields through adaptive fusion, consistently outperforms any single-scale variant. This highlights the importance of multi-scale integration: while individual scales capture specific temporal patterns, it is their combination that leads to a more robust and expressive representation, enabling superior forecasting accuracy across diverse datasets.

5   Conclusion and Future Work

This paper introduces MSCAN, a model for long-term multivariate time series forecasting, integrating Multi-Scale Dynamic Attention and Context-Aware Convolutional Attention for improved feature extraction and dependency modeling. Experiments on seven benchmark datasets demonstrate MSCAN's superior performance in MSE and MAE. Ablation studies confirm the effectiveness of MSDA and CACA, while robustness tests validate stability. Future work will focus on optimizing efficiency for long sequences, handling irregular sampling and missing data, and developing lightweight variants for real-time forecasting.

Acknowledgement. This work is supported by the Guangdong Provincial Education Science Planning Project (No. 2024GXJK140), and the Guangdong Province Quality Enhancement Project for the Construction of a Learning Society (No. JXYGC2024D226). The authors also acknowledge the support from the Innovation Research Team for Artificial Intelligence Application and the Research Center for Artificial Intelligence Application Innovation.

References

1. Passalis, N., Tefas, A., Kanniainen, J., Gabbouj, M., Iosifidis, A.: Deep adaptive input normalization for time series forecasting. IEEE Trans. Neural Netw. Learn. Syst. **31**(9), 3760–3765 (2020)
2. Zheng, W., Hu, J.: Multivariate time series prediction based on temporal change information learning method. IEEE Trans. Neural Netw. Learn. Syst. **34**(10), 7034–7048 (2023)
3. Wu, H., et al.: Timesnet: temporal 2d-variation modeling for general time series analysis. In: International Conference on Learning Representations (2023)
4. Cho, K., et al.: Learning Phrase Representations using RNN Encoder-Decoder for Statistical Machine Translation (2014)
5. Vaswani, A., et al.: Attention is all you need. Adv. Neural Inf. Process. Syst. **30** (2017)
6. Wu, H., Xu, J., Wang, J., Long, M.: Autoformer: decomposition transformers with auto-correlation for long-term series forecasting. Adv. Neural. Inf. Process. Syst. **34**, 22419–22430 (2021)
7. Nie, Y., Nguyen, N.H., Sinthong, P., Kalagnanam, J.: A time series is worth 64 words: long-term forecasting with transformers. In: International Conference on Learning Representations (2023)
8. Liu, Y., et al.: itransformer: inverted transformers are effective for time series forecasting. In: International Conference on Learning Representations (2024b)
9. Wang, S., et al.: Timemixer: decomposable multiscale mixing for time series forecasting. In: International Conference on Learning Representations (ICLR) (2024)
10. Liu, Y., Wu, H., Wang, J., Long, M.: Non-stationary transformers: exploring the stationarity in time series forecasting. Adv. Neural. Inf. Process. Syst. **35**, 9881–9893 (2022)
11. Zhu, S., Zheng, J., Ma, Q.: MR-transformer: multiresolution transformer for multivariate time series prediction. IEEE Trans. Neural Netw. Learn. Syst. **36**(1), 1171–1183 (2025)
12. Lim, B., Zohren, S.: Time-series forecasting with deep learning: a survey. Phil. Trans. R. Soc. A: Math. Phys. Eng. Sci. **379**(2194), 20200209 (2021)
13. Wang, Z., Ran, H., Ren, J., Sun, M.: PWDformer: deformable transformer for long-term series forecasting. Pattern Recogn. **147**, 110118 (2024)
14. Deihim, A., Alonso, E., Apostolopoulou, D.: STTRE: a spatio-temporal transformer with relative embeddings for multivariate time series forecasting. Neural Netw. **168**, 549–559 (2023)
15. Oreshkin, B.N., Carpov, D., Chapados, N., Bengio, Y.: N-BEATS: neural basis expansion analysis for interpretable time series forecasting (2020)
16. Salinas, D., Flunkert, V., Gasthaus, J., Januschowski, T.: DeepAR: probabilistic forecasting with autoregressive recurrent networks. Int. J. Forecast. **36**(3), 1181–1191 (2020)

17. Li, S., et al.: Enhancing the locality and breaking the memory bottleneck of transformer on time series forecasting. Adv. Neural Inf. Process. Syst. **32** (2019)
18. Zhou, T., Ma, Z., Wen, Q., Wang, X., Sun, L., Jin, R.: FEDformer: frequency enhanced decomposed transformer for long-term series forecasting. In: Proceedings of 39th International Conference on Machine Learning (ICML 2022) (2022)
19. Zhang, Y., Yan, J.: Crossformer: transformer utilizing cross-dimension dependency for multivariate time series forecasting. In: International Conference on Learning Representations (2023)

PAformer: Transformer with Learnable Period Detection and Periodic Attention for Multivariate Time Series

Meng Wan[1,2], Huan Hao[3], Yuxuan Bi[4], Jue Wang[2], Qi Su[5], Fang Liu[2(✉)],
Peng Shi[1(✉)], Xueyan Wei[3], Yangang Wang[2], Shulong Wang[6], and Helian Wu[6]

[1] University of Science and Technology Beijing, Beijing 100083, China
wanmengdamon@cnic.cn, pshi@ustb.edu.cn
[2] Computer Network Information Center, CAS, Beijing 100083, China
{wangjue,liufang,wangyg}@sccas.cn
[3] Binzhou Institute of Technology, Binzhou 256600, China
{haohuan,weixueyan}@wqucas.com
[4] North China Electric Power University, Baoding 071000, China
[5] Peking University, Beijing 100083, China
qiisuu@stu.pku.edu.cn
[6] Yunnan Hongqiao New Energy, Mengzi 661100, China
{wangshulong,wuhelian}@wqmail.cn

Abstract. Accurate forecasting of multivariate time series (MTS) is crucial across various domains. However, existing models often fail to effectively capture the complex periodic patterns across different variables, and struggle with utilizing periodic features in attention mechanism, which leads to uniformly distributed attention weights. To address these limitations, we introduce a novel Transformer model equipped with learnable period detection and periodic attention mechanisms. The combination of wavelet decomposition and convolution design can better extract the dominant period of each variable. The period-based Gaussian decay strategy can guide attention to relationships within the same position of each period. Experimental results show that our model significantly outperforms state-of-the-art attention-based models, particularly on datasets exhibiting notable periodic behavior.

Keywords: Multivariate Time Series Forecasting · Periodic Attention Mechanism · Period Detection · Wavelet Transform

1 Introduction

Time series forecasting is crucial in fields like finance [1], healthcare [2], and IoT [3], where accurate predictions are essential for decision-making and strategic planning. Traditional time series analysis primarily relied on statistical methods such as ARIMA and GARCH, and machine learning models like SVM and

---

F. Liu and P. Shi—Equal contribution.

T. Zhu et al. (Eds.): KSEM 2025, LNAI 15920, pp. 260–274, 2026.
https://doi.org/10.1007/978-981-95-3052-6_20

random forests. These methods are effective for modeling linear relationships but struggle with complex nonlinear patterns. With the rapid development of deep learning, time series forecasting has increasingly shifted towards deep learning models, which have shown unique advantages in handling nonlinearity and complex patterns.

Early deep learning models like Multilayer Perceptrons are used for time series modeling [4]. However, they struggle with long-term dependencies extraction. As deep learning techniques evolve, Transformer architectures with self-attention mechanisms have become powerful tools for time series forecasting. Transformer-based models, such as PatchTST [5] and Informer [6], perform exceptionally well in processing long time series data and demonstrate strong results across various forecasting tasks. In recent years, methods combining Graph Neural Networks (GNNs) and self-attention mechanisms for time series forecasting have also emerged. For example, the Hetero-GAT model [7] utilizes graph-based attention to capture relationships across time and space, although its applicability remains limited to specific scenarios. Despite significant advancements in MTS forecasting models, current methods still face key challenges when it comes to capturing complex periodic patterns [8,9]. These challenges are mainly focused on two aspects:

(1) **Difficulty in distinguishing independent periodic patterns:** Existing models, such as TimesNet [10] and SDformer [11], tend to use non-learnable mathematical methods like FFT to extract a uniform period for all variables, overlooking the unique periodic characteristics of each variable. As a result, these models struggle to capture multiple or complex periodic patterns, especially in datasets where the periodic behavior varies significantly between different variables [6,12]. Therefore, there is a critical need for models that can independently identify and utilize the unique periodic features of each variable.

(2) **Limitations in attention mechanism with periods:** Transformer-based models [13–15] typically design their attention mechanisms to globally model interactions between variables [16]. While these approaches can be effective in certain contexts, it often results in an overly uniform distribution of attention [17–19]. In scenarios where MTS data are rich in periodic features like Weather [20] and Solar [21], this can dilute the model's ability to focus on critical time segments that carry significant periodic information [22–24]. Thus, enhancing the attention mechanism to better focus on key periodic segments is essential for improving model performance [25].

To address these challenges, we propose a novel period-based model with three key innovations:

– We introduce a channel-specific periodic discovery method based on learnable wavelet decomposition. This approach can separate low-frequency and high-frequency components at multiple scales and identify dominant periodic features, allowing the model to independently capture the unique period of each channel.

- We design a periodic attention decay mechanism that dynamically adjusts attention weights using a Gaussian decay strategy. This mechanism aligns the attention distribution more closely with the periodic structure of the data, enabling the model to better focus on time segments with similar periodicity.
- We conduct experiments on multiple real-world time series datasets, and the periodic attention mechanism demonstrated its state-of-the-art (SOTA) results in complex forecasting tasks.

2   Related Work

2.1   Periodic Models

The periodic features in time series data are crucial for identifying underlying repetitive patterns. These periodic patterns not only enhance prediction accuracy but also optimize resource allocation and improve data analysis efficiency. Autoformer [26] calculates autocorrelation values to identify the periodic length of time series data, revealing periodic dependencies and further improving the model's predictive performance. TimesNet [10] converts one-dimensional time series into two-dimensional tensors and applies fast Fourier transform (FFT) to analyze frequency components, thereby determining the periodic length. PDF [27] introduces a multi-period decoupling module capable of capturing both short-term and long-term variations in two-dimensional time series. SparseTSF [28] employs down-sampling on the original series to focus on cross-period trend prediction, effectively extracting periodic features while minimizing model complexity and parameter size. However, these methods predominantly rely on traditional mathematical techniques for extracting periodic features. In MTS scenarios, capturing dynamic changes in cross-channel periodicity remains a significant challenge. Existing periodic extraction methods often struggle to handle interdependencies between multiple channels simultaneously, thereby limiting their applicability to complex time series data [29,30].

2.2   Attention Models

Transformer has emerged as a powerful framework for time series forecasting, driving progress in the study of attention mechanisms. Informer [6] introduces a sparse self-attention mechanism to prioritize dominant queries while incorporating self-attention distillation to reduce memory usage and mitigate the issue of high time complexity. Pyraformer [31] employs a multi-resolution pyramid attention mechanism to model time series as hierarchical structures, enabling the capture of multi-scale features. FEDformer [32] extends attention operations to the frequency domain by leveraging Fourier and wavelet transforms to extract frequency-domain features. PatchTST [5] focuses on computing relationships between different patches using a self-attention mechanism, while Pathformer [33] further integrates intra-patch and inter-patch attention across multiple scales to simultaneously model global and local dependencies. iTransformer [34] redefines the roles of the attention mechanism and feedforward networks, dedicating attention specifically to modeling inter-variable correlations. To address the issue of overly smooth attention distributions, SDformer [11] integrates spectral filtering transformations and dynamic directional attention to redistribute attention weights, thereby enhancing the heterogeneity of attention maps. Despite these advancements in the design of attention mechanisms, challenges remain in capturing periodic features specific to individual channels and optimizing attention distributions. In particular, research on leveraging periodic information to guide attention mechanisms is limited and lacks systematic solutions [35–38].

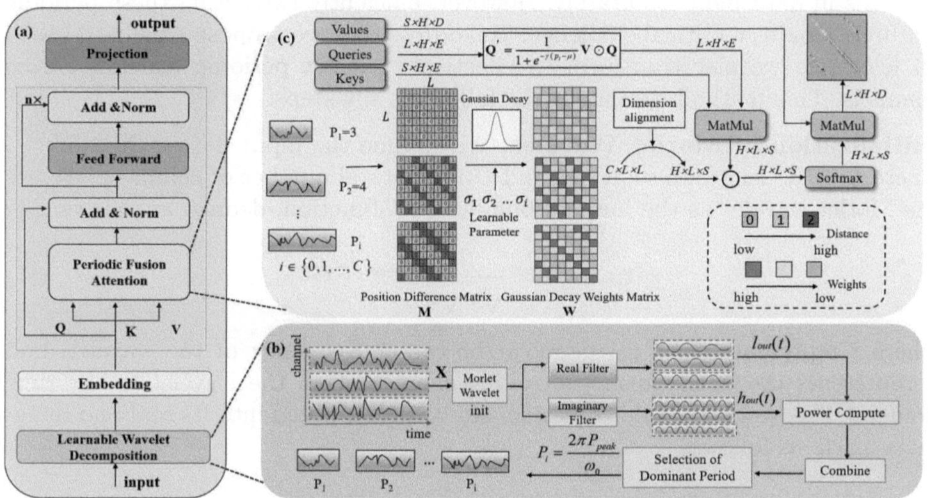

Fig. 1. The overall architecture of PAformer.

3   Methods

3.1   Framework

Figure 1 illustrates the overall framework of PAformer, which includes the LWT module, the PDA module, as well as embedding and projection operations. From a technical perspective, the input time series is first decomposed using the Morlet wavelet to generate real and imaginary filtered signals. Based on the power spectrum analysis, the dominant periods are extracted. The extracted periodic features are then fed into the PDA module, where a position difference matrix is constructed to capture the relative positional relationships, reflecting spatial differences. Subsequently, a Gaussian decay function is applied, and weights are computed using learnable parameters to generate a Gaussian decay weight matrix. This weight matrix is integrated into the attention mechanism, facilitating weighted fusion with Queries, Keys, and Values to capture and align periodic dependencies. The fused features are further enhanced through a feed-forward network and residual connections, and the final output is projected onto the desired dimensions via a projection operation. The framework effectively combines wavelet decomposition with the attention mechanism, efficiently capturing periodic patterns in time series while ensuring flexibility and expressive power.

3.2   Learnable Wavelet Decomposition

Periodic patterns are widely present in natural phenomena and time series. By capturing periodic information, it becomes possible to model the underlying patterns in data more accurately. However, efficiently extracting these periodic features remains a critical challenge. To address this, we propose a method based on learnable wavelet transform to effectively extract periodic features across channels. This method comprises the following key steps:

Initialization of Morlet Wavelet. We assume the input data is $\mathbf{X} \in \mathbb{R}^{L \times C}$, where L is the length of sequence and C is the total number of channels. We use the Morlet wavelet as the foundational wavelet function, defined as follows:

$$\psi(t; \omega_0, \sigma) = \frac{1}{\sqrt{\sigma\sqrt{\pi}}} e^{i\omega_0 t} e^{-\frac{t^2}{2\sigma^2}}, \tag{1}$$

where t represents time, ω_0 denotes the center frequency of the wavelet, and σ represents the bandwidth, controlling the spread of the wavelet in the time domain. The Morlet wavelet function can be decomposed into its real and imaginary parts as follows:

$$w_{\text{real}}(t) = \text{Re}(\psi(t; \omega_0, \sigma)) = \frac{1}{\sqrt{\sigma\sqrt{\pi}}} e^{-\frac{t^2}{2\sigma^2}} \cos(\omega_0 t), \tag{2}$$

$$w_{\text{imag}}(t) = \text{Im}(\psi(t; \omega_0, \sigma)) = \frac{1}{\sqrt{\sigma\sqrt{\pi}}} e^{-\frac{t^2}{2\sigma^2}} \sin(\omega_0 t). \tag{3}$$

To initialize the learning process, we generate learnable convolution kernels based on these Morlet wavelet filters, optimizing random perturbations during training.

Convolution Operation and Learnable Filters. The real and imaginary filters are applied through convolution operations. The outputs of these convolutions, $\mathbf{l}_{\text{out}}(t)$ and $\mathbf{h}_{\text{out}}(t)$, represent the filtered signals obtained by convolving the input signal $\mathbf{X}_t$ with the real and imaginary parts of the Morlet wavelet, respectively. These outputs capture the oscillatory components of the signal in the time-frequency domain. Specifically:

$$\mathbf{l}_{\text{out}}(t) = (\mathbf{X}_t * w_{\text{real}}(t)), \tag{4}$$

$$\mathbf{h}_{\text{out}}(t) = (\mathbf{X}_t * w_{\text{imag}}(t)), \tag{5}$$

where $\mathbf{X}_t$ represents the input signal at time t, and $*$ denotes the convolution operation. The symbols $w_{\text{real}}(t)$ and $w_{\text{imag}}(t)$ represent the real and imaginary filters, respectively, at time t.

The real and imaginary parts of the Morlet wavelet transform represent oscillatory behaviors in the time-frequency domain. By computing the power spectra of these components, we extract the signal's frequency characteristics. These filters are treated as learnable parameters, integrated into the end-to-end neural network model.

Extraction of Periodic Features. After the convolution operations, the power spectra of the signal are computed to identify periodic features:

$$P_{\text{real}}(t) = \mathbf{l}_{\text{out}}(t)^2, \tag{6}$$

$$P_{\text{imag}}(t) = \mathbf{h}_{\text{out}}(t)^2, \tag{7}$$

where $P_{\text{real}}(t)$ and $P_{\text{imag}}(t)$ represent the power of the real and imaginary components, respectively. These power values quantify the significance of the corresponding frequency components at time t.

To capture the full range of periodic components across different scales, we analyze the energy distribution of the power spectrum. By identifying peaks in the power spectrum across various scales, we can separate different periodic patterns, from global trends to localized oscillations.

Selection of Dominant Period. To determine the dominant periodicity in the signal, we analyze the power spectra $P_{\text{real}}(t)$ and $P_{\text{imag}}(t)$ over the entire time sequence. Peaks in these power spectra correspond to significant periodic components. Specifically, for each time step t, the peaks exceeding a predefined threshold are identified, and the scale S_{peak} corresponding to the highest peak is selected. The dominant period P_i of channel index $i \in \{0, 1, \ldots, C\}$ is then computed as:

$$P_i = \frac{2\pi S_{\text{peak}}}{\omega_0}, \tag{8}$$

where S_{peak} is the scale associated with the maximum value among the peaks found in $P_{\text{real}}(t)$ and $P_{\text{imag}}(t)$. This method ensures that the extracted period reflects both the global and localized periodic patterns within the signal.

3.3   Periodic Decay Attention

Existing attention mechanisms often face the problem of homogenization, where attention weight distributions are overly uniform. This makes it difficult for the model to effectively distinguish the importance of different positions or channels, limiting its ability to capture diverse information features in the data. To address this issue, this paper proposes a periodic decay attention module, which leverages periodic features to guide the attention distribution, significantly enhancing the prediction accuracy of PAformer. This method involves the following key steps:

Positional Difference Matrix. The position difference matrix can reflect the relative distances between different locations within the same period. For each period P_i, we calculate the corresponding position difference matrix $\mathbf{M} \in \mathbb{R}^{L \times L}$, where L is the sequence length. Each element of the $\mathbf{M}$ is defined as follows:

$$\mathbf{M}(j,k) = \min\left(|j-k|\mathrm{mod}P_i, P_i - (|j-k|\mathrm{mod}P_i)\right), \tag{9}$$

where j and k represent the row and column indices of the matrix.

As shown in Fig. 1(c), assuming $P_i = 4$, the calculated $\mathbf{M}(j,k)$ reflects the relative distances between different positions within a periodicity of 4. To facilitate understanding, the visualization highlights this relationship by representing elements with greater relative distances in darker colors and those with smaller distances in lighter colors, effectively illustrating the concept of relative positioning within the same period.

Gaussian Decay Weights Matrix. The Gaussian Decay Function is a method used to apply decay to weights in space or time. It is defined as follows:

$$w(x,\sigma) = \exp\left(-\frac{x^2}{2\sigma^2}\right), \tag{10}$$

where x is the input value; $w(x,\sigma)$ represent the weights at a given input x and standard deviation σ; The σ controls the rate of decay.

In periodic data, closer positions often exhibit stronger correlations, while the correlation gradually decreases with increasing distance. The Gaussian function, with its natural symmetry and rapid decay properties, is well-suited to describe this relationship. Unlike fixed weight assignments, Gaussian decay dynamically adjusts the parameter σ to adapt to the characteristics of different channels or data features. Therefore, We designed a Gaussian decay strategy that leverages the spatial decay characteristics of the Gaussian decay function. This strategy allows for learning the most suitable decay scale for each channel, Specifically, for each period P_i we calculate the corresponding Gaussian decay weights matrix $\mathbf{W} \in \mathbb{R}^{C \times L \times L}$. Each element of the $\mathbf{W}$ is computed as follows:

$$\mathbf{W}(j,k) = \exp\left(-\frac{\mathbf{M}(j,k)^2}{2\sigma_i^2}\right), \tag{11}$$

where σ_i is a learnable parameter representing the decay scale. This strategy effectively combines periodic positional information with weights, enhancing the influence of elements that are closer in terms of periodic alignment and diminishing the impact of those further apart.

As shown in Fig. 2 (a) the Gaussian decay curve intuitively illustrates how different standard deviations σ influence the weight distribution. Assuming $P_i = 5$, the position difference matrix reveals that in periodic structures, elements with smaller position differences have higher weights, while those with larger differences have lower weights. This highlights the role of periodic structures in guiding attention distribution. During actual training, σ is a learnable parameter that the model can automatically adjust based on the data characteristics to accommodate different periodic patterns. As visualized in Fig. 2 (b), the Gaussian

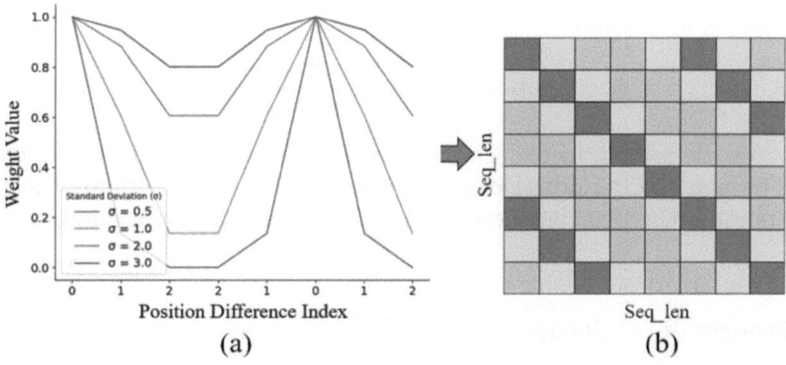

Fig. 2. Gaussian Decay Curve and Decay Matrix Illustration.

decay weight matrix demonstrates how weights gradually diminish with increasing distance, validating the strategy's effectiveness in concentrating attention on critical periodic positions while reducing the influence of out-of-period positions.

Period Guide Strategy. In the attention mechanism, the query vector $\mathbf{Q}$ plays a crucial role in guiding the attention. To improve the model's response to periodic patterns, we introduce a dynamic weights adjustment approach using periodic information. The periodic function $f(P)$ maps the variable's period P to weights adjustment factors, dynamically updating the weights of $\mathbf{Q}$. The function is defined as:

$$f(P_i) = \frac{1}{1 + e^{-\gamma(P_i - \mu)}}, \tag{12}$$

where γ and μ shape the function's curve. Specifically, the parameter γ controls the sensitivity of the adjustments to periodic features, while μ determines the center point of the weight adjustments. By introducing these two adjustable parameters, the function gains greater sensitivity and flexibility to meet the demands of various datasets. The weights adjustment matrix $\mathbf{W}'$ is computed as:

$$\mathbf{W}' = f(P) \cdot \mathbf{V}, \tag{13}$$

with V being a random matrix. The dynamic weight matrix $\mathbf{W}'$ enhances the responsiveness of the query vector $\mathbf{Q}$ to specific periodic features. The adjusted query vector Q' is obtained by:

$$\mathbf{Q}' = \mathbf{Q} \odot \mathbf{W}'. \tag{14}$$

We integrate the $\mathbf{W}$ with the adjusted attention score matrix to effectively incorporate periodic features into the attention calculation. The calculation formula is as follows:

$$\mathbf{Scores} = \mathbf{Q}'\mathbf{K}^{\mathbf{T}} \odot \mathbf{W}, \tag{15}$$

where $\odot$ represents element-wise matrix multiplication. **Scores** represents the adjusted attention score matrix. Therefore, the calculation formula for the attention weights A is as follows:

$$\mathbf{A} = \mathrm{Dropout}\left(\mathrm{Softmax}\left(\frac{\mathbf{Scores}}{\sqrt{d}}\right)\right), \tag{16}$$

where $\sqrt{d}$ is the scaling factor. Dropout reduces overfitting during the training phase. Through the Periodic Decay Attention, we leverage periodic features to guide attention distribution, thereby improves the prediction accuracy.

4 Experiments

4.1 Experimental Setup

Datasets. To comprehensively evaluate the performance of the model, we conducted experiments on 6 distinct public datasets: (1) The ETT dataset records 7 feature variables from two electricity transformers over the period from July 2016 to July 2018. For our analysis, we selected 2 representative subsets with different temporal resolutions, namely ETTh2 and ETTm2, where the former is recorded hourly and the latter every 15 min. (2) The PEMS dataset encompasses data from California's public transportation network, with a collection window set at 5-minute intervals. In this study, we focus on and report the results of the PEMS04 and PEMS08 subsets. (3) The Solar dataset documents the solar power output of 137 photovoltaic plants in 2006, with data sampled every 10 min. (4) The Weather dataset, sourced from the Weather Station of the Max Planck Institute for Biogeochemistry, includes 21 meteorological parameters updated every 10 min throughout 2020. The split ratios for all datasets align with the conventions widely accepted in most research studies [10,11,34].

Baselines and Settings. We select 7 popular models in MTS forecasting as the baseline for comparison, which include the variable attention-based models FEDformer [32], iTransformer [34] and SDformer [11], the periodic information-utilizing model TimesNet [10], as well as the well-performing models PatchTST [5], DLinear [39] and TiDE [40]. To ensure experimental fairness, we adhere to the experimental settings of iTransformer and TimesNet, conducting all experiments within the environment of PyTorch 2.1 and NVIDIA GeForce RTX 4090.

4.2 Main Results

As shown in Table 1, the results are evaluated by the MSE and MAE metrics. The results indicate that PAformer performs the best in the majority of cases, particularly on the Weather and PEMS datasets where periodicity is significant. Compared to the SOTA model iTransformer, PAformer achieves an MSE improvement of over 28.3% and an MAE improvement of over 17.2% on the average results across four prediction horizons on the PEMS dataset. The period-dominated attention mechanism, compared to variable-based modeling models like iTransformer and SDformer, demonstrates superior performance in forecasting tasks, more effectively guiding attention distribution. Additionally, PAformer utilizes a channel-based periodicity extraction method, achieving higher accuracy than other periodicity-based models.

Table 1. Multivariate time-series forecasting results, where the best results are in **bold**, the second best results are underlined.

Methods		PAformer MSE	PAformer MAE	SDformer MSE	SDformer MAE	iTransformer MSE	iTransformer MAE	PatchTST MSE	PatchTST MAE	TimesNet MSE	TimesNet MAE	TiDE MSE	TiDE MAE	DLinear MSE	DLinear MAE	FEDformer MSE	FEDformer MAE
Metric		MSE	MAE	MSE	MAE	MSE	MAE	MSE	MAE	MSE	MAE	MSE	MAE	MSE	MAE	MSE	MAE
PEMS04	12	**0.069**	**0.171**	0.104	0.215	0.080	0.188	0.105	0.224	0.087	0.195	0.219	0.340	0.148	0.272	0.138	0.262
	24	**0.079**	**0.183**	0.141	0.252	0.099	0.212	0.153	0.275	0.103	0.215	0.292	0.398	0.224	0.340	0.177	0.293
	48	**0.091**	**0.198**	0.220	0.317	0.131	0.245	0.229	0.339	0.136	0.250	0.409	0.478	0.355	0.437	0.270	0.368
	96	**0.106**	**0.216**	0.349	0.408	0.171	0.282	0.291	0.389	0.303	0.492	0.492	0.532	0.452	0.504	0.341	0.427
Weather	96	**0.166**	**0.208**	0.178	0.218	0.178	0.219	0.177	0.218	0.173	0.223	0.202	0.261	0.197	0.254	0.217	0.296
	192	**0.212**	**0.252**	0.227	0.261	0.260	0.259	0.225	0.259	0.219	0.263	0.242	0.298	0.237	0.294	0.276	0.336
	336	**0.272**	**0.296**	0.286	0.302	0.282	0.300	0.275	0.296	0.281	0.303	0.287	0.335	0.283	0.331	0.339	0.380
	720	0.354	**0.349**	0.361	0.351	0.358	0.350	0.354	0.348	0.357	0.352	0.351	0.386	**0.348**	0.383	0.403	0.428
Electricity	96	**0.135**	**0.230**	0.179	0.279	0.148	0.240	0.195	0.285	0.174	0.278	0.237	0.329	0.216	0.306	0.193	0.308
	192	**0.156**	**0.251**	0.192	0.290	0.168	0.259	0.199	0.289	0.199	0.302	0.236	0.330	0.215	0.309	0.201	0.315
	336	**0.177**	**0.271**	0.209	0.306	0.178	0.271	0.215	0.305	0.204	0.305	0.249	0.344	0.228	0.323	0.214	0.329
	720	**0.201**	**0.295**	0.235	0.326	0.210	0.300	0.256	0.337	0.286	0.361	0.284	0.373	0.263	0.354	0.246	0.355
Solar	96	**0.200**	**0.232**	0.227	0.251	0.203	0.237	0.234	0.286	0.255	0.290	0.312	0.399	0.291	0.377	0.242	0.342
	192	**0.229**	**0.256**	0.266	0.280	0.233	0.261	0.267	0.312	0.299	0.315	0.339	0.416	0.325	0.394	0.285	0.380
	336	**0.241**	**0.269**	0.281	0.291	0.248	0.273	0.295	0.318	0.318	0.334	0.368	0.430	0.352	0.416	0.282	0.376
	720	**0.245**	**0.273**	0.278	0.290	0.249	0.275	0.285	0.315	0.337	0.339	0.370	0.425	0.354	0.416	0.357	0.427
ETTh2	96	**0.297**	**0.346**	0.300	0.347	0.301	0.350	0.302	0.348	0.332	0.370	0.400	0.440	0.358	0.406	0.358	0.397
	192	**0.375**	**0.396**	0.379	0.398	0.380	0.399	0.388	0.400	0.402	0.415	0.528	0.509	0.484	0.479	0.429	0.439
	336	**0.416**	**0.428**	0.419	0.428	0.424	0.432	0.426	0.433	0.464	0.456	0.643	0.571	0.590	0.530	0.496	0.487
	720	**0.430**	0.445	0.430	**0.443**	0.430	0.447	0.431	0.446	0.453	0.461	0.874	0.679	0.833	0.654	0.463	0.474
ETTm2	96	**0.176**	**0.258**	0.189	0.274	0.185	0.272	0.179	0.264	0.188	0.268	0.207	0.305	0.195	0.294	0.203	0.287
	192	**0.240**	**0.301**	0.255	0.313	0.253	0.313	0.251	0.312	0.260	0.310	0.290	0.364	0.285	0.361	0.269	0.328
	336	**0.308**	**0.346**	0.318	0.353	0.317	0.352	0.311	0.346	0.321	0.349	0.377	0.422	0.392	0.433	0.325	0.366
	720	**0.404**	**0.402**	0.415	0.408	0.413	0.407	0.415	0.409	0.424	0.408	0.558	0.524	0.541	0.515	0.421	0.415

4.3 Ablation Study and Analysis

We conducted ablation experiments on the LWT module to verify its effectiveness. Since the periodic information learned by the LWT module relies on utilization by the PDA module, replacing the PDA module renders the LWT module ineffective, making it impossible to perform an independent ablation on the PDA module. In the W/O-LWT experiment, we replaced the LWT module with the fixed-period method from TimesNet. The experimental results are presented in Table 2, where the Electricity, Weather, and PEMS04 datasets exhibit pronounced periodic characteristics. The results show that when the period is fixed and not learnable, model performance degrades to varying degrees. On the PEMS04 dataset, the MSE decreased by an average of 4.6%, and the MAE decreased by an average of 3.4%. This validates the critical role of the proposed LWT module in learning periodic patterns.

4.4 Periodic Attention Analysis

By guiding the attention distribution with periodic features, we create the periodic patterns of datasets in the attention maps. As shown in Fig. 3(a), the atten-

Table 2. Comparison of PAformer and W/O-LWT on different datasets. The best results are in **bold**.

Dataset	Metric	PAformer				W/O-LWT			
		12/96	24/192	48/336	96/720	12/96	24/192	48/336	96/720
Electricity	MSE	**0.135**	**0.156**	**0.177**	**0.201**	0.136	0.158	0.180	0.204
	MAE	**0.230**	**0.251**	**0.271**	**0.295**	0.231	0.255	0.275	0.298
Solar	MSE	**0.200**	**0.229**	**0.241**	**0.245**	0.202	0.235	0.246	0.249
	MAE	**0.232**	**0.256**	**0.269**	**0.273**	0.237	0.262	0.272	0.277
PEMS04	MSE	**0.069**	**0.079**	**0.091**	**0.106**	0.071	0.081	0.095	0.114
	MAE	**0.171**	**0.183**	**0.198**	**0.216**	0.174	0.188	0.205	0.227
Weather	MSE	**0.166**	**0.212**	**0.272**	**0.354**	0.169	0.215	0.274	0.355
	MAE	**0.208**	**0.252**	**0.296**	**0.349**	0.210	0.254	0.300	0.352
ETTh2	MSE	**0.297**	**0.375**	**0.416**	**0.430**	0.299	0.379	0.420	0.432
	MAE	**0.346**	0.396	**0.428**	**0.445**	0.347	**0.396**	0.430	0.448

tion map produced by the existing attention mechanism exhibits a relatively uniform attention distribution, with smooth weights assignments, leading to a homogenized pattern in the attention map. Figure 3(b) displays a segment of data from the weather dataset, clearly showing daily periodicity with 48 time points per day. Figure 3(c) presents the attention map generated by our proposed periodic decay attention mechanism. Compared to Fig. 3(a) the attention distribution in Fig. 3(c) is more focused, effectively capturing the periodic feature in the data, especially where the key attention regions closely align with the periodic nodes. One reason is that points at the same periodic positions have higher similarity, resulting in higher attention scores.

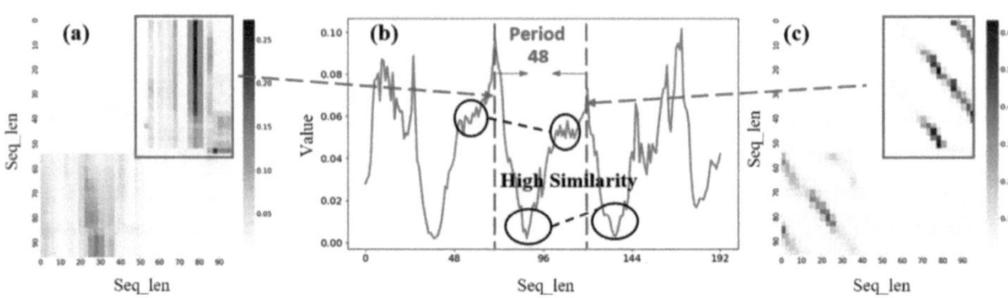

Fig. 3. The visualization of attention maps on Weather dataset.

4.5   Look-Back Window and Model Efficiency Analysis

We evaluate the model's memory efficiency and effectiveness in processing historical data for time series forecasting by adjusting the input time window length. Figure 4a compares the performance of different models under various look-back window settings. As the window length increases, most models show a decreasing MSE, indicating that longer historical data enhances forecasting accuracy. PAformer consistently achieves the lowest MSE across all settings. By incorporating a periodic attention mechanism, PAformer dynamically captures periodic patterns, maintaining stable performance, especially with longer windows. In contrast, TiDE exhibits performance fluctuations, while PatchTST and SDformer, though stable, do not surpass PAformer in accuracy.

Training time and memory usage are crucial for evaluating model efficiency. As shown in Fig. 4b, each circle's size represents memory usage, with models in the lower-left corner demonstrating better efficiency and predictive accuracy. PAformer stands out by achieving a low MSE with minimal training time. Conversely, TimesNet and TiDE consume excessive memory, while iTransformer and DLinear, though efficient, fall short in accuracy.

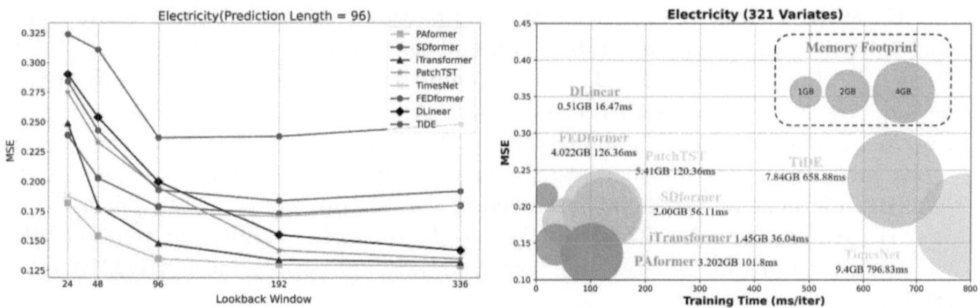

(a) Comparison of lookback window length L in {24,48,96,192,336}.

(b) Comparision of memory footprint, training time and MSE.

Fig. 4. Model performance comparison on the Electricity dataset.

5   Conclusion

In this paper, we introduce a learnable period detection strategy and a novel periodic attention design that improves MTS forecasting by effectively capturing periodic patterns across channels. In the future, we will combine our proposed methods with more transformer-based models and also try to extend to more other models based on Linear and convolutional neural network (CNN) design.

Acknowledgements. This work was supported by the National Key R&D Program of China (Grant No. 2023YFB3001803). This work was also supported by Open Competition Project of Binzhou Institute of Technology (GYY-JBGS-2024-ST-012). We thank VenusAI Platform (http://data.aicnic.cn) for kindly providing the GPU clusters for model training.

References

1. Cheng, D., Yang, F., Xiang, S., Liu, J.: Financial time series forecasting with multi-modality graph neural network. Pattern Recogn. **121**, 108218 (2022)
2. Kaushik, S., et al.: AI in healthcare: time-series forecasting using statistical, neural, and ensemble architectures. Front. Big Data **3**, 4 (2020)
3. Chen, Z., Chen, D., Zhang, X., Yuan, Z., Cheng, X.: Learning graph structures with transformer for multivariate time-series anomaly detection in iot. IEEE Internet Things J. **9**(12), 9179–9189 (2021)
4. Gamboa, J.C.B.: Deep learning for time-series analysis. arXiv preprint arXiv:1701.01887 (2017)
5. Nie, Y., Nguyen, N.H., Sinthong, P., Kalagnanam, J.: A time series is worth 64 words: long-term forecasting with transformers. In: The Eleventh International Conference on Learning Representations
6. Zhou, H., et al.: Informer: beyond efficient transformer for long sequence time-series forecasting. In: Proceedings of the AAAI Conference on Artificial Intelligence, vol. 35, pp. 11106–11115 (2021)
7. Jin, C., et al.: Hetgat: a heterogeneous graph attention network for freeway traffic speed prediction. J. Ambient Intell. Humanized Comput. 1–12 (2021)
8. Dang, Y., Zhang, Y., Wang, J.: A novel multivariate grey model for forecasting periodic oscillation time series. Expert Syst. Appl. **211**, 118556 (2023)
9. Cai, W., Liang, Y., Liu, X., Feng, J., Wu, Y.: Msgnet: learning multi-scale inter-series correlations for multivariate time series forecasting. In: Proceedings of the AAAI Conference on Artificial Intelligence, vol. 38, pp. 11141–11149 (2024)
10. Wu, H., Hu, T., Liu, Y., Zhou, H., Wang, J., Long, M.: Timesnet: temporal 2d-variation modeling for general time series analysis. arXiv preprint arXiv:2210.02186 (2022)
11. Zhou, Z., Lyu, G., Huang, Y., Wang, Z., Jia, Z., Yang, Z.: Sdformer: transformer with spectral filter and dynamic attention for multivariate time series long-term forecasting (2024)
12. Li, W., Guo, J.: Extraction of periodic signals in global navigation satellite system (GNSS) vertical coordinate time series using the adaptive ensemble empirical modal decomposition method. Nonlinear Process. Geophys. **31**(1), 99–113 (2024)
13. Ding, Y., Jia, M., Miao, Q., Cao, Y.: A novel time-frequency transformer based on self-attention mechanism and its application in fault diagnosis of rolling bearings. Mech. Syst. Signal Process. **168**, 108616 (2022)
14. Song, Z., Yu, J., Chen, Y.P.P., Yang, W.: Transformer tracking with cyclic shifting window attention. In: Proceedings of the IEEE/CVF Conference on Computer Vision and Pattern Recognition, pp. 8791–8800 (2022)
15. Chang, Y., Li, F., Chen, J., Liu, Y., Li, Z.: Efficient temporal flow transformer accompanied with multi-head probsparse self-attention mechanism for remaining useful life prognostics. Reliabil. Eng. Syst. Saf. **226**, 108701 (2022)
16. Yang, Z., Zhang, Q., Chang, W., Xiao, P., Li, M.: Egformer: an enhanced transformer model with efficient attention mechanism for traffic flow forecasting. Vehicles **6**(1), 120–139 (2024)
17. Irani Azad, M., Rajabi, R., Estebsari, A.: Nonintrusive load monitoring (NILM) using a deep learning model with a transformer-based attention mechanism and temporal pooling. Electronics **13**(2), 407 (2024)
18. de Santana Correia, A., Colombini, E.L.: Attention, please! a survey of neural attention models in deep learning. Artif. Intell. Rev. **55**(8), 6037–6124 (2022)

19. Ge, Q., Li, J., Wang, X., Deng, Y., Zhang, K., Sun, H.: Litetransnet: an interpretable approach for landslide displacement prediction using transformer model with attention mechanism. Eng. Geol. **331**, 107446 (2024)

20. Wawale, S.G., Bisht, A., Vyas, S., Narawish, C., Ray, S.: An overview: modeling and forecasting of time series data using different techniques in reference to human stress. Neurosci. Inf. **2**(3), 100052 (2022)

21. Takilalte, A., Harrouni, S., Mora, J.: Forecasting global solar irradiance for various resolutions using time series models-case study: Algeria. Energy Sources Part A: Rec. Utilizat. Environ. Effects **44**(1), 1–20 (2022)

22. Ning, Y., Kazemi, H., Tahmasebi, P.: A comparative machine learning study for time series oil production forecasting: arima, lstm, and prophet. Comput. Geosci. **164**, 105126 (2022)

23. Ren, Q., Li, Y., Liu, Y.: Transformer-enhanced periodic temporal convolution network for long short-term traffic flow forecasting. Expert Syst. Appl. **227**, 120203 (2023)

24. Zhao, X., Wang, N.: Enformer: encoder-based sparse periodic self-attention time-series forecasting. IEEE Access (2023)

25. Liao, X., Liu, Z., Zheng, X., Ping, Z., He, X.: Wind power prediction based on periodic characteristic decomposition and multi-layer attention network. Neurocomputing **534**, 119–132 (2023)

26. Wu, H., Xu, J., Wang, J., Long, M.: Autoformer: decomposition transformers with auto-correlation for long-term series forecasting. Adv. Neural. Inf. Process. Syst. **34**, 22419–22430 (2021)

27. Dai, T., et al.: Periodicity decoupling framework for long-term series forecasting. In: The Twelfth International Conference on Learning Representations (2024)

28. Lin, S., Lin, W., Wu, W., Chen, H., Yang, J.: Sparsetsf: modeling long-term time series forecastinfg with 1k parameters. arXiv preprint arXiv:2405.00946 (2024)

29. Kim, H., Yun, U., Vo, B., Lin, J.C.W., Pedrycz, W.: Periodicity-oriented data analytics on time-series data for intelligence system. IEEE Syst. J. **15**(4), 4958–4969 (2020)

30. Wen, Q., He, K., Sun, L., Zhang, Y., Ke, M., Xu, H.: Robustperiod: robust time-frequency mining for multiple periodicity detection. In: Proceedings of the 2021 International Conference on Management of Data, pp. 2328–2337 (2021)

31. Liu, S., et al.: Pyraformer: low-complexity pyramidal attention for long-range time series modeling and forecasting. In: International Conference on Learning Representations (2021)

32. Zhou, T., Ma, Z., Wen, Q., Wang, X., Sun, L., Jin, R.: Fedformer: frequency enhanced decomposed transformer for long-term series forecasting. In: International Conference on Machine Learning, pp. 27268–27286. PMLR (2022)

33. Chen, P., et al.: Multi-scale transformers with adaptive pathways for time series forecasting. In: International Conference on Learning Representations (2024)

34. Liu, Y., et al.: itransformer: inverted transformers are effective for time series forecasting. In: The Twelfth International Conference on Learning Representations (2023)

35. Qiu, J., Wang, B., Zhou, C.: Forecasting stock prices with long-short term memory neural network based on attention mechanism. PLoS ONE **15**(1), e0227222 (2020)

36. Chen, R., Yan, X., Wang, S., Xiao, G.: Da-net: dual-attention network for multivariate time series classification. Inf. Sci. **610**, 472–487 (2022)

37. Fu, E., Zhang, Y., Yang, F., Wang, S.: Temporal self-attention-based conv-lstm network for multivariate time series prediction. Neurocomputing **501**, 162–173 (2022)

38. Dong, Y., Xiao, L., Wang, J., Wang, J.: A time series attention mechanism based model for tourism demand forecasting. Inf. Sci. **628**, 269–290 (2023)
39. Zeng, A., Chen, M., Zhang, L., Xu, Q.: Are transformers effective for time series forecasting? In: Proceedings of the AAAI Conference on Artificial Intelligence, vol. 37, pp. 11121–11128 (2023)
40. Das, A., Kong, W., Leach, A., Mathur, S.K., Sen, R., Yu, R.: Long-term forecasting with tide: time-series dense encoder. Trans. Mach. Learn. Res. (2023)

ELS-GDR: Efficient Extraction of Long-Term Sequential Signals for Guiding Diffusion-Based Recommendation

Jianfang Wang$^{(\boxtimes)}$ iD, Zihao Wang iD, and Anunobi Victor Chibueze iD

School of Computer Science and Technology, Henan Polytechnic University, Jiaozuo 454000, China
wangjianfang@hpu.edu.cn, {212309010010,522309010004}@home.hpu.edu.cn

Abstract. Sequential recommendation (SR) aims to model users' dynamic interests over time and predict their next actions. However, existing sequential recommendation models based on conditionally guided diffusion still face two key challenges in long-term sequence modeling. First, excessive noise injection may disrupt the structure of target embeddings, thereby affecting recommendation accuracy and stability. Second, the high computational complexity of processing long sequences limits model efficiency. To tackle these challenges, we propose the Efficient Extraction of Long-Term Sequential Signals for Guiding Diffusion-Based Recommendation (ELS-GDR). We design ELS-GDR to effectively extract long-term sequential signals and enhance diffusion-based recommendation. Specifically, we incorporate an L2 normalized linear attention mechanism into the long-term sequential recommendation framework, significantly reducing computational complexity while capturing users' long-term behavioral patterns more effectively. We further introduce a bias noise strategy to improve the model's robustness against noisy interactions. Finally, we integrate a classifier-free guided diffusion mechanism to optimize the reverse denoising process, enhancing recommendation accuracy and personalization. Extensive experiments on three public datasets demonstrate that our method consistently outperforms existing approaches in both recommendation performance and computational efficiency.

Keywords: Sequential recommendation · Linear complexity · Diffusion models · L2 Normalization · Efficient Transformer

1 Introduction

In the era of information technology, sequential recommendation (SR) has emerged as a key technique for modeling user behavior sequences and predicting next-item interactions [1]. Early SR models relied on fixed vector representations of user histories, often augmented with contextual data [2–4]. However, such static representations fail to capture dynamic user preferences, limiting performance in complex scenarios [5]. Diffusion models (DMs) address this by progressively denoising interactions, improving long-term dependency modeling and recommendation quality [6]. DMs transform input data into noise and reconstruct it through an iterative denoising process, enabling effective modeling of complex distributions.

To enhance recommendation personalization, recent research has introduced conditionally guided diffusion mechanisms. These mechanisms utilize historical interactions as guidance signals in the denoising process, enabling the model to generate recommendations that align more closely with user preferences for both discrete user-item relationships and continuous latent representations [6].

Although guided diffusion models have improved recommendation performance, they still face two critical challenges:

Computational Complexity in Long Sequences: Existing methods often employ Transformer-based architectures to incorporate user interaction sequences as guidance in the reverse denoising process [7,8]. However, these approaches struggle to efficiently model long interaction sequences while reducing the complexity of the attention mechanism. Since the computational and memory cost of self-attention is $O\left(N^2\right)$ when the sequence length N greatly exceeds the item embedding dimension d, handling long sequences leads to substantial computational overhead [9].

Excessive Noise Injection: During the forward diffusion process, excessive noise may destabilize the model by disrupting the structure of target embeddings, ultimately degrading recommendation accuracy and stability.

To tackle these issues, we propose Efficient Extraction of Long-Term Sequential Signals for Guiding Diffusion-Based Recommendation (ELS-GDR). Our main contributions are as follows:

(1) We introduce an L2 normalized linear attention mechanism into the model architecture, reducing the complexity of attention from $O\left(N^2\right)$ to $O(N)$ in long-term sequential recommendation. Additionally, we incorporate explicit control signals into the diffusion process, enabling more effective sequence modeling.
(2) We propose a bias noise strategy and integrate classifier-free guided diffusion, optimizing the reverse denoising process and enhancing the model's robustness against noisy interactions.
(3) We perform comprehensive evaluations across three widely-used benchmark datasets, showing that our method achieves superior recommendation performance and improved computational efficiency compared to existing leading models.

2 Related Works

2.1 Sequential Recommendation

Existing sequential recommendation methods fall into two categories: deep learning-based and hybrid approaches. Deep learning models leverage neural networks to capture complex user behaviors—Recurrent Neural Networks (RNNs) for long-term dependencies [10], Convolutional Neural Networks (CNNs) for local patterns [11], Graph Neural Networks (GNNs) for user-item relations [12], and Transformers for self-attention-based modeling [13]. Hybrid approaches combine multiple techniques to address individual model limitations, such as causal inference for explainability [14] and contrastive learning for robust representations [2].

2.2 Diffusion Models

Diffusion models surpass GANs and VAEs in capturing multi-granularity features and generating high-quality, stably trained samples. Recent work introduces conditional guidance into recommendation, using external signals to steer the diffusion process. For example, Li et al. [6] extract key interests for reverse diffusion, Ma et al. [15] enhance historical information use, and Wang et al. [16] incorporate Transformers to improve sequential recommendation.

3 Methodology

As shown in Fig. 1, ELS-GDR consists of an L2-normalized linear attention mechanism and a guided diffusion model with bias noise, followed by inner product-based item retrieval.

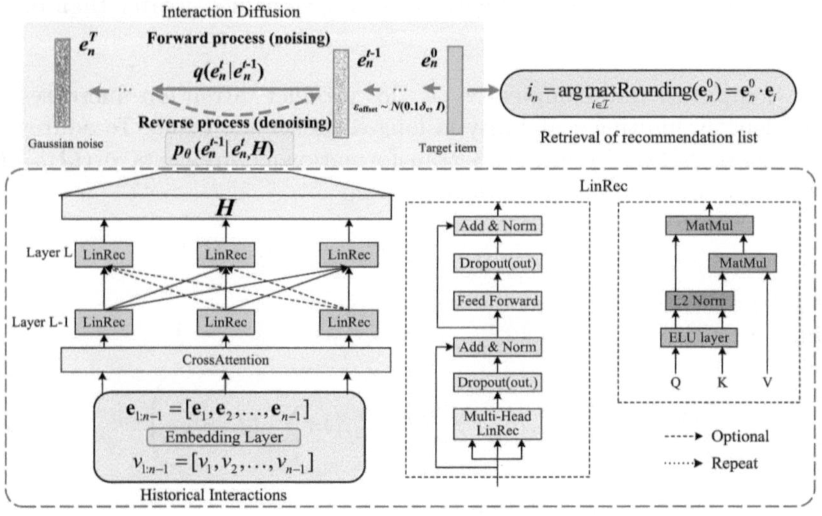

Fig. 1. The overall architecture of ELS-GDR.

3.1 L2 Normalized Linear Attention Mechanism

Embedding Layer. Given a discrete item set $\mathcal{I}$, a user's historical interaction sequence is denoted as $v_{1:n-1} = [v_1, v_2, \ldots, v_{n-1}]$, with v_n as the next item. The training data consists of all sequences $\mathcal{D} = \{[v_{1:n-1}, v_n]_m\}_{m=1}^{|\mathcal{D}|}$, while the test data is represented as $\mathcal{D}_t = \{[v_{1n-1}]_m\}_{m=1}^{|\mathcal{D}_m|}$.

We define an embedding matrix $\mathbf{M} \in \mathbb{R}^{|T| \times d}$, where d is the embedding dimension. Let N be the maximum sequence length. Trainable positional embeddings $\mathbf{P} \in \mathbb{R}^{N \times d}$ are added to the item embeddings to obtain the final sequence representations $\mathbf{e}_{1:n-1} = [\mathbf{e}_1, \mathbf{e}_2, \ldots, \mathbf{e}_{n-1}]$.

Transformer Layer. This section analyzes dot-product attention and its equivalence conditions, then introduces an efficient L2-normalized method that modifies the mapping and computation order to reduce complexity while preserving sequence modeling effectiveness.

Equivalence Conditions. The dot-product attention matrix is typically computed as:

$$\boldsymbol{A} = \rho\left(\boldsymbol{Q}\boldsymbol{K}^T\right)\boldsymbol{V}, \boldsymbol{B} = \rho\left(\boldsymbol{Q}\boldsymbol{K}^T\right), \tag{1}$$

where $\rho(\cdot)$ represents the scaled and row-wise Softmax-normalized attention matrix. The matrix $\boldsymbol{B}$ is characterized by the following two properties:

(1) Normalization property: The sum of elements in each row of $\boldsymbol{B}$ equals 1.
(2) Non-negativity property: All entries in $\boldsymbol{B}$ take values greater than or equal to zero.

The computational complexity of dot-product attention increases with sequence length, limiting scalability in long-sequence modeling. To address this, we decompose $\rho\left(\boldsymbol{Q}\boldsymbol{K}^T\right)$ into two transformation components $\rho_1(\boldsymbol{Q})\rho_2(\boldsymbol{K})^T$, resulting in a new computational formulation:

$$\boldsymbol{A}' = \rho_1(\boldsymbol{Q})\rho_2(\boldsymbol{K})^T\mathbf{V}, \boldsymbol{B}' = \rho_1(\boldsymbol{Q})\rho_2(\boldsymbol{K})^T, \tag{2}$$

where $\rho_1(\cdot)$ and $\rho_2(\cdot)$ represent different mappings.

Thus, the i-th row of $\boldsymbol{B}'$ can be expressed as:

$$\boldsymbol{B}'_i = \left(\sum_{j=1}^{d} Q_{ij}^{\rho}K_{1j}^{\rho}, \sum_{j=1}^{d} Q_{ij}^{\rho}K_{2j}^{\rho}, \mathrm{L}, \sum_{j=1}^{d} Q_{ij}^{\rho}K_{Nj}^{\rho}\right), \tag{3}$$

where $\boldsymbol{Q}^{\rho} = \rho_1(\boldsymbol{Q})$ and $\boldsymbol{K}^{\rho} = \rho_2(\boldsymbol{K})$.

Since $\boldsymbol{K}$ and $\boldsymbol{V}$ are $N \times d$ matrices, we can precompute transformation mappings $(\boldsymbol{K}^{\rho})^T \boldsymbol{V}$ to achieve $O\left(Nd^2\right)$ complexity. Additionally, by approximating long-sequence modeling through simplified transformation mappings $\rho_1(\cdot)$ and $\rho_2(\cdot)$, we can further reduce complexity to nearly linear $O(N)$. However, strictly ensuring the linear mapping satisfies the above equivalence conditions remains challenging.

L2 Normalization. We generalize the earlier constraints and define two transformation mechanisms that are required to adhere to the following specifications:

(1) $\rho_1(\cdot)$ and $\rho_2(\cdot)$ should be computationally efficient without incurring extra overhead.
(2) The mappings must retain the attention mechanism's recognition and stability for effective sequence representation learning.

We apply row-wise and column-wise L2 normalization to transform the i-th row of $\boldsymbol{Q}$, $\boldsymbol{Q}_i = (\boldsymbol{Q}_{i1}, ..., \boldsymbol{Q}_{id})$, and the j-th column of $\boldsymbol{K}$, $\boldsymbol{K}_j = (\boldsymbol{K}_{1j}, ..., \boldsymbol{K}_{Nj})^{\mathrm{T}}$, as follows:

$$
\begin{aligned}
\rho_1(\boldsymbol{Q}_i) &= \frac{\boldsymbol{Q}_i}{\sqrt{d}||\boldsymbol{Q}_i||_2} = \frac{1}{\sqrt{d}||\boldsymbol{Q}_i||_2}(\boldsymbol{Q}_{i1}, ..., \boldsymbol{Q}_{id}), \\
\rho_2(\boldsymbol{K}_j) &= \frac{\boldsymbol{K}_j}{\sqrt{N}||\boldsymbol{K}_j||_2} = \frac{1}{\sqrt{N}||\boldsymbol{K}_j||_2}(\boldsymbol{K}_{1j}, ..., \boldsymbol{K}_{Nj})^{\mathrm{T}},
\end{aligned}
\tag{4}
$$

where $|| \ ||_2$ denotes the L2 norm used for normalization.

We leverage the Cauchy-Schwarz inequality to ensure that the generated attention matrix B' satisfies the normalization property.

$$
\boldsymbol{Q}_{i1} + ... + \boldsymbol{Q}_{id} \leq \sqrt{d}||\boldsymbol{Q}_i||_2.
\tag{5}
$$

To ensure non-negativity of $\boldsymbol{B}'$, we use ELU instead of ReLU to avoid zero-gradient issues and preserve stable optimization.

The final computation process of the L2 normalized linear attention mechanism is given by:

$$
A'(\boldsymbol{Q}, \boldsymbol{K}, \boldsymbol{V}) = \rho_1(\text{elu}(\boldsymbol{Q})) \left(\rho_2(\text{elu}(\boldsymbol{K}))^T \boldsymbol{V}\right),
\tag{6}
$$

where the row transformation is denoted as $\rho_1(\boldsymbol{Q}_i) = \frac{1}{\sqrt{d}||\boldsymbol{Q}_i||_2}\boldsymbol{Q}_i$, where $\boldsymbol{Q}_i$ represents the i th row of $\boldsymbol{Q}$, and the column transformation is denoted as $\rho_2(\boldsymbol{K}_j) = \frac{1}{\sqrt{N}||\boldsymbol{K}_j||_2}\boldsymbol{K}_j$, where $\boldsymbol{K}_j$ represents the j-th column of $\boldsymbol{K}$.

3.2 Guided Diffusion for Item Generation

Bias Noise. Traditional diffusion models sample noise from $\mathcal{N}(0, \mathbf{I})$, but are sensitive to input shifts, reducing output diversity. To address this, we introduce bias noise sampled during training or forward diffusion.

$$
\epsilon_{\text{offset}} \sim \mathcal{N}(0.1\delta_c, \mathbf{I}),
\tag{7}
$$

where, δ_c represents a constant value, while a scaling factor of 0.1 is used to adjust the mean of the noise distribution.

Conditional Diffusion Model. Incorporating the bias noise strategy, the forward process in ELS-GDR iteratively adds Gaussian noise $\epsilon_{\text{offset}} \sim \mathcal{N}(0.1\delta_c, \mathbf{I})$ to the original data $\mathbf{e}_n^0$ until it becomes noise following a standard Gaussian distribution $\mathcal{N}(0, \mathbf{I})$. Specifically, this process recursively generates data $\mathbf{e}_n^t$ through the conditional distribution:

$$q\left(\mathbf{e}_n^t \mid \mathbf{e}_n^{t-1}\right) = \mathcal{N}\left(\mathbf{e}_n^t; \sqrt{1-\beta_t}\mathbf{e}_n^{t-1}, \beta_t \mathbf{I}\right),$$
$$\mathbf{e}_n^t = \sqrt{\bar{\alpha}_t}\mathbf{e}_n^0 + \sqrt{1-\bar{\alpha}_t}\epsilon, \tag{8}$$

where $\alpha_t = 1 - \beta_t, \bar{\alpha}_t = \prod_{s=1}^{t} \alpha_s, \epsilon \sim \mathcal{N}(0.1\delta_c, \mathbf{I})$, and β_t represent a set of predefined noise scales related to the timestep t.

The denoising process learns a parameterized inverse distribution $p_\theta\left(\mathbf{e}_n^{t-1} \mid \mathbf{e}_n^t\right)$, which, by Bayes' theorem, is given by:

$$p_\theta\left(\mathbf{e}_n^{t-1} \mid \mathbf{e}_n^t\right) = \mathcal{N}\left(\mathbf{e}_n^{t-1}; \boldsymbol{\mu}_\theta\left(\mathbf{e}_n^t, t\right), \boldsymbol{\Sigma}_\theta\left(\mathbf{e}_n^t, t\right)\right), \tag{9}$$

where $\boldsymbol{\mu}_\theta\left(\mathbf{e}_n^t, t\right)$ and $\boldsymbol{\Sigma}_\theta\left(\mathbf{e}_n^t, t\right)$ represent the mean and variance of the Gaussian distribution, respectively.

We estimate $\boldsymbol{\mu}_\theta$ via variational inference by maximizing the Evidence Lower Bound (ELBO), defined as:

$$\mathbb{E}\left[-\log p_\theta\left(\mathbf{e}_n^0\right)\right] \leq \mathbb{E}_q\left[-\log p\left(\mathbf{e}_n^t\right) - \sum_{t \geq 1} \log \frac{p_\theta\left(\mathbf{e}_n^{t-1} \mid \mathbf{e}_n^t\right)}{q\left(\mathbf{e}_n^t \mid \mathbf{e}_n^{t-1}\right)}\right] =: \mathcal{L}_{t-1}. \tag{10}$$

In Denoising Diffusion Probabilistic Models (DDPM), $\mathcal{L}_{t-1}$ is minimizing the KL divergence between $q\left(\mathbf{e}_n^{t-1} \mid \mathbf{e}_n^t, \mathbf{e}_n^0\right)$ and $p_\theta\left(\mathbf{e}_n^{t-1} \mid \mathbf{e}_n^t\right)$:

$$\mathcal{L}_{t-1} = D_{KL}\left(q\left(\mathbf{e}_n^{t-1} \mid \mathbf{e}_n^t, \mathbf{e}_n^0\right) \| p_\theta\left(\mathbf{e}_n^{t-1} \mid \mathbf{e}_n^t\right)\right). \tag{11}$$

Learning Phase. Applying a Transformer to the interaction sequence $\mathbf{e}_{1:n-1} = [\mathbf{e}_1, \mathbf{e}_2, \ldots, \mathbf{e}_{n-1}]$ yields the contextualized representation $\boldsymbol{H}^l \in \mathbb{R}^{N \times d}$:

$$\boldsymbol{H}^l = \text{Transformer}\left[\mathbf{e}_1, \mathbf{e}_2, \ldots, \mathbf{e}_{n-1}\right]. \tag{12}$$

Then, L2 normalized linear attention mechanism is applied to learn the representation, producing the encoded sequence representation H:

$$\text{head}_i = A'\left(\boldsymbol{H}^l\boldsymbol{W}_Q^{(i)}, \boldsymbol{H}^l\boldsymbol{W}_K^{(i)}, \boldsymbol{H}^l\boldsymbol{W}_V^{(i)}\right),$$
$$\text{MH}\left(\boldsymbol{H}^l\right) = \text{Concat}\left(\text{head}_1 \text{ L}, \text{thead}_h\right)\boldsymbol{W}_O,$$
$$\boldsymbol{S}^{l-1} = \text{LayerNorm}\left(\boldsymbol{H}^{l-1} + \text{Dropout}\left(\text{MH}\left(\boldsymbol{H}^{l-1}\right)\right)\right), \tag{13}$$
$$\boldsymbol{H}^l = \text{LayerNorm}\left(\boldsymbol{S}^{l-1} + \text{Dropout}\left(\text{FNN}\left(S_{l-1}\right)\right)\right),$$
$$\boldsymbol{H}^1 = \mathbf{e}_{1:n-1}; \boldsymbol{H} = \boldsymbol{H}^L\boldsymbol{W}_L + \boldsymbol{b}_L,$$

where $\boldsymbol{W}_Q^{(i)}, \boldsymbol{W}_K^{(i)}, \boldsymbol{W}_V^{(i)} \in \mathbb{R}^{d \times d}$ is the head weight matrix, $\boldsymbol{W}_O$ is the multi-head block weight matrix, LayerNorm is the layer normalization function, $\boldsymbol{H}^l$

represents the hidden values iteratively generated at layer $l(l = 1, \ldots, L)$ until reaching the final layer L, $\mathrm{FNN}(\ldots)$ represents the feed-forward network, $\boldsymbol{W}_L \in \mathbb{R}^{hd \times d}$ and $\boldsymbol{b}_L \in \mathbb{R}^d$ are the weight and bias parameters.

Next, conditional denoising is performed on the interaction sequence $\boldsymbol{H}$:

$$p_\theta \left(\mathbf{e}_n^{t-1} \mid \mathbf{e}_n^t, \boldsymbol{H} \right) = \mathcal{N} \left(\mathbf{e}_n^{t-1}; \boldsymbol{\mu}_\theta \left(\mathbf{e}_n^t, \boldsymbol{H}, t \right), \boldsymbol{\Sigma}_\theta \left(\mathbf{e}_n^t, \boldsymbol{H}, t \right) \right), \tag{14}$$

where the architecture of $\boldsymbol{\mu}_\theta \left(\mathbf{e}_n^t, \boldsymbol{H}, t \right)$ is a multi-layer perceptron (MLP).

Then, the guidance signal $\boldsymbol{H}$ is introduced to refine the conditional diffusion model Eq. (11) for the optimization objective L_{t-1}:

$$\mathcal{L}_{t-1} = D_{KI} \left(q \left(\mathbf{e}_n^{t-1} \mid \mathbf{e}_n^t, \mathbf{e}_{n-1}^0 \right) \| p_\theta \left(\mathbf{e}_n^{t-1} \mid \mathbf{e}_n^t, \boldsymbol{H} \right) \right). \tag{15}$$

Using the reparameterization trick, we predict the observed target samples $\mathbf{e}_n^0$ in the interaction sequence:

$$\boldsymbol{\mu}_\theta \left(\mathbf{e}_n^t, \boldsymbol{H}, t \right) = \sqrt{\bar{\alpha}_{t-1}} f_\theta \left(\mathbf{e}_n^t, \boldsymbol{H}, t \right) + \frac{\sqrt{\alpha_t} \left(1 - \bar{\alpha}_{t-1} \right)}{\sqrt{1 - \bar{\alpha}_t}} \epsilon, \tag{16}$$

which transforms Eq. (15) into an alternative form:

$$\mathcal{L}_{t-1} = \mathbb{E}_{\mathbf{e}_n^0, \epsilon} \left[\frac{\bar{\alpha}_{t-1}}{2\beta_t^{0\prime}{}_0} \left\| \mathbf{e}_n^0 - f_\theta \left(\sqrt{\bar{\alpha}_t} \mathbf{e}_n^0 + \sqrt{1 - \bar{\alpha}_t} \epsilon, \boldsymbol{H}, t \right) \right\|^2 \right] + C, \tag{17}$$

where $\mathbf{e}_n^0$ represents the target items in the interaction sequence.

Guided diffusion typically employs an auxiliary unconditional model, jointly trained via classifier-free guidance. With probability p_u, the condition H is replaced by a null label Φ, enabling unconditional learning during training.

Generation Phase. To adjust the impact of the guidance signal $\boldsymbol{H}$, we modify $f_\theta \left(\mathbf{e}_n^t, \boldsymbol{H}, t \right)$ as follows:

$$\tilde{f}_\theta \left(\mathbf{e}_n^t, \boldsymbol{H}, t \right) = (1 + w) f_\theta \left(\mathbf{e}_n^t, \boldsymbol{H}, t \right) - w f_\theta \left(\mathbf{e}_n^t, \Phi, t \right), \tag{18}$$

where w is a hyperparameter controlling the strength of H.

Based on Eq. (9), the single-step denoising process is formulated as:

$$\mathbf{e}_n^{t-1} = \frac{\sqrt{\bar{\alpha}_{t-1}} \beta_t}{1 - \bar{\alpha}_t} \tilde{f}_\theta \left(\mathbf{e}_n^t, \boldsymbol{H}, t \right) + \frac{\sqrt{\alpha_t} \left(1 - \bar{\alpha}_{t-1} \right)}{1 - \bar{\alpha}_t} \mathbf{e}_n^t + \sqrt{\tilde{\beta}_t} \mathbf{z}, \quad \mathbf{z} \sim \mathcal{N}(\mathbf{0}, \mathbf{I}). \tag{19}$$

This process is applied during inference to generate the final item $\mathbf{e}_n^0$.

Retrieval of Recommendation List. After generating the ideal item, we retrieve the top-K recommendations by computing inner products between $\mathbf{e}_n^0$ and all candidate embeddings $\mathbf{e}_i$, selecting those with the highest scores.

$$i_n = \arg\max_{i \in \mathcal{I}} \mathrm{Rounding} \left(\mathbf{e}_n^0 \right) = \mathbf{e}_n^0 \cdot \mathbf{e}_i. \tag{20}$$

4   Experiments

4.1   Experimental Setup

Datasets and Evaluation Metrics. We conduct experiments on three datasets: YooChoose [17], KuaiRec [18], and Zhihu [19]. The statistics are shown in Table 1. User interaction sequences are ordered by timestamp and partitioned into training, validation, and test subsets following an 8:1:1 proportion.

We evaluate performance using two standard metrics: Hit Ratio (HR@20) and Normalized Discounted Cumulative Gain (NDCG@20), where higher values indicate better recommendation performance.

Table 1. Dataset statistics.

Dataset	YooChoose	KuaiRec	Zhihu
#sequences	128,468	92,090	11,714
#items	9,514	7,261	4,838
#interactions	539,436	737,163	77,714

Baseline Comparisons. To assess the performance of ELS-GDR, we compare it with benchmark models in three categories: (1) traditional sequential models using deep networks and attention (e.g., SASRec [4], BERT4Rec [3], STOSA [5]); (2) self-supervised models with contrastive learning for robust representations (e.g., CL4SRec [2], ICLRec [20]); and (3) diffusion-based methods employing generative modeling (e.g., DiffuRec [7], DCRec [8], DimeRec [6]).

Implementation Details. We retain the latest 10 user interactions, padding shorter sequences for uniformity. For long-term recommendation $N/d > 1.5$, e.g., $d = 64$, we use up to 100 past items, ensuring $(n_i > d)$ via zero-padding. The model uses the AdamW optimizer with $L = 2$ Transformer layers, $h = 8$ heads, $d = 64$ embedding size, and $N = 100$ sequence length. Learning rates are tuned over $[0.01, 0.005, 0.001, 0.0005, 0.0001, 0.00005]$, with a 0.1 probability for unconditional training. The personalized guidance strength w is varied in $[0, 2, 4, 6, 8, 10]$.

4.2   Main Results

ELS-GDR is benchmarked against baselines, with results presented in Table 2.

(1) ELS-GDR consistently outperforms baselines, demonstrating its effectiveness in sequential recommendation. It uses L2-normalized linear attention to model long-term interactions and optimizes denoising with guided signals.

(2) Compared to deep learning and self-supervised models, ELS-GDR better captures user preferences by learning latent user-item distributions, enabling more personalized recommendations.

(3) ELS-GDR surpasses diffusion-based models due to its dynamic attention mechanism, which adaptively weights historical interactions. This makes it particularly effective for large-scale, long-term sequential recommendation tasks.

Table 2. Overall performance comparison.

Models	YooChoose		KuaiRec		ZhiHu	
	HR@20	NDCG@20	HR@20	NDCG@20	HR@20	NDCG@20
SASRec	0.0368	0.0163	0.0392	0.0332	0.0162	0.0061
BERT4Rec	0.0389	0.0162	0.0332	0.0123	0.0178	0.0067
STOTA	0.0374	0.0167	0.0415	0.0190	0.0167	0.0061
CL4Rec	0.0445	0.0186	0.0425	0.0201	0.0203	0.0074
ICLRec	0.0433	0.0184	0.0374	0.0177	0.0182	0.0065
DiffuRec	0.0447	0.0194	0.0382	0.0183	0.0171	0.0070
DCRec	0.0462	<u>0.0213</u>	0.0473	0.0209	0.0221	<u>0.0077</u>
DimeRec	<u>0.0469</u>	0.0205	<u>0.0495</u>	<u>0.0217</u>	<u>0.0224</u>	0.0072
ELS-GDR	**0.0484**	**0.0221**	**0.0519**	**0.0229**	**0.0237**	**0.0081**
#improve.	3.1%	3.7%	4.8%	5.5%	5.8%	5.1%

4.3   Ablation Study

To assess each component's impact, we perform an ablation study by comparing recommendation accuracy before and after their removal (Fig. 2). "w/o" denotes the removal of a module; "w/o all" removes both bias noise and attention; "w/o mn" removes only bias noise. The full ELS-GDR model serves as the baseline.

Comparing ELS-GDR with w/o mn shows that bias noise slightly improves robustness, despite introducing some noise. The performance gap between w/o mn and w/o all highlights the effectiveness of L2-normalized linear attention in stabilizing sequence representations and enhancing denoising guidance.

4.4   Analysis of Guidance Strength

To examine the impact of personalized guidance strength w on ELS-GDR, we conduct experiments with $w \in \{0, 2, 4, 6, 8, 10\}$ across three datasets. Using HR@20 as the evaluation metric, Fig. 3(a)–(c) show that ELS-GDR performs best at $w = 4$. When $w < 4$, performance improves with increasing w, indicating that moderate guidance enhances recommendation quality. However, when $w > 4$, performance declines as excessive guidance causes over-reliance on specific intent, lowering the quality of generated items.

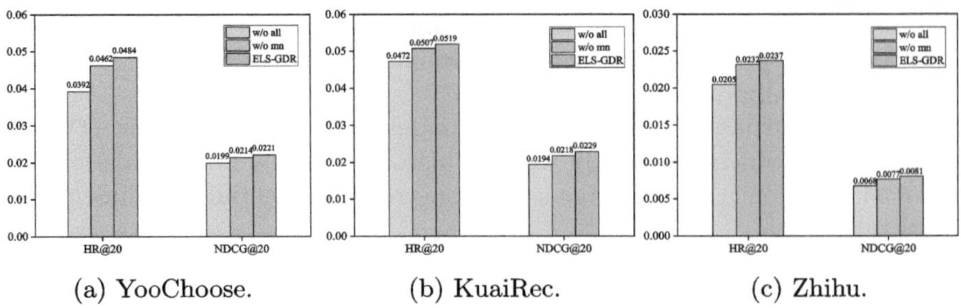

(a) YooChoose.   (b) KuaiRec.   (c) Zhihu.

Fig. 2. Ablation experiment results.

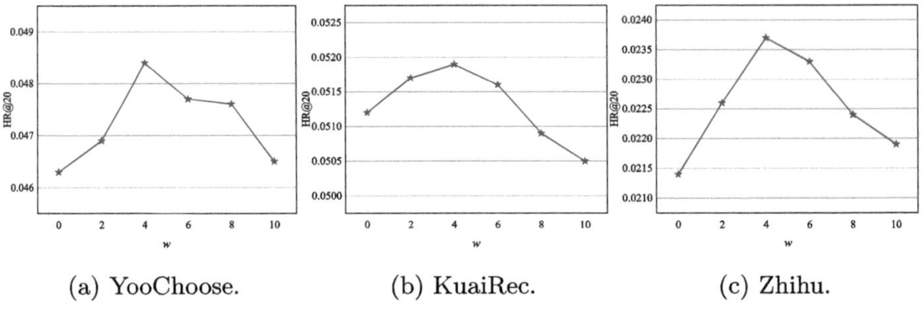

(a) YooChoose.   (b) KuaiRec.   (c) Zhihu.

Fig. 3. Experimental evaluation of classifier-free guidance sensitivity to w.

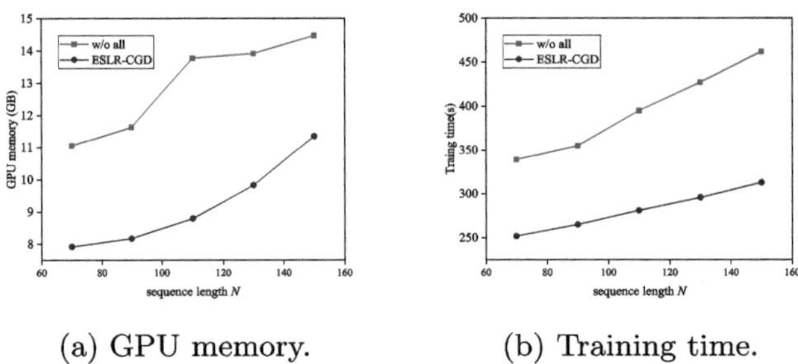

(a) GPU memory.   (b) Training time.

Fig. 4. Model efficiency in long-term sequential recommendation.

4.5 Efficiency in Long-Term Sequential Recommendation

To evaluate ELS-GDR's training costs for varying sequence lengths in long-term recommendation, we conduct experiments on KuaiRec with $N \in \{70, 90, 110, 130, 150\}$. As shown in Fig. 4(a) and Fig. 4(b), ELS-GDR consistently outperforms the w/o all configuration in computational efficiency. This confirms that L2 normalized linear attention effectively reduces training complexity, making it suited for real-world long-term sequential recommendation tasks.

5   Conclusion

We propose ELS-GDR, a novel recommendation model designed to reduce the high computational complexity of conditional diffusion models in long-term sequential tasks. By using L2 normalized linear attention, ELS-GDR decreases complexity from $O(N^2)$ to $O(N)$, improving efficiency. The model also incorporates an offset noise strategy and classifier-free guidance, enhancing robustness, stability, and generalization. Experimental results on three datasets (YooChoose, KuaiRec, and Zhihu) show significant improvements in recommendation accuracy with low computational costs. Future work will explore integrating multimodal knowledge to improve the adaptability and generalization capability of the model.

Acknowledgments. We sincerely appreciate the reviewers' constructive feedback and valuable suggestions.

Disclosure of Interests. The authors declare that there are no conflicts of interest associated with the content of this manuscript.

References

1. Yin, M., et al.: Dataset regeneration for sequential recommendation. In: KDD 2024, pp. 3954–3965. Association for Computing Machinery, New York (2024)
2. Xie, X., et al.: Contrastive learning for sequential recommendation. In: 2022 IEEE 38th International Conference on Data Engineering (ICDE), pp. 1259–1273 (2022)
3. Sun, F., et al.: Bert4rec: sequential recommendation with bidirectional encoder representations from transformer. In: Proceedings of the 28th ACM International Conference on Information and Knowledge Management, CIKM 2019, pp. 1441–1450. Association for Computing Machinery, New York (2019)
4. Kang, W.C., McAuley, J.: Self-attentive sequential recommendation. In: 2018 IEEE International Conference on Data Mining (ICDM), pp. 197–206 (2018)
5. Fan, Z., et al.: Sequential recommendation via stochastic self-attention. In: Proceedings of the ACM Web Conference 2022, WWW 2022, pp. 2036–2047. Association for Computing Machinery, New York (2022)
6. Li, W., et al.: Dimerec: a unified framework for enhanced sequential recommendation via generative diffusion models. Association for Computing Machinery, New York (2025)
7. Li, Z., Sun, A., Li, C.: Diffurec: a diffusion model for sequential recommendation. **42**(3) (2023)
8. Huang, H., Huang, C., Chang, X., Hu, W., Yao, L.: Dual conditional diffusion models for sequential recommendation. arXiv preprint arXiv:2410.21967 (2024)
9. Zhao, K., Zou, L., Zhao, X., Wang, M., Yin, D.: User retention-oriented recommendation with decision transformer. Association for Computing Machinery, New York (2023)
10. Hidasi, B., Karatzoglou, A., Baltrunas, L., Tikk, D.: Session-based recommendations with recurrent neural networks. CoRR abs/1511.06939 (2015)
11. Tang, J., Wang, K.: Personalized top-n sequential recommendation via convolutional sequence embedding. Association for Computing Machinery, New York (2018)

12. Liu, Y., Xia, L., Huang, C.: SelfGNN: self-supervised graph neural networks for sequential recommendation. Association for Computing Machinery, New York (2024)
13. Fan, X., Liu, Z., Lian, J., Zhao, W.X., Xie, X., Wen, J.R.: Lighter and better: low-rank decomposed self-attention networks for next-item recommendation. Association for Computing Machinery, New York (2021)
14. Wang, W., Zhang, Y., Li, H., Wu, P., Feng, F., He, X.: Causal recommendation: progresses and future directions. Association for Computing Machinery, New York (2023)
15. Lin, X., et al.: Discrete conditional diffusion for reranking in recommendation. In: Companion Proceedings of the ACM Web Conference 2024, WWW 2024, pp. 161–169. Association for Computing Machinery, New York (2024)
16. Wang, W., Tang, Y., Tian, K.: Leadrec: towards personalized sequential recommendation via guided diffusion. In: International Conference on Intelligent Computing, pp. 3–15. Springer, Cham (2024)
17. Ben-Shimon, D., Tsikinovsky, A., Friedmann, M., Shapira, B., Rokach, L., Hoerle, J.: Recsys challenge 2015 and the yoochoose dataset. Association for Computing Machinery, New York (2015)
18. Gao, C., et al.: Kuairec: a fully-observed dataset and insights for evaluating recommender systems. In: Proceedings of the 31st ACM International Conference on Information & Knowledge Management, CIKM 2022, pp. 540–550. Association for Computing Machinery, New York (2022)
19. Hao, B., et al.: A large-scale rich context query and recommendation dataset in online knowledge-sharing. arXiv abs/2106.06467 (2021)
20. Chen, Y., Liu, Z., Li, J., McAuley, J., Xiong, C.: Intent contrastive learning for sequential recommendation. In: Proceedings of the ACM Web Conference 2022, WWW 2022, pp. 2172–2182. Association for Computing Machinery, New York (2022)

EntiFA: Entity-Based Fine-Grained Adaptation for Knowledge Enhancement in Large Language Models

Dengkang Qin[1] and Zheng Chen[1,2(✉)]

[1] School of Information and Software Engineering, University of Electronic Science and Technology of China, Chengdu 610054, China
`202221090312@std.uestc.edu.cn, zchen@uestc.edu.cn`
[2] National Key Laboratory on Blind Signal Processing, Chengdu 610041, China

Abstract. Large Language Models (LLMs) often underperform on know-ledge-intensive tasks due to insufficient domain-specific information and a tendency to hallucinate. While knowledge graphs (KGs) offer structured and reliable information, integrating them into LLMs poses challenges related to semantic misalignment and inconsistent usage during text generation. To address these issues, we propose EntiFA, a fine-grained adaptation framework that dynamically integrates entity embeddings from KGs with the contextual representations of LLMs. EntiFA features a dual-tower architecture to align semantic spaces and a dynamic embedding fusion mechanism that operates throughout the generation process. By employing a parameter-efficient adaptation layer, EntiFA enables consistent and effective knowledge integration without compromising the model's original capabilities. Extensive experiments across multiple benchmarks show that EntiFA significantly outperforms existing methods in knowledge-intensive tasks, achieving superior accuracy and efficiency.

Keywords: Large Language Models · Knowledge Graphs · Knowledge Integration · Semantic Alignment

1 Introduction

Large Language Models (LLMs) have demonstrated remarkable capabilities across various tasks. However, their reliance on pre-trained knowledge often leads to limitations in domain-specific applications and potential hallucination issues when facing knowledge-intensive tasks. While knowledge graphs offer structured and reliable information that could potentially address these limitations, effectively integrating such external knowledge into LLMs remains challenging due to the semantic gap between different knowledge representations and the complexity of maintaining knowledge consistency during the generation process.

T. Zhu et al. (Eds.): KSEM 2025, LNAI 15920, pp. 287–299, 2026.
https://doi.org/10.1007/978-981-95-3052-6_22

Existing approaches to knowledge integration primarily follow two directions: knowledge-augmented pre-training and retrieval-augmented generation. The former requires substantial computational resources and often struggles with knowledge conflicts between pre-trained and newly integrated information. The latter, while more flexible, faces challenges in real-time knowledge retrieval and seamless integration. Moreover, most current methods focus solely on enhancing input prompts, neglecting the potential for knowledge injection during the autoregressive generation process, which can lead to inconsistent knowledge utilization across different generation steps.

To address these challenges, we propose **EntiFA**, a novel knowledge adaptation framework that dynamically fuses entity embeddings from knowledge graphs with LLMs' contextual representations. EntiFA employs a dual-tower model architecture to bridge the semantic gap between different knowledge representations and introduces a dynamic embedding fusion mechanism that operates throughout the entire generation process. This approach enables more effective and consistent knowledge integration while maintaining the model's original capabilities. Our key contributions are as follows:

- We introduce a novel dual-tower model architecture that effectively aligns the semantic spaces between LLM representations and knowledge graph embeddings, enabling more accurate and efficient knowledge integration.
- We develop a dynamic entity embedding fusion mechanism that operates during both encoding and decoding phases, ensuring consistent knowledge utilization throughout the entire generation process.
- We design a parameter-efficient adaptation layer that can be readily integrated into existing LLMs, demonstrating significant improvements across various knowledge-intensive tasks while maintaining computational efficiency.

2   Related Works

Recent advances in Large Language Models have highlighted a critical challenge: despite their impressive capabilities, these models often generate inaccurate content due to limited knowledge. To address this *hallucination* issue, researchers have explored integrating Knowledge Graphs (KGs) with LLMs. The integration of KGs into LLMs primarily follows two approaches:

Knowledge Integration During Pre-training. This approach incorporates KG information during the model's pre-training phase through three main methods: (1) embedding injection at the input layer [11], which enables joint learning but requires full model updates; (2) knowledge textualization, exemplified by K-BERT [10], which converts KG triples into training sentences; and (3) adapter-based integration [23], which introduces knowledge layers while keeping base model parameters frozen. Among these, CoLAKE [18] demonstrates an innovative approach by introducing a unified Word-Knowledge Graph that connects input text with knowledge subgraphs through entity alignment.

Knowledge Utilization During Inference. This approach focuses on real-time knowledge access and utilization. JointLK [19] represents a significant advancement in this direction, implementing dense bidirectional attention for joint reasoning between LLMs and KGs. Complementary methods include Contriever [7], which retrieves relevant Wikipedia passages, and KAPING [1], which focuses on KG triple retrieval for input augmentation. Additionally, numerous studies [3,8,24] have focused on integrating knowledge graphs with Retrieval-Augmented Generation (RAG) to enhance the reasoning capabilities of LLMs.

Current research trends favor approaches that can enhance LLM knowledge while maintaining model efficiency, particularly methods that do not require updating the entire model parameters. This direction promises more reliable and interpretable outputs while preserving computational practicality.

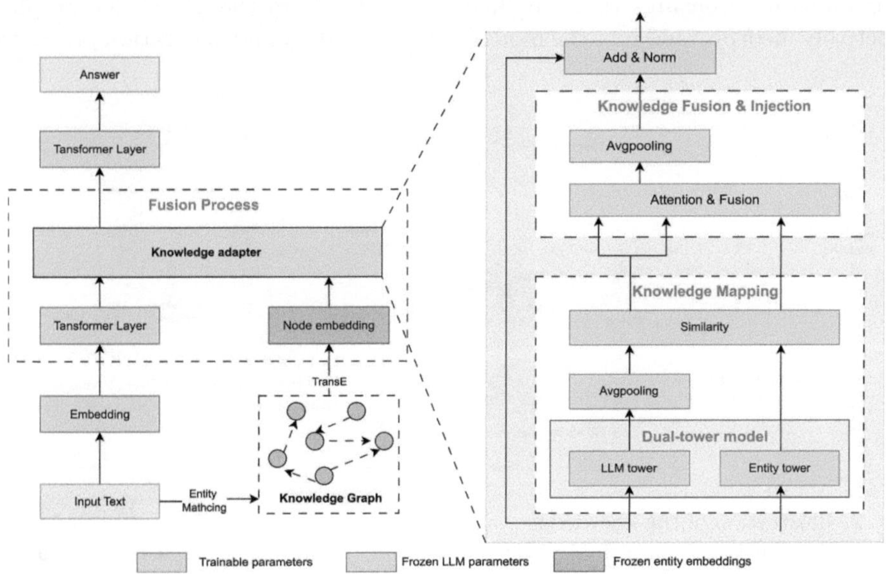

Fig. 1. Schematic architecture of the EntiFA adaptation framework. The EntiFA layer can be inserted between layers of an LLM. It consists of knowledge mapping, fusion, and injection.

3   Method

The EntiFA method designs a knowledge adaptation layer to be added to Large Language Models. This layer dynamically fuses the context embeddings in the model's hidden layers with entity embeddings from a knowledge graph by identifying entities within the input and generated text. This process facilitates the transformation of external non-parameterized knowledge into parameterized knowledge within the model.

Specifically, the schematic diagram of the knowledge-enhanced method based on entity embedding fusion is shown in Fig. 1, and the structure of the knowledge adaptation layer is illustrated in Fig. 2. By incorporating this knowledge adaptation layer, the model can leverage external structured knowledge more effectively, thereby enhancing its ability to generate accurate and contextually relevant outputs. The layer can be divided into two main modules:

Entity Matching and Knowledge Mapping. This module links tokens in the model's input and output with entities in the knowledge graph and maps the entity embedding space and the LLM representation space into a common semantic space.

Knowledge Fusion and Injection. In this module, the entity embeddings and text representations, now mapped to the same semantic space, are fused. This integration ensures that enriched knowledge from the knowledge graph is effectively incorporated into the model's understanding and generation processes.

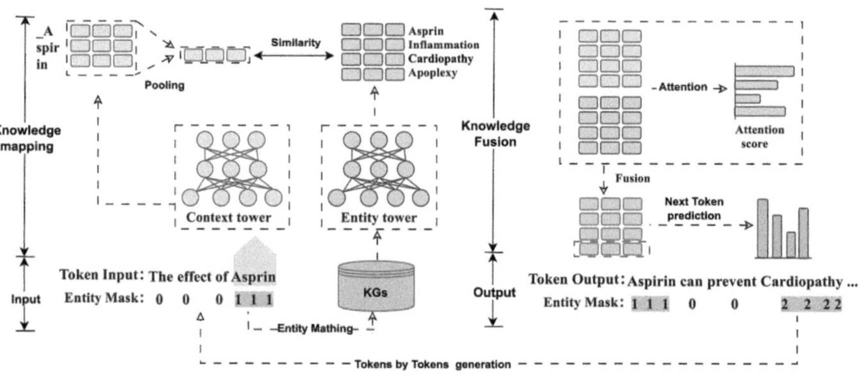

Fig. 2. Illustration of the knowledge mapping and fusion process. It includes candidate entity selection based on a dual-tower model, and the fusion of token representations and entity embeddings via attention mechanisms.

3.1 Entity Matching and Knowledge Mapping

The function of entity matching is to take a given input text and return the tokens that serve as candidate entities from a knowledge graph. For an input text sequence $X = \{x_1, x_2, \ldots, x_n\}$, the LLM first converts it into a token sequence $T = \{t_1, t_2, \ldots, t_m\}$, which serves as the input to the LLM. Previous research [12] has typically focused on performing a single round of entity matching and embedding fusion based solely on the input, neglecting the fact that tokens generated in an autoregressive manner may also possess entity characteristics. This oversight limits the enhancement of knowledge distribution probability during the generation process.

In this study, we predefined an entity vocabulary according to the KG, and marked the location of the entity. Define entity mask M, sequence $T = \{t_1, t_2, \ldots, t_m\}$, then the entity mask $M = \{m_1, m_2, \ldots, m_n\}$ can be expressed as the following formula:

$$M_i = \begin{cases} 0, & t_i \notin E \\ k, & t_i \in E \end{cases} \quad i = 1, 2, \ldots, n \tag{1}$$

where M_i indicates the location where the entity mask at t_i is used to mark the candidate entity token, and $k = 1, 2, \ldots, n$ represents the k-th different entity.

To address the issue of inconsistent semantic spaces between the two, this study introduces a dual-tower model (Deep Structured Semantic Model, DSSM) to achieve cross-space mapping. Define the text space $T \in \mathbb{R}^{d_t}$, where d_t represents the dimensionality of the LLM's hidden layer, and the knowledge space $K \in \mathbb{R}^{d_k}$, where d_k represents the dimensionality of the knowledge graph entity embeddings. The dual-tower model employs two separate but structurally similar encoders: a context encoder and an entity encoder. These encoders map the text space and knowledge space into a common target space $S \in \mathbb{R}^{d_s}$, where d_s is the dimensionality of the target space.

For each token t_i, its representation in the text space is given by the following formula:

$$h_i = \text{LLM}_{\text{encoder}}(t_i) \tag{2}$$

For each entity e_j in the knowledge graph, its initial representation is given by the following formula:

$$e_j = \text{KG}_{\text{encoder}}(e_j) \in K \tag{3}$$

where $\text{KG}_{\text{encoder}}(\cdot)$ represents the knowledge map entity embedding function.

Specifically, the context encoder receives the embedding of the input token as input and outputs the token in the target space as the following expression:

$$h_i' = \text{Context}_{\theta_c}(h_i) \in S \tag{4}$$

where $\text{Context}_{\theta_c}$ represents the context encoder function defined by the parameter θ_c.

Similarly, the entity encoder receives embeddings of entities from the KG as input and generates their corresponding representations in the target space, as shown in the following formula:

$$e_j' = \text{Entity}_{\theta_e}(e_j) \in S \tag{5}$$

where Entity_{θ_e} denotes the entity encoding function parameterized by θ_e. After this transformation, both the text representations and entity representations, which originally existed in different spaces, are now mapped into a common target space S.

Considering that a single entity may consist of multiple tokens, to more accurately represent the overall semantics of an entity comprised of several tokens, we employ an average pooling method. Assuming that the token sequence corresponding to entity e_j is represented in the target space as $H' = \{h'_1, h'_2, \ldots, h'_k\}$, the averaged representation of the entity is given by the following formula:

$$h'_j = \text{AvgPooling}(h'_1, \ldots, h'_k) \tag{6}$$

The cosine similarity is used to measure the correlation between the two, and the N candidate entities with the highest similarity are selected to be embedded for the next calculation. Considering that entity tokens may not directly map to any entities in the knowledge graph, a threshold is set, and only when the similarity score exceeds the preset threshold will it be considered that there is a valid knowledge mapping.

3.2 Knowledge Fusion and Injection

Knowledge fusion determines how effectively the original text embeddings can be combined with the injected knowledge graph entity embeddings. Considering that different tokens within a multi-token entity contribute variably to the overall semantics of the entity, this differential contribution should also be reflected during the knowledge fusion process. In this paper, we adopt an attention mechanism-based fusion approach to dynamically compute the importance weights of each token relative to its associated entity.

The method begins by calculating the attention matrix between the text embeddings $H' = \{h'_1, h'_2, \ldots, h'_k\}$ and the candidate entity embeddings $E' = \{e'_1, e'_2, \ldots, e'_n\}$ obtained from the previous step. This attention matrix serves as a weighting mechanism between the context token embeddings and the candidate entity embeddings, as shown in the following equation:

$$\text{Att} = \text{Softmax}\left(\frac{H'(E')^\top}{\sqrt{d_s}}\right) E' \tag{7}$$

Next, we apply average pooling and a linear transformation to Att to obtain the final fused result z_i, as shown in the following equation:

$$z_i = W_g\left(\text{AvgPooling}(\text{Att})\right) \tag{8}$$

Define h^l as the text representation from the decoder at the l-th layer of the LLM. In order to maintain consistency with the Pre-Norm mode adopted by the decoder and to mitigate issues of gradient vanishing or explosion, RMSNorm is applied to the input h^l received by the decoder. Finally, a learnable scaling factor α is introduced, allowing the fused representation to be further weighted and mixed with the original hidden states through a residual connection within the knowledge adaptation layer. This process achieves the fusion of the i-th token generated by the LLM with the entity embeddings, as shown in the following equation:

$$y_i = \alpha \cdot z_i + (1 - \alpha) \cdot h^l_i \tag{9}$$

By freezing the original LLM parameters and incorporating a knowledge adaptation layer between the LLM encoding layers, we exclusively train this additional layer to achieve parameter-efficient knowledge fusion and injection.

4 Experiments

4.1 Datasets and Setting

This section outlines the knowledge sources, benchmark datasets, and experimental settings used in our study.

For pre-training, we utilized **Wiki_stem**, an open-source corpus consisting of 676K STEM-related text segments extracted from Wikipedia articles. The data were carefully curated to ensure both domain specificity and textual quality.

To support knowledge integration, we employed three structured knowledge graphs for entity embedding generation. **WordNet** [13] is a lexical database that organizes English words into hierarchically structured synsets. **ConceptNet** [16] is a multilingual semantic network that encodes 28 million commonsense knowledge relationships. **Wikidata** [22] serves as a large-scale, cross-domain knowledge base supporting over 300 languages. Entity embeddings were generated using the TransE model, and for each question, up to five relevant entities were extracted based on semantic matching.

We evaluated the model across several benchmark datasets. **TriviaQA** [9] includes question-answer pairs derived from Wikipedia and web documents, serving as a testbed for closed-domain QA. **WebQuestionsSP** [26] is a knowledge-base QA dataset annotated with SPARQL queries, used to assess closed-book QA performance. **CommonsenseQA** [21] and **Social IQa (SIQA)** [15] are multiple-choice benchmarks that evaluate commonsense and social reasoning abilities, respectively, under zero-shot conditions. Finally, **BIG-Bench Hard (BBH)** [17] is a curated subset of BIG-Bench that includes challenging tasks requiring multi-step reasoning.

All datasets were preprocessed to maintain a consistent format and ensure input quality. For multiple-choice datasets, validation sets were used to evaluate the model's zero-shot performance. Experiments were conducted using 8 NVIDIA 3090 GPUs. To improve the model's sensitivity to entity-related information, we employed parameter-efficient training by introducing LoRA matrices into the Query-Key components of the attention layers, with a rank set to 16. Only the newly introduced adaptation layers were trained, while the original model parameters were kept frozen throughout the process.

4.2 Baseline Methods

We consider two categories of baseline methods for evaluating knowledge integration: retrieval-augmented generation (RAG) methods and knowledge graph entity embedding approaches. For the RAG category, we evaluate KAPING [1] and Contriever [7], both of which incorporate external structured knowledge during inference. Contriever is a dense retrieval model pre-trained on Wikipedia that enhances language model inputs by retrieving semantically similar triples from knowledge graphs and relevant Wikipedia passages. KAPING improves zero-shot performance on knowledge-intensive tasks by retrieving relevant triples from knowledge graphs and incorporating them as prefixed prompts to the input queries. Given the overlap between benchmarks and knowledge sources, both methods were evaluated using ConceptNet and WordNet to support multiple-choice question answering.

For knowledge graph entity embedding approaches, we adopt KnowLA [12] as a representative baseline. KnowLA enhances parameter-efficient finetuning of large language models by embedding lightweight adapters that inject structured knowledge directly into intermediate layers of the model. This enables dynamic and context-aware fusion of external information during inference. As KnowLA is the primary point of comparison for our proposed method, we follow the same setup and experimental protocol to ensure fair and consistent evaluation.

Table 1. Comparative evaluation of different knowledge enhancement methods on multiple-choice question answering tasks. Results demonstrate performance across **CommonsenseQA**, **SIQA**, and **BBH** benchmarks, with accuracy (Acc) and cross-entropy score (Score) metrics. #Parameter changes relative to base model are indicated.

Methods	#Parameters	CommonsenseQA		SIQA		BBH	
		Acc	Score	Acc	Score	Acc	Score
Qwen2.5	7B	64.12	43.29	54.24	45.09	37.75	25.09
Qwen2.5 ($r = 32$)	+0.5%	68.08	40.89	56.26	44.03	**43.45**	24.88
Contriever (WordNet)	+0.5%	67.15	46.09	53.58	46.13	–	–
Contriever(ConceptNet)		67.06	45.30	53.51	45.51	–	–
KAPING (WordNet)	+0.5%	67.21	45.91	53.51	45.89	–	–
KAPING (ConceptNet)		67.58	45.64	53.66	46.15	–	–
KnowLA (WordNet)		67.44	46.28	53.61	46.56	40.26	24.34
KnowLA (ConceptNet)	+0.55%	68.03	47.57	54.92	46.76	39.09	24.39
KnowLA (Wikidata)		66.73	47.19	54.22	46.81	41.25	24.29
EntiFA (WordNet)		67.10	46.82	**56.31**	45.97	42.47	24.90
EntiFA (ConceptNet)	+0.71%	68.73	**48.25**	55.34	**47.32**	**43.45**	**25.71**
EntiFA (Wikidata)		**69.80**	47.03	56.16	46.12	**43.45**	24.88

4.3 Experiments on Multi-choice QA

To evaluate the effectiveness of the knowledge adaptation layer, the experiments selected the original Qwen2.5 [25] model and the Qwen2.5 model further pretrained on the *Wiki_stem* dataset using the LoRA [6] method, denoted as Qwen2.5 (lora_rank = 32), as baselines. Both EntiFA and KnowLA methods use three knowledge graphs: WordNet, ConceptNet, and Wikidata. The specific experimental results and analysis are shown in Table 1.

Experimental results demonstrate that our proposed EntiFA method consistently outperforms baseline approaches across all three datasets. The Qwen2.5 (r = 32) model shows notable improvements over the original Qwen2.5-7B model. While KAPING performs better than Contriever among RAG methods, both show inferior results compared to Qwen2.5 (r = 32) on CommonsenseQA and SIQA. EntiFA exhibits superior performance compared to KnowLA when using the same knowledge graph, while maintaining compatibility with parameter-efficient methods like LoRA. With Wikidata integration, EntiFA improves accuracy on CommonsenseQA from 64.12% to 69.80% and on BBH from 37.75% to 43.45%. Interestingly, we observe different performance patterns across metrics: while EntiFA with Wikidata achieves the highest accuracy on CommonsenseQA (69.80%), EntiFA with ConceptNet consistently yields the highest cross-entropy scores across datasets. This divergence suggests that different knowledge graphs may offer complementary advantages: Wikidata's broad factual coverage may better support accurate answer selection, while ConceptNet's rich conceptual relationships might enhance the model's confidence in reasoning. These findings highlight the complexity of knowledge integration and suggest that different evaluation metrics may capture distinct aspects of model performance in knowledge-intensive tasks.

Table 2. Performance comparison on closed-book question answering tasks using WebQuestionsSP and TriviaQA benchmarks.

Methods	WebQuestionsSP	TriviaQA
Qwen2.5-7B	78.17	68.53
Qwen2.5-7B ($r = 16$)	82.98	71.41
Contriever (Wikipedia)	–	68.71
KAPING (Wikipedia)	–	66.05
KnowLA (WordNet)	78.30	68.81
KnowLA (ConceptNet)	80.96	70.02
KnowLA (Wikidata)	81.72	69.81
EntiFA (WordNet)	84.18	71.56
EntiFA (ConceptNet)	**84.75**	**71.81**
EntiFA (Wikidata)	82.98	71.65

4.4   Experiments on Closed-Book QA

The closed-book question answering experiment uses WebQuestionsSP and TriviaQA as two testing benchmarks to evaluate the ability of the knowledge adaptation layer. According to the answer matching strategy, the subtree labels provided by the component tree are used to extract all noun phrases from the text answers, calculate their similarity, and determine correctness based on a predefined threshold (e.g., 0.5). The test results are shown in Table 2.

Experimental results demonstrate that Qwen2.5-7B with LoRA fine-tuning ($r = 16$) outperforms the base model across both datasets, effectively mitigating hallucination issues. While Contriever$_{\text{Wikipedia}}$ shows marginal improvement over Qwen2.5-7B on TriviaQA, EntiFA combined with three knowledge graphs achieves superior performance on both TriviaQA and WebQuestionsSP. Notably, EntiFA surpasses both LoRA-based approaches and KnowLA, attributable to its dual-tower model for semantic space alignment and dynamic embedding fusion mechanism, which enables flexible entity integration during both training and inference stages.

4.5 The Impact of Base Models

In order to investigate the effectiveness of the knowledge adaptation layer across different base models, we conducted the same experiments using the LLaMA3-8B [4] model. The goal was to compare its performance with that of the Qwen2.5 model on the WebQuestionsSP and TriviaQA benchmarks after applying the EntiFA method and further pretraining on the Wiki_stem dataset, using consistent knowledge graph embeddings. The results are summarized in Table 3.

The experimental results demonstrate that the EntiFA method remains effective when applied to the LLaMA architecture. By fusing knowledge graph embeddings with the model's contextual representations through the dual-tower architecture, EntiFA enables efficient knowledge integration and enhanced performance.

Table 3. Performance evaluation of the EntiFA framework on the LLaMA3-8B architecture across WebQuestionsSP and TriviaQA benchmarks.

Methods	WebQuestionsSP	TriviaQA
LLaMA3-8B	71.34	63.64
LLaMA3-8B ($r = 16$)	76.07	63.55
EntiFA (WordNet)	78.17	65.93
EntiFA (ConceptNet)	**79.72**	65.45
EntiFA (Wikidata)	78.53	**66.13**

4.6 The Impact of Knowledge Graph Embedding Methods

In this study, we investigate the impact of different embedding models on knowledge injection within the entity embedding fusion framework. Utilizing five representative approaches-RESCAL [14], TransE [2], RotatE [20], Node2vec [5], and random embeddings as a baseline-we generate entity embeddings using ConceptNet, which demonstrated superior performance in earlier experiments.

These embeddings are integrated into the EntiFA framework and evaluated on the CommonsenseQA, SIQA, and BBH datasets. The detailed results are shown in Table 4.

The findings reveal that different embedding models exert varying levels of influence on model performance. Among them, TransE consistently outperforms others across most evaluation metrics, likely due to its strong generalization ability and compatibility with the design of our knowledge adaptation layer. In contrast, RotatE, despite its more complex vector representation, yields less favorable outcomes. Interestingly, performance differences between methods are relatively small, indicating that the EntiFA framework exhibits strong adaptability to diverse knowledge representations. During fine-tuning, it effectively aligns entity embeddings with Qwen2.5's semantic space, thus mitigating the risk of knowledge loss.

Table 4. Ablation study on the impact of different knowledge graph embedding methods in the EntiFA framework. Performance comparison across CommonsenseQA, SIQA, and BBH using accuracy and cross-entropy score.

Methods	CommonsenseQA		SIQA		BBH	
	Acc	Score	Acc	Score	Acc	Score
Random	66.52	46.35	53.12	45.42	41.25	24.12
Node2vec	67.85	47.42	54.28	46.51	42.34	24.98
TransE	**68.73**	48.25	**55.34**	**47.32**	**43.45**	**25.71**
RESCAL	68.25	**48.32**	54.82	46.95	**43.45**	25.38
RotatE	67.91	47.56	54.45	46.58	42.87	25.29

5   Conclusion

This paper presents **EntiFA**, a novel knowledge adaptation framework that effectively bridges the semantic gap between Large Language Models and knowledge graphs through dynamic entity embedding fusion. Extensive experiments across multiple benchmarks demonstrate the effectiveness of our approach.

EntiFA achieves significant improvements over baseline methods on various tasks, including multiple-choice question answering and closed-book QA. The framework exhibits robust compatibility with different knowledge graphs and embedding methods, showing particularly strong performance when utilizing ConceptNet and TransE embeddings.

Acknowledgements. This work was supported by National Key Laboratory on Blind Signal Processing (Grant No. 61424132024007003).

References

1. Baek, J., Aji, A.F., Saffari, A.: Knowledge-augmented language model prompting for zero-shot knowledge graph question answering. In: NLRSE, pp. 78–106 (2023)
2. Bordes, A., Usunier, N., Garcia-Duran, A., Weston, J., Yakhnenko, O.: Translating embeddings for modeling multi-relational data. In: Advances in Neural Information Processing Systems, vol. 26 (2013)
3. Edge, D., Trinh, H., Cheng, N., et al.: From local to global: a graph rag approach to query-focused summarization. arXiv preprint arXiv:2404.16130 (2024)
4. Grattafiori, A., Dubey, A., Jauhri, A., Pandey, A., et al.: The llama 3 herd of models. arXiv preprint arXiv:2407.21783 (2024)
5. Grover, A., Leskovec, J.: Node2vec: scalable feature learning for networks. In: KDD 2016, pp. 855–864. ACM (2016)
6. Hu, E.J., Shen, Y., Wallis, P., et al.: Lora: low-rank adaptation of large language models. In: Proceedings of the International Conference on Learning Representations, vol. 1, p. 3 (2022)
7. Izacard, G., et al.: Unsupervised dense information retrieval with contrastive learning. Trans. Mach. Learn. Res. (2022)
8. Ji, Y., et al.: Retrieval and reasoning on KGs: integrate knowledge graphs into large language models for complex question answering. In: Findings of the Association for Computational Linguistics: EMNLP 2024, pp. 7598–7610 (2024)
9. Joshi, M., Choi, E., Weld, D., Zettlemoyer, L.: Triviaqa: a large scale distantly supervised challenge dataset for reading comprehension, pp. 1601–1611 (2017)
10. Liu, W., et al.: K-BERT: enabling language representation with knowledge graph. In: Proceedings of the AAAI Conference on Artificial Intelligence, vol. 34, pp. 2901–2908 (2020)
11. Lu, Y., Lu, H., Fu, G., Liu, Q.: Kelm: knowledge enhanced pre-trained language representations with message passing on hierarchical relational graphs. In: DLG4NLP 2022 Workshop at ICLR, Seattle, Washington (2022)
12. Luo, X., Sun, Z., Zhao, J., Zhao, Z., Hu, W.: Knowla: enhancing parameter-efficient finetuning with knowledgeable adaptation, pp. 7153–7166 (2024)
13. Miller, G.A.: Wordnet: a lexical database for English. Commun. ACM **38**(11), 39–41 (1995)
14. Nickel, M., Tresp, V., Kriegel, H.P.: A three-way model for collective learning on multi-relational data. In: ICML 2011, pp. 809–816. Omnipress (2011)
15. Sap, M., Rashkin, H., Chen, D., Le Bras, R., Choi, Y.: Social IQA: commonsense reasoning about social interactions, pp. 4463–4473 (2019)
16. Speer, R., Chin, J., Havasi, C.: Conceptnet 5.5: an open multilingual graph of general knowledge. In: AAAI 2017, vol. 31 (2017)
17. Srivastava, A., Rastogi, A., Rao, A., et al.: Beyond the imitation game: quantifying and extrapolating the capabilities of language models. Trans. Mach. Learn. Res. **2023**(5), 1–95 (2023)
18. Sun, T., et al.: Colake: contextualized language and knowledge embedding. In: COLING 2020, Barcelona, Spain, pp. 3660–3670 (2020)
19. Sun, Y., Shi, Q., Qi, L., et al.: Jointlk: joint reasoning with language models and knowledge graphs for commonsense question answering. In: NAACL 2022, pp. 5049–5060 (2022)
20. Sun, Z., Deng, Z.H., Nie, J.Y., Tang, J.: Rotate: knowledge graph embedding by relational rotation in complex space. In: Proceedings of the 7th International Conference on Learning Representations (ICLR) (2019)

21. Talmor, A., Herzig, J., Lourie, N., Berant, J.: Commonsenseqa: a question answering challenge targeting commonsense knowledge, pp. 4149–4158 (2019)
22. Vrandecic, D., Krotzsch, M.: Wikidata: a free collaborative knowledgebase. Commun. ACM **57**(10), 78–85 (2014)
23. Wang, X., et al.: Kepler: a unified model for knowledge embedding and pre-trained language representation. Trans. Assoc. Comput. Linguist. **9**, 176–194 (2021)
24. Wu, W., Jing, Y., Wang, Y., Hu, W., Tao, D.: Graph-augmented reasoning: evolving step-by-step knowledge graph retrieval for LLM reasoning. arXiv preprint arXiv:2503.01642 (2025)
25. Yang, A., Yang, B., Zhang, B., Hui, B., et al.: Qwen2.5 technical report. arXiv preprint arXiv:2412.15115 (2025)
26. Yih, W., Richardson, M., Meek, C., et al.: The value of semantic parse labeling for knowledge base question answering. In: ACL 2016, pp. 201–206 (2016)

StressSentry-FHE: A Transformer-Based Privacy-Preserving Framework for Stress Detection Using Quantized Attention

Jichao Xiong[1], Jiageng Chen[1(✉)], Junyu Lin[1], Dian Jiao[1], Chunhua Su[2], and Weizhi Meng[3]

[1] School of Computer Science and Hubei Provincial Key Laboratory of Artificial Intelligence and Smart Learning, Central China Normal University, Wuhan, China
`jiageng.chen@ccnu.edu.cn`
[2] Department of Computer Science and Engineering, The University of Aizu, Aizuwakamatsu, Japan
[3] School of Computing and Communications, Lancaster University, Lancaster, UK

Abstract. Stress detection using physiological signals has emerged as a promising approach for monitoring mental health, yet current methods face significant challenges in preserving privacy while maintaining high accuracy. This paper introduces StressSentry-FHE, a novel privacy-preserving framework that leverages Fully Homomorphic Encryption (FHE) and Transformer-based architecture to analyze encrypted physiological data without compromising sensitive personal information. Our approach addresses critical limitations of existing models by: (1) implementing a specialized Transformer architecture that effectively captures complex inter-signal relationships and temporal dynamics across multiple physiological modalities including accelerometer, electrodermal activity, blood volume pulse, and temperature data; (2) developing FHE-compatible components through precision-preserving quantization strategies, numerically stable attention mechanisms, and efficient approximations for non-linear functions; and (3) delivering exceptional cross-subject generalization with 98.33% accuracy under General Partitioning and 96.06% accuracy with Leave-One-Subject-Out (LOSO) cross-validation on the WESAD 3-class dataset. Comparative analysis reveals that StressSentry-FHE significantly outperforms state-of-the-art approaches in both accuracy and privacy preservation, with only a modest 3.27% accuracy reduction when operating on fully encrypted data compared to plaintext inference. Our framework demonstrates that advanced deep learning architectures and robust privacy protection can be effectively combined for physiological signal analysis, establishing a new benchmark for secure affective computing in healthcare applications.

Keywords: Affective computing · Privacy-Preserving Large Language Models · Stress recognition · Privacy-Preserving Machine Learning

1   Introduction

Emotional regulation profoundly influences both psychological and physiological health. Positive emotions enhance well-being, immune function, and cardiovascular stability, while chronic negative emotions contribute to various disorders [22]. In today's high-pressure society, stress is pervasive—around one-quarter of individuals cite it as the main cause of mental health issues [10]. Prolonged stress impairs mental health and is linked to headaches, insomnia, and elevated cardiovascular risk [15]. Biologically, it persistently activates the neuroendocrine system, weakening immunity and increasing vulnerability to diseases including cancer [14]. Chronic stress also contributes significantly to depression, which can lead to suicidal behavior. Since 2020, anxiety and depression rates have surged globally, particularly among youth [12].

Safeguarding the privacy of physiological signals is essential in stress monitoring, as these data reflect not only stress levels but also sensitive health and emotional states [2]. Without proper protection, such data may be misused for psychological profiling, leading to discrimination in employment, insurance, and finance. Regulations like GDPR and HIPAA define physiological data as protected health information, making privacy a fundamental design requirement [18].

1.1   Related Work

Traditional stress recognition methods often rely on self-reported questionnaires, which are prone to subjective bias. Chronic stress can impair self-assessment, reducing reliability, while such assessments are also time-consuming and inefficient [1].

To overcome these drawbacks, recent studies have employed physiological signals and machine learning for objective stress detection. Sun et al. [24] proposed a deep learning method that extracts 123 features from raw physiological data, arranges them into 2D maps, and classifies them using a CNN-LSTM model. Deployed on a Coral Edge TPU, the system achieved 90.98% accuracy, validating its real-world applicability.

In another work, Sun et al. [23] designed an edge-based model for fear recognition using 2D feature maps derived from GSR, SKT, and BVP signals. Incorporating data augmentation and deep learning techniques, their model reached an F1-score of 88.07% and 89.12% accuracy on the WESAD dataset.

Liu et al. [13] introduced a Transformer-LSTM model using PPG signals, where CNNs extract local features, Transformers capture attention-based correlations, and LSTMs model temporal dependencies. This end-to-end framework achieved 92.27% accuracy in a three-class stress task.

Privacy preservation has also gained prominence. Firouzi et al. [8] proposed a federated learning-based stress monitoring system integrating IoT, AI, and blockchain. Using EDA, BVP, accelerometer, and temperature data, their system achieved 83.9% accuracy while safeguarding user privacy.

1.2 Our Contributions

While physiological signal-based stress detection has advanced, current methods often fail to capture complex inter-signal relationships and temporal dynamics. Moreover, privacy protection remains underexplored. We propose StressSentry-FHE—a Transformer-based model that processes multimodal physiological data entirely within the encrypted domain. Our key contributions include:

1. **Transformer-Based Signal Modeling:** StressSentry-FHE utilizes a tailored Transformer architecture to analyze accelerometer, EDA, BVP, and temperature signals. Self-attention effectively captures both temporal dependencies and cross-modal interactions, outperforming conventional approaches in representing emotional states.
2. **Strong Generalization:** Our model achieves 96.06% accuracy in the WESAD 3-class task under LOSO cross-validation and 98.33% under General Partitioning, demonstrating robustness across subjects and evaluation settings for practical stress monitoring.
3. **FHE-Compatible Design:** We address challenges of deploying Transformers under FHE via: (1) precision-preserving quantization, (2) stable attention approximations, and (3) efficient non-linear function replacements. These innovations enable accurate encrypted-domain computation with minimal precision loss, bridging advanced deep learning and privacy-preserving healthcare analytics.

2 Preliminary

2.1 Fully Homomorphic Encryption

Fully Homomorphic Encryption (FHE) represents a cryptographic breakthrough that enables computations to be performed directly on encrypted data without prior decryption. This capability ensures data privacy throughout the entire processing pipeline, making it particularly valuable for privacy-sensitive applications. FHE schemes can be categorized into three main types based on their mathematical foundations and design principles:

- **Integer Arithmetic Schemes:** These include Brakerski-Gentry-Vaikuntanathan (BGV) [4] and Fan-Vercauteren (BFV) [7], which are optimized for exact modular arithmetic over finite fields.
- **Boolean Circuit Schemes:** Represented by TFHE (Fast Fully Homomorphic Encryption over the Torus) [6], these schemes excel at bit-level operations and Boolean logic through efficient functional bootstrapping.
- **Approximate Computation Schemes:** Exemplified by Cheon-Kim-Kim-Song (CKKS) [5], these schemes support approximate arithmetic over real and complex numbers, suitable for floating-point operations.

The core operations in any FHE scheme are summarized in Table 1.

Table 1. Core Operations in Fully Homomorphic Encryption

Operation	Description
$\text{Enc}(PK, m) \rightarrow c$	Encrypts plaintext m with public key PK
$\text{Dec}(SK, c) \rightarrow m$	Decrypts ciphertext c with secret key SK
$\text{HomoAdd}(EK, c_1, c_2) \rightarrow c_{add}$	Encrypted addition: $c_{add} \approx \text{Enc}(PK, m_1 + m_2)$
$\text{HomoMul}(EK, c_1, c_2) \rightarrow c_{mul}$	Encrypted multiplication: $c_{mul} \approx \text{Enc}(PK, m_1 \times m_2)$

2.2 Challenges in Building Transformers with FHE

Implementing Transformer architectures with FHE presents several significant challenges that must be addressed:

- **Complex Non-linear Functions:** Transformers employ sophisticated non-linear operations that are particularly challenging to implement under FHE. Softmax requires exponentiation and division, which are difficult to compute homomorphically. Similarly, GeLU involves the error function, and Layer-Norm requires computing means, variances, and reciprocal square roots—all operations that are non-trivial in the encrypted domain.
- **Computational Overhead:** Homomorphic operations introduce substantial computational overhead compared to plaintext operations. A single homomorphic multiplication can be thousands of times slower than its plaintext counterpart. This overhead is particularly problematic for Transformers, which rely extensively on matrix multiplications in both attention mechanisms and feed-forward networks.
- **Noise Management:** Each homomorphic operation, especially multiplication, increases the noise level in ciphertexts. The deep structure of Transformer models, typically comprising multiple layers with several attention heads, creates a substantial multiplicative depth that challenges the noise management capabilities of FHE schemes and may require costly bootstrapping operations.

3 The StressSentry-FHE Model

This study utilizes the WESAD dataset [19], which contains physiological signals collected from Empatica E4 wristbands across 15 participants. We tackle the 3-class classification problem (neutral, stress, and amusement) by analyzing accelerometer (ACC), blood volume pulse (BVP), electrodermal activity (EDA), and temperature (TEM) signals, all of which exhibit distinctive patterns during different emotional states.

3.1 Data Processing Pipeline

Our data processing pipeline consists of three streamlined stages designed to transform raw physiological signals into discriminative features while minimizing computational overhead:

Signal Preprocessing: We apply Butterworth low-pass filtering to remove noise artifacts while preserving essential physiological patterns [20]. Signals are then segmented into non-overlapping 30-second windows to capture temporal stress response characteristics.

Feature Engineering: From each physiological modality, we extract statistical features including mean, standard deviation, and rate of change metrics. For ACC data, we compute the total acceleration magnitude to characterize physical activity intensity. For EDA, we decompose signals into phasic, tonic, and skin conductance response components using the cvxEDA method [9], as these components differentially reflect short and long-term stress responses. This process yields a comprehensive feature vector $\mathbf{X} \in \mathbb{R}^{54}$.

Dimensionality Reduction: To optimize computational efficiency for FHE implementation, we employ Recursive Feature Elimination to identify the most discriminative subset of features [16], reducing dimensionality from 54 to 12 dimensions, the resulting 12-dimensional feature vector serves as input to our privacy-preserving stress recognition model.

3.2 Design StressSentry-FHE with TFHE Encryption

Protecting user data privacy in stress recognition is crucial, as physiological signals contain sensitive personal health information. We introduce StressSentry-FHE, a Transformer-based model that enables secure stress detection with computations entirely within the encrypted domain using Fully Homomorphic Encryption (FHE). Figure 1 illustrates the system architecture.

Our framework directly addresses the FHE challenges identified in Sect. 2.2 through innovative algorithm design and efficient approximation techniques. The StressSentry-FHE model consists of two main components: (1) the Encrypted Feature Embedding module and (2) the Attention-based Classification module. These components form a sequential pipeline where Module 1 transforms raw physiological signals into encrypted feature representations, which are then processed by Module 2 to perform privacy-preserving attention-based classification. This architecture ensures that sensitive data remains encrypted throughout the entire computation process. We present the pseudocode for each component below.

Module 1 performs the initial processing by encrypting and quantizing raw physiological signals and transforming them into an embedded feature space suitable for the attention mechanism. The outputs from this module—standard and expanded feature representations—serve as inputs to Module 2, which implements the core Transformer operations. Module 2 performs query-key-value projections, attention score computation, and classification while maintaining

---

Algorithm 1. Module 1: Encrypted Feature Embedding

Require: Raw physiological signals $\mathbf{X} \in \mathbb{R}^{12}$, Public key PK
Ensure: Embedded feature representation $\mathbf{H}^{\mathrm{enc}} \in \mathbb{R}^{64}$
1: $\mathbf{X}^{\mathrm{enc}} \leftarrow \mathrm{Enc}(PK, \mathbf{X})$
2: $s \leftarrow \frac{\max(|\mathbf{X}|)}{2^{n_{\mathrm{bits}}-1}-1}$
3: $\mathbf{X}^{\mathrm{int}} \leftarrow \mathrm{round}\left(\frac{\mathbf{X}}{s}\right)$
4: $\mathbf{H}^{\mathrm{enc}} \leftarrow \sigma\left(\mathrm{HomoAdd}(EK, \mathrm{HomoMul}(EK, \mathbf{W}_{\mathrm{fc1}}^{\mathrm{enc}}, \mathbf{X}^{\mathrm{enc}}), \mathbf{b}_{\mathrm{fc1}}^{\mathrm{enc}})\right)$
5: $\mathbf{H}_{\mathrm{expanded}}^{\mathrm{enc}} \leftarrow \mathrm{Expand}(\mathbf{H}^{\mathrm{enc}})$
6: **return** $\mathbf{H}^{\mathrm{enc}}$, $\mathbf{H}_{\mathrm{expanded}}^{\mathrm{enc}}$

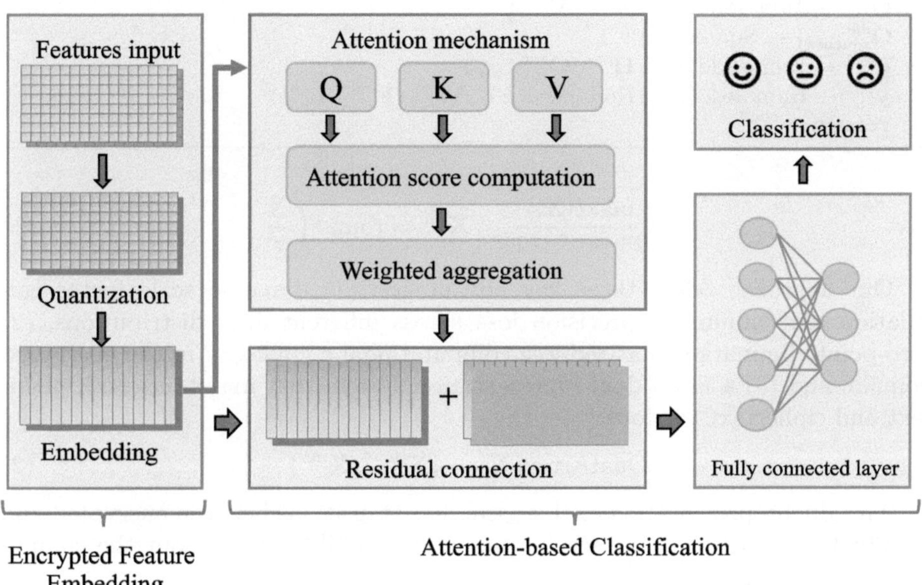

Fig. 1. Architecture of the StressSentry-FHE Model.

data in encrypted form. Our specialized FHE-Softmax implementation (line 6) enables attention mechanisms to operate securely with minimal precision loss. This sequential pipeline ensures privacy preservation while maintaining high classification performance.

Innovative FHE Components of StressSentry-FHE. Our Transformer-based model introduces several innovative components specifically designed to overcome the challenges of FHE-based neural networks while maintaining high accuracy for stress detection. These contributions include:

Precision-Preserving Quantization. To address the integer-only constraint of FHE operations, we designed a dynamic symmetric quantization scheme with $n_{\mathrm{bits}} = 6$:

Algorithm 2. Module 2: Attention-based Classification

Require: Embedded features $\mathbf{H}^{\text{enc}}$, Expanded features $\mathbf{H}^{\text{enc}}_{\text{expanded}}$, Encryption key EK
Ensure: Encrypted class probabilities $\mathbf{y}^{\text{enc}}$
1: $\mathbf{Q}^{\text{enc}} \leftarrow \text{HomoAdd}(EK, \text{HomoMul}(EK, \mathbf{W}^{\text{enc}}_q, \mathbf{H}^{\text{enc}}_{\text{expanded}}), \mathbf{b}^{\text{enc}}_q)$
2: $\mathbf{K}^{\text{enc}} \leftarrow \text{HomoAdd}(EK, \text{HomoMul}(EK, \mathbf{W}^{\text{enc}}_k, \mathbf{H}^{\text{enc}}_{\text{expanded}}), \mathbf{b}^{\text{enc}}_k)$
3: $\mathbf{V}^{\text{enc}} \leftarrow \text{HomoAdd}(EK, \text{HomoMul}(EK, \mathbf{W}^{\text{enc}}_v, \mathbf{H}^{\text{enc}}_{\text{expanded}}), \mathbf{b}^{\text{enc}}_v)$
4: $\mathbf{S}^{\text{enc}} \leftarrow \text{HomoMul}(EK, \mathbf{Q}^{\text{enc}}, \text{Transpose}(\mathbf{K}^{\text{enc}}))$
5: $\mathbf{S}^{\text{enc}}_{\text{scaled}} \leftarrow \text{HomoMul}(EK, \mathbf{S}^{\text{enc}}, \frac{1}{\sqrt{d_k}})$
6: $\mathbf{A}^{\text{enc}} \leftarrow \text{FHE-Softmax}(\mathbf{S}^{\text{enc}}_{\text{scaled}})$ // *The specific implementation is detailed in the Numerically Stable FHE-Softmax.*
7: $\mathbf{O}^{\text{enc}} \leftarrow \text{HomoMul}(EK, \mathbf{A}^{\text{enc}}, \mathbf{V}^{\text{enc}})$
8: $\mathbf{O}^{\text{enc}}_{\text{squeezed}} \leftarrow \text{Squeeze}(\mathbf{O}^{\text{enc}})$
9: $\mathbf{F}^{\text{enc}} \leftarrow \text{HomoAdd}(EK, \mathbf{H}^{\text{enc}}, \mathbf{O}^{\text{enc}}_{\text{squeezed}})$
10: $\mathbf{y}^{\text{enc}} \leftarrow \text{HomoAdd}(EK, \text{HomoMul}(EK, \mathbf{W}^{\text{enc}}_{\text{fc2}}, \mathbf{F}^{\text{enc}}), \mathbf{b}^{\text{enc}}_{\text{fc2}})$
11: **return** $\mathbf{y}^{\text{enc}}$

$$s = \frac{\max(|\mathbf{X}|)}{2^{n_{\text{bits}}-1} - 1}, \quad \mathbf{X}^{\text{int}} = \text{round}\left(\frac{\mathbf{X}}{s}\right) \tag{1}$$

Our approach offers three key advantages: (1) dynamic scale factor calculation that minimizes precision loss across different data distributions, (2) zero-point elimination that reduces computational complexity in the encrypted domain, and (3) a novel dual representation system that maintains both plaintext and ciphertext versions:

$$\text{DualArray}(\mathbf{X}) = \{\mathbf{X}^{\text{float}}, \mathbf{X}^{\text{int}}\} \tag{2}$$

This dual representation enables seamless transitions between encrypted and plaintext domains while preserving numerical stability throughout the computation pipeline.

Numerically Stable FHE-Softmax. The Softmax function presents significant challenges in FHE due to its reliance on exponentiation and division. We developed a decomposed implementation approach to construct the $FHE - Softmax()$ function, which is both compatible with FHE and numerically stable:

$$\mathbf{m}^{\text{enc}} = \text{Max}(\mathbf{S}^{\text{enc}}_{\text{scaled}}), \quad \mathbf{S}^{\text{enc}}_{\text{shifted}} = \text{HomoAdd}(EK, \mathbf{S}^{\text{enc}}_{\text{scaled}}, \text{Negate}(\mathbf{m}^{\text{enc}})) \tag{3}$$

$$\mathbf{E}^{\text{enc}} = \text{Exp}(\mathbf{S}^{\text{enc}}_{\text{shifted}}), \quad \mathbf{sum}^{\text{enc}} = \text{Sum}(\mathbf{E}^{\text{enc}}) \tag{4}$$

$$\mathbf{A}^{\text{enc}} = \text{HomoMul}(EK, \mathbf{E}^{\text{enc}}, \frac{1}{\mathbf{sum}^{\text{enc}}}) \tag{5}$$

This approach (1) enhances numerical stability by subtracting the maximum value before exponentiation, preventing overflow, (2) approximates non-FHE-friendly operations using only addition and multiplication, and (3) preserves the attention mechanism's semantic properties without compromising encryption security.

Simplified LayerNorm for FHE. Standard LayerNorm operations involve variance calculation and reciprocal square roots, which are expensive in FHE. Our model implements an efficient approximation:

$$\mu^{\mathrm{enc}} = \frac{1}{d}\sum_{i=1}^{d}\mathbf{X}_i^{\mathrm{enc}}, \quad \mathbf{X}_{\mathrm{norm}}^{\mathrm{enc}} = \mathrm{HomoAdd}(EK, \mathbf{X}^{\mathrm{enc}}, \mathrm{Negate}(\mu^{\mathrm{enc}})) \qquad (6)$$

By replacing the full normalization with mean-centering, we dramatically reduce computational complexity while maintaining the most critical aspect of normalization for transformer models. The model compensates for this simplification through learned weights in subsequent layers.

After model processing, the final encrypted prediction is decrypted with the secret key SK:

$$\mathbf{y} = \mathrm{Decrypt}(SK, \mathbf{y}^{\mathrm{enc}}), \quad \mathrm{state} = \arg\max(\mathbf{y}) \in \{0, 1, 2\} \qquad (7)$$

where $0, 1, 2$ represent neutral, stress, and amusement states.

By integrating these FHE-optimized components throughout our Transformer-based architecture, StressSentry-FHE successfully overcomes the computational challenges identified in Sect. 2.2 while ensuring physiological data remains fully encrypted during computation, thereby safeguarding user privacy with only minimal precision loss in detection accuracy.

4 Experimental Evaluation

This section systematically presents the experimental validation conducted to assess the effectiveness and stability of the proposed model. The WESAD 3-class dataset is selected as the benchmark dataset, given its widespread application in affective computing research. The primary focus of the experiment is to evaluate the model's classification performance across three distinct emotional states: neutral, stress, and amusement.

To ensure the reliability and comparability of the evaluation results, classification accuracy and F1-score are employed as the primary quantitative metrics. These metrics provide a comprehensive assessment of the model's overall performance and facilitate direct comparison with existing studies. All our experiments were performed on a Linux server equipped with two Intel Xeon Platinum 8352S CPUs (32 cores each, for a total of 128 threads) running at 2.20 GHz base frequency and up to 3.4 GHz turbo frequency. The system includes 251 GB of RAM and operates under Ubuntu 22.04.2 LTS with kernel version 6.5.0-18-generic.

4.1 Dataset Segmentation

To rigorously assess the generalization of StressSentry-FHE on the WESAD 3-class emotion dataset, two complementary data partitioning strategies are employed:

1. **General Partitioning (General):** The dataset is split into 80% training and 20% testing based on participant identity, ensuring no subject overlap to prevent data leakage and inflated performance.
2. **Leave-One-Subject-Out (LOSO):** Each participant is used as the test set once, with the remaining data for training. This cycle repeats for all subjects, offering a robust measure of generalizability to unseen individuals.

These strategies provide a balanced evaluation: General Partitioning reflects typical model performance, while LOSO assesses adaptability to new users. Their combination mitigates overfitting and aligns with best practices in physiological signal research, ensuring comprehensive validation across diverse populations.

4.2   Comparative Analysis

This section presents a comparative evaluation of the proposed StressSentry-FHE model against state-of-the-art (SOTA) stress recognition approaches. Performance is assessed using classification accuracy and F1-score under both general and LOSO settings. Benchmarked models include traditional machine learning algorithms (RF, DT, AB, KNN) and deep learning models (CNN, CNN-LSTM, Transformer-LSTM).

In addition to accuracy, data privacy preservation is examined by comparing StressSentry-FHE with encrypted and federated models. As shown in Table 2, our model consistently outperforms others across all metrics, achieving both high classification performance and strong privacy guarantees.

Table 2. Comparison of stress detection schemes on the WESAD dataset.

Scheme	Model	General		LOSO	
		ACC (%)	F1-score (%)	ACC ± STD (%)	F1-score ± STD (%)
Schmidt et al. [19]	RF, DT, AB, KNN	–	–	79.57 ± 0.93	68.85 ± 0.89
Bobade et al. [3]	ANN	–	–	84.32	78.71
Lai et al. [11]	Res-TCN	–	–	86.50 ± 7.94	83.01 ± 10.32
Sun et al. [23]	EfficientNet	89.12	88.07	84.09 ± 7.65	85.49 ± 6.84
Liu et al. [13]	Transformer-LSTM	92.27	91.5	–	–
Sun et al. [24]	CNN-LSTM	90.98	91.44	90.12 ± 4.94	88.59 ± 5.89
Firouzi et al. [8][†]	CNN	83.9[†]	84.7[†]	–	–
Ours[†]	**Transformer**	**98.33**[†]	**97.98**[†]	**96.06 ± 3.55**[†]	**94.76 ± 4.97**[†]

[†] Results obtained under encryption.

Traditional methods [3, 19] fall short in modeling the complexity and temporal nature of physiological signals, leading to limited performance. Deep learning models [11, 23, 24] offer improvements but rely on computationally expensive architectures or handcrafted features. While the Transformer-LSTM model [13] utilizes attention for local feature extraction, its unimodal reliance on PPG data hinders robustness in noisy or variable conditions.

Firouzi et al. [8] integrate federated learning with blockchain for privacy, but experience a substantial drop in accuracy under encryption. In contrast, StressSentry-FHE delivers superior accuracy (up to 98.33%) and generalization (LOSO: 96.06%) while preserving privacy through full homomorphic encryption.

By effectively capturing temporal and multimodal dependencies without expert-driven features, and maintaining high accuracy under encryption, StressSentry-FHE demonstrates strong potential for secure, real-world stress monitoring and personalized health applications.

4.3 Plaintext vs. Ciphertext

This section evaluates the performance trade-offs between plaintext and encrypted inference in the StressSentry-FHE model. Unlike the method proposed by Firouzi et al. [8], which uses federated learning to secure data during training, our model focuses on preserving privacy during real-time inference.

Fully Homomorphic Encryption (FHE) enables direct computation on encrypted data, ensuring algorithm-level privacy without exposing raw physiological features. Although FHE theoretically maintains accuracy, its limited support for only addition and multiplication requires quantization of complex components such as attention and SoftMax, potentially reducing precision.

To assess this, we compared model performance under plaintext and FHE inference using Leave-One-Subject-Out (LOSO) cross-validation. Metrics including accuracy, precision, recall, and F1-score are shown in Fig. 2, alongside training convergence, with 95% confidence intervals. These results illustrate the performance impact introduced by encryption.

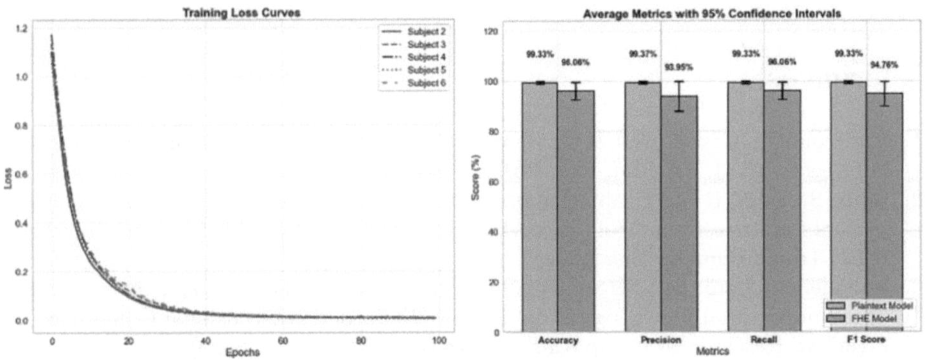

Fig. 2. Training Loss and Average Metrics Comparison.

Despite the privacy overhead, StressSentry-FHE shows only a 3.27% accuracy drop, notably lower than the 10.36% reported by Firouzi et al. [8]. Moreover, our model surpasses existing SOTA methods under both General Partitioning and LOSO settings in accuracy and F1-score, affirming its efficacy.

While FHE introduces computational latency—0.157 s for plaintext versus 26.65 s for ciphertext inference—this remains practical. Wearable devices such as Apple Watch typically sample physiological data every 1–10 min [17,21], making the delay acceptable even under frequent sampling scenarios.

5   Conclusion

This paper introduces StressSentry-FHE, a novel privacy-preserving framework for stress detection that integrates Transformer-based architecture with Fully Homomorphic Encryption. Our approach achieves state-of-the-art performance (98.33% accuracy under General Partitioning and 96.06% with LOSO validation) while ensuring physiological data remains encrypted throughout computation. The key innovations include precision-preserving quantization, FHE-compatible attention mechanisms, and efficient non-linear function approximations, which collectively enable sophisticated neural computations on encrypted data with only a modest 3.27% accuracy reduction compared to plaintext inference. By demonstrating that advanced deep learning architectures can maintain high performance under strong privacy constraints, StressSentry-FHE establishes a new benchmark for secure affective computing in healthcare applications. Future work will focus on reducing computational overhead and extending the framework to other physiological signal analysis tasks where privacy is paramount.

Acknowledgement. This work is financially supported by National Natural Science Foundation of China under Grant No. 12441102 and self-determined research funds of CCNU from the colleges' basic research and operation of MOE under Grant No. CCNU24ai010.

References

1. Andreou, E., Alexopoulos, E.C.: Perceived stress scale: reliability and validity study in Greece. Int. J. Environ. Res. Public Health (2011)
2. Betti, S., Lova, R.M.: Evaluation of an integrated system of wearable physiological sensors for stress monitoring in working environments by using biological markers. IEEE Trans. Biomed. Eng. (2018)
3. Bobade, P., Vani, M.: Stress detection with machine learning and deep learning using multimodal physiological data. In: 2020 Second International Conference on Inventive Research in Computing Applications (ICIRCA) (2020)
4. Brakerski, Z., Gentry, C.: (leveled) fully homomorphic encryption without bootstrapping. ACM Trans. Comput. Theory (TOCT) (2014)
5. Cheon, J.H., Kim, A., Kim, M., Song, Y.: Homomorphic encryption for arithmetic of approximate numbers. In: Takagi, T., Peyrin, T. (eds.) ASIACRYPT 2017. LNCS, vol. 10624, pp. 409–437. Springer, Cham (2017). https://doi.org/10.1007/978-3-319-70694-8_15
6. Chillotti, I., Gama, N.: TFHE: fast fully homomorphic encryption over the torus. J. Cryptol. (2020)

7. Fan, J., Vercauteren, F.: Somewhat practical fully homomorphic encryption. Cryptology ePrint Archive (2012)
8. Firouzi, F., Jiang, S.: Fusion of IoT, AI, edge–fog–cloud, and blockchain: challenges, solutions, and a case study in healthcare and medicine. IEEE Internet Things J. (2022)
9. Greco, A., Valenza, G.: cvxEDA: a convex optimization approach to electrodermal activity processing. IEEE Trans. Biomed. Eng. (2016)
10. Hosseini, E., Fang, R.: Emotion and stress recognition utilizing galvanic skin response and wearable technology: a real-time approach for mental health care. In: 2023 IEEE International Conference on Bioinformatics and Biomedicine (BIBM) (2023)
11. Lai, K., Yanushkevich, S.N.: Intelligent stress monitoring assistant for first responders. IEEE Access (2021)
12. Liang, Y., Liu, L.: Identifying emotional causes of mental disorders from social media for effective intervention. Inf. Process. Manage. (2023)
13. Liu, Z., Shi, Z.: Mental stress detection using PPG signals based on transformer-LSTM model. In: 2024 IEEE International Conference on Bioinformatics and Biomedicine (BIBM) (2024)
14. McEwen, B.S.: Brain on stress: how the social environment gets under the skin. Proc. Natl. Acad. Sci. (2012)
15. McEwen, B.S., Stellar, E.: Stress and the individual: mechanisms leading to disease. Arch. Internal Med. (1993)
16. Misra, P., Yadav, A.S.: Improving the classification accuracy using recursive feature elimination with cross-validation. Int. J. Emerg. Technol. (2020)
17. Nelson, B.W., Allen, N.B.: Accuracy of consumer wearable heart rate measurement during an ecologically valid 24-hour period: intraindividual validation study. JMIR mHealth uHealth (2019)
18. Protection, F.D.: General data protection regulation (GDPR). Intersoft Consulting, Accessed in October (2018)
19. Schmidt, P., Reiss, A.: Introducing wesad, a multimodal dataset for wearable stress and affect detection. In: Proceedings of the 20th ACM International Conference on Multimodal Interaction (2018)
20. Setz, C., Arnrich, B.: Discriminating stress from cognitive load using a wearable EDA device. IEEE Trans. Inf. Technol. Biomed. (2010)
21. Shcherbina, A., Mattsson, C.M.: Accuracy in wrist-worn, sensor-based measurements of heart rate and energy expenditure in a diverse cohort. J. Personalized Med. (2017)
22. Shu, L., Xie, J.: A review of emotion recognition using physiological signals. Sensors (2018)
23. Sun, J., Portilla, J.: A deep learning approach for fear recognition on the edge based on two-dimensional feature maps. IEEE J. Biomed. Health Inform. (2024)
24. Sun, J., Portilla, J.: Negative emotion recognition based on physiological signals using a CNN-LSTM model. In: 2024 IEEE International Conference on Bioinformatics and Biomedicine (BIBM) (2024)

Dual Attention Transformer
with Multi-scale Perception
for Multivariate Time Series Forecasting

Fengjie Li, Wu Peng, Mingyu Zhang, Miao Wang$^{(\boxtimes)}$, and Hong Zhang$^{(\boxtimes)}$

School of Cyber Security and Computer, Hebei University, Baoding, China
202370019072@stumail.hbu.edu.cn, {wm,hzhang}@hbu.edu.cn

Abstract. Multivariate time series (MTS) forecasting plays a critical role across various domains. Recent advancements in deep learning, particularly transformer-based methods, have shown promising results. These methods partition time series into patches and treat them as tokens to capture complex temporal patterns. However, two key challenges remain: effectively modeling multi-scale temporal dependencies and accurately capturing inter-variable relationships. Existing models typically adopt a single-scale patch division strategy, overlooking the inherently multi-scale nature of time series, which is crucial for precise forecasting. Additionally, these models either fully mix all channels or process them independently, failing to explicitly emphasize inter-variable dependencies. To address these limitations, we propose the Multi-scale Perception Dual Attention Transformer (DTMP). DTMP leverages periodic information to segment time series into multiple scales and adaptively selects the most suitable scale for each instance. To enhance temporal modeling, we introduce a dual attention mechanism that separately captures global and local dependencies. Furthermore, given that inter-variable dependencies may vary across different scales, we incorporate graph structure learning at each scale and employ graph convolution to model scale-specific variable interactions. Extensive experiments on multiple real-world datasets demonstrate the superior forecasting performance of DTMP, highlighting its effectiveness in capturing both multi-scale temporal dependencies and inter-variable relationships.

Keywords: Multivariate time series forecasting · Transformer · Dual attention · Multi-scale modeling

1 Introduction

Time series forecasting is crucial in finance, meteorology, and energy management, yet traditional methods struggle with complex nonlinear relationships and long-term dependencies [1]. Recently, Transformer-based models have emerged as a powerful alternative, effectively capturing dependencies across all time steps

© The Author(s), under exclusive license to Springer Nature Singapore Pte Ltd. 2026
T. Zhu et al. (Eds.): KSEM 2025, LNAI 15920, pp. 312–324, 2026.
https://doi.org/10.1007/978-981-95-3052-6_24

and achieving superior long-term forecasting performance [2]. However, their self-attention mechanism incurs quadratic complexity in both time and space, limiting scalability. To address this, various approaches introduce sparse or hierarchical attention mechanisms [3–5], yet they fundamentally rely on pointwise attention. PatchTST [6] highlights that single time steps provide limited semantics, making it difficult to extract reliable dependencies. Consequently, Transformer-based models may underperform compared to simpler MLP architectures [7]. To mitigate this, PatchTST segments time series into patches as input tokens, while Crossformer [8] employs a dimension segmentation embedding method. Although patch-based Transformer models have demonstrated excellent performance, we believe two challenges remain. The first challenge lies in modeling multi-scale temporal correlations. Traditional approaches often use fixed sampling frequencies or patch sizes, which may not generalize well across datasets. Real-world time series exhibit overlapping periodicities, such as seasonal variations and economic cycles, necessitating adaptive multi-scale modeling. Moreover, multi-scale dependencies extend beyond patch segmentation to both local and global temporal interactions [9]. Simply projecting patches into the Transformer space may weaken local feature extraction, reducing information utilization. Thus, attention should also be directed to dependencies within patches. The second challenge is capturing inter-variable dependencies in multivariate time series (MTS). Existing Transformer-based models primarily focus on temporal dependencies while overlooking inter-variable correlations [3, 4, 10]. These models embed data points from the same time step into a single token, disregarding their distinct physical meanings. While some studies explicitly model inter-variable dependencies [2, 8], PatchTST [6] and Petformer [11] argue that channel independence improves robustness to distribution shifts [12]. However, we contend that channel mixing fails primarily due to its inability to capture complex variable relationships, which may vary across temporal scales. Viewing MTS as graph signals, Graph Neural Networks [13, 14] provide a promising solution for modeling inter-variable dependencies. Yet, most GNN-based models rely on predefined graph structures or learn single-scale graphs [15], limiting adaptability and performance.

To address key challenges in multivariate time series forecasting—namely, modeling complex variable-wise correlations and capturing temporal patterns across multiple scales—we propose a Dual Attention Transformer with Adaptive Multi-scale Perception (DTMP). Inspired by the mixture of experts (MoE) paradigm [16], DTMP allocates different model components to distinct temporal scales for specialized pattern extraction. The model consists of four key modules: a periodicity-aware scale selection module, a graph structure learning and convolution module, a temporal dual-attention module, and a multi-scale aggregation module. To adaptively select meaningful scales, we apply Fast Fourier Transform (FFT) to identify dominant frequencies, reconstruct scale-specific signals, and mix them with the original series via a gated network that learns scale weights. For each scale, DTMP decouples time-variable dependencies: variable-wise correlations are modeled through learned adjacency matrices and graph convolutions; temporal dependencies are captured using a dual-attention mechanism that separately learns local (intra-patch) and global (inter-patch) patterns, effectively covering short-term fluctuations and long-term trends. The attention across time points is computed independently with shared weights, incurring minimal overhead. Finally, a multi-scale aggregation module integrates information across all scales, unifying temporal and variable dependencies into a cohesive forecasting representation. DTMP thus systematically addresses the core challenges through a tailored, multi-scale architectural design. In summary, our contributions are as follows:

(1) We propose DTMP, a novel architecture that jointly models variable and temporal dependencies from a multi-scale perspective.
(2) We design a periodicity-driven adaptive module to select relevant time scales and construct scale-specific graphs for variable correlation modeling.
(3) We introduce a dual-attention mechanism to separately capture global and local temporal patterns.
(4) Extensive experiments on multiple real-world datasets demonstrate DTMP's superior accuracy and robustness compared to state-of-the-art baselines.

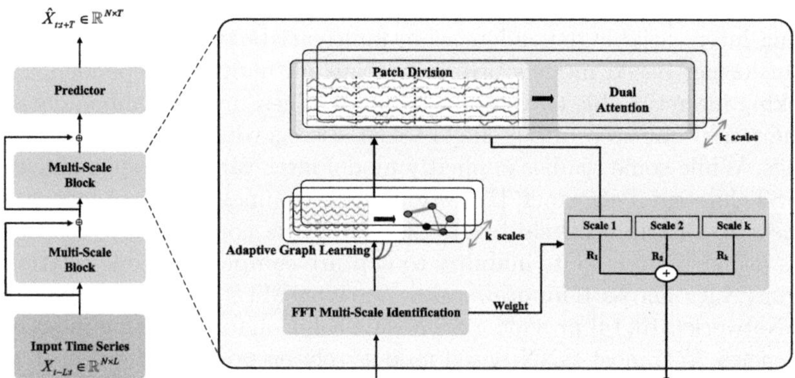

Fig. 1. Overall structure of DTMP.

2   Methodology

2.1   Problem Definition

Given a multivariate time series input $X_{t-L:t} = \{x_{t-L}, x_{t-L-1}, ...x_{t-1}\} \in \mathbb{R}^{N \times L}$ with N variables and look-back window L, we aim to predict future values $\hat{X}_{t:t+T} = \{x_t, x_{t+1}, ..., x_{t+T-1}\} \in \mathbb{R}^{N \times T}$ over horizon T. We use a graph $G = \{V, X, \{A^k\}\}$ to describe the inter-variable dependencies in MTS, where nodes V represent variables, $X \in \mathbb{R}^{N \times L}$ denotes the values of the time series, and $\{A^k\}_{k=1}^{K}$ are learnable adjacency matrices, each representing dependencies at different time scales, enabling a comprehensive modeling of interactions across various temporal granularities.

2.2   Model Architecture

Our proposed DTMP is illustrated in Fig. 1. The multi-scale module is the core component of our model, comprising four main parts: (a) Multi-scale recognition and selection module focuses on identifying periodic patterns in the data and computing the weights for the experts corresponding to each scale. (b) Graph learning and convolution module involves learning adaptive graphs to capture the relationships between different variables and applying convolution operations accordingly. (c) Dual attention transformer module utilizes a dual attention mechanism to effectively capture dependencies both between and within patches. (d) Multi-scale fusion module is responsible for fusing information from different scales based on the computed weights to enhance the overall predictive capability of the model. The following sections provide a detailed description of each module.

2.3   Multi-scale Adaptive Recognition and Selection

The intrinsic characteristics of different time series may make certain time scales more suitable for prediction tasks. Using a single scale or manually selecting one may not capture the true correlations, especially when considering multiple scales. We believe that periodic information within the series is key for optimal multi-scale partitioning and selection. Thus, we use FFT to transform the time series from the time domain to the frequency domain:

$$
\begin{aligned}
A &= \mathrm{Avg}(\mathrm{Amp}(\mathrm{FFT}(X))), \\
\{f_1, ..., f_k\} &= \underset{f_* = \{1, ..., \lfloor \frac{L}{2} \rfloor\}}{\mathrm{argTopK}} (A), \\
x_{per} &= \mathrm{IFFT}(\{f_1, ..., f_k\}, A, \phi),
\end{aligned}
\tag{1}
$$

where $\mathrm{FFT}(\cdot)$ represents the Fast Fourier Transform, $\mathrm{Amp}(\cdot)$ denotes the computation of the amplitude value, $A \in \mathbb{R}^L$ represents the computed amplitudes for each frequency, averaged over the number of variables N. The j-th value of A, denoted as A_j, represents the strength of the periodic basis function for frequency j, corresponding to a period length of $\lceil \frac{L}{j} \rceil$. To extract significant periodic information and avoid meaningless high-frequency noise, we select the top k amplitude values, thus obtaining the k most important frequencies $\{f_1, ..., f_k\}$ and their corresponding amplitudes $\{A_{f_1}, ..., A_{f_k}\}$, where k is a hyperparameter. $\mathrm{IFFT}(\cdot)$ denotes the inverse Fourier Transform, which captures the periodic patterns X_{per}.

We combine the original data X with the periodic patterns along the time dimension and apply a linear transformation to obtain the mixed sequence: $X_{mix} = Linear(X + X_{per})$, where $X_{mix} \in \mathbb{R}^d$. We introduce D experts, each representing a different scale, and select the k most relevant ones for the task. An adaptive scale selection module, similar to a gating network, assigns weights to each scale. To ensure load balancing and prevent the model from overfocusing on a few scales, we add a noise term to introduce randomness, calculated as follows:

$$\mathcal{R}(X) = \mathrm{Softmax}(X_{mix}W_g + \epsilon \cdot \mathrm{Softplus}(X_{mix}W_{noise})), \tag{2}$$

where $\mathcal{R}(\cdot)$ represents the weight distribution, W_g and $W_{noise} \in \mathbb{R}^{d \times D}$ are learnable weight parameters, D is the number of experts, i.e., the number of the candidate scales, and ϵ denotes standard normalization.

2.4 Graph Learning and Convolution

Before inputting the multivariate time series data into the dual-attention module, we model variable dependencies using a graph neural network. Since these dependencies vary across scales, we use a separate adjacency matrix for each scale to learn these relationships. The adjacency matrix is learned end-to-end, initialized randomly, allowing the model to capture dependencies without prior knowledge. For each scale, we employ a graph structure learning method similar to MTGNN [15] to capture one-way dependencies between variables.

$$\begin{aligned}
M_1 &= \tanh(E_1\theta_1), \\
M_2 &= \tanh(E_2\theta_2), \\
A &= \mathrm{ReLU}(M_1(M_2)^T - (M_1)^T M_2).
\end{aligned} \tag{3}$$

Here, $E_1, E_2 \in \mathbb{R}^{N \times d_{\mathrm{node}}}$ denote randomly initialized and trainable node feature matrices, d_{node} represents the dimensionality of node features. The matrix $A \in \mathbb{R}^{N \times N}$ serves as the learned adjacency matrix, capturing the unidirectional dependencies among variables. $\theta_1, \theta_2 \in \mathbb{R}^{1 \times 1}$ correspond to model parameters, associated respectively with sender and receiver features.

We utilize the MixHop graph convolutional operator [17] to capture correlations between variables, which enhances the node feature representation by repeatedly mixing feature representations of neighbors at different distances, thereby capturing more complex graph structural information:

$$H = \sigma \left(\big\|_{j \in p} A^j X \right) W, \tag{4}$$

where the hyperparameter p is a set of integer adjacency powers, A^j represents the adjacency matrix A raised to the power of j, $\|$ denotes column-wise concatenation, and $W \in \mathbb{R}^{(L \times p) \times L}$ is a learnable parameter. Through graph convolution, we blend information across various variables, explicitly capturing the dependencies between them.

2.5 Dual Attention

Based on a given time scale, we transform the original time series $X \in \mathbb{R}^{L \times d}$ into $\{X^1, X^2, \ldots, X^P\}$, where $X^i \in \mathbb{R}^{S \times d}$, $P = \lceil L/s \rceil$ denotes the number of patches, and S represents the patch size. To capture both local (within-patch)

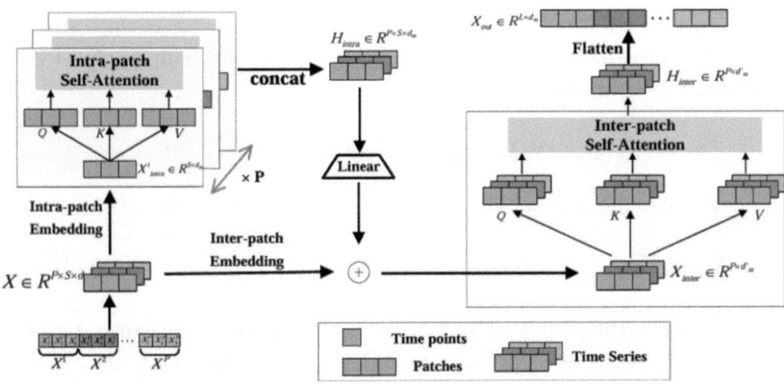

Fig. 2. The framework of Dual Attention.

and global (across-patch) temporal dependencies, we propose a dual attention mechanism, as shown in Fig. 2. First, attention is computed within each patch and fused with the original patches. Then, attention is calculated across patches. Since intra-patch attention uses shared network weights, the added complexity is negligible. We use a channel-wise independent approach, similar to PatchTST [6], for input sequences into the dual attention module, but we uniquely capture variable dependencies through graph convolution beforehand. For simplicity, we describe the mechanism using a single variable.

Intra Attention. First, we compute the attention across various time points within each patch. We embed this patch along the feature dimension d into d_m, yielding $X^i_{intra} = X^i W_{intra} + E_{intra} \in \mathbb{R}^{S \times d_m}$, where $W_{intra} \in \mathbb{R}^{d \times d_m}$ represents a fully connected layer, and $E_{intra} \in \mathbb{R}^{S \times d_m}$ denotes trainable positional encoding. Each patch X_{intra} is mapped to three feature spaces, namely Query Q^i_{intra}, Key K^i_{intra}, and Value V^i_{intra}. The computations for these features are as follows:

$$Q^i_{intra} = X^i_{intra} W_{Q_{intra}}, \quad K^i_{intra} = X^i_{intra} W_{K_{intra}}, V^i_{intra} = X^i_{intra} W_{V_{intra}}.$$

$$(5)$$

Next, we use the self-attention mechanism to model the temporal dependencies within each patch, and we concatenate all patches after computing attention, which integrates the surrounding local information, to obtain a sequence with the same shape as the original data, as shown below:

$$Attn^i_{intra} = Softmax(\frac{Q_{intra}(K_{intra})^T}{\sqrt{d_m}}),$$

$$H^i_{intra} = Attn^i_{intra} V_{intra},$$

$$H_{intra} = Concat(H^1_{intra}, ..., H^P_{intra}),$$

$$(6)$$

where $H^i_{intra} \in \mathbb{R}^{S \times d_m}$, and $H_{intra} \in \mathbb{R}^{P \times S \times d_m}$. **Inter Attention.** Similarly, we first embed and rearrange the series for inter-patch attention: $X_{inter} =$

$XW_{inter} + E_{inter}$, where $X_{inter} \in \mathbb{R}^{P \times d'_m}$, and $d'_m = S \times d_m$. Additionally, we project the intra-patch attention into the inter-patch space and mix them through a linear projection:

$$X_{inter} = X_{inter} + FC(H_{intra}) \in \mathbb{R}^{P \times d'_m}. \tag{7}$$

Next, we compute the query, key, and value for inter-patch attention:

$$Q_{inter} = X_{inter} W_{Q_{inter}}, \quad K_{inter} = X_{inter} W_{K_{inter}}, V_{inter} = X_{inter} W_{V_{inter}}. \tag{8}$$

We compute the inter-patch attention, which not only captures the temporal dependencies between patches from a global perspective but also includes the details within each patch. This comprehensive approach significantly aids in the accurate understanding of the entire time series, as shown below:

$$Attn_{inter} = Softmax(\frac{Q_{inter}(K_{inter})^T}{\sqrt{d_m}}), \quad H_{inter} = Attn_{inter} V_{inter}, \tag{9}$$

where $H_{inter} \in \mathbb{R}^{P \times d'_m}$, finally flatten into $X^i_{out} \in \mathbb{R}^{L \times d_m}$ as the output.

2.6   Multi-scale Fusion and Output Layer

To obtain the final multi-scale representation, the most straightforward approaches are either to directly concatenate each scale's representation or to aggregate them through global pooling. However, these methods fail to consider the specific impact of each scale on the final prediction results. Empirically, small-scale perspectives are more crucial for short-term predictions, while large-scale perspectives provide more accurate predictions for long-term forecasting. Therefore, we designed an adaptive aggregator to dynamically select and integrate information from different scales, ensuring optimal feature extraction for both short-term and long-term forecasting. Additionally, to avoid meaningless scale sizes, we chose the top k weighted scales for fusion:

$$X_{out} = \sum_{i=1}^{K} TopK(R_i(X_{mix}))F_i(X^i_{out}), \tag{10}$$

where $\text{Topk}(\cdot)$ selects the k scales with the highest weights and sets the weights of the remaining scales to zero, R_i represents the weights of scale i calculated above, and $F_i(\cdot)$ is a linear layer that aligns features of different scales by projecting them into the same hidden space.

After obtaining the sequence representation through the MultiscaleBlocks, we utilize a linear projection layer to derive the final prediction results:

$$\hat{X} = FC(X_{out}), \tag{11}$$

where $\hat{X} \in \mathbb{R}^{T \times N}$, N is the number of variables and T is the prediction window length. We use the Mean Squared Error (MSE) loss to measure the discrepancy between the predicted values and the actual values. The overall loss function is obtained by averaging the loss across N variables. The optimization objective is as follows:

$$\mathcal{L} = \frac{1}{N} \sum_{i=1}^{N} |\hat{X}^i - X^i|_2^2. \tag{12}$$

Table 1. Statistics of datasets

Dataset	Timestamps	Variables	Sample Rate
Weather	52696	21	10 min
Traffic	17544	862	hourly
Electricity	26304	321	hourly
ETTh1&ETTh2	17420	7	hourly
ETTm1&ETTm2	69680	7	15 min
Solar-Energy	52560	137	10 min

3 Experiments

Datasets. We conducted experiments on eight real-world datasets from various domains, including ETT (4 subsets), Weather, Electricity, Traffic [4], and Solar-Energy [1]. Their summarized information is shown in Table 1.

3.1 Forecasting Results

In this section, we conduct experiments to evaluate our model's forecasting performance against state-of-the-art deep forecasters.

Baselines. We carefully select 9 widely recognized forecasting models as our benchmark, including (1) Transformer-based methods: PatchTST [6], Cross-former [8], FEDformer [5], Informer [3], Autoformer [4], iTransformer [2]; (2)Linear-based method: DLinear [7]; and (3) TCN-based methods: TimesNet [9], MTGNN [15].

Implementation Details. Our model utilizes Adam as the optimizer, initializing with a learning rate of 10^{-3}. We use mean square error(MSE) and mean absolute error (MAE) as evaluation metrics. All training and testing procedures were executed on an NVIDIA GeForce RTX 4090 GPU using the PyTorch framework. To ensure equitable comparison with the baselines, we maintain a consistent input length of $L = 96$ and evaluate performance across prediction lengths

320   F. Li et al.

Table 2. Multivariate time series forecasting results. The values in bold indicate the best performance, and the underlined values indicate the second-best performance. A lower MSE/MAE indicates a more accurate prediction.

Method		DTMP (Ours)		iTransformer (2024)		CrossFormer (2023)		PatchTST (2023)		MTGNN (2021)		Informer (2021)		DLinear (2023)		TimesNet (2023)		Autoformer (2021)		FEDformer (2022)	
Metric		MSE	MAE	MSE	MAE	MSE	MAE	MSE	MAE	MSE	MAE	MSE	MAE	MSE	MAE	MSE	MAE	MSE	MAE	MSE	MAE
Weather	96	**0.168**	**0.205**	0.174	0.214	0.181	0.231	0.177	0.218	0.171	0.231	0.300	0.384	0.195	0.253	0.172	0.220	0.266	0.336	0.217	0.296
	192	**0.205**	**0.246**	0.221	0.254	0.219	0.275	0.224	0.258	0.215	0.274	0.598	0.544	0.239	0.299	0.219	0.261	0.307	0.367	0.276	0.336
	336	**0.262**	**0.280**	0.278	0.296	0.274	0.332	0.277	0.297	0.266	0.313	0.578	0.523	0.282	0.333	0.280	0.306	0.359	0.395	0.339	0.380
	720	**0.337**	**0.330**	0.358	0.347	0.356	0.387	0.350	0.345	0.344	0.375	1.059	0.741	0.352	0.390	0.365	0.359	0.419	0.428	0.403	0.428
Traffic	96	0.501	**0.286**	0.425	0.288	0.528	0.290	0.492	0.324	0.532	0.307	0.719	0.391	0.648	0.396	0.593	0.321	0.613	0.388	0.587	0.366
	192	0.520	**0.290**	0.446	0.296	0.540	0.303	0.487	0.303	0.534	0.312	0.696	0.379	0.613	0.386	0.617	0.336	0.616	0.382	0.604	0.373
	336	0.521	**0.291**	0.453	0.304	0.568	0.315	0.505	0.317	0.540	0.335	0.777	0.420	0.614	0.383	0.629	0.336	0.622	0.337	0.621	0.383
	720	0.544	**0.302**	0.495	0.312	0.602	0.358	0.542	0.337	0.557	0.343	0.864	0.472	0.655	0.405	0.640	0.350	0.660	0.408	0.626	0.382
Electricity	96	**0.155**	**0.248**	0.158	0.250	0.254	0.347	0.180	0.264	0.211	0.305	0.274	0.368	0.194	0.276	0.168	0.272	0.201	0.317	0.186	0.302
	192	**0.173**	0.259	0.181	**0.253**	0.261	0.353	0.188	0.275	0.225	0.319	0.296	0.386	0.193	0.279	0.184	0.289	0.222	0.334	0.197	0.311
	336	**0.181**	**0.275**	0.188	0.269	0.273	0.364	0.206	0.291	0.247	0.340	0.300	0.394	0.206	0.294	0.198	0.300	0.231	0.338	0.213	0.328
	720	0.233	**0.307**	0.225	0.317	0.303	0.388	0.247	0.328	0.287	0.373	0.373	0.439	0.241	0.328	**0.220**	0.320	0.254	0.361	0.233	0.344
ETTh1	96	0.391	0.402	0.386	0.405	0.429	0.440	0.394	0.408	0.440	0.450	0.865	0.713	0.392	0.405	0.384	**0.402**	0.449	0.459	**0.376**	0.419
	192	0.443	0.433	0.441	0.436	0.494	0.482	0.446	0.438	0.449	0.433	1.008	0.792	0.441	0.436	0.436	**0.429**	0.500	0.482	**0.420**	0.448
	336	0.475	0.469	0.487	**0.458**	0.570	0.546	0.501	0.466	0.598	0.554	1.107	0.809	0.501	0.478	0.491	0.469	0.521	0.496	**0.459**	0.465
	720	**0.475**	**0.473**	0.503	0.491	0.563	0.621	0.500	0.488	0.685	0.620	1.181	0.865	0.538	0.526	0.521	0.500	0.514	0.512	0.506	0.507
ETTh2	96	0.320	**0.342**	0.297	0.349	0.632	0.547	**0.294**	0.343	0.496	0.509	3.755	1.525	0.331	0.381	0.340	0.374	0.358	0.397	0.346	0.388
	192	**0.353**	**0.392**	0.380	0.400	0.876	0.663	0.378	0.394	0.716	0.616	5.602	1.931	0.432	0.435	0.402	0.414	0.456	0.452	0.429	0.439
	336	**0.358**	**0.390**	0.428	0.432	0.924	0.702	0.382	0.410	0.718	0.614	4.721	1.835	0.441	0.451	0.452	0.452	0.482	0.486	0.496	0.487
	720	0.415	0.439	0.427	0.445	1.390	0.863	**0.412**	**0.433**	1.161	0.791	3.647	1.625	0.564	0.578	0.462	0.468	0.515	0.511	0.463	0.474
ETTm1	96	**0.320**	0.359	0.334	0.368	0.428	0.444	0.324	0.361	0.381	0.415	0.672	0.571	0.342	0.370	0.338	**0.357**	0.505	0.475	0.379	0.419
	192	0.370	**0.375**	0.377	0.391	0.445	0.468	**0.362**	0.383	0.442	0.451	0.795	0.669	0.383	0.394	0.374	0.387	0.553	0.496	0.426	0.441
	336	**0.392**	**0.397**	0.426	0.420	0.533	0.519	0.399	0.410	0.475	0.475	1.212	0.871	0.413	0.414	0.410	0.411	0.621	0.537	0.445	0.459
	720	0.487	0.450	0.491	0.459	0.728	0.655	**0.461**	**0.466**	0.531	0.507	1.166	0.823	0.472	0.452	0.478	0.450	0.671	0.561	0.543	0.490
ETtm2	96	**0.176**	**0.251**	0.180	0.264	0.197	0.321	0.177	0.260	0.240	0.343	0.365	0.453	0.186	0.279	0.187	0.267	0.255	0.339	0.203	0.287
	192	**0.239**	**0.296**	0.250	0.309	0.326	0.375	0.248	0.306	0.398	0.454	0.533	0.563	0.266	0.339	0.249	0.309	0.281	0.340	0.269	0.328
	336	**0.298**	**0.325**	0.311	0.348	0.372	0.421	0.304	0.342	0.568	0.555	1.363	0.887	0.332	0.376	0.321	0.351	0.339	0.372	0.325	0.366
	720	0.407	0.409	0.412	0.407	0.410	0.448	**0.403**	**0.397**	1.072	0.767	3.379	1.338	0.462	0.455	0.408	0.403	0.433	0.432	0.421	0.415
Solar	96	0.210	0.246	**0.203**	**0.237**	0.310	0.331	0.234	0.286	0.294	0.307	0.236	0.259	0.290	0.378	0.250	0.292	0.884	0.711	0.242	0.342
	192	0.238	0.266	0.233	**0.261**	0.734	0.725	0.267	0.310	0.338	0.341	**0.217**	0.267	0.320	0.398	0.296	0.318	0.834	0.692	0.285	0.380
	336	0.258	0.280	**0.248**	**0.273**	0.720	0.735	0.290	0.315	0.357	0.369	0.249	0.283	0.353	0.415	0.319	0.330	0.941	0.723	0.282	0.376
	720	0.260	0.288	0.252	**0.275**	0.769	0.765	0.289	0.317	0.431	0.445	**0.241**	0.317	0.356	0.413	0.338	0.337	0.882	0.717	0.357	0.427
1st Count		**15**	**20**	6	6	0	0	5	3	0	0	2	0	0	0	1	2	0	0	3	0

$T \in \{96, 192, 336, 720\}$. Our model is configured with two stacked Multiscale-Blocks, where each MultiscaleBlock incorporates five experts and their patch sizes are $\{8, 12, 16, 24, 32\}$. We select the top 3 optimal patch sizes for fusion.

Main Results. The experimental results, shown in Table 2, demonstrate that our model outperforms others in most cases. Specifically, DTMP achieves the best average results across multiple prediction lengths on five datasets and the second-best on three others. Notably, compared to the state-of-the-art model iTransformer, our approach reduces MSE by 5.7% and MAE by 4.7% on Weather, highlighting its effectiveness. Although TimesNet also incorporates multi-scale periodic information, its convolutional backbone is not optimized for time series, limiting its ability to capture global dependencies. This explains why its performance is inferior to ours. PatchTST, the first to introduce the patch concept for multivariate time series, only uses a fixed scale for segmentation, while our model utilizes multi-scale segmentation to capture different perspectives. Furthermore,

PatchTST's channel-independent approach may not be optimal. In contrast, we learn an adjacency matrix for each scale to fully capture variable dependencies. Lastly, while CrossFormer and MTGNN model dependencies using attention and graph neural networks respectively, they focus on a single scale, overlooking the fact that inter-variable relationships vary across scales.

3.2   Ablation Studies

To comprehensively evaluate the effectiveness of each module in DTMP, we conducted ablation experiments with several variants:

W/O Inter: This variant removes the cross-segment attention mechanism, making the model focus solely on local features.

W/O Intra: This variant eliminates the intra-segment attention mechanism.

W/O Adaptive: This variant removes adaptive scale selection, using a fixed single-scale perspective to model the sequence, specifically with patch sizes of 16 and 32.

W/O Graph: This variant excludes the graph structure learning and graph convolution modules, instead adopting a purely channel-independent strategy.

Table 3 presents the results of the ablation experiments. It is evident that each module contributes to performance improvements. Specifically, the absence of Inter Attention significantly deteriorates the results, highlighting the critical importance of global dependencies for long-term forecasting. Additionally, Intra attention aids prediction results, indicating the necessity of modeling intra-patch details. The improvement brought by the graph convolution layer suggests that explicitly learning the relationships among variables outperforms the simple channel-independent and channel-mixing strategies. The results without the adaptive multi-scale selection module emphasize the importance of multi-scale modeling for time series prediction. Each of these modules is indispensable, collectively achieving optimal forecasting performance for multivariate time series.

Table 3. Ablation experiment results. The result is obtained by taking the average of the predicted lengths {96,192,336,720}.

Dataset	Weather		Electricity		Traffic	
Metric	MSE	MAE	MSE	MAE	MSE	MAE
DTMP	**0.243**	**0.265**	**0.185**	**0.272**	**0.522**	**0.292**
w/o Inter	0.271	0.281	0.214	0.305	0.561	0.326
w/o Intra	0.258	0.277	0.215	0.297	0.544	<u>0.309</u>
w/o adaptive-64	<u>0.251</u>	0.278	<u>0.206</u>	0.288	0.539	0.310
w/o adaptive-32	0.252	<u>0.276</u>	0.210	<u>0.281</u>	<u>0.529</u>	0.311
w/o graph	0.258	0.281	0.212	0.299	0.545	0.321

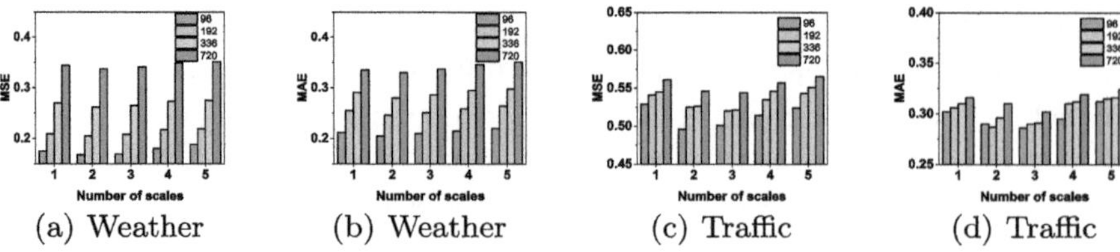

(a) Weather   (b) Weather   (c) Traffic   (d) Traffic

Fig. 3. The impact of the number of selected fusion scales on the prediction results.

3.3 Parameter Sensitivity

To investigate the impact of multiple scale perspectives, we evaluated DTMP using different numbers of scales. Figure 3 presents the results on the Weather and Traffic datasets. It is evident that the best performance is achieved with 2–3 scales, effectively capturing the complex relationships within the sequences, including temporal and variable dependencies. When the number of scales is further increased, performance does not improve, likely due to the incorporation of irrelevant scales, which can lead to overfitting as a result of an excessive number of parameters.

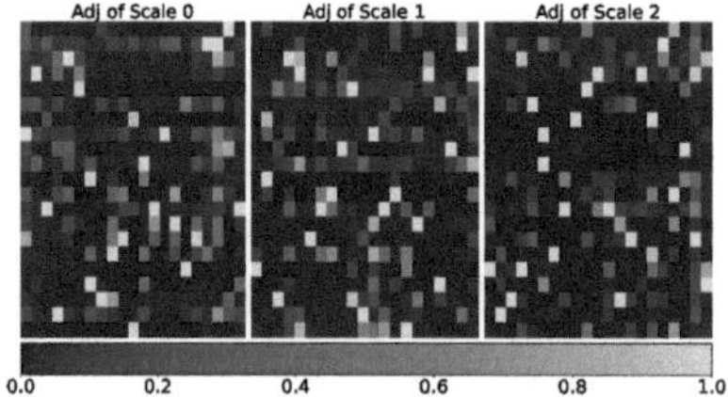

Fig. 4. Heat maps of adjacency matrices learned at different scales.

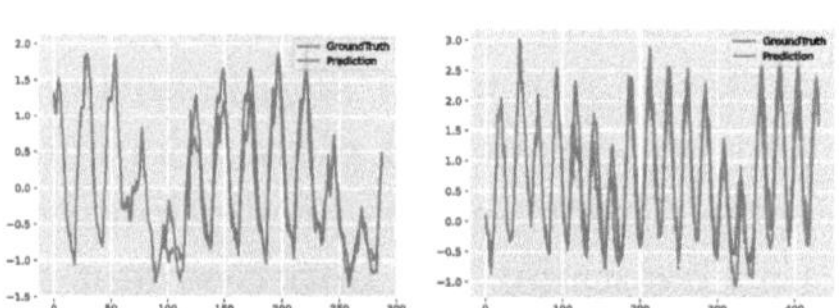

Fig. 5. Forecasting visualization.

3.4 Visualization

Figure 4 shows the heatmaps of adjacency matrices learned at three different scales on the Weather dataset, revealing how variable dependencies change across scales. As the scale shifts, correlations between variables can switch from positive to negative, supporting our hypothesis. Figure 5 visualizes the results for two random variables at predicted lengths of 192 and 336, where our model effectively captures both short-term cyclical and long-term trend patterns. This is due to our multi-scale approach, which allows the model to capture complex temporal patterns.

4   Conclusion and Future Work

We propose the Dual Attention Transformer with Adaptive Multi-Scale Perception (DTMP) for multivariate time series forecasting. DTMP addresses key challenges in existing methods, such as modeling multi-scale temporal dependencies and capturing variable dependencies. By using a periodic information-based approach for scale selection and a dual attention mechanism, it effectively captures both short-term periodic and long-term trend features. Graph structure learning and graph convolution enhance variable dependency modeling. Extensive experiments demonstrate the model's superior performance. Future work will focus on improving adaptive scale selection, exploring variable dependencies, and integrating interpretability.

References

1. Lai, G., Chang, W.-C., Yang, Y., Liu, H.: Modeling long-and short-term temporal patterns with deep neural networks. In: The 41st International ACM SIGIR Conference on Research & Development in Information Retrieval, pp. 95–104 (2018)
2. Liu, Y., et al.: itransformer: inverted transformers are effective for time series forecasting. arXiv preprint arXiv:2310.06625 (2023)
3. Zhou, H., et al.: Informer: beyond efficient transformer for long sequence time-series forecasting. In: Proceedings of the AAAI Conference on Artificial Intelligence, vol. 35, pp. 11106–11115 (2021)
4. Wu, H., Xu, J, Wang, J, Long, M.: Autoformer: decomposition transformers with auto-correlation for long-term series forecasting. In: Advances in Neural Information Processing Systems, vol. 34, pp. 22419–22430 (2021)
5. Zhou, T., Ma, Z., Wen, Q., Wang, X., Sun, L., Jin, R.: Fedformer: frequency enhanced decomposed transformer for long-term series forecasting. In: International Conference on Machine Learning, pp. 27268–27286. PMLR (2022)
6. Nie, Y., Nguyen, N.H., Sinthong, P., Kalagnanam, J.: A time series is worth 64 words: long-term forecasting with transformers. arXiv preprint arXiv:2211.14730 (2022)
7. Zeng, A., Chen, M., Zhang, L., Xu, Q.: Are transformers effective for time series forecasting? In: Proceedings of the AAAI Conference on Artificial Intelligence, vol. 37, pp. 11121–11128 (2023)
8. Zhang, Y., Yan, J.: Crossformer: transformer utilizing cross-dimension dependency for multivariate time series forecasting. In: The Eleventh International Conference on Learning Representations (2022)
9. Wu, H., Hu, T., Liu, Y., Zhou, H., Wang, J., Long, M.: Timesnet: temporal 2D-variation modeling for general time series analysis. In: The Eleventh International Conference on Learning Representations (2022)
10. Kitaev, N., Kaiser, Ł., Levskaya, A.: Reformer: the efficient transformer. arXiv preprint arXiv:2001.04451 (2020)
11. Lin, S., Lin, W., Wu, W., Wang, S., Wang, Y.: Petformer: long-term time series forecasting via placeholder-enhanced transformer. arXiv preprint arXiv:2308.04791 (2023)
12. Han, L., Ye, H.-J., Zhan, D.-C.: The capacity and robustness trade-off: revisiting the channel independent strategy for multivariate time series forecasting. IEEE Trans. Knowl. Data Eng. (2024)
13. Kipf, T.N., Welling, M.: Semi-supervised classification with graph convolutional networks. arXiv preprint arXiv:1609.02907 (2016)

14. Shao, Z., Zhang, Z., Wang, F., Xu, Y.: Pre-training enhanced spatial-temporal graph neural network for multivariate time series forecasting. In: Proceedings of the 28th ACM SIGKDD Conference on Knowledge Discovery and Data Mining, pp. 1567–1577 (2022)
15. Wu, Z., Pan, S., Long, G., Jiang, J., Chang, X., Zhang, C.: Connecting the dots: multivariate time series forecasting with graph neural networks. In: Proceedings of the 26th ACM SIGKDD International Conference on Knowledge Discovery & Data Mining, pp. 753–763 (2020)
16. Shazeer, N., et al.: Outrageously large neural networks: the sparsely-gated mixture-of-experts layer. arXiv preprint arXiv:1701.06538 (2017)
17. Abu-El-Haija, S., et al.: Mixhop: higher-order graph convolutional architectures via sparsified neighborhood mixing. In: International Conference on Machine Learning, pp. 21–29. PMLR (2019)

Uncertainty-Aware Prototype Semantic Decoupling for Text-Based Person Search in Full Images

Zengli Luo[1], Canlong Zhang[1,2]($\boxtimes$), Zhixin Li[1,2], Zhiwen Wang[3], and Chunrong Wei[1]

[1] Key Lab of Education Blockchain and Intelligent Technology, Ministry of Education, Guangxi Normal University, Guilin 541004, China
{lizx,weicr,clzhang}@gxnu.edu.cn
[2] Guangxi Key Lab of Multi-source Information Mining and Security, Guangxi Normal University, Guilin 541004, China
[3] School of Electronic Engineering, Guangxi University of Science and Technology, Liuzhou 545006, China
wzw69@gxust.edu.cn

Abstract. Text-based pedestrian search (TBPS) in full images aims to locate a target person in uncropped images using natural language queries. However, in complex scenes with multiple pedestrians often lead to ambiguous detections and misalignment between language and vision. To address these challenges, we propose **UPD-TBPS**, a novel framework composed of three modules: Multi-granularity Uncertainty Estimation (MUE), Prototype-based Uncertainty Decoupling (PUD), and Cross-modal Re-identification (ReID). MUE reduces early-stage detection ambiguity via confidence-scored multi-view queries. PUD decouples multi-level visual semantics and mines coarse-to-fine prototypes to guide grounding. ReID leverages uncertainty-aware features to improve final retrieval. Experiments on two TBPS benchmarks adapted to full-image settings demonstrate the effectiveness of our framework.

Keywords: Uncertainty-Aware Learning · Text-Based Person Search · Prototype Semantic Decoupling

1 Introduction

Text-based pedestrian search in full images is more applicable to real-world scenarios than traditional methods [1,2], especially when textual queries are the only available cues. However, full-scene scenarios introduce challenges such as complex backgrounds, dynamic environments, and pedestrian occlusion [1,3]. These challenges can be summarized as: (1) overcoming the difficulty of pedestrian detection in complex scenes that traditional object detection methods struggle with, (2) reducing the uncertainty in identifying multiple detected

T. Zhu et al. (Eds.): KSEM 2025, LNAI 15920, pp. 325–337, 2026.
https://doi.org/10.1007/978-981-95-3052-6_25

pedestrians, and (3) bridging the modality gap between text and images in traditional text-based pedestrian retrieval. Despite recent efforts [3,4], research on text-based person search in full images remains limited. Current methods are still hindered by architectural limitations, face challenges in achieving accuracy and robustness in complex scenes and cross-modal matching.

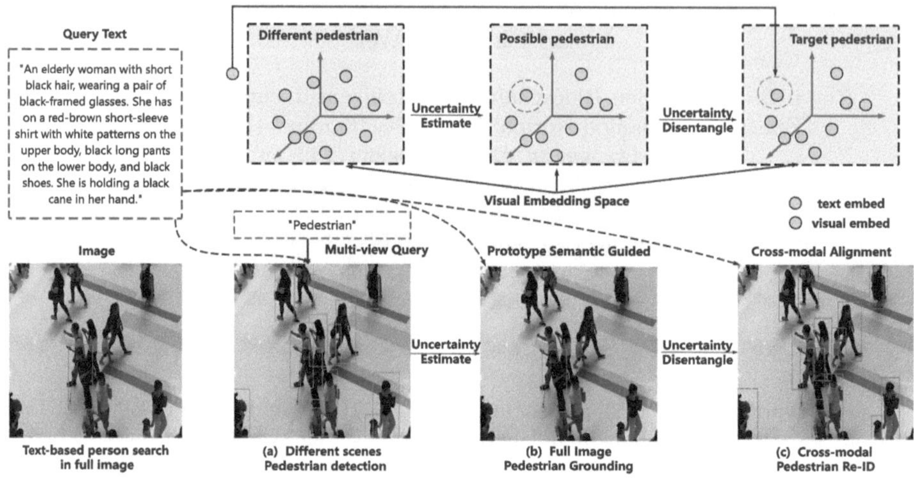

Fig. 1. Illustration of text-based person search in full images task.

To address the above challenges, we propose a novel strategy (as show in Fig. 1), which decomposes the full images text-based pedestrian search task into three key sub-tasks: (a) pedestrian detection in diverse scenes, (b) pedestrian identity recognition within the full image, and (c) cross-modal pedestrian re-identification. Correspondingly, we present the novel Uncertainty-driven Estimation and Decoupling framework (UPD-TBPS) that estimates and decouples uncertainty to retrieve the target pedestrian from multiple potential candidates based on semantic queries within complex, full-scene images. Pedestrian detection (Fig. 1(a)) aims to localize all potential persons in diverse full-image scenarios. However, variations in viewpoint and occlusion introduce significant input-level uncertainty, making accurate detection challenging [5]. Therefore, we introduce a **Multi-granularity Uncertainty Estimation (MUE)** module, which performs coarse screening and confidence assignment via multi-view queries, thereby enhancing detection robustness in the early stage. Pedestrian identification (Fig. 1(b)) aims to ground the described pedestrian among all proposals, where matching ambiguity and semantic misalignment remain major obstacles. To address this, we develop a **Prototype-based Uncertainty Decoupling (PUD)** module, which disentangles visual semantics and leverages both class-level and instance-level prototypes to guide fine-grained grounding while reducing uncertainty in cross-modal matching. Pedestrian re-identification (ReID)

(Fig. 1(c)) aims to select the correct pedestrian among all candidates across full scenes. A significant challenge is bridging the semantic gap between textual and visual modalities while managing uncertainty across modules to identify the target pedestrian [6]. Therefore, we develop the **ReID** module, which fuses textual and visual embeddings, leveraging uncertainty cues from both MUE and PUD for reliable retrieval. Our contributions can be summarized as follows: (1) We propose **UPD-TBPS**, a novel framework for text-based pedestrian search in full images, which explicitly models and decouples uncertainty throughout detection and matching stages. (2) We design three key modules: **MUE** for uncertainty-aware pedestrian detection, **PUD** for semantic-aligned identity recognition, and **ReID** for uncertainty-integrated cross-modal retrieval. (3) Extensive experiments on two public benchmarks demonstrate the superiority of UPD-TBPS over state-of-the-art methods in both accuracy and robustness.

2   Related Work

Accurate pedestrian detection for TBPS in full images is a key challenge in text-based pedestrian search (TBPS). Existing detection strategies typically follow either single-stage or two-stage designs. Single-stage methods offer faster inference by combining detection and feature learning, while two-stage approaches achieve higher precision through region proposals and refined matching. Recent works [1] explore anchor-free detectors and Transformer-based architectures to enhance robustness, but they are still limited by the complex backgrounds and semantic ambiguity in full-image settings.

In the context of TBPS [3], several methods have addressed partial challenges such as cross-modal discrepancy and semantic ambiguity. For example, prototype-based feature alignment [7] and uncertainty-aware representations [5] improve robustness to noisy descriptions or visual variation. Yet, these solutions typically tackle modality alignment or uncertainty modeling in isolation and are limited in handling real-world, full images scenarios. Therefore, our work introduces a unified Transformer-based framework that explicitly models multi-level uncertainty, integrates semantic prototypes, and aligns visual-textual modalities for robust target retrieval in cluttered environments.

3   Method

3.1   Preliminary

Figure 2 illustrates the overall workflow of the proposed UPD-TBPS framework, which aims to perform person search on uncropped full images using textual descriptions. To this end, UPD-TBPS progressively narrows the search space and improves retrieval precision through three interdependent submodules. We denote $\mathbf{F}_v$ as visual features extracted from full images using a trainable collaborative visual encoder, and $\mathbf{F}_t$ as textual features obtained from a 12-layer BERT-based encoder [8]. These features are subsequently processed through three key modules: MUE, PUD, and ReID. Each submodule is designed to address the three specific subtasks in full-image TBPS, as illustrated in Fig. 1.

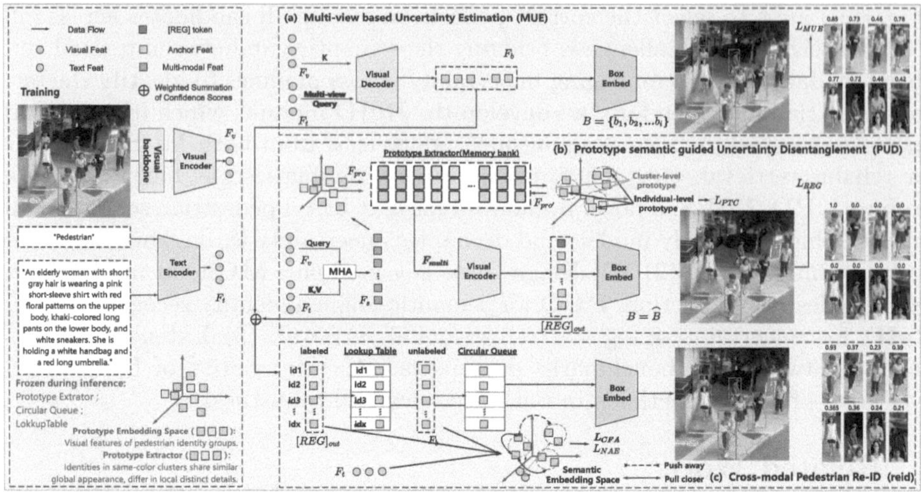

Fig. 2. Overview of the proposed UPD-TBPS framework. It consists of three key components: (a) Multi-Granularity Uncertainty Estimation (MUE), (b) Prototype-Guided Uncertainty Disentanglement (PUD), and (c) Cross-Modal Pedestrian Re-Identification (ReID).

3.2   Multi-granularity Based Uncertainty Estimation

We adopt a trainable and separable collaborative framework based on a disentangled visual-text encoder-decoder. Different from traditional pedestrian detection methods [3] that are limited by dense queries, our design integrates multi-granularity textual queries with visual features to search for all potential targets in a full image. We first fuse global and local visual features $\mathbf{F}_v$ with textual features $\mathbf{F}_t$ and input them into a visual decoder, where visual features serve as Keys and textual features as Queries. This yields a set of bounding box features $\mathbf{F}_b$ corresponding to all potential targets mentioned in the query. A bounding box embedding module [9] then transforms $\mathbf{F}_b$ into a set of predicted boxes $\mathbb{B} = \{b_1, b_2, \ldots, b_N\}$, where each $b_i = \{c_i, l_i\}$ includes a class prediction c_i and a location prediction l_i. We then use the Hungarian Algorithm to align predicted boxes $\mathbb{B}$ with ground-truth boxes $\hat{\mathbb{B}} = \{\hat{b}_1, \hat{b}_2, \ldots, \hat{b}_j\}$, resulting in the following matching loss:

$$L_{\text{MUE}}(\mathbb{B}, \hat{\mathbb{B}}) = \sum_{i=1}^{N} \left[-\log p_{\sigma(i)}(c_i) + L_{\text{box}}(l_i, \hat{l}_{\sigma(i)}) \right], \tag{1}$$

where $\sigma(i)$ is the optimal match index. The bounding box loss L_{box} consists of the L1 loss and the generalized IoU loss:

$$L_{\text{box}}(l_i, \hat{l}_i) = L_{\text{IoU}} + \|l_i - \hat{l}_i\|_1. \tag{2}$$

3.3 Prototype-Semantic Guided Uncertainty Disentanglement

Different from the method based on uncertainty disentanglement of prototype semantics [7], this module learns both instance-level and class-level prototypes to construct multi-granularity representations $\mathbf{F}_{\mathrm{multi}}$ for the ReID module. By combining fine-grained hard negative mining with class-level abstraction, the module proceeds through: (1) salient semantic feature extraction, (2) prototype mining and aggregation, and (3) visual-textual feature refinement with bounding box regression. Here we first compute salient semantic features via a multi-head attention (MHA):

$$\mathbf{F}_s = \mathrm{MHA}(\mathbf{F}_v, \mathbf{F}_t). \tag{3}$$

and generate refined visual features using a similarity-based scaling factor:

$$t = \exp\left(-\frac{(1 - S(\mathbf{F}_v, \mathbf{F}_s))}{2\mu^2}\right), \tag{4}$$

where $S(\cdot)$ denotes projected similarity and μ is a learnable parameter. MHA suppresses background noise and highlights target-related features. Refined features $\mathbf{F}\mathrm{pro}$ are assigned to the nearest prototype p_j in the prototype set $\mathbf{P} = p_i i = 1^k$ based on Euclidean distance. A contrastive loss aligns visual prototypes and text embeddings bidirectionally:

$$L_{\mathrm{PTC}} = \frac{L_{\mathrm{proto2t}} + L_{\mathrm{t2proto}}}{2}, \tag{5}$$

where each loss term optimizes similarity distributions between matched/unmatched pairs:

$$L_{\mathrm{proto2t}} = -\frac{1}{K} \sum_{i=1}^{K} \log \frac{\exp(\mathrm{sim}(p_i^m, t_i^m)/\tau)}{\sum_{j=1}^{K} \exp(\mathrm{sim}(p_i^m, t_j^m)/\tau)}, \tag{6}$$

$$L_{\mathrm{t2proto}} = -\frac{1}{K} \sum_{i=1}^{K} \log \frac{\exp(\mathrm{sim}(p_i^m, t_i^m)/\tau)}{\sum_{j=1}^{K} \exp(\mathrm{sim}(p_j^m, t_i^m)/\tau)}, \tag{7}$$

During training, instance-level features are clustered into prototype centers forming a memory bank Q_{proto} (updated with a stop-gradient strategy [10]). Hierarchical aggregation yields refined instance-level features, which are mapped to Q_{proto} for inference and used to retrieve prototype-aligned candidates. Next, $\mathbf{F}_{\mathrm{pro}}$ is fused with $\mathbf{F}_t$ via element-wise multiplication to generate the multi-modal representation:

$$\mathbf{F}_{\mathrm{multi}} = \tan(\mathbf{F}_{\mathrm{pro}}) \odot \mathrm{rank}(\mathbf{F}_t), \tag{8}$$

which is passed into the visual decoder for regression token refinement:

$$[\mathrm{REG}]_{\mathrm{out}} = VE\left([\mathrm{REG}]_{\mathrm{in}}, \mathbf{F}_{\mathrm{multi}}, \theta_v\right), \tag{9}$$

Then we have the regression loss consists of L_1 and generalized IoU loss:

$$L_{\mathrm{REG}} = L_1(B, \hat{B}) + L_{\mathrm{GIoU}}(B, \hat{B}), \tag{10}$$

Therefore, the overall loss for this module is:

$$L_{\mathrm{PUD}} = L_{\mathrm{PTC}} + L_{\mathrm{REG}}. \tag{11}$$

3.4   Cross-Modal Pedestrian Re-Identification

In ReID module, feature alignment and discrimination are key to optimizing visual and textual embeddings. We employ stepwise optimization to improve model efficiency and accuracy. Bounding box features $\mathbf{B}$, extracted and processed from the image modality by the cooperative visual decoder, yield $[\text{REG}]_{\text{out}}$ features. These are combined with textual features $\mathbf{F}_t$ and sent to a Lookup Table and Circular Queue for Norm-Aware Embedding Learning [11].

Meanwhile, the model improves cross-modal alignment through Spatial Distance Matrix learning [2] at the class level and Image-Text Contrast learning at the instance level. To align image regions with textual descriptions, the model calculates the Cosine similarity $sim([\text{REG}]_{\text{out}}, \mathbf{F}_t)$ and converts it into probability distributions using a softmax function with temperature ρ. Based on these probabilities, we have the class level loss for the image-to-text direction:

$$L_{\text{t2i}} = KL(p_{ij} \parallel q_{ij}) = \frac{1}{N} \sum_{i=1}^{N} \sum_{j=1}^{N} p_{ij} \log \frac{p_{ij}}{q_{ij} + \epsilon}, \tag{12}$$

where p_{ij} is the matching probability between image region i and textual description j, q_{ij} is the ground-truth probability, and ϵ is a small constant to prevent numerical instability. Similarly, the text-to-image direction is calculated in the same way, resulting in:

$$L_{\text{class-l}} = L_{\text{i2t}} + L_{\text{t2i}}. \tag{13}$$

The instance-level loss maximizes the similarity of positive samples while minimizing the similarity of negative samples:

$$L_{\text{ins-l}} = -\log \left(\frac{\exp\left(s_{ii}/\epsilon\right)}{\exp\left(s_{ii}/\epsilon\right) + \sum_{j \neq i} \exp\left(s_{ij}/\epsilon\right)} \right), \tag{14}$$

where s_{ij} represents the cosine similarity between the i-th visual feature $\mathbf{F}_b^i$ and the j-th textual feature $\mathbf{F}_t^j$, and ϵ is a temperature parameter that adjusts the "sharpness" of the similarity distribution. Then we have the corresponding cross-modal feature alignment loss:

$$L_{\text{CFA}} = L_{\text{class-l}} + L_{\text{ins-l}}. \tag{15}$$

In addition, we adopt the norm-aware embedding [11] to enhance feature discrimination. Specifically, this method uses lookup tables and circular queues to unify features, ensuring better consistency across different modalities. The NAE method utilizes L_2 normalization and learnable scaling to refine the visual features $\mathbf{F}_b$. The refined textual features $\mathbf{N}_t$ and visual features $\mathbf{F}_b$ are sent to the Lookup Table (LUT) and Circular Queue (CQ) for further processing:

$$L_{\text{NAE}} = \text{OIM}(\mathbf{F}_b, \mathbf{N}_t, \text{LUT}, \text{CQ}), \tag{16}$$

where LUT stores features with known identities, and CQ is a circular queue for features with unknown identities. Therefore, the loss for the ReID module is:

$$L_{\text{ReID}} = L_{\text{CFA}} + L_{\text{NAE}}. \tag{17}$$

3.5   Training and Inference

To balance the contributions of different components during training, we adopt a normalized adaptive loss formulation. Specifically, the total loss is defined as:

$$L_{\text{total}} = \frac{\alpha_1 L_{\text{MUE}} + \alpha_2 L_{\text{PUD}} + \alpha_3 L_{\text{ReID}}}{\alpha_1 + \alpha_2 + \alpha_3}, \tag{18}$$

where $\alpha_1, \alpha_2, \alpha_3$ are dynamic weighting factors that adjust the influence of each loss term. This strategy can ensure that no single component dominates training and that the model adaptively emphasizes more uncertain or challenging tasks as needed.

During inference, the lookup table and circular queue in the PUD and ReID modules are frozen. The query text is input into the BERT model to extract textual features $\mathbf{Q}_t \in \mathbb{R}^{1 \times 256}$. Similarly, the image is input into the visual backbone and visual decoder to extract visual features $\mathbf{G}_i \in \mathbb{R}^{n \times 256}$, which are then passed to the MUE and PUD modules. The MUE module outputs a set of candidate bounding boxes $\mathbf{B}_{\text{MUE}}$ and their corresponding confidence scores $\mathbf{C}_{\text{MUE}}$. The PUD module outputs another set of candidate bounding boxes $\mathbf{B}_{\text{PUD}}$ and their corresponding confidence scores $\mathbf{C}_{\text{PUD}}$. The final prediction is obtained by fusing the confidence scores of the candidate boxes from the MUE and PUD modules. Specifically, for a candidate box b_i from the MUE module and a candidate box b_j from the PUD module, if their IoU exceeds a predefined threshold, the two boxes are considered a match, and their combined score R_{ij} is calculated as:

$$R_{ij} = \alpha \cdot c_i + \beta \cdot c_j, \tag{19}$$

where c_i and c_j are the confidence scores of b_i and b_j, respectively. Finally, all matched candidate boxes are ranked by R_{ij}, and the box with the highest score is selected as the final prediction.

4   Experiments

4.1   Implementation Details

We conduct experiments on two benchmark datasets: CUHK-SYSU-TBPS [3] with 11,206 training images (15,080 boxes, 5,532 IDs) and 2,900 queries, and PRW-TBPS [3] with 5,704 images (14,897 boxes, 483 IDs) and 2,056 queries. Each box in CUHK-SYSU-TBPS is paired with two/one textual descriptions for training/query, and vice versa in PRW-TBPS. Following [3], we use mAP and CMC top-K as evaluation metrics.The IoU threshold is set to 0.5.

Visual Backbone. We uses the backbone of Faster R-CNN [12] extract global visual features from full-scene images. These features serve as input to the collaborative visual encoder, implemented as a DETR-style encoder-decoder [9]. The combination enables effective spatial reasoning and avoids reliance on dense region proposals.

Collaborative Encoding. To model complex spatial and semantic dependencies, we adopt a DETR-style encoder-decoder architecture as the collaborative visual decoder. The DETR design allows for query-based decoding and avoids hand-crafted anchor design, making it well-suited for sparse pedestrian retrieval under complex scenes. Images are resized to 640×640 and trained with SGD for 100 epochs (initial learning rate 0.0001, decayed ×10 after 60 epochs) and a batch size of 32. For the PUD module, we set the prototype size to 2048, embedding dimension to 256, temperature to 0.07, and the circular queue size to 5,000 (known IDs)/500 (unknown).

4.2   Comparison with State-of-the-Art Methods

We evaluate our approach against a range of state-of-the-art text-based person search methods on CUHK-SYSU-TBPS and PRW-TBPS. As shown in Table 1, our method achieves the best top-1 accuracy of 57.95% on CUHK-SYSU-TBPS and delivers competitive performance across all metrics. On PRW-TBPS, although MACA [4] slightly outperforms in mAP, our method achieves better top-5 and top-10 accuracy, indicating more robust ranking in large-scale retrieval.

The methods chosen for comparison span several key paradigms in text-based person search. OIM [13] provides a foundational joint detection-identification framework using Online Instance Matching loss. NAE [11] improves upon this by introducing norm-aware embeddings to enhance feature discrimination in cross-modal scenarios. BSL [3] captures contextual dependencies within textual inputs to improve alignment. SDRPN [3] represents a more recent direction that integrates semantic information directly into region proposals. MACA [4] further pushes performance through a memory-driven coarse-to-fine alignment strategy. These methods collectively cover the spectrum of region proposal strategies, cross-modal matching techniques, and prototype-based learning, making them suitable points of comparison for evaluating the effectiveness and generalizability of our uncertainty-driven framework.

4.3   Ablation Study

Effectiveness of Each Component. Table 2 presents the impact of different components in our framework. Replacing RPN with our MUE module (MUE+OIM+BERT) leads to consistent improvements, increasing the mAP from 41.28% to 46.79% and top-1 accuracy from 36.91% to 41.14% on CUHK-SYSU-TBPS. On PRW-TBPS, the mAP improves from 9.27% to 10.39%, and top-1 from 12.21% to 15.13%, demonstrating the effectiveness of MUE in early-stage candidate filtering. Adding Norm-Aware Embedding (MUE+NAE+BERT) further enhances performance, boosting top-1 accuracy to 44.81% on CUHK-SYSU-TBPS and 16.05% on PRW-TBPS by improving identity discrimination.

Incorporating the PUD module (MUE+PUD+OIM+BERT) yields larger gains, with mAP rising to 51.45% and top-1 to 47.25% on CUHK-SYSU-TBPS, and mAP/top-1 reaching 14.63% and 20.97% on PRW-TBPS.

Table 1. Comparisons on CUHK-SYSU-TBPS and PRW-TBPS.

Methods	CUHK-SYSU-TBPS				PRW-TBPS			
	mAP	top-1	top-5	top-10	mAP	top-1	top-5	top-10
OIM [13]+BiLSTM	23.74	17.41	38.48	49.21	4.58	6.66	16.33	22.99
NAE+BiLSTM	23.48	16.62	38.45	49.66	5.20	7.54	17.21	24.11
BSL+BiLSTM	26.91	20.97	42.31	52.31	3.60	6.42	15.41	22.46
OIM [13]+BERT	43.39	36.59	62.03	72.66	8.52	14.44	30.68	39.77
NAE+BERT	45.70	39.14	64.62	74.34	9.20	14.44	31.55	39.91
BSL+BERT	48.39	40.83	67.52	76.86	10.70	16.82	34.86	45.36
SDRPN [3]	50.36	49.34	74.48	82.14	11.93	21.63	42.54	52.99
MACA [4]	**57.77**	52.03	76.71	83.79	**18.18**	33.25	52.87	61.93
Ours	57.43	**57.95**	**77.36**	**84.83**	17.56	**37.54**	**53.55**	**62.67**

Further integrating instance-level prototype learning (MUE+PUD*+OIM+ BERT) raises top-1 to 52.39% (CUHK-SYSU-TBPS) and 24.81% (PRW-TBPS).

Our full model, which combines MUE, PUD with instance-level learning, and NAE, achieves the best overall performance: 57.43% mAP and 57.95% top-1 on CUHK-SYSU-TBPS, and 17.56% mAP and 37.54% top-1 on PRW-TBPS, confirming the complementary benefits of each module across different stages.

Analysis on Different Confidence Levels during Inference. Table 3 shows that both datasets achieve the best overall performance when the confidence fusion parameter β is set to 0.5. This suggests that a balanced contribution from both MUE and PUD modules yields the most effective retrieval results, while relying too heavily on either module (*e.g.*, $\beta = 0.0$ or $\beta = 1.0$) leads to performance degradation. Although slight differences exist across datasets, the overall trend remains consistent. From the qualitative results in Fig. 5, we observe that in datasets with smaller or more occluded targets (e.g., PRW-TBPS), assigning relatively more confidence to early-stage proposals (lower β) can help mitigate missed detections and improve robustness.

Analysis on Different Gallery Size on CUHK-SYSU-TBPS. In Fig. 3, as the gallery size of CUHK-SYSU-TBPS increases from 50 to 4000, our method consistently outperforms others in both mAP and top-1 metrics. Although performance slightly decreases with the increasing gallery size, our method maintains advantage overall.

4.4 Visualization

Figure 4 illustrates the clustering results of image and text features before and after prototype semantic learning at the instance level. Prior to applying the PUD module, image and text representations exhibit poor alignment, with Davies-Bouldin indices of 0.896 and 0.923, respectively. After training, these

Table 2. Ablation study on CUHK-SYSU-TBPS and PRW-TBPS. (* indicates instance-level prototype semantic learning.)

Methods	CUHK-SYSU-TBPS				PRW-TBPS			
	mAP	top-1	top-5	top-10	mAP	top-1	top-5	top-10
RPN+BERT+OIM [13]	41.28	36.91	64.92	71.85	9.27	12.21	27.90	37.53
MUE+OIM [13]+BERT	46.79	41.14	65.75	73.42	10.39	15.13	39.23	46.06
MUE+NAE+BERT	49.15	44.81	68.34	77.56	12.51	16.05	42.56	47.34
MUE+PUD+OIM [13]+BERT	51.45	47.25	72.89	80.65	14.63	20.97	47.89	52.27
MUE+PUD+NAE+BERT	53.79	48.95	73.54	81.75	16.75	21.89	49.22	53.76
MUE+PUD*+OIM [13]+BERT	54.95	52.39	75.63	82.89	17.04	24.81	50.55	56.02
Ours	**57.43**	**57.95**	**77.36**	**84.83**	**17.56**	**37.54**	**53.55**	**62.67**

Table 3. Performance Comparison of Different Confidence Levels (β) during Inference on CUHK-SYSU-TBPS and PRW-TBPS. The table presents the performance (mAP, top-1, top-5, and top-10) under varying confidence levels.

Confidence Level (β)	CUHK-SYSU-TBPS				PRW-TBPS			
	mAP	top-1	top-5	top-10	mAP	top-1	top-5	top-10
$\beta = 0.0$	52.88	50.72	73.71	81.32	12.51	16.05	42.56	47.34
$\beta = 0.3$	56.32	53.49	76.35	83.80	17.76	26.13	51.34	56.97
$\beta = 0.5$	**57.43**	**57.95**	**77.36**	**84.83**	**17.56**	**37.54**	**53.55**	**62.67**
$\beta = 0.8$	55.22	54.71	75.16	82.03	15.76	28.47	52.58	57.07
$\beta = 1.0$	53.04	51.58	72.96	80.42	13.41	22.58	45.96	49.64

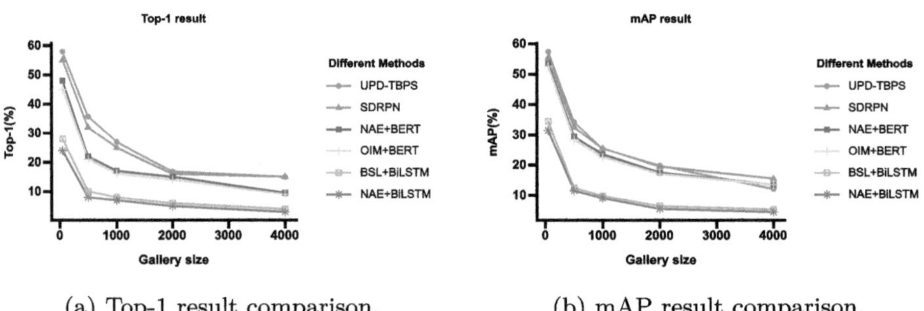

(a) Top-1 result comparison.   (b) mAP result comparison.

Fig. 3. Top-1 result and mAP result comparison with different gallery sizes of CUHK-SYSU-TBPS. The left subfigure (a) shows the Top-1 result, while the right subfigure (b) shows the mAP result.

indices decrease by 6.8% (image) and 11.5% (text), indicating improved feature compactness and enhanced cross-modal consistency. Figure 5 presents qualitative retrieval examples on the CUHK-SYSU-TBPS and PRW-TBPS datasets. Cor-

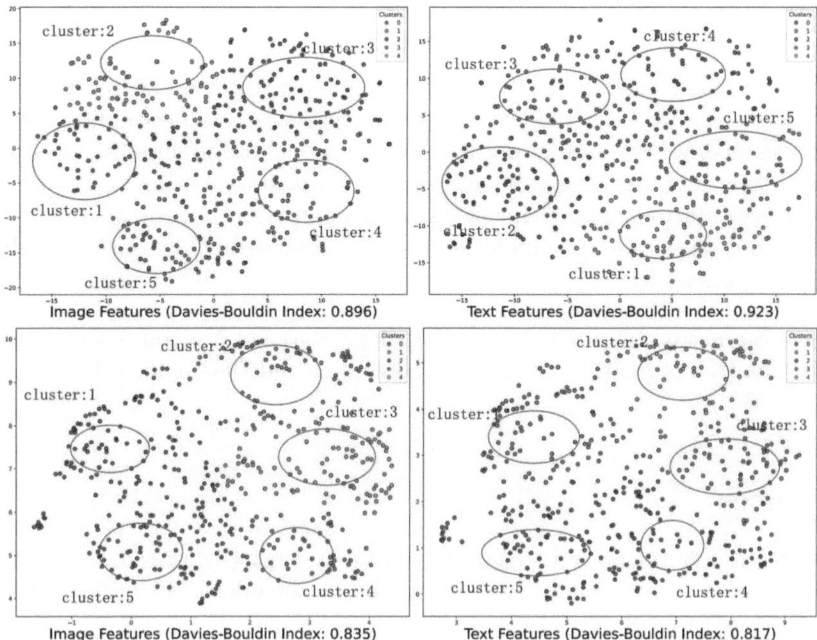

Fig. 4. Comparison of image and text features before and after prototype semantic learning at the instance level (top: before, bottom: after).

Fig. 5. Case studies of text-based person search in full images on CUHK-SYSU-TBPS and PRW-TBPS datasets.

rectly retrieved targets are shown in red bounding boxes, while incorrect ones are highlighted in green. UPD-TBPS effectively captures fine-grained semantic cues from textual queries. However, challenges persist in PRW-TBPS due to small target sizes and occlusions, suggesting future directions for model enhancement.

5   Conclusion

In this paper, we introduce UPD-TBPS, a text-based person search framework in full images that leverages uncertainty quantification and decoupling. By integrating cluster-level and individual-level prototypes through semantic decoupling and prototype learning. Experiments demonstrate its superior robustness and accuracy over state-of-the-art methods on benchmarks. Future work will focus on optimizing cross-modal re-identification and addressing occlusion to enhance real-world applicability.

Acknowledgement. This work is supported by National Natural Science Foundation of China (No. 62266009), Guangxi Key Research and Development Program (No. AB25069418).

References

1. Niu, K., Liu, Y., Long, Y., Huang, Y., Wang, L., Zhang, Y.: An overview of text-based person search: recent advances and future directions. IEEE Trans. Circuits Syst. Video Technol. (2024)
2. Jiang, D., Ye, M.: Cross-modal implicit relation reasoning and aligning for text-to-image person retrieval. In: Proceedings of the IEEE/CVF Conference on Computer Vision and Pattern Recognition, pp. 2787–2797 (2023)
3. Zhang, S., et al.: Text-based person search in full images via semantic-driven proposal generation. In: Proceedings of the 4th International Workshop on Human-centric Multimedia Analysis, pp. 5–14 (2023)
4. Su, L., Quan, R., Qi, Z., Qin, J.: MACA: memory-aided coarse-to-fine alignment for text-based person search. In: Proceedings of the 47th International ACM SIGIR Conference on Research and Development in Information Retrieval, pp. 2497–2501 (2024)
5. Jung, M.C., Zhao, H., Dipnall, J., Gabbe, B., Du, L.: Uncertainty estimation for multi-view data: the power of seeing the whole picture. Adv. Neural. Inf. Process. Syst. **35**, 6517–6530 (2022)
6. Wei, Z., Zhang, Z., Wu, P., Wang, J., Wang, P., Zhang, Y.: Fine-granularity alignment for text-based person retrieval via semantics-centric visual division. IEEE Trans. Circuits Syst. Video Technol. (2024)
7. Tang, W., Li, L., Liu, X., Jin, L., Tang, J., Li, Z.: Context disentangling and prototype inheriting for robust visual grounding. IEEE Trans. Pattern Anal. Mach. Intell. (2023)
8. Devlin, J., Chang, M.W., Lee, K., Toutanova, K.: BERT: pre-training of deep bidirectional transformers for language understanding. In: Proceedings of NAACL-HLT, vol. 1, p. 2 (2019)
9. Lin, M., et al.: DETR for crowd pedestrian detection. arXiv preprint arXiv:2012.06785 (2020)
10. Van Den Oord, A., Vinyals, O., et al.: Neural discrete representation learning. Adv. Neural Inf. Process. Syst. **30** (2017)
11. Chen, D., Zhang, S., Yang, J., Schiele, B.: Norm-aware embedding for efficient person search. In: Proceedings of the IEEE/CVF Conference on Computer Vision and Pattern Recognition, pp. 12615–12624 (2020)

12. Ren, S., He, K., Girshick, R., Sun, J.: Faster R-CNN: towards real-time object detection with region proposal networks. IEEE Trans. Pattern Anal. Mach. Intell. **39**(6), 1137–1149 (2016)
13. Xiao, T., Li, S., Wang, B., Lin, L., Wang, X.: Joint detection and identification feature learning for person search. In: Proceedings of the IEEE Conference on Computer Vision and Pattern Recognition, pp. 3415–3424 (2017)

Scale Margin Loss for Object Detection

Yuxuan Cheng[1], Yanjun Zhang[2], Leo Yu Zhang[3],
Donglong Chen[1(✉)], and Yuming Fang[4]

[1] Beijing Normal-Hong Kong Baptist University, Beijing, China
{chengyuxuan,donglongchen}@uic.edu.cn
[2] University of Technology Sydney, Sydney, Australia
Yanjun.Zhang@uts.edu.au
[3] Griffith University, Brisbane, Australia
leo.zhang@griffith.edu.au
[4] Jiangxi University of Finance and Economics, Nanchang, China
fa0001ng@e.ntu.edu.sg

Abstract. Object detection models trained on natural data often face challenges with scale imbalance, where objects of different sizes provide varying levels of useful features. Larger objects typically contain richer and more detailed information, while smaller objects often lack sufficient distinctive features and are more prone to being overwhelmed by background noise. This imbalance can push models into suboptimal learning states. While the model effectively locates meaningful features for larger objects, it may fail to locate noisy features for smaller objects. To address this issue, we proposed a scale margin loss motivated by reducing models' overfitting degree for small objects. By adding a set of regularization terms, our scale margin loss can better locate noisy features for small objects, making the model's overall generalization ability closer to the optimal. We tested our method with the state-of-the-art object detection models on two benchmarking datasets. The experiments demonstrate the effectiveness of our methods with 1.42%+ Average Precision on MS COCO and 3.37%+ Small Object Average Precision on VOC. Codes are available at https://github.com/Andisyc/ScaleMargin.

Keywords: Object detection · Scale Imbalance · Margin-based Loss Function

1 Introduction

Object detection plays a crucial role in computer vision, with applications ranging from facial recognition and person re-identification to aerial photography. However, detectors trained on real-world data often struggle with the scale imbalance problem, which can significantly degrade their performance in practical applications.

Recent research identifies that both box-level and feature-level imbalances [19] contribute to the scale imbalance problem. Box-level imbalance occurs when objects of different scales are unevenly distributed, leading to a shortage of objects at specific scales. Feature-level imbalance means that larger objects have more useful features, leading to longer training time and better generalization performance.

A generic intuition addressing the box-level imbalance is to enhance the models' representation ability. The feature pyramid [7,13,16] constructs multi-level representations to improve model performance across multi-scale objects. TridentNet [11] and POD [20] introduce scale-invariant branches to handle multi-scale objects more effectively. Mosaic [1] improves multi-scale object performance by creating college fashion images. DST [3] improves small objects performance by reducing the average scale of these college fashion images.

Fig. 1. An image from VOC *train2007*. The blue box indicate ground truth bounding box. The red box indicate the predication bounding box. Although both objects belong to the *person* class, large object have significantly more features than small object. This phenomenon leads to a significant decrease in the accuracy of prediction box localization for small objects. (Color figure online)

Despite significant progress in addressing the box-level imbalance problem, feature-level imbalance has not been fully studied. As shown in Fig. 1, small objects are easily overwhelmed by the background due to the lack of useful features. As a result, while the model is still capturing features for large objects, it tends to consider featureless parts of small objects as the background, leading to degraded performance.

In this work, we aim to improve performance in multi-scale complex scene by reducing the fitting-degree of useful features learned by the model at various scales. To achieve this, we maintain elevated loss values for small objects, which incentivizes the model to learn more discriminative features. In particular, we proposed a scale margin loss which adds a set of regularization terms to adjust the margin for objects across scales, slowing down converging speed of smaller objects. This approach ensures that the model continues to extract meaningful features from large objects while mitigating overfitting to useful features from small objects. Moreover, this approach can not only be seamlessly transferred to different models, but can also be used together with multi-scale data augmentation techniques like Mosaic [1].

In summary, our contributions are two-fold:

- We proposed a scale margin loss motivated by reducing the influence of useful features learned by the model. Additionally, we introduced a controller to adjust the regularization strength during training, allowing us to identify the suitable regularization strength.
- We evaluated the effectiveness of our methods on COCO and VOC using Faster R-CNN and YOLOX, respectively. Our method achieved improvements of +1.42% and +1.18% *Average Precision* on Faster R-CNN-101, and +3.37% and +0.19% *Small Object Average Precision* on YoloX-S, compared to baseline and state-of-the-art methods, all under the 0.5 IoU threshold.

2   Related Work

2.1   Scale Imbalance Problem

Existing methods to address the scale imbalance problem focused on data augmentation and loss function design. Data augmentation aims to create richer scale variations. For instance, Image Pyramid methods, such as SNIP [24] and SNIPER [25], construct multi-scale inputs but incur heavy computation burden. Multi-Scale augmentation techniques, such as RICAP [26] and Mosaic [1], introduce multi-scale training but ignore the different optimization requirements for different scales. Dynamic Scale Training [3] takes a step further, providing extra optimization strength for small objects by reducing the average scale of images.

The core intuition behind loss function design methods is to assign more weight to small objects during optimization. Focal Loss [14] prevents easy sample overwhelming hard samples by decreasing the loss contribution of well-trained objects. Scale Adaptive [18] adjusts weights based on the ratio of small objects in each batch, whereas Scale Balance [23] assigns weights according to the number of predicted bounding boxes. However, these methods maintain a constant weighting strategy throughout training and cannot distinguish between well-trained and poorly trained samples within the same scale.

2.2   Margin Based Loss Function

The margin principle has proven to be effective in numerous areas, including few-shot learning [10], facial recognition [4], and class imbalance [21]. Large Margin Softmax [17] was proposed to enforce the feature learned by the model to have intra-class compactness and inter-class separability. LDAM [2] demonstrated that generalization performance can be improved by increasing the margin between minor classes and major classes. Asymmetric Margin Loss [12] enhanced segmentation performance for foreground classes by pushing the decision boundary toward the background class. However, these methods are all focused on the class imbalance problem. To our best knowledge, no margin-based approach has yet applied to tackle the scale imbalance problem.

3   Methodology

3.1   Problem Setup

Let x denote an input object and y the corresponding label. Following LDAM's [2] definition, we consider a dataset $\{(x_i, y_i)\}_{i=1}^{n}$ where we divide all objects into n scale intervals. For a model $f : \mathbb{R}^d \to \mathbb{R}^q$ that outputs a q number of logits, the margin of an object (x, y) is defined as the distance between the correct logit value and the largest incorrect logit:

$$\gamma(x, y) = f(x)_y - \max_{z \neq y} f(x)_z. \tag{1}$$

Assuming that the i-th scale has v number of objects, we define the average margin of the i-th scale, $\bar{\gamma}_i$, as follows:

$$\bar{\gamma}_i = \frac{1}{v} \sum_{j=1}^{v} \gamma_{ij}(x_{ij}, y_{ij}). \tag{2}$$

Clearly, $\bar{\gamma}_i$ represents the Euclidean distances between the i-th scale objects and the decision boundary [17]. The larger the margin values, the better the model learns toward objects.

Let F denote a family of hypothesis scale. $C(F)$ can be denoted as the complexity of the family of hypothesis scales. Following the definitions in [8,9,27], when the train-set distribution and the test-set distribution are the same, the generalization upper bound can be defined as Eq. 3:

$$\text{test error} \lesssim \frac{1}{k} \sum_{i=1}^{k} \frac{1}{\bar{\gamma}_i} \sqrt{\frac{C(F_i)}{n_i}}, \tag{3}$$

where we use $\lesssim$ to hide low-order terms. γ_i denote the average margin of i-th scale objects on train set in training, n_i denote the object number of i-th scale, and k denote the total scale number.

Data collected from the natural world often exhibit rich scale variation, in which object feature reduces as scale decrease. This phenomenon makes over-parameterized networks prone to overfitting small objects. Without losing generality, we calculated scale-wise AP_i and $\bar{\gamma}_i$ on VOC, where $i \in [s, m, l]$ under 0.5 IoU threshold. Then we made two observations:

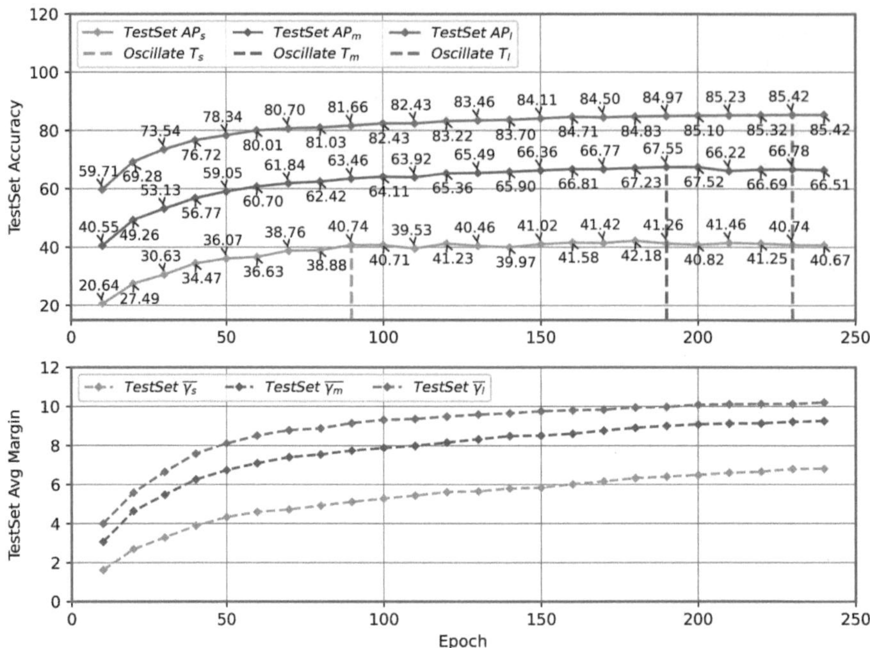

Fig. 2. Scale-wise average precisions and average margins on VOC *test2007* based on the YoloX-S. The object scale follows the MSCOCO definition: s $\in [0, 32^2]$, m $\in [32^2, 96^2]$, l $\in [96^2, \infty]$. *Oscillate* T_i indicates the time at which the AP_i for the i-th scale begins to oscillate instead of continuing to increase.

1. *Different Best Generalization Time Across Scales*: As shown in the upper sub-figure in Fig. 2, on the test set, the accuracy of the small objects AP_s starts to oscillate at 90 epoch, while the accuracy of the middle objects AP_m and the accuracy of the large objects AP_l continues to increase until 190 epoch and 230 epoch.
2. *TestSet Objects' Average Margin Continues to Increase*: As shown in the bottom sub-figure in Fig. 2, the average test margin $\bar{\gamma}_{test}$ of objects from all scales continues to increase. From Eq. 3, the test error should continue to decrease. However, AP_s start to oscillate at 90 epoch.

Based on the observations above, we found that the traditional classification generalization upper bound is inadequate to describe the generalization behavior of object detection. This is because object detection requires localization (identifying whether an area belongs to the object) beyond classification.

Large objects usually have more useful features. Taking the *person* class as an example, large objects tend to have more details about the face, torso, and limbs, causing the components of large objects to be distinguished by detectors from the background easier than smaller objects.

In contrast, smaller objects normally have noisy features and are relatively indistinguishable from the background for detectors. The detector may consider certain parts of small objects as background and exclude them when generating prediction bounding boxes, as shown in Fig. 1. In other words, the detector may become overly focused on salient features and struggle to handle noisy features. This phenomenon implies a set of missing regularization terms across scale.

3.2   Scale Margin Loss

To address the problem above, we propose to add a set of regularization terms δ_i for object margins across different scales during training. Smaller objects will receive more regularization strength. Following cross entropy loss, our scale margin loss $\mathcal{L}_{scm}$ is defined as:

$$\mathcal{L}_{scm}(x_i, y_i) = -\log \frac{e^{z_{iy} - \delta_i}}{e^{z_{iy} - \delta_i} + \sum_{j \neq y} e^{z_{ij}}}, \tag{4}$$

where $i \in \{1, \ldots, n\}, j \in \{1, \ldots, q\}$.

Here, n denotes the total scale number, q denotes the total class number, and $z_i = f(x_i)$ denotes the output logits of an object from i-th scale.

Compared to reweighting-based methods, our scale margin loss is more fine-grained. Our scale margin loss depends on the object logits output by the model, whereas reweighting-based methods only depend on scale partitioning.

3.3   Regularization Strength Controller

Intuitively, we understand that δ_i should decrease as the size of the object increases. However, determining an appropriate value for δ_i is inherently challenging. To address this, we initialized the training process with a relatively large regularization parameter, δ_i^0. Subsequently, a controller is employed to gradually reduce the regularization term, δ_i^t, throughout the training process until convergence is achieved.

$$f(t, \delta_i^0) = \delta_i^0 \times (\frac{1 - \delta_i^T}{1 - e^{-2}} \times (1 - e^{\frac{-2}{T}(T-t)}) + \delta_i^T), \tag{5}$$

where t denotes the current iteration number, and T denotes the maximum iteration number. δ_i^0 and δ_i^T are the starting value and the final value of the i-th scale δ_i in training.

In this way, we can prevent the model from suffering from excessive regularization strength and reaching a lower point on the loss landscape.

Table 1. Comparison results on COCO and VOC.

Dataset	Depth	Method	AP	AP_{50}	AP_{75}	AP_s	AP_m	AP_l
COCO	Faster-RCNN-50	Baseline	30.39	49.20	32.27	16.11	32.66	39.97
		LDAM [2]	30.33	49.16	31.99	16.28	32.67	39.61
		Scale Adaptive [18]	29.41	47.48	31.11	15.20	31.08	38.48
		Scale Balance [23]	30.87	49.68	33.25	16.46	33.32	40.18
		Scale Margin	**31.39**	**50.57**	**33.64**	**16.51**	**34.19**	**40.70**
	Faster-RCNN-101	Baseline	32.27	51.08	34.74	17.37	35.06	42.31
		LDAM [2]	32.32	51.34	34.87	17.73	34.97	42.23
		Scale Adaptive [18]	31.35	49.71	33.69	16.39	33.89	42.04
		Scale Balance [23]	32.65	51.32	35.00	**18.10**	35.50	42.60
		Scale Margin	**33.36**	**52.50**	**35.75**	17.85	**36.27**	**43.56**
VOC	YoloX-Small	Baseline	54.86	77.84	**60.04**	40.80	67.51	85.09
		LDAM [2]	**55.12**	77.93	59.83	40.21	67.11	85.22
		Scale Adaptive [18]	54.85	77.81	59.94	40.91	67.08	**85.38**
		Scale Balance [23]	55.01	78.02	59.94	43.98	66.77	85.25
		Scale Margin	55.03	**78.34**	60.00	**44.17**	**67.58**	85.08
	YoloX-Large	Baseline	60.91	81.34	65.93	46.89	70.58	86.76
		LDAM [2]	58.84	80.52	64.93	46.39	70.29	86.01
		Scale Adaptive [18]	**60.71**	80.71	**66.24**	45.91	70.33	86.68
		Scale Balance [23]	60.13	80.82	64.88	46.65	69.69	86.76
		Scale Margin	60.64	**81.37**	65.58	**47.30**	**70.66**	**86.86**

4　Experiments

4.1　Experimental Settings

We tested our methods with two-stage (Faster-RCNN [22]) and one-stage (YoloX [6]) detectors on MS COCO [15] and Pascal VOC [5] datasets.

Evaluation Metrics. We evaluate AP, AP_{50} and AP_{75} for overall performance, refering to the mean average precision of all objects with all IoU thresholds, 0.5, and 0.75 IoU thresholds. We evaluated AP_s, AP_m, and AP_l for small, middle, and large object performance under the 0.5 IoU threshold. Following COCO definitions, $s \in [0, 32^2]$, $m \in [32^2, 96^2]$, $l \in [96^2, \infty]$.

Comparison Methods. Apart from the baseline, we compared our method with Scale Adaptive [18], Scale Balance [23], and LDAM [2]. Scale Adaptive reweights the loss based on the ratio of large to small objects in each batch, while Scale Balance uses the number of predicted boxes for reweighting. LDAM improves minor classes performance by adjusting the margin between different classes according to their sample ratios.

Hyper-parameters. For regularization terms δ_i where $i \in \{s, m, l\}$, we simply set $\delta_s = 1$, $\delta_m = 0.5$, $\delta_l = 0.25$ in experiments.

For the controller, we set δ_i^T as 0. With $\delta_s^0=1$, $\delta_m^0 = 0.5$, and $\delta_l^0 = 0.25$ at the beginning of training.

For Faster-RCNN, we use SGD with learning rate as 0.02 and weight decay as 5e−4. The learning rate scheduler is *WarmupCosineLR* and the maximum iteration is 90000. No data augmentation is applied.

For YoloX, we use SGD with learning rate of 0.01 and weight decay as 5e−4. The learning rate scheduler is *YoloxWarmcos* and the maximum epoch is 250. The mosaic range is $[0.1, 2]$. No other data augmentation is applied.

Table 2. Comparison results of Focal Loss with RetinaNet.

Dataset	Depth	Method	AP	AP_{50}	AP_{75}	AP_s	AP_m	AP_l
VOC	ResNet-50	Baseline	51.05	75.99	53.99	23.70	59.25	84.42
		Class-Wise	50.60	76.10	53.49	**23.88**	58.99	84.54
		Scale-Wise	**51.08**	**76.65**	**54.86**	22.29	**59.44**	**84.73**
	ResNet-101	Baseline	53.32	77.56	56.98	21.80	60.40	85.44
		Class-Wise	53.36	77.92	57.30	23.18	60.94	**85.58**
		Scale-Wise	**53.58**	**77.95**	**58.19**	**23.27**	**61.45**	85.28
COCO	ResNet-50	Baseline	30.97	48.38	32.86	16.94	34.42	39.03
		Class-Wise	30.79	48.23	32.47	17.47	34.22	38.97
		Scale-Wise	**31.05**	**48.59**	**32.94**	**17.67**	**34.45**	**39.37**
	ResNet-101	Baseline	**32.89**	50.76	34.88	18.23	36.87	41.51
		Class-Wise	32.67	50.70	34.62	**18.49**	36.73	41.04
		Scale-Wise	32.88	**50.83**	**35.01**	18.39	**36.91**	**41.70**

4.2   Performance Evaluation

FasterRCNN on COCO. We first evaluated our method with Faster-RCNN [22] on COCO [15]. As shown in Table 1, our scale margin loss improved AP_{50} +1.37% compared to baseline on ResNet-50 backbone. Meanwhile, our scale margin loss improved AP_s +0.4%, AP_m +1.53%, and AP_l +0.73% compared to baseline. On ResNet-101 backbone, our scale margin loss improved AP_{50} +1.42%, AP_s +0.48%, AP_m +1.21%, and AP_l +1.25% compare to the baseline.

YoloX on VOC. Next, we evaluated our method with YoloX [6] on VOC [5]. As shown in Table 1, on YoloX-S, our scale margin loss improved AP_{50} +0.5% and AP_s +3.37% compared to the baseline. Meanwhile, our scale margin loss improved AP +0.32% and AP_s +0.19% compared to the scale balance loss. On YoloX-L, our scale margin loss improved AP_s +0.41% compared to the baseline. Moreover, our scale margin loss improved AP_s +0.65% and AP_m +0.97% compared to the scale balance loss.

Scale-Wise Focal Loss. We also extend our design ethos to the focal Loss [14]. The higher accuracy of the large objects often results in it falling to the right side of the focal loss curve. However, poorly trained large objects should be subjected to a stronger optimization strength.

Therefore, we decrease γ values as the scale increases. This allows the loss value of large objects to be slightly increased. We set $\gamma_s = 2$, $\gamma_m = 1.25$, $\gamma_l = 1$ in experiments. As shown in Table 2, our scale-wise focal loss exhibits superiority over class-wise focal loss on different benchmarks.

Controller for Data Augmentation. Finally, we test our controller on DST 3. We incorporate our controller into the DST so that the initialization probability of data augmentation decreases in training. As shown in Table 3, our controller improves DST on all COCO sizes.

Table 3. Controller for DST with RetinaNet on COCO.

Method	Dataset Size	AP	AP_{50}	AP_{75}	AP_s	AP_m	AP_l
Baseline	Full	34.87	54.25	36.97	21.38	38.98	43.61
DST [3]	Full	36.30	55.52	38.81	23.02	40.60	45.39
+ Controller	Full	**37.26**	**56.89**	**39.47**	**24.33**	**41.69**	**46.71**
Baseline	Half	36.64	55.98	39.05	23.03	40.59	46.90
DST [3]	Half	36.48	55.83	38.75	23.62	40.68	45.99
+ Controller	Half	**37.34**	**56.86**	**39.86**	**23.64**	**41.56**	**47.14**
Baseline	Quar	28.22	45.38	28.95	14.53	30.75	36.37
DST [3]	Quar	36.35	55.65	38.72	23.08	40.51	45.07
+ Controller	Quar	**37.27**	**56.85**	**40.14**	**23.77**	**41.70**	**46.67**

4.3   Performance Analysis

Assuming a model f outputs q number logit values for an object (x, y), the vertical axis represents the correct class logit $f(x)_y$, while the horizontal axis is the maximum wrong class $\max_{z \neq y} f(x)_z$. The yellow line in Fig. 3 marks the decision boundary, where the correct class logit equals the maximum wrong logit.

Then we move the decision boundary upward along the vertical axis by a distance of Δ units for n times. The new decision boundaries can be defined as:

$$f(x)_y = \max_{z \neq y} f(x)_z + \Delta * n. \tag{6}$$

When Δ is set to 5, we divide the entire figure into five belt areas: $[-\infty, 0]$, $[0, 5]$, $[5, 10]$, $[10, 15]$, and $[15, 20]$. Then we distribute all small object predictions from the baseline and our scale margin loss, as shown in Fig. 3.

As shown in Fig. 3, our method not only improves the localization accuracy of small objects, but also increases the classification accuracy of small objects.

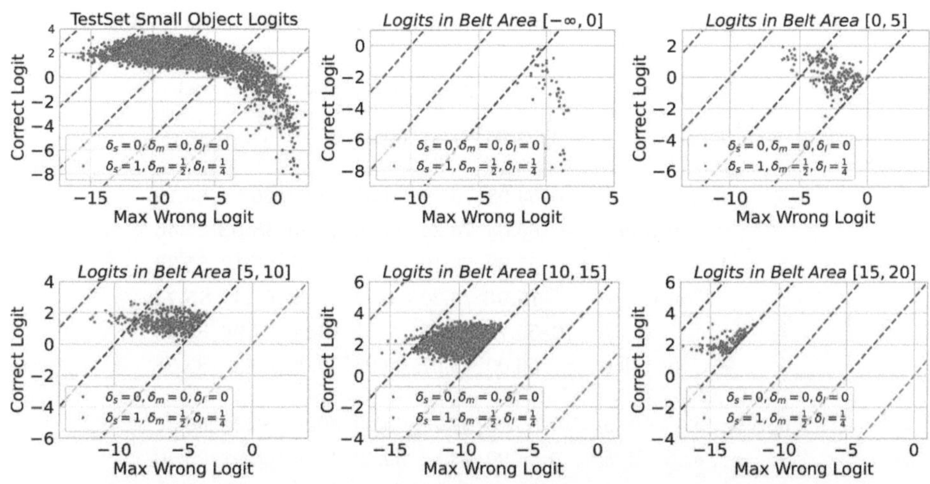

Fig. 3. The distribution of small object prediction logits on the VOC *test2007*. The yellow line represents the decision boundary, where the correct class logit is equal to the maximum wrong class logit. The gray line indicate the decision boundaries that have been moved n times by Δ units each time, where $\Delta = 5$. The areas between the blue line represent the belt areas. Objects located on the upper left side of the decision boundary are correctly classified, while those on the lower right side are classified incorrectly. (Color figure online)

4.4   Ablation Study

To effectively search for a appropriate set of regularization terms δ_i, we first used the controller to find a suitable starting value for δ_s in training. Next, we performed a grid search to determine the suitable δ_m and δ_l in VOC with YoloX-S. In grid search, we gradually decreased the value 0.25 at each step.

As shown in Table 4, although excessive regularization strength can negatively impacted the model performance, the controller is able to prevent the model from falling into a sub-optimal generalization point.

We then conducted a grid search for scale-wise regularization terms. As shown in Table 4. Ultimately, we found that the set of regularization terms δ_s, δ_m and δ_l achieved the best AP of 78.34% and AP_s of 44.17%.

Table 4. Grid Search of Scale Margin Loss with YoloX-S on VOC.

Parameters	AP	AP_{50}	AP_{75}	AP_s	AP_m	AP_l
$\delta_s = 0,\ \delta_m = 0,\ \delta_l = 0$	54.86	77.84	60.04	40.80	67.51	85.09
$\delta_s = 3,\ \delta_m = 0,\ \delta_l = 0$	54.98	78.01	59.81	42.94	66.81	85.19
+ Controller	55.03	78.24	59.76	42.43	**68.03**	85.46
$\delta_s = 2,\ \delta_m = 0,\ \delta_l = 0$	55.32	78.16	60.35	42.37	67.12	85.33
+ Controller	**55.93**	78.26	**61.21**	41.28	67.43	**85.71**
$\delta_s = 1,\ \delta_m = 0,\ \delta_l = 0$	55.13	78.15	59.75	43.08	67.96	85.45
+ Controller	56.00	78.07	60.95	39.90	66.84	85.57
$\delta_s = \frac{3}{4},\ \delta_m = 0,\ \delta_l = 0$	55.00	77.71	60.03	40.51	66.32	85.35
$\delta_s = \frac{2}{4},\ \delta_m = 0,\ \delta_l = 0$	54.90	78.17	59.40	41.54	66.91	85.40
$\delta_s = \frac{1}{4},\ \delta_m = 0,\ \delta_l = 0$	54.85	77.74	59.67	41.45	66.38	85.10
$\delta_s = 1,\ \delta_m = \frac{1}{4},\ \delta_l = 0$	55.01	77.67	59.95	41.41	66.96	85.23
$\delta_s = 1,\ \delta_m = \frac{2}{4},\ \delta_l = 0$	54.94	78.08	59.38	42.08	67.21	85.59
$\delta_s = 1,\ \delta_m = \frac{3}{4},\ \delta_l = 0$	55.00	78.07	60.11	40.73	67.43	85.36
$\delta_s = 1,\ \delta_m = 1,\ \delta_l = 0$	55.02	77.81	60.27	41.71	67.09	84.87
$\delta_s = 1,\ \delta_m = \frac{2}{4},\ \delta_l = \frac{1}{4}$	55.03	**78.34**	60.00	**44.17**	67.58	85.08
$\delta_s = 1,\ \delta_m = \frac{2}{4},\ \delta_l = \frac{2}{4}$	54.81	77.97	60.00	42.68	67.26	85.02

5   Conclusion

We observed that objects of different scales exhibited varying optimal generalization times during training. This occurs because objects of different scales possess varying levels of useful features. These feature-level differences cause overfitting on useful features in smaller objects. To address this issue, we proposed the scale margin loss. By incorporating regularization terms into object margins, we mitigated overfitting in smaller objects, thereby enhancing the model's generalization performance. However, the relationship between the regularization term δ and object scales remains unclear, and we leave this issue for future work.

Acknowledgements. This work is supported in part by Guangdong Provincial Key Laboratory of IRADS (2022B1212010006), Guangdong and Hong Kong Universities "1+1+1" Joint Research Collaboration Scheme, Guangdong Basic and Applied Basic Research Foundation (2024A1515011274), Guangdong Province General Universities Key Field Project (New Generation Information Technology) (2023ZDZX1033), and UIC Research Grant (UICR04202401-21).

References

1. Bochkovskiy, A., Wang, C.Y., Liao, H.Y.M.: YOLOv4: optimal speed and accuracy of object detection. arXiv preprint arXiv:2004.10934 (2020)
2. Cao, K., Wei, C., Gaidon, A., Arechiga, N., Ma, T.: Learning imbalanced datasets with label-distribution-aware margin loss. In: Advances in Neural Information Processing Systems, vol. 32 (2019)
3. Chen, Y., et al.: Dynamic scale training for object detection. arXiv preprint arXiv:2004.12432 (2020)
4. Deng, J., Guo, J., Xue, N., Zafeiriou, S.: ArcFace: additive angular margin loss for deep face recognition. In: Proceedings of the IEEE/CVF Conference on Computer Vision and Pattern Recognition, pp. 4690–4699 (2019)
5. Everingham, M., Van Gool, L., Williams, C.K., Winn, J., Zisserman, A.: The pascal visual object classes (VOC) challenge. Int. J. Comput. Vision **88**, 303–338 (2010)
6. Ge, Z., Liu, S., Wang, F., Li, Z., Sun, J.: YOLOx: exceeding yolo series in 2021. arXiv preprint arXiv:2107.08430 (2021)
7. Ghiasi, G., Lin, T.Y., Le, Q.V.: NAS-FPN: learning scalable feature pyramid architecture for object detection. In: CVPR, pp. 7036–7045 (2019)
8. Kakade, S.M., Sridharan, K., Tewari, A.: On the complexity of linear prediction: Risk bounds, margin bounds, and regularization. In: Advances in Neural Information Processing Systems, vol. 21 (2008)
9. Koltchinskii, V., Panchenko, D.: Empirical margin distributions and bounding the generalization error of combined classifiers. Ann. Stat. **30**(1), 1–50 (2002)
10. Li, B., Yang, B., Liu, C., Liu, F., Ji, R., Ye, Q.: Beyond max-margin: class margin equilibrium for few-shot object detection. In: Proceedings of the IEEE/CVF Conference on Computer Vision and Pattern Recognition, pp. 7363–7372 (2021)
11. Li, Y., Chen, Y., Wang, N., Zhang, Z.: Scale-aware trident networks for object detection. In: ICCV, pp. 6054–6063 (2019)
12. Li, Z., Kamnitsas, K., Glocker, B.: Analyzing overfitting under class imbalance in neural networks for image segmentation. IEEE Trans. Med. Imaging **40**(3), 1065–1077 (2020)
13. Lin, T.Y., Dollár, P., Girshick, R., He, K., Hariharan, B., Belongie, S.: Feature pyramid networks for object detection. In: CVPR, pp. 2117–2125 (2017)
14. Lin, T.Y., Goyal, P., Girshick, R., He, K., Dollár, P.: Focal loss for dense object detection. In: Proceedings of the IEEE International Conference on Computer Vision, pp. 2980–2988 (2017)
15. Lin, T.-Y., et al.: Microsoft COCO: common objects in context. In: Fleet, D., Pajdla, T., Schiele, B., Tuytelaars, T. (eds.) ECCV 2014. LNCS, vol. 8693, pp. 740–755. Springer, Cham (2014). https://doi.org/10.1007/978-3-319-10602-1_48
16. Liu, S., Qi, L., Qin, H., Shi, J., Jia, J.: Path aggregation network for instance segmentation. In: CVPR, pp. 8759–8768 (2018)
17. Liu, W., Wen, Y., Yu, Z., Yang, M.: Large-margin softmax loss for convolutional neural networks. arXiv preprint arXiv:1612.02295 (2016)
18. Lv, R., Wang, X., Yang, T.: Small object detection with scale adaptive balance mechanism. In: 2020 15th IEEE International Conference on Signal Processing (ICSP), vol. 1, pp. 361–365. IEEE (2020)
19. Oksuz, K., Cam, B.C., Kalkan, S., Akbas, E.: Imbalance problems in object detection: a review. IEEE PAMI **43**(10), 3388–3415 (2020)
20. Peng, J., Sun, M., Zhang, Z., Tan, T., Yan, J.: POD: practical object detection with scale-sensitive network. In: ICCV, pp. 9607–9616 (2019)

21. Ren, J., Yu, C., Ma, X., Zhao, H., Yi, S., et al.: Balanced meta-softmax for long-tailed visual recognition. In: Advances in Neural Information Processing Systems, vol. 33, pp. 4175–4186 (2020)
22. Ren, S., He, K., Girshick, R., Sun, J.: Faster R-CNN: towards real-time object detection with region proposal networks. IEEE Trans. Pattern Anal. Mach. Intell. **39**(6), 1137–1149 (2016)
23. Shuang, K., Lyu, Z., Loo, J., Zhang, W.: Scale-balanced loss for object detection. Pattern Recogn. **117**, 107997 (2021)
24. Singh, B., Davis, L.S.: An analysis of scale invariance in object detection snip. In: CVPR, pp. 3578–3587 (2018)
25. Singh, B., Najibi, M., Davis, L.S.: Sniper: efficient multi-scale training. In: Advances in Neural Information Processing Systems, vol. 31 (2018)
26. Takahashi, R., Matsubara, T., Uehara, K.: RICAP: random image cropping and patching data augmentation for deep CNNs. In: Asian Conference on Machine Learning, pp. 786–798. PMLR (2018)
27. Wei, C., Ma, T.: Improved sample complexities for deep neural networks and robust classification via an all-layer margin. In: International Conference on Learning Representations (2019)

Enhancing Fundus Image-Based Glaucoma Screening via Dynamic Global-Local Feature Integration

Yuzhuo Zhou[1], Chi Liu[2(✉)], Sheng Shen[3], Siyu Le[1], Liwen Yu[1], Sihan Ouyang[1], and Zongyuan Ge[4]

[1] Minzu University of China, Beijing, China
[2] Faculty of Data Science, City University of Macau, Taipa, Macao SAR, China
`chiliu@cityu.edu.mo`
[3] Design and Creative Technology Vertical, Torrens University Australia, Adelaide, NSW, Australia
[4] Faculty of Information Technology, Monash University, Melbourne, VIC, Australia

Abstract. With the advancements in medical artificial intelligence (AI), fundus image classifiers are increasingly being applied to assist in ophthalmic diagnosis. While existing classification models have achieved high accuracy on specific fundus datasets, they struggle to address real-world challenges such as variations in image quality across different imaging devices, discrepancies between training and testing images across different racial groups, and the uncertain boundaries due to the characteristics of glaucomatous cases. In this study, we aim to address the above challenges posed by image variations by highlighting the importance of incorporating comprehensive fundus image information, including the optic cup (OC) and optic disc (OD) regions, and other key image patches. Specifically, we propose a self-adaptive attention window that autonomously determines optimal boundaries for enhanced feature extraction. Additionally, we introduce a multi-head attention mechanism to effectively fuse global and local features via feature linear readout, improving the model's discriminative capability. Experimental results demonstrate that our method achieves superior accuracy and robustness in glaucoma classification.

Keywords: Glaucoma Detection · Feature Fusion · Dynamic Window

1 Introduction

Glaucoma is a major ocular pathology and one of the leading causes of irreversible blindness worldwide. Early screening is an effective strategy for detecting glaucomatous alteration in its initial stages, facilitating timely intervention before substantial visual impairment occurs. Fundus photography plays a key role in early glaucoma screening due to its non-invasive nature and cost-effectiveness. The recent integration of AI into automated fundus image analysis has demonstrated remarkable potential in this field, achieving accuracy levels comparable to or even surpassing those of human ophthalmologists. This

T. Zhu et al. (Eds.): KSEM 2025, LNAI 15920, pp. 351–363, 2026.
https://doi.org/10.1007/978-981-95-3052-6_27

advancement holds substantial promise for improving global eye care systems and is increasingly being adopted in clinical practice.

In glaucoma screening, traditional methods primarily rely on the visual assessment of fundus images by clinicians. This process is highly subjective, as it is heavily influenced by the clinicians' individual background knowledge and clinical experience. As shown in the Fig. 1, the delineation of the cup-disc boundary is of critical importance, and is commonly identified at the first bend of small blood vessels within the OC. However, this cup-disc boundary does not have fixed, predefined criteria, as the locations vary across the diverse structures of the small blood vessels among patients. This delineation is entirely subjective. Such subjectivity extends beyond cup-disc boundary delineation to multiple aspects of the diagnostic process, including the identification of subtle ocular lesions in fundus images, variations in imaging quality, and the assessment of lesion severity. These subjective factors contribute to substantial inconsistencies in segmenting criteria and glaucoma diagnosis, undermining the reliability of the overall screening process.

To mitigate clinician subjectivity and enhance the accuracy of glaucoma diagnosis, there have been increasing attempts to apply AI for fundus image-based glaucoma screening. These AI methods classify patients as 'referable' or 'non-referable' based on the detected disease status in their fundus images. The primary objective is to enable AI to capture robust pathological features associated with early-stage glaucoma through a deep feature encoder. As illustrated in Fig. 1, the clinical criteria incorporates early indicators of the disease, including small splinter hemorrhages on the OD and defects in the retinal nerve fiber layer, which are typically located at the superotemporal or inferotemporal margin. However, these margins do not have fixed predefined boundaries, as their locations vary across cases. A major limitation of existing deep encoders is their inability to account for the natural variability present in real-world data [12], thereby restricting their accuracy and efficiency in handling diverse image qualities and fused datasets [17]. These deep encoders lack a dynamic mechanism to adaptively determine the optimal receptive region for accurate defect detection. Moreover, most approaches [7,8] rely on global fundus images as input, often overlooking local details critical to detecting glaucomatous alterations, which primarily manifest around the OC and OD. Including irrelevant regions can increase the encoder's susceptibility to global imaging noise, such as overexposure and shadows. Nevertheless, global imaging noise is less prevalent in the OC and OD areas, whereas the presence of co-existing ocular diseases with pathological defects outside these regions may further degrade the encoder's performance. Therefore, effectively integrating global and local branches to develop a robust deep feature representation that generalizes across various image qualities and datasets warrants further exploration.

To address the inherent limitations of deep encoders, we propose a cross-attention three-branch model. Our model can capture the inherent fuzziness of the cup-disc boundary, reflecting the uncertainty in clinical decision-making. The model consists of three branches: the global branch, the local branch, and the

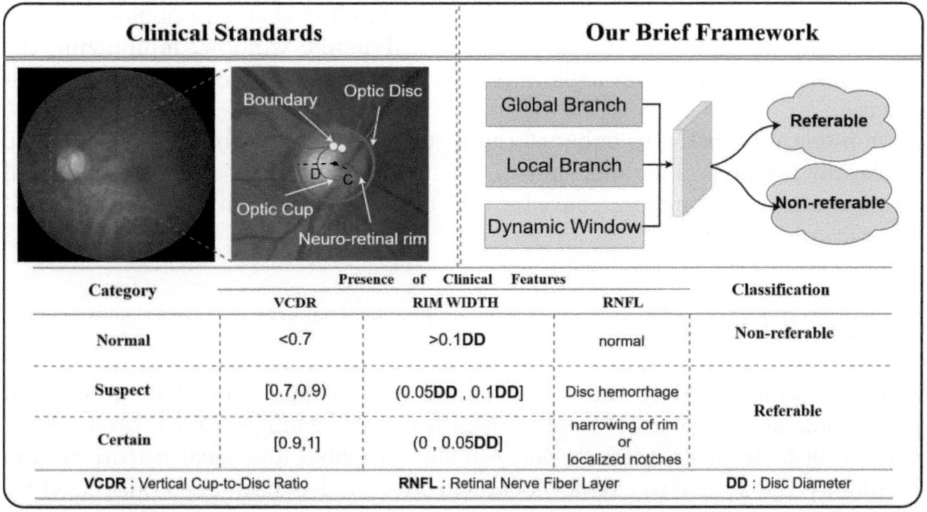

Category	Presence of Clinical Features			Classification
	VCDR	RIM WIDTH	RNFL	
Normal	<0.7	>0.1**DD**	normal	Non-referable
Suspect	[0.7,0.9)	(0.05**DD** , 0.1**DD**]	Disc hemorrhage	Referable
Certain	[0.9,1]	(0 , 0.05**DD**]	narrowing of rim or localized notches	
VCDR : Vertical Cup-to-Disc Ratio		**RNFL** : Retinal Nerve Fiber Layer		**DD** : Disc Diameter

Fig. 1. The motivation of our method: Detecting glaucoma with aligning with clinical standards.

dynamic window mechanism (DWM)-based local branch. The global branch captures spatial features at a global level, while the local branch extracts features from the region of interest (ROI). The DWM, as the core component of our model, automatically selects the optimal receptive fields across entire images. Similar to the second branch, it belongs to the local branches but introduces a dynamic selection process. The optimal receptive fields are determined by computing the maximum and total scores of each feature map. Using these scores, we compute the centers of selected patches and determine the boundaries of the selected fields based on the scales of the receptive regions, which are localized through the top-left and bottom-right corner indices of the selected receptive patch. Moreover, we integrate a convolutional block attention mechanism (CBAM) [15] to mitigate the information redundancy inherent in traditional convolutional neural networks. By leveraging the channel attention and the spatial attention, our model not only enhances feature extraction across various channels and spatial regions but also minimizes the impact of irrelevant features in the surrounding regions identified by DWM. By incorporating DWM and CBAM, the third branch effectively mitigates the uncertainty in clinical margin decision-making. The experiments demonstrate that our model reduces reliance on individual clinical experience, fostering a more objective and robust determination of the cup-disc boundary and significantly improving the accuracy of glaucoma diagnosis. Our main contributions are summarized as follows:

1. We propose a cross-attention three-branch model to capture the inherent fuzziness of the cup-disc boundary in glaucoma screening, addressing the uncertainty in clinical decision-making.

2. We introduce DWM into a patch selection module that autonomously identifies the optimal receptive fields using a dynamic window, minimizing the likelihood of focusing on irrelevant information and improving feature localization.
3. We integrate CBAM to enhance the feature extractor's ability to select deep relevant features. This mechanism ensures our approach's performance and robustness, guaranteeing consistent effectiveness across diverse model architectures.

2   Related Work

Accurate Glaucoma detection is becoming increasingly crucial in automated ophthalmologic diagnosis. Recently, deep learning techniques have been widely adopted [9] to improve model's performance in global and local feature fusion. To enhance the ability to extract local features, models have been optimized for segmenting the OC and OD, capturing deeper local features and mitigating deviations caused by the diversity of unseen datasets. Li et al. [10] improved model performance in OC and OD segmentation by utilizing a disc proposal network and a cup proposal network in conjunction with an end-to-end region-based deep convolutional neural network. Similarly, Huang et al. [7] proposed a dynamic-local learning module incorporating deformable convolution, which enhances the ability to focus on local features from low-resolution medical images. Xu et al. [16] further designed interest mechanisms to localize the OC and OD.

Due to the complexity of fundus feature extraction, attention-based mechanism have gained increasing attention within the academic community. Salam et al. [13] designed an autonomous glaucoma detection algorithm that integrates structural and non-structural features using machine learning. Sinthanayothin et al. [14] utilized color contrast to enhance the capacity for OD localization. Guo et al. [6] proposed a neural network named CP-FD-UNet++, which incorporates input and feature maps at different scales, while their proposed IFOV model extracts hidden visual features from the gray-level co-occurence matrix. However, since Guo et al.'s method addresses multiple scales of feature maps, it does not specifically focus on receptive field localization.

3   Method

3.1   Overall of the Method

Figure 2 provides an overview of our cross-attention three-branch model, which processes retinal images as input. The Global Branch extracts spatial features from entire images, while the Local Branch consists of two sub-branches designed to extract local features from informative regions. To segment the ROI, we use a pretrained model from Fu et al. [3]. This pretrained model incorporates spatial constraints, equivalent augmentation, and cup proportion balancing, demonstrating a high performance in delineating the boundaries of OC and OD across a large-scale datasets.

Additionally, We employ a DWM to automatically select the optimal receptive regions, including the vasculature surrounding OC and OD. To further enhance feature extraction, we utilize ResNet as the backbone and optimize it with CBAM, naming our network as ResNet152-CBAM. The ROI and selected receptive regions are then passed to our two sub-branches which focus on local features and generate two local-feature embeddings. By integrating the global embeddings with the local embeddings from both sub-branches, the fused embeddings are delivered to the classier for the identification of 'referable' or 'non-referable' cases.

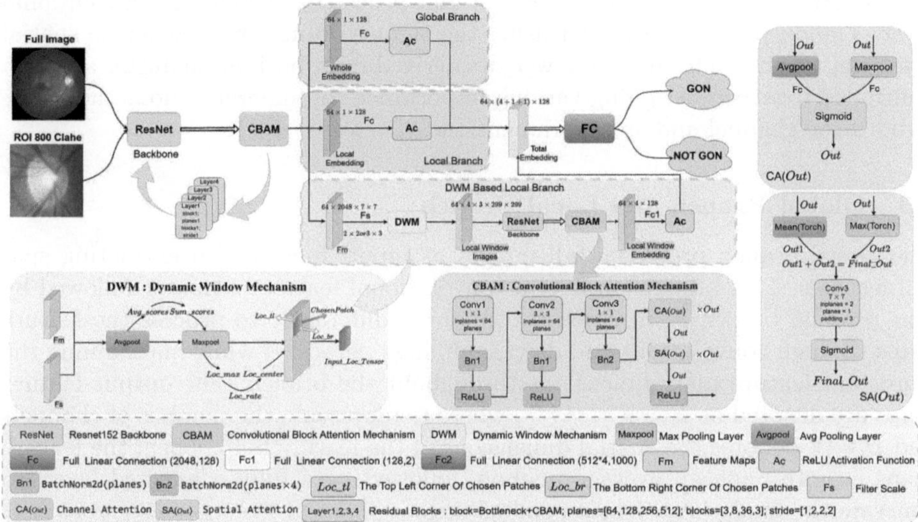

Fig. 2. The architecture of our model. Global branch extracts global features and Local branch extracts subtle feature from local patches selected by **DWM**. The feature fusion method fuses the global feature embeddings and local feature embeddings for the classification.

3.2 ResNet152-CBAM

Our network, Resnet152-CBAM, incorporates an attention mechanism to enhance feature extract by focusing on the most relevant information in both channel and spatial dimensions. To further improve the feature extraction, we integrate another CBAM as a post-process module to refine the extracted features. Specifically, we introduce two additional attention mechanisms into the fundamental block of the ResNet backbone. The Channel Attention Mechanism highlights the most informative feature channels. It consists of a full connected layer that includes two convolutional layers and an activation layer. The first convolutional layer reduces the number of output channels while the second convolutional layer restores the number of input channels, thereby reducing computational complexity. The mechanism begins by applying adaptive maximum pooling and average pooling to the input feature map. The results of these pooling operations are then processed through the full connected layer, where they are integrated and normalized using the sigmoid function to generate channel-attention weights.

Spatial Attention Mechanism directs the network's attention to spatially important regions within the feature maps. It computes the maximum and average values along the channel dimension of the feature maps. These values are concatenated along an extra dimension and processed through a convolutional layer. The output is normalized using the sigmoid function to generate spatial attention weights. The attention weights derived from both mechanisms are then multiplied together, assigning varying importance to different regions the image in both the channel and spatial dimensions.

3.3   Global Branch and Local Branch

The global branch processes full images as input, focusing on extracting spatial features. This branch employs a convolutional feature extractor followed by four residual blocks. Each block is configured differently to process the feature maps through convolutions and downsampling operations while maintaining the consistent feature map dimensions throughout the branch. The output feature maps are denoted as $F \in \mathbb{R}^{C \times H \times W}$, where C represents the number of channels and $H \times W$ denotes the spatial dimensions of the feature map. Then, the feature maps pass through an average pooling, followed by a fully connected layer, to generate the final global feature embeddings.

The second sub-branch, the local branch, fully utilizes local features extracted from the ROI, which processes segmented ROI as input. The feature maps, after passing through the final convolutional layer, are represented as $F_1 \in \mathbb{R}^{C \times H \times W}$. Similar to the global branch, F_1 is further processed to generate local feature embeddings, encapsulating both spatial and structural information. Ultimately, the global and local embeddings are integrated with embeddings from the third branch to facilitate the downstream classification task.

3.4   DWM Based Local Branch

Our second sub-branch is responsible for extracting additional potential information from automatically selected regions. We design an automatic coordinating strategy that utilizes the feature maps F of entire images to calculate a fixed number of locations containing the optimal receptive patches. The process begins by inputting F into an average pooling operation, resulting in a score filter of size $H_f \times W_f$. Let p denote the proposal size of each entire image; we then compute the size of score patches $H_s \times W_s$ and obtain the total score S_{sum} by summing all the average scores S_a. To localize the center of each patch, we identify the maximum score V_{max} within each patch and compute its location using

$H_{max} = L_{flat}/W_s$ and $W_{max} = L_{flat} \bmod W_s$, where L_{flat} denotes the index of V_{max} in the flatten total score maps. The identified patch locations are then mapped back to the original entire image coordinates. The height H_{loc} of each patch in the original image is computed by $H_{loc} = (2 \times H_{max} + H - H_s + 1)/(2 \times H)$ while the width W_{loc} is computed as $W_{loc} = (2 \times W_{max} + W - W_s + 1)/(2 \times W)$.

Next, to determine the optimal receptive regions, we prior compute loc_max, the locations of the maximum values of the total scores within the flatten images. Then, let fm_h denote the height of image maps, fm_w denote the width, H and W respectively denote the height and width of images, the height rate **loc_rate_h** and the width rate **loc_rate_w** are calculated as follows. The central locations **loc_center** are computed based on loc_rate_h and loc_rate_w. After compute the rate of height and width, let H_p and W_p denote the size of corresponding patches. With the size of patches, the top left corner **loc_tl** and the bottom right corner **loc_br** of chosen patches will be calculated by following two functions. Based on the determined center and four corners of the optimal receptive patches within the entire images, the target patches are segmented out and the most relevant patches are selected by ranking the scores. These selected patches are then reshaped to an adaptive size and fed into our network. The resulting output feature maps are denoted as $\sum_{i=1}^{p} F_{2i} \in \mathbb{R}^{C \times H \times W}$. These feature maps are processed through average pooling followed by a fully connected layer to obtain the second set of local feature embeddings. Finally, the embeddings are integrated with the global and local embeddings, and the final feature embeddings are delivered to the downstream classifier for the final prediction.

$$loc\_rate\_h = \frac{2 \times loc\_max[:,0] + fm\_h - H + 1}{2 \times fm\_h} \tag{1}$$

$$loc\_rate\_w = \frac{2 \times loc\_max[:,1] + fm\_w - W + 1}{2 \times fm\_w} \tag{2}$$

$$loc\_tl = \left(loc\_center[:,0] - \frac{H_p}{2}, loc\_center[:,1] - \frac{W_p}{2} \right) \tag{3}$$

$$loc\_br = \left(loc\_center[:,0] + \frac{H_p}{2} + (H_p\%2), loc\_center[:,1] + \frac{W_p}{2} + (W_p\%2) \right) \tag{4}$$

4   Experiments

4.1   Experiment Environment

Datasets. The dataset used in our experiment is the Rotterdam EyePACS AIROGS dataset [1], which contains a large collection of color fundus images from diverse subjects across multiple sites, representing a heterogeneous ethnic population. Our training dataset consists of 36,803 images, including 9,284 referable and 27,519 non-referable samples. The testing dataset comprises 1,999 images, with 488 referable and 1,511 non-referable samples. Additionally, we

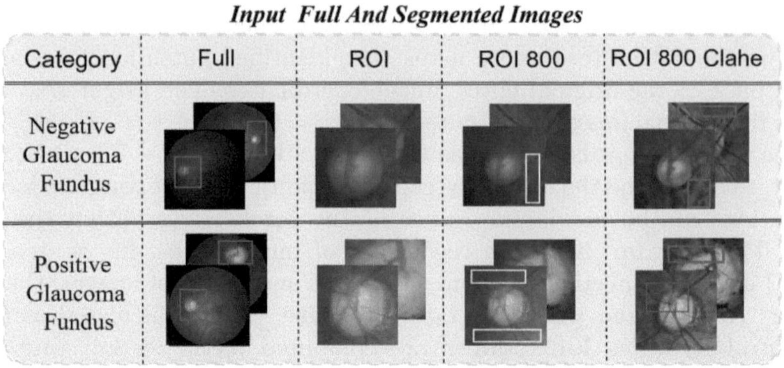

Input Full And Segmented Images

Category	Full	ROI	ROI 800	ROI 800 Clahe
Negative Glaucoma Fundus				
Positive Glaucoma Fundus				

Fig. 3. The samples both contain full images, segmented ROI, ROI 800 (in a higher view) and **ROI 800 Clahe (Contrast Limited Adaptive Histogram Equalization)** which is our final input. **Red boxes** mark the target region ROI, **Yellow boxes** are used to mark the effect of higher view and **Blue boxes** mark the improving image contrast. (Color figure online)

segment ROI from the full images to create a separate dataset, as illustrated in Fig. 3. During the training and testing process, ROI 800 Clahe is selected as the final input, as it demonstrates superior performance in enhancing ROI features by improving image contrast. This preprocessing step helps mitigate variations caused by differences in equipment or environmental factors, thereby playing a crucial role in improving the overall performance of our model.

Model Structures. We design three comparative neural network for this binary classification task:

1. Patch5Model: A three - branch model that uses ResNet152 backbone.
2. Branch2CBAM: A cross - attention two - branch model that utilizes ResNet152 equipped with CBAM.
3. Branch3CBAM: A cross - attention three - branch model based on ResNet152 backbone with CBAM.

The full and ROI images are loaded as model input in [64, 6, 3, 224, 224]. To simulate real-world conditions and enhance model robustness, we apply random horizontal flip, vertical flip, color jitter, and Gaussian blur during training. These augmentations expose the model to diverse fundus images. The enhanced data is then normalized and resized to [64, 6, 3, 299, 299] to meet Branch3CBAM input requirements. In the network, full and ROI data are processed into feature maps of size [64, 2048, 7, 7], with output embeddings of [64, 2048]. The local window regions in the third branch are determined based on these feature maps. Full images and filter scales $S = [3,3]$ and [2,2] are used to compute optimal receptive regions, with patch sizes in [224, 224] and [112, 112]. Average scores are computed in [7, 2048, 5, 5] and [7, 2048, 6, 6] using avg_pool2d, with total scores sized [7, 1, 5, 5] and [7, 1, 6, 6].

W and H are respectively in choice of [5,6]. After flatting the total scores into the size of $[7, W \times H]$, the maximum value and index of the total scores are processed into maximum locations in size of [7, 2]. Then the total scores are delivered into max_pool2d, the maximum pool of torch functional module. To localize the optimal receptive patches, we compute the height and width rates of receptive patches to the entire images. After computing the center of the receptive patches, we calculated the indices of the top-left corner and bottom-right corner within the flatten entire images. By combining the former two corner vectors, the optimal receptive regions can be obtained and the final shape of the input location tensors are [7, 6, 4].

The local window images, obtained based on the calculated locations within full images, are embedded into local window embeddings in size of $[64 \times 4, 3, 299, 299]$. Ultimately, all the embeddings are fused into the final embeddings in size of $[64 \times (4 + 1 + 1), 128]$ which are fed into a full connected layer with the output of the final classification task.

Parameter Settings. The optimizer parameters are configured as follows: the initial learning rate is 0.001 for the first 10,000 iterations. The Adam optimizer uses a momentum term of 0.9 and a batch size of 64. For logging and check-pointing, the loss is recorded in TensorBoard every 400 iterations. Results are saved every 2,000 iterations, and checkpoints are stored every 10 epochs, with training resuming from the latest checkpoint starting at epoch 1.

4.2   Evaluation Metrics

To compare the performance of our cross-attention three-branch model with Patch5Model and Branch2CBAM, we use the following evaluation metrics: 1) average precision (AP): measures the ability to distinguish referable from non-referable images. 2) area under the curve (AUC): evaluates classification performance across various sensitivity-specificity trade-offs. 3) accuracy (Acc): represents overall classification correctness between referable and non-referable samples. 4) sensitivity (Sen): assesses the model's ability to identify referable samples. 5) specificity (Spe): measures the model's ability to correctly classify non-referable samples. 6) F1-score ($F1$): balances precision and recall, providing a trade-off between sensitivity and specificity.

4.3   Result Analysis

Figure 4 illustrates the exact performances of both Branch3CBAM and the baseline model in the classification tasks, presenting the detailed confusion matrix and highlighting the TP, TN, FP, FN. Branch3CBAM achieves higher accuracy in identifying referable samples, but makes slightly more mistakes while identifying non-referable samples. This trade-off in Branch3CBAM performance may be given rise to the employed cross-attention mechanism compared to the baseline. The increased complexity of model architecture enables the model to capture

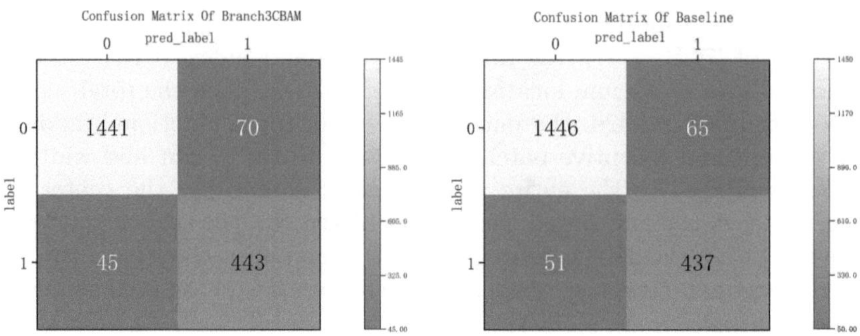

Fig. 4. The predicted results of our proposed model.

more potential features from referable samples while simultaneously introducing more noise when processing non-referable images.

Table 1. Evaluation Metrics For Comparative Methods

Models	Evaluation Metrics					
	AP	AUC	Acc	F1	Sen	Spe
Patch5Model	0.954	0.982	0.941	0.883	0.895	0.957
Branch2CBAM	0.947	0.981	0.928	0.866	0.957	0.919
Branch3CBAM	0.955	0.982	0.942	0.885	0.908	0.954

To ensure an optimal layout, the evaluation metrics for the comparative methods are detailed in Table 1, providing a quantitative assessment of their classification performances. 1) AP: Branch3CBAM achieves an AP of 0.955, which is slightly higher than Patch5Model's 0.954 and much higher than Branch2CBAM's 0.947, indicating that Branch3CBAM is better at identifying positive samples. 2) AUC: Branch3CBAM achieves an AUC of 0.982446, which is almost identical to Patch5Model's AUC 0.982417 while Branch3CBAM outperforms Branch2CBAM (0.981). This indicates that the third branch using DWM further enhances the model's discriminative power. 3) Acc: Branch3CBAM has an Acc of 0.942, higher than both Patch5Model (0.941) and Branch2CBAM (0.928), showing that Branch3CBAM retains high accuracy while benefiting from the model complexity and deeper feature extracting method. 4) $F1$: Branch3CBAM achieves an $F1$ score of 0.885, slightly higher than Patch5Model (0.883) and much better than Branch2CBAM (0.866), highlighting Branch3CBAM's superior performance in balancing *precision* and *recall*. 5) Sen: Branch3CBAM's Sen (0.908) is better than Patch5Model (0.895). However, the sensitivity of Branch3CBAM is lower than Branch2CBAM (0.957). This is likely due to the increased complexity of model architecture which might introduce slight over-fitting to dominant pattern, leading to the reducing sensitivity. 6)

Spe: Branch3CBAM achieves a specificity of 0.954, surpassing Branch2CBAM (0.919), but slightly lower than Patch5Model (0.957). This marginally lower specificity compared to Patch5Model may result from CBAM which enhances subtle together with less discriminate features, leading to an increased false positive rate. Nevertheless, compared to Branch2CBAM, the introduction of our third sub-branch in application of DWM allows better negative sample recognition.

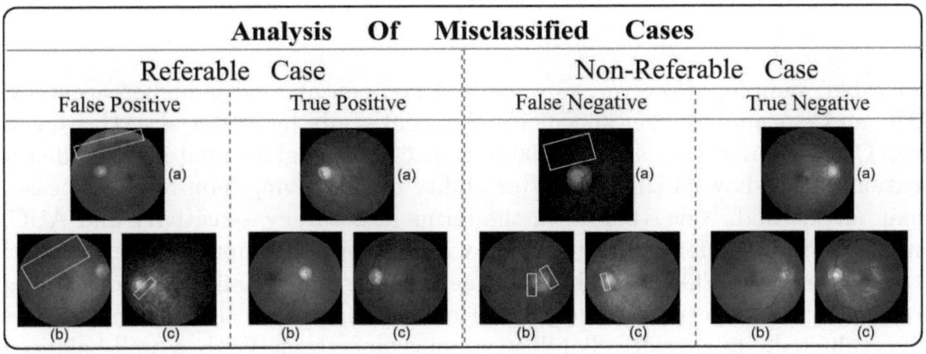

Fig. 5. Figure 5 illustrates the misclassifications in both 'referable' and 'non-referable' categories. **Yellow boxes** highlight the regions where various factors may misdirect the model to make errors potentially. (Color figure online)

To better understand the sources of misclassification in distinguishing between 'referable' and 'non-referable' cases, we present misclassified samples alongside correctly classified ones for comparison in Fig. 5. For the referable cases, misclassification in Figure (a) may be attributed to poor exposure and low resolution, while Figure (b) might be affected by noise from other ocular diseases. Figure (c) demonstrates an uncertain optic cup-disc boundary, which could have led to misprediction. In the non-referable cases, the misclassification in Figure (a) is likely due to the insufficient highlight in the picture. Figure (b) also exhibits an ambiguous cup-disc boundary, similar to the issue in referable cases. Figure (c) may be misclassified due to its low resolution in imaging the small blood vessels while the correctly classifies samples in the rightmost column all have clear and well-defined vessel structures.

Table 2 presents a comparison of the latest deep - learning - based methods for glaucoma detection on public and private datasets. To compare the performance of all the latest methods, we select the evaluation metrics, including accuracy, sensitivity, specificity and AUC. Notably, out method achieves the highest accuracy among all the methods, indicating the superior overall performance of our proposed method in glaucoma detection. Compared to VGG19 TL proposed by Gomez et al. [5], our proposed method surpasses their method in all four metrics. For Diaz et al. [2] who utilizes the CNN method: Xception, our method achieves slight low sensitivity (90.78 vs 93.46), generating more wrongs while missing

Table 2. Performance comparison with the latest detection methods

Author	Method	Acc	Sen	Spe	AUC
Gomez et al. [5]	VGG19 TL	88.05	87.01	89.01	94
Diaz et al. [2]	Pre-trained CNN model: Xception	89.77	93.46	85.80	96.05
Liu et al. [11]	Deep CNN architecture	92.7	87.9	96.5	97
Gheisari et al. [4]	VGG16 with Long Short-Term Memory	–	95	96	99
Proposed Method	Resnet152-CBAM-3B with DWM	94.25	90.78	95.37	98.24

'referable' samples. However, our method compensates with higher accuracy, AUC and especially higher specificity. A recent study by Liu et al. [11], using a deep CNN architecture, showed a 96.5 in specificity in glaucomatous disc identification which shows a slightly better ability of identifying 'non-referable' cases than our method. Nevertheless, in the terms of accuracy, sensitivity and AUC, our methods outperforms their method with conspicuous improvement. Gheisari et al. [4] employs VGG16 with a designed memory mechanism, demonstrating great sensitivity, specificity, and AUC. However, since its accuracy is not explicitly evaluated, its overall reliability remains uncertain. With a well-balanced performance across all metrics while all the scores surpass 90, our proposed method, ResNet152-CBAM-3B with DWM, achieves remarkable harmonization and stability, ensuring its reliability in glaucoma detection.

5   Conclusion

In this work, we propose a cross-attention three-branch model that integrates the CBAM and DWM. The third branch, introducing DWM, complements the global and local branches, which are limited by their fixed focus on specific regions, thereby addressing uncertainty in cup-disc boundary determination. CBAM enhances the network by incorporating channel and spatial attention mechanisms, enabling adaptation to complex retinal imaging scenarios. Experimental results demonstrate that Branch3CBAM outperforms other models with greater stability and higher accuracy, even when handling images of varying resolutions and inconsistent quality from multiple imaging devices. For future work, we aim to develop a more generalizable module to enhance efficiency and accuracy in glaucoma detection, particularly for datasets representing diverse racial and geographical populations.

Acknowledgement. This work was supported by the National Natural Science Foundation of China (Grant No. 62402009), and the Science and Technology Development Fund of Macao under Grant 0013-2024-ITP1.

References

1. De Vente, C., et al.: Airogs: artificial intelligence for robust glaucoma screening challenge. IEEE Trans. Med. Imaging **43**(1), 542–557 (2023)
2. Diaz-Pinto, A., Morales, S., Naranjo, V., Köhler, T., Mossi, J.M., Navea, A.: CNNs for automatic glaucoma assessment using fundus images: an extensive validation. Biomed. Eng. Online **18**, 1–19 (2019)
3. Fu, H., Cheng, J., Xu, Y., Wong, D.W.K., Liu, J., Cao, X.: Joint optic disc and cup segmentation based on multi-label deep network and polar transformation. IEEE Trans. Med. Imaging **37**(7), 1597–1605 (2018)
4. Gheisari, S., et al.: A combined convolutional and recurrent neural network for enhanced glaucoma detection. Sci. Rep. **11**(1), 1945 (2021)
5. Gómez-Valverde, J.J., Antón, A., Fatti, G., Liefers, B., Herranz, A., Santos, A., Sánchez, C.I., Ledesma-Carbayo, M.J.: Automatic glaucoma classification using color fundus images based on convolutional neural networks and transfer learning. Biomed. Opt. Express **10**(2), 892–913 (2019)
6. Guo, F., Li, W., Tang, J., Zou, B., Fan, Z.: Automated glaucoma screening method based on image segmentation and feature extraction. Med. Biol. Eng. Comput. **58**(10), 2567–2586 (2020). https://doi.org/10.1007/s11517-020-02237-2
7. Huang, W., Liao, X., Chen, H., Hu, Y., Jia, W., Wang, Q.: Deep local-to-global feature learning for medical image super-resolution. Comput. Med. Imaging Graph. **115**, 102374 (2024)
8. Jalili, J., et al.: Glaucoma detection and feature identification via GPT-4V fundus image analysis. Ophthalmol. Sci. 100667 (2024)
9. Ju, Y., Jia, S., Ke, L., Xue, H., Nagano, K., Lyu, S.: Fusing global and local features for generalized AI-synthesized image detection. In: 2022 IEEE International Conference on Image Processing (ICIP), pp. 3465–3469. IEEE (2022)
10. Li, F., et al.: Joint optic disk and cup segmentation for glaucoma screening using a region-based deep learning network. Eye **37**(6), 1080–1087 (2023)
11. Liu, S., et al.: A deep learning-based algorithm identifies glaucomatous discs using monoscopic fundus photographs. Ophthalmol. Glaucoma **1**(1), 15–22 (2018)
12. Rosano, M., Furnari, A., Gulino, L., Santoro, C., Farinella, G.M.: Image-based navigation in real-world environments via multiple mid-level representations: fusion models, benchmark and efficient evaluation. Auton. Robot. **47**(8), 1483–1502 (2023)
13. Salam, A.A., Khalil, T., Akram, M.U., Jameel, A., Basit, I.: Automated detection of glaucoma using structural and non structural features. Springerplus **5**(1), 1–21 (2016). https://doi.org/10.1186/s40064-016-3175-4
14. Sinthanayothin, C., Boyce, J.F., Cook, H.L., Williamson, T.H.: Automated localisation of the optic disc, fovea, and retinal blood vessels from digital colour fundus images. Br. J. Ophthalmol. **83**(8), 902–910 (1999)
15. Woo, S., Park, J., Lee, J.Y., Kweon, I.S.: Cbam: convolutional block attention module. In: Proceedings of the European Conference on Computer Vision (ECCV), pp. 3–19 (2018)
16. Xu, Y., et al.: Efficient optic cup localization based on superpixel classification for glaucoma diagnosis in digital fundus images. In: Proceedings of the 21st International Conference on Pattern Recognition (ICPR2012), pp. 49–52. IEEE (2012)
17. Yuan, S.A., Wang, Z., He, F.L., Zhang, S.W., Zhao, Z.Y.: GFHANet: global feature hybrid attention network for salient object detection in side-scan sonar images. IEEE Access (2024)

BackdoorHunter: Poisoned Training Data Removal via Contrastive Responses Under Pruned Models

Rixi Liang, Shuai Zhou$^{(\boxtimes)}$, Mingxu Zhu, Chi Liu, and Minfeng Qi

City University of Macau, Macao, China
{D24091110122,shuaizhou,D23090101934,chiliu,mfqi}@cityu.edu.mo

Abstract. Backdoor attacks pose a severe threat to deep neural networks (DNNs) by injecting malicious triggers into training data, allowing attackers to manipulate model predictions while maintaining normal behavior for regular users. To address this, we propose a proactive defense method called PMRF (pruning-based segmentation & Mutual Reinforcement Filtering). Our approach filters out backdoor samples before model training by leveraging the behavioral differences between clean and backdoor samples under pruned models. PMRF can be integrated with most post-training defense methods, effectively mitigating backdoor threats. We evaluate our method on the CIFAR-10 dataset (with a poisoning rate of 0.3%) against four attacks using VGG16 and ResNet18 models. Experimental results demonstrate the robustness of PMRF across various attack scenarios. For instance, on the ResNet-18 architecture, the clean data accuracy (ACC) only drops from 91.71% to 91.24%, while the attack success rate (ASR) decreases significantly from 100% to 1.33%, substantially mitigating the threats of backdoor attacks.

Keywords: Backdoor Attack · Proactive Defense · Poisoning data · Pruning · Deep Neural Networks

1 Introduction

With the rapid development of artificial intelligence (AI) and its widespread applications across various domains, the security of AI systems has garnered increasing attention [28]. In recent years, backdoor attacks have emerged as a highly stealthy attack method, posing a severe threat to deep neural networks (DNNs) [4]. When the trigger is not activated, backdoor attacks do not affect the model's normal usage or performance [26]. However, once the trigger is activated, the attack can manipulate the model's output with an extremely high attack success rate (ASR) [1,6,8], forcing the model to classify inputs into the attacker-specified class while disregarding the true physical meaning of the data. For instance, in computer vision tasks, a model may misclassify an image with a trigger into a predefined class chosen by the attacker [10,11,16].

T. Zhu et al. (Eds.): KSEM 2025, LNAI 15920, pp. 364–379, 2026.
https://doi.org/10.1007/978-981-95-3052-6_28

Current mainstream backdoor attacks, such as BadNet, Blend, TaCT, and Trojan, exhibit both high attack success rates and strong stealthiness. Due to the massive scale of training datasets, manually removing poisoned samples is nearly infeasible, resulting in significant damage to neural networks and posing a serious threat to model security [3,17,27].

Existing backdoor defense techniques can be broadly categorized into three main types: 1) Data preprocessing, which reduces the impact of poisoned samples through data cleaning or augmentation but often relies on the attacked model exhibiting distinct behaviors (e.g., latent separability) to differentiate poisoned from clean samples [2–5,20,22]. However, in practice, these backdoor features may be inherently weak (e.g., at low poisoning rates), leading to method failure or performance degradation [5,9,22], and may result in a significant reduction in certain class data; 2) Model-based defenses, which include regularization to limit model complexity, backdoor removal through pruning, fine-tuning, or model distillation, and defensive distillation using a teacher model to guide backdoor-resistant training; and 3) Backdoor detection, which designs algorithms to identify backdoor features based on empirical knowledge. [12,26] However, these detection methods are prone to false positives and false negatives, and their effectiveness can be compromised by adaptive attacks that deliberately suppress backdoor features [18,20].

These methods have notable limitations: data preprocessing cannot fully eliminate poisoned samples, model-based defenses often degrade performance or require additional data to restore it, and backdoor detection struggles with varying datasets, where features may differ significantly [20]. To address these challenges, we propose a novel proactive defense strategy, PMRF (pruning-based segmentation & Mutual Reinforcement Filtering), which leverages a cooperative mechanism of structured pruning and behavioral clustering. Our approach uses model pruning to identify data that can still be correctly classified in an incomplete neural network, while behavioral clustering employs a clean model trained on clustered clean data to detect misclassified anomalies and a poisoned model (with weak classification ability but strong poisoned data identification capability) trained on clustered poisoned data to identify poisoned samples. By combining these two techniques, PMRF effectively narrows the scope of suspicious data and enhances the identification of poisoned samples. Our method is simple to implement, requiring neither data preprocessing nor model regularization. During behavioral clustering, it automatically extracts features and identifies suspicious data based on these features during verification. The filtered clean data can be directly used to train a secure model.

Our main contributions can be summarized as follows:

1. We propose a novel pre-training backdoor defense mechanism that detects and removes poisoned samples from training datasets before model training begins. Unlike traditional post-training defense methods that mitigate backdoor effects after model deployment, our approach proactively eliminates backdoor threats at their source, introducing a new defense paradigm in the machine learning pipeline.

2. We introduce a technically innovative approach by leveraging the distinctive behavioral differences between clean and poisoned samples under structured pruning. Specifically, we observe that poisoned samples exhibit consistent classification stability across multiple pruned models due to their reliance on trigger features, while clean samples show unstable performance due to disrupted feature extraction. This insight enables effective identification and isolation of poisoned data.
3. Our method is assumption-free and orthogonal to existing defense strategies, enhancing its applicability and compatibility. It does not rely on prior knowledge of attack types, trigger patterns, or model architectures, making it a versatile solution that can be seamlessly integrated with other defense methods to strengthen overall backdoor resilience.
4. We validate the effectiveness of our method through extensive experiments across diverse backdoor attack types (e.g., BadNet, Blend) and model architectures (e.g., VGG, ResNet). Our results demonstrate that the proposed defense reduces the attack success rate (ASR) to as low as 0.67% while maintaining high clean accuracy (ACC) above 85%, outperforming existing methods in both robustness and efficiency.

2   Related Work

Backdoor attack defense has become a prominent research focus in the field of deep learning security, with existing methods primarily categorized into backdoor detection [19], robust training [7,13,21,24], and backdoor removal [14,15,23]. However, these approaches often suffer from significant limitations.

2.1   Post-Hoc Detection via Model Features

Many prior studies adopt a post-hoc workflow [19], where the defender passively allows the attack to occur by training a backdoor model through a standard training process. This approach relies on the assumption that the backdoor model will naturally exhibit distinguishable features, such as differences in latent representations, which can then be used to differentiate between clean and poisoned samples [2,5,20,22]. However, this passive method has significant drawbacks. The features exhibited by the backdoor model may be subtle or easily suppressed by attackers, making them unreliable for consistent detection [18,20]. As a result, this approach often fails to provide robust defense against sophisticated attacks.

2.2   Robust Training

Robust training methods focus on enhancing model resilience against backdoor attacks during the training phase. These approaches typically involve techniques such as data augmentation, adversarial training, or regularization to reduce the model's reliance on backdoor triggers [7,21,24]. However, robust training often comes at the cost of degraded performance on clean data, and its effectiveness can vary depending on the attack type and model architecture [14,21].

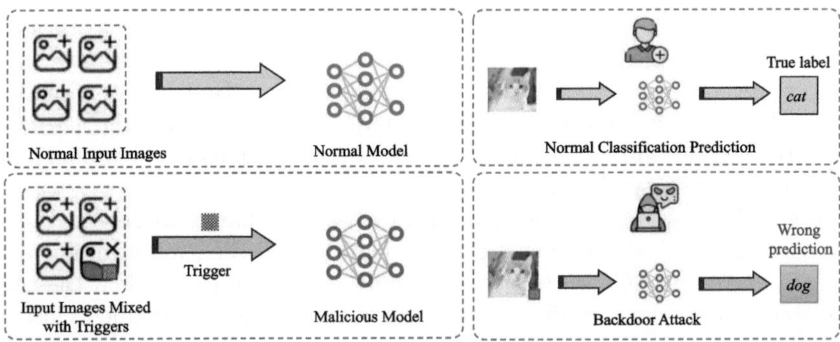

Fig. 1. Illustration of a backdoor model's behavior under different scenarios.

2.3   Backdoor Removal

Backdoor removal techniques aim to eliminate backdoors from an already compromised model, often through methods like pruning, fine-tuning, or model distillation [14,24,25]. While these methods can reduce the attack success rate, they typically require additional clean data to restore model performance and may not fully eliminate all backdoor effects, especially for complex triggers [23,25]. Further discussion on specific approaches and their challenges will be included in future revisions.

2.4   Discussion

Our proposed PMRF (pruning-based segmentation & Mutual Reinforcement Filtering) integrates structured random pruning with data mutual reinforcement filtering, offering a proactive defense strategy that filters poisoned samples before model training. PMRF places suspicious data into a "honeypot" model, where it is screened by observing anomalous behaviors. This approach can be combined with most post-training defense methods to further enhance filtering capabilities. PMRF is simple to implement, and significantly reduces the attack success rate (ASR) while maintaining stable defense performance across various attack types.

3   Threat Model

To clearly define the scope of our study, we elaborate on the threat model by specifying the assumptions, capabilities, and objectives of both the attacker and the defender in the context of backdoor attacks against deep neural networks (DNNs).

3.1   Attacker's Assumptions

The attack occurs before the model training phase, where the attacker aims to compromise the integrity of the deep learning model by injecting backdoor vulnerabilities. Specifically, the attacker can inject a certain proportion of poisoned samples into the training dataset. These poisoned samples may employ various trigger patterns, such as localized triggers (e.g., BadNet) or global triggers (e.g., Blend). The attacker's goal is to make the model learn the association between the trigger and a specific label, thereby manipulating the model's inference behavior, as shown in Fig. 1.

The attacker's objectives are twofold: on the one hand, to ensure that the backdoored model performs normally on clean inputs (i.e., maintaining a high clean data accuracy, ACC); on the other hand, to ensure that, when the trigger is activated, the model classifies inputs into the attacker's predefined class (i.e., achieving a high attack success rate, ASR).

3.2 Defender's Goal

The defender aims to proactively identify and remove suspicious samples from the training dataset before training models, ensuring that the filtered dataset used for training is free of backdoor data (i.e., achieving a low attack success rate, ASR).

4 Methodology

4.1 Method Overview

In this paper, we propose a defense method, termed PMRF (pruning-based segmentation & Mutual Reinforcement Filtering), to prevent from backdoor attacks. This method initially screens suspicious data using a structured random pruning strategy. After that, we further identify and remove backdoor samples through a mutual reinforcement filtering mechanism involving clean and poisoned models. PMRF significantly reduces the attack success rate (ASR) while incurring only a minimal loss of clean data, thereby effectively protecting the model from backdoor attacks.

4.2 Pruning-Based Segmentation

The core of PMRF lies in leveraging the behavioral differences between poisoned and clean samples under pruned models to distinguish them. Specifically, we design the following steps:

Multi-round Pruning Verification. When fixing the number of pruned layers and the pruning ratio, we repeat model pruning for k times. This process generates k pruned models. These pruned models are then used to distinguish between poisoned and clean samples based on the classification results.

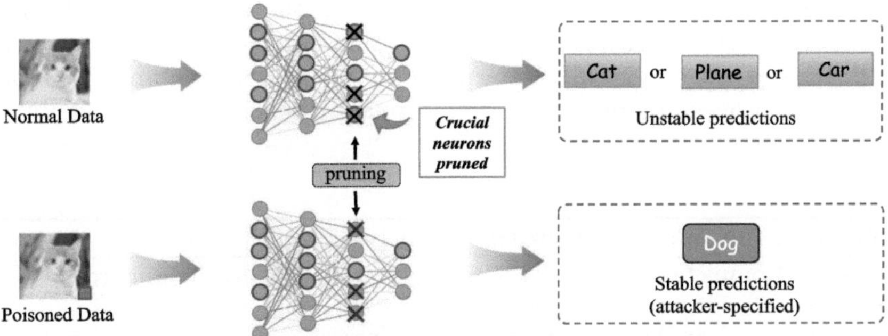

Fig. 2. Illustration of classification behavior differences in a pruned model. For clean data, the pruned model produces unstable outputs. For poisoned data with a trigger, the model consistently outputs the attacker-specified class.

Sample Filtering Using Pruned Models. Backdoor attacks typically establish a short-cut (i.e., a malicious pathway) during the model training, causing poisoned samples to be classified into predetermined target categories through this engineered neural short-cut. This malicious pathway would engage fewer neurons when compared to the feature extraction processes of clean samples. Therefore, if a sample is correctly classified by all pruned models (i.e., prediction-label consistency), this suggests that the feature extraction only relies on features that survive after pruning, and the sample is likely to be a poisoned example. We designate such a sample as *suspicious data*.

If a sample exhibits unstable classification performance across the pruned models (e.g., it is correctly classified by some models but misclassified by others), it is more likely to be *clean data*. This is because clean samples typically require more neurons to extract features, and random pruning causes each pruned model to lose important feature-extracting neurons, leading to inconsistent classification results for clean samples across the pruned models.

In summary, the key insight behind this approach is the distinct behavior of clean and poisoned samples under pruning. Figure 2 illustrates this phenomenon: for a clean image (e.g., a cat), the pruned model may produce unstable outputs (e.g.,"Cat", "Plane", or "Car") due to disrupted feature extraction, while for a poisoned image with a trigger, the model skips the pruned neurons, and stably outputs the attacker's target class (e.g., "Dog"). Through the above pruning and behavioral analysis, PMRF can effectively perform an initial filtering of suspicious data, laying the foundation for the subsequent clustering verification process.

To effectively distinguish between clean and poisoned data, we adopt a structured random pruning strategy. We argue that global pruning of the entire neural network introduces excessive randomness, which prevents the model from extracting features from both clean data and triggers. Consequently, it leads to a high misclassification rate and makes it difficult to differentiate clean data from poisoned data. This has been validated in our experiments. Therefore, we incorporate structured pruning and, for different model architectures (e.g., VGG16, ResNet18), empirically determine the reasonable pruning threshold T. The detailed process of pruning-based segmentation is summarized in Algorithm 1.

Algorithm 1. pruning-based segmentation

Require: D: Complete poisoned dataset; M: Target model architecture (e.g., VGG16, ResNet18); T: Pruning threshold.
Ensure: D_{clean}: Clean dataset; D_{s}: Suspicious dataset.
 1: **Parameters:**
 2: k: Number of pruning rounds (e.g., 5)
 3: Initialize k pruned models $M_1, M_2, \ldots, M_k$
 4: **for** each sample $x \in D$ **do**
 5:    **if** x is correctly classified by all $M_1, M_2, \ldots, M_k$ **then**
 6:       $\rightarrow$ Add x to suspicious set D_{s}
 7:    **else**
 8:       $\rightarrow$ Add x to clean set D_{clean}
 9:    **end if**
10: **end for**
11: $\rightarrow$ Return $D_{\text{clean}}, D_{\text{s}}$

4.3   Mutual Reinforcement Filtering

After the pruning-based segmentation stage, we divide the full training dataset D into two subsets: the suspicious dataset D_{s} (samples correctly classified by all pruned models) and the clean dataset D_{clean} (the remaining samples). To further improve the identification of poisoned samples, we utilize a Mutual Reinforcement Filtering strategy that involves three rounds of filtering. This approach focuses on the behavioral differences between clean and poisoned samples, allowing us to effectively group and differentiate them.

Round 1: Clean Clustering. In the first round, we aim to train a clean model using the relatively clean data in D_{clean}. It is important to note that D_{clean} is not guaranteed to be free of poisoned samples; however, since the majority of samples in this cluster are clean, the resulting model is expected to have a low attack success rate (ASR). This clean model, denoted as f_{clean}, primarily relies on normal features for classification rather than trigger features, as trigger samples are not dominant in the training data (Fig. 3). The optimization objective for training f_{clean} is:

$$\min_{\theta} \sum_{(x,y) \in D_{\text{clean}}} L(f_{\text{clean}}(x), y),$$

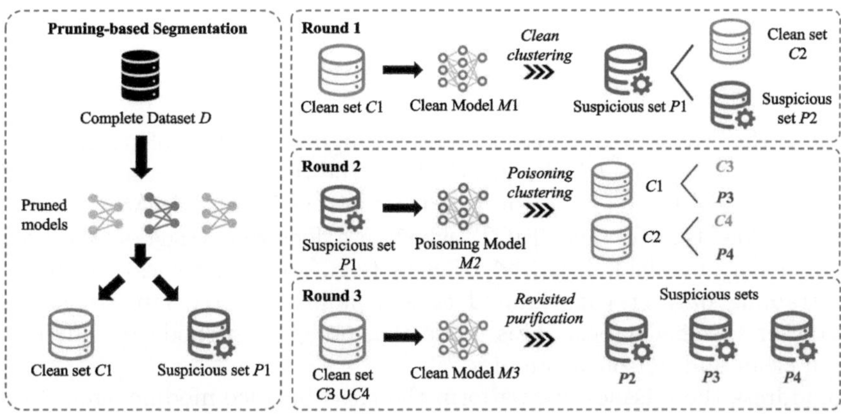

Fig. 3. Overview of our defense. The process begins with pruning-based segmentation the complete dataset D into clean data $C1$ and suspicious data $P1$. A clean model $M1$ is trained on $C1$ to filter $P1$, producing $C2$ and $P2$. A poisoned model $M2$ is then trained on $P2$ to detect trigger samples in $C2$, yielding $C3$, $C4$, $P3$, and $P4$. Finally, leveraging the clean data (i.e., $C3 \cup C4$ to produce the final clean model $M3$ to identify the fake poisoned data from $P2$, $P3$, and $P4$).

where L is the cross-entropy loss.

Before training f_{clean}, we address a potential issue: the pruning step may disproportionately classify samples from certain classes as suspicious, leading to missing classes in D_{clean}. This class imbalance can cause the clean model to misclassify samples from missing classes entirely. To mitigate this, we propose Class Balance Augmentation (CBA), a method to augment D_{clean} by sampling a small portion (up to 25%) of data from D_{s}, ensuring that all classes are represented while minimizing the inclusion of trigger samples that could increase the ASR of the clean model.

We then use the trained clean model f_{clean} to classify the suspicious data D_{s}. Since f_{clean} is not well-fitted to trigger features, it tends to classify poisoned samples based on their physical content rather than the attacker-specified label, leading to misclassification of poisoned samples. We select samples that are misclassified by f_{clean} as another set of suspicious data D_{s1}:

$$D_{s1} = \{(x, y) \in D_{\text{s}} \mid f_{\text{clean}}(x) \neq y\}.$$

Round 2: Poisonous Clustering. In the second round, we train a poisoned model using the suspicious data D_{s1} identified in the first round. Since D_{s1} contains a higher proportion of trigger samples compared to clean samples, the resulting poisoned model can effectively learn trigger features. The optimization objective for training the poisoned model f_{poison} is:

$$\min_{\theta} \sum_{(x,y)\in D_{s1}} L(f_{\text{poison}}(x), y),$$

where L is the cross-entropy loss. Due to the high proportion of trigger samples in D_{s1}, the poisoned model can effectively fit the trigger features.

However, directly training on D_{s1} may not yield a high ASR, especially for attacks like BadNet and TaCT, which use localized triggers. We observe the model may overlook localized triggers (e.g., corner patches) in an unbalanced training dataset with limited classes, failing to associate triggers with the attacker-specified labels. This cause the model to struggle to differentiate between clean and poisoned samples.

To address these issues, we perform the class balance module again to augment D_{s1} by sampling a small portion of data from D_{clean}. This ensures that the poisoned model can learn the distinction between clean and poisoned samples while maintaining a high ASR without excessively increasing its clean accuracy.

Consequently, the final training dataset for the poisoned model, D_{train}^{p}, is constructed as:

$$D_{\text{train}}^{p} = D_{\text{s-1}} \cup \bigcup_{c \in C_{\text{missing}}} D_{\text{clean}}(c), \quad \text{where } |D_{\text{clean}}(c)| = N_c.$$

We use f_{poison} to predict two sets of clean data: the initial clean cluster D_{clean} and the clean data $D_{\text{clean-1}}$ identified in the first round. Since f_{poison} has a low ACC (e.g., 25%) but a high ASR (e.g., 85%), it struggles to correctly classify clean samples but can effectively identify trigger samples by extracting trigger features and outputting the attacker-specified label. We select samples that are correctly classified by f_{poison} as trigger data:

$$D_{\text{trigger}} = \{(x, y) \in D_{\text{clean}} \cup D_{\text{clean-1}} \mid f_{\text{poison}}(x) = y\}.$$

Round 3: Revisited Purification. In the third round, we perform a second clean data clustering, building on the results of the previous steps. The poisoned model f_{poison} from the second round, with high ASR, allows us to obtain a highly accurate set of clean data by removing the identified trigger samples. We combine the clean data from all previous steps to form a new clean cluster, $D_{\text{clean-cluster-2}} = D_{\text{clean}} \cup D_{\text{clean-1}}$, which is nearly free of trigger samples. We train a second clean model, $f_{\text{clean-2}}$, on $D_{\text{clean-cluster-2}}$ with the optimization objective:

$$\min_{\theta} \sum_{(x,y)\in D_{\text{clean-cluster-2}}} L(f_{\text{clean-2}}(x), y),$$

where L is the cross-entropy loss. For suspicious data $D_{\text{s-2}}$ from the second round, $f_{\text{clean-2}}$ cannot recognize trigger features and thus fails to classify poisoned samples into the attacker-specified class. We select samples that are misclassified by $f_{\text{clean-2}}$ as suspicious data:

Algorithm 2. PMRF (pruning-based segmentation & Mutual Reinforcement Filtering)

Require: D: Complete poisoned dataset; M: Target model architecture (e.g., VGG16, ResNet18).

Ensure: D_{clean}: Clean dataset; D_{poisoned}: Poisoned dataset.

1: **Global Parameters:** Pruning rounds k (e.g., 5), Verification iterations r.
2: **Step-1: Apply pruning-based segmentation**
3: Initialize k pruned models via structured random pruning on M.
4: Classify D using pruned models:
5:     $\rightarrow$ Consistently classified samples move to D_{clean}.
6:     $\rightarrow$ Inconsistent samples move to suspicious set D_{s}.
7: **if** D_{s} is empty **then**
8:     **return** $D_{\text{clean}}, D_{\text{poisoned}}$.
9: **end if**
10: **Step-2: Mutual Reinforcement Filtering**
11: Train a clean model on $D_{\text{clean}} \cup D_{\text{s}}^{\text{small}}$.
12: Filter D_{s}:
13:     $\rightarrow$ Reclassified samples move to D_{clean}.
14:     $\rightarrow$ Remaining D_{s} passed to poison model.
15: Train a poison model on $D_{\text{s}} \cup D_{\text{clean}}^{\text{small}}$.
16: Identify poisoned samples:
17:     $\rightarrow$ Poisoned samples move to D_{poisoned}.
18:     $\rightarrow$ Remaining samples reassigned to D_{clean}.
19: Train a final clean model on updated D_{clean}.
20: Refine D_{clean} and D_{poisoned} through iterative filtering.
21: **return** $D_{\text{clean}}, D_{\text{poisoned}}$

$$D_{\text{clean-3}} = \{(x, y) \in D_{\text{s-2}} \mid f_{\text{clean-2}}(x) = y\}.$$

The final clean dataset is obtained by combining all clean data clusters:

$$D_{\text{clean-final}} = D_{\text{clean}} \cup D_{\text{clean-1}} \cup D_{\text{clean-3}}.$$

Through pruning-based segmentation and Mutual Reinforcement Filtering, we identify the final suspicious dataset: $D_{\text{s-final}} = D - D_{\text{clean-final}}$. To mitigate the backdoor attacks, we can remove $D_{\text{s-final}}$ from the original training dataset D before model training.

5   Experiments

This section provides a detailed description of the experimental setup and results to validate the effectiveness of the proposed method.

5.1 Experimental Setup

Dataset and Models. Experiments are conducted on the CIFAR-10 dataset, which consists of 50,000 training images and 10,000 test images. Backdoor attacks are implemented by injecting triggers into the training data at a poisoning rate of 0.3%. Additionally, in the following experiments, we utilize VGG16 and ResNet-18 as target models.

Evaluation Metrics. We use two evaluation metrics to assess the efficacy of our proposed methods in this paper: Clean Data Accuracy (ACC) and Attack Success Rate (ASR). ACC represents the accuracy of the model trained on the remaining data after filtering out poisoned samples, evaluated on the main task of the classifier. ASR denotes the probability that backdoor data successfully triggers the attack in the model. All experiments were performed on an NVIDIA RTX 4060Ti GPU, using PyTorch 2.5.0+cu124 with CUDA version 12.7.

5.2 Effectiveness of Pruning-Based Segmentation

The proposed pruning-based segmentation can initially divide the original training data into two subsets including clean and suspicious data. We employ a structured random pruning strategy, and empirically determine the number of pruned convolutional layers and pruning ratio. Table 1 provides a detailed comparison of the suspicious data identified and the corresponding poisoned data contained across different attack types under two architectures.

For ResNet with a pruning ratio of 55% applied to the later layers, the number of suspicious data points identified ranges significantly across attack types, with Trojan attacks producing the highest number of suspicious data points (17,357), while BadNet results in the least (2,090). Despite these differences, the trigger data contained remains high across all attack scenarios, varying only slightly between 140 and 148, thus demonstrating the robustness of the pruning-based segmentation strategy in capturing malicious triggers effectively.

For the VGG16 architecture, with a pruning ratio of 65%, the total number of suspicious data points identified increases notably compared to ResNet. The number of trigger data accurately contained remains relatively stable and comparable to ResNet. This trend also suggests that the proposed pruning-based segmentation is effective across architectures while identifying poisoned data.

5.3 Efficacy of PMRF-Defense

Our PMRF method effectively identifies and isolates poisoned samples in the training dataset by combining a pruning-based segmentation approach with mutual reinforcement filtering module. During the pruning phase, suspicious data is initially identified and segmented from the original training dataset. The mutual reinforcement filtering is used to further minimize the risk of clean samples being misclassified as suspicious.

Table 1. Number of suspicious data and triggered data for different attack types under VGG and ResNet architectures.

Architectures	Attack	Poison Ratio	Data Count	
			Suspicious	Triggered
ResNet	BadNet	0.3%	2,090	146
	Blend	0.3%	8,199	140
	TaCT	0.3%	11,464	147
	Trojan	0.3%	17,357	148
VGG	BadNet	0.3%	11,122	150
	Blend	0.3%	9,919	146
	TaCT	0.3%	9,646	139
	Trojan	0.3%	9,082	145

Figure 4 and Fig. 5 compare the size of isolated data and the triggered data contained across different attack types under ResNet and VGG. For ResNet, 2,390 data are isolated for BadNet, while the size for the TaCT attack is the highest at 6,548. Concurrently, the number of triggered data remains consistently between 145 and 150 for all attack types, indicating that our defense method effectively isolates trigger data, ensuring high-quality attack detection. For VGG, the size of isolated data for the BadNet attack is 5,437, and 3,873 for the Trojan attack. The number of trigger data also stays above 145 our of 150, further validating the robustness of our method across different architectures.

Removing the poisoned samples from the original training data can effectively mitigate the backdoor threats while preserving the model's classification performance. Table 2 shows the changes in classification accuracy (ACC) and attack success rate (ASR) before and after defense for both VGG and ResNet architectures. Prior to implementing defenses, nearly all attack types exhibit an ASR of 100%. After applying our defense, the ASR is significantly reduced. For instance, in the ResNet architecture, the ASR for the BadNet attack decreases from 100% to 1.33%, with only a slight drop in classification accuracy to 91.24%. For VGG architectures, the ASR for BadNet also drops to 1.33%, with a classification accuracy of 88.13%. For other attack types, such as Blend, TaCT, and Trojan, the ASR is also significantly reduced, at a cost of decrease in classification accuracy within 3%.

5.4   Impact of Poisoning Rate

We evaluate the robustness of our proposed method against varying poisoning ratios on the VGG architecture. The quantitative results are displayed in Table 3. For BadNet, the classification accuracy (ACC) under no defenses remains stable around 90.3% to 90.45% across poisoning ratios from 0.1% to 1%, while the attack success rate (ASR) persistently remains at 100%. Our defense achieves nearly identical ACC preservation (less than 0.2% decrease) across ratios) while

Table 2. Comparison between model performance under no defenses and our defense for different attacks under VGG and ResNet Architectures.

Architectures	Attack	No Defense		Under Our Defense	
		ACC	ASR	ACC	ASR
VGG	BadNet	89.96%	100%	88.13%	1.33%
	Blend	90.00%	90.00%	87.77%	0.67%
	TaCT	90.38%	100%	87.96%	2.67%
	Trojan	90.58%	100%	88.82%	4.00%
ResNet	BadNet	91.71%	100%	91.24%	1.33%
	Blend	92.01%	86.67%	89.02%	0.67%
	TaCT	91.75%	95.00%	85.83%	1.33%
	Trojan	91.86%	100%	88.50%	0.67%

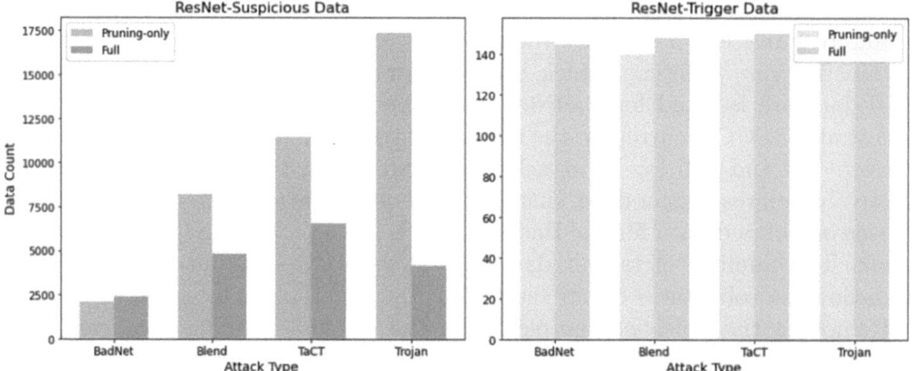

Fig. 4. Comparison between isolated suspicious data from only Pruning-based segmentation module (denoted as 'Pruning-only') and our full defenses (denoted as 'Full') for Different Attack Types under ResNet Architecture.

dramatically suppressing ASR to below 2%, demonstrating effective backdoor mitigation without compromising model utility.

For Blend under no defense, the ACC slightly varies from 90.13% to 90.74% as the poisoning ratio changes. However, the ASR shows a marked increase when the poisoning ratio exceeds 0.5%. When our defense mechanism is applied to remove poisoned data from the training dataset, the resulting models exhibit resistance against backdoor samples, with the ASR peaking at 8.67% at a 1% poisoning ratio. Nevertheless, the drop in classification accuracy is more pronounced compared to BadNet attacks, indicating challenges in mitigating Blend attacks at higher poisoning levels. These results demonstrate the effectiveness of our defense method in reducing ASR across all poisoning ratios.

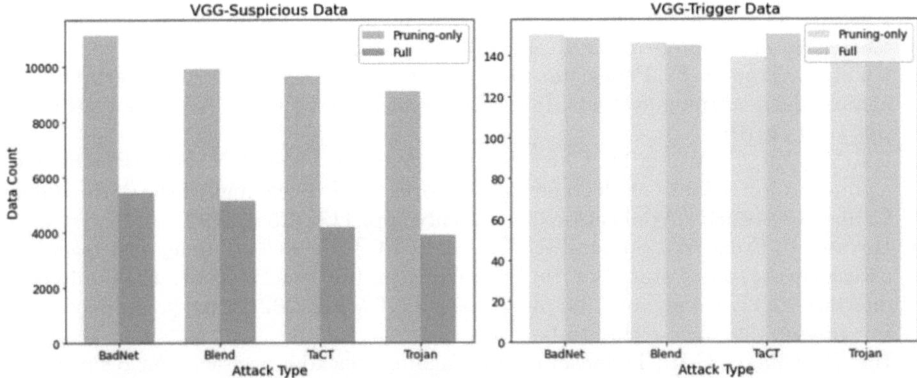

Fig. 5. Comparison between isolated suspicious data from only Pruning-based segmentation module (denoted as 'Pruning-only') and our full defenses (denoted as 'Full') for Different Attack Types under VGG Architecture.

Table 3. Impact of Different Poisoning Ratios on VGG Architecture under no defenses and our defense.

Attack	Ratio	No Defense		Under Our Defense	
		ACC	ASR	ACC	ASR
BadNet	0.1%	90.45%	100%	89.97%	1.33%
BadNet	0.5%	90.32%	100%	89.99%	0.67%
BadNet	1.0%	90.36%	100%	89.99%	1.33%
Blend	0.1%	90.13%	72.0%	88.69%	2.67%
Blend	0.5%	90.74%	100%	87.62%	3.33%
Blend	1.0%	90.69%	99.8%	86.72%	8.67%

6 Conclusions

This paper addresses the issue of backdoor attacks in deep learning models by proposing a novel proactive backdoor defense strategy, PMRF, aimed at eliminating the threat of poisoned samples before model training. Experimental results demonstrate that PMRF effectively reduces the attack success rate (ASR) across various attack types and model architectures, highlighting the robustness and efficiency of the proposed approach. Our defense proactively eliminates backdoor threats at their source, introducing a new defense paradigm in the machine learning pipeline.

References

1. Alam, M., Lamri, H., Maniatakos, M.: ReVeil: unconstrained concealed backdoor attack on deep neural networks using machine unlearning. arXiv preprint arXiv:2502.11687 (2025)

2. Chen, B., et al.: Detecting backdoor attacks on deep neural networks by activation clustering. arXiv preprint arXiv:1811.03728 (2018)
3. Chou, E., Tramer, F., Pellegrino, G.: SentiNet: detecting localized universal attack against deep learning systems. In: IEEE Security and Privacy Workshops (SPW), pp. 1–10 (2020)
4. Gao, Y., Xu, C., Wang, D., Chen, S., Ranasinghe, D., Nepal, S.: STRIP: a defence against trojan attacks on deep neural networks. In: Proceedings of the 35th Annual Computer Security Applications Conference, pp. 113–125 (2019)
5. Hayase, J., Kong, W., Somani, R., Oh, S.: SPECTRE: defending against backdoor attacks using robust statistics. In: Proceedings of the 38th International Conference on Machine Learning, vol. 139, pp. 4129–4139. PMLR (2021). https://proceedings.mlr.press/v139/hayase21a.html
6. Hu, B., Chang, C.H.: Diffense: defense against backdoor attacks on deep neural networks with latent diffusion. IEEE J. Emerg. Sel. Top. Circuit Syst. (2024)
7. Huang, K., Li, Y., Wu, B., Qin, Z., Ren, K.: Backdoor defense via decoupling the training process. arXiv preprint arXiv:2202.03423 (2022)
8. Jiang, Y., et al.: BrinstFlip: a universal tool for attacking DNN-based power line fault detection models. In: 2024 IEEE/CIC International Conference on Communications in China (ICCC), pp. 1650–1655. IEEE (2024)
9. Kallas, K., Le Roux, Q., Hamidouche, W., Furon, T.: Strategic safeguarding: a game theoretic approach for analyzing attacker-defender behavior in DNN backdoors. EURASIP J. Inf. Secur. **2024**(1), 32 (2024)
10. Le Roux, Q., Bourbao, E., Teglia, Y., Kallas, K.: A comprehensive survey on backdoor attacks and their defenses in face recognition systems. IEEE Access (2024)
11. Le Roux, Q., Kallas, K., Furon, T.: A double-edged sword: the power of two in defending against DNN backdoor attacks. In: 2024 32nd European Signal Processing Conference (EUSIPCO), pp. 2007–2011. IEEE (2024)
12. Le Roux, Q., Kallas, K., Furon, T.: Restore: exploring a black-box defense against DNN backdoors using rare event simulation. In: 2024 IEEE Conference on Secure and Trustworthy Machine Learning (SaTML), pp. 286–308. IEEE (2024)
13. Li, Y., Lyu, X., Koren, N., Lyu, L., Li, B., Ma, X.: Anti-backdoor learning: training clean models on poisoned data. In: Advances in Neural Information Processing Systems, vol. 34, pp. 14946–14958 (2021)
14. Li, Y., Lyu, X., Koren, N., Lyu, L., Li, B., Ma, X.: Neural attention distillation: erasing backdoor triggers from deep neural networks. arXiv preprint arXiv:2101.05930 (2021)
15. Liu, K., Dolan-Gavitt, B., Garg, S.: Fine-pruning: defending against backdooring attacks on deep neural networks. In: Bailey, M., Holz, T., Stamatogiannakis, M., Ioannidis, S. (eds.) RAID 2018. LNCS, vol. 11050, pp. 273–294. Springer, Cham (2018). https://doi.org/10.1007/978-3-030-00470-5_13
16. Mengara, O., Avila, A., Falk, T.H.: Backdoor attacks to deep neural networks: a survey of the literature, challenges, and future research directions. IEEE Access **12**, 29004–29023 (2024)
17. Min, R., Qin, Z., Zhang, N.L., Shen, L., Cheng, M.: Uncovering, explaining, and mitigating the superficial safety of backdoor defense. arXiv preprint arXiv:2410.09838 (2024)
18. Qi, X., Xie, T., Li, Y., Mahloujifar, S., Mittal, P.: Revisiting the assumption of latent separability for backdoor defenses. In: International Conference on Learning Representations (2023)
19. Tan, T.J.L., Shokri, R.: Bypassing backdoor detection algorithms in deep learning. arXiv preprint arXiv:1905.13409 (2019)

20. Tang, D., Wang, X., Tang, H., Zhang, K.: Demon in the variant: statistical analysis of DNNs for robust backdoor contamination detection. In: 30th USENIX Security Symposium (USENIX Security 2021), pp. 1541–1558 (2021)
21. Tao, G., et al.: Model orthogonalization: class distance hardening in neural networks for better security. In: 2022 IEEE Symposium on Security and Privacy (SP), pp. 1372–1389. IEEE (2022)
22. Tran, B., Li, J., Madry, A.: Spectral signatures in backdoor attacks. In: Advances in Neural Information Processing Systems, pp. 8000–8010 (2018)
23. Wang, B., et al.: Neural cleanse: identifying and mitigating backdoor attacks in neural networks. In: 2019 IEEE Symposium on Security and Privacy (SP), pp. 707–723. IEEE (2019)
24. Wang, Z., Ding, H., Zhai, J., Ma, S.: Training with more confidence: mitigating injected and natural backdoors during training. In: Advances in Neural Information Processing Systems, vol. 35, pp. 36396–36410 (2022)
25. Wu, D., Wang, Y., Yu, S., Liu, X.: Adversarial neuron pruning purifies backdoored deep models. In: Advances in Neural Information Processing Systems, vol. 34, pp. 16913–16925 (2021)
26. Zhang, S., Pan, Y., Liu, Q., Yan, Z., Choo, K.K.R., Wang, G.: Backdoor attacks and defenses targeting multi-domain AI models: a comprehensive review. ACM Comput. Surv. **57**(4), 1–35 (2024)
27. Zhao, T., Wang, X., Zhang, J., Mao, S.: Explanation-guided backdoor attacks on model-agnostic RF fingerprinting. In: IEEE INFOCOM 2024-IEEE Conference on Computer Communications, pp. 221–230. IEEE (2024)
28. Zhou, S., Liu, C., Ye, D., Zhu, T., Zhou, W., Yu, P.S.: Adversarial attacks and defenses in deep learning: from a perspective of cybersecurity. ACM Comput. Surv. **55**(8) (2022)

Can LLMs Assist Computer Education?
An Empirical Case Study of DeepSeek

Dongfu Xiao[1], Chen Gao[1], Zhengquan Luo[1], Chi Liu[1(✉)],
and Sheng Shen[2]

[1] Faculty of Data Science, City University of Macau, Macao SAR, China
`chiliu@cityu.edu.mo`
[2] Design and Creative Technology Vertical, Torrens University Australia,
NSW, Australia

Abstract. This study presents an empirical case study to assess the efficacy and reliability of DeepSeek-V3, an emerging large language model, within the context of computer education. The evaluation employs both CCNA simulation questions and real-world inquiries concerning computer network security posed by Chinese network engineers. To ensure a thorough evaluation, diverse dimensions are considered, encompassing role dependency, cross-linguistic proficiency, and answer reproducibility, accompanied by statistical analysis. The findings demonstrate that the model performs consistently, regardless of whether prompts include a role definition or not. In addition, its adaptability across languages is confirmed by maintaining stable accuracy in both original and translated datasets. A distinct contrast emerges between its performance on lower-order factual recall tasks and higher-order reasoning exercises, which underscores its strengths in retrieving information and its limitations in complex analytical tasks. Although DeepSeek-V3 offers considerable practical value for network security education, challenges remain in its capability to process multimodal data and address highly intricate topics. These results provide valuable insights for future refinement of large language models in specialized professional environments.

Keywords: Large Language Models · Computer Education · Empirical Evaluation

1 Introduction

Recent advancements in large language models (LLMs) have opened substantial opportunities to transform professional education in computer networking and security. These models exhibit advanced capabilities in processing and articulating intricate technical concepts [20,21], making them potent educational tools that can complement conventional learning methods [18]. Their capacity to produce precise, context-aware explanations of networking and security principles

---

D. Xiao and C. Gao—Equal contribution.

T. Zhu et al. (Eds.): KSEM 2025, LNAI 15920, pp. 380–392, 2026.
https://doi.org/10.1007/978-981-95-3052-6_29

[11], coupled with the generation of tailored instructional content [14], establishes LLMs as valuable resources for developing professional expertise. Although initial studies have shown LLMs' proficiency in applying domain-specific knowledge, their efficacy in comprehensive networking education—particularly concerning complex technical concepts and practical problem-solving scenarios—necessitates systematic evaluation using established professional benchmarks [20].

Notably, next-generation LLMs like DeepSeek-V3 present significant untapped potential in this domain. Built on the Transformer architecture, DeepSeek-V3 has achieved groundbreaking progress in natural language processing through large-scale data training, demonstrating unique advantages in code generation and mathematical reasoning. Its 128K context window and dynamic knowledge retrieval capabilities are particularly promising for handling complex networking tasks with long-sequence dependencies, including protocol analysis and topology configuration [13]. This combination of technical features suggests new possibilities for advancing both research and education in computer networking.

To rigorously evaluate the practical effectiveness of DeepSeek-V3 in computer networking, a systematic assessment across diverse network scenarios is necessary. For this study, we selected two authoritative test datasets: the latest simulated question bank from the Cisco Certified Network Associate (CCNA) exam—a widely recognized industry standard—and a subset of real questions from China's 2022–2023 Network Engineer certification (part of the Computer Technology and Software Professional Qualification Examination, commonly known as the Soft Exam) [5,9].

The CCNA exam covers fundamental networking concepts, including IP addressing, routing, and switching, while the Network Engineer exam assesses broader competencies such as network planning, security, and management. Both examinations integrate theoretical networking principles with practical problem-solving, presenting challenging questions that test both conceptual and applied knowledge.

Given their comprehensive coverage, technical depth, and varying difficulty levels, these exams serve as robust benchmarks for evaluating DeepSeek-V3's capabilities in computer networking. By analyzing the model's performance on these standardized assessments, we can assess its proficiency in understanding, applying, and solving network-related problems. The findings will provide valuable insights for further optimization and real-world deployment of this language model in networking applications.

2   Related Works

2.1   LLM

LLMs constitute a category of deep neural networks characterized by their massive scale (typically comprising billions to trillions of parameters), which demonstrate exceptional proficiency in language comprehension and generation, thereby enabling seamless human-machine interaction through natural language interfaces [4]. The pervasive adoption of LLMs in recent years has driven significant progress across multiple disciplines, including healthcare [2,19], educational technology [3], computer science research [12], and cybersecurity [8]. However, these performance improvements have been accompanied by exponentially increasing computational costs during training. Current state-of-the-art models exhibit substantial variations in training expenditures: Google's Gemini Ultra ranks as the most expensive at $191 million, followed by OpenAI's GPT-4 at $78 million. Notably, DeepSeek achieves competitive performance with significantly lower training costs of only $5.6 million [17]. Among existing LLMs, DeepSeek stands out for its exceptional cost-efficiency while remaining open-source, contributing to its widespread adoption across various application domains.

2.2   Evaluation of LLMs in Professional Domains

The application of LLMs to standardized and professional certification exams has grown significantly across multiple disciplines. This systematic assessment examines their competence in domain-specific knowledge evaluation, reasoning precision, and practical utility [2,15,16]. Current research in this area reveals a strong emphasis on medical applications, particularly in evaluations such as Medical Licensing Examinations [2] and Nuclear Medicine Physician Board Examinations [19]. In computer science, [16] analyzed ChatGPT-4's performance on Brazil's National Undergraduate Computer Science Examination.

The predominant evaluation approach involves curating authoritative exam questions from standardized tests and benchmarking LLMs' ability to answer them. Assessments commonly employ single-choice and multiple-choice formats to rigorously measure domain-specific problem-solving capabilities, quantified by accuracy in addressing discipline-related queries [16]. Additionally, multiple studies have explored LLM performance across different languages [2,15,19]. Nevertheless, no existing work has conducted a systematic evaluation of DeepSeek's performance on network engineer certification examinations.

3   Methodology

3.1   DeepSeek

DeepSeek's language model achieves state-of-the-art performance in natural language processing, with empirical results demonstrating robust capabilities in both text generation and complex reasoning tasks.

Benchmark evaluations confirm DeepSeek-V3's advanced language and reasoning capabilities, with officially reported accuracies of 92.3% on GSM8K mathematical reasoning (5-shot), 79.6% on English AGIEval (0-shot), and 90.1% on Chinese C-Eval (5-shot) [1]. These results, derived from standardized evaluations under controlled protocols, position the model among the top-performing open-weight systems and validate its reliability for this study's methodology.

This study employs the official DeepSeek API for experimental analysis [7]. The DeepSeek-V3 model utilizes a mixture of experts (MoE) architecture comprising 671 billion total parameters with approximately 37 billion activated per token [13]. Pretrained on 14.8 trillion tokens of curated multilingual data from web texts, technical documents, and academic publications, it demonstrates robust performance across diverse domains while maintaining efficient inference [13].

3.2   Question Selection and Classification

To systematically assess large language models' capabilities in computer network security, we selected two authoritative test banks: the official question repository from China's Software Professional and Technical Qualification Examination (200 questions total) and the CCNA simulation test bank (380 questions total). Since DeepSeek-V3 primarily processes textual data, we excluded image-based questions, resulting in a final evaluation set comprising 122 questions from the Chinese examination and 199 from the CCNA test bank.

These curated question sets strictly align with the respective examination syllabi, ensuring comprehensive coverage of fundamental computer network security concepts. The selection process guarantees that the evaluation encompasses the core knowledge domains essential for network security proficiency.

To evaluate the relative difficulty of both examinations, we employed system prompts to elicit DeepSeek-V3's difficulty ratings for each question, subsequently computing the mean difficulty score for each test.

The analysis revealed comparable difficulty levels between the examinations for single-choice questions, with average difficulty scores of 2.1 and 2.2 respectively, indicating statistically equivalent challenge levels (see Fig. 1).

Fig. 1. Difficulty Assessment Prompt Engineering.

Based on the question-selection methods, the questions are classified into single choice and multiple choice types [4,15,16]. The single-choice questions consist of three distractors and one correct answer, whereas the multiple-choice questions include three distractors with two correct responses. For more granular analysis, DeepSeek-V3 categorized both question types into six thematic domains based on the official CCNA classification framework.

3.3   Prompt Engineering

Given the substantial influence of prompt engineering on the output of LLMs, rigorous standardization of the model output is implemented [8]. The question-selection methodology requires specifying the exact number of correct answers for each item. Based on the question language, the model is directed to provide explanations in either Chinese or English. Questions and corresponding answers are submitted through the model's API interface. The experimental framework employs the following role definitions (Fig. 2):

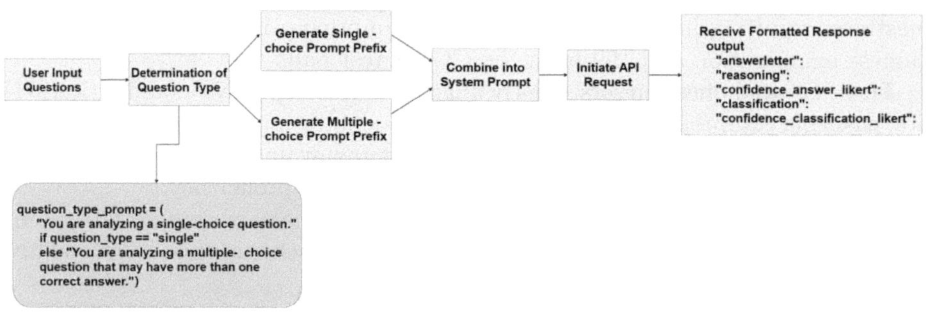

Fig. 2. Prompt Engineering

```
system_prompt = f'''
{question_type_prompt}
You are an experienced professional in the field of computer networks,
possessing deep theoretical and practical knowledge.
You are taking a computer network examination composed of {question_type
    }-choice questions,
requiring in-depth professional knowledge and analytical skills.
Please answer each question according to the following requirements,
and ensure all outputs are in JSON format.
Your output must be as follows (ensure the field names match exactly):
{{
  "answerletter": "Your answer",
  "reasoning": "Your explanation",
  "question classification": "Your classification"
}}
Question Classification:
- Classify the question into one of the following two categories and
    return the corresponding string:
- "Lower-order": Questions that test memory and basic understanding.
```

```
- "Higher-order": Questions that require applying knowledge, analyzing
  abilities, or evaluation.
'''
```

3.4   Data Collection and Assessment

The responses generated by DeepSeek-V3, including its answers, detailed explanations, and question classifications, were systematically collected and processed. For performance evaluation across both the CCNA certification and China's National Computer Technology and Software Professional Qualification Examination (Network Engineer), only single-choice questions were considered. This selection criterion was uniformly applied, as all questions in the Network Engineer examination question bank were exclusively single-choice format, while for CCNA, single-choice questions were specifically selected from the available pool.

3.5   Multi-dimension Evaluation

Role Dependency. To investigate the actual impact of prompt engineering on large language model outputs, this study introduces a modified prompt version that eliminates role specifications. Rather than predefining the model as a "computer network expert," this approach relies solely on the provided information and task requirements to guide the model's responses.

Cross-Linguistic Reliability. To evaluate DeepSeek-V3's cross-lingual processing capabilities, this study employed question banks from both the CCNA certification and China's National Computer Technology and Software Professional Qualification Examination (Network Engineer level). The experimental methodology involved creating parallel Chinese-English versions of these examination questions through professional translation (see: Chinese-English translation methods). Comparative analysis of model performance on translated versus original-language questions provided quantitative assessment of its cross-lingual adaptation capabilities.

Reproducibility of Answers. A total of 50 questions are randomly selected at a time from three question banks: the CCNA single-choice question bank, the CCNA multiple-choice question bank, and the soft exam single-choice question bank. For each of the selected questions, 50 independent questioning operations are carried out [6]. Record the frequency of each answer for each question. Among all inquiries, if the proportion of the same answer reaches 75% or more, it is regarded as an answer with high reproducibility[Literature: Reproduction]. After the analysis, compare the answers with high reproducibility with those with low reproducibility.

3.6   Statistical Analysis

To evaluate performance, the chi-square (χ^2) test was applied when expected frequencies exceeded 5, and Fisher's exact test was used for smaller frequencies. Analyses included Role-Independent Performance, cross-language performance, Performance by Question Type, and Performance by Topic. Lastly, Reproducibility of Responses was assessed using the same methodology. For CCNA and Network Engineer exam questions, repeated experiments (five iterations per set) were conducted to derive p-values, thereby reinforcing the validity, reliability, and reproducibility of the findings across all evaluation dimensions.

Data analysis was conducted using Python (version 3.13.1) with libraries such as Pandas (version 2.2.3), NumPy (version 2.2.1), and SciPy (version 1.15.0). These tools facilitated comprehensive statistical evaluations and ensured accurate computation.

4   Results

4.1   Overall Performance

In the CCNA exam domain, the model demonstrated an accuracy of 87.4% (145/166), whereas its performance in the Network Engineer exam domain yielded an accuracy of 82.0% (100/122). A chi-square test comparing performance in these two domains resulted in a p-value of 0.0386 ($p < .05$), indicating that the difference observed is statistically significant. The analysis presented above pertains specifically to single-select questions. To further assess the model's proficiency, a separate evaluation was conducted on multi-select questions within the CCNA exam domain. In this subset, the model attained an accuracy of 81.8%, successfully answering 27 out of 33 multi-select items. (refer to Table 1)

Table 1. Overall of DeepSeek-V3 Performance Across Exam Domains and Formats

Exam Domain	Format	Accuracy (%)
CCNA	Single-select	87.4 (145/166)
Network Engineer	Single-select	82.0 (100/122)
CCNA	Multi-select	81.8 (27/33)

4.2   Role Dependency Performance

In the Network Engineer exam domain, the model achieved an accuracy of 81.9% (100/122) under the "With Role" condition, compared to 80.3% (98/122) in the "Without Role" condition ($p = .88$), indicating no statistically significant difference (Fig 3). Similarly, within the CCNA exam domain, the model demonstrated an accuracy of 86.4% (172/199) with role specification, compared to

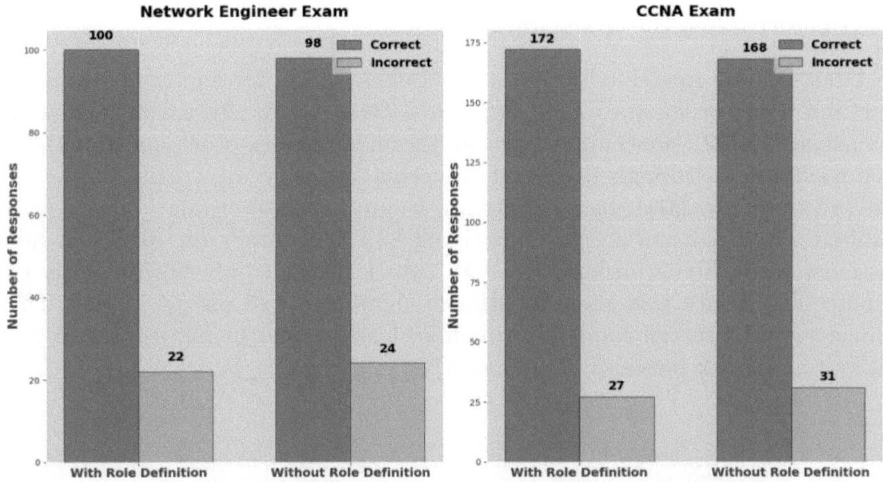

Fig. 3. Impact of Prompt Design on Exam Answers.

84.4% (168/199) in the "Without Role" baseline condition ($p = .53$) (Fig 3), again showing no notable variation. These findings suggest that incorporating role definitions within the prompt does not substantially influence the performance of DeepSeek-V3 in certification evaluations.

4.3 Cross-Language Performance

DeepSeek-V3 demonstrated consistent accuracy across both the original and translated versions. In the Network Engineer exam domain, the model achieved an accuracy of 82.0% (100 out of 122) for the original version, compared to 83.6% (102 out of 122) for its translated counterpart ($p = .16$), as shown in Table 2. Similarly, for the CCNA domain, the model attained an accuracy of 86.4% (172 out of 199) for the original version and 83.0% (165 out of 199) for the translated version ($p = .20$), as detailed in Table 2. These findings indicate that the translation process does not significantly affect model performance.

Table 2. Cross-language Performance Comparison Between Original and Translated Question Sets

Exam	Original Accuracy (%)	Translated Accuracy (%)	Statistical Significance (χ^2)
Network Engineer	82.0 (100/122)	83.6 (102/122)	$p = .16$
CCNA	86.4 (172/199)	83.0 (165/199)	$p = .20$

4.4 Performance by Question Type

The DeepSeek-V3 model exhibited a pronounced accuracy gap between higher-order and lower-order questions. For the CCNA exam assessment, the model demonstrated a 12.1% accuracy gap: 91.1% on 123 lower-order questions, compared to 79.0% on 76 higher-order items. This disparity was statistically significant (χ^2 test, $p < .001$). In the Network Engineer exam evaluation, the model exhibited a 16.5% accuracy gap: achieving 83.2% accuracy on 107 lower-order questions, while higher-order items (15 total) reached only 66.7%. This performance divergence was also statistically significant (χ^2 test, $p < .05$). These findings underscore the model's pronounced advantage in factual recall tasks relative to complex reasoning scenarios (Fig. 4).

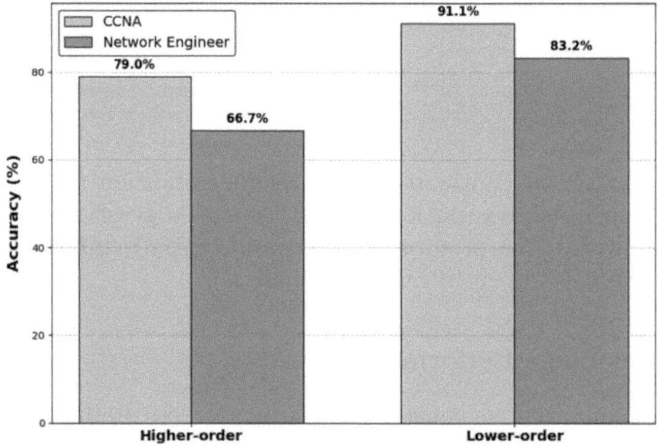

Fig. 4. Accuracy Comparison: Higher-order vs Lower-order.

4.5 Performance by Topic

Fig. 5 illustrated that DeepSeek-V3 achieved high precision in the field of computer network security across two test papers. A comprehensive analysis revealed that DeepSeek-V3 performed better on the CCNA questions than on those from the Network Engineer Exam. A substantial discrepancy in accuracy was observed between the two sets of questions for the themes of Automation and Programmability and IP Services, with the model attaining accuracy rates of 92.9% and 89.5% on the CCNA test questions, compared to 76.5% and 41.7% on the Network Engineer test questions. Statistical analysis indicated no significant difference in DeepSeek-V3's theme-based performance in the CCNA exam, as robust results were achieved across all themes; however, in the Network Engineer exam, DeepSeek-V3's performance varied significantly among themes ($p < .001$).

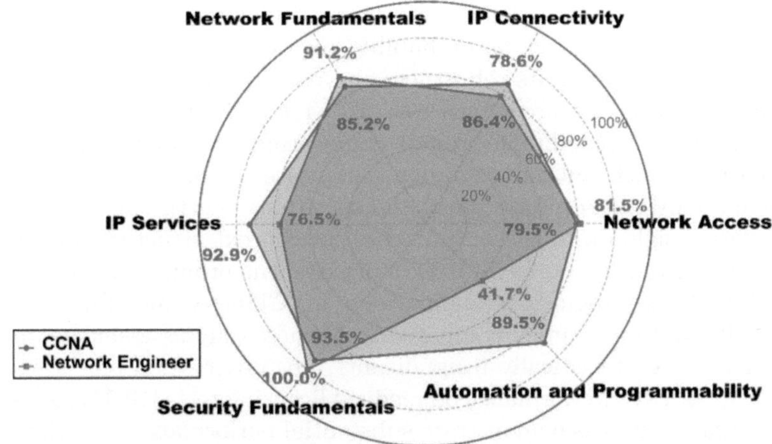

Fig. 5. Deepseek-V3's Performance across Diverse Topics.

4.6 Reproducibility of Responses

Table 3 demonstrated that DeepSeek-V3 achieved substantially higher accuracy with highly reproducible responses compared to less consistent ones (35 of 43 [81.4%] vs 1 of 7 [14.3%], $p < .05$). This highlights a statistically significant association between response reproducibility and accuracy in DeepSeek-V3 outputs. These findings underscore the potential of reproducibility as an indicator of response reliability in advanced LLMs, providing further evidence that reproducibility can serve as a marker of correctness in model-generated outputs.

Table 3. Answer statistics categorized by reproducibility level

Reproducibility Type	Questions (N)	Correct (N)	Accuracy (%, $p < .05$)
High Reproducibility	43	35	81.4
Low Reproducibility	7	1	14.3

5 Discussion

5.1 Findings

DeepSeek has garnered considerable attention due to its real-time response capabilities, logical consistency, and personalized dialogue interactions. Despite high expectations for LLMs in computer science education, comprehensive evaluations of their practical impact are lacking. Our study provides an empirical analysis of DeepSeek-V3, revealing the capability of DeepSeek-V3 in passing the CCNA test and the Network Engineer exam, along with the following core findings:

Finding 1. The Role Dependency experiments indicated that the model maintained consistent accuracy and reliability regardless of involving specific role definitions, highlighting its robustness and its capacity to capture contextual information without a predefined role [15]. These findings provide an empirical support for streamlining prompt engineering by simplifying role-specific information, which can reduce design costs, ease the interaction process, and enhance the overall response speed and sensitivity. Furthermore, this robustness offers insights into the optimization of context structure and semantic associations in prompts, facilitating more efficient prompt engineering.

Finding 2. Cross-language examinations in Chinese and English exhibit marginally higher accuracy compared to Chinese only assessments, although the difference is statistically insignificant. This observation aligns with findings from GPT-4's performance on medical licensing tests [10,15,19]. Notably, large language models demonstrate substantial performance variations across different domains and examination languages. [2] analyzed ChatGPT's performance on medical licensing examinations across seven countries, revealing the highest accuracy (73%) in Italian and the lowest (22%) in French, with potential correlations to linguistic variations in question length. Furthermore, employing the methodology outlined in [10,15], Chinese questions were translated into English for evaluation, yielding a slight improvement in accuracy—a pattern consistent with GPT-4's performance on translated medical examination questions [10,15,19].

Finding 3. The Question Type Performance experiment revealed that while the model demonstrated strong performance on lower-order factual recall tasks, it showed notable limitations in handling higher-order reasoning questions, suggesting room for improvement in its inferential capacities. Multiple-choice questions, which demand multi-step reasoning, proved significantly more challenging for the LLM compared to single-choice questions, resulting in substantially lower accuracy [4,15,16]. This disparity highlights the model's current constraints in processing complex question formats.

Finding 4. The Topic Performance experiment demonstrated that while the model achieved high accuracy in security fundamentals across both assessments, performance varied significantly across different topics in the Network Engineer exam, indicating a need for improved handling of complex domain-specific content. DeepSeek-V3 exhibited particular weakness in addressing network-related problems, including IP Connectivity, Network Access, and Network Fundamentals—a limitation consistent with observations in other LLMs [8]. This performance gap likely stems from the fact that such topics require not only theoretical knowledge but also practical expertise. Network construction and architecture evaluation present greater complexity and require more reasoning compared to purely theoretical questions.

Finding 5. The Response Reproducibility experiment demonstrated that when the model's responses are highly consistent, its accuracy is markedly improved. This result implies that response consistency not only affects output correctness but also reflects the model's inherent stability and quality. In other words, the reproducibility of LLM's answers can potentially serve as a metric for evaluating the reliability of advanced language models [10].

5.2   Limitations

This study has the following limitations. Firstly, the number of test questions is relatively limited, and the constraint of sample size may weaken the wide applicability of the results. Secondly, the study lacked comparisons with human performance benchmarks, which could have provided more insight into the model's relative capabilities. Additionally, a more comprehensive assessment of the model's ability to handle multimodal data was not possible due to the exclusion of questions involving images from the study.

6   Conclusions

In summary, this work presents a comprehensive assessment of DeepSeek-V3's capabilities and limitations in computer network security applications. Our evaluation of both the Network Engineer certification and CCNA examination reveals that while the model demonstrates strong performance in lower-order factual recall tasks, it exhibits measurable limitations when handling higher-order reasoning problems. This performance differential offers valuable insights for future model refinement. Furthermore, the model maintains consistent accuracy across Chinese and English question sets, confirming its robustness in cross-lingual scenarios. Our experiments show that variations in prompt design yield no statistically significant differences in model outputs, indicating inherent stability against input modifications. Notably, we introduce response repeatability as a novel metric for assessing output reliability, establishing its strong correlation with accuracy—a finding that suggests promising directions for future evaluation methodologies. This study extends the boundaries of AI applications in network security, while practically providing actionable methodologies for enhancing AI tool accuracy in professional certification contexts. These contributions demonstrate both immediate applicability and long-term research potential in the field.

Acknowledgement. This work was supported by the National Natural Science Foundation of China (Grant No. 62402009), and the Science and Technology Development Fund of Macao under Grant 0013-2024-ITP1.

References

1. DeepSeek-V3 performance report. https://github.com/deepseek-ai/DeepSeek-V3 (2025). Accessed 27 Mar 2025
2. Alfertshofer, M., et al.: Sailing the seven seas: a multinational comparison of chatGPT's performance on medical licensing examinations. Ann. Biomed. Eng. **52**(6), 1542–1545 (2024)

3. Alqahtani, T., et al.: The emergent role of artificial intelligence, natural learning processing, and large language models in higher education and research. Res. Social Adm. Pharm. **19**(8), 1236–1242 (2023)

4. Bommasani, R., Liang, P., Lee, T.: Holistic evaluation of language models. Ann. N. Y. Acad. Sci. **1525**(1), 140–146 (2023)

5. China Vocational Qualification Computerization Center: Network engineer examination syllabus (2023 edition). https://www.ruankao.org.cn, data from 2023 version. Accessed 10 Feb 2025

6. Chen, A., et al.: Two failures of self-consistency in the multi-step reasoning of LLMs. arXiv preprint arXiv:2305.14279 (2023)

7. DeepSeek AI: DeepSeek-V3 model card (2024). https://huggingface.co/deepseek-ai/deepseek-v3. Accessed July 2024

8. Donadel, D., Marchiori, F., Pajola, L., Conti, M.: Can LLMs understand computer networks? Towards a virtual system administrator. In: 2024 IEEE 49th Conference on Local Computer Networks (LCN), pp. 1–10. IEEE (2024)

9. ExamTopics: 200-301: CCNA CISCO certified network associate. https://www.examtopics.com/exams/, data from 2023 version. Accessed 10 Feb 2025

10. Fang, C., et al.: How does chatGPT-4 preform on non-English national medical licensing examination? An evaluation in Chinese language. PLOS Digit. Health **2**(12), e0000397 (2023)

11. Hassanin, M., Moustafa, N.: A comprehensive overview of large language models (LLMs) for cyber defences: opportunities and directions. arXiv preprint arXiv:2405.14487 (2024)

12. Hou, X., et al.: Large language models for software engineering: a systematic literature review. ACM Trans. Softw. Eng. Methodol. **33**(8), 1–79 (2024)

13. Liu, A., et al.: DeepSeek-V3 technical report. arXiv preprint arXiv:2412.19437 (2024)

14. Liu, C., Xie, X., Zhang, X., Cui, Y.: Large language models for networking: workflow, advances and challenges. IEEE Netw. (2024)

15. Liu, M., et al.: Performance of chatGPT across different versions in medical licensing examinations worldwide: systematic review and meta-analysis. J. Med. Internet Res. **26**, e60807 (2024)

16. Mendonça, N.C.: Evaluating chatGPT-4 vision on Brazil's national undergraduate computer science exam. ACM Trans. Comput. Educ. **24**(3), 1–56 (2024)

17. Mikhail, D., et al.: Performance of DeepSeek-R1 in ophthalmology: an evaluation of clinical decision-making and cost-effectiveness. medRxiv pp. 2025–02 (2025)

18. Raihan, N., Siddiq, M.L., Santos, J.C., Zampieri, M.: Large language models in computer science education: a systematic literature review. In: Proceedings of the 56th ACM Technical Symposium on Computer Science Education V. 1, pp. 938–944 (2025)

19. Ting, Y.T., et al.: Performance of chatGPT incorporated chain-of-thought method in bilingual nuclear medicine physician board examinations. Digit. Health **10**, 20552076231224070 (2024)

20. Xu, H., et al.: Large language models for cyber security: a systematic literature review. arXiv preprint arXiv:2405.04760 (2024)

21. Zhang, J., et al.: When LLMs meet cybersecurity: a systematic literature review. Cybersecurity **8**(1), 1–41 (2025)

Privacy-Preserving Federated Learning via Homomorphic Adversarial Networks

Wenhan Dong[1], Chao Lin[3(✉)], Xinlei He[1(✉)], Shengmin Xu[3], and Xinyi Huang[2]

[1] Hong Kong University of Science and Technology (Guangzhou), Guangzhou, Guangdong, China
wdong768@connect.hkust-gz.edu.cn, xinleihe@hkust-gz.edu.cn
[2] Jinan University, Guangzhou, Guangdong, China
[3] Fujian Normal University, Fuzhou, Fujian, China
linchao91@fjnu.edu.cn

Abstract. Privacy-preserving federated learning (PPFL) aims to train a global model for multiple clients while maintaining their data privacy. However, current PPFL protocols exhibit one or more of the following insufficiencies: considerable degradation in accuracy, the requirement for sharing keys, and the need for cooperation during key generation or decryption processes. As a mitigation, we develop the first protocol that utilizes neural networks to implement PPFL, incorporating an Aggregatable Hybrid Encryption scheme tailored to the needs of PPFL. We name these networks as *Homomorphic Adversarial Networks* (HANs), which demonstrate that neural networks are capable of performing tasks similar to multi-key homomorphic encryption (MK-HE) while solving the problems of key distribution and collaborative decryption. Our experiments show that HANs are robust against privacy attacks. Compared with non-private federated learning, experiments conducted on multiple datasets demonstrate that HANs exhibit a negligible accuracy loss (at most 1.35%). Compared to traditional MK-HE schemes, HANs increase the encryption aggregation speed by 6,075 times while incurring a 29.2× increase in communication overhead.

Keywords: Privacy Protection · Homomorphic Encryption · Homomorphic Adversarial Networks · Aggregatable Hybrid Encryption

1   Introduction

Federated Learning (FL) has emerged as a promising paradigm for collaborative model training without direct data sharing [18,24]. While initially believed to preserve privacy [20,34], recent studies have revealed vulnerabilities in FL, demonstrating that gradients can potentially leak sensitive training data [6,14,25,38].

C. Lin and X. He—Equal contribution.

T. Zhu et al. (Eds.): KSEM 2025, LNAI 15920, pp. 393–404, 2026.
https://doi.org/10.1007/978-981-95-3052-6_30

To prevent data reconstruction in FL settings, researchers have been exploring various strategies, notably differential privacy (DP) [13,16,31] and homomorphic encryption (HE) [7,23,29,32,35,36]. DP stands out for its computational efficiency but may potentially reduce the performance of the FL model.

Regarding HE, although it preserves the model's performance, it may compromise the data privacy of all honest participants if a client conspires with an external attacker to share the key (collusion attacks) [5,11].

To mitigate this problem, Multi-Key Homomorphic Encryption (MK-HE) [7] has been proposed, which is designed to prevent collusion attacks without compromising the model's performance. However, the implementation of MK-HE introduces its challenges, such as cooperation during key generation or decryption processes [26]. These issues underscore the persistent dilemma faced in FL, how to find the right trade-off between data privacy and the practical constraints of model performance, as well as resource allocation.

To address these challenges, we propose Homomorphic Adversarial Networks (HANs), a novel privacy-preserving approach that leverages neural networks to emulate the behavior of MK-HE (comparisons shown in Table 1). HANs are designed to optimize encryption and aggregation tasks without the need for traditional key distribution or collaborative decryption, thus significantly simplifying deployment in FL scenarios. The HANs framework employs an Aggregable Hybrid Encryption (AHE) scheme, which synthesizes the advantages of both symmetric and asymmetric cryptography while addressing their respective limitations in the context of FL. The proposed AHE scheme introduces three cryptographic primitives: *KeyGen*, *Enc*, and *Aggregate*, each tailored to meet the specific demands of distributed training environments.

HANs offer several key advantages over traditional privacy-preserving techniques in FL. Unlike MK-HE, HANs do not require a cumbersome key distribution process or collaborative decryption, making implementation more straightforward and practical. Furthermore, HANs exhibit strong resistance to collusion attacks, even in scenarios where the majority of participants are compromised. The use of efficient One-Time Pad (OTP) and Privacy-Preserving Update (PPU) mechanisms further safeguards sensitive information, providing a robust privacy-preserving solution for FL environments.

Table 1. Comparisons of HANs with other privacy-preserving federated learning Methods

Feature	DP	HE	MK-HE	HANs
Low Accuracy Loss	×	✓	✓	✓
No Key Distribution Required	✓	×	×	✓
No Collaborative Decryption	✓	✓	×	✓
Strong Collusion Attack Resistance	✓	×	✓	✓
Low OTP Overhead	N/A	×	×	✓
Irreversible Ciphertext	N/A	×	×	✓

Contributions. Our contributions are as follows.

1. We pioneered the use of neural networks to emulate MK-HE algorithms, enabling efficient encryption and aggregation in FL through the proposed AHE scheme. In addition, we introduce the PPU mechanism to enhance privacy guarantees. The AHE approach utilizes private key encryption to generate an irreversible ciphertext, providing new insights into neural network-based cryptography in FL.
2. The HANs framework effectively balances privacy, performance, and efficiency by eliminating the need for collaborative decryption and key sharing. Our approach allows for the use of OTP and PPU with minimal cost while ensuring privacy, even if $N - 2$ clients collude with the server.
3. We designed a multi-stage training strategy to balance security and usability. Empirical evaluations demonstrate that AHE-based HANs are practical in FL scenarios, showing only 1.35% accuracy loss compared to non-private FL, while improving encryption aggregation speed by 6,075 times, with a 29.2-fold increase in communication overhead.

2 Related Work

2.1 Privacy-Preserving Federated Learning (PPFL)

Differential Privacy is a frequently utilized tool for privacy protection. These studies [2,13,15,17,28,30] have utilized DP to secure data and user privacy. However, if there is a need to prevent the reconstruction of data, the inclusion of DP can significantly compromise the accuracy of the models.

Homomorphic Encryption enables computations on ciphertexts, producing encrypted results. Several studies [4,8,11,35] have explored its application in privacy-preserving FL. However, traditional HE schemes rely on key-sharing assumptions, assuming no collusion between the *Server* and *Clients* [4].

To mitigate collusion risks, MK-HE allows multiple parties to use distinct keys for encryption, with decryption requiring collaborative involvement. While this approach enhances security, it introduces additional computational overhead during key generation and decryption, necessitating collaboration among clients. SecFed [5], an innovative FL framework, integrates MK-HE with trusted execution environments to improve computational efficiency and safeguard multi-user privacy.

2.2 Cryptography Based on Generative Adversarial Networks

In recent years, the use of neural networks, particularly Generative Adversarial Networks (GANs), for encryption has emerged as a promising direction in cryptography research. [1] proposed a method to learn symmetric encryption protocols based on GANs.

They used two neural networks for encryption and decryption respectively, and introduced an attacker network to evaluate security. Subsequent works built upon this foundational research, further refining the approach [3,21,22,27].

While these works have significantly contributed to the application of neural networks in cryptography, they still face certain limitations. Primarily, they focus on message encryption without addressing homomorphic computation. Moreover, they do not adequately tackle the challenges of key distribution or negotiation, which are crucial aspects of practical cryptographic systems.

Inspired by these studies, particularly their loss function design and the application of GANs in training encryption neural networks, we propose HANs to address the limitations as mentioned earlier and provide an enhanced solution for privacy protection within the FL context.

3   HANs System Definition

We propose HANs, which leverage the AHE algorithm to meet the privacy-preserving requirements of FL.

3.1   Design Concept of AHE

This AHE scheme, tailored for PPFL, uses private keys for encryption and public keys for aggregation, protecting individual client data while enabling efficient aggregation without relying on trusted third parties. The key concepts of AHE are as follows:

- *Public key*: A public key used for computing the aggregated plaintext.
- *Private key*: Confidential key for encrypting original ciphertext.
- *Original plaintext*: The plaintext containing gradient information from a single client, which other clients or servers should not access.
- *Original ciphertext*: The ciphertext that corresponds to the original plaintext and is encrypted by a private key.
- *Aggregated plaintext*: The combined gradient information derived from multiple original ciphertexts and their corresponding public keys. In PPFL contexts, this aggregated plaintext may be shared openly among all participants.
- *Original model*: The initial HANs model distributed to clients by servers or third parties. It is potentially vulnerable to information leakage due to the absence of fully trusted distributors.
- *Private model*: The result of applying PPU to the original model. Each client securely stores their private model, treating it with the same confidentiality as private keys.

AHE primitives differ from traditional cryptography. We will clarify the capabilities and significance of the following attack methods in the AHE context:

- *Ciphertext-only attack (COA)*: The attacker analyzes only the ciphertext, knowing it was encrypted using AHE but without knowledge of the specific HANs model.
- *Known-model attack (KMA)*: Attacker knows the ciphertext is AHE-encrypted and has access to the original model parameters, but not the private model parameters. This corresponds to known-plaintext attacks and chosen-plaintext attacks in traditional cryptography.

– *Chosen-ciphertext attack (CCA)*: Not applicable in AHE as the encryptor cannot derive plaintext from ciphertext.

3.2   Definition of AHE

Here we further define the algorithms of AHE. It is worth noting that both the private and public keys are always real numbers rather than integers. This significantly expands key space of AHE, thereby enhancing the security of the algorithm.

1. $(pk, sk) \leftarrow \mathrm{KeyGen}(\kappa)$. Generates a public key pk and private keys $sk = \{sk_A, sk_B\}$.
2. $c \leftarrow \mathrm{Enc}(m, sk_A, sk_B, \psi)$. Encrypts real number $m \in [-\psi, \psi]$ using two private keys sk_A and sk_B.
3. $m_{\mathrm{agg}} \leftarrow \mathrm{Agg}\left(\{c_i\}_{i=1}^n, \{pk_i\}_{i=1}^n\right)$. Aggregates n ciphertexts and outputs the sum of the plaintexts.

Each private key consists of two real numbers, sk_A and sk_B, generated from a security parameter κ. The aggregated result only reveals the sum of the plaintexts, ensuring security as individual ciphertexts cannot be reversed.

3.3   Usability in Modeling

In traditional HE schemes like CKKS, the error introduced by HE must be relatively small compared to the ciphertext modulus [9]. However, in the context of PPFL, our criteria can be somewhat relaxed. Our primary objective is to ensure that the difference between the homomorphically aggregated values m_{agg} and the actual value m_{real} does not significantly affect the model's overall performance. Specifically, we require the original model to have high performance, so that after undergoing the PPU phase, it can maintain an acceptable level of performance.

3.4   Threat Model in AHE Setting

Attack Process. The adversary aims to exfiltrate the dataset of client D_i through a three-step process:

1. **Step 1:** The adversary intercepts the encrypted messages c_i and public keys pk_i transmitted between clients and the server during the PPFL process. $\mathrm{intercept}(\cdot)$ is an interception method capable of capturing all information transmitted through a communication channel: $(c_i, pk_i) \leftarrow \mathrm{intercept}(\cdot)$, where $c_i = \mathrm{Enc}(\theta_i, sk_{iA}, sk_{iB}, \psi)$ where θ_i represent model of $client_i$
2. **Step 2:** Currently, no existing technology can extract plaintext information by solely analyzing the ciphertext c of HANs. Consequently, an attacker attempting a COA would be unsuccessful. Instead, the attacker would likely

resort to a KMA. To break the ciphertext, they would utilize the original model to train two models $crack_1(\cdot)$ and $crack_2(\cdot)$.

Detailed descriptions of these architectures and information on how to obtain them will be provided in the following section. We use θ_{attack} to represent model parameters cracked by the attacker: $\theta_i^{attack1} \leftarrow crack_1(c_i, pk_i)$ and $\theta_i^{attack2} \leftarrow crack_2(c_i)$

3. **Step 3:** Using the cracked information, the adversary attempts to reconstruct the dataset of client D_i. $reconstruct(\cdot)$ is an algorithm capable of reconstructing datasets based on gradients: $D_i^{attack} \leftarrow reconstruct(\theta_i^{attack})$.

An attack is deemed successful if, upon reconstruction, either one of the two datasets by the adversary is similar to the authentic client dataset:

$$Attack\ successful. \Leftrightarrow D_i^{attack1} \simeq D_i \ \cup \ D_i^{attack2} \simeq D_i$$

It is imperative to note that we protect our private model parameters with confidentiality equivalent to that of private keys. We assume attackers cannot access these private model parameters, just as they cannot access private keys.

3.5 Pseudo N-1 Collusion Attacks

In addition to attacks and challenges targeting the model's inherent encryption capabilities, the unique characteristics of HANs may lead to two types of pseudo N-1 collusion attacks. These attacks attempt to overcome the limitations of traditional N-2 collusion attacks by leveraging additional information to achieve an effect approximating N-1 collusion. However, due to the PPU mechanism, their effectiveness remains significantly limited. The basic attacks are:

1. **Pseudo N-1 Collusion Attack based on Original Model (PCAOM):** In this attack, the adversary uses another trusted client's original model to substitute for that client's private model. This is a KMA where the attacker attempts to simulate collusion among N-1 clients by using the publicly available original model, while in reality only N-2 clients are colluding.
2. **Pseudo N-1 Collusion Attack based on Public Dataset (PCAPD):** attack utilizes the noisy public datasets information generated during the PPU process. The attacker uses this public data to approximate the behavior of another trusted client, thereby achieving an effect similar to N-1 collusion. This is an enhanced version of a COA.

3.6 PPU

To further enhance privacy protection, we have designed a PPU process, which includes two stages:

- **CPPU:** The CPPU stage aims to reduce model exposure risks in multi-party collaboration. Each client combines its private data with noisy public datasets from others to create a noise training set for model updates.

– **IPPU:** In the IPPU stage, clients enhance security by performing multiple independent updates using only private data.

The PPU process balances privacy protection and model performance. Although the update process may lead to a slight decrease in model performance, the combination of CPPU and IPPU effectively enhances the overall security of the system.

4   Experimental Analysis

This section aims to validate the accuracy, security, and efficiency of HANs. All experiments were conducted using an A800 GPU.

To improve experimental efficiency, we ensured that the encryption model structure used by each client was consistent. However, the attacker models were allowed to vary in structure to accommodate different attack strategies.

The encryption model consists of linear layers, convolutional layers, and residual blocks. The initial linear layer expands the dimensionality of the plaintext and private keys, while the convolutional layers obscure the relationship between them. Multiple residual blocks further enhance the complexity of the input transformation, and the output layer compresses the data to the target ciphertext length. The attacker models mirror the architecture of the encryption model, with input dimensions adjusted to accommodate the ciphertext input.

4.1   Training Optimization and PPU Enhancements

For the encryption model, lower **Average** and **Maximum Differences** indicate better performance. For attackers, higher **Average** signify greater difficulty in data reconstruction.

The results show that Atk 1 faces greater challenges in data reconstruction compared to Atk 2, likely due to the added complexity from public key information. Even with increased complexity in Atk 1 (Dbl) and Atk 2 (Dbl), their performance improvements were marginal, suggesting that simply increasing model complexity is insufficient to break HANs' encryption mechanism.

The PPU process further enhanced security. Both CPPU and IPPU stages progressively increased the difficulty for attacker models, as evidenced by higher average and maximum differences. The narrowing performance gap between standard and double versions of the attacks further underscores the limitations of relying solely on increased model complexity to breach HANs' security.

Overall, these results demonstrate the stability and attack resistance of the encryption model across different scenarios, showing that it effectively resists attempts to enhance attack success through increased computational complexity. While these metrics offer valuable insights into model performance and security, they do not provide absolute thresholds for meeting system goals. Therefore, further investigation in practical FL scenarios is necessary to evaluate the performance and security of HANs fully.

Table 2. Aggregation differences and their impact on FL accuracy using the HANs Model

	MNIST	FashionMNIST	CIFAR-10
Accuracy difference	+0.48%	−0.27%	−1.35%
Average difference	0.0047	0.0056	0.0097
Standard deviation of average difference	0.0003	0.0006	0.0016
Maximum differences	0.1219	0.1904	0.2941
Standard deviation of Maximum differences	0.0367	0.0461	0.0623

4.2 Performance and Security Analysis of HANs in FL

Table 2 presents a comparison between traditional additive aggregation and HANs aggregation on the MNIST [10], FashionMNIST [33], and CIFAR-10 [19].

The **Accuracy difference** shows the impact of HANs on model performance. On MNIST, there is a 0.48% accuracy improvement, which could be due to the additional noise introduced during aggregation acting as a form of regularization on simpler datasets. However, there is a slight drop in accuracy for FashionMNIST (−0.27%) and CIFAR-10 (−1.35%).

The **Average difference** and **Maximum differences** quantify the discrepancies between parameters aggregated using HANs and traditional methods. Despite larger differences in some parameters, overall model performance remains nearly unaffected, demonstrating that HANs can maintain strong model performance while ensuring privacy.

To validate the security of our proposed scheme, we employ simple models in conjunction with the original DLG attack. While recent research has advanced to more complex models and efficient reconstruction techniques [12,37], the use of DLG on simpler models is sufficient for our security verification purposes.

We evaluated HANs' defense against DLG attacks using the MNIST dataset, which is known to be vulnerable [38]. The original DLG attacks demonstrated high efficacy in scenarios without HANs protection, whereas the introduction of HANs encryption resulted in the complete failure of dataset reconstruction attempts.

4.3 Resistance to Pseudo N-1 Collusion Attacks

In evaluating the security of HANs, we conducted experiments on pseudo N-1 collusion attacks.

These attack methods attempt to simulate the effect of N-1 collusion attacks, but their effectiveness is significantly limited due to the PPU mechanism. The experimental results show that after implementing PPU, PCAOM has a MAD of 0.31067, while PCAPD has a MAD of 0.30340, indicating that the PPU mechanism effectively enhanced the system's security. Notable differences between the estimated and original values can be observed, ranging from 0.15399 to 0.41589.

This further confirms the effectiveness of HANs in resisting these advanced attacks.

The similar performance of both attack methods suggests that the PPU mechanism successfully limits the amount of potentially leaked information, thereby enhancing the overall security of the system.

Table 3. Performance metrics of HANs (results based on 1000 experiments)

Batch Size	Encryption Time	Aggregation Time	Key Generation Time
100,000	0.019554 s ($\pm$0.001629)	0.017444 s ($\pm$0.000108)	0.000028 s ($\pm$0.000008)
200,000	0.035329 s ($\pm$0.000027)	0.035380 s ($\pm$0.000013)	0.000029 s ($\pm$0.000008)
300,000	0.053281 s ($\pm$0.003922)	0.053462 s ($\pm$0.004456)	0.000031 s ($\pm$0.000012)

4.4 Operating Efficiency

To evaluate the computational efficiency of HANs, we conducted a series of experiments assessing encryption time, aggregation time, and communication overhead across various scenarios. Table 3 shows the performance metrics of HANs for different batch sizes.

The encryption time for a batch size of 200,000 (0.035329 s) is less than 2 times that of 100,000 (0.019554 s), indicating that for smaller batch sizes, the GPU's computational capacity is not fully utilized. Therefore, we use the encryption and aggregation times for the batch size of 300,000 to extrapolate the performance for 3,000 ciphertexts.

Our results demonstrate that HANs significantly outperforms SecFed in terms of computational efficiency. For a batch of 3,000 ciphertexts, HANs completes encryption and aggregation in just 0.00107 s, compared to SecFed's 6.5 s. This represents a remarkable 6,075-fold speedup, highlighting the exceptional computational efficiency of our approach. The significant improvement in computational efficiency comes at a cost, specifically a 29.2-fold increase in communication overhead compared to SecFed.

The dramatic performance improvement can be attributed to HANs' ability to leverage GPU parallel computing capabilities, a benefit inherent to its neural network-based architecture. This allows HANs to efficiently process large volumes of parameters simultaneously, resulting in significantly reduced computation time.

While these results are promising, it is essential to acknowledge the inherent limitations in our comparative analysis. As the pioneering approach using neural networks for MK-HE, our comparison with traditional methods encounters certain constraints. The reported 6.5-second runtime for SecFed may underestimate its operational complexity, as additional procedures, such as multiple refresh operations, could potentially extend its execution time, potentially amplifying

HANs' efficiency gains. Conversely, the lack of information about SecFed's GPU acceleration capabilities, and the potential challenges in adapting their scheme to GPU, prevents us from replicating their results in an equivalent computing environment, introducing some uncertainty into comparative findings.

5 Conclusion

This work introduces Homomorphic Adversarial Networks (HANs) with Aggregatable Hybrid Encryption for Privacy-Preserving Federated Learning (PPFL). HANs leverage neural networks to emulate multi-key homomorphic encryption, offering a novel approach that balances privacy, performance, and efficiency. Our method enables independent key generation and aggregation without collaborative decryption, while resisting N-2 client collusion. The innovative Privacy-Preserving Update mechanism enhances security through private model updates, effectively mitigating potential vulnerabilities in the initial public model. Experimental results demonstrate HANs' ability to maintain model accuracy within 1.35% of non-private federated learning. HANs also significantly outperform traditional multi-key homomorphic encryption schemes, achieving a 6,075-fold increase in computational efficiency. The introduction of these neural network-based protocols not only improves the practical implementation of PPFL but also opens new research directions in federated learning privacy protocols and neural network-based cryptography.

Acknowledgements. This work was supported by the National Natural Science Foundation of China under Grant 62402109, Grant 62425205, Grant U21A20466, Grant 62372108, and Education Bureau of Guangzhou Municipality under Grant 2024312049.

References

1. Abadi, M., Andersen, D.G.: Learning to protect communications with adversarial neural cryptography. arXiv preprint arXiv:1610.06918 (2016)
2. Abadi, M., et al.: Deep learning with differential privacy. In: Proceedings of the 2016 ACM SIGSAC Conference on Computer and Communications Security, pp. 308–318 (2016)
3. An, Y., Zebing, H., Cai, H., Ji, Z.: CNNs-based end-to-end asymmetric encrypted communication system. Intell. Converged Netw. 4(4), 313–325 (2023)
4. Aono, Y., Hayashi, T., Wang, L., Moriai, S., et al.: Privacy-preserving deep learning via additively homomorphic encryption. IEEE Trans. Inf. Forensics Secur. **13**(5), 1333–1345 (2017)
5. Cai, Y., Ding, W., Xiao, Y., Yan, Z., Liu, X., Wan, Z.: SecFed: a secure and efficient federated learning based on multi-key homomorphic encryption. IEEE Trans. Dependable Secure Comput. **21**, 3817–3833 (2023)
6. Carlini, N., Chien, S., Nasr, M., Song, S., Terzis, A., Tramer, F.: Membership inference attacks from first principles. In: 2022 IEEE Symposium on Security and Privacy (SP), pp. 1897–1914. IEEE (2022)

7. Chen, H., Dai, W., Kim, M., Song, Y.: Efficient multi-key homomorphic encryption with packed ciphertexts with application to oblivious neural network inference. In: Proceedings of the 2019 ACM SIGSAC Conference on Computer and Communications Security, pp. 395–412 (2019)
8. Chen, Y., Qin, X., Wang, J., Chaohui, Yu., Gao, W.: FedHealth: a federated transfer learning framework for wearable healthcare. IEEE Intell. Syst. $35(4)$, 83–93 (2020)
9. Cheon, J.H., Kim, A., Kim, M., Song, Y.: Homomorphic encryption for arithmetic of approximate numbers. In: Takagi, T., Peyrin, T. (eds.) ASIACRYPT 2017. LNCS, vol. 10624, pp. 409–437. Springer, Cham (2017). https://doi.org/10.1007/978-3-319-70694-8_15
10. Deng, L.: The MNIST database of handwritten digit images for machine learning research. IEEE Signal Process. Mag. $29(6)$, 141–142 (2012)
11. Fang, H., Qian, Q.: Privacy preserving machine learning with homomorphic encryption and federated learning. Future Internet $13(4)$, 94 (2021)
12. Geiping, J., Bauermeister, H., Dröge, H., Moeller, M.: Inverting gradients-how easy is it to break privacy in federated learning? Adv. Neural. Inf. Process. Syst. 33, 16937–16947 (2020)
13. Geyer, R.C., Klein, T., Nabi, M.: Differentially private federated learning: a client level perspective. arXiv preprint arXiv:1712.07557 (2017)
14. Hitaj, B., Ateniese, G., Perez-Cruz, F.: Deep models under the GAN: information leakage from collaborative deep learning. In: Proceedings of the 2017 ACM SIGSAC Conference on Computer and Communications Security, pp. 603–618 (2017)
15. Rui, H., Guo, Y., Li, H., Pei, Q., Gong, Y.: Personalized federated learning with differential privacy. IEEE Internet Things J. $7(10)$, 9530–9539 (2020)
16. Iyengar, R., Near, J.P., Song, D., Thakkar, O., Thakurta, A., Wang, L.: Towards practical differentially private convex optimization. In: 2019 IEEE Symposium on Security and Privacy (SP), pp. 299–316. IEEE (2019)
17. Kim, M., Günlü, O., Schaefer, R.F.: Federated learning with local differential privacy: trade-offs between privacy, utility, and communication. In: ICASSP 2021-2021 IEEE International Conference on Acoustics, Speech and Signal Processing (ICASSP), pp. 2650–2654. IEEE (2021)
18. Konečný, J., McMahan, H.B., Ramage, D., Richtárik, P.: Federated optimization: distributed machine learning for on-device intelligence. arXiv preprint arXiv:1610.02527 (2016)
19. Krizhevsky, A., Hinton, G., et al.: Learning Multiple Layers of Features from tiny Images (2009)
20. Qinbin Li, Q., et al.: A survey on federated learning systems: vision, hype and reality for data privacy and protection. IEEE Trans. Knowl. Data Eng. 35, 3347–3366 (2021)
21. Li, Z., Yang, X., Shen, K., Zhu, R., Jiang, J.: Information encryption communication system based on the adversarial networks foundation. Neurocomputing 415, 347–357 (2020)
22. Luo, X., Chen, Z., Tao, M., Yang, F.: Encrypted semantic communication using adversarial training for privacy preserving. IEEE Commun. Lett. $27(6)$, 1486–1490 (2023)
23. Madi, A., Stan, O., Mayoue, A., Grivet-Sébert, A., Gouy-Pailler, C., Sirdey, R.: A secure federated learning framework using homomorphic encryption and verifiable computing. In: 2021 Reconciling Data Analytics, Automation, Privacy, and Security: A Big Data Challenge (RDAAPS), pp. 1–8. IEEE (2021)

24. McMahan, B., Moore, E., Ramage, D., Hampson, S., y Arcas, B.A.: Communication-efficient learning of deep networks from decentralized data. In: Artificial Intelligence and Statistics, pp. 1273–1282. PMLR (2017)

25. Melis, L., Song, C., De Cristofaro, E., Shmatikov, V.: Exploiting unintended feature leakage in collaborative learning. In: 2019 IEEE Symposium on Security and Privacy (SP), pp. 691–706. IEEE (2019)

26. Park, J., Lim, H.: Privacy-preserving federated learning using homomorphic encryption with different encryption keys. In: 2022 13th International Conference on Information and Communication Technology Convergence (ICTC), pp. 1869–1871. IEEE (2022)

27. Pattanayak, S., Ludwig, S.A.: Encryption based on neural cryptography. In: Abraham, A., Muhuri, P.K., Muda, A.K., Gandhi, N. (eds.) HIS 2017. AISC, vol. 734, pp. 321–330. Springer, Cham (2018). https://doi.org/10.1007/978-3-319-76351-4_33

28. Rahman, M.A., Rahman, T., Laganière, R., Mohammed, N., Wang, Y.: Membership inference attack against differentially private deep learning model. Trans. Data Priv. **11**(1), 61–79 (2018)

29. Shi, Z., Yang, Z., Hassan, A., Li, F., Ding, X.: A privacy preserving federated learning scheme using homomorphic encryption and secret sharing. Telecommun. Syst. **82**(3), 419–433 (2023)

30. Triastcyn, A., Faltings, B.: Federated learning with Bayesian differential privacy. In: 2019 IEEE International Conference on Big Data (Big Data), pp. 2587–2596. IEEE (2019)

31. Wei, K., et al.: Federated learning with differential privacy: Algorithms and performance analysis. IEEE Trans. Inf. Forensics Secur. **15**, 3454–3469 (2020)

32. Wibawa, F., Catak, F.O., Kuzlu, M., Sarp, S., Cali, U.: Homomorphic encryption and federated learning based privacy-preserving CNN training: Covid-19 detection use-case. In: Proceedings of the 2022 European Interdisciplinary Cybersecurity Conference, pp. 85–90 (2022)

33. Xiao, H., Rasul, K., Vollgraf, R.: Fashion-MNIST: a novel image dataset for benchmarking machine learning algorithms. arXiv preprint arXiv:1708.07747 (2017)

34. Yang, Q., Liu, Y., Chen, T., Tong, Y.: Federated machine learning: concept and applications. ACM Trans. Intell. Syst. Technol. (TIST) **10**(2), 1–19 (2019)

35. Zhang, C., Li, S., Xia, J., Wang, W., Yan, F., Liu, Y.: {BatchCrypt}: efficient homomorphic encryption for {Cross-Silo} federated learning. In: 2020 USENIX Annual Technical Conference (USENIX ATC 20), pp. 493–506 (2020)

36. Zhang, X., Fu, A., Wang, H., Zhou, C., Chen, Z.: A privacy-preserving and verifiable federated learning scheme. In: ICC 2020-2020 IEEE International Conference on Communications (ICC), pp. 1–6. IEEE (2020)

37. Zhao, B., Mopuri, K.R., Bilen, H.: IDLG: Improved Deep Leakage from Gradients. arXiv preprint arXiv:2001.02610 (2020)

38. Zhu, L., Liu, Z., Han, S.: Deep leakage from gradients. In: Advances in Neural Information Processing Systems, vol. 32. Curran Associates Inc. (2019)

SoMORE: Social Context-Aware MLLM
for Video Character Search

Xin Kou[1], Wenjun Peng[2], and Tong Xu[1]([envelope])

[1] State Key Laboratory of Cognitive Intelligence, University of Science and
Technology of China, Hefei, China
xink@mail.ustc.edu.cn, tongxu@ustc.edu.cn
[2] Alibaba Group, Hang Zhou, China
pengwj@mail.ustc.edu.cn

Abstract. Video character search is a fundamental yet challenging task
in video understanding due to pose variations, occlusions, and style differences that reduce feature discriminability. Existing techniques are often
constrained by traditional training and testing frameworks as well as
homogeneous training data. These methods fail to capture the identity
information embedded in the high-level semantics of complex or cross-
domain, which means statistical distribution discrepancy between queries
and training corpus, scenarios, leading to significant performance degradation. The emergence of multimodal large language models (MLLMs)
has introduced a potential solution to this problem. Although MLLMs
are not particularly adept at person retrieval due to differences in pre-
training tasks, their powerful general semantic understanding and reasoning capabilities can aid in exploring identity information in complex social scenarios. Building on this, we propose a novel framework,
Social MultimOdal RE-identification (SoMORE). Specifically, we guide
the MLLM to extract visual features of individuals that are highly relevant to identity recognition. By leveraging the deep semantic understanding and reasoning capabilities of the MLLM, we then explore the relationships between individuals to provide richer prior knowledge. Ultimately,
these relationships enable us to connect the query individual with the
gallery individuals, aggregating identity cues from related gallery subjects to enhance the robustness of person features. Experimental results
demonstrate that, compared to traditional models, SoMORE not only
excels in complex scenarios but also achieves state-of-the-art (SOTA)
performance on the defined cross-domain problem.

Keywords: MLLM · Multimodal Learning · Person Search · Person
Re-identification · Heuristic Search

1   Introduction

Video character search is a fundamental task in the field of computer vision,
aiming to accurately identify individuals appearing in videos. This facilitates

© The Author(s), under exclusive license to Springer Nature Singapore Pte Ltd. 2026
T. Zhu et al. (Eds.): KSEM 2025, LNAI 15920, pp. 405–416, 2026.
https://doi.org/10.1007/978-981-95-3052-6_31

person-centric video understanding and supports a wide range of downstream applications. Early works [1,2] focused on closed-world scenarios [3] with homogeneous and continuous behaviors, like surveillance. However, with the development of social media and the increasing diversity of video content, a growing number of person re-identification tasks [4,5] are focusing on detecting individuals in more complex scenarios, where variations in target person attributes such as posture, clothing, along with external interferences like occlusion and lighting, often make it challenging to achieve reliable accuracy. Moreover, modern videos exhibit substantial stylistic diversity, and recent detection models often show limited cross-dataset generalizability due to overfitting on stylistic variances. This highlights the necessity of evaluating cross-domain performance, where a distribution discrepancy exists between training and testing data, particularly in open-world settings.

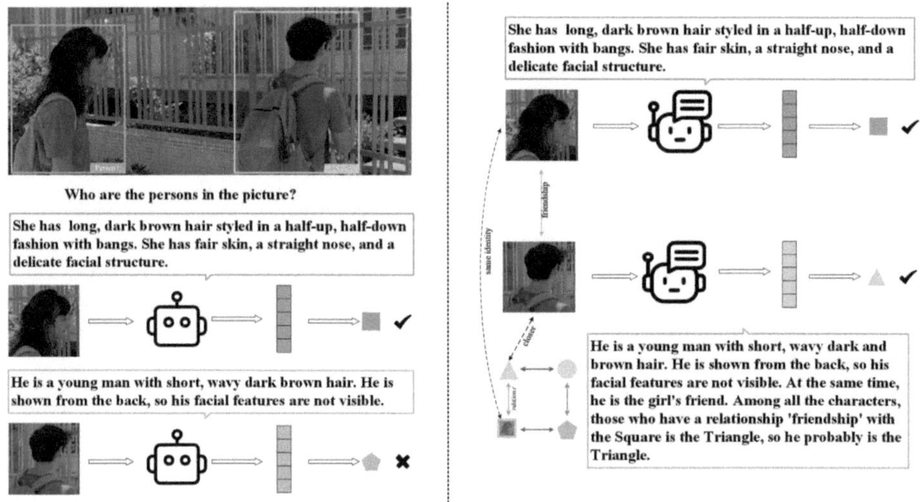

Fig. 1. Illustration of enhancing character representation using social relationships. (Left) Only visual features of the characters are used, and the results are affected by their poses. (Right) Social features are incorporated. Different shapes represent different identities, and solid lines in different colors represent different relationships.

Recent works have improved detection accuracy by incorporating external cues, such as camera perspectives [2] or the influence of clothing [6], but they remain limited by the closed-world assumption. In open-world scenarios, an individual's identity is defined not only by visual features but also by their social identity, such as their profession and relationships with others. As shown in Fig. 1, Person 1 can be accurately identified through visual features, but Person 2 is shown from the back. And we know from the scene that Person 1 and Person 2 are friends, the possible range for Person 2 is significantly narrowed. Traditional methods struggle to comprehend high-level identity information in complex scenarios, leading to generalization gaps in open-world settings. The emergence of MLLMs provides new approaches for exploring the multifaceted nature of individual characteristics, thanks to their strong semantic comprehension and generalization ability. However, directly deploying them for identity-specific detection often underperforms due to a misalignment with fine-grained ReID objectives. Fully leveraging the potential of these powerful models for ReID remains an urgent challenge.

In light of the above, we propose Social MultimOdal RE-identification (SoMORE) to utilize MLLM to integrate visual features and structured social-semantic relationships to enhance identity features in complex scenarios. Leveraging the deep semantic understanding and reasoning capabilities of MLLMs, we are able to explore the relationships between individuals more effectively. By combining visual features and relational information, the resulting identity features are more robust. Experimental results confirm the pivotal role of MLLMs in relational reasoning, enabling accurate identification under complex and cross-domain conditions. Evaluations on real-world datasets validate the framework's superiority in open-world retrieval tasks.

2   Related Works

2.1   Person Re-identification

Person Re-Identification (ReID) aims to retrieve target individuals from videos or images by extracting discriminative identity features. OSNet [1] uses a lightweight CNN with dynamic multi-layer feature fusion to enhance representation learning. TransReID [2] introduces a Jigsaw module for robust features via patch shuffling and a Side Information Embedding module to reduce camera-view variation. CLIPReID [7] further improves multimodal alignment by optimizing identity-specific text tokens, leveraging CLIP's semantic understanding for ReID.

The ReID methods described above predominantly target closed-world scenarios through visual-centric designs [3], leading to suboptimal performance in open-world tasks characterized by complex camera shifts and stylistic diversity. To overcome this difficulty, [5] introduces the Dynamic Relation Weight Module and Co-occurrence Miner to build a social relationship network, demonstrating that social networks play a positive role in identity recognition. Inspired by this, we propose enhancing identity representation by incorporating the relationships between individuals.

2.2   Multimodal Large Language Models

Multimodal large language models (MLLMs) [8–12] extend LLMs by aligning multimodal data into a unified feature space processed through LLMs, enabling versatile cross-modal applications. MLLM-generated representations capture rich semantics and excel in downstream tasks have been demonstrated in [13]. So recent work [14] tried to use MLLMs to solve re-identification task. But they often emphasize the visual comprehension capacity of MLLMs while overlooking identity-related semantics inherent in open-world scenarios. Therefore, we try to leverage MLLMs' high-level semantic understanding capability to extract features from both visual and abstract perspectives, providing new insights into their potential applications.

3   Method

MLLMs have shown strong cross-modal understanding and reasoning capabilities: (1) explicit extraction of fine-grained visual-semantic features, (2) implicit inference of social interactions from context. By combining visual and relational features, we can enhance the robustness of identity representations.

3.1   Overall Framework

In the video character search task, given a video (including frames and text), query Regions of Interest(RoIs) and gallery RoIs, the goal is to retrieve galleries that share the same identity as each query. As shown in the Fig. 2, the proposed architecture consists of three parts. First, the Visual Feature Extraction Module uses MLLMs to extract stable visual features of individuals for subsequent matching. Meanwhile, the Social Relationships Extraction Module utilizes the semantic understanding capabilities of MLLMs to identify social roles and interaction patterns among individuals, selecting relationship graphs among gallery individuals based on scene context. Finally, in the Multi-clue Features Fusion Module, we select the query individual with the highest identity probability as a bridge between the query and the galleries. By leveraging indirect social relationships, we construct a graph that connects query and galleries to get social features. The final representation is obtained by integrating the extracted social features with the visual features.

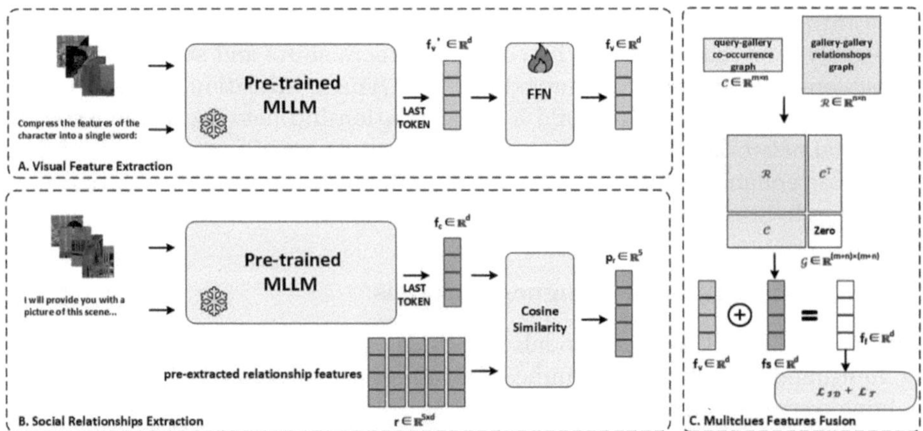

Fig. 2. Overall architecture of our model.

3.2   Visual Feature Extraction

Given the RoIs of the query and gallery, we use a frozen MLLM as the visual encoder. Since MLLMs are not specifically designed for ReID tasks, the features they directly extracts are not sufficiently distinctive. Therefore, we guide MLLM with prompts to focus on key identity-related information, enabling it to extract more fine-grained visual features. We experimented with various prompts from different perspectives. Due to the specific nature of MLLM's pretraining tasks, we found that guiding the model to compress the person's features into a single word yields better results. The prompt is as follows:

Prompt:⟨IMG⟩image⟨/IMG⟩ *. Compress the features of the character into a single word:*

We denote the last token vector of the final layer as $f'_v \in \mathbb{R}^d$. And the final visual representation $f_v \in \mathbb{R}^d$ is computed as follows:

$$f_v = FFN(f'_v) \tag{1}$$

where $FFN(\cdot)$ refers to two fully connected layers with bias terms.

3.3   Social Relationships Extraction

The identity of a character is determined not only by physical traits but also by social interactions. Based on the setup in previous work [5], we categorize all relationships in the video into five types: working, kinship, hostile, friendship and couple. We use a MLLM to obtain relationship features by taking the last token vector from the output layer, forming the social relationship matrix $\mathbf{r} \in \mathbb{R}^{5 \times d}$.

Next, given the background image of the scene and textual information (e.g., screen-bullet comments and subtitles), we concatenate these with a prompt to instruct the MLLM to predict relationships between individuals.

Prompt: I will provide the scene's image, dialogue, and comments. Please figure out the social relationships in it. ⟨IMG⟩ ⟨TEXT⟩

The last token vector from the output layer is taken as the scene's contextual representation, $f_c \in \mathbb{R}^d$. Cosine similarity is then employed to quantify the similarity between each relationship and the scene context. The similarity scores are subsequently mapped to the range $[0, 1]$ to represent the probabilities of different social relationships.

$$\mathbf{p_r} = \sigma(COS(f_c, \mathbf{r})) \tag{2}$$

where $\sigma(\cdot)$ and $COS(\cdot)$ are element-wise operation.

For each video, a predefined social relationship graph $\mathbf{R} \in \mathbb{R}^{n \times n}$ is constructed, where n represents the number of gallery characters. This graph can be extended to a multi-graph of $\mathbb{R}^{n \times n \times 5}$. The relevant portion of the graph, corresponding to the most likely relationships in the scene, is then extracted and denoted as $\mathcal{R} \in \mathbb{R}^{n \times n}$.

3.4   Multi-clue Features Fusion

After completing the two previous modules, we obtain the visual features of the query characters $\mathbf{Q} \in \mathbb{R}^{m \times d}$, the visual features of the gallery characters $\mathbf{G} \in \mathbb{R}^{n \times d}$, and the social relationship graph $\mathcal{R} \in \mathbb{R}^{n \times n}$ representing the relationships between the galleries. Next, we will compute the social features and fuse them with the queries' visual features to obtain the final representation.

We first compute the squared Euclidean distance matrix $\mathcal{D} \in \mathbb{R}^{m \times n}$ between the query-gallery pairs.

$$\mathcal{D} = diag(\mathbf{Q} \cdot \mathbf{Q}^T) \cdot \mathbf{1}_n + \mathbf{1}_m \cdot diag(\mathbf{G}^T \cdot \mathbf{G}) - 2\mathbf{Q} \cdot \mathbf{G}^T \tag{3}$$

where $diag(\mathbf{Q} \cdot \mathbf{Q}^T) \in \mathbb{R}^{m \times 1}$ and $diag(\mathbf{G}^T \cdot \mathbf{G}) \in \mathbb{R}^{n \times 1}$ represent row-wise L2-norm squared vectors, and $\mathbf{1}_m$ and $\mathbf{1}_n$ are all-ones vectors..

To ensure that smaller Euclidean distance corresponds to higher similarity, we normalize $\mathcal{D}$ and take its negative to obtain the matrix $\mathbf{S} \in \mathbb{R}^{m \times n}$.

$$s_{ij} = \frac{\mu_i - d_{ij}}{\sigma_i} \tag{4}$$

where s_{ij} and d_{ij} are the elements of $\mathbf{S}$ and $\mathcal{D}$, respectively, and μ_i and σ_i denote the mean and standard deviation of the i-th row of $\mathcal{D}$.

Finally, a softmax is used to transform $\mathbf{S}$ into a probability matrix $\mathbf{P} \in \mathbb{R}^{m \times n}$.

$$\mathbf{P} = Softmax(\mathbf{S}) \tag{5}$$

To associate query and gallery identities, we select an anchor node (e.g., Person 1 in Fig. 1) from the most similar query-gallery pair in $\mathbf{P}$. Since Person 1 and Person 2 appear in the same scene, the similarity probability between Person 1 and the galleries can be used as the co-occurrence probability for Person 2 with the galleries. Based on this, we construct a co-occurrence graph $\mathcal{C} \in \mathbb{R}^{m \times n}$ and combine it with the relationship graph $\mathcal{R}$ to form a unified graph $\mathcal{G} \in \mathbb{R}^{(m+n) \times (m+n)}$.

$$\mathcal{G} = \begin{pmatrix} \mathcal{R} & \mathcal{C}^T \\ \mathcal{C} & \mathbf{0} \end{pmatrix} \tag{6}$$

In graph $\mathcal{G}$, the second-order neighbors of query nodes encapsulate the potential social features of the corresponding query individual. As illustrated in the previous example, q_1 and g_1 exhibit maximal identity correspondence, and the relationship between g_1 and g_2 is r_i, while the relationship between q_1 and q_2 is also r_i. This social relationship implies that q_2 and g_2 are likely to share the same identity. To reinforce such node similarities, we implement feature aggregation from second-order neighbors using a graph convolution operation:

$$\mathbf{F}^{(k)} = \mathbf{D}^{-\frac{1}{2}} \mathcal{G} \mathbf{D}^{-\frac{1}{2}} \mathbf{F}^{(k-1)} \tag{7}$$

where calligraphic letters represent the adjacency matrix corresponding to the graph, $\mathbf{D}$ is the degree matrix of graph $\mathcal{G}$. $\mathbf{F}^{(k)} \in \mathbb{R}^{(m+n) \times d}$ is the results of aggregating visual features from k-th layer.

Under this setting, $\mathbf{F}^{(0)}$ and $\mathbf{F}^{(2)}$ contain visual (f_v) and social (f_s) features, respectively. Following [5], the final identity features are computed as:

$$w = \frac{p_a}{\sum \hat{p_r}} \tag{8}$$

$$\mathbb{F}_f = w\mathbf{F}^{(2)} + (1 - w)\mathbf{F}^{(0)} \tag{9}$$

where p_a is the anchor node's identity confidence, and $\hat{p_r}$ represents social relationship probabilities. The weight w adaptively balances social and visual features: lower p_a or richer social connections decrease w, emphasizing visual cues.

Following the ReID community, we use cross-entropy loss and triplet loss to train the model.

4   Experiment

4.1   Experimental Settings

Dataset. To address the Video Character Search task, the dataset must include the RoIs of individuals, video frames, textual information, and relationship graphs. Following [5], we use two datasets: Social-Bilibili and Social-Movienet [15]. The dataset statistics is presented in the Table 1.

Table 1. Dataset statistics for SocialBilibili and SocialMovienet

Statistics	SocialBilibili			SocialMovienet		
	Train	Test	Gallery	Train	Test	Gallery
#images	11461	1989	375	14462	5991	79
#characters	325	50	375	59	20	79
#frames	183376	31824	6016	144606	59904	790
#subtitles	53637	9368	1510	49191	21358	282
#comments	184866	32003	6080	-	-	-

Evaluations. We evaluate the model's performance using two widely adopted metrics in re-ID research: Cumulative Matching Characteristic Rank@k (CMC-R_k) and mean Average Precision (mAP). Additionally, to better assess the model's ability to retrieve the hardest positive sample, we utilize the mean Inverse Negative Penalty (mINP) [3].

4.2   Experimental Results

To assess the generalization ability of the models, we evaluate their performance when there are stylistic or contextual discrepancies between the training and test sets by exchanging SocialBilibili and SocialMovienet test sets, which

Table 2. Overall performance comparison between our method and baseline methods on standard ReID task. The best results are highlighted in bold, while the second-best results are underlined.

Method	SocialBilibili			SocialMovienet		
	mAP	mINP	R1	mAP	mINP	R1
MLFN [16]	55.7	34.6	72.0	30.6	20.6	40.0
ResNet [17]	61.2	35.8	82.0	42.1	22.2	65.0
OSNet [1]	64.6	38.2	80.0	49.1	21.2	75.0
OSNet-AIN [18]	65.1	39.7	86.0	45.3	20.9	80.0
TP-Resnet [4]	59.5	36.2	78.0	44.8	21.7	75.0
MLLMReID [14]	57.9	34.7	80.0	45.8	21.3	75.0
NFormer [19]	63.8	36.3	80.0	37.8	20.7	65.0
ViT [20]	76.5	49.1	90.0	59.4	23.0	_90.0_
TranReID [2]	79.9	51.2	90.0	_62.3_	**24.6**	_90.0_
TP-ViT [4]	68.1	40.3	86.0	59.2	24.1	**95.0**
SCPS-L [4]	80.9	52.6	90.0	57.9	23.9	80.0
SCPS-P [4]	81.0	53.1	90.0	58.9	24.1	80.0
SoCo [5]	**82.8**	**56.3**	_94.0_	**63.6**	_24.5_	**95.0**
SoMORE(Ours)	_81.5_	_54.5_	**96.0**	60.0	22.0	_90.0_

is defined as cross-domain performance. **Movinet → Bilibili** refers to using the SocialMovienet train set and the SocialBilibili test set, while **Bilibili → Movienet** denotes the reverse configuration.

As Tables 2 and 3 show, our method matches state-of-the-art SoCo [5] on standard ReID tasks while outperforming existing methods in cross-domain performance. For instance, under Movinet to Bilibili transfer, it surpasses baselines by at least 25.7%, 14.1%, and 22.0% in terms of mAP, mINP, and Rank-1 accuracy (R1), respectively. These results suggest that most traditional models tend to extract features that are heavily influenced by the stylistic characteristics of the specific dataset, leading to considerable performance degradation when applied to test sets with different styles or contexts. In contrast, the features extracted by our method exhibit superior robustness, demonstrating broad applicability for diverse ReID scenarios.

4.3   Ablation Study

Module Ablation Analysis: We conducted an evaluation to assess the contribution of the FFN and social features on the SocialBilibili dataset. Table 4 shows that removing the social features causes performance degradation across all evaluation metrics, which means social context provides critical cues for distinguishing identities in complex environments. Furthermore, FFN alignment

Table 3. Overall performance comparison between our method and baseline methods on cross-domain ReID task.

Method	Movinet → Bilibili			Bilibili → Movienet		
	mAP	mINP	R1	mAP	mINP	R1
MLFN [16]	28.5	32.1	48.0	40.9	22.0	75.0
TP-ResNet [4]	37.2	26.3	46.0	28.9	20.4	60.0
TransReID [2]	50.5	31.0	74.0	38.3	20.5	75.0
TP-ViT [4]	50.4	31.0	72.0	38.4	20.5	75.0
MLLMReID [14]	46.3	28.9	65.0	40.6	21.7	70.0
SCPS-L [4]	52.5	35.2	64.0	36.2	21.3	50.0
SCPS-P [4]	53.5	35.8	66.0	52.4	**23.7**	75.0
SoCo [5]	47.9	29.4	74.0	47.5	22.4	85.0
SoMORE(Ours)	**79.2**	**49.9**	**96.0**	**59.3**	21.8	**90.0**

further enhances performance by bridging the gap between MLLM pretraining objectives and ReID task requirements, optimizing feature adaptation.

Table 4. The Performance on dataset SocialBilibili with different modules.

f_s	FFN	mAP	mINP	R1
✗	✗	76.6	45.4	96.0
✗	✓	78.4	48.4	**98.0**
✓	✗	79.3	48.3	96.0
✓	✓	**81.5**	**54.5**	96.0

Base Model Ablation Analysis: We ablate social features and trainable parameters to evaluate the zero-shot ReID capabilities of MLLMs as visual encoders. The results in the Table 5 show that even without additional training or auxiliary methods, the models still achieve good performance, which strongly demonstrates the significant potential of MLLM for ReID tasks. LLaVA's inferior performance (likely due to lacking Chinese fine-tuning data) and minor inter-model variations highlight the impact of pretraining strategies, like divergent pretraining datasets and task designs, on downstream adaptation efficacy. This underscores the importance of multilingual alignment and task-aware pretraining for generalizable visual representations.

4.4 Case Study

We will demonstrate the effectiveness of our method through a specific case. In Fig. 3, part a) shows the main character relationship diagram from the movie *Se7en*. In part b), there are images and subtitle information depicting

Table 5. The performance of different base models.

Base Model	SocialBilibili			SocialMovienet		
	mAP	mINP	R1	mAP	mINP	R1
Qwen-VL [8]	50.7	27.9	72.0	**44.2**	20.3	80.0
VisualGLM [10]	47.8	**29.6**	64.0	41.7	**20.9**	70.0
Deepseek-VL [11]	**51.0**	28.8	**86.0**	38.9	20.3	**90.0**
InternLMX [12]	43.7	27.5	62.0	34.2	20.3	60.0
LLaVa [9]	28.6	25.3	24.0	20.9	20.2	20.0

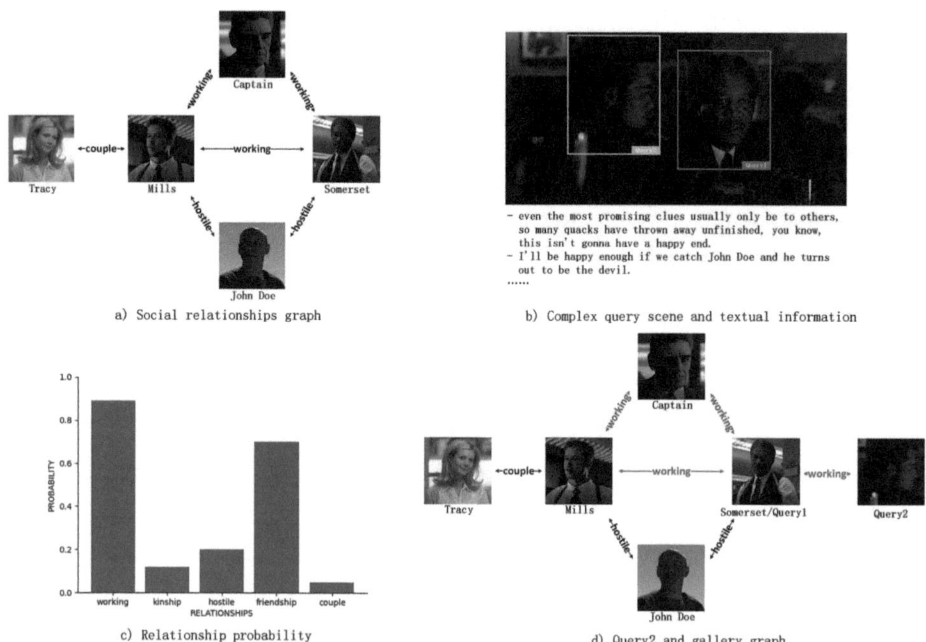

Fig. 3. Example from movie Se7en.

Query1 and Query2 conversing in a room. Since the camera focuses on Query1, visual information confirms Query1 as Somerset, while Query2 appears blurred and difficult to identify. As shown in part c), the MLLM infers that the most likely relationship between Query1 and Query2 is *working*. Thus, when identifying Query2, the search scope is narrowed to characters who share a *working* relationship with Somerset. Aggregating the visual features of these relevant characters as part of Query2's identity features enhances the robustness of the final representation. This method leverages the semantic understanding capabilities of MLLMs; however, it is highly dependent on the context length. When textual information is insufficient or semantically misleading, the MLLM may misinterpret relationships, thereby reducing the similarity between Query and the target

Gallery. The impact of this issue may diminish as the comprehension capabilities of MLLMs improve, but it remains a problem worthy of exploration.

5   Conclusion

In this paper, we explored the application of MLLM in video character retrieval task and introduced a person search framework called Social MultimOdal RE-identification (SoMORE). First, we employed MLLM to generate distinctive visual features of characters and predict relationship information among individuals in complex scenarios. Subsequently, a GNN leveraged visual and relational clues to adaptively weight and aggregate visual and social information, generating robust individual representations. This significantly enhanced the model's generalization capability. Experimental results on two real-world datasets demonstrated that our method outperformed traditional ReID approaches and achieves SOTA performance in cross-domain scenarios.

Acknowledgments. This work was supported in part by the grants from National Natural Science Foundation of China (No.62222213, U22B2059)

References

1. Zhou, K., Yang, Y., Cavallaro, A., Xiang, T.: Omni-scale feature learning for person re-identification. In: 2019 IEEE/CVF International Conference on Computer Vision (ICCV), pp. 3701–3711 (2019). https://doi.org/10.1109/ICCV.2019.00380
2. He, S., Luo, H., Wang, P., Wang, F., Li, H., Jiang, W.: TransReid: transformer-based object re-identification. In: 2021 IEEE/CVF International Conference on Computer Vision (ICCV), pp. 14993–15002 (2021). https://doi.org/10.1109/ICCV48922.2021.01474
3. Ye, M., Shen, J., Lin, G., Xiang, T., Shao, L., Hoi, S.C.H.: Deep learning for person re-identification: a survey and outlook. IEEE Trans. Pattern Anal. Mach. Intell. **44**(6), 2872–2893 (2022). https://doi.org/10.1109/TPAMI.2021.3054775
4. Li, D., et al.: Social context-aware person search in videos via multi-modal cues. ACM Trans. Inf. Syst. **40**(3) (2021). https://doi.org/10.1145/3480967
5. Peng, W., He, W., Xu, D., Xu, T., Zhu, C., Chen, E.: Social context-aware GCN for video character search via scene-prior enhancement. In: 2023 IEEE International Conference on Multimedia and Expo (ICME), pp. 2609–2614 (2023). https://doi.org/10.1109/ICME55011.2023.00444
6. Bao, Y., Zheng, H., Zhang, X., Zhan, K., Zhang, P.: Identity semantic correspondence for cloth-changing person re-identification. In: 2024 International Joint Conference on Neural Networks (IJCNN), pp. 1–8 (2024). https://doi.org/10.1109/IJCNN60899.2024.10651092
7. Li, S., Sun, L., Li, Q.: Clip-Reid: exploiting vision-language model for image re-identification without concrete text labels. AAAI 2023/IAAI 2023/EAAI 2023, AAAI Press (2023). https://doi.org/10.1609/aaai.v37i1.25225
8. Bai, J., et al.: QWEN-VL: a versatile vision-language model for understanding, localization, text reading, and beyond. arXiv preprint arXiv:2308.12966 (2023)

9. Liu, H., Li, C., Wu, Q., Lee, Y.J.: Visual instruction tuning. In: Oh, A., Naumann, T., Globerson, A., Saenko, K., Hardt, M., Levine, S. (eds.) Advances in Neural Information Processing Systems, vol. 36, pp. 34892–34916. Curran Associates, Inc. (2023)

10. Du, Z., et al.: GLM: general language model pretraining with autoregressive blank infilling. In: Muresan, S., Nakov, P., Villavicencio, A. (eds.) Proceedings of the 60th Annual Meeting of the Association for Computational Linguistics (Volume 1: Long Papers), pp. 320–335. Association for Computational Linguistics, Dublin, Ireland (2022). https://doi.org/10.18653/v1/2022.acl-long.26, https://aclanthology. org/2022.acl-long.26/

11. Lu, H., et al.: DeepSeek-VL: towards real-world vision-language understanding. ArXiv **abs/2403.05525** (2024). https://api.semanticscholar.org/CorpusID: 268297008

12. Dong, X., et al.: InterNLM-XCOMPOSER2: mastering free-form text-image composition and comprehension in vision-language large model. arXiv preprint arXiv:2401.16420 (2024)

13. Xu, D., et al.: Large language models for generative information extraction: a survey. Front. Comp. Sci. **18**(6), 186357 (2024)

14. Yang, S., Zhang, Y.: MLLMREID: multimodal large language model-based person re-identification. arXiv preprint arXiv:2401.13201 (2024)

15. Huang, Q., Xiong, Yu., Rao, A., Wang, J., Lin, D.: MovieNet: a holistic dataset for movie understanding. In: Vedaldi, A., Bischof, H., Brox, T., Frahm, J.-M. (eds.) ECCV 2020. LNCS, vol. 12349, pp. 709–727. Springer, Cham (2020). https://doi. org/10.1007/978-3-030-58548-8_41

16. Chang, X., Hospedales, T.M., Xiang, T.: Multi-level factorisation net for person re-identification. In: 2018 IEEE/CVF Conference on Computer Vision and Pattern Recognition, pp. 2109–2118 (2018). https://doi.org/10.1109/CVPR.2018.00225

17. He, K., Zhang, X., Ren, S., Sun, J.: Deep residual learning for image recognition. In: Proceedings of the IEEE Conference on Computer Vision and Pattern Recognition, pp. 770–778 (2016)

18. Zhou, K., Yang, Y., Cavallaro, A., Xiang, T.: Learning generalisable omni-scale representations for person re-identification. IEEE Trans. Pattern Anal. Mach. Intell. **44**(9), 5056–5069 (2022). https://doi.org/10.1109/TPAMI.2021.3069237

19. Wang, H., Shen, J., Liu, Y., Gao, Y., Gavves, E.: NFormer: robust person re-identification with neighbor transformer. In: 2022 IEEE/CVF Conference on Computer Vision and Pattern Recognition (CVPR), pp. 7287–7297 (2022). https://doi. org/10.1109/CVPR52688.2022.00715

20. Dosovitskiy, A.: An image is worth 16x16 words: Transformers for image recognition at scale. arXiv preprint arXiv:2010.11929 (2020)

A Multimodal Feature Fusion Method for Analyzing Children's Interests

Guangjie Chang⬡, Pengfei Wang ⬡, Xiugang Gong$^{(\boxtimes)}$ ⬡, Yikang Liu⬡, and Zhihui Dong⬡

School of Computer Science and Technology, Shandong University of Technology, Zibo 255000, Shandong, China
gong_xg@sdut.edu.cn

Abstract. Analyzing children's interests aids parents and educators in understanding their needs and preferences, facilitating more personalized educational guidance and support. Traditional methods like observation, interviews, and questionnaires are widely used but are subjective, time-consuming, and lack precision. Emotion computing methods based on single physiological features are insufficient to describe complex interest states comprehensively. This study proposes a multimodal feature fusion method for analyzing children's interests, integrating facial expressions, eye openness, expression change intensity, head posture, and EEG signals. A Multi-scale Hybrid Attention Weight Concatenation Network (MHAWCN) is employed to predict interest states. It uses multi-scale convolutional operations and hybrid attention mechanisms to comprehensively extract physiological features. The Attention Weight Concatenation Module (AWCM) adjusts focus on different features, enhancing accuracy and robustness. The algorithm achieved 89.87% accuracy on a self-built dataset and 93.4% on the PAMAP2 dataset, demonstrating robustness and generalization capability.

Keywords: Children's Interest Analysis · Multimodal Feature Fusion · Attention Mechanism

1 Introduction

Childhood is a critical period for individual development, where the formation of interests and learning preferences significantly influences motivation and cognitive growth [1–3]. Research on children's interest analysis aims to enhance educational outcomes and advance intelligent, personalized education systems [4, 5]. Traditional methods like questionnaires (pioneered by Francis Galton [6]), observation [7, 8], and interviews [9] remain widely used but face challenges such as subjectivity, time constraints, and children's limited articulation skills. To address these limitations, wearable devices enabling physiological data collection (e.g., skin conductance, heart rate, EEG signals [10]) have emerged as objective alternatives. However, relying on single physiological features—such as facial expressions (affected by lighting and developmental variability [11]), head pose (influenced by habits [12]), eye aspect ratio (EAR, impacted by blinks and lighting

© The Author(s), under exclusive license to Springer Nature Singapore Pte Ltd. 2026
T. Zhu et al. (Eds.): KSEM 2025, LNAI 15920, pp. 417–430, 2026.
https://doi.org/10.1007/978-981-95-3052-6_32

[13]), or expression intensity (EI, variable across individuals [14])—proves insufficient due to environmental interference, developmental differences, and inability to pinpoint focus objects. Thus, multimodal approaches are essential for accurate interest analysis.

Multimodal feature fusion, which combines data from multiple modalities to boost model performance and generalization, has made significant progress recently [15]. In children's interest analysis, a single physiological feature can't fully reflect interest states, making multimodal feature fusion essential. For instance, EEG signals show concentration but not the specific focus, while head pose indicates attention direction. Frequent head movement or deviation from the activity area may mean distraction. Combining EEG and head pose can more accurately determine if a child is distracted. Also, facial expressions and their intensity offer insights into emotional states, with higher intensity suggesting stronger emotions. Thus, integrating multimodal features enables a more comprehensive and accurate analysis of children's interest states. In recent years, multimodal technology has been used in interest analysis. For example, Ziwang Fu et al. proposed the NHFNet to handle non-homogeneous multimodal information, enhancing low-level visual and audio features via a fusion module with attention aggregation, and then high-level text semantic features using cross-modal attention for effective interest analysis [16]. Wen Zuoqian et al. put forward a BiLSTM-VGG-16 network with an attention mechanism for text and image information analysis in movie reviews [17]. Tan Xiao et al. combined LightGBM and DeepFM to fuse text, image, and structured video features for interest prediction [18]. Taekeun Hong et al. used a CNN model to classify SNS post images and an RNN model to classify text data, combining text and image features to predict user interests [19]. Weiren Hao et al. utilized a GA-BP neural network to integrate children's family income, gender, age, and other feature information for predicting children's interest development directions [20]. Despite its theoretical potential for children's interest analysis, multimodal fusion technology faces challenges like high data collection costs, algorithm complexity, and interdisciplinary collaboration difficulties, and thus hasn't been widely applied in children's interest analysis based on physiological features [21].

This study introduces a multimodal feature fusion approach for children's interest analysis. Physiological features are converted into vectors and input into the MHAWCN, which employs hybrid attention mechanisms and an attention weight concatenation module to assign different weights to various features, enhancing feature extraction efficiency and accuracy. This design boosts interest recognition's accuracy and robustness. The MHAWCN's performance was tested by comparing it with other multimodal fusion models, and it outperformed them on children's interest and PAMAP2 datasets. High-quality children's interest datasets are vital for recognition. However, privacy issues with children's physiological data and the complexity of interdisciplinary research involving psychology, education, and sociology limit relevant projects and dataset development and sharing [22]. This study built a children's interest dataset with physiological features (facial expressions, eye openness, expression intensity, head pose, EEG signals) and interest labels from eight children under 14, totaling 785 entries. Guardian consent was obtained to ensure ethical and privacy compliance [23].

This study's main contributions are proposing the MHAWCN for children's interest recognition, which integrates a hybrid attention mechanism and AWCM to fuse multimodal features like facial expressions, eye openness, expression intensity, head pose, and EEG signals, thus enhancing recognition robustness and accuracy. It also constructed a children's interest dataset with 785 samples containing various physiological features and corresponding interest labels, providing a basis for physiological-feature-based interest analysis. Additionally, by combining psychology, education, and computer science knowledge, this study put forward a children's interest recognition method via multimodal feature fusion. This method converts children's physiological features into vectors for input into the MHAWCN network for interest analysis, supporting the development of personalized educational technologies.

The paper is organized as follows. Section 2 reviews related work, covering the attention mechanisms (spatial and channel) and the method for collecting children's multi-modal physiological features. Section 3 describes the datasets: the self-built children's interest dataset and the PAMAP2 dataset. Section 4 introduces the proposed children's interest recognition network. Section 5 presents experiments and results, testing the algorithm on both datasets. Section 6 concludes the work and outlines future research directions.

2 Related Work

2.1 Attention Mechanism Modules

The channel attention module enhances the feature representation of key channels [24]. Its overall structure is illustrated in Fig. 1.

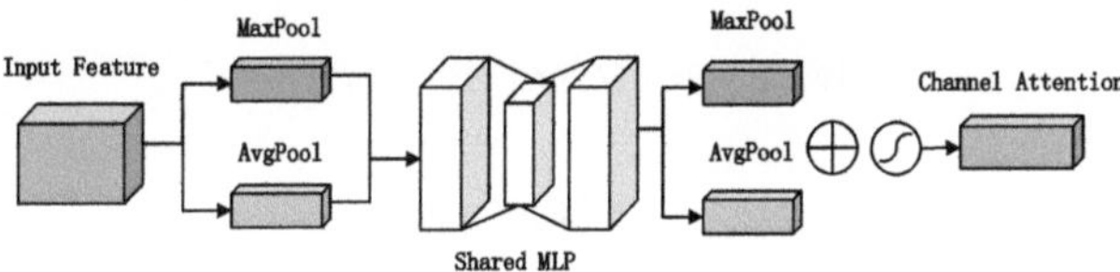

Fig. 1. Structure diagram of channel attention module.

The channel attention module enhances key channels by first applying global max and average pooling to the input feature map, generating two vectors representing maximum and average features per channel. These are fed into a shared fully connected layer to learn attention weights. The weights are combined using a Sigmoid function and multiplied with the original feature map, emphasizing relevant channels and suppressing irrelevant ones. The input F and output $F_{channel}$ are computed as shown in Eqs. (1)–(4).

$$F_{cavg} = Avgpool(F) \tag{1}$$

$$F_{cmax} = Maxpool(F) \tag{2}$$

$$W_c(F) = \delta(MLP(F_{cavg}) + MLP(F_{c\,\max})) \tag{3}$$

$$F_{channel} = W_c(F) \otimes F \tag{4}$$

The spatial attention module highlights the importance of different spatial locations in the feature map [25]. Its overall structure is illustrated in Fig. 2.

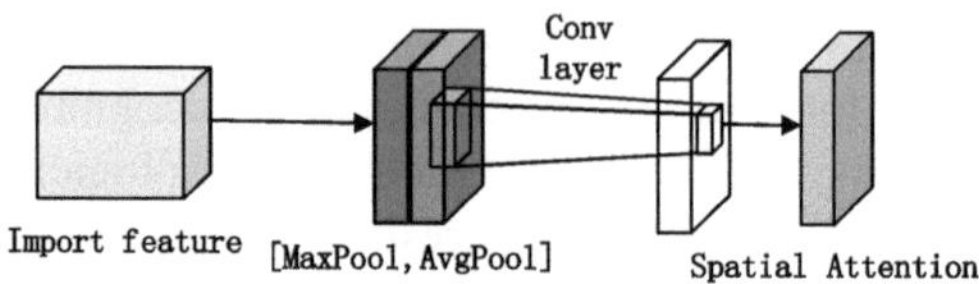

Fig. 2. Structure diagram of the spatial attention module.

The spatial attention module processes the input channel-attention feature map by applying max and average pooling along the channel dimension, generating multi-scale features. These are concatenated and passed through a convolutional layer with a Sigmoid activation to produce spatial attention weights. The weights are applied to the original feature map, emphasizing important regions and reducing irrelevant ones. The input F and output $F_{spatial}$ are computed as shown in Eqs. (5)–(9).

$$F_{savg} = Avgpool(F) \tag{5}$$

$$F_{smax} = Maxpool(F) \tag{6}$$

$$F_{concat} = Concat(F_{savg}, F_{smax}) \tag{7}$$

$$W_s(F) = \delta(Conv(F_{concat})) \tag{8}$$

$$F_{spatial} = W_s(F) \otimes F \tag{9}$$

2.2 Multimodal Feature Collection in Children

In this study, children's facial images were captured by a front-facing camera at 0.01-s intervals. Due to children's activity, some images had off-center or blurred faces. A Haar-based classifier was used for face detection, cropping off-center faces and discarding blurred frames to ensure data quality. The Multi-scale Asymmetric Convolutional Neural Network (MACNN) was employed for expression recognition, which uses multi-scale convolutional kernels and asymmetric layers to enhance feature extraction and robustness. After training, asymmetric layers can be converted to standard convolutions, improving efficiency. MACNN effectively handles the complexity of children's expressions, providing reliable recognition performance. For each valid facial image frame, MACNN identifies the expression and records probabilities for seven basic categories. Every 5 s, the average probabilities of these expressions are calculated and combined into a 7-dimensional feature vector.

The dlib library was used to collect eye openness and expression intensity features. The library's 68-point facial landmark detection model enables accurate localization of facial features. Left and right eye openness (leftEAR and rightEAR) were calculated using the Euclidean distances between corresponding key points, as shown in Eqs. (10) and (11). Expression intensity (EI) was calculated using four key points (40, 43, 55, 49) and is shown in Eq. (12). For each frame with a clear face, these metrics were recorded, and their averages were calculated every 5 s. The averages of left and right eye openness and expression intensity were combined into a 3-dimensional feature vector.

$$leftEAR = \frac{||P_{38} - P_{42}|| + ||P_{39} - P_{41}||}{2 \cdot ||P_{37} - P_{40}||} \tag{10}$$

$$rightEAR = \frac{||P_{44} - P_{48}|| + ||P_{45} - P_{47}||}{2 \cdot ||P_{43} - P_{46}||} \tag{11}$$

$$EI = \frac{2 \cdot ||P_{49} - P_{55}|||}{||P_{40} - P_{49}|| + ||P_{43} - P_{55}||} \tag{12}$$

Head pose is a key physiological feature reflecting attention and emotional states. This study used keypoint detection and 3D spatial transformation to capture head pose data. A 3D facial model with six keypoints—left eye corner, right eye corner, nose tip, left mouth corner, right mouth corner, and chin—was defined. During data collection, the dlib library extracted six keypoints (37, 46, 31, 49, 55, and 9) from each frame with a clear face. Using OpenCV's solvePnP function, these 2D keypoints were converted into 3D head pose information, deriving a rotation vector. This vector was then transformed into Euler angles—pitch, yaw, and roll—representing head rotation. The average values of these angles were calculated every 5 s and combined into a 3-dimensional feature vector as the final head pose representation.

For convenient EEG data collection from children, the Tao Glass Application Module (TGAM), a portable EEG device, was used. TGAM employs a unipolar lead method, placing one electrode on the scalp and another on the earlobe to measure and amplify the potential difference, capturing EEG signals. The TGAM module collects Delta, Theta, Alpha (low/high), Beta (low/high), and Gamma (mid/low) waves, each with specific frequency ranges and physiological meanings. This study investigates the link between brainwave intensities and children's interest. Using the TGAM device, intensities of Delta, Theta, low/high Alpha, low/high Beta, and mid/low Gamma waves were recorded every 0.1 s. Every 5 s, the average intensities were calculated and combined into an 8-dimensional feature vector as the EEG representation.

3 Dataset Description

3.1 Children's Interest Dataset

To address the lack of physiological-based datasets in children's interest analysis, this study developed a dataset capturing various physiological features, such as facial expressions, head posture, eye openness, brainwaves, and expression intensity changes. Following the WHO definition of children (under 14 years), data from eight eligible subjects were collected, including their physiological features and interest states during activities.

To comprehensively consider children's interests and improve the objectivity of dataset annotation, this study adopts judgments from three parties: children, guardians, and recorders. If at least two parties deem the child interested in the activity, the data is labeled as "interested"; otherwise, it's labeled as "not interested". A total of 785 data entries were collected and annotated. The header, data length, and description of the Children's Interest Dataset are shown in Table 1.

Table 1. The header, data length, and description of the Children's Interest Dataset.

Header	Data length	Description
Facial Expression Feature	3	Probability Concatenation of Seven Basic Emotions
Eye Openness and Expression Intensity Feature	3	Concatenation of *leftEAR*, *rightEAR* and *EI*
Head Pose Feature	7	Concatenation of pitch, yaw and roll
EEG Feature	8	Concatenation of Eight Types of EEG Intensity
Children's Interest Situation	1	Whether children are interested in the current activity

3.2 PAMAP2 Dataset

The PAMAP2 dataset, released by ETH Zurich in 2012, is a multivariate dataset designed for human activity monitoring and classification using wearable sensors. It includes data from 9 subjects performing 18 activities, ranging from static to dynamic [28].

During collection, subjects wore 3 IMUs and a heart rate monitor. Each IMU recorded temperature, 3D acceleration, 3D gyroscope, and 3D magnetometer data at 100 Hz. The dataset's columns include timestamps, activity IDs, heart rate, and sensor measurements. Details like headers, data length, and descriptions are provided in Table 2.

Table 2. The header, data length, and description of the PAMAP2 Dataset.

Header	Data length	Description
timestamp	1	Data Recording Time (seconds)
activityID	1	Current Activity
heart rate	1	Heart Rate (beats per minute)
IMU hand	16	Hand Inertial Measurement Unit (IMU)
IMU chest	16	Chest Inertial Measurement Unit (IMU)
IMU ankle	16	Ankle Inertial Measurement Unit (IMU)

The PAMAP2 dataset includes 18 activity types, such as lying, sitting, standing, walking, running, cycling, climbing stairs, household chores, and sports. It has 12 mandatory and 6 optional activities. Due to the dataset's large size and many null values, this study uses 22,590 entries from Subject 101 covering the 12 mandatory activities to test the MHAWCN algorithm's performance.

4 Deep Learning Network for Analyzing Children's Interests

4.1 Multi-scale Convolutional Unit

Multi-scale convolution is a CNN technique that extracts features from images or signals at different scales. It uses convolution kernels of varying sizes to capture both local and global information. A multi-scale convolutional unit has parallel pathways, each with kernels of different scales. The extracted features are combined into a unified representation.

This study develops a multi-scale convolutional framework to efficiently extract key features from complex data. It focuses on four types of features: head pose, eye openness, facial expression, and EEG signals. Convolutional kernels are designed to match the length of each physiological feature, as shown in Fig. 3. Feature vectors are processed using kernels of varying sizes to generate feature maps, enabling a comprehensive analysis of the input data.

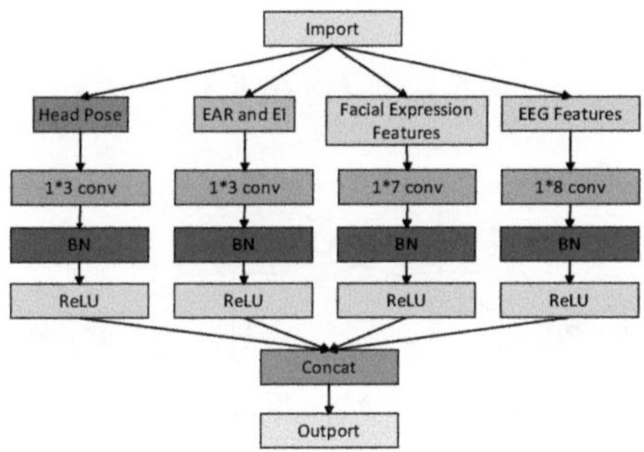

Fig. 3. Structure diagram of multi-scale convolution unit.

The multi-scale convolutional unit features four parallel branches with kernels of sizes 1×3, 1×3, 1×7, and 1×8, processing the input feature vector to extract feature maps that are concatenated for the final output, with computations detailed in Eqs. (13)–(17).

$$F_1' = ReLU(BN(Conv(F_1, K_{1\times3}) + b_1)) \tag{13}$$

$$F_2' = ReLU(BN(Conv(F_2, K_{1\times3}) + b_2)) \tag{14}$$

$$F_3' = ReLU(BN(Conv(F_3, K_{1\times7}) + b_3)) \tag{15}$$

$$F_4' = ReLU(BN(Conv(F_4, K_{1\times8}) + b_4)) \tag{16}$$

$$F_{concat} = Concat(F_1', F_2', F_3', F_4') \tag{17}$$

The multi-scale convolutional unit extracts features at multiple scales from inputs F_1–F_4 using kernels of various sizes to produce F_1'–F_4', which are then aggregated into F_{concat}, enhancing analysis accuracy.

4.2 Hybrid Attention Mechanism Unit

The hybrid attention module combines channel and spatial attention to process 1D features, with SE and SA blocks processing input F to produce output Fout. This structure is shown in Fig. 4, and the computations are detailed in Eqs. (18)–(22).

$$F_c = SEBlock(F) \tag{18}$$

$$F_{c2} = SEBlock(F \otimes F_c) \tag{19}$$

$$F_s = SABlock(F) \tag{20}$$

$$F_{s2} = SABlock(F \otimes F_s) \tag{21}$$

$$F_{out} = F_{c2} \oplus F_{s2} \tag{22}$$

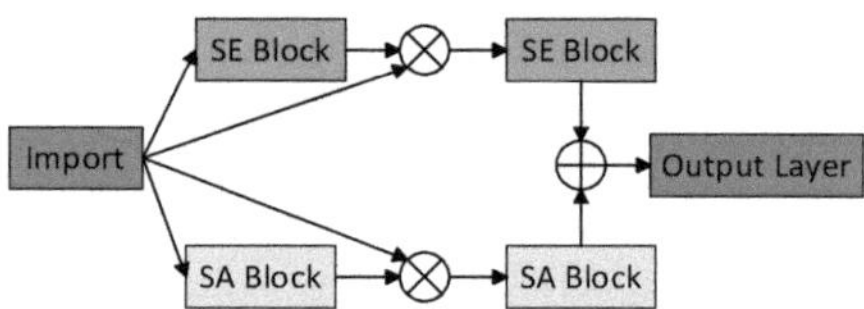

Fig. 4. Structure diagram of the hybrid attention module.

4.3 AWCM

The AWCM enhances the multi-scale convolutional unit by assigning learnable weights to different-path features, focusing on key physiological ones. It initializes weights (all at 1), normalizes them via softmax, multiplies each weight by its input tensor, concatenates the results, and outputs F_{out}, enabling dynamic multi-path info integration. The structure is shown in Fig. 5, and the computation is detailed in Eqs. (23)–(25).

$$a = [a_1, a_2, \ldots, a_n](a_i = 1) \tag{23}$$

$$w = soft\max(a) \tag{24}$$

$$F_{out} = concat(w_1 \cdot F_1, w_2 \cdot F_2, \ldots, w_n \cdot F_n) \tag{25}$$

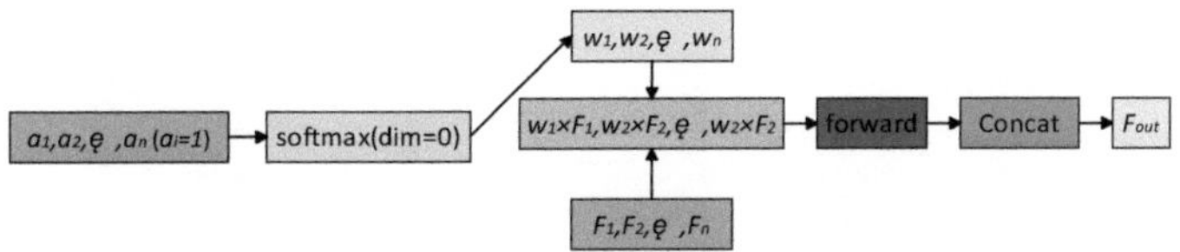

Fig. 5. Structure diagram of AWCM.

4.4 MHAWCN Network

To overcome traditional deep learning networks' limitations in children's interest analysis, such as poor feature extraction and low accuracy, this chapter proposes the MHAWCN. It uses multi-scale convolution to extract physiological features and a hybrid attention mechanism to improve accuracy and robustness. The MA Block is the hybrid attention module, and AWCM is the adaptive weighted concatenation module. The architecture of the MHAWCN network is illustrated in Fig. 6.

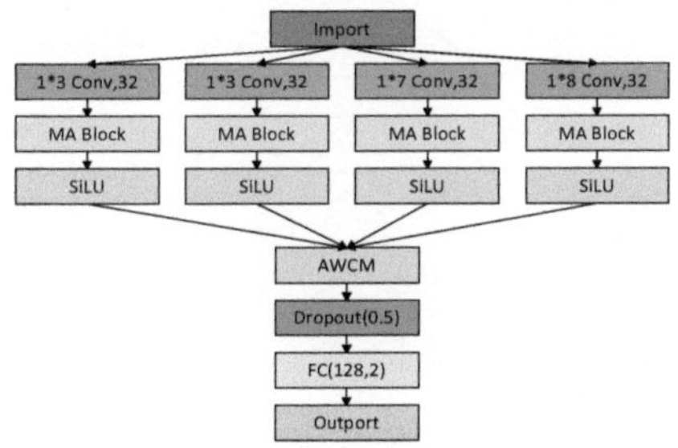

Fig. 6. Structure diagram of the MHAWCN.

5 Results

The algorithm was validated with 10-fold cross-validation on a self-built dataset and tested on PAMAP2. Model performance was assessed using a confusion matrix and ROC curve to tell interested from uninterested categories.

5.1 Experimental Environment

The experiments used Python 3.8, PyTorch 1.7.1, and CUDA 11.0 for model building and training on a Linux system with an Intel Xeon Silver 4114 CPU, 252 GB RAM, and a Tesla P100 GPU with 16 GB VRAM.

5.2 Recognition Results and Analysis of the Children's Interest Dataset

The confusion matrices for MHAWCN and DNN on the children's interest dataset are presented in Fig. 7, with correct classifications indicated on the diagonal and misclassifications shown off-diagonal.

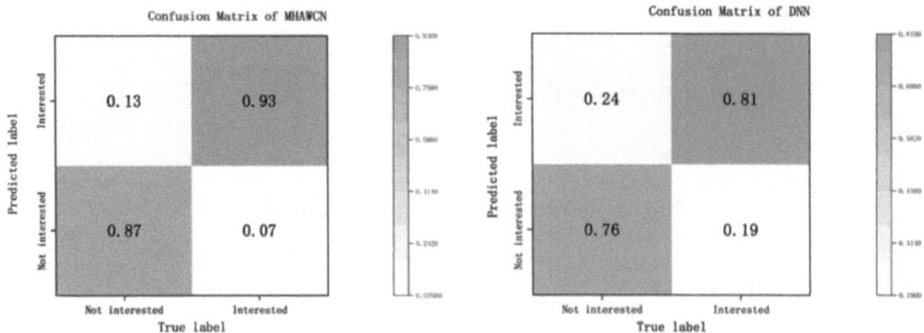

Fig. 7. Confusion Matrices of MHAWCN and DNN on the Children's Interest Dataset.

MHAWCN outperforms DNN, improving recognition accuracy by 11% for "not interested" and 12% for "interested" (Fig. 7), and ROC curves with AUC (Fig. 8) show its better category distinction ability.

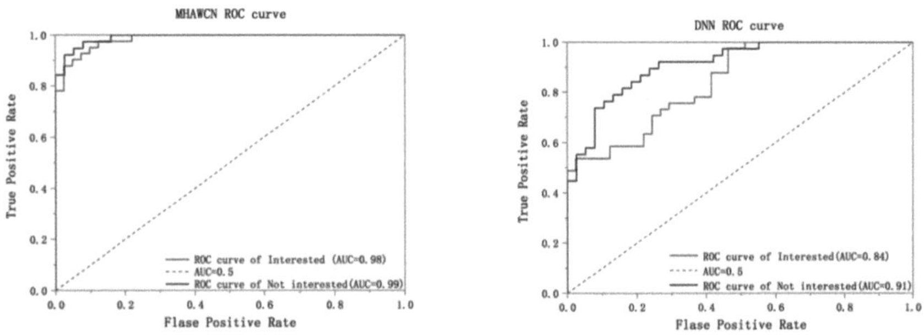

Fig. 8. ROC Curves of MHAWCN and DNN for Identifying Children's Interests.

MHAWCN outperforms DNN with ROC curves above the diagonal and higher AUC (0.14 for "interested", 0.08 for "not interested"), and achieves the highest accuracy of 89.87% on the children's facial expression dataset as shown in Table 3.

Table 3. Recognition accuracy of different algorithms on the children's interests dataset.

Algorithms	Accuracy (%)
DNN	78.48
CNN + RNN	87.34
BiLSTM-VGG-16	86.08
LightGBM + DeepFM	84.81
BP-GA	83.54
NHFNet	88.61
MHAWCN	89.87

To analyze the contributions of different MHAWCN modules to performance improvement in child interest analysis, ablation experiments were done on a child-interest dataset, with results in Table 4.

Table 4. Ablation experimental results of MHAWCN on the children's interests dataset.

Model	Accuracy (%)
DNN	78.48
MHAWCN without MA block	87.34
MHAWCN without AWCN	82.27
Complete MHAWCN	89.87

The ablation experiments indicate that the complete MHAWCN model achieves the highest accuracy of 89.87% on the children's interests dataset, demonstrating that its MA and AWCN modules effectively boost performance.

5.3   Recognition Results and Analysis of the PAMAP2 Dataset

The MHAWCN algorithm was evaluated on the PAMAP2 dataset, with results shown in Fig. 9, demonstrating improved recognition accuracy.

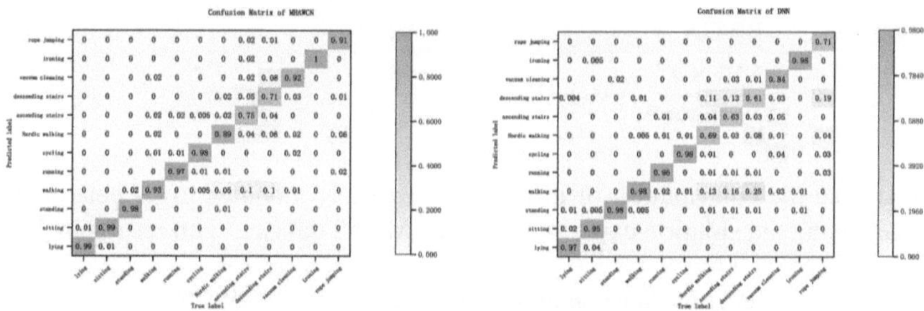

Fig. 9. Confusion matrix of DNN and MHAWCN on PAMAP2 dataset.

MHAWCN outperforms DNN in human activity recognition on the PAMAP2 dataset, especially for Nordic walking and rope jumping, with a 20% accuracy improvement. It achieves 93.4% accuracy, a 5.79% increase over DNN's 87.61%. Figure 10 shows MHAWCN's ROC curve on the PAMAP2 dataset.

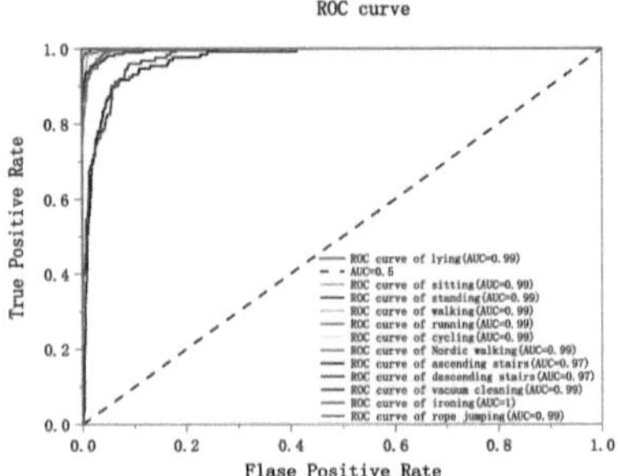

Fig. 10. ROC curve of MHAWCN for identifying PAMAP2 dataset.

Figure 10 shows MHAWCN's ROC curve on the PAMAP2 dataset, with AUC values over 0.9 for all 12 activities, indicating high accuracy. MHAWCN also outperforms other algorithms on this dataset, as shown in Table 5, demonstrating strong robustness and generalization.

Table 5. Recognition accuracy of different algorithms on PAMAP2 dataset.

Algorithms	Accuracy (%)
DNN	87.61
CNN + RNN	92.38
BiLSTM-VGG-16	92.82
LightGBM + DeepFM	93.09
BP-GA	92.91
NHFNet	93.04
MHAWCN	93.40

To analyze the contribution of different MHAWCN modules to its generalization boost, we conducted ablation experiments on PAMAP2 dataset, with results in Table 6.

Table 6. Ablation experimental results of MHAWCN on the PAMAP2 dataset.

Model	Accuracy (%)
DNN	87.61
MHAWCN without MA block	92.96
MHAWCN without AWCN	90.91
Complete MHAWCN	93.40

The ablation experiments on the PAMAP2 dataset reveal that the complete MHAWCN model yields the highest accuracy of 93.40%. This indicates that the combination of MA and AWCN modules significantly enhances its generalization capability.

In summary, MHAWCN uses multi-scale convolution to efficiently extract children's physiological features at different spatial scales. Its hybrid attention mechanism combines channel and spatial attention, enabling the network to focus on both dimensions for comprehensive feature extraction, improving robustness. Additionally, the AWCM automatically adjusts attention weights, emphasizing key features and suppressing irrelevant information, further enhancing accuracy and robustness.

6 Conclusions

This study proposes a multi-modal feature fusion method using MHAWCN to analyze children's interests, integrating physiological features like facial expressions, eye openness, and EEG signals. MHAWCN extracts multi-scale features, combines channel and spatial attention for comprehensive analysis, and uses AWCM to focus on key features, achieving 89.87% accuracy on a self-built dataset and 93.4% on PAMAP2, outperforming other algorithms. Limitations include a small dataset and potential biases, and its complexity may limit real-time use. Future work will expand the dataset, optimize the model, explore more features, and test the method in real-world educational settings for personalized learning.

Acknowledgments. This study was funded by the Shandong Provincial Natural Science Foundation of P.R China (Grant Number: ZR2020QF06), the 2024 Shandong Province Graduate Elite and High-quality Professional Degree Teaching Case Library project (Grant Number: SDYAL2024100), as well as the Shandong University of Technology Teaching Reform Research Project (Research and Case Design on Cultivating the Thinking of Shifting from "Solving Problems" to "Solving the Right Problems") (Project Number: 4053/222063).

Disclosure of Interests. Authors have no competing interests.

References

1. Qi, D., Shen, J.: International and national children development research in the last decade: visualization analysis based on citespace. Soc. Work Manage. **20**(6), 39–49, 59 (2020)
2. Wang, Y.P., Dong, Q.: Research on brain plasticity: current status and progress. J. Beijing Normal Univ. Soc. Sci. edn. (3), 7 (2007). (in Chinese)
3. Tetzlaff, L., Schmiedek, F., Brod, G.: Developing personalized education: a dynamic framework. Educ. Psychol. Rev. **33**, 863–882 (2021)
4. Piaget J.: The origins of Intelligence in Children, vol. 438. International University Press, New York (1952)
5. Vygotsky, L.S.: The development of higher psychological functions. Sov. Rev. **18**(3), 38–51 (1977)
6. Redvaldsen, D.: Francis Galton and the early days of eugenics. In: A History of British Eugenics since 1865. Medicine and Biomedical Sciences in Modern History, pp. 3–22. Palgrave Macmillan, Cham (2024)
7. Westland, J.C.: Information loss and bias in likert survey responses. PLoS ONE **17**(7), e0271949 (2022)

8. Zhang, Y.B.: Reshaping the sociological imagination of the observation method. China Soc. Sci. Today (2020). (in Chinese)

9. Ren, Y.M., Li, R., Tang, S., et al.: Qualitative interview study on public awareness and participation in pediatric clinical trials: analysis of methodological characteristics. Peking Union Med. College J. **14**(5), 1076–1083 (2023). (in Chinese)

10. Olivas, G., et al.: Detecting change in engineering interest in children through machine learning using biometric signals. In: 2021 Machine Learning-Driven Digital Technologies for Educational Innovation Workshop, Monterrey, Mexico, pp. 1–7 (2021)

11. Guo, X.X.: Research on student classroom concentration analysis system based on micro-expression recognition. Master's thesis, Yunnan Normal University, Kunming, China (2019). (in Chinese)

12. Zhang, C., et al.: Multimodal intelligence: representation learning, information fusion, and applications. IEEE J. Sel. Top. Sig. Process. **14**(3), 478–493 (2020)

13. Liang, Y.H., Wu, Q.L., Cao, L.J.: Research on eye state detection algorithm based on multi-feature fusion. J. Comput. Technol. Dev. **31**(2), 97–100 (2021). (in Chinese)

14. Ren, J.: Comprehensive evaluation of student concentration based on machine vision. Master's thesis, North China University of Technology, Beijing, China (2020). (in Chinese)

15. Ni, J., Bai, Y., Zhang, W., Yao, T., Mei, T.: Deep equilibrium multimodal fusion. arXiv:2306.16645 (2023)

16. Fu, Z.W., et al.: NHFNET: a non-homogeneous fusion network for multimodal sentiment analysis. In: 2022 IEEE International Conference on Multimedia and Expo (ICME). IEEE, New York (2022). ISBN 978-1-6654-8563-0

17. Wen, Z.Q., Zhang, Y.H.: Multimodal movie review sentiment analysis with attention mechanism. J. Intell. Comput. Appl. **13**(11), 44–48 (2023). (in Chinese)

18. Tan, X., Sun, Q. M., Qu, Z. J.: Personalized video recommendation method based on multimodal feature fusion. J. Intell. Comput. Appl. **10**(12), 209–213 (2020). (in Chinese)

19. Hong, T., Choi, J.A., Lim, K., et al.: Enhancing personalized ads using interest category classification of SNS users based on deep neural networks. Sensors **21**, 199 (2021)

20. Hao, W., Kong, C.: Orientation and triage of preschool students' interest development based on deep learning model. Appl. Math. Nonlinear Sci. **9**(1), 1–20 (2024)

21. Luo, Z., Zheng, C., Gong, J., et al.: 3DLIM: intelligent analysis of students' learning interest by using multimodal fusion technology. Educ. Tech. Res. Dev. **28**, 7975–7995 (2023)

22. Earnshaw, R.: Interdisciplinary research and development—opportunities and challenges. Technol. Des. Arts Opportunities and Challenges **20**(6), 40857–40860 (2020)

23. Hester, D.M., Miner, S.A.: Consent and assent in pediatric research. Pediatr. Clin. North Am. **71**(1), 83–92 (2024)

24. Hu, J., Shen, L., Albanie, S., Sun, G., Wu, E.: Squeeze-and-excitation networks. IEEE Trans. Pattern Anal. Mach. Intell. **42**(8), 2011–2023 (2020)

25. Zhu, X., Cheng, D., Zhang, Z., et al.: An empirical study of spatial attention mechanisms in deep networks. In: 2019 IEEE/CVF International Conference on Computer Vision (ICCV), Piscataway, NJ. IEEE (2020)

26. Wang, P., Gong, X., Guo, Q., Chang, G., Du, F.: Children's expression recognition based on multi-scale asymmetric convolutional neural network. Int. J. Adv. Comput. Sci. Appl. **15**(7) (2024)

27. Kazemi, V., Sullivan, J.: One millisecond face alignment with an ensemble of regression trees. In: IEEE Conference on Computer Vision and Pattern Recognition (CVPR), Piscataway, NJ. IEEE (2014)

28. Reiss, A., Stricker, D.: Introducing a new benchmarked dataset for activity monitoring. In: The 16th IEEE International Symposium on Wearable Computers (ISWC), Piscataway, NJ. IEEE (2012)

Seaformer: An Adaptive Forecasting Framework for Multi-source Heterogeneous Ocean Observation Data

Yingdi Xu[1,2], Xiang Li[1,2(✉)], Lu Wu[1,2(✉)], Xiaoning Wang[1,2], Zhigang Zhao[1,2], and Jian Zhang[1,2]

[1] Key Laboratory of Computing Power Network and Information Security, Ministry of Education, Shandong Computer Science Center (National Supercomputer Center in Jinan), Qilu University of Technology (Shandong Academy of Sciences), Jinan, China
`1983039949@qq.com`, `W1807291@163.com`
[2] Shandong Provincial Key Laboratory of Computing Power Internet and Service Computing, Shandong Fundamental Research Center for Computer Science, Jinan, China
`{xiangli,wul,zhaozhg,zhangjian01}@sdas.org`

Abstract. Ocean observation data forecasting is crucial for environmental monitoring and climate research. Although pre-training has shown great potential in enhancing model forecasting capabilities and alleviating data scarcity, existing pre-training methods struggle with multivariate forecasting due to the inconsistency in the number and types of variables observed at different marine monitoring stations. To address this issue, we propose a framework, Seaformer, which consists of two key stages: univariate pre-training and multivariate fine-tuning. In the pre-training stage, the model learns general temporal patterns from large-scale univariate data, providing strong prior knowledge for downstream tasks. During the fine-tuning stage, the model leverages a dynamic channel encoding layer and a sparse dependency graph structure to flexibly adapt to varying input dimensions and effectively capture key inter-variable dependencies. Experimental results demonstrate that the proposed method achieves superior forecasting accuracy and strong cross-site adaptability under both sufficient and limited data conditions.

Keywords: Ocean Observation Data · Forecasting · Univariate Pre-training · Multivariate Fine-tuning · Pre-trained Model

1 Introduction

With the intensification of global climate change and marine environmental pollution, the role of ocean observation data in environmental monitoring and ecological protection has become increasingly important [12]. Data such as temperature and salinity collected through ocean buoys and sensors not only can reflect the health of marine ecosystems but also reveal their complex relationships with climate change and pollution. Accurately forecasting these data is crucial for understanding ecosystem dynamics, identifying environmental risks, and formulating ecological conservation policies.

In the field of ocean observation data forecasting, although traditional statistical methods have achieved a certain level of success, they exhibit limitations in handling complex nonlinear relationships. In contrast, while machine learning methods demonstrate better capabilities in processing nonlinear relationships, they typically focus on analyzing individual variables. In recent years, deep learning techniques, particularly transformer models, have gradually become important tools for time series analysis due to their powerful self-attention mechanisms and parallel processing capabilities, which offer valuable insights for ocean observation data forecasting.

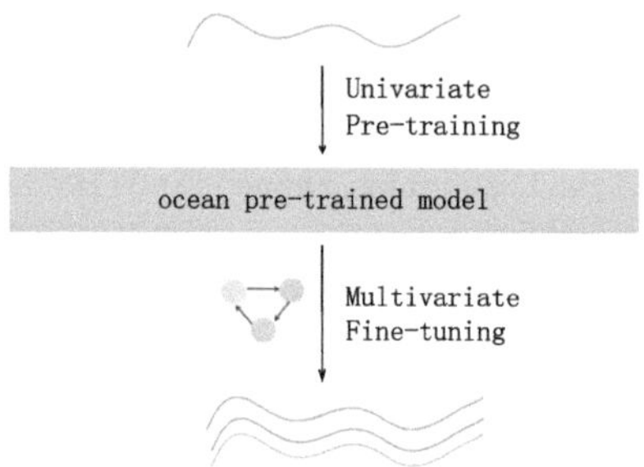

Fig. 1. Workflow Diagram: The framework is first pre-trained on large-scale univariate ocean data to learn general representations, and then fine-tuned on specific stations to capture inter-variable dependencies.

Given the remarkable success of large language models in text and vision, building a pre-trained model for ocean data is both feasible and valuable. By leveraging large-scale ocean datasets, such a model can learn underlying patterns and features, enabling accurate forecasting even with limited samples. However, existing pre-training frameworks typically fix the number of input channels during the pre-training stage, which in turn determines the number of channels in the fine-tuning stage. This design poses limitations for ocean observation data, as the number of variables often varies across different observation sites. Consequently, such approaches usually require building separate models for each site, significantly restricting the scalability and practicality of the models. Additionally, many stations suffer from data scarcity, making it difficult for models trained from scratch to learn meaningful representations, thereby impeding their forecasting performance. In this context, we propose a framework which includes two key stages: univariate pre-training and multivariate fine-tuning, as shown in Fig. 1. The main contributions of this paper are as follows:

1. We utilize a single-channel pre-training strategy, which allows a unified model to be trained across stations with varying numbers of variables, eliminating the need for separate models and enabling effective forecasting even under limited data conditions.

2. During fine-tuning, the number of input channels of the model is no longer limited by those used in the pre-training stage. A channel encoding layer is introduced to adapt to inputs with arbitrary numbers of variables, effectively addressing the heterogeneity of ocean data.

3. We evaluated the model's performance under ample data conditions at five ocean observation sites, and conducted tests under limited data conditions at one site. Experimental results demonstrate superior forecasting accuracy and cross-station adaptability compared to baseline methods.

2   Related Work

2.1   Forecasting Methods for Ocean Observation Data

Statistical models like ARIMA and SARIMA have been widely used in ocean data forecasting, such as predicting long-term temperature trends [5], sea surface temperature changes [10], and significant wave height [14]. Although traditional statistical methods are effective in ocean data forecasting, they are limited by data assumptions and struggle to handle complex nonlinear data.

To address nonlinearity, machine learning methods like Support Vector Machines (SVM) and Backpropagation (BP) Neural Networks have been introduced. Hybrid models combining ARIMA with SVM or BP show improved performance [1,9]. Moreover, Multi-Layer Perceptrons (MLP) outperform ARIMA in forecasting accuracy due to better nonlinear modeling [2]. Although machine learning methods can handle nonlinear relationships, they typically analyze single variables and overlook the complex interactions among multiple variables.

In the field of ocean forecasting, deep learning methods like convolutional neural networks (CNNs), recurrent neural networks (RNNs), and their variants (such as LSTM) have been widely applied, significantly improving the modeling accuracy of dynamic changes in ocean temperature and salinity [6]. For instance, Na et al. combined CNN and LSTM to enhance long-term chlorophyll-a concentration forecasting [8]. Recently, Transformer-based models like Informer [19], Autoformer [13], and FEDformer [20] have shown strong capabilities in long-sequence forecasting.

2.2   Unsupervised Training Methods for Time Series

Common unsupervised learning tasks include reconstruction-based methods. For example, Ma et al. introduced a DAE-based model for learning representations of incomplete time series [7]. Hou et al. proposed a token-based pretraining model that pretrains a transformer encoder using a random masked token strategy to forecast traffic flow time series [4]. Zhao et al. designed a bidirectional transformer encoder to model temporal dependencies in traffic flow time series [18]. Zhang et al. introduced a cross-reconstruction transformer that pretrains using a cross-domain masked reconstruction task to model time series relationships [16]. In addition, SimMTM [3] and UP2ME [17] have demonstrated strong performance across various domains, but they fundamentally rely on a multi-channel pre-training and multi-channel fine-tuning strategy, where the number of channels used during pre-training determines the number of channels required during fine-tuning. Since the types and quantities of variables differ across ocean observation stations, this strategy necessitates building a separate model for each station, which significantly limits its practical applicability.

3   Methodology

Inspired by the above mentioned UP2ME framework, we propose a method that transitions from univariate pre-training to multivariate fine-tuning (Fig. 2). Unlike UP2ME, our approach uses single-channel inputs during the pre-training phase to build a unified model and can adapt to inputs with arbitrary numbers of variables during the fine-tuning stage.

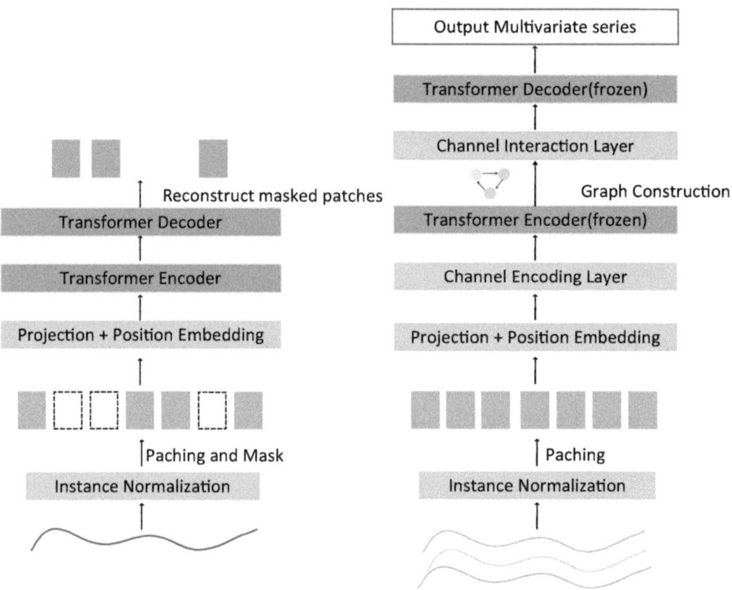

Fig. 2. Model Architecture. Left: Univariate pre-training. The architecture learns temporal representations by reconstructing masked sequences during pre-training. Right: Multivariate fine-tuning. A channel encoding layer and a sparse graph are used to capture dependencies among arbitrary numbers of variables.

3.1   Univariate Pre-training

Addressing the heterogeneity of ocean observation data is challenging during pre-training, so we put off this issue to the fine-tuning stage. To circumvent this problem in the pre-training stage, we employ single-channel pre-training with an adaptable window length strategy.

Adaptable Window Length Strategy. During pre-training, each univariate time series is first divided into nonoverlapping patches of length P. We define a set of candidate patch numbers $\{n_1, n_2, \ldots, n_s\}$, and create separate data loaders for each candidate patch number n_j. Each loader generates data windows of length $L_j = n_j \times P$. During training, a loader is randomly selected from a sampled pool to produce batches of length L_j. To accommodate memory constraints and training efficiency, the pool of candidate patch numbers can either be fixed or dynamically sampled, enabling flexible control over training window lengths and computational resource usage.

Single-Channel Reconstruction Pre-training. The segmented time series patches are embedded into the model's feature space via linear projection, with positional embeddings. Next, a portion of patches is randomly masked, forcing model to infer miss information. The unmasked patches are fed into the encoder to capture underlying temporal patterns. The encoder consists of Transformer layers and models the complex dependencies among different time steps in the time series through self-attention, extracting valuable contextual information. These encoded unmasked patches, along with learnable tokens representing the masked patches, are fed into a decoder. The decoder utilizes the contextual information provided by the encoder and the presence markers of the masked patches to reconstruct the original patches.

3.2 Multivariable Fine-Tuning

During the fine-tuning phase, we freeze the core parameters of the model. By introducing a learnable channel encoding layer, we dynamically adapt to inputs with any number of variables, effectively addressing the inconsistency in variable types and quantities across different observation sites in oceanic data.

Channel Encoding Layer. The model designs a flexible channel encoding mechanism that enables processing an arbitrary number of input variables. Specifically, the original input tensor with shape $[\text{batch}_{size}, \text{num}_{vars}, \text{seq}_{len}]$ is first reshaped into a pseudo-univariate form $[\text{batch}_{size} \times \text{num}_{vars}, \text{seq}_{len}]$, enabling the reuse of the pre-trained single-variable encoder based on the masked autoencoder structure. To introduce variable identity semantics, the model assigns a unique channel identifier to each variable and maps it to a learnable channel embedding vector via an embedding layer. The formula is defined as:

$$\text{Channel\_Embedding}(c) = \mathbf{e}_c \in \mathbb{R}^{d_{\text{model}}}, \quad c \in \{1, 2, \ldots, d_{\text{dim}}\}$$

where c denotes the channel index of the variable, and $\mathbf{e}_c$ is the corresponding embedding vector serving as a unique identifier. During encoding, the model employs a masked Transformer encoder to process temporal patch representations, ultimately restoring the flattened structure into a four-dimensional tensor $[\text{batch}_{size}, \text{num}_{vars}, \text{patch}_{num}, d_{\text{model}}]$, providing a structured foundation for subsequent inter-variable interaction modeling.

Sparse Dependency Graph. During training, we extract the encoded patch representations of each channel and perform max pooling across the patch dimension to obtain a compact representation for each channel. These pooled representations are then used to compute a cosine similarity matrix S:

$$S_{m,n} = \frac{h_m \cdot h_n}{\|h_m\|\|h_n\|} \tag{1}$$

This matrix reflects the similarities among the channels. Finally, based on the correlation matrix S, we construct the sparse dependency graph G:

$$G = \text{topK}(S, rC) \, \Lambda \, \text{KNN}(S, r) \tag{2}$$

where r is a hyperparameter representing the maximum neighborhood size for each channel, and C denotes the total number of channels in the dataset.

Channel Interaction Layer. The channel interaction layer consists of two main parts: temporal dependency modeling and channel dependency modeling. First, standard Transformer layers are utilized to model the time series of each channel, capturing their temporal characteristics:

$$H^{(\text{time},k)}_{:,c} = \text{Transformer}(H^{(\text{channel},k-1)}_{:,c}), \forall c \tag{3}$$

Among them, $H^{(\text{channel},k-1)}_{:,c}$ represents the temporal sequence representation of channel c at layer $k-1$. Subsequently, based on the sparse dependency graph G, the sparse interdependencies among channels are modeled through graph Transformer layers to further enhance the interaction among channels:

$$H^{(\text{channel},k)}_{i,:} = \text{Graph\_Transformer}(H^{(\text{time},k)}_{i,:}, G), \forall i \tag{4}$$

Among them, $H^{(\text{time},k)}_{i,:}$ represents the representation of all channels at time step i in layer k. After $K \geq 1$ Channel Interaction Layers, finally, the deep feature representations $H^{(\text{channel, K})}$ are input to the decoder, generating forecasted values.

4   Experiments

4.1   Experiment Setting

During the pre-training phase, we set the batch size to 128, the learning rate to 1e-4, the dropout rate to 0.0, the patch length to 12, and the masking ratio to 0.5. In the fine-tuning phase, the batch size is set to 16, the learning rate to 1e-5, the dropout rate to 0.2, the patch length to 12, and the number of training epochs to 20. To validate the model's generalization ability, we pre-trained the model using data from 10 sites and additionally selected data from 5 independent sites for testing. The testing is divided into two stages: first, fine-tuning with sufficient data using the full dataset from 5 sites; second, fine-tuning with limited data by selecting one site and using 2000 and 4000 samples, respectively. The experiments cover both single-step and multi-step (12 steps) predictions, with mean squared error (MSE) and mean absolute error (MAE) as evaluation metrics. The experimental environment is based on Python 3.10 and PyTorch 2.0.1, with pre-training conducted on NVIDIA V100 GPUs and fine-tuning and inference performed on NVIDIA T4 GPUs.

4.2   Datasets

Our research is based on the Copernicus Global Ocean-In-Situ Near-Real-Time Observations dataset[1], which is maintained by the French Ifremer Center. This dataset comprises 22 subsets, covering a wide range of oceanographic variables. We primarily use the mooring buoy data subset MO. During the pre-training phase, we selected observation data from 10 sites globally, encompassing various ocean environmental factors such as temperature, salinity, and dissolved oxygen, totaling approximately 1 million records. For the fine-tuning phase, we additionally selected data from 5 sites, including variables such as temperature, seawater density, and chlorophyll, amounting to approximately 200,000 records.

4.3   Results

To comprehensively evaluate the performance of the proposed model, we benchmarked it against cutting-edge time series forecasting models, which include Informer (Zhou et al., 2021) [19], Autoformer (Wu et al., 2021) [13], FEDformer (Zhou et al., 2022) [20], Transformer (Vaswani, 2017) [11], DLinear (Zeng et al., 2023) [15], and SimMTM (Dong et al., 2023) [3].

We first tested these models on single-step and multi-step (12-step) forecasting using sufficient data from 5 sites. Table 1 presents the performance of our model compared to baseline models under sufficient-sample conditions for single-step and multi-step (12-step) forecasting. Bolded values indicate the best results, and underlined values represent the sub-optimal outcomes. From the tables, it can be seen that our model demonstrates a significant advantage in both key metrics, MSE and MAE, whether in single-step or multi-step forecasting. This indicates that our model can exhibit excellent predictive accuracy and stability when handling large-scale data, especially maintaining high performance in multi-step forecasting.

After validating the model's forecasting capability on sufficient samples, we further evaluated its adaptability and generalization under few-shot conditions. We conducted few-shot fine-tuning on station 5 using 2,000 and 4,000 samples. Both single-step and multi-step (12-step) forecasting tasks were tested to assess stability under limited data. As shown in Table 2, the results indicate that our model consistently outperforms baselines in both MSE and MAE.

---

[1] https://data.marine.copernicus.eu/product/INSITU_GLO_PHYBGCWAV_ DISCRETE_MYNRT_013_030/description.

Table 1. Comparison of single-step and multi-step forecasting performance of our model and baseline models under sufficient-sample conditions.

Methods		Autoformer		Informer		FEDformer		Transformer		DLinear		SimMTM		Seaformer	
Metric		MSE	MAE	MSE	MAE	MSE	MAE	MSE	MAE	MSE	MAE	MSE	MAE	MSE	MAE
Single-step Forecasting															
station1	DOX1	0.1751	0.2989	0.0869	0.2090	0.1306	0.2450	0.0292	0.1086	0.0471	0.1282	0.0302	0.1092	**0.0117**	**0.0558**
	TUR4	0.1095	0.1876	0.1609	0.2284	0.1341	0.2043	0.0644	0.1191	0.0817	0.1192	0.0641	0.0893	**0.0560**	**0.0807**
station2	TEMP	0.1583	0.2474	0.1563	0.2410	0.1781	0.2610	0.1289	0.1944	0.1245	0.1636	0.1158	0.1598	**0.1082**	**0.1386**
	PSAL	0.2776	0.3976	0.1331	0.2488	0.3541	0.4365	0.1118	0.2180	0.0997	0.1803	0.0944	0.1768	**0.0772**	**0.1378**
	DENS	0.2417	0.3323	0.2115	0.2858	0.2845	0.3603	0.1722	0.2258	0.1711	0.2034	0.1593	0.1941	**0.1465**	**0.1706**
station3	TEMP	0.3383	0.4302	1.2626	0.9036	0.2489	0.3456	1.0097	0.7852	0.0642	0.2014	0.0269	0.1031	**0.0163**	**0.0879**
	PSAL	0.2563	0.2773	0.2959	0.3220	0.1874	0.1638	0.1814	0.1718	0.1385	0.1085	0.1266	0.0671	**0.1264**	**0.0624**
	DOX1	1.0933	0.8502	0.7834	0.7284	0.4154	0.5087	0.4814	0.5237	0.2197	0.3563	0.1167	0.2462	**0.0914**	**0.2164**
	CHLT	1.5557	0.5470	1.5369	0.3987	1.4157	0.3934	1.4887	0.4201	0.4988	0.2147	0.4177	0.1830	**0.3972**	**0.1562**
	OSAT	1.5310	0.9822	0.6563	0.6643	0.4546	0.5312	0.4176	0.4797	0.2289	0.3644	0.1202	0.2511	**0.0918**	**0.2176**
station4	TEMP	0.0311	0.1344	0.0111	0.0824	0.0361	0.1448	0.0032	0.0430	0.0004	0.0133	0.0015	0.0296	**0.0003**	**0.0118**
	DOX1	0.3609	0.4682	0.1132	0.2588	0.1183	0.2605	0.0349	0.1322	0.0336	0.1215	0.0525	0.1662	**0.0311**	**0.1139**
station5	TEMP	0.0380	0.1441	0.0884	0.2423	0.0555	0.1705	0.0175	0.1008	0.0109	0.0734	0.0045	0.0417	**0.0019**	**0.0268**
	PSAL	0.2824	0.3545	0.5287	0.5201	0.3533	0.4432	0.1700	0.2696	0.2291	0.2942	0.1698	0.2471	**0.0735**	**0.1239**
Multi-step (12-step) Forecasting															
station1	DOX1	0.1889	0.3113	0.0967	0.2183	0.1313	0.2539	0.0484	0.1300	0.0698	0.1569	0.0483	0.1288	**0.0381**	**0.1030**
	TUR4	0.1335	0.2151	0.1672	0.2278	0.1275	0.2018	0.0776	0.1230	0.0920	0.1307	0.0818	0.1086	**0.0760**	**0.0983**
station2	TEMP	0.1652	0.2475	0.1707	0.2513	0.1876	0.2631	0.1446	0.1971	0.1435	0.1845	0.1287	0.1721	**0.1271**	**0.1612**
	PSAL	0.2844	0.3974	0.1573	0.2671	0.3693	0.4505	0.1265	0.2173	0.1278	0.2183	0.1202	0.2112	**0.1042**	**0.1784**
	DENS	0.2532	0.3334	0.2351	0.3003	0.3024	0.3689	0.1971	0.2360	0.1977	0.2315	0.1800	0.2174	**0.1750**	**0.2002**
station3	TEMP	0.3310	0.4225	1.2486	0.8949	0.2616	0.3544	0.5742	0.5685	0.1435	0.3018	0.0658	0.1661	**0.0524**	**0.1508**
	PSAL	0.2299	0.2448	0.3007	0.3257	0.1830	0.1564	0.1707	0.1559	0.1747	0.1371	0.1448	0.0943	**0.1435**	**0.0933**
	DOX1	0.9519	0.7749	0.8571	0.7532	0.4761	0.5419	0.7203	0.6737	0.3606	0.4589	0.2901	0.4017	**0.2664**	**0.3841**
	CHLT	1.5735	0.5087	1.5256	0.3961	1.4582	0.4003	1.4481	0.4170	0.7024	0.2567	0.6365	0.2368	**0.5013**	**0.1931**
	OSAT	1.0048	0.7836	0.7294	0.6897	0.5073	0.5586	0.6833	0.6521	0.3783	0.4705	0.3062	0.4137	**0.2791**	**0.3935**
station4	TEMP	0.0364	0.1441	0.0134	0.0888	0.0391	0.1507	0.0046	0.0503	0.0035	0.0395	0.0040	0.0450	**0.0028**	**0.0338**
	DOX1	0.4571	0.5237	0.2022	0.3320	0.2777	0.3961	**0.1317**	**0.2472**	0.1367	0.2513	0.1477	0.2696	0.1434	0.2521
station5	TEMP	0.0482	0.1613	0.0930	0.2502	0.0709	0.1939	0.0191	0.1034	0.0257	0.1165	0.0144	0.0688	**0.0084**	**0.0540**
	PSAL	0.3818	0.3804	0.6995	0.5476	0.5535	0.5177	0.2471	0.3127	0.3906	0.3473	0.3398	0.3249	**0.2154**	**0.2508**

Table 2. Comparison of single-step and multi-step forecasting performance of our model and baseline models under few-shot conditions for station 5.

Methods		Autoformer		Informer		FEDformer		Transformer		DLinear		SimMTM		Seaformer	
Metric		MSE	MAE	MSE	MAE	MSE	MAE	MSE	MAE	MSE	MAE	MSE	MAE	MSE	MAE
Single-step Forecasting															
2000	TEMP	0.2149	0.3408	1.2414	0.9507	0.1930	0.3023	0.2082	0.3354	0.1085	0.1969	0.0696	0.1459	**0.0070**	**0.0476**
	PSAL	0.6924	0.5773	1.1677	0.9100	1.0393	0.7703	0.6347	0.5683	0.5064	0.4553	0.3382	0.3937	**0.0387**	**0.1058**
4000	TEMP	0.2518	0.3745	0.4894	0.5911	0.3420	0.3986	0.3156	0.4502	0.1105	0.2068	0.0299	0.0990	**0.0131**	**0.0478**
	PSAL	1.6599	0.6153	2.6421	1.1296	2.2088	0.7350	1.0809	0.5476	1.2374	0.5254	0.6057	0.2852	**0.1023**	**0.0870**
Multi-step (12-step) Forecasting															
2000	TEMP	0.2064	0.3381	1.2410	0.9554	0.2217	0.3264	0.2737	0.3561	0.1482	0.2384	0.0966	0.1663	**0.0285**	**0.0850**
	PSAL	0.7725	0.6275	1.2332	0.9395	1.0336	0.7709	0.8713	0.6670	0.6877	0.5431	0.4383	0.4370	**0.1527**	**0.2062**
4000	TEMP	0.3061	0.3993	0.4674	0.5766	0.3595	0.4011	0.2848	0.4182	0.1361	0.2527	0.0435	0.1124	**0.0320**	**0.0827**
	PSAL	1.8539	0.6704	2.5953	1.1137	2.2443	0.7427	1.4277	0.5975	1.6610	0.5783	0.9165	0.3431	**0.4357**	**0.1830**

Bolded and underlined values denote the best and sub-optimal results, respectively. These findings confirm the model's strong forecasting performance and robustness under both sufficient and few-shot settings.

To visually demonstrate the forecasting performance of our model, we conducted a comparative visualization with the sub-optimal method using station 1 as a case study. Figure 3 presents both the single-step and multi-step (12-step) forecasting results for the station. These visual comparisons clearly demonstrate that our model achieves the closest fit to ground-truth values throughout the forecasting process, significantly outperforming the sub-optimal baseline. To further demonstrate the effectiveness of the model under few-shot conditions, we conducted a comparative visualization of single-step and multi-step (12-step) forecasting between our model and the sub-optimal model using 2000 samples. Figure 4 presents both the single-step and multi-step (12-step) forecasting

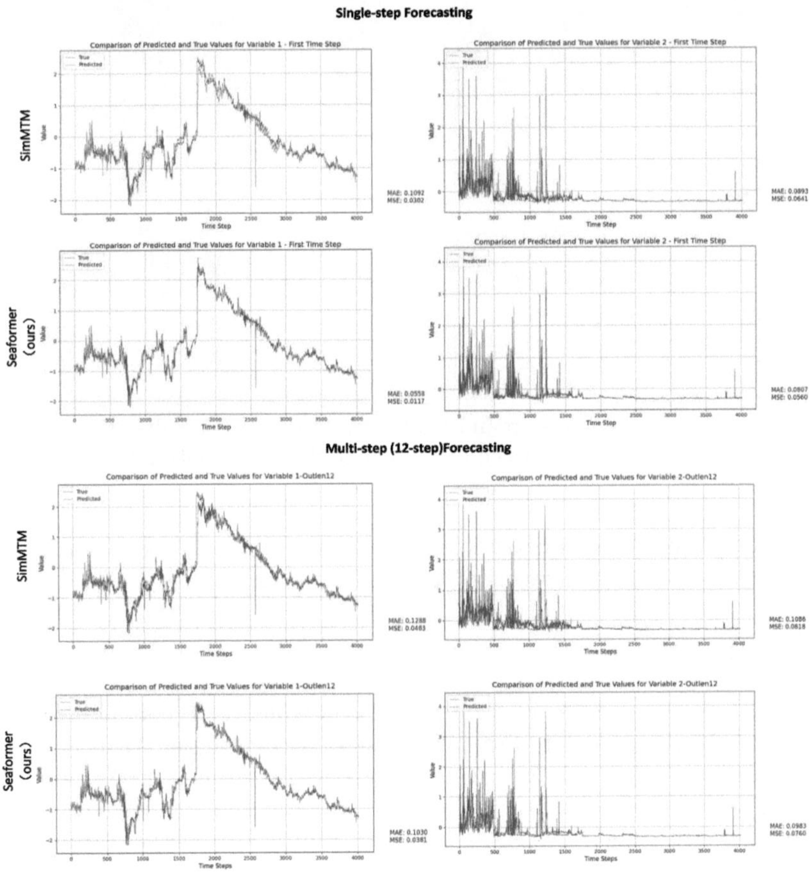

Fig. 3. Visualization of single-step and multi-step forecasting results at Station 1 with sufficient samples: comparison between our model and sub-optimal model.

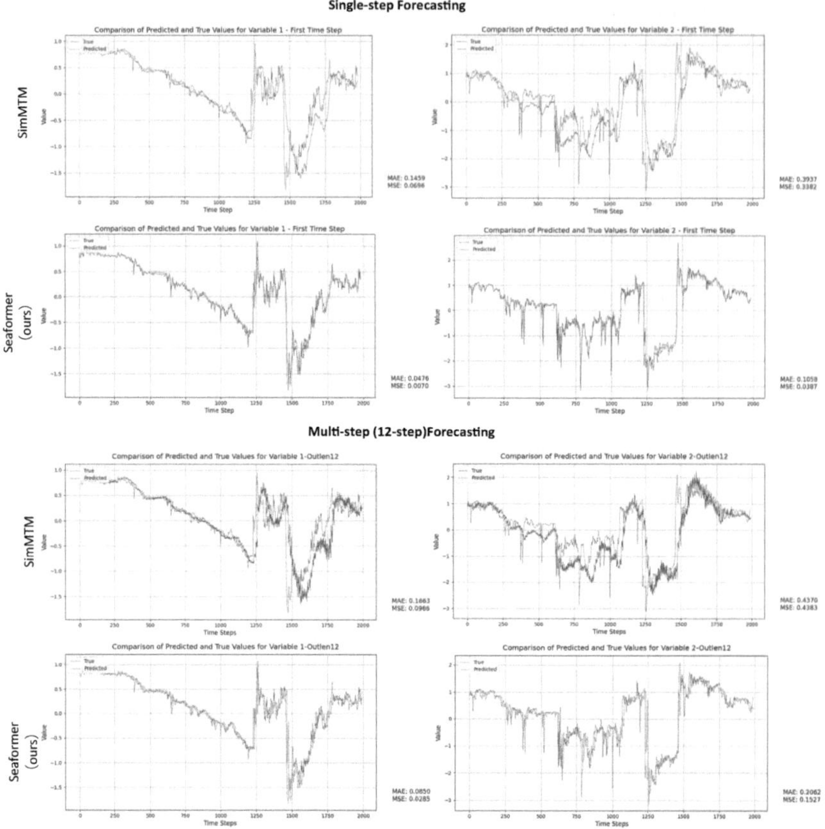

Fig. 4. Visualization of single-step and multi-step forecasting results at station 5 with limited samples: comparison between our model and the sub-optimal model.

results. These visual comparisons clearly indicate that our model outperforms the sub-optimal baseline in terms of forecasting accuracy.

4.4   Ablation Study

To validate the effectiveness of each model component, we conducted ablation experiments. As shown in Fig. 5(a), we compared the average MSE across variables for station 3 between the pre-training plus fine-tuning setting and direct training. The results demonstrate that pre-training significantly improves the model's adaptability and forecasting accuracy. Figure 5(b) further compares forecasting performance under three variable relationship modeling strategies. The model that ignored variable relationships performed the worst, while the sparse graph structure achieved the best accuracy with the lowest average MSE. The fully connected graph structure yielded sub-optimal results. These findings high-

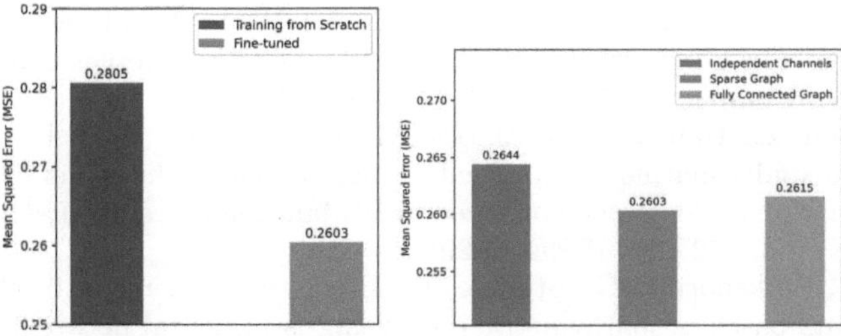

Fig. 5. Ablation study of pre-training and graph structure at Station 3. Subfigures show: (a) Forecasting performance comparison between fine-tuning after pre-training and training from scratch; (b) Comparison of forecasting performance with different graph structures.

light the existence of meaningful inter-variable dependencies in ocean observation data and confirm that modeling these relationships can enhance forecasting performance.

5   Conclusion

Our framework demonstrates strong effectiveness and generalization in ocean data forecasting, particularly under limited data conditions. During pre-training, the model captures universal temporal patterns in ocean data. During fine-tuning, it adapts to varying input dimensions and models inter-variable dependencies. In future work, we aim to scale training to larger ocean datasets and incorporate spatiotemporal features to further enhance performance.

Acknowledgments. This work was supported by the Major Innovation Project for the Integration of Science, Education, and Industry of Qilu University of Technology (Shandong Academy of Sciences) (2024GH24, 2023JBZ02), the Jinan '20 New Colleges and Universities' Funded Project (202333043), the Key Research and Development Program of Shandong Province (Major Scientific and Technological Innovation Project) (2024CXGC010111) and the Taishan Scholars Program (NO. tspd20240814).

References

1. Chen, X., Li, Q., Zeng, X., Zhang, C., Xu, G., Wang, G.: A hybrid arima-gabp model for predicting sea surface temperature. Electronics **11**(15), 2359 (2022)
2. Chi, Y.N.: Time series modeling and forecasting of monthly mean sea level (1978–2020): Sarima and multilayer perceptron neural network. Int. J. Data Sci. **3**(1), 45–61 (2022)
3. Dong, J., Wu, H., Zhang, H., Zhang, L., Wang, J., Long, M.: Simmtm: a simple pre-training framework for masked time-series modeling. Adv. Neural. Inf. Process. Syst. **36**, 29996–30025 (2023)

4. Hou, L., Geng, Y., Han, L., Yang, H., Zheng, K., Wang, X.: Masked token enabled pre-training: a task-agnostic approach for understanding complex traffic flow. IEEE Trans. Mob. Comput. **23**(12), 11121–11132 (2024)
5. Hu, Y., Pan, Z., Han, Z., Lin, Z., Tao, Z.: Forecasts for the fish migration and fishing time under marine environment changes based on the arima model. In: 2020 2nd International Conference on Economic Management and Model Engineering (ICEMME), pp. 352–355. IEEE (2020)
6. Jörges, C., Berkenbrink, C., Stumpe, B.: Prediction and reconstruction of ocean wave heights based on bathymetric data using lstm neural networks. Ocean Eng. **232**, 109046 (2021)
7. Ma, Q., Zheng, J., Li, S., Cottrell, G.W.: Learning representations for time series clustering. Advances in neural information processing systems **32** (2019)
8. Na, L., Shaoyang, C., Zhenyan, C., Xing, W., Yun, X., Li, X., Yanwei, G., Tingting, W., Xuefeng, Z., Siqi, L.: Long-term prediction of sea surface chlorophyll-a concentration based on the combination of spatio-temporal features. Water Res. **211**, 118040 (2022)
9. Nawi, W., et al.: Improved of forecasting sea surface temperature based on hybrid arima and support vector machines models. Malaysian J. Fundamental Appl. Sci. **17**(5), 609–620 (2021)
10. Rosmiati, R., Liliasari, S., Tjasyono, B., Ramalis, T.: Development of arima technique in determining the ocean climate prediction skills for pre-service teacher. In: Journal of physics: Conference series, vol. 1731, p. 012072. IOP Publishing (2021)
11. Vaswani, A., et al.: Attention is all you need. Advances in neural information processing systems **30** (2017)
12. Von Schuckmann, K., et al.: The copernicus marine environment monitoring service ocean state report. J. Operational Oceanography **9**(sup2), s235–s320 (2016)
13. Wu, H., Xu, J., Wang, J., Long, M.: Autoformer: decomposition transformers with auto-correlation for long-term series forecasting. Adv. Neural. Inf. Process. Syst. **34**, 22419–22430 (2021)
14. Yang, S., Zhang, Z., Fan, L., Xia, T., Duan, S., Zheng, C., Li, X., Li, H.: Long-term prediction of significant wave height based on sarima model in the south china sea and adjacent waters. IEEE Access **7**, 88082–88092 (2019)
15. Zeng, A., Chen, M., Zhang, L., Xu, Q.: Are transformers effective for time series forecasting? In: Proceedings of the AAAI Conference on Artificial Intelligence, vol. 37, pp. 11121–11128 (2023)
16. Zhang, W., Yang, L., Geng, S., Hong, S.: Cross reconstruction transformer for self-supervised time series representation learning (2022). arXiv preprint arXiv:2205.09928
17. Zhang, Y., Liu, M., Zhou, S., Yan, J.: Up2me: Univariate pre-training to multivariate fine-tuning as a general-purpose framework for multivariate time series analysis. In: Forty-first International Conference on Machine Learning (2024)
18. Zhao, L., Gao, M., Wang, Z.: St-gsp: Spatial-temporal global semantic representation learning for urban flow prediction. In: Proceedings of the Fifteenth ACM International Conference on Web Search and Data Mining, pp. 1443–1451 (2022)
19. Zhou, H., Zhang, S., Peng, J., Zhang, S., Li, J., Xiong, H., Zhang, W.: Informer: Beyond efficient transformer for long sequence time-series forecasting. In: Proceedings of the AAAI Conference on Artificial Intelligence, vol. 35, pp. 11106–11115 (2021)
20. Zhou, T., Ma, Z., Wen, Q., Wang, X., Sun, L., Jin, R.: Fedformer: Frequency enhanced decomposed transformer for long-term series forecasting. In: International conference on machine learning. pp. 27268–27286. PMLR (2022)

Hybrid Kolmogorov-Arnold and Graph Attention Networks for Gold Price Forecasting Under Uncertainty

Dat Le[1]($^{(\boxtimes)}$) , Sutharshan Rajasegarar[1] , Wei Luo[1] , Thanh Thi Nguyen[2] , and Maia Angelova[3]

[1] School of Information Technology, Deakin University, Geelong, Australia
{d.le,wei.luo}@deakin.edu.au
[2] Faculty of Information Technology, Monash University, Clayton, Australia
thanh.nguyen9@monash.edu
[3] Aston Digital Futures Institute, Aston University, Birmingham, UK
angelovm@aston.ac.uk

Abstract. Accurate gold price forecasting is essential for financial decision making, particularly in volatile economic environments. Traditional time series models such as ARIMA and Transformers often struggle to capture the complex and dynamic dependencies between macroeconomic variables. To address these challenges, we propose KAN-GAT, a novel hybrid forecasting framework that integrates Kolmogorov-Arnold Networks (KAN) with Graph Attention Networks (GAT). The KAN module captures non-linear relationships among financial indicators, while GAT refines predictions by modeling temporal dependencies through graph-based learning. Experimental evaluations on real-world financial data—including gold prices, USD Index, oil prices, and inflation rates, demonstrate that the KAN-GAT significantly outperforms state-of-the-art models, achieving a MAPE of 2.75 ± 0.17, compared to 11.32 ± 15.19 by KAN, 8.22 ± 3.46 by GAT, 9.56 ± 1.77 by N-HiTS, 20.94 ± 9.20 by N-BEATS, and 31.00 ± 1.76 by Transformers. Additionally, KAN-GAT reduces RMSE to 2.94 ± 0.37 and MAE to 2.28 ± 0.15, achieving a statistically significant improvement over baseline methods. These findings highlight the effectiveness of our proposed hybrid approach in financial forecasting and establish KAN-GAT as a powerful tool for capturing complex market dynamics.

Keywords: KAN · GAT · Gold price · Time series · Residual learning

1 Introduction

The global financial markets have experienced unprecedented volatility since 2020, posing significant challenges in forecasting commodity prices, particularly gold [14]. Accurate prediction of gold prices has become increasingly complex due to abrupt shifts driven by economic instability, fluctuating macroeconomic indicators such as the U.S. Dollar Index (USDI) and oil price [10,11]. In such volatile

T. Zhu et al. (Eds.): KSEM 2025, LNAI 15920, pp. 443–454, 2026.
https://doi.org/10.1007/978-981-95-3052-6_34

contexts, traditional forecasting methods like Autoregressive Integrated Moving Average (ARIMA) struggle to effectively capture the intricate and dynamic interdependencies among multiple influencing factors [13].

Recent advancements have led to sophisticated forecasting approaches, such as Transformers [9], Neural Basis Expansion Analysis for Time Series Forecasting (N-BEATS) [15], Neural Hierarchical Interpolation for Time Series Forecasting (N-HiTS) [2], and Time Series Mixer (TSMixer) [5], which effectively capture complex temporal patterns. Transformers leverage attention mechanisms to identify important sequential dependencies but may exhibit sensitivity to abrupt data shifts. N-BEATS and N-HiTS utilize deep architectures to model hierarchical temporal patterns but can require extensive data and computational resources, limiting their adaptability to rapidly changing market conditions. Similarly, TSMixer efficiently models structured temporal data but may lack sufficient flexibility when encountering high volatility.

Literature highlights the benefits of hybrid forecasting models incorporating residual correction techniques to further enhance forecasting accuracy. For example, Iterative Residual Forecasting methods iteratively refine forecasts by addressing residuals from previous models [17]. Hybrid models combining classical forecasting techniques with error correction have recursively modeled residuals, significantly improving forecast reliability [16]. Approaches such as Residual Recurrent Neural Networks (R2N2) integrate linear models with Recurrent Neural Networks, effectively capturing both linear and nonlinear dependencies in multivariate series [1].

In line with these developments, this study proposes a novel forecasting framework that combines the adaptive kernel modeling strengths of Kolmogorov-Arnold Networks (KAN) [12] with the dynamic attention-driven relational modeling of Graph Attention Networks. Graph Attention Networks (GAT) [26] have proven effective in dynamically modeling temporal and structural relationships, offering interpretability through attention mechanisms. However, GAT models can be sensitive to noise and may struggle with capturing intricate non-linear patterns in highly volatile datasets. Conversely, Kolmogorov-Arnold Networks (KAN) excel at modeling complex non-linear interactions due to adaptive kernel-based architectures but lack explicit capabilities for modeling sequential and relational dependencies [19]. Therefore, combining GAT with KAN (KAN-GAT) addresses these limitations by simultaneously capturing complex non-linearities through adaptive kernels and modeling dynamic temporal and structural dependencies via graph attention mechanisms. Consequently, the proposed KAN-GAT framework enhances predictive robustness, adaptability, and accuracy under market volatility and uncertainty, representing a significant advancement over traditional and recent baseline models in multivariate time series forecasting.

The main contributions of this research, specifically focused on gold price forecasting, are as follows:

- **Novel hybrid forecasting model:** We propose a KAN-GAT framework as shown in Fig. 1, integrating Kolmogorov-Arnold Networks (KAN) with

Graph Attention Networks (GAT), explicitly tailored for accurate gold price prediction under volatile financial market conditions.

- **Enhanced forecasting accuracy:** Our proposed KAN-GAT model effectively captures complex non-linear relationships and dynamic temporal dependencies inherent in gold price movements, significantly improving predictive accuracy in environments characterized by uncertainty and volatility.
- **Comprehensive evaluation and benchmarking:** We extensively evaluate the KAN-GAT model against state of the art forecasting methods, demonstrating its superior robustness, adaptability, and forecasting accuracy specifically within the gold price prediction context.

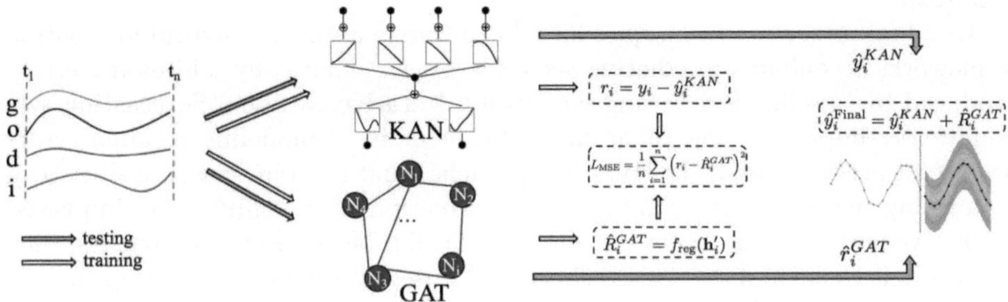

Fig. 1. Overview of the proposed KAN-GAT forecasting framework. The Kolmogorov-Arnold Network (KAN) first learns complex non-linear relationships from multivariate input features—including gold price (g), oil price (o), USD index (d), and inflation rate (i)—to produce baseline forecasts $\hat{y}_i^{KAN}$. The residual errors $r_i = y_i - \hat{y}_i^{KAN}$ are then used to train a Graph Attention Network (GAT), which builds a temporal graph over sliding windows and learns to predict corrections $\hat{R}_i^{GAT}$. The final forecast is obtained by integrating the KAN prediction with the GAT-estimated residual: $\hat{y}_i^{\text{Final}} = \hat{y}_i^{KAN} + \hat{R}_i^{GAT}$. This hybrid architecture enables dynamic error refinement and improves predictive accuracy.

2   Related Work

This section reviews existing literature on Kolmogorov-Arnold Networks, Graph Attention Networks, and residual correction methods in hybrid forecasting frameworks.

KAN [12] have emerged as powerful neural network architectures capable of adaptively modeling complex non-linear relationships in various data domains. Unlike conventional neural networks, KAN leverages adaptive kernel functions that dynamically adjust their shape and scale based on input data, enhancing the ability to model intricate relationships and ensuring greater flexibility and accuracy. KAN has already demonstrated promising results in diverse forecasting scenarios, such as economic indicators, financial markets, and environmental systems [21]. Despite these advantages, KAN models alone are limited in capturing explicit temporal or structural relationships, making them potentially less effective in scenarios characterized by complex sequential dependencies [18].

GAT [20] have gained significant popularity due to their capability of dynamically capturing relationships within graph-structured data through attention mechanisms. GAT effectively learns node importance and interaction patterns, improving performance in various tasks, such as node classification, link prediction and temporal forecasting [25,27]. Specifically, GAT has demonstrated superior performance in capturing temporal dependencies and providing interpretable results due to its attention-weighted structure. However, GAT models can be sensitive to noise and may struggle to accurately model complex nonlinear patterns inherent in highly volatile datasets, such as financial time series data [22].

Residual correction techniques have been widely applied in hybrid forecasting frameworks to enhance predictive accuracy by systematically addressing errors produced by baseline forecasting models [6]. Iterative Residual Forecasting systematically improves forecast accuracy by recursively modeling residual errors from prior predictions [4,17]. Hybrid approaches that combine classical statistical forecasting methods with residual error correction have significantly improved predictive performance across various domains [7]. More recent approaches, such as Residual Recurrent Neural Networks [1], integrate linear forecasting models with recurrent neural networks to effectively capture linear and complex nonlinear patterns, achieving robust performance in multivariate forecasting tasks.

Recent advancements in deep learning have led to the development of powerful neural network-based forecasting models that aim to improve predictive performance across a variety of time series applications. N-BEATS [15] introduced a purely MLP-based architecture with hierarchical basis expansion layers, achieving state-of-the-art results in time series decomposition-based forecasting. N-HiTS [2] extended this approach by integrating hierarchical interpolation for multiscale forecasting, further improving adaptability to different time frequencies. Meanwhile, TSMixer [5] leverages MLP-based temporal mixing layers to capture complex dependencies in sequential data.

Transformer-based architectures have also emerged as a dominant approach in time series forecasting. Time Series Transformers [9] and related attention-based models have demonstrated strong performance in long-range forecasting tasks. However, despite their success, these models struggle with highly volatile financial data due to their reliance on self-attention mechanisms, which may not effectively model short-term fluctuations. Additionally, computational inefficiency remains a concern for large-scale forecasting tasks.

While these models have achieved significant improvements, they often fail to fully leverage graph-based dependencies in financial time series data. This gap motivates the hybrid integration of KAN and GAT, where KAN effectively models non-linear financial relationships, while GAT captures temporal dependencies and structural interactions, leading to more accurate and robust financial forecasting.

3   Methodology

The proposed KAN-GAT forecasting framework integrates Kolmogorov-Arnold Networks (KAN) and Graph Attention Networks (GAT) to enhance gold price prediction. The methodology involves five sequential steps, described as follows:

3.1   Sliding Window Dataset Construction

To capture temporal dependencies, we construct a dataset of input-output pairs using a sliding window approach. For a given window size W, the i-th training sample is defined as:

$$X_i = [x_{t_i-W+1}, x_{t_i-W+2}, \ldots, x_{t_i}], \quad y_i = x_{t_i+1} \tag{1}$$

where x_t is the multivariate time series at time step t, and $X_i \in \mathbb{R}^d$ is the flattened and normalized feature window of dimension d. Here, the subscript i indexes the training samples, each derived from a unique window ending at time t_i.

3.2   Baseline Forecasting with KAN

The Kolmogorov-Arnold Network (KAN) models complex non-linear mappings between the input window X_i and the forecast target y_i. The baseline forecast is given by:

$$\hat{y}i^{KAN} = \phi \left(\sum j = 1^n \alpha_j \psi_j(X_i) + b \right) \tag{2}$$

where $\psi_j(\cdot)$ are adaptive spline basis functions applied to each dimension of X_i, α_j are learnable weights, b is a bias term, and $\phi(\cdot)$ is an optional activation function (e.g., identity or ReLU). The residual between the true target and the KAN forecast is:

$$r_i = y_i - \hat{y}_i^{KAN} \tag{3}$$

These residuals are used to supervise the GAT-based correction model, while at test time, r_i is unavailable.

3.3   Residual Correction with GAT

To enhance forecast accuracy, we train a Graph Attention Network (GAT) to learn a residual correction function using graph-structured samples.

Temporal Graph Construction: We define a temporal graph $\mathcal{G} = (\mathcal{V}, \mathcal{E})$, where each node $v_i \in \mathcal{V}$ represents a sample X_i, and edges $e_{ij} \in \mathcal{E}$ connect temporally adjacent windows (e.g., i to $i+1$).

Node Features and Residual Supervision: Each node is initialized with the normalized input X_i. During training, the model is supervised to predict the residual r_i:

$$\text{Node features:} \quad \mathbf{h}_i = X_i, \quad \text{Supervision:} \quad r_i = y_i - \hat{y}_i^{KAN} \tag{4}$$

Graph Attention Mechanism: The attention score between nodes i and j is computed as:

$$e_{ij} = \text{LeakyReLU}(\mathbf{a}^T[W\mathbf{h}i\|W\mathbf{h}j]), \quad \alpha ij = \frac{\exp(eij)}{\sum_{k \in N(i)} \exp(e_{ik})} \tag{5}$$

where W is a shared linear transformation and $\mathbf{a}$ is a trainable attention vector. Node embeddings are updated as:

$$\mathbf{h}'i = \sigma\left(\sum j \in N(i)\alpha_{ij}W\mathbf{h}_j\right) \tag{6}$$

The predicted residual is given by:

$$\hat{r}i^{GAT} = f\text{reg}(\mathbf{h}'_i) \tag{7}$$

The model is optimized via MSE loss:

$$L_{\text{MSE}} = \frac{1}{n}\sum_{i=1}^{n}(r_i - \hat{r}_i^{GAT})^2 \tag{8}$$

3.4   Final Forecast Integration and Evaluation

The final forecast is computed by correcting the KAN baseline with the GAT-predicted residual:

$$\hat{y}_i^{\text{Final}} = \hat{y}_i^{KAN} + \hat{r}_i^{GAT} \tag{9}$$

During training, r_i is computed using ground truth y_i to supervise the GAT. During inference, only X_i and the KAN baseline prediction $\hat{y}_i^{KAN}$ are used; the ground truth y_i is never accessed.

4   Experiments

In this section, we describe the experimental procedures employed to evaluate the effectiveness of the proposed KAN-GAT model for gold price forecasting.

4.1   Data Preparation

The dataset used in this research comprises daily financial data collected from January 2020 to March 2025, as described in Fig. 2. Specifically, we included:

- Gold prices (represented by the GLD ETF) obtained from Yahoo Finance.
- U.S. Dollar Index (USDI), also sourced from Yahoo Finance.
- Inflation rates retrieved from the Federal Reserve Economic Data (FRED).
- Oil prices (WTI crude futures) sourced from Yahoo Finance.

The collected dataset was normalized using Min-Max scaling and then segmented into training (80%) and testing (20%) sets. The sliding window technique was applied to create sequences of historical data as model inputs.

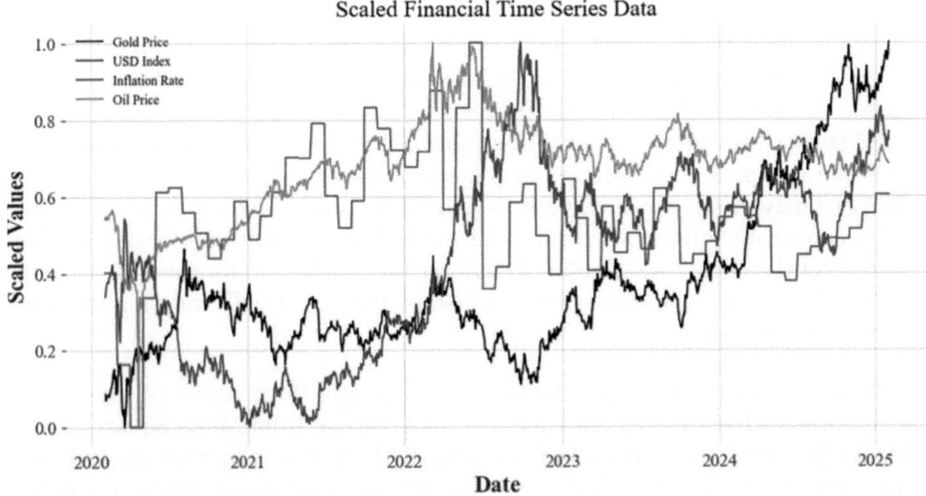

Fig. 2. Scaled financial time series data from 2020 to 2025, including Gold Price, USD Index, Inflation Rate, and Oil Price. All values are normalized for comparison. The figure illustrates the dynamic relationships among key financial indicators. Gold prices exhibit an overall upward trend, influenced by inflation surges and USD Index fluctuations, showcasing an inverse correlation with the USD. Oil prices demonstrate volatility, impacting inflationary pressures, while inflation follows a stepwise pattern. The dataset highlights gold's role as a safe-haven asset, reacting to macroeconomic changes, making it crucial for forecasting models like KAN-GAT.

4.2 Experimental Setup

The experimental framework includes training and evaluating our KAN-GAT model against multiple advanced forecasting baselines: Transformer, N-BEATS, N-HiTS, and TSMixer. All models were trained and evaluated under identical conditions to ensure fair comparison. Key hyperparameters were carefully selected through preliminary experimentation:

- **Window Size (W):** 12 trading days (approximately two weeks).
- **KAN Parameters:** Embedding dimension of 64, adaptive kernels with grid = 1, and polynomial order $k = 2$.
- **GAT Parameters:** Embedding dimension of 64, 32 hidden units per attention head, and 2 attention heads. The Adam optimizer was employed with a learning rate of 0.01, trained over 100 epochs.

For evaluation, we conduct experiments **10 times** with different random seeds to ensure the robustness of our results. We compare the performance of KAN-GAT against the following state-of-the-art forecasting models:

- **Transformers:** [23] A deep learning model leveraging self-attention mechanisms to capture long-term dependencies in time series data.

- **N-BEATS**: [15] A deep neural network architecture utilizing basis expansion layers to model both trend and seasonality in forecasting.
- **N-HiTS**: [2] An extension of N-BEATS that introduces hierarchical interpolation for improved multi-scale time series forecasting.
- **TSMixer**: [5] A novel model that applies MLP-based temporal mixing layers to learn complex dependencies in sequential data.
- **KAN Only**: Uses the Kolmogorov-Arnold Network without residual correction, capturing non-linear interactions but lacking explicit temporal modeling.
- **GAT Only**: Employs Graph Attention Networks for forecasting without KAN, leveraging graph-based relationships but potentially missing intricate non-linear dependencies.

The performance of each model is evaluated using three standard forecasting metrics: Mean Absolute Percentage Error (MAPE) [8], Root Mean Squared Error (RMSE) [3], and Mean Absolute Error (MAE) [24]. These metrics measure the accuracy and robustness of forecasting models by quantifying prediction errors relative to actual values. The proposed KAN-GAT method is assessed using these same metrics to determine its effectiveness in capturing non-linear dependencies and temporal dynamics. In addition to error metrics, we conduct a statistical significance analysis using the paired t-test to compare KAN-GAT with baseline models.

5   Results and Comparison

Table 1 and Fig. 3 present the comparative performance of multiple forecasting models for gold price prediction, evaluated using three key metrics: MAPE, RMSE, and MAE. Lower values indicate higher predictive accuracy.

The results demonstrate that the proposed **KAN-GAT** model significantly outperforms all baseline methods, achieving the lowest MAPE (2.75 ± 0.17), RMSE (2.94 ± 0.37), and MAE (2.28 ± 0.15). This confirms its superior capability in capturing complex non-linear dependencies and dynamic temporal relationships.

Among the baseline models, **GAT** and **N-HiTS** exhibit the best performance, with GAT achieving MAPE of 8.22 ± 3.46 and N-HiTS recording 9.56 ± 1.77. However, both models still lag behind KAN-GAT, indicating that while GAT effectively models temporal dependencies, it benefits significantly from the residual correction provided by KAN. Similarly, N-HiTS performs better than other deep learning models but lacks the dynamic adaptability of graph-based learning.

Conversely, **Transformers** and **TSMixer** struggle to maintain accuracy, showing the highest errors across all metrics. Transformers, despite their long-range dependency modeling capabilities, exhibit a high MAPE of 31.00 ± 1.76, suggesting they may be less effective for volatile financial data. TSMixer also underperforms, likely due to its inability to effectively capture hierarchical temporal interactions.

The **KAN-only** model, while outperforming Transformers and TSMixer, displays substantial variance (MAPE: 11.32 ± 15.19), indicating instability in its predictions. This highlights the necessity of integrating GAT for residual correction to improve accuracy and robustness.

Overall, these findings confirm that combining KAN's non-linear adaptability with GAT's temporal learning in the **KAN-GAT** framework provides substantial accuracy improvements, making it the most effective model for gold price forecasting. The best results are highlighted in red.

Table 1. Performance comparison of forecasting models on gold price prediction.

Metrics	Transformers	N-BEATS	N-HiTS	TSMixer	KAN	GAT	**KAN-GAT**
MAPE	31 ± 1.76	20.94 ± 9.20	9.56 ± 1.77	20.73 ± 5.12	11.32 ± 15.19	8.22 ± 3.46	*2.75 ± 0.17*
RMSE	26.08 ± 1.33	17.56 ± 7.84	8.62 ± 1.75	17.35 ± 4.11	11.44 ± 12.27	7.37 ± 3.00	*2.94 ± 0.37*
MAE	23.13 ± 1.27	15.56 ± 6.95	7.24 ± 1.39	15.38 ± 3.77	9.60 ± 12.23	6.44 ± 2.79	*2.28 ± 0.15*

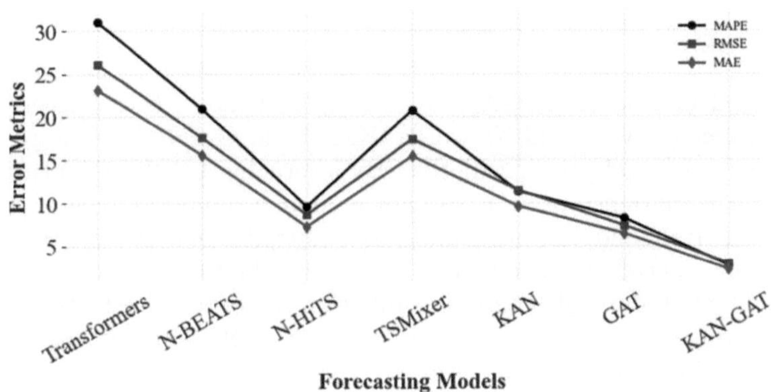

Fig. 3. Comparative evaluation of forecasting models for gold price prediction.

Table 2 presents the results of paired t-tests conducted to evaluate whether the improvements achieved by the proposed **KAN-GAT** model are statistically significant compared to baseline forecasting models. The null hypothesis assumes no significant difference between the compared models, while the alternative hypothesis posits that KAN-GAT outperforms each respective baseline.

The results show that KAN-GAT exhibits a highly significant improvement over all models, with p-values of 0.0000 in most cases, indicating an extremely low probability that the observed differences are due to random variation. The large negative t-statistics suggest substantial performance differences in favor of KAN-GAT.

The most significant difference is observed between KAN-GAT and KAN (-95.12, p = 0.0000), confirming that integrating GAT for residual correction significantly improves predictive accuracy compared to using KAN alone. Similarly, KAN-GAT vs GAT (-60.91, p = 0.0000) highlights that while GAT captures temporal dependencies, it benefits significantly from the enhanced non-linearity modeling of KAN. Comparisons with Transformers (-46.36, p = 0.0000), N-HiTS (-11.81, p = 0.0000), N-BEATS (-5.920, p = 0.0002) and TSMixer (-10.60, p = 0.0000) further establish the superiority of KAN-GAT in gold price forecasting.

Overall, the results confirm that the performance gains of KAN-GAT over all baselines are statistically significant, reinforcing its effectiveness as the most robust forecasting approach in this study.

Table 2. Statistical significance test (t-test) results comparing KAN-GAT with baseline models

Metric	KAN	GAT	Transformers	N-BEATS	N-HiTS	TSMixer
t-statistic	-95.12	-60.91	-46.36	-5.920	-11.81	-10.60
p-value	0.0000	0.0000	0.0000	0.0002	0.0000	0.0000

6   Conclusion

This study introduced KAN-GAT, a novel hybrid forecasting framework that combines Kolmogorov-Arnold Networks (KAN) and Graph Attention Networks (GAT) to enhance gold price prediction. By leveraging KAN for capturing complex non-linear relationships and GAT for modeling temporal dependencies, our approach effectively addresses the limitations of traditional forecasting methods.

Extensive experiments conducted on real-world financial data—including gold prices, USD Index, oil prices, and inflation rates—demonstrate that KAN-GAT significantly outperforms state-of-the-art models. Our approach achieves a MAPE of 2.75 ± 0.17, outperforming KAN (11.32 ± 15.19), GAT (8.22 ± 3.46), TSMixer (20.73 ± 5.12), N-BEATS (20.94 ± 9.20), N-HiTS (9.56 ± 1.77), and Transformers (31.00 ± 1.76). Furthermore, RMSE and MAE reductions to 2.94 ± 0.37 and 2.28 ± 0.15, respectively, validate its robustness. Statistical significance tests confirm that KAN-GAT's improvements are highly significant.

These results highlight the effectiveness of hybrid residual correction in financial forecasting, particularly in volatile economic conditions. Future work could extend this framework to other financial assets and explore additional enhancements, such as incorporating real-time market sentiment or expanding the graph structure to capture multi-source dependencies. KAN-GAT sets a new benchmark in financial time series forecasting, offering a powerful and adaptive approach for capturing complex market dynamics.

While KAN-GAT delivers strong forecasting performance, it has limitations, such as reliance on fixed hyperparameters and sensitivity to market variations. Future work will explore extending it to multi-asset forecasting, incorporating real-time sentiment or macroeconomic signals, and improving generalization through self-supervised or meta-learning techniques.

References

1. Ceni, A., Gallicchio, C.: Residual echo state networks: residual recurrent neural networks with stable dynamics and fast learning. Neurocomputing **597**, 127966 (2024)
2. Challu, C., Olivares, K.G., Oreshkin, B., Ramirez, F., Canseco, M., Dubrawski, A.: NHITS: Neural hierarchical interpolation for time series forecasting. Proc. AAAI **37**, 6989–6997 (2023)
3. Diebold, F., Mariano, R.: Comparing predictive accuracy. J. Bus. Econ. Stat. **13**(3), 253–263 (1995)
4. Elahi, U., Khalid, Z., Kennedy, R.A., McEwen, J.D.: Iterative residual fitting for spherical harmonic transform of band-limited signals on the sphere: Generalization and analysis. In: 2017 International Conference on Sampling Theory and Applications (SampTA), pp. 470–474. IEEE (Jul 2017). https://doi.org/10.1109/sampta.2017.8024463
5. Gobato Souto, H., Heuvel, S.K.: Tsmixer and realized volatility prediction. Available at SSRN (2024)
6. Goel, H., Melnyk, I., Banerjee, A.: R2N2: residual recurrent neural networks for multivariate time series forecasting. CoRR abs/1709.03159 (2017). http://arxiv.org/abs/1709.03159
7. Han, J., Zeng, P.: Residual bilstm based hybrid model for short-term load forecasting in buildings. J. Build. Eng. **99**, 111593 (2025). https://doi.org/10.1016/j.jobe.2024.111593, https://www.sciencedirect.com/science/article/pii/S2352710224031619
8. Hyndman, R., Koehler, A.: Another look at measures of forecast accuracy. Int. J. Forecast. **22**, 679–688 (2006)
9. Islam, S., Elmekki, H., Elsebai, A., Bentahar, J., Drawel, N., Rjoub, G., Pedrycz, W.: A comprehensive survey on applications of transformers for deep learning tasks. Expert Syst. Appl. **241**, 122666 (2024)
10. Li, M., Zhu, Y., Shen, Y., Angelova, M.: Clustering-enhanced stock price prediction using deep learning. World Wide Web **26**(1), 207–232 (2023)
11. Li, Y., Du, Q.: Oil price volatility and gold prices volatility asymmetric links with natural resources via financial market fluctuations: Implications for green recovery. Resour. Policy **88**, 104279 (2024)
12. Liu, Z., et al.: Kan: Kolmogorov-arnold networks. arXiv preprint arXiv:2404.19756 (2024)
13. Majumder, M.M.R., Hossain, M.I.: Limitation of arima in extremely collapsed market: A proposed method. In: 2019 International Conference on Electrical, Computer and Communication Engineering (ECCE), pp. 1–5. IEEE (2019)
14. Mohammadi, V., Fallah Shams, M.F., Zomorodian, G.: The gold market bubble and its contagion to the stock market. Int. J. Nonlinear Anal. Appl. **15**(4), 149–158 (2024)
15. Oreshkin, B.N., Carpov, D., Chapados, N., Bengio, Y.: N-BEATS: Neural basis expansion analysis for interpretable time series forecasting. arXiv preprint arXiv:1905.10437 (2019)
16. Ren, J., Wu, S.: Two-stage hybrid models for enhancing forecasting accuracy on heterogeneous time series (2025). https://arxiv.org/abs/2502.08600
17. da Silva, E.G., de Mattos Neto, P.S., de Oliveira, J.F.: Hybrid system for time series using iterative residual forecasting models. In: 2019 8th Brazilian Conference on Intelligent Systems (BRACIS), pp. 872–877. IEEE (2019)

18. Somvanshi, S., Javed, S.A., Islam, M.M., Pandit, D., Das, S.: A survey on kolmogorov-arnold network. arXiv preprint arXiv:2411.06078 (2024)
19. Vaca-Rubio, C.J., Blanco, L., Pereira, R., Caus, M.: Kolmogorov-arnold networks (kans) for time series analysis. arXiv preprint arXiv:2405.08790 (2024)
20. Veličković, P., Cucurull, G., Casanova, A., Romero, A., Lio, P., Bengio, Y.: Graph attention networks. arXiv preprint arXiv:1710.10903 (2017)
21. Viktoratos, I., Tsadiras, A.: Advancing real-estate forecasting: A novel approach using kolmogorov-arnold networks. Algorithms **18**(2), 93 (2025)
22. Vrahatis, A.G., Lazaros, K., Kotsiantis, S.: Graph attention networks: a comprehensive review of methods and applications. Future Internet **16**(9), 318 (2024)
23. Wen, Q., et al.: Transformers in time series: a survey. arXiv preprint arXiv:2202.07125 (2022)
24. Willmott, C.J., Matsuura, K.: Advantages of the mean absolute error (mae) over the root mean square error (rmse) in assessing average model performance. Climate Res. **30**(1), 79–82 (2005)
25. Zeng, X., Ji, G., Zhou, Y., Li, H., Wei, T.: Multi-load forecasting for integrated energy systems based on gat-mtl. J. Eng. **2025**(1), e70050 (2025)
26. Zhang, Z., Chen, Y., Wang, H., Fu, Q., Chen, J., Lu, Y.: Anomaly detection method for building energy consumption in multivariate time series based on graph attention mechanism. PLoS ONE **18**(6), e0286770 (2023)
27. Zhou, H., He, T., Ong, Y.S., Cong, G., Chen, Q.: Differentiable clustering for graph attention. IEEE Trans. Knowl. Data Eng. **36**(8), 3751–3764 (2024)

Author Index

T. Zhu et al. (Eds.): KSEM 2025, LNAI 15920, pp. 455–457, 2026.
https://doi.org/10.1007/978-981-95-3052-6